The Vineyard
of Liberty

THE

AMERICAN EXPERIMENT

The Vineyard of Liberty

By

James

MacGregor

Burns

VINTAGE BOOKS

A DIVISION OF RANDOM HOUSE

NEW YORK

First Vintage Books Edition, August 1983
Copyright © 1982 by James MacGregor Burns
All rights reserved under International and Pan-American
Copyright Conventions. Published in the United States by
Random House, Inc., New York, and simultaneously in
Canada by Random House of Canada Limited, Toronto.
Originally published by Alfred A. Knopf in 1982.

Owing to limitations of space, all acknowledgments
of permission to use illustrations and maps will be found
following the index.

Library of Congress Cataloging in Publication Data
Burns, James MacGregor.
The vineyard of liberty.
Includes bibliographical references and index.
1. United States—Politics and government—1783–1865.
I..23 Title.
II. Title: The American experiment.
E302.1.B86 1983   320.973   83-3506
ISBN 0-394-71629-9

Manufactured in the United States of America

To the vital cadres of history—
the archivists, librarians, research assistants,
and secretaries
—who make possible the writing of history

I sought in my heart to give myself unto wine; I made me great works; I builded me houses; I planted me vineyards; I made me gardens and orchards, and pools to water them; I got me servants and maidens, and great possessions of cattle; I gathered me also silver and gold, and men singers and women singers, and the delights of the sons of men, and musical instruments of all sorts; and whatsoever mine eyes desired I kept not from them; I withheld not my heart from any joy. Then I looked on all the works that my hands had wrought, and behold! all was vanity and vexation of spirit! I saw that wisdom excelleth folly, as light excelleth darkness.

From *Ecclesiastes,*
as quoted by Thomas Jefferson, 1816

Contents

PART III · Liberty and Equality

PART IV · The Empire of Liberty

PART V · Neither Liberty Nor Union

*Historical maps of the United States will be found
following pages 10 and 416.*

The Vineyard
of Liberty

The Vineyard

As Americans gained their liberty from Britain in the 1780s, they had only the most general idea of the great lands stretching to the west. But the scattered reports from explorers had indicated abundance and diversity: a huge central plain and valley drained by a river four thousand miles long; beyond that, an endless series of mountain ranges rising to rocky peaks and interspersed with burning deserts; and then a final mountain range sloping down to a green coastal fringe on the Pacific. There were stories of boundless physical riches in the bottomlands of the rivers, the herds of buffalo stretching for hundreds of miles, primeval forests so thick that migrating geese could fly over them for a thousand miles and never see a flash of sunlight on the ground below.

People living in the thirteen states in the east savored these reports, but they savored even more the diversity and abundance of their own regions. They too could boast of lush valleys and lofty mountain ranges, ample farmlands and invigorating climate. New Hampshire farmers could still be battling blizzards while Virginians saw their first tobacco plants breaking through the red soil. And their own explorers spoke of the matchless beauties of the east. One of these was Thomas Pownall, an eminently practical young Englishman who had helped plan the war against the French and Indians, and in the 1750s had been rewarded with the governorship of Massachusetts.

A tireless traveler along the seaboard and into the mountains, Pownall set about making a map of the "middle British colonies." A no-nonsense type, he ended his map at the Mississippi and dismissed most of the topography of central Pennsylvania as "Endless Mountains." But Pownall, in doing his work, was constantly distracted by the charm and luxuriance of the land he charted—the wild vines and cherries and pears and prunes; the "flaunting Blush of Spring, when the Woods glow with a thousand Tints that the flowering Trees and Shrubs throw out"; the wild rye that sprouted in winter and appeared green through the snow; above all, by the autumn leaves: the "Red, the Scarlet, the bright and the deep Yellow, the warm Brown," so flamboyant that the eye could hardly bear them.

Pownall was eager for Americans to learn from European experience with the cultivation of crops. But he was cautious about trying to transplant

3

European vines to the American climate, with its extremes of dry and wet, its thunderous showers followed by "Gleams of excessive Heat," when the skins of "Exotic grapes" might burst. Better, he said, that Americans try to cultivate and meliorate their native vines, small and sour and thick-skinned though the grapes be. Given time and patience, even these vines could grow luxuriant and their grapes delicious.

*   *   *

Some ten thousand years ago or more, big-game hunters from Siberia crossed over the Bering Strait and pushed down along an ice-free corridor through Canada to the grasslands below. These were the first Americans. As they fanned out to the south and east they hunted down and killed countless bison, mastodons, mammoths, and other game with their grooved spears. It took the descendants of these onetime Mongols about a hundred and fifty years to reach the present-day Mexican border and the Atlantic coast, and another six hundred to cross the Isthmus into South America. By that time, they had killed off almost all the big game and had mainly turned to growing maize and other grains.

By the 1780s, Americans living along the Atlantic—immigrants from the opposite direction, the east—had lived with the Indians, as they were misnamed, for a century and a half. Whites tended either to idealize red people as noble savages or to fear and despise them as shiftless, thieving, cruel, ignorant, and Godless. Actually, the Indians were as polyglot and diverse in character as were the European Americans three centuries after Columbus had arrived in the New World with his ship's company of Spaniards, Italians, Irishmen, and Jews.

At this time, all the land west of the Mississippi—and hence the Indians occupying it—lay under the dominion of Spain. The French had once owned much of the plains to the immediate west of the Mississippi, and the Russians had infiltrated down the Pacific coast, so that to varying degrees the Indians felt the impact of three European cultures. Closest to Spanish influence were the theocratic Pueblos of present-day New Mexico and Arizona, including the Hopi clinging to the crests of high mesas and the Rio Grande Pueblos with their adobe houses. In the northwest, stretching up to present-day British Columbia and Alaska, the Kwakiutl, Nootka, and other tribes typically lived off fishing, hunting, and berrying. Residing in plank houses, they fashioned totem poles as family crests and maintained a class system consisting of chiefs, commoners, and slaves. These northwestern people, backed up against precipitous mountain ranges, felt close to the sea. "When the tide is out," said the Nootka, "the table is set."

The great expanse of land running from the plateau of Idaho and Montana through the plains to the prairie region of the upper midwest was occupied by a variety of tribes that one day would become famous: the Blackfeet, Crows, Sioux, and Cheyenne of the plains, and the Pawnees, Osage, and Illinois of the prairies. The more eastern of these peoples farmed and lived in permanent villages, from which they might hunt buffalo. The farther west a tribe lived, the more likely it was to be nomadic, dependent on horses for travel, buffalo for meat, and tipis for shelter. Plains Indians had a reputation for being warlike.

Yet the first Americans defied generalization. Some, like the Kwakiutl, had sharply defined classes based on ostentatious possession of wealth; others, like the Zuñi, did not. Some were religious and others not, and the religions embraced an enormous variety of gods, priests, rites, practices, and forms of magic. Many, though not all, were creative in crafts, art, and music. Their personalities and cultures varied widely. One scholar has differentiated among the controversial Pueblos, the egocentric northwest coast men, the manly-hearted plains people, the aggressive but insecure Iroquois.

Indians had no common speech. When Europeans arrived with their own dozen or so languages, American Indians were speaking in at least two thousand separate tongues. Few Indians of one speech could understand that of others; the languages were mutually unintelligible. Within four centuries, at least half of those languages would be extinct—in part because the tongues carrying them were to be silenced for good.

The plight of the first Americans in the east was far different, in the 1780s, from that of the Indians in the central and western regions. The hand of the Spanish in the great west, and of the French in the Mississippi Valley, had been relatively light; they were mainly explorers and trappers, soldiers, missionaries. The seaboard settlers had come to settle and to stay —often on the tribal lands of the Indians. Almost from the start, a civil war had existed between native and new Americans—a civil war less of arms than of disease. Two little islands told the story. "When the English first settled Martha's Vineyard in 1642," Howard Zinn writes, "the Wampanoags there numbered perhaps three thousand. There were no wars on that island, but by 1764, only 313 Indians were left there. Similarly, Block Island Indians numbered perhaps 1,200 to 1,500 in 1662, and by 1774 were reduced to fifty-one."

By 1790, most of the Indians on tideland and piedmont had died or been killed off or confined to reservations. In Maine, a small village of Penobscots lay on the edge of the unmapped wilderness between the white settlements and British Canada. Except for the Herring Ponds and Wampanoags, still largely undisturbed on Cape Cod, only a handful of purebloods remained from the tribes of southern New England. New Jersey and South Carolina also maintained reservations for a few hundred red people, while just over a thousand Delawares, Munsees, and Sopoones held the north branch of the Susquehanna River in Pennsylvania.

Pioneers in most states had driven the Indians away from the edge of the frontier, but in New York a famous confederation still stood between the white communities and the unvanquished western tribes. The six Iroquois nations—Mohawks, Senecas, Cayugas, Onondagas, Oneidas, and Tuscaroras—had been powerful allies of the British for more than a century. Chiefs like Joseph Brant moved with assurance in both white and Native societies; he met with noblemen and dined off crystal in his own fine mansion, yet donned the traditional deerskin mantle to lead his people against the rebelling Americans. But many of the rank-and-file Iroquois suffered for their loyalty to the Crown. When British defeat brought the burning of their frame houses and orchards, many fled to Canada. By 1790 only four thousand of these tribesmen remained within the United States.

Beyond the Iroquois lived the Great Lakes tribes: Miamis, Wyandots, Shawnees, and a dozen others. These forest Indians resembled the natives whom the first colonists encountered upon the Atlantic shore almost two hundred years earlier. They dwelt in substantial houses of bark and plastered straw set upon a framework of poles. While the women tended fields of corn and pumpkins, the men hunted deer for the larder, and beaver to trade for guns, axes, and trinkets. The civil war between white and Native Americans burned fiercely as these red warriors exchanged depredations and murders with the struggling settlements on the north bank of the Ohio. The Indians received British aid, but the white Americans had more devastating allies—disease and whiskey.

While the forest tribes of the north slowed the white advance, the five southern nations seemed capable of halting it altogether. Years of desultory warfare between northern and southern Indians had left a no-man's-land between the Ohio and Tennessee rivers into which white settlers moved in force during the 1780s, but in the rich lands between the Mississippi and the Altamaha the power of the Chickasaws, Choctaws, Cherokees, Creeks, and Seminoles remained unbroken. The United States government recognized the strength of these southern tribes. To the Cherokees, Congress promised that they might "send a deputy of their own choice, whenever they think fit, to Congress," an offer tantamount to statehood under the Articles of Confederation. Congress also deferred to the Creek-Seminole confederacy, whose six thousand warriors constituted the largest standing army in North America outside of the Spanish Empire.

These braves could hardly doubt their ability to protect their land against the white men advancing from the east.

* * *

The population center of the United States in 1790 lay twenty-three miles east of Baltimore. Of the four million persons in the original thirteen states at this time, the vast majority lived on farms within a hundred miles or so of the Atlantic. The population of the country towns was remarkably uniform, running typically between one and three thousand souls, for farming imposed its own restrictions on numbers. A few seeming metropolises did exist—Philadelphia with 42,000 inhabitants, New York with 33,000, Boston 18,000, and Charleston 16,000. But 95 percent of the people dwelt in towns with fewer than 2,500 persons.

Looking west, people living along the Atlantic coast in the 1780s saw a fragmented and vulnerable America. Somewhere beyond the Appalachians lay a small fringe of frontier dwellers and new settlers in a land that might still be coveted by Britain or France or some other European power. Beyond the Mississippi stretched a great unexplored territory claimed by the Spanish king. Sticking out from the southeast was Florida—not merely claimed but possessed by Spain—and between Georgia and Florida lay almost impassable swamps. The northern boundary of Maine was in dispute with Britain. Of the country's 820,000 square miles, less than a third was settled. Western Pennsylvania and New York were wilderness.

Americans were united by common fears of Indians and foreigners, shared rural needs and environments, memories of the Revolution, a powerful belief in independence and liberty—but little else. Of the four million, about 750,000 were black, and of these, 700,000 were slaves and the rest "free." Slavery had been largely abolished in the North during and after the Revolutionary period, but many indentured servants were in a state of virtual, if temporary, bondage. A full-bodied caste system existed in the South, with black slaves at the bottom of the steeply graded pyramid. Americans were not yet drawn together by a common experience of liberty, equality, and fraternity.

Nor were Americans, though overwhelmingly Protestant, drawn together by a common religious view. In 1775, Congregationalists were estimated to number around 575,000 souls, Anglicans 500,000, Presbyterians 410,000, the German churches 200,000, Dutch Reformed 75,000, Baptists and Roman Catholics 25,000 each, Methodists 5,000, and Jews 2,000. From the start the colonies had been alive with religious controversies, doctrinal disputes, sectarian splits and secessions, revivalism and evangelism, the importation of new creeds and dogmas from Europe, along with their carriers—alive also with rationalistic, deistic, and atheistic counterattacks on religion. Roman Catholics early gained a foothold in Maryland and elsewhere, but could not win their political and religious rights against the overpowering Protestant majority. Only one force united all these believers, disbelievers, mystics, pietists, schismatics, dissenters, establishmentarians and disestablishmentarians: a belief in religious liberty.

The long Atlantic coastal plain, with its multitude of rivers and swamps, tended to keep Americans apart, and transport hardly made up for it. In 1790 many sections of the country had no real roads at all; what might be shown on maps as highways were often little more than bridle paths or blazed trails. Stagecoaches and heavy wagons could travel only on highways connecting major cities. A few roads—notably the Wilderness Road through the Cumberland Gap into Kentucky—penetrated the mountain barriers to the west. Bostonians had just completed in the late 1780s a great engineering feat in the Charles River Bridge, then the longest in the world. But many rivers and most streams had no bridges at all and had to be forded.

Setting out on a journey, a man carried not "American" currency but the most common coin, the Spanish "milled dollar" or "piece of eight." Or he might possess English pounds and pence, or French guineas, or Portuguese johannes or "joes." Visiting Virginia, he would be wise to acquire paper notes called "tobacco money"—public warehouse receipts for the tobacco placed there. Everywhere the traveler's paper banknotes would be regarded with suspicion. If he wanted to feel at home away from home, his best resort might be either the local church or the tavern. The latter—named perhaps the Bag o' Nails or the Goat and Compass or the Silent Woman—would serve familiar grog, and a lot of it. Americans loved to drink. An estimated four million gallons of rum, brandy, and strong spirits was imported in 1787, along with a million gallons of wine and three million gallons of molasses, for making rum—all aside from the fruits of local vineyards.

Cutting across all the differences and divisions was the most fundamental of all—that between North and South. The two areas diverged in climate, farm economy, and social system, and in dependence on slaves. The ties between Charleston and London and between Boston and London were closer than those between Charleston and Boston. "I am not a Virginian but an American," Patrick Henry had declaimed when the Revolution broke out. But he was always a Southerner.

Americans had saving graces—a sense of humor, a degree of tolerance, a love of song. They delighted in their tall stories, practical jokes, high jinks. When Congregationalist John Thayer returned from Rome a converted Roman Catholic and held a mass in Boston, the local Protestants did not chase him out of town; rather, they were so curious about the ceremony that they bought tickets to attend. And everywhere Americans expressed their joys and sorrows in song.

In the mission of San Carlos, near Monterey, a mass might be said outdoors under bells swinging from a beam, or a young man might sing to his sweetheart in an adobe hut, under a thatched roof:

> Lo que digo de hoy en día,
> Lo que digo le sostengo,
> Yo no vengo a ver si puedo,
> Yo no vengo a ver si puedo,
> Yo no vengo a ver si puedo,
> Sino porque puedo, vengo!

On the banks of the upper Missouri, an Omaha chief, leading a peace delegation to the neighboring Sioux, celebrated his mission in verse:

> Shub'dhe adhinhe ondonba i ga ho . . .
> Shub'dhe adhinhe ondonba i ga ho . . .
> Shaonzhinga ha, dhadhu anonzhin ondonba ga, he . . .
> Wakonda hidheg'dhon be dho he . . . dhoe.

On a northern river a French-born voyageur, paddling back with his furs and dreaming of the old Norman homestead, drowsily hummed:

> Fringue, fringue sur la rivière,
> Fringue, fringue sur l'aviron.

In his Virginia mansion a tobacco planter stood by the window and sang an old Scots ballad:

> Oh! send Laurie Gordon hame,
> And the lad I daurna name;
> Though his back be at the Wa',
> Here's to him that's far awa'.

In Salem the congregation hymned from the old *Bay Psalm Book:*

> The earth Jehovahs is,
> And the fullness of it:
> The habitable world, & they
> That thereupon doe sit. . . .

From the slave quarters of a South Carolina plantation came the deep, throaty lament:

> De night is dark, de day is long,
> And we are far from home.
> Weep, my brudders, weep!

A

MAP

of the

UNITED STATES

— *of* —

AMERICA

As settled by the Peace of

1783.

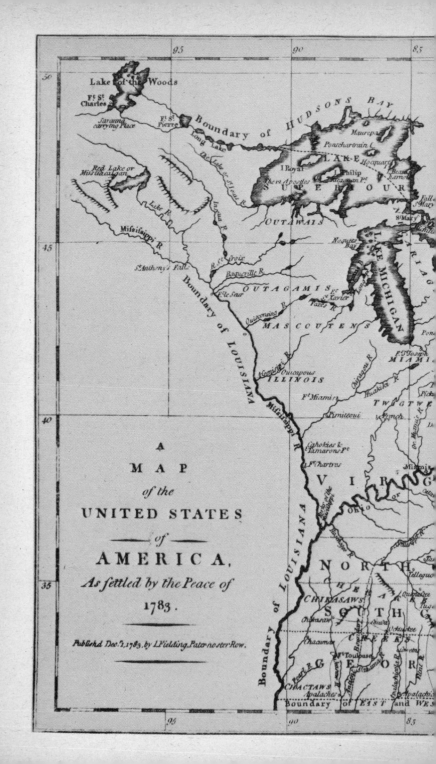

A
MAP
of the
UNITED STATES
of
AMERICA,
As settled by the Peace of
1783.

Publish'd Dec.ʳ 1,1783, by I.Fielding, Paternoster Row.

PART I
Liberty and Union

CHAPTER 1

The Strategy of Liberty

W*estern Massachusetts, late January 1787.* Down the long sloping shoulders of the Berkshire Mountains they headed west through the bitter night, stumbling over frozen ruts, picking their way around deep drifts of snow. Some carried muskets, others hickory clubs, others nothing. Many wore old Revolutionary War uniforms, now decked out with the sprig of hemlock that marked them as rebels. Careless and cocksure they had been, but now gall and despair hung over them as heavy as the enveloping night. They and hundreds like them were fleeing for their lives, looking for places to hide.

These men were rebels against ex-rebels. Only a few years before, they had been fighting the redcoats at Bunker Hill, joining General Stark in the rout of the enemy at Bennington, helping young Colonel Henry Knox's troops pull fifty tons of cannon and mortars, captured from the British at Ticonderoga, across these same frozen wastes. They had fought in comradeship with men from Boston and other towns in the populous east. All had been revolutionaries together, in a glorious and victorious cause. Now they were fighting their old comrades, dying before their cannon, hunting for cover like animals.

The trouble had been brewing for years. Life had been hard enough during the Revolution, but independence had first brought a flush of prosperity, then worse times than ever. The people and their governments alike struggled under crushing debts. Much of the Revolutionary specie was hopelessly irredeemable. People were still paying for the war through steep taxes. The farmers in central and western Massachusetts felt they had suffered the most, for their farms, cattle, even their plows could be taken for unpaid debts. Some debtors had been thrown into jail and had languished there, while family and friends desperately scrounged for money that could not be found.

Out of the despair and suffering a deep hatred had welled in the broad farms along the Connecticut and the settlements in the Berkshires. Hatred for the sheriffs and other minions of the law who flung neighbors into jail. Hatred for the judges who could sign orders that might wipe out a man's entire property. Hatred for the scheming lawyers who connived in all this, and battened on it. Hatred above all for the rich people in Boston, the merchants and bankers who seemed to control the governor and the state legislature. No single leader mobilized this hatred. Farmers and laborers rallied around local men with names like Job Shattuck, Eli Parsons, Luke Day. Dan Shays emerged as the most visible leader, but the uprising was as natural and indigenous as any peasants' revolt in Europe. The malcontents could not know that history would call them members of "Shays's Rebellion." They called themselves Regulators.

Their tactic was simple: close up the courts. Time and again, during the late summer and early fall of 1786, roughhewn men by the hundreds crowded into or around courthouses, while judges and sheriffs stood by seething and helpless. The authorities feared to call out the local militia, knowing the men would desert in droves. Most of the occupations were peaceful, even jocular and festive, reaching a high point when debtors were turned out of jail. Most of these debtors were proud men, property owners, voters. They had served as soldiers and junior officers in the Revolution. They were seeking to redress grievances, not to topple governments. Some men of substance—doctors, deacons, even judges—backed the Regulators; many poor persons feared the uprisings. But in general, a man's property and source of income placed him on one side or the other. Hence the conflict divided town and country officials, neighbors, even families.

Then, as the weather turned bitter in the late fall, so did the mood of the combatants. The attitude of the authorities shifted from the implacable to the near-hysterical. Alarmists exaggerated the strength of the Regulators. Rumors flew about that Boston or some other eastern town would be attacked. A respectable Bostonian reported that "We are now in a State of anarchy and confusion bordering on a Civil War." Boston propagandists spread reports that British agents in Canada were secretly backing the rebels. So the Regulators were now treasonable as well as illegal. The state suspended habeas corpus and raised an army, but lacking public funds had to turn to local "gentlemen" for loans to finance it. An anonymous dissident responded in kind:

"This is to lett the gentellmen of Boston [know?] that wee Country men will not pay taxes, as the think," he wrote Governor Bowdoin in a crude, scrawling hand. "But Lett them send the Constabel to us and we'll nock him down for ofering to come near us. If you Dont lower the taxes we'll pull down the town house about you ears. It shall not stand long then or else they shall be blood spilt. We country men will not be imposed on. We fought of our Libery as well as you did. . . ."

Country people and city people had declared for independence a decade before. They had endorsed the ideals of liberty and equality proclaimed in the declaration signed by John Adams and others. But now, it seemed, these ideals were coming to stand for different things to different persons. Fundamental questions had been left unresolved by the Revolution. Who would settle them, and how?

THE GREAT FEAR

Through the autumn weeks of 1786, George Washington had been savoring the life that he had hungered to return to years earlier, during the bleak days of Boston, Valley Forge, Germantown. Mornings he came downstairs past the grandfather's clock at the turning, strode through the long central hall and out the far door, to stand on the great porch and gaze at the Potomac flowing a mile wide below him, and at the soft hills beyond. Later he usually "rid" to the plantations that flanked the mansion, fields called Muddy Hole, Dogue Run, and Ferry, where he closely supervised his white work hands and his slaves—"the People," he liked to call them —as they planted the fall crops of wheat and rye, "pease" and Irish potatoes. As commanding a figure as ever, with his great erect form and Roman head, he would readily dismount to supervise rearrangement of his plows and harrows breaking up the soil sodden with the heavy rains of that autumn.

On returning to the mansion he might find a goodly company of neighbors, or of old political and military comrades from distant parts; these he entertained in a manner both friendly and formal. After the years of harrowing struggle with Britain and of earlier bloody combat against Frenchmen and Indians, with the possibility of slave uprisings often in mind, Washington luxuriated in the sense of order that enveloped Mount Vernon, with its formal gardens, greenhouses, deer park, and graceful drives. He took heart also in the political calm that now seemed to have settled on Virginia. Then the news of disturbances to the north came crashing in on this serenity. Washington's first reaction was of sheer incredulity.

"For God's sake tell me what is the cause of all these commotions," he implored a friend late in October; "do they proceed from licentiousness, British-influence disseminated by the Tories, or real grievances which admit of redress." If the latter, why were the grievances not dealt with; if the former, why were the disturbances not put down? "Commotions of this sort, like snow-balls, gather strength as they roll, if there is no opposition in the way to divide and crumble them." Most mortifying of all to the general was the likely reaction in London; the Tories had always said that the Americans could not govern themselves, and how London would scoff at this anarchy.

Anxiously Washington tried to discern what was actually happening in Massachusetts. Distrusting the vague and conflicting reports in the newspapers, he depended heavily on his old companion-in-arms General Henry Knox, who had been asked by Congress to investigate the disorders. The rebels would annihilate all debts public and private, Knox warned Washington, and pass agrarian laws that would make legal tender of unfunded paper money. "What, gracious God, is man!" Washington cried out to another friend, "that there should be such inconsistency and perfidiousness in his conduct? It is but the other day, that we were shedding our blood to obtain the . . . Constitutions of our own choice and making; and now we are unsheathing the sword to overturn them." He felt that he must be under the illusion of a dream.

An impudent rebellion, an impotent Congress, a jeering Europe—these were the catalysts for George Washington, and hundreds of others like him, who believed that national independence and personal liberty could flourish only under conditions of unity and order. If government could not check these disorders, Washington wrote James Madison, "what security has a man for life, liberty, or property?" It was obvious that, in the absence of a stronger constitution, "thirteen Sovereignties pulling against each other, and all tugging at the federal head will soon bring ruin on the whole." No one knew better than the commanding general of the Continental armies the price of division and weakness in Congress, and he had been as little impressed by the nation's leadership in the years since the war.

Washington saw one sign of hope. In September, commissioners from five of the middle states had met in Annapolis to discuss vexing restrictions on commerce among them. They had proposed a larger convention to be held in Philadelphia in May of the coming year. But what could such a convention accomplish, given the strange fears and distempers abroad in the land?

*   *   *

In London, in the fall of 1786, John and Abigail Adams also waited anxiously for news from Massachusetts. As American minister to the Court of St. James's, Adams presided over a large house in Grosvenor Square near Hyde Park, which Abigail pictured to her relatives back home as rather like Boston Common, only "much larger and more beautified with trees." Maddening weeks passed without word from home, across the wayward Atlantic; then a fever of excitement took over the house when the butler or a footman brought a tray full of letters to the little room, off the formal drawing room, that Abigail Adams had made into a parlor. Tea and toast would turn cold as the family tore open their letters and drank in family and political news.

The political news seemed more and more clouded. Not only was Congress as irresolute and slow-moving as ever, but the unrest in Massachusetts appeared to be getting out of hand. What in earlier letters had been termed "disturbances" now were verging on anarchy and civil war. The state authorities seemed helpless to put down the commotion; the legislature dawdled, and the governor, reported Adams' son John Quincy from Harvard, was called the "Old Lady." His friends left John Adams in no doubt about the true nature of the rebels. They were violent men who hated persons of substance, especially lawyers. Some were of the most "turbulent and desperate disposition," moving from town to town to enflame the locals. They would annihilate the courts, and then all law and order. Among the leaders there were no persons of reputation or education. Not one of Adams' correspondents sympathized with the rebels, or even explained their hardships, except as the result of speculation and prodigality.

Isolated in London's winter smoke and fogs, Adams seethed in his frustration. This was *his* state that was setting such a bad example; it was the state, in fact, of whose constitution he was the main author. But there was something he could do, even in London; he could warn his countrymen of the dangers ahead. "The Sedition in Massachusetts," Abigail Adams wrote John Quincy at Harvard, "induced your Poppa to give to the World a book" contending that "salutary [?] restraint is the vital Principal of Liberty," that turbulence could bring only coercion.

A sense of desperate urgency possessed Adams. He had to rebut the erroneous notions of such men as Tom Paine and the French thinker Turgot; he had to demolish false ideas before his fellow Americans made further decisions about their system of government. Snatching every available minute from his official duties, barring his study door to all but his wife, surrounding himself with the works of the greatest philosophers and historians, he scribbled so quickly that his hand turned sore, so fast that his work was disorganized, strewn with errors, packed with badly translated quotations. But it was also a powerful argument that the new institutions in America must be built properly to last thousands of years; that free government, with all its woes, was superior to even the wisest monarchy; that the tendency of republics to turbulence could be curbed by a system of checks and balances within government; and that men were equal in the eyes of God and under the law but manifestly unequal—and always would be—in beauty, virtue, talents, fortune.

Aware that he himself, with his medium height, balding pate, and pointed features set oddly in a soft and rounded head, hardly met the popular image of the leader, Adams had no doubt that he possessed the wisdom and virtue necessary to the natural aristocracy that republics too must zealously protect.

*   *   *

In Paris, in the spacious town house that he had rented on the Champs-Elysées, just within the city wall, the American minister, Thomas Jefferson, pondered early reports of the disturbances in Massachusetts. He felt not so much alarmed as mildly embarrassed, for he did not expect independent farmers to disrupt law courts and abolish debts—or so he had explained to European friends.

Later that fall more portentous reports arrived, and Jefferson hardly knew whether to be more concerned about the alarums or the alarmists. The Adamses in London in particular seemed to want to share their concern with Jefferson. He enjoyed cordial relations with both. He had taken a great fancy to the sprightly and knowledgeable Abigail; he and John had toured English towns and estates earlier that year. Although the Virginian had been more interested in the layout of roads and ponds and in contraptions like an Archimedes' screw for raising water, and the Bostonian more attracted to places where Englishmen had fought for their rights—Adams had actually dressed down some people in Worcester for neglecting the local "holy Ground" where "liberty was fought for"—the two men had got along famously.

Still, Jefferson was uneasy at the turn that his correspondence with the Adamses was taking. John had reassured him in November, stating that the Massachusetts Assembly had laid too heavy a tax on the people, but that "all will be well." But in January, when the Shaysites seemed more threatening, Abigail wrote a letter that troubled him. "Ignorant, wrestless desperadoes, without conscience or principals, have led a deluded multitude to follow their standard, under pretense of grievances which have no existance but in their immaginations. Some of them were crying out for a paper currency, some for an equal distribution of property, some were for annihilating all debts. . . . Instead of that laudible spirit which you approve, which makes a people watchfull over their Liberties and alert in the defense of them, these mobish insurgents are for sapping the foundation, and distroying the whole fabrick at once. . . ." Jefferson knew that Abigail was speaking for John as well as herself. Indeed, her views were shared in varying degrees by the most important leaders in America—by Washington, John Jay, Rufus King, Alexander Hamilton, by powerful men in every state.

Jefferson, almost alone among America's leadership, rejected this attitude toward insurgency. The spirit of resistance to government was so important that it must always be kept alive. It would often be exercised wrongly, but better wrongly than not exercised at all.

"I like a little rebellion now and then," he wrote Abigail Adams late in February 1787. "It is like a storm in the Atmosphere." Yet he knew that the problem was not this simple. He did not really approve of rebellion, certainly not a long and bloody one; he simply feared repression more. The solution, he felt, lay in better education of the people and in the free exchange of ideas. Unlike Washington, he believed in reading the newspapers, not because the press was all that dependable, but because a free press was vital to liberty. If he had to choose, he said, he would prefer newspapers without a government to a government without newspapers. Still, Jefferson had to recognize that liberty was impossible without order, just as one day he would prefer to run a government without certain newspapers. The problem now was to reconcile liberty—and equality too —with authority. As summer approached, he wondered whether the planned convention in Philadelphia could cope with this problem that had eluded so many previous constitution-makers.

But he would not yield to the panic over rebellion. Had they not all been revolutionaries? Months later, he was still taking the line he had with the Adamses:

"The tree of liberty must be refreshed from time to time with the blood of patriots and tyrants. It is its natural manure."

* * *

Back in western Massachusetts, in January 1787, people were suffering through the worst snowstorms they could remember. But weather could not stop the insurrection. For months both government men and Regulators had been eyeing the arsenal at Springfield, with its stores of muskets and ammunition. Late in January, Captain Shays led one thousand or more of his men, in open columns by platoons, toward the arsenal. General William Shepard, commanding the "loyal" troops, sent his aide to warn the Regulators to stop. Shays's response was a loud laugh, followed by an order to his men, "March, God damn you, march!" March they did, their muskets still shouldered, straight into Shepard's artillery. A single heavy cannonade into the center of Shays's column left three men dead and another dying, the rest in panic. In a few seconds the rebels were breaking rank and fleeing for their lives.

What now? The Regulators were not quite done. Those who gathered in friendly Berkshire towns after the long flight west calculated that the mountain fastness to the north and the long ranges stretching south provided natural havens for guerrilla resistance. But they underrated the determination of the government to stamp out the last embers of rebellion. The well-armed militia ranged up and down the county, routing the rebels. Hundreds of insurgents escaped into New York and Vermont, whence they sent raiding parties into Berkshire towns.

One of these towns was Stockbridge, where people had been divided for months over the insurgency. For hours the rebels roamed through the town, pillaging the houses of prominent citizens and "arresting" their foes on the spot. At the house of Judge Theodore Sedgwick, an old adversary, they could not find the judge but they encountered Elizabeth Freeman, long known as "Mum Bett." Arming herself with the kitchen shovel, Mum let them search the house but forbade any wanton destruction of property, all the while jeering at their love for the bottle. She had hidden the family silver in a chest in her own room. When a rebel started to open it, she shamed him out of it, according to a local account, with the mocking cry, "Oh, you had better search that, an old nigger's chest!—the old nigger's as you call me."

Soon the raiders streamed out of town to the south. They had time to free some debtors from jail and celebrate in a tavern. Then the militiamen cornered them in the woods, killing or wounding over thirty of them.

The uprising was over. Some Regulators felt that they had gambled all and lost all. As it turned out, they had served as a catalyst in one of the decisive transformations in American history. Though their own rebellion had failed, they had succeeded in fomenting powerful insurrections in people's minds. Rising out of the grass roots of the day—out of the cornfields and pasturelands of an old commonwealth long whipped by religious and political conflict—they had challenged the "system" and had rekindled some burning issues of this revolutionary age:

When is rebellion justified? Granted that Americans had the right to take up arms against the Crown, which had given them taxation but no representation, were people who felt cheated of their rights justified in a *republic* in turning to bullets rather than ballots?

If decisions were indeed to be made by ballots, how would ballots count? By majority rule—by a majority of the voters in an election or of their representatives in a legislature? Or would the minority be granted special rights and powers in order to protect elites against the populace? And under either system would all people—all adult men, women, poor persons, Indians, black people—have an equal voice and vote?

If the rebellion had touched people's basic fears about their safety and security, what price stability and unity? The response of the social and political elites to the rebellion was drastic: build a stronger national government that could cope with domestic unrest and fend off foreign foes. What local and regional rights would be swallowed up in the new Leviathan? Would precious personal liberties be engulfed by the new federal government? Or might they be better protected and enhanced by it?

If the immediate goal was a wider union, what was the ultimate purpose and justification of this union? Was it essentially for internal harmony and national defense? Humankind had higher needs—for individual liberty and self-expression, for a sense of sharing and fraternity, for the equal rights and liberties proclaimed in the Declaration of Independence. How would such aspirations and expectations be fulfilled?

To these questions Americans—rebels and elites, common and uncommon—would bring vast experience, a big stock of common sense, a large assortment of misconceptions and prejudices, boundless optimism, and a quality less evident in some of the older nations of Europe: a willingness to experiment. Americans were accustomed to being tested, in their churches, on their farms, out in the wilderness. They were used to trying something, dropping it, and trying something else. They were good at figuring, probing, calculating, reasoning things out. The American people, Alexander Hamilton would soon be writing, must decide "the important question, whether societies of men are really capable or not of establishing good government from reflection and choice, or whether they are forever destined to depend for their political constitutions on accident and force." Americans were willing to test themselves on this issue.

Some Americans thought of their country, or at least of their new young republic, as a received design, as a sanctified destiny, as a sacred mission for a selected people. Others saw it as a venture in trial and error, as a gamble, above all as an experiment. Sacred Mission or Grand Experiment —by what yardstick, by what purposes or principles or moral values, would American leadership be measured?

A RAGE FOR LIBERTY

In Philadelphia, in early 1787, Benjamin Franklin busied himself with adding some rooms to his house on High (later named Market) Street. Now eighty-one, he found dealing with glaziers, stonecutters, timber merchants and coppersmiths a bit fatiguing, but, as he wrote a friend in France, building was an "Old Man's Amusement" and "Posterity's advantage." He still had time for his main pleasures: cribbage, playing with his grandchildren, exercising with his dumbbell, and reading while soaking in his boot-shaped copper tub. Surrounding him were mementos from his years as a printer, Philadelphia politician and official, colonial agent in London, spokesman in Paris for the new nation. His library, to which he would retreat from the children's tumult, was lined ceiling-high with books from Europe and America, including his own world-famous *Poor Richard's Almanack.* He made use of his own inventions too—his "Franklin stove," a freestanding fireplace, lightning rods atop the house, and a mechanical device to pick books off the top shelves, a device later adapted for use by grocers to reach cans and boxes.

In his years in France, Franklin had become an international celebrity, so popular that crowds followed him as he passed along Paris streets. He had returned to Philadelphia in 1785 to equal acclaim. Cannon boomed; bells rang out; the town fathers waited on him; and shortly, he was elected president of Pennsylvania. He did not cut a dramatic figure; visitors found "a short, fat trunched old man in a plain Quaker dress, bald pate, and short white locks," often sitting hatless under a mulberry tree in his garden on a warm day. But mentally he was as acute and wide-ranging as ever, shifting easily in correspondence and conversation from politics to diplomacy to types of thermometers to agriculture to gossip to the constitutional questions that would arise at the convention to be held in Philadelphia in the spring.

Despite the gout and kidney stone that tormented him, the patriarch occasionally made his way about town, often in a sedan chair. Much of Philadelphia was a monument to him. He could proceed down High Street toward the public landing on the river, passing nearby Christ Church, which he had served thirty years earlier as a manager of a lottery to raise money for the steeple. On the way back he could observe Presbyterian churches and Friends' meeting houses he had often attended. Or he could head over to the American Philosophical Society, which he had helped found and over which he had presided for years. If he chose to turn down High Street in the opposite direction, he might come to City Hall on the corner of Fifth and Chestnut and then to the Library Company, the first subscription library in America, which he had conceived in 1731. If he turned right at the corner of Fifth and Chestnut, he encountered the long façade of Independence Hall, the most famous building in the city, indeed in America.

To this building—formerly the State House—Franklin's life also had been linked. Here he had been a delegate to the Second Continental Congress, where he supported the petition to the King for a redress of grievances, drew up a plan of union, and organized the first post office; it was Franklin, naturally, who was appointed the first postmaster general. In this building too he had signed the Declaration of Independence, after serving on the drafting committee with Adams and Jefferson and others. Here he was alleged to have said, "We must, indeed, all hang together, or most assuredly we shall all hang separately." Franklin was in Paris when the Articles of Confederation were signed in this building but now he was back, and in the spring of 1787 Independence Hall was being readied for the grandest occasion of all—the convening of the Constitutional Convention.

Atop Independence Hall stood the Liberty Bell, which had rung out the news of the signing of the Declaration of Independence and of Revolutionary War victories. The tocsin had had a flawed existence. It had been cast in England, for no colony could make a bell like this, weighing over a ton. It was cracked on arrival and had to be crudely recast by a local firm. It was spirited out of Philadelphia and ignominiously submerged in a New Jersey river when the redcoats threatened the city. But now it was back in place, and still girdled by a noble sentiment: "Proclaim Liberty throughout the land, and to all the inhabitants thereof."

*   *   *

Proclaim Liberty! No bell need ring it out; the idea had transfixed Americans for generations, and never more than in the last twenty years. Liberty had been the clangorous rallying cry against the British. It was the Sons of Liberty who had denounced the Stamp Act, conducted funerals of patriots killed in street brawls, tarred and feathered Tory foes and American renegades. It was the Liberty Poles around which the Sons had assembled to pledge their sacred honor to the cause, the Liberty Tree in Boston from which they had hanged Tory officials in effigy, only to see the redcoats cut down the noble elm and convert it into firewood. Although Liberty was not the only goal for Americans in the 1770s and 1780s—they believed also in Independence, Order, Equality, the Pursuit of Happiness—none had the evocative power and sweep of Liberty, or Freedom—two terms for the same thing. To preserve liberty was the supreme end of government.

Liberty, indeed, was more than a cause or a symbol; it was a possession and a passion. Sober men referred to the "sweets of liberty"; it was a treasure, a "precious jewel." No wonder Alexander Hamilton spoke darkly of the "rage for liberty." If liberty had an uncertain future in America, it had emerged from a glorious past in England. Once upon a time, it was thought, liberty had flourished among the Saxons, a simple and virtuous people, only to be assaulted by the barbaric Norman invaders. Liberty had flowered and wilted in other countries, as in Denmark and Italy. It was almost crushed out in England. So liberty was not only precious but pure, virginal, vulnerable. It must be rescued in the New World from its chains in the Old.

Liberty was many-sided. The ideal of liberty of conscience—the most sacred, the most unalienable liberty of all—had been fired and burnished in the crucibles of colonial experience. Many Americans had fled religious oppression in Europe only to find religious establishments somehow surviving in the New World. They were usually mild compared to the British, perhaps, but even in America clerics seemed to plot against a man's liberty. In one New England town the Baptists, claiming to be the first settlers, balked at paying taxes to support the established Congregationalist church. The Congs, as the disrespectful called them, had then rallied at the town meeting, outvoted the Baptists, and confiscated their property, on the ground that the Baptists were raging schismatics, their church "a sink" for the "filth of Christianity."

Victories for religious tolerance were all the sweeter for this. During the First Continental Congress in 1774 John Adams and other Massachusetts delegates were invited to Carpenters' Hall to do "a little business." On being seated, they discovered facing them across a long table some solemn Baptists flanked by Quakers who looked even more somber under their broad-brimmed beavers. John Adams found himself trying to explain how the Massachusetts men squared their establishment of religion with their paeans to liberty. The grandest victory of all came a month before the Declaration of Independence, when Virginia passed a Declaration of Rights calling for "free exercise of religion according to the dictates of conscience."

An equally vital liberty was freedom of the press. Despite the vaunted liberations in the New World, free and unlicensed newspapers hardly existed for the first hundred years after Plymouth. The first free newspaper, appearing in Boston in 1690, was promptly suppressed. Newspaper editors fought for their rights against colonial governors; in 1735 John Peter Zenger was jailed on a charge of criminal libel, for his attacks on the colonial government, only to win his freedom after a brilliant defense. At the age of sixteen Benjamin Franklin was claiming in the *New-England Courant,* the editor of which—Ben's brother James—was already in jail, that there was "no such Thing as publick Liberty, without Freedom of Speech; which is the Right of every Man, as far as by it, he does not hurt or controul the Right of another." It should suffer no other check. Whoever would overthrow the liberty of a nation must begin by subduing free speech and the free press.

Liberty had to be grounded, according to practical Americans like Franklin, in something real and dependable, namely the right to hold property. Not only was "property surely a right of mankind as really as liberty," in John Adams' words; each buttressed the other. Property—especially his house and land and tools—was something a man could fall back on, if liberty was threatened; it was the threat of loss of property through foreclosures, leaving them as less than free men, that had so enflamed the Massachusetts Regulators. Yet the close marriage of liberty and property seemed, in the eyes of some sharp observers, to embrace a potential evil, or at least a strain. Could property become the enemy of liberty? Must society, "to secure the first of blessings, *liberty,*" strangle wealth, the first offspring of liberty, to safeguard liberty itself? A member of the Continental Congress summed up the "sad dilemma in politics": if the people forbade wealth, it would be through regulations "intrenching too far upon civil *liberty.*" But if wealth was allowed to accumulate, "the syren *luxury*" would follow on its heels and contaminate the whole society.

The ugliest form of property in America in the 1780s was slavery. Nothing posed so sharply the issue of the nature of liberty, of the relationship of liberty and property, of the linkage and tension between liberty and equality, as the 700,000 Negroes in the seaboard South, 96 percent of whom were slaves, or the 50,000 in New England, over a fifth of whom were slaves. And nothing was more embarrassing for Americans who boasted of their liberties and compared them to the tyranny of benighted Europe.

"How is it," Samuel Johnson growled, "that we hear the loudest *yelps* for liberty among the drivers of negroes?"

Preachers, editors, and a few politicians, especially in the northern states, made the same charge of hypocrisy. By the mid-seventies, slavery was under attack in some northern areas as a cruel and un-Christian institution, but only Pennsylvania achieved an act of gradual abolition. Despite all the oratory, the other states could not act, or would not. The institution of slavery survived, essentially intact, both the Revolution and the Articles of Confederation.

Still, American whites somehow were able collectively to love liberty, recognize the evils of slavery, and tolerate slavery, all at the same time. The spreading stain of bondage did not blot out the American self-image of a chosen people engaged in a grand experiment. In the seventeenth century the colonists had carried the "spirit of Liberty" from England, where it had been perverted and corrupted, to the wilderness, where it had taken root and flowered. "To our own country," Americans were told, "must we look for the biggest part of that liberty and freedom that yet remains, or is to be expected, among mankind." This self-image battened on enlightened Europe's view of a people, "in the vigour of youth," as Richard Price put it, "inspired by the noblest of all passions, the passion for being free." This people, virile and virtuous if a bit rustic and bumptious, basked in its sense of a special mission. "The Eyes of Europe, nay of the World," proclaimed South Carolina's President John Rutledge, "are on America."

Such was the sustaining, the elevating, the euphoric self-image of most Americans during the Revolution and for a few years after. Then came a time of disillusionment and, by 1787, a pervasive feeling that the new nation had fallen into "evils and calamities" that were precipitating a profound crisis.

On the face of it, the crisis was simply the Confederation's seeming ineffectiveness and near-paralysis. Even in their private correspondence men like Washington, Hamilton, and Madison spoke in the most urgent terms of the lack of a strong central government. The "mortal diseases of the existing constitution," Madison wrote Jefferson in March 1787, ". . . are at present marked by symptoms which are truly alarming, which have tainted the faith of the most orthodox republicans, and which challenge from the votaries of liberty every concession in favor of stable Government not infringing fundamental principles." By this time, Gordon Wood found, most reformers were seeking some change in the structure of the central government as the best, and perhaps the only, solution to the nation's problems. Anti-Federalists of the day—and some historians since—contended that the failures of the Confederation were grossly exaggerated and its successes, such as the return of some prosperity, minimized. But few Americans perceived these achievements, and if they did, the successes led to heightened expectations that were soon to be crushed in the turmoil of early 1787.

A far more profound crisis—a crisis of mind and morality—lay behind the failure of institutions, centering in the palpable need for liberty and the increasing doubts and confusion over it. Five years after the Revolution Americans were discovering that it was not enough to apotheosize liberty; it was increasingly necessary to define it, and to see its linkages with other values. What kind of liberty? Whose liberty? Protected by whom, and against whom? Above all, how did liberty relate to other great aims? Some Americans felt that the pursuit of liberty ultimately would safeguard other values, such as order and equality; others saw order and authority as prior goals in protecting liberty.

The crisis of liberty was often seen too as a crisis of property. Thus John

Quincy Adams, who was by no means a young fogy, devoted his Harvard graduation speech of 1787 to a dramatic portrait of a nation in which the "violent gust of rebellion" had hardly passed and the people were groaning under the burden of "accumulated evils" such as luxury and dissipation, but where the root problem appeared to be a decline in the punctual observance of contracts and in that public credit upon which historically "the fabric of national grandeur has been erected."

By the mid-1780s both sides were disillusioned. The pursuers of liberty feared that the nabobs were conspiring to restrict their freedom, perhaps in that ominous constitutional convention to be held in Philadelphia; in any event, the achievement of liberty had not brought them more prosperity or security or equality. Those who hungered for order and stability were in even greater despair. The capture of the Rhode Island legislature by cheap-money men, unrest in other states, the fear of violence at the hands of Indians and even slaves, the inability of government to maintain order, and above all the shocking rebellion in Massachusetts—all these were warnings that liberty was safe neither under the state governments nor under the Confederation. Glumly they recalled the apparent lessons of history: that republics had disintegrated as they descended the fateful road marked by steps leading from LIBERTY to DISORDER to ANARCHY to POPULAR DESPOTISM and finally to TYRANNY.

*   *   *

Historians are wary of the notion that, at a critical point in history, a heroic figure, galloping to the rescue, snatches victory from the jaws of defeat and changes the destiny of a nation. In real life the hero's horse loses a shoe and he fails to arrive; or if he does arrive, it is at the wrong place at the wrong time, and it makes no difference anyway. Historians are especially skeptical of the decisive role of intellectual heroes. The intellectual may not be able to find his horse in the first place, or may have neglected to have it shod; in any event, intellectuals are part of a long, complex, and tumultuous stream of innovation, conflicts, and borrowings of ideas, a process in which individual influence is usually hard to identify. Yet if any American may be included in that small company that plays a critical role at a pivotal point in history, it was James Madison, who almost literally did gallop across the New Jersey flatlands in 1787 to take the lead in confronting and resolving, for a time at least, the dilemma of "liberty versus order."

Madison's leadership would have been impossible without magnificent collegiality from brilliant thinkers and actors, impossible without magnificent "followership" from the people who would one day vote to accept or reject the new constitution. The generation of Americans coming into leadership in the late 1780s had gone through a series of laboratory exercises of unmatched diversity. Collectively they had experimented with British rule in its many forms, with a variety of state constitutions, with revolutionary regimes during the War of Independence. They had tried weak executives and strong, governors appointed by the Crown, by the legislatures, by the "better people" in councils or upper chambers, by "all the people," by various combinations thereof. They had tried bicameral legislatures and unicameral; legislatures elected in a variety of ways, under a variety of suffrage arrangements, holding a variety of legislative, executive, and even judicial powers. They had experimented with conventions that sprang directly from the people and bypassed legislatures.

These men, self-conscious and thoughtful experimenters, had not merely observed the laboratory exercises; they had conducted them, suffered from them, learned from them. Madison himself had helped draft the Virginia Constitution of 1776; served in the Continental Congress for three years and in the Virginia House of Delegates for two; and attended the Annapolis Convention. By 1787 he was back in Congress, now convened in New York. Many of his colleagues could boast of even broader experience, including service in executive and military establishments.

Learning illuminated experience. Rarely has a generation of activists been so thoroughly schooled in classical political thought as that of Madison and Adams. For them the works of the Greeks and Romans constituted neither dead languages nor dead learning. Many read Montesquieu in his own language. They liked to cite the great English thinkers—Hobbes and Locke and Hume—against English rule itself. Polemicists clinched their arguments by citing chapter and verse. The result of the ferment was an outpouring of broadsides, sermons, addresses, and above all pamphlets. "Almost every American pen" was at work, it was noted. Even "peasants and their housewives in every part of the land" had begun "to dispute on politics and positively to determine upon our liberties." To a degree perhaps hardly matched in Western history, Americans of the 1780s *thought* their way through a thicket of political problems—and then acted.

Others matched Madison in their grasp of these problems, but no one equaled him in preparations for the convention in Philadelphia. A man of both action and thought, he had busied himself in New York City during the spring helping to win congressional authorization of a convention to revise the Articles of Confederation, then organizing a caucus of fellow Virginians and sorting out his own thoughts. To Jefferson in Paris he wrote a long analysis of the need for reform, resorting to their private code when he touched on controversial matters. Madison kept George Washington closely informed of events; he was pleased to have the general's endorsement of the need for "thorough reform of the present system," and even more pleased to learn that Washington, after much wavering, had decided to attend the convention. Sensing that Governor Edmund Randolph was too busy with state affairs to bone up on national constitution-making, Madison carefully coached him on tactics and substance, and urged him to get to Philadelphia early so that the Virginians could help prepare some "materials" for the other delegates, even if it meant that Mrs. Randolph, who was pregnant, could not accompany her husband.

Madison failed to organize the whole delegation. Patrick Henry had been elected to it and had declined, for the reason, Madison conjectured, that he would feel freer to oppose the new charter if he disliked it. George Mason, another delegate, was less politically ambitious than Henry, but Madison suspected him of anti-Federalist tendencies.

Madison had spent many a long evening in New York refining his own views, jotting them down in his small, even handwriting. It was easy for him to list the faults of the Confederation—weakness, instability, and inability to control the factious, rambunctious states—and he did so in a three-thousand-word essay bluntly entitled "Vices of the Political System of the U. States." But what would take the Confederation's place? By the time Madison left Manhattan early in May and took the open boat that ferried him over to Paulus Hook, he had fashioned a plan that would provide the central strategy for the delegates who would assemble in Philadelphia.

The journey itself provided Madison with occasions for reflection. As his boat plowed slowly across the mouth of the Hudson he could see packets and schooners bearing products—Madeira and rum, perhaps, or machinery and ironware—that would be taxed as imports from abroad not by the Confederation but by New York State. Traveling across the pleasant New Jersey countryside in his towering, deep-bellied stagecoach, the "American Flyer," he could reflect that in New Jersey too the farmers and debtors had compelled the state legislature to issue paper money. Pulling up at the Nassau Tavern in Princeton the first evening of the trip, he must have recalled earlier days when he and the other students crowded around the stages to hear the latest news from New York and Philadelphia. He might have recalled too his first reading in Aristotle and Polybius, Locke and Montesquieu. Out of the writings of such men, out of his own and his comrades' political experiences, Madison had forged his theories of government.

Fundamental to these theories was an assumption that men inevitably tended toward conflict and struggle. The latent causes of faction, he had concluded, were sown in the nature of man. "All civilized societies," he had written in New York that spring, "are divided into different interests and factions, as they happen to be creditors or debtors—rich or poor—husbandmen, merchants or manufacturers—members of different religious sects—followers of different political leaders—inhabitants of different districts—owners of different kinds of property, &c &c." Even where there was no actual basis for conflict, frivolous and fanciful differences could excite passionate hatreds.

How protect liberty and order against these factions? Especially under a republican government, where the majority of the people was supposed to rule, how thwart a majority united by some passion or interest from crushing minority or individual rights? Faith? Doctrine could lead to dogma and then to oppression. Enlightened self-interest? Leaders with vision would not always be at the helm. Public opinion? The average man —even the average legislator—pursued local interests. Did a Rhode Island assemblyman, Madison asked, care what France or even Massachusetts thought of his paper money?

How then control selfish factions, oppressive local majorities, popular follies and passions? Madison's answer went straight to the heart of the grand strategy of the men who would come to be known as Federalists. The solution was not to try to remove the causes of faction, for a free society would always produce differences among men and a good republican must respect those differences. The solution was to dilute the power and passion of local factions by enlarging the sphere of government into a nation of many regions, interests, and opinions. Like a careful cook, Madison would blend indigestible lumps and fiery spices in the blander waters of a large pot.

It was this plan to "enlarge the sphere" that Madison brought to Philadelphia in his luggage as the "Flyer" rattled over the pebble stones of Chestnut Street and pulled up at the Indian Queen Tavern.

Philadelphia: The Continental Caucus

The eager Madison was the first delegate to show up; no one else arrived for ten days. He had time to settle into rooms in Mary House's celebrated lodgings at Fifth and Market, to talk tobacco prices with the local merchant who handled the crop from Madison's fields at Montpelier, to pay a visit to Benjamin Franklin, and to work on final details of the plan that Governor Randolph would present to the convention. The delegates straggled in over the next few weeks, most of them after long and hard journeys. General Charles C. Pinckney brought his young bride with him from

Charleston; both of them had been miserably seasick as their packet beat its way up the coast to Delaware Bay. Elbridge Gerry of Massachusetts also brought his young wife, along with their infant child, despite Yankee doubts about the pestilent fevers of southern cities like Philadelphia; shortly, he sent them off to stay with in-laws in New York City. William Samuel Johnson of Connecticut had traveled mainly overland, south on the post road along the Connecticut River, through the populous area around Hartford, and then down the much-traveled Boston Post Road along the coastline into Manhattan, whence he probably followed the same route as Madison into Philadelphia. Johnson had stopped in Hartford long enough to collect two hundred pounds from the state treasury for his expenses, and in New York to receive news that he had been chosen president of the newly reorganized Columbia College. Delegates from New Hampshire did not arrive for eight weeks because, it was rumored, the state was too poor to pay their expenses. Delegates from Rhode Island did not arrive at all, because the legislators of Little Rhody were as suspicious of the convention delegates as the delegates were contemptuous of them and their cheap-money ways.

On May 13 there was a great commotion outside Mrs. House's lodging house: General Washington had arrived, escorted by the City Light Dragons and hailed by the pealing of the Liberty Bell, the booming of artillery, the flashing of sabers, and the huzzahs of a great throng. Mrs. House had tidied up her best rooms for the general, only to see the financier Robert Morris carry him off to his fine brick mansion, leaving her to hope that she could fill the rooms with Baptists, Cincinnati, or abolitionists, who were also then conventioneering in the nation's first city.

Washington had to wait twelve fretful days before a quorum was present, but Madison helped fill the time with caucus meetings of the Virginia delegates at the Indian Queen—to form, as Mason put it, "a proper correspondence of sentiments."

The Virginians got off to a good start when the assembly finally convened on May 25, a rainy Friday. Washington was unanimously elected president of the convention on the nomination of Morris and with the backing of Franklin, Washington's only rival for world fame—a nice expression of unity at the start. Madison secured a seat up front, where he took a leading role in debate and, at the same time, kept the best and fullest record of the proceedings. He soon impressed the delegates with his lucid, low-voiced exposition of constitutional and political problems; he blended together, a Georgia delegate noted, "the profound politician with the scholar." The prudent delegates devoted two days to laying out rules and procedures, the most important of which was absolute secrecy about the debates. During these days they had an opportunity to begin taking the measure of their associates.

What manner of men were these? The "bar of history" has rendered changing verdicts during two centuries of hindsight. For a hundred years or more the Framers were virtually deified, or seen at least as Olympians rising above petty self-interest and local prejudice to produce what Prime Minister William Gladstone would call, on the occasion of the Constitution's centennial, "the most remarkable work known to me in modern times to have been produced by the human intellect, at a single stroke (so to speak), in its application to political affairs." Then, in the iconoclastic Progressive era of the early twentieth century, the heroes were pulled off their pedestals and found to be crass conservatives who wanted to curb agrarian radicals and debtors, men of property who calculated that their holdings of land and securities and slaves would be safer under a national government judiciously removed from direct control by the masses. Interpretation followed interpretation. Marxists saw the Framers as products of class background and interest. Political theorists viewed them as ideologues responding to the dominant values of the time. Recently, political "realists" have analyzed them as state politicos maneuvering in the convention for regional advantage. Others have regarded them as nationalists and continentalists, still others as bold engineers engaged in a grand experiment. Two centuries later, the jury of history has rendered no final verdict from among these various theories.

How did the men of Philadelphia view themselves? To see them as they appeared to one another in that hot chamber in the Pennsylvania State House is to raise them from immortality to mortality. All of them were unabashedly and even proudly *political* men to some degree, or they would not have been chosen by their state legislatures. Most of them were ambitious. Clinton Rossiter estimated that as a group they had had more political experience than any gathering of the leaders of a newly independent nation at any time in history. They were mainly youngish, averaging in their early forties. Almost all were wealthy, or at least comfortably off. Most were from established families. They had the correct formal education: nine were products of (now) Princeton, four each of William and Mary and Yale, three each of Harvard and (now) Columbia.

At least a dozen were planters or farmers on a big scale; another dozen, lawyers; still another dozen, state officeholders; and some were all three of these. Most had married women of social standing. Over a third owned slaves. They were almost all at least nominally religious, ranging from robust Christians to the tolerantly ecumenical or broadly secular. Most were war veterans, or at least had known military life.

The poor, the back-country people, the agrarian debtors, the uneducated, the non-voters, and of course women, Indians, and blacks were inconspicuously unrepresented.

So this was a convention of the well-bred, the well-fed, the well-read, and the well-wed. But the men of Philadelphia were neither solely defined nor wholly confined by these identities. Transcending these interests and occupations and affiliations was their sense of a compelling goal, a strategy to achieve that goal, and a host of notions about how to make that strategy work. The delegates did not see themselves as merely landowners or merchants or lawyers. They conceived of themselves as engaged in a grand "experiment"—a word they often used—the outcome of which would shape their nation's destiny, and hence their own and their posterity's, for decades to come. They saw themselves—in a word they would never have used—as pragmatists, as men thinking their way through a thicket of problems, in pursuit of that goal.

That goal was liberty—liberty with order, liberty with safety and security, liberty of conscience, liberty of property, liberty with a measure of equality, but above all, liberty. They defined this term in many different ways, they had varying expectations of it, they differed over its relationship to other values, and later these differences would help spawn a series of tragedies. But conflict over this supreme goal did not deter the delegates at the time. Rather, liberty served as a unifying symbol and goal around which practical men could rally. Reading the convention debates, some historians have remarked on the absence of ideological conflict. The Framers did not need to argue over ideology; they had their ideology of liberty, with all its kindling power and glowing, confusing, contradictory implications for the future.

And even as the delegates gathered, further news from Massachusetts caused them to fear all the more for the future of liberty. Beaten on the field of battle in the winter, the rebels in the spring had turned to the state elections despite an act disqualifying former Regulators from voting for a year. The "malcontents" helped defeat Governor Bowdoin for re-election and replaced him with the more populistic John Hancock. "Shaysites" picked up seats in the state senate in April and the lower house in May. Madison warned that the election crisis would bring "wicked measures" from the Massachusetts legislature. To some, the spring news was worse than the winter's: it was easy to castigate men who took up arms, but what about men who took up *ballots?*

If the Framers by and large were agreed on the goal of liberty and the nature of the threat to it, the strategy of protecting and augmenting it posed a potentially more divisive challenge. Almost all the Framers shared Madison's crucial premise that liberty and order and property could not be safeguarded by relying on education or religion or the basic goodness of man; liberty must be protected and expanded through the careful building of *institutions.* Almost all agreed that liberty and order were in danger from popular movements or legislative majorities in the states and hence that the new institutions necessary to protect liberty, and the order and stability without which liberty could not survive, must be *national* in scope and power. But all agreed too that the new national government would be a government elected by, representative of, and responsible to, the *people* —it would be, in short, a *republic.*

And here was the rub. If the people were ultimately to control, what would stop radical and "leveling" popular majorities from taking over the new national government as they had threatened to do in certain states? What would stop the "scum," as conservatives like Benjamin Rush liked to call the malcontents, from rising to the top of the national stew as well as the local? It was in confronting this problem—how to solve, on a national basis, republican ills with republican remedies, as Madison put it— that the genius of the Framers was most sorely tested.

The Virginians' answer to this problem lay at the heart of the plan that Governor Randolph presented to the delegates on the first day of real business, May 29. Randolph, gaining the initiative that Madison hoped for, put the "Virginia Plan," as it came to be called, first on the agenda and thus made it the point of departure for the deliberations. Randolph's audience anticipated his proposals that the Articles of Confederation be "corrected & enlarged," that the new national legislature consist of two chambers; that a national executive be chosen by the legislature; that a national judiciary be established. But many were disturbed when Randolph proposed that the new Congress be empowered "to negative all laws passed by the several States, contravening in the opinion of the National Legislature the articles of Union," and if necessary use military force to back up that negative.

The delegates at the moment could hardly see Madison's logic—or at least the logical extension of his belief in checks and balances—that the national government must have a check on state governments just as each branch of government would have a check on the others. All the delegates could envisage was a radical threat to the very existence of their constituencies. And all they could see was Randolph—himself the governor of a state —threatening to submerge New Jersey and New Hampshire and the other proud little republics in a great national pool. Did the Virginians really want this? When Randolph reiterated his proposals the following day, Charles Pinckney rose to ask whether the governor "meant to abolish the State Governments altogether."

Randolph did not, of course, but the gauntlet had been thrown down. For the next two weeks the Virginians and their allies—James Wilson of Pennsylvania, along with several of the South Carolina delegation and others—pressed their arguments, while their opponents questioned them and attacked them whenever they could get the floor. Madison demonstrated his parliamentary skills in keeping control of the agenda; when he sensed that it would be premature for the assembly to discuss representation of the slave population in Congress, he smoothly moved that that matter be postponed.

The Virginians had powerful assistance from other delegates. The Pennsylvanians were especially helpful, especially prestigious, and especially nationalistic. Franklin, though so feeble that he sometimes asked others to speak his sentiments for him, intervened at critical moments. James Wilson, a Philadelphian born and educated in Scotland, had helped lead the cause of independence and later had become heavily involved—some said overextended—in banking and business investments. Portrayed by William Pierce of South Carolina, who wrote down pithy evaluations of his colleagues, as a "fine genius . . . well acquainted with Man and . . . all the passions that influence him," and as "no great Orator" but "clear, copious, and comprehensive," Wilson took an almost uncompromising position for a powerful national government. He was supported by the two wealthy and sophisticated Morrises, Robert and Gouverneur, and by several other members of a strong delegation, including Thomas Fitzsimmons, a merchant and banker and one of two Catholics among the delegates.

A noted man at the convention was the head of the Delaware delegation, John Dickinson, a distinguished lawyer, member of several Congresses, and the author of *Letters from a Farmer in Pennsylvania,* a widely read tract, in the years just prior to the Revolution, on the proper and improper powers of Parliament. Massachusetts could not send its ablest sons to the convention—John Adams was in London, Samuel Adams was aging, James Bowdoin bereft of his governorship, General Knox in New York serving as Secretary of War—but the Bay State was nevertheless able to contribute four gifted moderate nationalists: Nathaniel Gorham of Charlestown, Caleb Strong of Northampton, Rufus King of Newburyport, and Elbridge Gerry of Marblehead. This quartet was matched in prestige and articulateness by South Carolina's trio of the experienced planter-lawyer John Rutledge, the eminent lawyer-general Charles Cotesworth Pinckney, and his second cousin Charles Pinckney, deeply experienced in law, politics, and soldiering for a man still in his twenties. The strangest delegation was New York's, consisting of the ambitious continentalist Alexander Hamilton "chaperoned"—and outvoted—by two cautious anti-Federalists.

On the face of it, the cardinal question facing the convention seemed simple: how much power to yield to the new federal government at the expense of the states? This "division of powers" was closely related, however, to "separation of powers." How should power be divided up among the legislative, executive, and judicial branches of the new federal government? And these two questions were related in turn to extraordinarily complex issues of representation: by what persons should members of the two houses of Congress, the executive, and the judiciary be appointed or elected, for terms of what length, and with what checks or vetoes upon one another? And attitudes toward all these questions were closely affected by delegates' calculations of local and regional advantage; by personal experience, interest, and ideology; by concern for the likely impact of the new constitution on issues such as slavery, western expansion, foreign relations, economic policy; by faith—or lack of it—in the people's intelligence and in majority rule. The delegates had to think in terms of literally hundreds of possible permutations and combinations, with every new decision possibly upsetting positions previously arrived at.

The Virginia Plan provided a focus that helped avert parliamentary anarchy. Day after day Madison and his allies mustered the votes to put through major parts of their program, at least provisionally. By the second week of June, however, the opponents of the Virginia Plan were organizing a counterattack. The immediate issue was the most divisive that faced the convention: how the small states and the big states would be represented in Congress. And this issue was inseparable from the question of how much power Congress would wield.

On June 15 William Paterson of New Jersey rose to join battle—a gentleman of "about 34 ys. of age, of a very low stature," Pierce noted, and of rather modest appearance and presence, but "one of those kind of Men whose powers break in upon you, and create wonder and astonishment." He offered a counterplan to the Virginians', supported by men who were less famous throughout America than delegates like Madison and Hamilton, but well known and highly regarded in their states, nonetheless: men like Roger Sherman, a Connecticut politician, self-taught lawyer, Yale treasurer; Luther Martin, Princeton graduate, a lawyer, a patriot, but tending toward both the bottle and the battological; John Lansing of Albany, owner of a vast tract of land in upstate New York, a friendly, good-looking man who generally took the anti-nationalist line. Paterson and his colleagues seemed to challenge the Virginia Plan on almost every point, especially in their plea for a new national Congress of one chamber that would represent the large and the small states equally.

With the issue of confrontation clear, the convention moved on to new heights of oratory and argumentation. Emotions rose to such a pitch that there were veiled warnings of walkouts, and indeed of a separation of states and disintegration of the Union. But the convention was never in serious danger. The New Jersey Plan had accepted the major premises of the Virginia Plan: expanded power for the national government; the authority of that government to act directly on individuals and not merely on states; the national executive to have coercive authority over the states if necessary to enforce the law. Committees of compromising politicians were set up and the rival plans were adjusted to each other. Historians have generally written that the "Connecticut compromise" came to the rescue of the beleaguered convention, but in fact the main feature of the compromise —election of an upper chamber on the basis of equality between large and small states, and election of a lower chamber through popular representation—had been foreshadowed in the convention deliberations almost from the start. It was a natural compromise, granting both the Virginians and the New Jerseyites the kind of representation they wanted.

Because the vast majority of the delegates were so agreed on one fundamental concept, further agreements were reached during the remaining weeks of the convention. That concept was checks and balances. One might have expected the proponents of both plans to be disgruntled by the final compromise, because each chamber of Congress was given an absolute veto over the other, which meant that a "small state" Senate might block a "large state" House of Representatives, or vice versa. But neither side seemed to have this fear, mainly because all they wanted for their small states or large states was a "negative veto" to protect their existing liberties, not a positive power to join with other branches to use government in attempts to expand people's liberties. This attitude and this decision would come back to haunt the future conduct of American public affairs.

It was also because of this fundamental agreement between large- and small-staters that the convention was able to resolve, for the time being at least, some of the other knotty problems before it. One of these was the national executive. The issue arose early in the convention, and it soon became clear that the delegates had highly mixed feelings about the mechanics of the executive. After Charles Pinckney called for a "vigorous executive" but feared that it might exercise powers over "peace and war" more appropriate to a monarchy, and after Wilson moved that the executive consist of a single person, a considerable pause ensued, and Rutledge remarked on the "shyness of gentlemen" on this subject. They were less shy than uncertain. Sherman considered the "Executive magistracy" to be nothing more than an agency for carrying out the will of the new Congress. Gerry wanted a council annexed to the executive, "in order to give weight and inspire confidence." Randolph condemned "a unity in the Executive" as the "foetus of monarchy." Wilson replied: No, it would be the best safeguard against tyranny. Madison suggested mildly that before choosing between a unity and a plurality in the executive, they might fix the extent of executive authority.

On this matter too, the delegates' differences were largely on points of detail. Certainly the executive should have some kind of veto over the legislative; should exercise initiative and assume responsibility in the making of foreign policy; should possess considerable control over his own executive branch, through the appointive power and the like. The President would be given authority to conduct war as Commander in Chief, but not the unilateral power to declare or make war; he would have no general prerogative to exercise emergency powers, although it was assumed he would act for the national self-defense. The Framers argued at length over some of these questions but did not sharply disagree, because they all wanted to grant the President a balanced and limited set of powers within the overall framework of the strategy of checks and balances.

The men of Philadelphia showed a far less firm grasp on the question of how to elect the executive. Knowing today the crucial differences between the parliamentary and presidential forms of government, we read the convention debates almost suspensefully as the delegates teeter back and forth between selection of the President by Congress and election by the state legislatures or by the voters. The delegates were more impressed by the dilemma than by the drama. Gerry opposed legislative selection of the President on the ground that Congress and the presidential candidates would constantly "intrigue" and "bargain and play into one another's hands."

In the end, the Framers decided on a jerry-built institution called the electoral college, designed to create a bulwark between the aroused passions of the people and the office of the chief executive and, in the spirit of the checks and balances, to make the executive and legislative branches responsible to different constituencies. The common assumption that George Washington would be the first President nourished agreement on the presidential election process.

On the national judiciary, most of the delegates were agreed as to its general shape and role but divided over mechanics. The judicial power would be vested in one supreme tribunal, and Congress would have authority to establish inferior federal courts. The question of the reach of the judiciary was left obscure; most delegates assumed, however, that the Supreme Court would at least be able to invalidate acts of the states and probably also acts of Congress. Both powers would fit neatly into the checks and balances strategy. So should the manner of choosing the judges, though here the delegates disagreed. In one early session, James Wilson opposed congressional selection on the grounds that "Experience shewed the impropriety of such appointmts. by numerous bodies," according to Madison's notes. "Intrigue, partiality, and concealment were the necessary consequences." But "Mr. Rutlidge was by no means disposed to grant so great a power to any single person. The people will think we are leaning too much towards Monarchy." Madison was inclined to give the power to the Senate. Franklin "in a brief and entertaining manner" reminded the delegates of the "Scotch mode"—lawyers were given the power to nominate, and they always selected the ablest "in order to get rid of him, and share his practice [among themselves]." Eventually the delegates took advantage of the planned separate entities of the President and the Senate, the first of whom would propose, and the second confirm, appointments to the Supreme Court for life.

On the festering and rankling issue of slavery the delegates compromised from start to finish. Indeed, the delegates were already compromised before the start of the convention, for the "federal ratio" of three-fifths "representation" for slaves had been established under the Confederation and still reflected a crude balance of sections, ideology, and interests. Facing the delegates was not merely the stark issue of slavery itself; intertwined with it was the question of whether representation should be based on persons alone or also on property. Not only Southerners but Northerners like Rufus King and Gouverneur Morris believed in extra representation for property, and in the eyes of the law slaves were property, not persons.

For these white men the black man was always a brooding and unsettling presence (the black woman, even more than the white woman, was beyond the pale, beyond calculation). For the black man, the white man deciding on slave representation could be a cause only of sardonic reflection. For the issue never was slave representation, slave votes, slave power; it was whether slaves would not count in the representation of the South at all, or whether a *slave owner* would enjoy a three-fifths increment of representation for every slave he owned. On this latter choice the slave could reflect that he had been granted three-fifths symbolic manhood. William Paterson told the delegates bluntly that slaves were "no free agents, have no personal liberty, no faculty of acquiring property, but on the contrary, are themselves property" and hence like other property "entirely at the will of the master."

For the black man, exclusion from the reach of liberty and equality, even on solemn occasions glorifying liberty and equality for "all men," was already an old story. In his first draft of the Declaration of Independence, Thomas Jefferson had indicted King George for the horrors of the slave trade, only to have this clause struck out from the final draft on the insistence of South Carolinians and other seacoast Southerners. And even in Massachusetts, where slaves had been "freed," emancipation was accomplished by judicial decree rather than legislative action. What white workers really wanted, in Donald Robinson's words, "was not the emancipation of the slaves, but their removal from the state."

Throughout the heated debates that followed, the three-fifths formula stuck. Another seeming compromise was reached on the issue of the slave trade: abolition not before 1808, with a powerful extradition clause written into the Constitution. What the delegates did not do was more important than what they did: "they did not themselves outlaw slavery," Rossiter noted, "nor in any way seek to mitigate its effects; they did not give Congress the power to outlaw slavery in the states; they made provision neither to help nor hinder free Negroes in the attempt to win the status and rights of citizenship." The reason was obvious to all: a stronger stand on slavery would probably have led to rejection of the Constitution in the South, and eventually to disunion.

Union and order and national strength were far more important to most of the Framers than were the rights or liberties of black men and women. For only in union and order, most of them believed, could their own liberties be protected.

And so the men of Philadelphia persevered through the hot July and August days, filling out the details now that the grand design had been set in the Connecticut compromise, sawing boards to make them fit, as Benjamin Franklin said. Some of the boards required much sanding and smoothing, as the delegates thrashed out irksome but vital aspects of the relations between the national and state governments, the enumerated powers of Congress, the jurisdiction of the courts, the reach of impeachment, the amending clause, and procedures for ratifying the Constitution itself. They endured hundreds of roll-call votes as they polished clause after clause of the new charter. They debated the "details" of the Constitution as if they foresaw that someday vital outcomes would turn on such matters as the availability of impeachment or the scope of judicial review. They deliberated as if the eyes of the world were on them. "With Grave Anxiety, my dear friend, I wait for the Result of the Convention," Lafayette had written John Jay, who was keeping in touch with delegates from his post in New York. Hour after hour the delegates toiled, six days a week, with hardly a break, except for a ten-day recess during which a committee on detail consolidated the work of the convention, while the rest of the delegates dined out, tackled their correspondence, took excursions into the countryside, and went fishing. Philadelphia offered few temptations; nights were given over to further talk in taverns and in the delegates' hot and crowded quarters.

There were diversions. One was the spectacle of Alexander Hamilton taking the floor for six hours one day to orate brilliantly on the need for a powerful national government and a President of almost monarchical cast. The delegates listened avidly, then returned to their mundane carpentry. Another was John Fitch's steamboat, which the inventor demonstrated down at the river. Watching the ungainly, heaving, panting contraption, the delegates could hardly have dreamed that steam would transform the very society and economy they were seeking to tame.

CHAPTER 2

The Third Cadre

T HE story has often been told of the final conciliatory moment of the convention, on September 17—of Benjamin Franklin's remark, as the last members were signing, that during the vicissitudes of the proceedings he had often looked at the president's chair, on which a sun happened to be painted, and wondered whether it was a rising or a setting sun; but now, he said, he knew that it was rising. The delegates later repaired to the City Tavern on Second Street near Walnut, where they "dined together," Washington reported, "and took a cordial leave of each other."

Nevertheless, the convention adjourned amid extensive disagreements and misgivings. Three delegates—Randolph, Mason, and Gerry—refused to put their names on the document. Others signed mainly to present a show of unity. A number of delegates lamented especially the absence of a bill of rights. When Charles Pinckney and Elbridge Gerry had proposed in convention that the "liberty of the Press should inviolably be observed," Sherman had replied, "It is unnecessary—the power of Congress does not extend to the Press," and the proposal was voted down. Sherman's argument had sat badly; how could a constitution fashioned to protect liberty omit a guarantee of liberty? Still, delegates felt that this omission and other failures in the charter could be remedied through extensive use of the amendment process that they had fashioned so carefully. Some calculated that adding a bill of rights could be made the price of accepting the new charter.

Still, the delegates had passed a hard test of leadership in Philadelphia. The question in the fall of 1787 was whether these leaders could pass the far harsher test of winning support for the new charter in the ratifying conventions to be held in the states. At the start, prospects looked good for the "friends of the Constitution." They were led by Madison, Hamilton, Wilson, and others who had demonstrated their political skills year after year, in struggle after struggle. They had both an evocative symbol and a stalwart leader in George Washington. They had access to clergymen, editors, state officials. They could boast of a reserve team of leaders who had not attended the convention but who matched the Federalists at Philadelphia in their political experience and acumen—men like John Adams of Boston and London, Thomas Jefferson of Charlottesville and Paris, John Jay of New York, John Marshall and Edmund Pendleton of Virginia, Dr. Benjamin Rush of Pennsylvania, Edward Rutledge and Henry Laurens of South Carolina.

The Federalist plan was to push quickly through Congress, in which they were well represented, a resolution transmitting the draft Constitution on to the states with a recommendation in favor of ratification. But the national legislature, still cautious to the point of inertia, would not commit itself; and the Federalists had to be satisfied with a resolution that the document "be transmitted to the several legislatures in order to be submitted to a convention of delegates chosen in each state by the people thereof." Richard Henry Lee of Virginia complained to his fellow anti-Federalist George Mason that the Federalists had made much of the Congress *unanimously* transmitting the Constitution to the states, "hoping to have it mistaken for an unanimous approbation of the thing . . . [but] no approbation was given." The Federalist tacticians also saw to it that the legislatures *had* to call conventions in their states, and that the Constitution would go into effect—for the ratifying states—after endorsement by conventions in any nine of the thirteen states. The new order would not wait for unanimity.

For a time the critics of the Constitution seemed thrown off balance by the Federalist momentum. But the anti-Federalists had a general strategy too. If the strength of the Federalists lay in their power to dominate the central and secret conclave in Philadelphia, that of their foes was to rally the opposition in the separate states. If the strength of the Federalists lay also in possessing a positive plan that would catalyze the amorphous political groupings in America, that of their foes was to unite the opponents of the Constitution, despite their own disagreements, in efforts to delay, amend, or repudiate the charter in the battle arenas of the states. The anti-Federalists were not overawed by the eminence of their leading opponents. One of them, annoyed by the incessant prating about the demigods of Philadelphia, remarked that he would not make invidious comments about their characters, "but I will venture to affirm, that twenty assemblies of equal number might be collected, equally respectable both in point of ability, integrity, and patriotism." The foes of the Constitution could point to their own leadership in the convention—Mason, Gerry, and the others —and to their remarkable second team throughout the country, with state leaders such as Richard Henry Lee, Governor George Clinton of New York, Samuel Adams, and above all, the formidable Patrick Henry of Virginia.

Among the Federalist leaders, none was more active than Alexander Hamilton, now barely thirty-two years old. During the summer of 1787, as Robert Yates and John Lansing returned from Philadelphia and spread rumors that a consolidated national government was being contrived, he fell into a row with Governor Clinton, who was already busy rallying the opposition in New York State. Hamilton was at his worst in this encounter. Choosing the dangerous pseudonym "Caesar," indulging freely in personal attacks, he took such an elitist position in favor of a strong national government, in which popular passions would be curbed to defend the people's own liberties, that he confirmed the anti-Federalists' worst suspicions. So Hamilton turned to a mere cerebral approach—a collaborative series of reasoned and trenchant essays on the Constitution, to be published in New York newspapers, and he had the wit to involve in this enterprise James Madison and John Jay, both of whom were in New York City at this time. By late October, Hamilton had struck off the first number of the *Federalist*—written, it has been said, on a vessel proceeding up the Hudson—in which the author called for moderation and then went on to argue that "a dangerous ambition more often lurks behind the specious mask of zeal for the rights of the people, than under the forbidding appearance of zeal for the firmness and efficiency of government." The vigor of government was essential, he argued, to the "security of liberty."

It was a remarkable collaboration. So agreed were the authors on their ends and their means, so similar was their background in ancient and contemporary classics, that readers could not recognize the particular author of a paper. Hamilton evidently had hoped that the three authors could meet regularly at his house at the corner of Broadway and Wall Street to unify the papers, but the trio were all too busy for this. He wisely chose Jay, still Secretary of Foreign Affairs, to write on foreign policy, Madison to philosophize on the shape and structure of the new government, and himself to demonstrate the inadequacies of the Confederation —a subject on which Hamilton viewed himself as an expert.

The authors wrote in secrecy, using the benign pseudonym "Publius"; Washington was one of the few to know something about the authorship. Throughout the late fall and winter of 1787–88 the papers appeared in the New York *Packet* on Tuesdays and Fridays and in the *Independent Journal* Wednesdays and Saturdays. Another newspaper ran some of the essays, but dropped the series after anti-Federalists aroused pressure from subscribers. So avidly were the essays sought after by "politicians and persons of every description," the publishers John and Archibald McLean reported, that they issued a collected edition in March 1788, long before the end of the struggle over ratification.

Not even the enthusiastic McLeans could guess that a later publisher would be able to say with good reason that the *Federalist* was "America's greatest contribution to political philosophy." What attracted attention to the papers even at the time was the enlarged vision and the sophisticated analysis that the authors brought to their pitch for the new system. Although the essayists—especially Madison—drew heavily on their own earlier writings, they seemed to grow intellectually as they struck off the papers, sometimes as the printer waited impatiently.

Madison obviously liked his own earlier comments about the human tendency of liberty toward factionalism; the need nonetheless to protect liberty and find some other way to curb faction, which was sown in the very nature of man; the many varieties of faction, including the frivolous but most of all the economic ("the various and unequal distribution of property"). He contended still that the *causes* of faction could not be removed, and hence the only remedy was to control its *effects,* and that this could be accomplished by submerging factions in a wider sphere—namely, under a new, strong, national government. These ideas appeared in the 10th paper.

But Madison went far beyond his earlier writings intellectually in facing the supreme dilemma—the possibility that powerful factions, whether minority or majority, might capture the new national government just as they had come close to dominating state governments. No one has ever described the ultimate remedy—separation of House, Senate, executive, and judiciary, with each branch responsible to its own unique, competing constituency—as cogently and compellingly as Madison did in the 51st paper. "To what expedient then," he asked after a long survey of the dilemma, "shall we finally resort for maintaining in practice the necessary partition of power among the several departments, as laid down in the constitution? The only answer that can be given is, that as all these exterior provisions are found to be inadequate, the defect must be supplied, by so contriving the interior structure of the government, as that its several constituent parts may, by their mutual relations, be the means of keeping each other in their proper places." Each department must be as separate as possible, with a will of its own. Then came the imperishable words:

"But the great security against a gradual concentration of the several powers in the same department, consists in giving to those who administer each department the necessary constitutional means and personal motives to resist encroachments of the others. The provision for defence must in this, as in all other cases, be made commensurate to the danger of attack. Ambition must be made to counteract ambition. The interest of the man must be connected with the constitutional rights of the place. It may be a reflection on human nature, that such devices should be necessary to controul the abuses of government. But what is government itself but the greatest of all reflections on human nature? If men were angels, no government would be necessary. If angels were to govern men, neither external nor internal controuls on government would be necessary. In framing a government which is to be administered by men over men, the great difficulty lies in this: You must first enable the government to controul the governed; and in the next place oblige it to controul itself. A dependence on the people, is no doubt, the primary controul on the government; but experience has taught mankind the necessity of auxiliary precautions."

It was Madison's capacity to combine deep political and psychological understanding—as in his summary statement of the strategy of "supplying by opposite and rival interests, the defect of better motives"—that would justify his reputation as both the intellectual and political father of the Constitution.

The Anti-Federalists

The opponents of the Constitution still declined to yield to this Federalist display of political and intellectual power. They had their own strength to fall back on, their own networks of friendly preachers, politicians, and newspaper editors. The anti-Federalist leaders were far less celebrated nationally than Washington, Franklin et al., but Madison himself was struck by the large number of "respectable names" he found among his adversaries. They had their own ideological strategy—to charge the framers of the Constitution with not only ignoring the needs of liberty but actively conspiring against it—and they polished their political tactics of dividing and eviscerating their adversaries as the struggle over the Constitution dissolved into numberless state and local encounters, so that the great national issue would be sucked into the whirlpools of local and state politics. Attacking parts of the Constitution rather than the whole charter, the anti-Federalists demanded not the repudiation of Philadelphia but the right of state conventions to pass amendments to the Constitution and in effect to gain a *second* convention. Nothing distressed the Framers more than this prospect. To return to Philadelphia for another session would throw them on the defensive, inundate them in a sea of incompatible amendments, and produce a far weaker national charter. The Federalists would accept *recommendations* for the new Congress under the Constitution to consider, but amendments to the existing draft—never!

And so the issue was put to the American people in the late fall of 1787

—put not to a great mass public, though large numbers of voters would turn out to elect state convention delegates, put not to small national or state elites, though established leaders would exercise heavy influence in many of the contests, but put to about 1,200 delegates who would be elected to the state conventions in hundreds of tiny contests across the thousand-mile length of the American states. A first cadre in Philadelphia had written a charter; a second cadre of state leadership was quick to join the battle; now the issue would depend on a third cadre, composed largely of local politicians from the American backlands—the western counties, the farm area, the piedmont, the mountain valleys—as well as from the urban and cosmopolitan areas. These men must analyze a complex document, follow the debates in press and pulpit and public house, and manage also to get elected as delegates. The future of the republic would turn on the perspicacity and vision of country politicians, circuit-riding lawyers, money-minded men of commerce, cracker-barrel philosophers—on a critical mass of men who would have to lift their sights above gables and chimney pots and see their way into the possibilities of nationhood.

The Federalists exulted over smashing victories in several of the smaller states that acted early on ratification. The Delaware convention voted unanimously for the new charter on December 7, 1787, followed by similar votes in the New Jersey and Georgia delegations within a month. But Pennsylvania had acted in the meantime, and the fate of the Constitution in this big state, considered to be heavily pro-Federalist, warned the friends of the Constitution that trouble lay ahead. In no state had the charter been more intensely debated than in Pennsylvania, with its plethora of newspapers and of printers eager to publish pamphlets and broadsides. In no state was the press more one-sidedly pro-Federalist, nor were so many thousands of petitions submitted in behalf of the new plan of government. But the anti-Federalists were organized too, prepared to employ the tactics of dissection and delay, and they seized on a procedural incident to pose a moral argument against the Framers.

The incident came the day after the Congress, still sitting in New York City, voted to transmit the Constitution to the states. An express rider galloped through the night to put the resolution into the hands of the Pennsylvania Assembly, with its impatient Federalist majority. The opponents of the Federalists were also prepared, armed with a provision of the Pennsylvania constitution that required two-thirds of the members, rather than the usual majority, to make up a quorum. When the Assembly met that morning the Federalists found the enemy absent—hence no quorum.

Indignant, the majority ordered the sergeant at arms to "collect the absent members." The sergeant and his minions proceeded to track down the errant assemblymen in the streets and boardinghouses of Philadelphia. Two men were finally cornered, hustled by the sergeant and some zealous citizens into the Assembly hall, and thrust into their seats. When one made a bolt for the door, his way was blocked by a mob. Armed now with their quorum, the Federalists pushed through a measure for the election of convention delegates within six weeks and the holding of the convention two weeks after that.

It was a skirmish won by the Federalists, at the risk of losing the battle. Reading about the affair in the newspapers or in letters from Philadelphia, anti-Federalists charged that the Framers were trying to shove the new instrument through without adequate popular discussion. Why the rush? The Pennsylvania Federalists, sure of their majority, pressed ahead in the hope that Pennsylvania would be the first large state to ratify the Constitution. Obscured by the clamor was the fact that the Pennsylvanians were conducting an intensive and searching analysis of the charter throughout the fall, in the long process of calling the convention, choosing a new Assembly, electing convention delegates, and debating the Constitution in the convention. In mid-December the convention voted to ratify the Constitution, 46–23, but the Federalist cause was tarnished again when rioting broke out in Carlisle, where James Wilson was burned in effigy and hundreds of militiamen advanced on the town with a threat to liberate political prisoners.

It was no surprise that Wilson—the only delegate to the national constitutional convention who took part in the Pennsylvania ratifying convention —should have exhibited his brilliance as he marshaled support for the charter. The test was whether the "average" person could adequately cope with a document of such complexity. Robert Whitehill was typical of the plain-spoken, clear-minded men from all parts of the country who stood up and debated with the more celebrated. The new Constitution, he told his fellow delegates, would lead to a consolidated government dangerous to the people's liberties. The words "We the people of the United States," he said, proved that "the old foundation of the Union is destroyed, the principle of confederation excluded, and a new unwieldy system of consolidated empire is set up upon the ruins of the present compact between the states . . . It is declared that the agreement of nine states shall be sufficient to carry the new system into operation, and, consequently, to abrogate the old one. Then, Mr. President, four of the present confederated states may not be comprehended in the compact;

shall we, sir, force these dissenting states into the measure?" Wilson and the other Pennsylvania delegates had been authorized to strengthen the Confederation Congress but "they have overthrown that government which they were called upon to amend." So forcefully did Whitehill—long viewed as a run-of-the-mill politician—pose the issue of liberty under the new Constitution that Wilson, in answering him, argued on Whitehill's ground.

With the ratifications by four middle and southern states, the epicenter of the struggle moved north as New England states prepared to hold conventions. Delegates gathered in the imposing Hartford State House during the first week of January for a session that the ruling Federalists planned to convert into a demonstration of strong leadership, as a model for the Yankees farther north. A demonstration it was, as the friends of the Constitution massed their strength in the convention, 128–40, while the anti-Federalists complained that they had been "brow beaten by many of those Cicero'es as they think themselves & others of Superior rank" who had indulged in "Shuffleing & Stamping of feet, caughing Halking Spitting & Whispering."

Massachusetts would be a different story. In no state save Virginia did the two sides seem so well matched at every level of leadership. A solid phalanx of Federalists—former Governor Bowdoin, Theodore Sedgwick of Stockbridge fame, Fisher Ames, Francis Dana, and three delegates fresh from Philadelphia—confronted a locally prestigious cohort of anti-Federalists such as Elbridge Gerry, Speaker of the Massachusetts House of Representatives James Warren, and, it was expected, the renowned Samuel Adams with his riding friend Governor John Hancock.

Gerry especially was to be feared: he had served in the constitutional convention, he had heard all the arguments, he had rejected the charter. Adams was an enigma. A Harvard graduate, an organizer of the Sons of Liberty, agitator for independence, longtime politician, he was both ideologue and wire puller, both a government man and an agitator for the cause of liberty against government. Hancock was a trimmer. The first delegate to sign the Declaration of Independence, the first governor of the state of Massachusetts, he had become immensely popular in Boston, where he was probably the richest man of his generation, and in the hinterland, on which he had bestowed free Bibles in abundance. Arrayed behind the noted leaders of both sides was the "third cadre" of county and local politicians, lawyers, judges, convention delegates, and others who had sharpened their political rhetoric and perceptions in twenty years of almost continuous disputes over issues of revolution, independence, Regulation, state constitution making, and now constitution ratifying for the nation.

Gerry opened with a letter to the Massachusetts legislature that intoned the familiar litany of the dangerous blending of executive, legislative, and judicial power, lack of provision for rotation of office, senators virtually appointed for life—but returned again and again to charges of lack of protection for rights of conscience, liberty of the press, trial by jury—in short, the lack of a bill of rights. Gerry's style was "too sublime and florid" for certain of the "common people," some Albany Federalists said. But his attack on the alleged chicanery, intrigue, duplicity, and imbecility of the framers of the Constitution opened the Massachusetts struggle on a note of rancor.

Boston—commercial, cosmopolitan, seafaring, internationalist Boston —was a hotbed of Federalist agitation. Most of its eight newspapers steadily praised the new Constitution, ranging from sober analysis of its provisions to castigations of its opponents as ignorant, shortsighted, weak-headed, bad-hearted, *wicked*. It was an age of invective, and few paid particular attention when a Federalist denounced opponents as "blind, positive, conceited sons of bitches" who deserved roasting in hell. When the *American Herald* broke the press phalanx and attacked the Constitution, Federalist merchants pulled out their advertising and Federalist readers canceled their subscriptions. Why should we finance attacks on our own opinions? one of them asked.

The opponents of the Constitution in Massachusetts were part of a nationwide network, though far less extensive than the Federalists'. As if he needed any coaching, Samuel Adams received letters from Richard Henry Lee urging that the new Constitution "be bottomed upon a Declaration or bill of Rights." Lee felt free to press his views on Adams because he had "long toiled with you my dear friend in the Vineyard of liberty . . ." Like the Federalists, critics of the Constitution had their own pulpits —the town meetings that would elect convention delegates from the country areas of Massachusetts, often with instructions on how to vote. Anti-Federalist feeling ran strong in scores of towns in western and central Massachusetts, where the grievances that erupted in Shays's Rebellion (as it had come to be called)—and the memories of its suppression—still rankled. Sometimes the Federalists prevailed in the hinterland only to be accused of ramming the Constitution down the "throats of others" in the spirit of Pennsylvania. In Sheffield the leading Federalist was accused of a hat trick: "Instead of seting it"—the hat for collecting ballots—"fair & open on the Table as usual," he "held it in his Left hand Pressed Close to his breast . . ." The pattern of seacoast Federalism and inland opposition also appeared in Maine, then part of Massachusetts. The election of convention delegates reflected this split. Federalists scored so heavily in eastern towns that Gerry himself was beaten in Cambridge, and James Warren in Milton, but a "cloud" of anti-Federalists were elected inland, and Adams and Hancock won in Boston.

In mid-January—just a year after troops had moved west to subdue Shays and his men—350 delegates were arriving in Boston by carriage and sleigh. The meeting house on Milk Street had been enlarged to seat several hundred spectators, with a special gallery for newspaper reporters. The audience watched a Federalist minority led by skillful publicists and parliamentarians outmaneuver an apparent anti-Constitution majority. Evidently considering Gerry safer within the convention hall than outside, the friends of the Constitution acquiesced in a motion by Samuel Adams that Gerry be permitted a seat on the floor to supply information "that *possibly* had Escaped the memory of the other Gentlemen of the general Convention." The Federalists treated Gerry so rudely, however, that he quit the floor in a huff. Without him the anti-Federalist leadership seemed to falter, though some of the country delegates performed brilliantly.

Samuel Nasson, a Maine saddler and storekeeper, rose to "beg the indulgence" of the convention while he made "a short apostrophe to liberty. O, liberty! thou greatest good! thou fairest property! With thee I wish to live, with thee I wish to die!" He shed a rhetorical tear over the perils to which liberty was exposed, first at the hands of British tyranny and now before the power of Congress. Nasson and his colleague John Taylor peppered the Federalists with more prosaic objections too: questions about the Constitution's mechanics, attacks on its concessions to slavery, and arguments in favor of the annual election of legislators.

Still facing the possibility of defeat, the friends of the Constitution adopted the stratagem of accepting their opponents' most convincing amendments—especially those relating to the absence of a bill of rights—and of urging that they be proposed not as the condition of ratifying the Constitution but as amendments recommended to the future Congress. Further, the Federalists induced John Hancock—on the promise, it was said, of supporting him for Vice-President of the new Union, or even for President, if Virginia stayed out—to offer this amendment procedure to the convention.

The dismayed anti-Federalists, now turning to the tactic of delay, moved that the convention adjourn so that the towns could discuss the proposed amendments. This effort failed by a lopsided vote. The convention then ratified the Constitution with the recommended amendments, 187–168, a narrow vote that gave the Federalists pause. They had possessed the advantage of the ablest leadership, strong press support, backing from Congregationalist leaders, the symbolism of George Washington and of Union. The anti-Federalists, on the other hand, suffered from faltering leadership at the top and some bad luck. Yet the foes of the Constitution had almost won, testifying to the strength of their leadership corps at the grass roots. The country politicians and farmers and lawyers had risen to the challenge, sometimes to heights of oratory. The near-defeat also warned the Federalists that the American hinterland was still to be heard from.

And heard it was, all across New England. In New Hampshire during January, meeting after meeting in the hilly upland towns elected anti-Federalist delegates to that state's convention. Viewing the proceedings, a man in Maine reported that "it is with them as it was with us the Country Members Mostely against the Traiding Towns for it." The seaboard towns were not numerous enough to counteract the interior. The New Hampshire Federalists, seizing on a device they had denounced elsewhere, managed to stave off defeat by gaining a recess of the convention until June. In Rhode Island the country leaders in the legislature spurned a convention and called a popular referendum, which the Federalists boycotted; their adversaries won overwhelmingly. This was in late March, the nadir of hopes for the new charter.

Support for the Constitution was much warmer toward the south. In Maryland in April the Federalist near-oligarchy won overwhelming control of the convention in the delegate elections and arranged for a brief sitting, where they allowed their foes to talk, declined to debate against them, brushed aside recommendatory amendments, ratified the Constitution by a 63–11 vote, and adjourned—all in four working days. In South Carolina the delegate elections produced the usual split between the seacoast and the western counties, with Charleston almost solidly pro-Constitution. Just as effectively as their counterpart in Maryland, but with more elegance, the Federalist oligarchy arranged to hold the ratifying convention in Charleston, where in May they plied country delegates with sherry and Madeira, squelched an effort to postpone the session until October, accepted some recommendatory amendments, and won ratification by a 149–73 vote. In both cases the anti-Federalist leadership failed to measure up to its opponents.

On June 21, 1788, the postponed New Hampshire convention approved the charter by a close vote, the ninth ratification. The new Constitution was now in effect. The Federalists did little celebrating, however, since two key states had not acted: Virginia, the link between north and south and the home of Washington and other heroes; and New York, the hinge between the middle and northern states, and a vital commercial center, with its great port and long, slow-flowing river.

THE COURSE IS SET

No state surpassed Virginia in its array of talent on both sides of the ratification struggle. Its celebrated leaders—Washington, Madison, Randolph, and Mason—were flanked by a leadership corps of hardly less esteem—John Marshall, Henry Lee, and Edmund Pendleton—for the Constitution. Poised against them were Richard Henry Lee, James Monroe, William Grayson, John Tyler, and Benjamin Harrison, but towering over the anti-Federalist group was Patrick Henry, impassioned orator, oracle of liberty, first governor of the state of Virginia.

At fifty-two Henry—bespectacled and slightly stooped, his thinning hair topped by a nomadic wig—had lost a little of his fire. But he still drew crowds when word flashed through the countryside that he was speaking in the local courthouse. As a recent settler in Prince Edward County, Henry had close connections with Kentuckians coming from southern Virginia who were convinced that Northerners would jeopardize settlement of the vast lands to the west. They feared men like John Jay, who had made supine agreements with Spain, holder of the southern Mississippi. Patrick Henry, a bowed figure in clothes made on his own loom, set off for Richmond at the end of May in a simple, topless gig.

He did not disappoint the spectators gathered in Richmond. As in other states, Federalist leaders, better prepared than their foes, quickly gained control of the organization and agenda of the convention. But nothing could control Henry. Stating flatly that he considered himself to be his fellow Virginians' "sentinel over their rights, liberty, and happiness," he sought to pre-empt the supreme issue of liberty for the anti-Federalists. "The rights of conscience, trial by jury, liberty of the press, all your immunities and franchises, all pretensions to human rights and privileges are rendered insecure, if not lost, by this change," he told the congregation. "Liberty, the greatest of earthly possessions—give us that precious jewel, and you may take everything else! But I am fearful I have lived long enough to become an old-fashioned fellow. Perhaps an invincible attachment to the dearest rights of man may, in these refined, enlightened days, be deemed old-fashioned; if so, I am contented to be so. . . ."

Some able Federalists were ready to answer Henry—Governor Randolph, who at last had come down on the side of the Constitution, Pendleton, Henry Lee, and a rising young lawyer from Richmond, John Marshall. But the center of attention was James Madison. The congressman had remained in New York throughout the winter, writing a string of Federalist papers, tending to what little business Congress had, and indefatigably planning tactics and exchanging intelligence with friends throughout the states. He had supposed he might not need to attend the Virginia convention, until he was warned that Henry and his allies were inflaming the public against the Constitution.

Madison was even threatened at home. An anti-Federalist candidate had announced for convention in Madison's county; "his unwared Labours Riding his Carquits [circuit] & the Instruments he makes use of to Obtain his Election," a friend wrote Madison, "misrepresents things in such Horred carrecters that the weker clas of the people are much predegessed agains it. . . . amoungs his Friends appears, in a General way the Baptus's, the Prechers of that Society are much alarm'd fearing Relegious liberty is not Sufficiently secur'd. . . ." Madison had returned home and beaten this opponent by a four-to-one vote.

Now he was facing the formidable Henry, without Henry's oratorical power. In a low voice that sometimes failed to carry to the packed hall, he bluntly confronted Henry's main argument. "He told us, that this constitution ought to be rejected, because it endangered the public liberty, in his opinion, in many instances." He wished the honorable gentleman would give details rather than vague assertions, Madison went on. "He has suggested that licentiousness has seldom produced the loss of liberty; but that the tyranny of rulers has almost always effected it. Since the general civilization of mankind, I believe there are more instances of the abridgment of the freedom of the people, by gradual and silent ancroachments of those in power, than by violent and sudden usurpations: but, on a candid examination of history, we shall find that turbulence, violence, and abuse of power, by the majority trampling on the rights of the minority have produced factions and commotions, which, in republics, have more frequently than any other cause, produced despotism." Madison went on to specify the various means whereby nations had lost their liberties.

It took all the resources the Federalists could muster—not only Madison's matchless knowledge of the letter and spirit of the Constitution, but Randolph's new support for the charter, the bluntness of "Light-Horse Harry" Lee, advice from out-of-state eminences such as the two Morrises from Pennsylvania, and the pervading sense that the spirit of George Washington was present—to keep Henry and his stalwarts from cutting into the slight margin that the friends of the Constitution had gained in the election of the convention delegates. One anti-Federalist viewed the convention as evenly divided, with "one half of her crew hoisting sail for the land of *energy,* and the other looking with a longing aspect on the shore of *liberty.* " Day after day the delegates debated every major aspect of the charter.

A timely concession by the Federalists swung the balance. Yielding to Henry's impassioned calls for the protection of liberty, Madison and his allies accepted recommendations for a number of amendments that would constitute a bill of rights, including freedom of religion, speech, and assembly; no excessive bail or cruel and unusual punishment; and retention of the jury system. It was the Massachusetts formula, and it convinced wavering delegates in Richmond as it had earlier in Boston.

Unappeased, Henry took the floor for a climactic assault. Amid darkening skies outside and the crackling of thunder, he warned of the "awful immensity of the dangers" in the Constitution, castigated Randolph, and clung to his role of sentinel of liberty.

The Federalist ranks held firm, but the convention was still closely divided between tidewater and northern counties for ratification, and southern Virginia and Kentucky opposed. The decision lay with the sixteen delegates from the Alleghenies, between the Shenandoah Valley and the upper Ohio. These frontiersmen appreciated the philosophical arguments for liberty—their leader, George Jackson of Clarksville, had taught himself to read by painstakingly working his way through Coke and Blackstone—but they made their choice on grounds of practical local interests: a strong federal government, they hoped, would clear their lands of Indians. The Allegheny men voted 15–1 in favor; the Constitution passed 88–80.

The Federalists did not celebrate with abandon; it had been too close-run a thing. And it would have been impossible without the presence of Washington at Mount Vernon. James Monroe wrote Jefferson: "Be assured his influence carried this government."

The climax of the ratification struggle was now approaching in New York, where the ratifying convention was already in session. In many respects this struggle paralleled those in other states: the same rough split between the commercial-cosmopolitan leaders on the urban seacoast and the rural and small-town politicians in the interior; the same lively debate dominated by criticism of the absence of a bill of rights; the same division within, as well as between, cadres of leadership. But in New York State the Federalists were supported not only by the coastal interests but also by the great patroons and landlords in the Hudson Valley, and their opponents by laborers, tenants, artisans, and small tradespeople, led by their champion, Governor George Clinton. The convention would be another showdown—perhaps the final one—between Clinton and Hamilton.

A "self-made man," the son of an Irish immigrant, George Clinton had served as a lieutenant of rangers in the French and Indian wars and as a brigadier general in the Revolution. Not yet fifty, he had already had a long career in political office, including ten years as governor of New York. As in other states, the two rivals were flanked by able leaders—Hamilton by John Jay, Chancellor Livingston, James Duane, Isaac Roosevelt; Clinton by John Lansing, General John Lamb, and, not least, Melancton Smith, a prominent merchant-lawyer.

Both sides had thrown themselves into the battle for convention delegates. The anti-Federalists in New York City organized the Federal Republican Committee, which distributed widely copies of Mercy Warren's attack on the Constitution. They were accused of "daily going about to poison the Tenants" on the large estates. Each side hinted secession—the anti-Federalists of New York State from the Union, the Federalists of New York City from the state. Hamilton himself was not above ethnic politics. In a campaign broadside he was one of fifty-five New Yorkers who assured "Friends and Countrymen, that the SCOTSMEN of this City, with very few Exceptions, are friendly to the New Plan of Government." Each side bombarded the other in the press. A Clintonian complained that the opposition "instead of arguments, spit out a dozen mouthful of names, epithets, and interjections in a breath, cry Tory! Rebel! Tyranny! Centinel! Sidney! Monarchy! Misery! George the Third! Destruction! Arnold! Shays! Confusion! & c. & c."

The election results had mirrored the city-hinterland split; the Federalists won heavily in the four lower counties of the state, the anti-Federalists sweepingly elsewhere. Clinton, prudently running from both the city and Poughkeepsie, lost in the former and won in the latter. He had astutely arranged for the convention to be held in Poughkeepsie, away from the contaminating influence of Manhattan. But the voters seemed to be turning against the Federalists. The "elections have gone wrong," Hamilton wrote Gouverneur Morris even before the final results were in.

By June 16, when two sloops left New York City for Poughkeepsie, one carrying Federalists and the other opposition delegates, Hamilton and his friends knew that only a heroic effort could salvage a convention victory. "How are the mighty fallen!" a Clintonian gloated; not since the Revolution had the "well *born*" seemed so lacking in influence. But this view did not allow for Federalist talent. In Poughkeepsie, Hamilton gave the virtuoso performance of his career. While Clinton stayed mainly in the background, letting Melancton Smith lead the anti-Federalists in debate, Hamilton dominated the floor and still found time to buttonhole and proselytize delegates in Poughkeepsie's taverns and boardinghouses. He was waiting for the word from Virginia, and had arranged for riders to bring the tidings in relays of horses. After the express rider burst in on the convention with news of Virginia's ratification, John Jay could write Washington, "I congratulate you my dear Sir! . . . That Event has disappointed the Expectations of Opposition here, which nevertheless continues pertinacious."

The pertinacious Clintonians were not to be stampeded; they still had the votes. By now it was becoming clear to Hamilton that he could win ratification only by isolating the opposition extremists who were insisting on conditional amendments from moderates who might settle for recommendatory amendments. Hamilton had to step carefully between wings of his own party—Madison was insisting that the Constitution required "one adoption *in toto* and *for ever*"—in exploiting potential division among his foes. A number of Clintonians were won over on the promise that the host of amendments they had proposed, including bill of rights liberties, would be sent to other states with a plea for a second constitutional convention. Ratification with these non-binding amendments was voted through on July 26, by a vote of 30–27; the Federalists had recruited just enough support. Jay, whose conciliatory tactics contrasted with Hamilton's asperity, had played a key role in reaching out to wavering anti-Federalists.

The collapse of the Clintonians is still shrouded in some obscurity. Perhaps it was Hamilton's seizure of the middle ground, or the renewed threat of secession by New York City, or some failure of nerve or will, or the realization, after Virginia, that New York without ratification would be economically and politically isolated in the new Union. The end came quietly, without histrionics or serious recriminations.

If the Poughkeepsie convention ended calmly, it was the quiet of the eye of the storm. Elsewhere New Yorkers were aroused and pugnacious. An anti-Federalist parade in Albany on the Fourth of July had ended in a bloody, drunken brawl, with a dozen or so casualties. Later in the month a Federalist mob in New York City broke into a printer's shop, spilled ink, and upset type cases, closing down an opposition newspaper. Next day a great Federalist parade made its way up Broadway. Carpenters and shipyard workers towed a magnificent miniature ship they had made, its full canvas rippling in the wind and brushing the buildings on both sides of the street. The ship was named *Alexander Hamilton* and a heroic effigy of the young leader stood in the prow. At some point, however, Hamilton's arm was broken off—the arm that held aloft a copy of the Constitution. What kind of omen was this?

VICE AND VIRTUE

Mercy Otis Warren would have savored this omen, if she had heard of it. As a dramatist who had amused Bostonians with her satirical portraits of Massachusetts Tories, she would have delighted even more in caricaturing Hamilton—a true-blue native Tory, in her view—as a would-be dictator with an arm of straw. As a political writer, she welcomed the chance to inveigh against the foes of liberty.

Of all the "women of the republic" who had a pervasive private role in public affairs, Mercy Warren was perhaps the most remarkable, save for her good friend Abigail Adams. Almost sixty at the time of the Philadelphia convention, she had grown up in a family deeply immersed in the revolutionary currents of the 1770s. Denied—as a female—a formal education, she sat in on her brother's lessons, explored an uncle's library, and took part in vigorous family debates. Her idolized older brother, James Otis, had helped tutor her in politics until he was set upon by British crown officers, sabered on the head, and left deranged. Married to James Warren —a Plymouth merchant and farmer—and the mother of five sons, she had somehow found time to write verse and a half-dozen dramas. Her stock characters probably never saw the stage, for Massachusetts forbade theatrical performances; it is believed that Mercy Warren the playwright never saw a play.

Family duties and Boston blue laws, however, were not the main bar to her political expression; it was rather the solidly established idea that woman's place was in the home. Few men in Massachusetts had a better right than Mercy Warren to serve in the state's ratifying convention, but it was inconceivable that she or any other woman would attend that or any other convention, just as it was barely conceivable that women would help elect the male delegates who did attend. Mercy Warren did not challenge this masculinism. What she did was to explore the farther political reaches of the domain of the home.

A woman could write there, and Mercy Warren composed copious letters to the statesmen of the day, as well as her political plays and tracts. She could educate her sons in republican ideas and virtue; she was lucky in that all five sons grew to adulthood, unlucky in that she and her husband survived all but two of them. Even more, she could begin to construct for less advantaged women, in Linda Kerber's words, "a rationale that would permit women to attend to political matters without abandoning their domestic responsibilities, as men did." During the Revolution and after, women had often used the right of petition—a right that implied the subordination of the petitioner. Mercy Warren attacked establishments also with the play, the broadside, and the pamphlet—and it was a pamphlet she employed against the proposed Constitution. Confiding her authorship to her good friend the British historian Catharine Macauley, she used the pseudonym "A Columbian Patriot."

She began with a dire prediction: someday, when Americans would be asked what had become "of the flower of their crop, and the rich produce of their farms," they would answer as had the *Man of La Mancha*, "The Steward of 'my Lord has seized and sent it to *Madrid,'*" or more literally, tax collectors of the new national government had seized that produce and transmitted it to the *"Federal City."* Columbian Patriot went on to a blistering attack on the "many-headed monster"—its centralizing tendencies, dangerous blending of legislative and executive functions, excessive judicial power, congressional control of elections, its provision for standing armies, "the nursery of vice and the bane of liberty." She castigated the charter even more for its lacks—no provisions for rotation in office or for annual elections, and above all no bill of rights. Nor did she like the way the Constitution was drawn up in "secret conclave," or the method of ratification.

Over and over—at least a score of times—Mercy Warren portrayed the Constitution as a direct threat to liberty, freedom, personal rights. That the new government might *protect* individual rights appeared to carry no weight with her. The way to keep government safe was to tie it directly to the popular will, through frequent elections, rotation in office, and local and states' rights. Anticipating Jefferson, she wrote that the "most indubitable enemy to the publick welfare" was not sedition but despotism.

In essence, Mercy Warren was a majoritarian who would depend on the wisdom and virtue of the electorate. That such an electorate would not include a single woman did not seem to disturb her. Far more significant was her faith in popular government at a time when she had to recognize, as a daughter of Puritans and Calvinists, that vice was deeply seated in the "breasts of Americans." She quoted with approval the Abbé de Mably's observation that "the virtues and vices of a people when a revolution happens in their government, are the measure of the liberty or slavery they ought to expect—An heroic love for the publick good, a profound reverence for the laws, a contempt of riches, and a noble haughtiness of soul, are the only foundations of a free government." But all around her Mercy Warren saw sycophancy, intrigue, preferment, corruption, insolence of office, and other weaknesses of character.

"Liberty delights the ear and tickles the fond pride of man," she wrote Catharine Macaulay about this time, "but it is a jewel much oftener the plaything of his imagination than a possession of real stability." A person acquiring it today "probably will barter it the next hour as a useless bauble to the first officious master that will take the burthen from his shoulders." Mercy Warren saw tendencies toward vice mainly in the people who were coming to be known as Federalists. But what if the *populace as a whole,* on which she depended for majority rule and representative government, should also develop tendencies toward selfishness, obsequiousness, expensive pleasures, and the like? A republic was critically dependent on *virtue* in the great populace that had power under the republic. It was this question that Madison and the others confronted so brilliantly in their "Federalist papers"—and that Mercy Warren failed to deal with in her "anti-Federalist" paper.

*   *   *

The Framers had to play on a far more complex constitutional chessboard than did Mercy Warren. She—and most of the anti-Federalists— wanted to protect and nurture liberty and equality mainly by keeping government relatively weak, small, open, and close to the people. The Framers calculated in terms of a multi-dimensional set of ends and means. They too wanted to safeguard liberty and equality—but not an unbridled liberty or a leveling equality. They wanted to create also a governmental structure that would prevent tyranny from developing within it and hence would provide no moral justification for the Shayses of the land to mount a rebellion against it. They wanted a system of representation that would respond to the legitimate needs of the people but curb their passions and their greed. They wanted to gain safety for their fledgling republic and security for its people by creating a broader union, strengthening the federal government, and charging it with the duties of maintaining external defense and internal harmony. They wanted to combat vice and encourage virtue among both leaders and followers.

In planning against tyranny the Framers had to recognize that it took many forms—tyranny of opinion, governmental tyranny, tyranny by a popular majority. They could thwart the first of these by opposing an established church or any other monopolistic fount of opinion, by safeguarding religious and political liberty in the state bills of rights and in the national bill of rights that would be added to the Constitution—in short, by safeguarding political and social pluralism. They could thwart the second kind of tyranny through ensuring the right to vote, frequent elections, and specific procedures such as impeachment and judicial appeal. But the third kind of tyranny—majority tyranny—was far harder to guard against, because of the Framer's fundamental commitment to rule by popular majorities. How could a constitution thwart an oppressive majority bent on taking control of government? The solution was several-fold: a federal system, so that such a threatening majority would have to seize control of both the federal government and a host of state governments—a daunting prospect to any demagogue; staggered elections for President, House, and Senate, so that a majority could not seize control all in one swoop; an elaborate separation of powers, so that a majority winning one office, such as the presidency, would face a Senate or House in hostile hands. Thus conflict was built into a fragmented government to prevent majority tyranny.

Still, representation posed the most challenging intellectual problem for the Framers. They wanted to achieve a balance of interests in government without risking disruption or oppression by excessive factionalism. How achieve this in a *republic* representing the *public?* They could not rely on the balance of orders and classes that was understood to protect liberty in Britain and elsewhere. As Charles Pinckney reminded his fellow delegates at Philadelphia, the new republic would "contain but one order . . . the order of Commons." They could not depend on the wisdom and prudence of the people as a whole, because they saw popular majorities as well as elites all too prone toward selfishness, rashness, aggrandizement, and hostility to other people's liberties. The basic solution was to pass the expressed interests and passions of the voting populace through a filter of overlapping and mutually checking representative processes and bodies— again, staggered elections, separation of powers, accountability of rulers to fragmented, conflicting, competing, and overlapping voting constituencies, and all the rest of the formidably intricate system of eviscerated powers and checks and balances. In order to govern, representatives would have to bargain with one another ceaselessly in a vast system of brokerage and accommodation that would give something to everybody—liberty to the individual, desired laws or appropriations to groups, and governmental balance and stability to the whole.

If the separation of powers among and within the three federal branches was the most exacting intellectual problem for the Framers, the new division of powers between the federal and state governments was the toughest political one. Too many people made the simple equation—the more centralized a government, the greater its threat to liberty. Too many shared Mercy Warren's fear of the "hydra-headed monster" in "federal city" sinking its fangs into the states. For their part the Framers feared that the states might be taken over by local demagogues or overzealous majorities. They could not forget Shays and his threat to Massachusetts. The Framers' most telling argument was that all Americans would gain far more safety and security from foreign threats—from the great powers lodged on their frontiers—under a stronger national government. The basic issue was settled by compromise—in 1787 and for centuries thereafter.

The more the two sides argued over process and power in these grand debates, the more they appealed to purpose and principle. To what ends were all these means directed? Both sides invoked the Declaration of Independence and its call for the supreme values of liberty and equality. But what kind of liberty and equality? Equal political liberty? Individual economic opportunity? These were considered necessary but far from adequate. Government must be strong enough to protect individual liberty but not strong enough to suppress it—but what kind of government was that? In ancient times liberty had meant the right to participate in government; now it meant freedom from government—was that progress? The grand debates did little to clarify these grand issues. And the issue that would become the grandest question of them all—the extent to which government should interfere with some persons' liberties in order to grant them and other persons more liberty and equality—this issue lay beyond the intellectual horizons of virtually all the debaters of the time.

If the questions were not settled, the battle was—the "Feds" had won at Philadelphia. In winning they had imposed on themselves and others an enormously heavy burden of leadership. Under the new system, men must become expert brokers and dexterous improvisers so that they could operate successfully across the many vertical and horizontal boundaries separating governments. They must be masterly transactional leaders. But at times when people felt that they had lost their way, or needed new goals, leaders would have to transcend brokerage and provide a sense of unity and direction. And in times of real crisis, when people's fundamental wants and needs, aspirations and expectations, were unmet, and when people hungered for action—any action—the system would depend on men who could reshape the political and intellectual environment; in short, the new Constitution must not altogether inhibit masterful transforming leadership.

But the Framers wanted even more than this—they wanted *virtue* in both leaders and citizens. By virtue they meant at the least good character and civic concern; at the most—with Abbé de Mably—a heroic love for the public good, a devotion to justice, a willingness to sacrifice comfort and riches for the public weal, an elevation of the soul. One reason the Framers believed in representation was that it would refine leadership, acting as a kind of sieve that would separate and elevate the more virtuous elements. Others—most notably Jefferson—believed that virtue must be nurtured at the bottom, among the "little republics" of the states, where, as he wrote later, "every man is a sharer in the direction of his ward-republic, or of

some of the higher ones, and feels that he is a participator in the government of affairs, not merely at an election one day in the year, but every day;
where there shall not be a man in the State who will not be a member of
some one of its councils, great or small, he will let the heart be torn out
of his body sooner than his power wrested from him by a Caesar or a
Bonaparte." Thus Jefferson proposed local public forums where the
"views of the people," in Jean Yarbrough's words, "could be refined
through deliberation *before* they were made known to their representatives." The people, in short, would refine and elevate themselves; it was
on the civic virtue of this cadre that the moral leadership of higher cadres
would be founded.

In late 1788, however, it was the top cadre—the fifty or so national
leaders and nationally known state leaders who had written or indirectly
shaped the Constitution—who had the power and responsibility of leadership. Now that they had won a constitution, they must win a government.
This meant organizing elections and choosing leaders at the same time
that they were creating the offices the winners would occupy. If the federal
leadership seemed undaunted by their tasks, it was in part because they
had agreed so closely, planned so creatively, built so carefully. It was even
more because they were not proclaiming a thousand-year Reich but rather
inaugurating an experiment and expecting a period of trial and testing.
They were undertaking a set of experiments in majority rule, minority
rights, balanced representation, separation of powers, checks and balances. They were beginning the profoundest experiment of all—that of
forming a "more perfect Union," in order to "establish Justice, insure
domestic Tranquility, provide for the common defense, promote the general Welfare, and secure the Blessings of Liberty" to themselves and their
posterity.

CHAPTER 3

The Experiment Begins

═══════════

Around ten o'clock on the morning of April 16, 1789, George Washington and two companions climbed up into a carriage standing outside the great hall at Mount Vernon. One of these fellow travelers was his aide David Humphreys, the other Charles Thomson, longtime secretary of the Congress then meeting in New York City. Two days earlier Thomson had ridden into Mount Vernon to inform Washington of his election as President of the United States.

"I have now, sir, to inform you," Thomson had said at the climax of his short announcement, "that the proofs you have given of your patriotism and of your readiness to sacrifice domestic separation and private enjoyments to preserve the liberty and promote the happiness of your country did not permit the two Houses to harbour a doubt of your undertaking this great, this important office to which you are called not only by the unanimous vote of the electors, but by the voice of America. . . ."

Now the President-elect was leaving Mount Vernon with little ceremony. Indeed, he wrote in his diary, he was departing with "a mind oppressed with more painful and anxious sensations" than he could express, but ready to answer his country's call. Evidently few witnessed the leave-taking. Since Washington's carriage had to cut north through Muddy Hole Farm before turning northeastward toward Alexandria, and since he had only recently instructed his plantation manager that all able-bodied laborers, male or female, were to work diligently from dawn to dark, slaves working in the tobacco fields must have looked up, comprehending or not, as the carriage sped by.

Two hours later the little party pulled up in the busy town on the banks of the Potomac. "Federal to a man," Washington had called Alexandria not long before, and now the Alexandrians had political as well as personal reasons to greet their old neighbor. Indeed, the President-elect found himself among creditors as well as friends. A few weeks earlier he had borrowed £500 in Alexandria—something "I never expected to be driven to—that is, to borrow money on interest," owing to "short crops and other causes," including the expenses of his trip to New York. But now he was being escorted to Mr. Wise's tavern for a celebratory dinner. Toast after toast—thirteen in all—punctuated the meal, and if Alexandrians followed their custom, each lifting of glasses was followed by the boom of cannon. Along with the new toasts to the people of the United States and to the federal Constitution, "may it be fairly tried," and the conventional toasts to the Congress, friendly nations, heroes of the Revolution, there were salutes of a more pointed nature:

"May party spirit subside, and give place to universal zeal for the public good" . . . BOOM!

"May religion, industry, and economy constitute the national character of the United States" . . . BOOM!

"The American ladies; may their manners accord with the spirit of the present government" . . . BOOM!

A sugary tribute to Washington by the mayor brought an address of saccharine modesty by the general.

Next day Washington, his escorts, and his carriage were ferried across the Potomac to Georgetown. There, and at Spurrier's Tavern that evening, and in Baltimore next day, guards of honor met and fell in with him—a tribute that, along with the felicitous addresses, pleased the President-elect but so delayed him that he resolved from then on to start his daily journey at sunrise and travel all day long. He could not forget that Congress was awaiting him. Among the officers who greeted him he often found comrades from wartime, and his route lay near old bivouacs and battles, but the general seemed more occupied with thoughts of the tasks ahead than with remembrances of the darker days hardly more than a decade past.

At the outskirts of Philadelphia the military escort gave way to outpourings of persons who crowded around the general's carriage. When Washington, seated on a superbly caparisoned white horse, crossed the Susquehanna, he found "every fence, field, and avenue" lined with cheering onlookers. Twenty thousand people choked the central streets of the city. In Trenton—another reminder of earlier, sadder times—matrons and girls scattered blossoms before him as they sang a specially composed ode beginning "Welcome, mighty Chief!" and ending "Strew your Hero's way with flowers!" In Princeton and New Brunswick and Elizabeth Town large throngs turned out amid clamorous church bells and thunderous salutes.

The little procession out of Mount Vernon was turning into a triumphal promenade of democracy. A people frustrated by years of war and uncertainty and hardship, a people starved for leadership and direction, citizens denied the power of directly choosing their President and often denied any vote at all—these persons were now voting with lungs and legs for their leader, a man on a white horse, a republican hero.

A gleaming new barge festooned with red curtains, its twenty-six oars manned by the finest pilots in New York, rowed Washington across Newark Bay toward Manhattan. A long tail of sloops and smaller craft formed as the barge moved off the Battery on Staten Island. A familiar tune sounded across the water from a sloop crowded with singers; it was "God Save the King," with the words changed to form an ode to Washington. A Spanish warship, its yards manned and rigged and bedecked with the colors of nations, fired off a salute. As the barge neared the southern end of Manhattan Island, Washington could make out masses of people crowded along the waterfront and stretching up the streets behind. Once the barge was secured, the general mounted carpeted steps to receive a delegation of officials headed by Governor Clinton. A parade was formed, but it had such trouble threading its way through the cheering crowd that it took half an hour to move from the dock to the Franklin House at 3 Cherry Street, assigned to the President-elect.

Washington was emotionally satiated. He wrote in his diary: "The display of boats . . . the decorations of the ships, the roar of cannon, and the loud acclamations of the people . . . filled my mind with sensations as painful (considering the reverse of this scene, which may be the case after all my labors to do good) as they are pleasing."

A week later—on April 30, 1789—Washington left Cherry Street in a grand coach drawn by four horses, preceded by troops and accompanied by carriages filled with officials. He was wearing a dark brown suit of "superfine American Broad Cloths" that he had seen advertised in the New York *Daily Advertiser;* white stockings and shoes with silver buckles; and a steel-hilted dress sword. Milling crowds surrounded the procession. Along Queen Street to Great Dock Street, then north toward Wall Street and along Broad Street the long column wound its way to Federal Hall, an imposing building with its massive Doric columns. There, in the handsome Senate chamber, John Adams had been encouraging a last-minute debate over protocol—how should the President and the members of the lower house be greeted? There had been much reference to English practice, to the annoyance of republicans present. By the time Washington entered the crowded chamber, Adams seemed almost speechless. But finally he led the President-elect out of the chamber onto a small, partly enclosed portico overlooking Broad and Wall.

A great cheer broke out from below. Chancellor Livingston administered the oath of office; Washington, looking grave, repeated the words and then lifted the Inaugural Bible to his lips.

"It is done!" Livingston cried out, and turning to the crowd, shouted, "Long live George Washington, President of the United States!" Above the roar of the crowd and the chorus of church bells came the thunder of salutes from the Battery and the harbor. Washington bowed, turned back into the Senate chamber, seated himself next to the Vice-President, waited until the senators and representatives took their seats, and rose to deliver his Inaugural Address. His voice trembled a bit, his words at times came slowly and indistinctly, he seemed not to know what to do with his hands, but he sounded a note of profound eloquence. After the usual modest disclaimers and supplications to the "Almighty Being who rules over the Universe," he came to the heart of the matter:

"There is no truth more thoroughly established, than that there exists in the œconomy and course of nature, an indissoluble union between virtue and happiness, between duty and advantage, between the genuine maxims of an honest and magnanimous policy, and the solid rewards of public prosperity and felicity: Since we ought to be no less persuaded that the propitious smiles of Heaven, can never be expected on a nation that disregards the eternal rules of order and right, which Heaven itself has ordained; And since the preservation of the sacred fire of liberty, and the destiny of the Republican model of Government, are justly considered as *deeply,* perhaps as *finally* staked, on the experiment entrusted to the hands of the American people."

THE FEDERALISTS TAKE COMMAND

And now to the task of governing. The "old general"—still only fifty-seven—and the politicians who would launch the new republic had been gathering slowly in New York throughout the winter. The alchemy of ambition and duty had brought to the temporary capital hordes of job applicants along with elected legislators. One man who had not been eager for his job was George Washington. So often, indeed, had he informed friends during the past year that he preferred to stay in private life, and would take on public service only if duty absolutely required it, that he might have been fighting his own personal devil—a relish less of power than of fame and acclaim and deference. He had not raised a hand to influence the electors of 1789. He announced in his Inaugural Address that he would renounce any presidential salary—perhaps out of a fear of tainting his image of patriotic disinterestedness.

Washington's election had gone so smoothly as to arouse no controversy. Electors had been chosen in popular elections in some states, by legislatures in others, and by other methods in several others; in New York the two houses fell into a quarrel over procedure and chose no electors at all. But wherever or however they were chosen, the electors acted on only one mandate—to cast their ballot for the Revolutionary leader.

The vice-presidency was a different matter. Shrewd politicians had already sized up the office as vibrant with hope but barren of power. Still, the post had interested leading candidates, the most notable of whom was John Adams, who with Abigail had returned to their beloved Braintree home after their public service abroad. Vowing even more insistently than Washington that he preferred tending his farm to another stint of politics, he yet watched narrowly as the vice-presidential jockeying began. Washington made clear that while he esteemed Adams, he would be happy to accept whomever the electors chose to choose. Into this little political vacuum Alexander Hamilton moved with gusto. He could not deny Adams' experience and distinction, but he had long disliked his frigid and dogmatic ways, his civilian suspicion of the military during the Revolution (in which Adams had not served as a soldier), and his only slightly veiled coolness to General Washington.

Hamilton's weapon was right at hand: by warning friends in Pennsylvania, Connecticut, and elsewhere that Adams might actually beat out Washington for the presidency, and playing on fears that a thwarted Adams might become the pawn—or the head—of anti-Federalists, Hamilton persuaded a number of electors to withhold their second-choice votes from the Bostonian. Adams won the office, but his 34 votes fell far short of the unanimous 89 that Washington won. Belatedly he discovered that Hamilton had engineered the "dark and base intrigue." Throwing away votes was a breach of honor, a perjury. He would get revenge. He would "drag out to public infamy both dupers and dupes" and "make those men repent of their rashness." But Adams would have to wait.

Choosing the first Congress had also been conflict-ridden and a bit manipulative. State legislatures met for the double task of choosing senators and setting up districts for electing representatives. Once again the pros and cons of the Constitution were argued across the land, as anti-Federalists backed candidates who would seek to amend the Constitution, perhaps even convene a second constitutional convention.

Nowhere were the contests watched more closely than in Virginia. While Washington followed developments closely but silently from Mount Vernon, and Madison apprehensively from New York, Patrick Henry in Richmond rallied his followers, and dominated the selection of two senators and the rejection of Madison for the upper chamber. He engineered an appeal to Congress for an immediate second convention, and helped draw the lines for the new congressional districts in a manner that would put Madison in an anti-Federalist district. This "Henry-mander" antedated the famous "Gerrymander" in Massachusetts.

Though fearful of seeming too eager for election and afflicted with piles,

Madison returned home by stagecoach and two-wheeled chair. There he found himself pitted against a rising young politician, James Monroe. The two rivals were longtime friends, however, and agreed to tour the district together to debate the issues. Madison picked up votes by granting that additional safeguards to liberty, in a bill of rights, were necessary; and his firm backing for religious freedom helped him with the Baptist vote. His defeat of Monroe—their friendship continued unimpaired—helped Virginia send a majority of pro-Federalist representatives to New York.

Federalists won in most of the other states too, though in some cases only after a pitched battle. In Pennsylvania as elsewhere, continuing dispute over the Constitution closely affected the elections. Pennsylvanians demonstrated that they knew election artifice too; the pro-Constitution leaders put through an election law calling for the statewide rather than districtwide election of representatives, on the calculation that they would do better statewide. Both sides "ticketed" candidates and took stands on the Constitution at "conventions" or conferences before the final voting. And both sides appealed to the crucial German vote.

When the elections finally ended, it was clear that Washington would have a pro-Administration majority—though the general's direct influence on the outcome was minimal, except perhaps in Virginia.

By April the new men were settling into their New York City houses and hostelries. Invited by Governor Clinton to stay at the Governor's House, Washington had politely declined, adding that he would hire lodgings until a presidential house could be provided. To Madison he explained that he wished not to be placed *early* in a situation where he must entertain. In fact, Washington wanted a house and style befitting his station. Toward the end of May, Martha Washington arrived from Mount Vernon, after a trip that had turned out to be a kind of triumphal procession of its own. Soon she was cultivating close relationships with Administration wives, especially with Abigail Adams. The Adamses had taken a somewhat run-down but pleasant house on Richmond Hill, from which Abigail gazed with rapture at the "noble" Hudson, dotted with small boats bearing produce to Manhattan. Madison settled back into the Manhattan life he had known for years. Hamilton and Jay had homes convenient to Federal Hall, the temporary location of Congress.

Congress—the "first wheel of the government," Washington called it—had got off to a dull start on March 4, 1789, after a long wait for newly elected senators and representatives to make their way to New York through the winter snow. Not until early April was a quorum finally mustered in the House. The Senate was enlivened by a dispute between its presiding officer, John Adams, and a Pennsylvania democrat, William Maclay. Puffed up a little by his new status, "His Rotundity," as some critics called Adams, seemed almost obsessed by questions of parliamentary practice and protocol, especially English practice and protocol. Maclay, a frontier lawyer, tall and broad and rustic, scoffed at his pretensions and punctilio and concluded that New Englanders were too parochial to get along with anyone save their close neighbors.

Matters came to a head when Adams wished to refer to the President's Inaugural Address as "his most gracious speech." Maclay rose. "Mr. President, we have lately had a hard struggle for our liberty against kingly authority. The minds of men are still heated: everything related to that species of government is odious to the people. The words prefixed to the President's speech are the same that are usually placed before the speech of his Britannic Majesty. I know they will give offense." He moved that they be struck out. Adams professed to be astonished: he was for a dignified and responsible government; if he had thought during the Revolution it would come to this, he never would have drawn his sword. A weeks-long quarrel then developed in the Senate over the President's title—should he be referred to as "His Highness" or "His Elective Highness," or the like? Good republicans claimed to be shocked by such monarchical instincts. Despite Adams' admonition that a man could be "President" of *any* little organization, the final title would be simply "The President of the United States."

The tripartite structure of the new federal government was completed in September 1789, when Congress passed the Judiciary Act establishing a Supreme Court to consist of a Chief Justice and five associates, three circuit courts, and thirteen district courts. Washington soon nominated John Jay, who was acting as Secretary of State until Jefferson's arrival, as the first Chief Justice of the United States. An immensely experienced man as a legislator, former chief justice of New York, and diplomat, Jay was widely regarded as learned and judicious, but by the end of the 1780s he was seen by republicans as an arch-Federalist who believed in British precedents, centralized government, and presidential power. While Washington called the new judicial department the "key-stone of our political fabric," Jay found major cases slow in coming and spent many months working with his fellow justices to set up circuits, designate judges to ride them, appoint clerks, and ensure that the new federal judges would be received in the states with proper respect.

President and Congress were engaged in the everyday business of government as well. They could hardly escape it; problems of taxes, imports, Indians, foreign relations engulfed them. Washington started out with only two assistants, David Humphreys and Tobias Lear, but soon he had to recruit several other aides. Hamilton worked closely with him on political matters, Madison on legislative. Washington did not have to construct a federal executive from scratch. The Confederation had bequeathed him a Foreign Office run by John Jay and two clerks, a Treasury Board with no treasury, and a War Department with no war. A scattering of federal officers—lighthouse keepers, postmasters, tax collectors, troop commanders, diplomats—manned a long thin line of federal power. Washington's major appointments were geographically balanced—Thomas Jefferson of Virginia (still in Paris) for Secretary of State, Alexander Hamilton of New York for Secretary of the Treasury, his old comrade-in-arms Henry Knox of Massachusetts for Secretary of War, another Virginian, Edmund Randolph, for Attorney General.

The middle and minor offices gave Washington, Adams, and the department heads the most trouble. Little had they anticipated the stream of job applicants and applications into New York. Washington had to fend off jobseekers months before the electors were even due to meet. The Administration leaders knew how to deal with place-warmers, but many jobseekers were overqualified, if anything, and some were personal friends and even family members. To Adams applied General Benjamin Lincoln, of Shays's Rebellion fame, Samuel Otis, Robert Treat Paine, and his close friend and adopted "brother," Richard Cranch. When his and Abigail's good friend Mercy Warren wrote poignantly on behalf of her husband, Adams responded that he had no patronage and, if he had, neither her children nor his own could be sure of it. Similarly, President Washington wrote to his nephew Bushrod Washington, a young lawyer hankering to be appointed United States district attorney for Virginia, that he was too inexperienced for the post, that the President must stand on principle against nepotism, and that as a practical matter he could not be partial to friends and relations, "for the eyes of Argus are upon me."

It was with relief as well as pride that the President of the United States could write to Gouverneur Morris, on October 13, 1789, that the "national government is organized. . . ."

*   *   *

Two days later, the President left on a formal tour of the "Eastern" states—Connecticut, Massachusetts, and New Hampshire. He had "hope of perfectly reestablishing my health," he wrote Jefferson, which a "series of indispositions"—mainly anthrax—"has much impaired." How a trip into the New England states, in a carriage jolting over rocky roads and disgorging its passengers at every large river and quagmire, could restore haleness only a military man and plantation rider could understand.

Actually, Washington had other reasons for his journey: he wanted to make a show of federal authority and leadership among people who had not yet fully accepted the new Constitution; and he was curious about agriculture and manufacturing and the "face of the Country." Accompanied by Hamilton, Knox, and Jay for some distance out of the city, he continued with his retinue of two secretaries and six servants.

It was rainy, that first day, and the road was rough and stony as the party proceeded through New Rochelle and Mamaroneck, but Washington was impressed by the droves of fine beef cattle and the flocks of sheep on the way to the New York market, the Indian corn and pumpkins lying yet ungathered in the fields, and widow Haviland's "neat and decent Inn" in Rye, where they put up for the night. But next day, crossing over into Connecticut, he was even more taken by the superb landscapes on the road from Stamford to Norwalk and Fairfield, though saddened by "the Destructive evidences of British cruelty"—burned-out houses with gaunt chimneys still standing. He noted that vessels of seventy-five tons or so could make their way up rivers to many of the towns through which he passed. The ports served mainly a coastal and West Indian trade, as local farmers bartered their grain and meat for imported articles.

Washington took the lower road into New Haven and hence missed the usual delegation braced to greet him with flowery speeches of welcome, but he found a bustling town with several Episcopalian and Congregational churches, a number of manufactories, and Yale College, then numbering 120 students. Among those welcoming him were members of the small elite who ran the town, merchants, clerics, and college faculty, but this Federalist political leadership was already beginning to meet opposition. At the bottom of the social ladder was a body of slaves—over four hundred in New Haven County—who worked mainly in fields and households but also helped in lumbering, whaling, and fishing. The slave trade, but not slavery, had been abolished in Connecticut. President Ezra Stiles of Yale would found an antislavery society the year after Washington's visit.

Daily the Virginia planter noted the quality of the crops, the nature of the roads, the number of bushels of wheat or corn the farmers were getting from their acres, the gristmills and sawmills, the quality of the food and beds in the taverns. In Wallingford he was fascinated to "see the white Mulberry growing, raised from the seed, to feed the silkworm," he wrote in his diary. "We also saw samples of lustring"—a glossy, heavy silk— "(exceeding good) which had been manufactured from the Cocoon raised in this Town, and silk thread very fine. This, except the weaving, is the work of private families, without interference with other business, and is likely to turn out a beneficial amusement."

Hartford had furnished Washington with his inaugural suit, and the President was eager to see Colonel Wadsworth's "Woolen Manufactory." Escorted by the colonel himself, he found a lively establishment that, after years of coping with untutored workers, inadequate machinery, and heavy mortgages, was now producing 5,000 yards of woolen goods a year at $5 a yard. Washington had been trying to encourage Americans to buy clothes made in the United States, but he had to admit that domestic "Broadcloths" were not of the best quality, though good enough, as were the "Cassimeres" and serges. Indeed, he purchased a suit of broadcloth to be sent to him in New York. Hartford also had cotton and paper mills, and a glass factory that had fallen on hard times and whose losses had to be made up through a lottery.

Hugging the western bank of the Connecticut River, and moving across the state border into Massachusetts, the President proceeded through more rain into Springfield, a town in many ways like Hartford. While dinner was being readied at the famous tavern of Zeno Parsons, Washington toured the federal arsenal—probably the same one that Shays's men had attacked less than two years before. He found the brick powder magazine in good repair and the powder dry.

The next morning he headed along another rocky road, through forests of pine and oak, to Palmer and Spencer and Worcester. Isaac Jenks's tavern in Spencer, which Washington noted down as a "pretty good Tavern," was fairly typical of the inns in which Washington stayed; it charged 14p for tea, cider, punch, lodgings, and a dinner of roast beef, vegetables, and tankards of ale. Washington found the supper "only passable," but "one could scarcely complain."

Through his carriage window, Washington constantly studied the unfolding countryside. He had noted a "great equality in the People" as he passed through Connecticut and the Connecticut Valley. "Few or no opulent men—and no poor. . . ." The land was generally more stony and sandy as he traveled east through Massachusetts. Rocky and hilly and infertile indeed was much of New England land, resulting in steady migration to more fructuous country to the west. Parents and children labored in the fields from dawn to dusk during the long spring and summer days. The small farm, a historian observed, was an unsurpassed school for boyhood but an intellectual prison for manhood.

Welcoming escorts multiplied as Washington and his party passed through Worcester and neared Boston. Doubtless he expected the usual protocol as he entered that metropolis, but he could hardly have anticipated the mock comedy that ensued. Both the town fathers of Boston and the state authorities of Massachusetts—the latter headed by the redoubtable lieutenant governor, old Sam Adams—were at hand at the Boston line to greet the President. An unseemly quarrel broke out between city and state as to who held the right to offer the welcome. While the President waited, mounted officials crowded in around him, endangering children who were to take part in the ceremony; only after Washington climbed upon his horse and threatened to ride off did the state officials give way to the local.

Worse was to come. Washington had declined John Hancock's invitation to stay at the Governor's House on the ground that he had resolved on leaving New York not to put private individuals to any trouble; and he had declined to review the state militia on the ground that he should not establish even the faintest precedent of a President reviewing a *state's* troops. Whether out of personal pique or out of his own anti-Federalist proclivities, Governor Hancock, pleading an attack of the gout, failed to call on the President after Washington was settled in his lodgings. The President, in turn, promptly canceled his earlier acceptance of Hancock's invitation to dine, and settled down to dinner in his own lodgings with John Adams. President or governor had to yield, and it was the governor. Next day four husky men carried Hancock, swathed in bandages, and profuse with apologies, across Washington's threshold.

Behind these seemingly trivial episodes lay momentous conflicts over the respective powers and status of the federal and state governments, and behind those conflicts lay even deeper issues of principle and power. It was not surprising that a contest between state and local officials, and a showdown between national and state officials, should take place in Boston, for in no city in the nation had passions run so high, or memories of past battles continued more unclouded. With its many newspapers, its associations of tradesmen, its numerous churches, its humane societies, its great number of factories making dozens of products, Boston sustained a vigorous political culture. And Boston could boast of Harvard, next door in Cambridge. Founded in 1636, Harvard had more than sixty years' lead over Yale (1701) and more than a century over Brown (1764) and Dartmouth (1769). College curricula had broadened after the Revolution to include extensive studies in the natural and physical sciences, modern foreign languages, law, rudimentary social science, and even a premedical program for future doctors.

North of Boston was one of the most developed stretches on the American coast. After a final, exhausting tour of a cotton duck mill, a playing card factory ("63,000 pr. of Cards in a year," Washington noted), and huge French gunships in Boston Harbor, Washington struck out north over the famous bridge in Charlestown. Rapidly he moved through Lynn, which claimed to turn out 175,000 pairs of shoes a year; through Marblehead, where eight hundred men and boys and over a hundred vessels were engaged in fishing; through Salem, already a historic town, now exporting fish and lumber in the East India trade; to Beverly. In this last town the President visited John and George Cabot's cotton manufactory and studied for some time the precision machinery that could spin eighty-four threads at a time, double and twist threads for particular cloths, wind cotton from the spindles and prepare it for the warp, and turn out what seemed to the President to be superior cotton goods. He made no mention of the Beverly labor force in his diary; in Boston he had noted that "girls of Character" along with "daughters of decayed families" worked ten hours a day on a piece-rate basis. Some girls turned the wheels for twenty-eight looms, while others were spinning with both hands, the flax fastened to their waists.

Soon Washington was off again, to Newburyport, in the northeastern corner of Massachusetts, and to Portsmouth, New Hampshire, twenty miles beyond. Both these towns were noted for shipbuilding. New England shipbuilders bragged that their vessels, while smaller than English or European, sailed faster, beat well to the windward, could hug the shores better, and were generally safer. But the Yankees admitted that they had sold a lot of ships, especially before the Revolution, that had not been constructed of seasoned timber. Hemp, cordage, sailcloth, fittings, and much else were often imported from Europe. The problem in both cases, shipbuilders contended, was capital. Thus New Hampshire had iron ore and ironworks, but they were not sufficiently developed. Builders knew that they should season their timber, as the English did, but they could not afford to store it for long months before use. Portsmouth had taverns, ropeworks, a sawmill—but no bank.

After a boat ride around the Portsmouth anchorage, a brief stop in Kittery, Maine—his farthest point north—and more entertainment, receptions, and addresses, the President started back toward New York. He was weary of travel, and the return trip seemed long and trying—especially because of the New England ban on Sunday travel—but there were some diversions. In Andover he visited a small private school and in Lexington he viewed the Green, "the spot on which the first blood was spilt in the dispute with Great Britain, on the 19th of April, 1775." The President could observe interesting contrasts in the Andover and Lexington schools. Phillips Academy of Andover had opened in 1778 in a "rehabilitated carpenter's shop." Its several dozen students boarded with local families, paid a modest entrance fee, and studied such an array of "the Liberal Arts, Sciences, or Languages as opportunity and ability may hereafter admit." Lexington had a "free school," but not altogether free; pupils had to pay a small charge and furnish two feet of wood annually for the fire. There was a separate "Dame's School" for girls, who had far less educational opportunity than boys. New England was still the only region that could claim anything resembling a public school system. Massachusetts had just established a district-by-district school system, but sparsely settled areas were ill served. Teaching consisted mainly of memorization, recitation, and repetition.

On Friday, November 13, 1789, Washington was back in New York, where he found Martha and the rest of the family well. There was a towering pile of mail.

THE NEW YORKERS

The national government had begun its life in a noble building surrounded by stir and squalor.

Federal Hall was the hub of government. Even in 1789 this was already a historic place. Built as City Hall at the start of the century, it had housed New York's Revolutionary government until the British Navy arrived off Staten Island. It was here that the Provincial Congress had met, and here that General Washington had made a famous speech in which he assured New Yorkers worried about a military dictatorship that he and his soldiers would "rejoice with you in that happy hour when the establishment of American Liberty" would enable the soldiers to return to their private stations. The Confederation Congress had met in this hall, and now the first Congress of the United States occupied its remodeled rooms. Each house had its chamber. The representatives met in a spacious octagonal room with fireplaces and large windows, under Ionic columns and pilasters. Their chairs and desks ranged semicircularly facing the Speaker's chair. The Senate chamber was smaller, and superbly carpeted and marbled.

Outside pounded the beat of people's daily lives and work. In the area of Broad and Wall streets, the day would start with the cry of "Milk, ho! Milk, ho!" from milkmen or milkmaids who brought their produce by boat from Long Island or New Jersey and now carried it in two buckets hanging from a yoke. Then there might come chimney sweeps calling out "Sweep, ho! Sweep ho!" After that might appear knife grinders, lamp menders, orange girls, ragmen, wood vendors, all with their distinctive cries. Hogs rooted through the garbage-clogged gutters, cows wandered up and down Broadway, horses' hooves clattered on the cobbled streets. People bustled out of boardinghouses and into taverns and groceries, into the shops of tailors, cobblers, tobacconists, wigmakers, haberdashers, hatters, attorneys. Sometimes the racket was so great that it drowned out the debate in Congress and forced the closing of windows in Federal Hall.

At the close of their deliberations each day, senators and representatives threaded their way through the clamorous streets to coffeehouses, taverns, and boardinghouses. Turning left down Wall Street would take the hungry lawmaker past the Bank of New York to Tontine's, where he would find food and drink and also encounter brokers trading in securities and in loaf sugar, Jamaica rum, and other commodities. Or he could stroll down Broad Street—as wide as its name suggested—to Fraunces' Tavern and then on to Battery Park and South Ferry. More often he would turn west from Federal Hall and head toward the newly rebuilt Trinity Church and then move north on Broadway toward Maiden Lane and the theater and recreation districts. Along the way he had a choice of taverns to stop by for newspapers, gossip, and travelers' reports from Philadelphia and Boston.

Packed into this area of barely one-half square mile was the political leadership of the young nation and the financial center of much of the Northeast. The most celebrated leader, George Washington, lived and worked at 39 Broadway; after ten months at his Cherry Street house, he decided to move to a more commodious and convenient mansion downtown. While professing to disdain "the glare which hovers around the external trappings of elevated office," he continued to work hard and with relish at establishing the presence of the presidency.

A formal procession by the President to Federal Hall to address Congress was a sight to behold: two uniformed military aides on prancing white horses, then Washington's magnificent coach-and-six, followed by another aide and then by carriages containing the Chief Justice and cabinet members. Afternoons, when his work was done and the weather seemed fine, Washington promenaded on the Battery along with other notables. His Friday-evening receptions were rather stiff and formal, but his social dinners were the talk of the town—especially the one at which a lady's ostrich plumes caught fire from a chandelier and were rescued by an aide-decamp. On social occasions the President would enter dressed in black velvet and satin, his diamond knee buckles gleaming, his wig well powdered, a military hat on his head, and a dress sword hanging at his side.

Secretary of the Treasury Hamilton lived at 58 Wall Street at about this time, Secretary of State Jefferson on Maiden Lane, Secretary of War and

Mrs. Knox on lower Broadway, where Attorney General Randolph and his wife also resided. The John Jays, who were second only to the Washingtons as social arbiters of the federal capital, had a three-story dwelling farther north on Broadway. The cabinet members worked at home or in law offices; there was no central executive headquarters. John and Abigail Adams continued to enjoy their Richmond Hill mansion on the southeast corner of Varick and Charlton streets, amid old oaks and flowering shrubs. Most of the government clerks, copiers, attorneys, customs house employees, and military officers, along with congressmen with lesser social connections, lived in rented rooms and boardinghouses throughout southern Manhattan.

Sundays the President set an example for his Administration officials by worshipping at Trinity Church, once it had been restored after a devastating fire. While Trinity was being rebuilt the President attended St. Paul's Chapel, farther up Broadway, where he had a pew. Samuel Provoost, bishop of New York and chaplain of Congress, conducted special services at the church. Trinity had a political history: "pro-Tory" leaders had tried to keep control of the church after the Revolution, but their Loyalist rector had been ousted by patriots, who then installed Provoost.

New Yorkers also worshipped at Dutch Reformed, Presbyterian, and German Calvinist Reformed churches. Quakers were a small but influential sect. During English rule Catholics had worshipped secretly in a Jesuit father's home, but after the Revolution, buoyed by the repeal of anti-Catholic measures, Father William O'Brien raised funds in Mexico and elsewhere to build St. Peter's Church. Jews too had suffered disabilities during the colonial period, and many had fled to Philadelphia during the British occupation, but now they were returning and building a small but enduring congregation under the leadership of Rabbi Gershom Mendes Seixas.

Taverns, groggeries, and porterhouses—over four hundred in the whole city—vastly outnumbered the churches, but these were far more than tippling havens. They served as public meeting houses, polling places, club and society headquarters, centers for news about ships, foreign events, commodity prices. Taverns catered to all tastes, prices, and classes. Some were the scenes of formal entertainments and public celebrations, attended by the fashionable; the City Tavern, on Broadway, was respectable enough to house court sessions. Others offered—illegally—games of cards and dice, billiard tables, shuffleboards, and cockfighting. Some hotels and taverns provided board and lodging for eight dollars a week.

The rich found their entertainments in formal balls and dinners, three o'clock tea parties, summer drives down Broadway to the Battery breezes.

The theater, though undistinguished, attracted the socially prominent, not least George Washington. Music, equally undistinguished, was also patronized by the social elite. Peter Van Hagen, a skillful violinist who had taken political refuge from Holland, taught their children, promoted concerts, and wrote compositions for the theater. The wealthy commissioned portraits of themselves. Washington sat for the noted portraitist John Trumbull on several occasions.

The Revolution had hardly altered old class lines. Thirty years after the British evacuated New York an observer was identifying "three distinct classes": the first of divines, lawyers, physicians, principal merchants, and propertied persons; the second of small merchants, retail dealers, clerks, petty officials; and the third of "inferior orders of people." Upper-class ladies advertised their standing by their dress: elaborate coiffures, costly silk gowns, hooped skirts, enormous hats. The poor found their amusements in traveling acrobats, jugglers, and comedians, in circuses, menageries, and equestrian shows, in waxworks, freaks, and "natural curiosities" from exotic places, inventors' mechanical contrivances.

Outdoors, people of all classes could attend horse racing near Bowery Lane, hunt small game in woods and swamps over on the west side, fish off Sandy Hook, bathe in the East and North (Hudson) rivers, take excursions to Long Island and Governors Island. On snowy winter days they could skate on Collect Pond two blocks off Broadway or ride sleds and sleighs on the rutted snow. In all seasons promoters offered fistfights and eye-gouging as attractions. Thousands attended the baiting of bulls, dogs, bears, even panthers. Gangs of young toughs, flaunting names like "Smith's Fly" and "Broad Way," fought one another with stones and slingshots.

New York City in 1790 was a Federalist town. Anti-Federalists had considerable weight in state politics, with George Clinton now in his fourteenth year as governor, and a potentially strong Republican movement was organizing in New York City, but during the year and a half that the national government was headquartered in Manhattan, it was the Federalist command post of the nation. For more than a century Manhattanites had been experiencing a remarkably intensive, competitive, factious, and increasingly sophisticated political life. The New Yorkers around Washington had become expert in the Federalist style of politics. Now they had new advantages: the momentum of the new Constitution and government, the patriotic glow that surrounded Washington, a clear sense of the program and policies they wanted from the new government. These were youthful and vigorous men. Hamilton was thirty-four at the time of Washington's inaugural, Jay forty-four, Rufus King thirty-four. They had the backing of influential newspapers, the most notable of which was John Fenno's *Gazette of the United States*. And the Federalists had access to money, for the city was an expanding financial center.

The Bank of New York, founded by Hamilton and others in the mid-1780s, by 1791 was paying stock dividends of 7 percent and lending money to the city, state, and federal governments. Men of wealth were joining to found other financial institutions, as "Bancomania" began to sweep the city. Banks helped fuel a robust expansion of commerce and manufacturing in New York. Many merchant princes and shipowners lived on State Street overlooking the Battery; from their homes and offices they could watch the signal flags on top of Dongan Hills and gather the first intelligence on cargo vessels starting their passage through the Narrows. By 1790 exporters were shipping out of the city each year over $2 million worth of wheat, flour, beef and pork, furs, raw hides, lumber, and livestock.

The habits of the New York merchants reminded a visiting English actor of his friends back home. "They breakfasted at eight or half past, and by nine were in their counting houses, laying out the business of the day; at ten they were on their wharves, with aprons round their waists, rolling hogsheads of rum and molasses; at twelve at market, flying about as dirty and as diligent as porters; at two back again to the rolling, heaving, hallooing and scribbling. At four they went home to dress for dinner; at seven, to the play; at eleven, to supper, with a crew of lusty Bacchanals who would smoke cigars, gulp down brandy, and sing, roar, and shout in the thickening clouds they created, like so many merry devils, till three in the morning. At eight, up again, to scribble, run, and roll hogsheads. . . ."

Manufacturing was not far advanced in New York by 1790, but individual craftsmen turned out hats, chairs, cabinets, coaches, and rope. By 1790 a new factory on Liberty Street off Broadway employed 130 spinners and 14 weavers. One of the spinners was Samuel Slater, who soon would move to Pawtucket, Rhode Island, to found the first successful cotton factory in America.

New York City's biggest resource, however, lay in its people, in their numbers, variety, vigor, and talents. In 1790, with a population of 33,000, New York City had overtaken Philadelphia's 28,500 (exclusive of suburbs), thus becoming the largest city in the nation. The city was already turning into the human salmagundi of the new nation. Its numbers included about 29,700 whites, 2,400 slaves, and 1,100 "free persons other than whites." Old Dutch families with names like Verplanck, Beekman, and Stuyvesant were still prominent in the city's social and financial affairs. So many exiles from France had settled in Manhattan that newspapers printed some advertisements in their language. Germans and British—especially Irish—

were landing by the boatload, sometimes 400 at a time, in the "slips" protruding from lower Manhattan.

Inevitably old families, immigrants, and free black persons tended to settle in their own communities and organize their own societies. It did not take the Irish long to establish the Friendly Sons of St. Patrick. Black people soon formed Protestant churches of various denominations. Scots held their parades and their flings. But these were all communities, not feudal enclaves. The Dutch, to be sure, were accused of segregating themselves along the Hudson in their yellow brick houses, from which they watched the changes in the city through "rolling waves of smoke from their melancholy pipes," and Irish Catholics experienced the usual suspicion; but New York did not yet contain a ghetto for blacks, Jews, Irish, or any other race or nationality.

Leaders tended more to build bridges among communities than to seal them off. It was not surprising that the political and economic notables of the city were in close touch; living so closely together in the crowded city, they could hardly avoid bumping into one another in law offices, taverns, shops, or in the street. The social elite mingled at the theater, horse races, charity balls, the President's receptions, splendid parties in their mansions. The first families were considerably interrelated. Hamilton was married to the daughter of Philip Schuyler, the general and politico who had been an inspiration for the young Hamilton. James Duane, New York's first federal district judge, had married into the influential Livingston family, as had Postmaster General Samuel Osgood, who was also related to the Clintons. John Jay's wife was a Livingston.

Group leaders outside the social elite reached out to the rest of the city. Rabbi Gershom Mendes Seixas not only led the Jewish community but had served as a Columbia College trustee and a leader in education. Another Seixas helped found the New York Stock Exchange. Free blacks in Manhattan had built their own church and congregation and Samuel Fraunces, a West Indian, opened the tavern bearing his name. At Fraunces' Tavern General Washington had bidden farewell to his officers after the Revolution. "Black Sam," as Philip Freneau called him, won such a reputation as a good manager and as a connoisseur of wine that President Washington installed him in his Manhattan household as steward. Fraunces' daughter Phoebe became the Washingtons' housekeeper. She was lucky; aside from socially prominent ladies who were active in charity, most women found few channels of opportunity or influence.

A nondescript, two-story "Wigwam" on Broad Street was doubtless the best mixing place in Manhattan for all but the most fashionable. Here met the Society of St. Tammany. Founded hardly two weeks after Washington's inauguration, Tammany at this time was a benevolent and fraternal organization dedicated to liberty, patriotism, and republicanism. Its goals, a New York newspaper reported, were "the smile of charity, the chain of friendship, and the flame of liberty." While the society attracted both Federalists and anti-Federalists, it was a clear reaction against the high Federalists and the detested Cincinnati, a fraternal society of Revolutionary officers, who retaliated by dubbing the Wigwam the "Pig Pen."

In place of social distinctions—or was it to mock them?—Tammany leaders took the titles of Grand Sachem, Sagamore (master of ceremonies), and Wiskinskie (doorkeeper). Men of the middle and working classes were welcome as members; if ex-officers dominated the Cincinnati, former enlisted men found a haven in the Wigwam. Fraternity was embellished in strong drink, but Tammany's sons loved above all to parade. Wearing buck tails in their hats as symbols of liberty, often sporting full Indian regalia and war paint, the tribes marched to public ceremonies in solemn procession. On initiating new members the brothers sang out their credo:

> Sacred's the ground where Freedom's found,
> And Virtue stamps her name;
> Our hearts entwine at Friendship's shrine,
> And Union fans the flame. . . .

Tradesmen were especially active in Tammany. The first Grand Sachem, William Mooney, was a paperhanger and upholsterer. Another charter member, John Stagg, served as president of the General Society of Mechanics and Tradesmen. Lacking unions or any kind of working-class organization, mechanics and laborers might join Stagg's society or Tammany, but neither was politically militant in 1790. Workers probably found more rousing republican talk at one of their favorite taverns, Martling's on Nassau Street.

Cincinnati and Tammany, white and black, Quaker and Jew, merchant and tough—all these were New Yorkers. Somehow, in fine mansions and reeking grog houses, amid a jungle of crooked streets, shop fronts, hitching posts, refuse piles, dingy stoops, amid the sledges and derricks and carts and barrows of construction sites, amid the smells of hogs and goat manure and outhouses, and out of the pushing and hauling of ambitious legislators, aroused interest groups, rival factions, elitist manipulations—the government of a young republic emerged. It is impossible to measure the effect of its New York environment on the nature of that new government. But it must have been of some significance that the men who were drawing up new tariffs, spending, taxing, banking, and other financial measures lived, worked, and played cheek by jowl with merchants, financiers, shipowners, tradesmen, ferry and stagecoach operators, real estate speculators, commodities investors, importers and exporters—of some significance, in short, that the new government was born in a bawling, innovative, expansive, competitive society, in an ugly-beautiful, capitalistic and cosmopolitan environment.

THE FEDERALIST THRUST

Washington's travels had brought him face to face with tens of thousands of his fellow citizens. His magisterial appearance, his clothes and equipage, his superb *presence* in ceremonial situations, and above all, his ability to seem to hover far above the squalid politics of party and parochialism—all this delighted many Americans and alarmed others. Among the most pleased was John Adams, who had a profound, even philosophical faith in "the efficacy of pageantry." Ceremony was necessary to secure the authority and dignity of government; but even more, the people wanted it. Even in the meanest families, Adams said, "you will find these little distinctions, marks, signs, and decencies which are the result of nature, feeling, reason which are policy and government in their places as much as crowns and tiaras, ceremonies, titles, etc., in theirs."

Washington wanted government—especially this new, frail, vulnerable government—to be respectable and dignified. It was for this reason, and because he appeared increasingly to enjoy display for its own sake, that he drove about Manhattan with a carriage and six cream-colored horses; kept fourteen white servants and seven slaves in his house on Broadway; put on large and elaborate dinners, with powdered lackeys standing by; ordered champagne and claret by the dozens of dozens. Occasionally he rode about town on a white steed with leopard-skin housing and saddlecloth bound in gold.

The President and his fellow Federalists held full command of the government, substantive as well as symbolic. At least half of the members of the first Congress had taken part in forming and adopting the Constitution; over half the members of the 1787 convention were serving as administrators, legislators, or judges in the new government. These men were not Federalists in a formal or party sense; they were Federalists because they had wanted a government that could act quickly and decisively for the whole nation, especially in promoting banking, commerce, and industry. What they had conceived in the summer of '87 they now wished to nurture, to provide with flesh and bone.

This was the work not of one man, not of Washington or Hamilton or Madison alone, but of a large fraternity. They had their differences; some were more concerned with commerce, others with banking and credit, others with manufacture. Later, these and other differences would harden and deepen. But now the leaders were united on the need for rapid economic development of the new nation. And they had the votes in both the first and second sessions of the Congress.

James Madison had made economic policy the very first order of business in the first session when on April 8, 1789—three weeks before the nation even had a President—he stood up in the House of Representatives and called for an economy that was balanced, equitable, and above all independent of control by other nations. For these ends, and also to raise badly needed revenue, and to promote manufacturing, he proposed an elaborate system of duties. Those first tariff measures—like countless others that would follow in the next two centuries—aroused a furious and interminable debate. Senators and representatives sprang to the protection of their local interests. Rum, beer, molasses, sugar, cocoa, coffee suddenly became hot political items, as tea had been sixteen years before. In jousting with some of his old comrades and with rising young men such as Fisher Ames of Massachusetts, in coping with faction in the House, and in facing up to the opposition of the Senate, Madison the practical legislative leader was also confronting Madison the "speculative philosopher" who had led in fashioning a federal government of limited, balanced, and checked powers.

Throughout the first year of Congress members were clamoring to get on with the major task of securing the credit of the new United States. Public creditors, especially in Pennsylvania, were demanding support of the national credit, and a committee of sixteen in the House backed them up. This was all the encouragement needed by Hamilton, who had become Secretary of the Treasury in mid-September 1789, to prepare reports on the broadest dimensions of the American economy. Hamilton saw a vital need to honor debts, quicken the national economy through expanded currency and credit, and strengthen the Union by giving businessmen, as well as the educated and professional persons, a vested interest in the political and financial strength of the new government.

As lively, generous, and charming as ever, at least within his own circle, Hamilton continued to impress his fellow politicians with his habit of command, his eloquence, his darting imagination, his ability to stick to principle despite concessions to expediency. He had not only an instinct for leadership but a theory of it. He believed that the leader must risk and dare, venture and strive; that great men could influence history; that the mass of people could not act on their own, but only in response to forceful initiatives and bold innovations from a few men; that in his own case, he could lead best not by appealing to the masses—an idea he detested—but by galvanizing his immediate followers, who in turn would carry his purposes and ideas to the people. Hamilton was the supreme political venturer; consciously or not, a biographer noted, he seemed to follow Machiavelli's case for boldness: "for fortune is a woman, and it is necessary, if you wish to master her, to conquer her by force; and it can be seen that she lets herself be overcome by the bold rather than by those who proceed coldly." Hence fortune, like a woman, was a friend to the young, because they mastered her with greater ferocity. And Hamilton was young.

Certainly his Report on Public Credit was audacious. Not only did he repudiate the idea of repudiating the debt, on the ground that failure to repay was a rejection of public morality and an invitation to anarchy or despotism. He also proposed that the federal government assume the states' debts contracted during the Revolution, as well as those of the Confederation. And—most provocative of all—he urged that those presently holding securities, rather than the original buyers, be compensated. Thus the foreign and domestic debt would be funded at par, allowing creditors to swap depreciated securities for new interest-bearing bonds at face value. The bearers of these securities had a property right in them, Hamilton said, as in "their houses or their lands, their hats or their coats." Hamilton had not dreamed up his proposals out of his fertile imagination alone. He had drawn heavily from European and especially British experience, from the writings of philosophers and economists, from extensive correspondence with other leaders, including James Madison. He had won the backing of the President, who had commended the resolve for support of the public credit in his January message to Congress.

It was not enough. The House of Representatives was so dubious about the forthcoming report, and so wary of Hamilton's persuasiveness with a small body of his peers, that he was not permitted to introduce the report in person, or to answer questions. Soon his proposal to pay off current securities holders was opening partly healed wounds. All the old fears of a dominating national government, of a moneyed elite, of a paradise for speculators, were revived. It was the people against the money men. "America, sir," cried James Jackson of Georgia, "will not always think as is the fashion of the present day; and when the iron hand of tyranny is felt, denunciations will fall on those who, by imposing this enormous and iniquitous debt, will beggar the people and bind them in chains." For weeks a steaming debate occupied the House. Hamilton, always the realist, could not have been surprised by a revival of the old issues that had divided Federalists and anti-Federalists. But he was astonished when Madison—Madison, his collaborator on the *Federalist;* Madison, his partner in conceiving and setting up the new government—turned against major parts of his report. A "perfidious desertion" of principles Madison had sworn to defend, this seemed to Hamilton. But the two men had been drawn into different political and philosophical orbits since the days of the *Federalist;* they now held clashing views over the nature, role, and scope of government.

Dominating the debate too was the politics of sectionalism, for the Southerners, and especially the Virginians, felt that Hamilton's proposals favored "Eastern" interests over their own. And it was the politics of sectionalism that also rescued the bill. By July, Hamilton's forces had sustained a series of setbacks in Congress. The arrival of "anti-Federalist" congressmen from North Carolina after that state's belated ratification further darkened Hamilton's prospects. Now the political gambler decided to play a strong card. For months New Yorkers, Philadelphians, and Southerners had been jockeying over possession of the permanent site of the nation's capital. Hamilton now decided to offer support for a "southern" location in exchange for support of his proposals.

It was not easy for the New Yorker to make this concession. He had dreamed of seating the federal government permanently amid the banking and trading community of Manhattan; moreover, he would have to modify his proposals further if the Southerners were to accept the deal. But once Hamilton did decide, the deal was made almost overnight. In August 1790 the essence of Hamilton's Report on Public Credit was approved by Congress, though by a narrow margin. And the capital would move to Philadelphia for ten years, and then be relocated permanently on the banks of the "Potoumac."

With the nation's credit narrowly assured, to Hamilton's satisfaction but at no little political cost, he moved forward resolutely to the linchpin of his grand economic design—establishment of a powerful national bank. In this field too, the young Secretary was no novice. He had studied with admiration the august Bank of England; he had read the great economists, including Adam Smith, whose *Wealth of Nations* his sister-in-law sent him from abroad; he had been deeply involved in New York banking. In December 1790, Hamilton submitted to the President and to the Congress the second of his carefully drawn reports. Typically he took not a narrow banking approach but a broad fiscal one. Crucial to his plan was assigning to the new bank power over the issuance of bank notes. Money, Hamilton had long argued, was the lifeblood of the economy, and he calculated that a central bank would be strong enough to maintain the necessary supply of money without letting matters get out of hand. The nation's capital would be augmented by increasing the amount of notes in circulation, by providing wider use of individual notes, and by collecting individual deposits. At the heart of the plan was a marriage of government and private bankers. The two were so intertwined, in a system of mutual support, that the one was financially and legally implicated with the other. To ensure that the bank would not fall into improper hands—that is, into the hands of radicals who would pump out paper money—Hamilton provided for private stockholders to control most of the stock in the bank and appoint the great majority of directors.

Once again Congress split into warring factions, as Washington glumly watched the further erosion of his government of national unity. The most fiery issue was private control of the bank. The agrarians in Congress raised the old warnings of corruption, control by the rich and wellborn, higher taxes, a mania of speculation. Some also complained that Hamilton's reports were simply too intricate and complex to be understandable. But part of Hamilton's task was the education of a people who were still dominated by the notions of small-town economics; and Hamilton's journalistic supporter John Fenno answered for him:

> The Secretary makes reports
> Where'er the House commands him;
> But for their lives, some members say
> They cannot understand him.
> In such a puzzling case as this
> What can a mortal do?
> 'Tis hard for ONE to find REPORTS
> And understanding too.

Many of the more moderate Republicans and anti-Federalists had to grant Hamilton's case for a national bank and a stronger system of currency and credit; they too were concerned about the supply and stability of money. Some of them fell back on the constitutional issue—all the more appropriately, perhaps, now that Congress was meeting in Philadelphia, at the site of the constitutional convention itself. The attack on the proposed bank's constitutionality was led by Madison himself. Speaking in his quiet precise way, but with unsurpassed authority, he reviewed the Constitution and found in it no "power to incorporate a bank"—no power under the authority to lay and collect taxes, none under the power to borrow money, none under the power "to pass all laws necessary and proper to carry into execution those powers." He reviewed at length the writing and the ratifications of the Constitution and concluded that "the power exercised by the bill was condemned by the silence of the Constitution; was condemned by the rule of interpretation arising out of the Constitution; was condemned by its tendency to destroy the main characteristic of the Constitution; was condemned by the expositions of the friends of the Constitution . . . ; was condemned by the apparent intention of the parties which ratified the Constitution; was condemned by the explanatory amendments proposed by Congress themselves to the Constitution; and he hoped it would receive its final condemnation by the vote of this House."

It did not. Beating off crippling amendments, facing down the charges of the irrepressible Jackson that the bill would help the mercantile interests at the expense of "the farmers, the yeomanry of the country," surmounting almost solid southern opposition, the Federalists held their ranks firmly enough to pass the bill in its essentials. The problem indeed seemed to lie less in Congress than in the President himself. Washington had been troubled by the arguments of his fellow Virginian Madison. Always—and proudly—dependent on the advice of men he respected, the President referred the question of constitutionality to two other Virginians, the Secretary of State and the Attorney General. Both Jefferson and Randolph promptly agreed with Madison that the Constitution gave the federal government no power to establish a banking corporation and that no such authority could be implied in any power expressly given. Washington turned back to Hamilton.

The Secretary rose supremely to the occasion. Undaunted by the constitutional authorities arrayed against him, he wrote one of the notable state papers in American history, boldly laying out a broad construction of the Constitution, calling the bank vital to the collection of taxes and the regulation of trade and other functions clearly within the ambit of federal authority, and—even more sweeping—arguing in effect that the federal government as a sovereign entity had the right to use all means "necessary and proper" to realizing such objectives as were not forbidden by the Constitution. His state paper, written with verve and passion, was a direct link between Hamilton the nationalist of 1787 and the Hamiltonian system that the Secretary was seeking to establish. If sustained, his position could be a precedent for later constitutional decisions. But would Washington sustain it? The President, Hamilton had once said, "consulted much, resolved slowly, resolved surely." Now Washington, delaying as long as he could, resolved in favor of Hamilton and signed the bank bill.

Though this was a striking victory for Hamilton, the bank still represented only one part of the Federalist thrust in America's political economy. The House of Representatives had also asked the Secretary of the Treasury for a plan "for the encouragement and promotion of such manufacturers as will tend to render the United States independent of other nations for essential, particularly for military supplies." As usual, Hamilton interpreted his mandate in the broadest terms, and in December 1791, after almost two years of collecting and analyzing economic data, he submitted to Congress nothing less than an economic plan for the United States. Protection of struggling young industries—a central concern for the congressmen—was only a part of the plan, and the smaller part to boot. Hamilton and his brilliant Assistant Secretary, Tench Coxe, took an elaborate inventory of the nation's capacities and needs, evaluated its existing and potential manpower, machinery, energy resources such as water power, and proposed economic measures that would guarantee the nation's economic unity and industrial power for decades to come. His key proposals were for a variety of governmental aids to business, ranging from bounties for inventions and subsidies to business, to modernized transport and other internal improvements.

Hamilton did not feel bound by dogma; he borrowed from Adam Smith while rejecting most of his laissez-faire philosophy. Nor was he handicapped by sentiment. Coldly but approvingly he evaluated the potential of labor by women and children in factories. Better off there than on the farm! He counted especially on the availability of women for the cotton factories.

It was a superb piece of economic planning. But did it reach the fundamental wants and needs, hopes and expectations of the great mass of Americans, especially in the hinterland, and of the rival politicians who would respond to those basic needs?

*   *   *

Thousands of Americans indeed did not see Hamilton's program as meeting their deepest needs and hopes. Their primary concerns were rather the religious and political liberties that had brought their forefathers to America, liberties that had received some protection under state bills of rights, liberties they wanted to protect against any possible threat from the new federal government.

Madison turned to drafting a bill of rights as quickly as he could in the first Congress, partly in response to the intense demand, partly to head off anti-Federalists who were pressing for a second general convention. Why not use the new amending process? Madison asked. This alternative required passage by a two-thirds vote in both House and Senate and endorsement by three-quarters of the states—a cumbersome procedure, but Madison was confident that the groundswell of support for a bill of rights would push the amendments through. First he and his colleagues in the House had to deal with more than two hundred amendments submitted by state ratifying conventions. These made up a mixed bag. Many simply wanted to restrict federal power in general. A few were *anti-*civil liberties;

thus from New England came one claim that the prohibition of religious tests in the Constitution would enable "Jews, Turks and infidels" to infest the new government. Others were eloquent on the popular demand for procedural and substantive rights. Out of the grist House leaders refined seventeen amendments. After Senate consideration, a conference between senators and representatives to adjust differences, and consideration by state legislatures, ten amendments emerged. Two of them—the ninth and tenth—reaffirmed the reservation of rights to the states and to the people. Others would secure the right of people to bear arms, to be secure in their homes, to enjoy a host of procedural rights in courts and outside. But the heart of the Bill of Rights lay in the bold and absolute provisions of the first article:

Congress shall make no law respecting an establishment of religion, or prohibiting the free exercise thereof; or abridging the freedom of speech, or of the press; or the right of the people peaceably to assemble, and to petition the Government for a redress of grievances.

The amendments were ratified by the end of 1791. The American people had their Bill of Rights. What would they do with it?

Newspaper editors knew what to do with it. By 1790 the nation had almost a hundred newspapers, most of them weeklies, but a few semi-weeklies and eight dailies. Pressed down a page at a time on a crude block of type by human labor, printed on rough rag paper with a drab grayish or bluish cast, produced at the rate of about two hundred copies an hour, these two- or four-page newssheets were not much to look at. Many papers were short-lived, as editors found they could not make up with job printing for lack of subscribers, high costs of paper and mailing. But these newspapers had an immense vitality. They played up foreign and national news at the expense of local, in part because filching material from foreign newspapers and quoting verbatim from congressional debates were cheap ways of filling their columns. The result was the spread of an immense amount of political news throughout the states.

These newspapers were by no means "objective." While few editors published their views as editorials, their biases so infused their news columns as to stamp most papers as clearly Federalist or Republican. Many editors were themselves politicians, or unabashedly sponsored and even financed by politicians. The most famous of these arrangements came to be Jefferson's sponsorship of Philip Freneau's *National Gazette* and Hamilton's of John Fenno's *Gazette of the United States.* Hamilton saw to it that his *Gazette* received printing contracts from the Treasury Department; and Jefferson arranged for the publication of his *Gazette* by providing Freneau with a State Department post that allowed for plenty of time off. Each stung by the gibes in the other man's paper, both Hamilton and Jefferson appealed to Washington, who admonished his two cabinet members to make "mutual yieldings." Neither Hamilton nor Jefferson would yield. They were operating amid rising political tensions. The editors were not encouraging a politics of accommodation. Raucous, venal, often libelous, yet committed and strong-minded, they went their way, now shielded by the Bill of Rights.

The early 1790s were indeed a period of political tumult, but even more, of political paradox. George Washington presided over a government of national unity, but his administration was rife with internal conflict. Men addressed one another face to face or in correspondence in the most exquisitely courteous terms—one gentleman writing to another would end his letter, even if he hated his correspondent, with a painfully written out "I have the honor to be with the highest respect, sir, Your most Obedt. & mot: hble Servant"—but public political discourse was conducted in the most extreme language. The men around Washington were building a national governmental structure in a cooperative, soldierly, and workmanlike way, yet they differed violently over banks, tariffs, slavery, fiscal policy, foreign policy, presidential power, congressional prerogative, the permanent location of the national capital, and over a multitude of philosophical issues, such as representation, revolution, responsibility, and the protection of liberty.

Above all, political leaders at local, state, and national levels were buttressing freedoms of speech and press and assembly, without a clear concept of just how these liberties related to the role of government and opposition, faction and interest, majority and minority party. The leaders in fact feared, spurned, and despised the idea of faction and party even as they took part in factions and shaped embryonic parties. They did not consider and firmly articulate the role of government party and opposition party. Leaders as varied in outlook as Washington, Paine, Adams, Jefferson, and Henry agreed on one thing—the evil of organized factional or party opposition. Such an opposition, indeed, took on a strongly sinister, subversive cast, and became an alien threat to republican government and hence something to be extirpated. The political leadership, in short, had no theory of party. Hence the future of parties would be shaped far more by events than by design.

One of the more benign of these events occurred in May 1791, when Jefferson and Madison took off on a "botanical expedition" up the Hudson. After tarrying in New York City a couple of days, they left for Albany by carriage and boat. New York Federalists eyed them narrowly. What could these two Republicans be up to? Practical politicians could not believe it, but the two Virginians were actually interested mainly in the flowers and fish, the trees, game, insects, soil, streams, lakes, scenery, and battlefields rather than in the political flora and fauna. However, they probably did visit Governor Clinton in Albany, before pursuing their journey up Lake George to Champlain, down through Vermont to Bennington, overland to the Connecticut Valley, and finally across the Sound to Long Island. They had a chance to compare notes on Republican politics in the "Eastern" states, and doubtless word seeped out to the surrounding countryside that the celebrated Virginians had passed through.

It was evident that as long as George Washington stayed in office political conflict would be kept within bounds, and by late 1792 it was evident that he would be President for another four years. He had talked much about quitting after his first term, but when leaders in the different factions urged him to run again—"North & South will hang together, if they have you to hang on," Jefferson told him—the President allowed electors to be chosen for him. His popularity was still at a high pitch, and he had bolstered it even more when he took a sea voyage to Rhode Island, where he spoke in favor of tolerance to representatives of the Jewish Congregation of Newport, and when he toured Georgia and the Carolinas in 1791. He carried the electoral college unanimously the following year. John Adams was also re-elected, but once again votes were diverted from him, this time mainly by Republicans. Washington, managing as always to stay above the election battle, did not intervene to help his Vice-President.

The hero worship for Washington had its limits. When it was proposed in Congress that the head of the President be stamped on the new coin of the United States, republicans warned of monarchical tendencies and future Caesars, Neros, and Caligulas, and the move was defeated. Instead Congress ordered that the coins be adorned with the female figure of LIBERTY.

THE DEADLY PATTERN

George Washington seemed to be a relaxed and happy man at the ball given in his honor on the occasion of his sixty-second birthday, ten days before the second inaugural. With military bearing and punctilio, he marched in with Martha Washington at his side, to the airs of "The President's March." He liked the Philadelphia belles who were there, he liked the words "Long live the President" in Latin or French they had woven into their hair bandeaux, and he liked his old friends from Revolutionary days, among whom he moved easily, remembering old campaigns and humorous war stories. Political talk he brushed aside. Precisely at the moment of the ball's end, he and the First Lady rose, the band struck up a reprise of "The President's March," and the couple paraded out, amid cheers.

The President had good reason to feel content. He had wanted above all to nurture and symbolize a united nation, and he seemed to have done so, in appointing a balanced Cabinet, in his travels, and always in furbishing his carefully shaped image of benign authority. He had followed up his northeastern tour with a journey to the South in the spring of 1791, where as usual he had been showered with endless tributes but where he had also talked with farmers and woodsmen in the taverns along the way. He concluded: "Tranquility reigns among the people."

The man who took the oath of office ten days later, however, seemed a changed man, almost an angry man. He proceeded to the Senate alone in a coach, entered the chamber with minimal ceremony, gave an address of 136 words in which he said that if he knowingly violated the Constitution he should be impeached and upbraided, took the oath of office, and returned to his residence. The reason, rumor had it, was an attack in Freneau's *National Gazette* on the birthday ball as a "monarchical farce" promoted by sinister types close to the President and opposed to freemen's liberties. More likely, the attack reminded Washington of more basic divisions in the country—of the party and factional rivalries that had broken out even within his official family, the hostility to Hamilton's excise tax out in the hinterland, the battles between the first Americans and the settlers that erupted fitfully along the long frontier to the west.

Increasingly the West was exciting the interest of the public and posing problems for the government. Settlers were moving toward the Ohio and the Mississippi, with the help of the land speculators. About the time of Washington's first inaugural certain citizens of Pennsylvania and New Jersey were receiving, on a confidential basis, an "invitation" that read:

"Several Gentlemen who propose to make settlements in the Western Country mean to reconnoitre & survey the same the ensuing winter. All farmers, Tradesmen &c of good characters, who wish to unite in this scheme & to visit the Country under my direction, shall be provided with boats & provisions for the purpose, free of expence, on signing an agreement. . . . The boats which will be employed on this expedition are proposed to be from 40 to 60 feet long, to row with 20 oars each, & to carry a number of Swivels. Each man to provide himself with a good firelock or rifle, ammunition & one blanket or more if he pleases. Such as choose tents or other conveniences must provide them themselves. Every person who accompanies me on this undertaking shall be entitled to 320 acres of land, at ⅛ of a dollar per acre. . . . All persons who settle with me at New Madrid,

& their posterity will have the free navigation of the Mississippi & a Market at New Orleans free from duties for all the produce from their lands, where they may receive payment in Mexican Dollars for their flour, tobacco &c. . . ."

Buffalo and other game would be plentiful in the area, it was promised; settlers would be helped in clearing ground, building a house, and obtaining livestock; schoolmasters would be engaged and ministers encouraged to come. The new city would be built on a high bank of the Mississippi, near the mouth of the Ohio, in the "richest & most healthy part of the Western Country."

This kind of advertisement was helping swell a vast movement of population over the Appalachians and into the West. Amid intense state jealousies and fierce political combat, the original states had been adjusting to the pressures of western expansion. Before and after the Revolution, Virginians and Marylanders were moving as far as the forks of the Ohio, joining Pennsylvanians and others. New Englanders and New Yorkers were also moving west. After the Revolution the streams of settlers swelled to torrents.

State lands were reorganized as people legislated with their feet. In 1783 Virginia had agreed to cede its lands north of the Ohio, provided it could reserve for itself a district to satisfy military grants made during the Revolution. Virginia had held back its land south of the Ohio, which would be organized as the state of Kentucky. In 1785 Massachusetts gave up its claim to a stretch of land crossing the (present) states of Michigan and Wisconsin, and the following year Connecticut ceded some of its western land, withholding a tract in northern Ohio—the Western Reserve—for the relief of Connecticut victims of destruction of property by the British. Other states too let go of their lands, which gave to the Confederation—and later to the United States—a huge public domain.

Into this domain swarmed the settlers, crowding the roads year after year, especially during the months of spring to fall, moving singly, by families, or by groups. Usually it was a family, its belongings packed into one covered wagon, leading a horse or cow or mule. Others traveled by two-wheeled carts, still others on horseback or even on foot. With luck they could boat down rivers, but sometimes luck failed, as overloaded craft upset in rapids or "savages" shot arrows from the high banks. Preceding, accompanying, or following the migrants were other possible dangers—claim jumpers, squatters and fugitives from justice, merchants and other middlemen looking for quick profits in monopolistic situations, and land sellers and speculators not unwilling to lure poor farmers and mechanics west with grandiose promises of cheap land, rich harvests, and big money.

On the face of it, the "invitation" to New Madrid looked like such a real estate scheme.

But James Madison put a far more ominous gloss on the document when he sent a copy of it to George Washington late in March 1789. "It is the most authentic & precise evidence of the Spanish project that has come to my knowledge." The Spanish project! For decades Spaniards, Frenchmen, and Englishmen had contended for control of the lower Mississippi. For years Americans on the southwest frontier had chafed under Spanish control of the lower Mississippi and had resented the Northeasterner who seemed to care so little about settlers' rights in the Southwest. Patrick Henry, trying to mobilize Kentuckians against the 1787 Constitution, charged that the new federal government would surrender navigation of the Mississippi to Spain in exchange for concessions that would mean little to the frontiersmen. James Wilkinson, a Revolutionary War general, actually accepted Spanish gold in return for information and other services to the Spanish. By the end of the 1780s the Southwest was a conspiracy theorist's heaven, alive with intrigue, suspicion of the new federal government, and plots for secession. Land speculators were believed to be aiding and abetting the conspiracies.

The question of the Southwest was one more flammable issue in the politics of the 1790s, and one more stimulus to party rivalry, with Republicans generally more sympathetic to southwestern fears and hopes than were Federalists based in the Northeast. The Southwest intensified rather than transcended political conflict. And the Southwest—indeed the whole frontier from Florida through the Southwest and up through the Northwest to the Canadian border in the Northeast—involved another "foreign power" who aroused among some Americans the deepest anxieties and hatreds of all—the American Indian.

*   *   *

For years the main device for dealing with this "foreign power" had been the treaty, as in the case of the Cherokees, Choctaws, and Chickasaws in the South in the mid-1780s. "The principle was adopted of considering the Indians as foreign and independent powers, and also as proprietors of lands," John Quincy Adams wrote later. "As independent powers, we negotiated with them by treaties; as proprietors, we purchased of them all the land which we could prevail on them to sell; as brethren of the human race, rude and ignorant, we endeavored to bring them to the knowledge of religion and of letters."

This sentiment was typical of the ambivalent policy of Americans toward Indians—paying for the Indians' land as they ousted them, uplifting them as they uprooted them. Washington and other Federalist leaders rejected the policy many frontiersmen called for—all-out conquest of the Indians. They chose policies of negotiation, a show of liberality, guarantees of protection from encroaching whites, trade, and education. The Northwest Ordinance of 1787, passed by Congress in one of its final and most important actions under the Confederation, stated that the "utmost good faith shall always be observed towards the Indians; their lands and property shall never be taken from them without their consent . . ." and "laws founded in justice and humanity shall, from time to time, be made, for preventing wrongs being done to them, and for preserving peace and friendship with them. . . ."

Noble words—and genuinely meant by many of those who uttered or legislated them—but the frontiersmen and settlers hardly heard and rarely heeded these words; their actions were based on practical needs for more land, on fear and suspicion of the "redskin," on the latest scalping incident, no matter who provoked it. Inevitably, the fierce combat that followed led to bigger battles.

It was the same old deadly pattern of white advance, Indian defense, white retaliation. In 1790 Kentucky militiamen and federal regulars burned deserted Indian villages near the Maumee River in Ohio; later a combined force of Chippewas, Miamis, Shawnees, Ottawas, and other tribes, under the leadership of Chief Little Turtle, slaughtered six hundred men commanded by General Arthur St. Clair. Vengeance was delayed when Washington invited fifty chiefs of the Six Iroquois Nations, old allies of the British but also friendly to the Americans, to journey to Philadelphia for a parley. The whites wished to awe the Indians with their wealth and numbers, satisfy some of the minor Indian grievances, and persuade them to go as emissaries to Little Turtle. After a month of being wined and dined in the best Philadelphia style, the guests were flattered but not deceived. Their chief, Red Jacket, suggested that since the red men were being manipulated by both Britain and the United States, only an agreement between the two powers would bring order to the frontier. But he did promise to try to soothe his western brethren.

That task fell to Captain Hendrick Aupaumut, a Mohican chief who had served under Washington at the Battle of White Plains. To the Delawares, one of Little Turtle's allies, Aupaumut pictured Washington's policy of friendship. Since the Americans now had their own liberty, "now they endeavor to lift us up . . . from the ground, that we may stand up and walk ourselves." The British, on the other hand, would just cover them "with blanket and shirt every fall," so that they would remain "on the ground and could not see great way."

Little Turtle's followers, however, already felt uplifted enough by their victories, and what they could see close at hand was not liberty but more encroachment. They would not yield. Then came the vengeance: Three years after St. Clair's disaster, General Anthony Wayne decimated Ottawas, Shawnees, and other Indians at the Battle of the Fallen Timbers. Next year a thousand red men from thirteen tribes gathered at Fort Greenville, Ohio, and ceded over 25,000 square miles of eastern and southern Ohio for $25,000 in goods and a $9,500 annuity.

Whether standing fast and dying, retreating west, or remaining to barter and be educated in white ways, Indians might well wonder how they were making out on the other side of the American experiment. They may have read a hint of the future on the medal that General Washington had conferred on Red Jacket: it depicted the general in martial array presenting a peace pipe to an Indian chief while, in the background, a white man broke the land with a plow.

*   *   *

News of Wayne's victory came to President Washington not in Philadelphia but twenty-five miles to the northwest, where he was conducting his own war, not against red men but against whites. With him was Alexander Hamilton, who more than any other man was the cause of the trouble.

As part of the Secretary's plan to fund the national debt, Congress had in 1790 imposed a small excise tax on the production of liquor, as well as on such other genteel indulgences as snuff and sugar loaf. From the start, anti-Federalist congressmen had denounced the whiskey excise as "odious, unequal, unpopular, and oppressive" and predicted that it would "convulse the Government." Even though Washington had moved to ease Hamilton's tax, Pennsylvania farmers west of the Alleghenies were not to be mollified. They had long been "intoxicated with liberty," a French traveler had noted, and their definition of liberty was freedom from the tax collector. This particular levy they loathed. With the Mississippi closed off to western trade, the farmers made more profits from shipping wheat and rye over the mountains in liquid form rather than bulk. The excise had to be paid in cash, which was so scarce in the western counties that jugs of home brew were used for currency. Worst of all, since the tax was levied at the still head, farmers had to pay tax on what they saved for their own refreshment. In practice, the home brewers were masterly at foiling the tax men, whether state or federal, but it was the *principle* of the thing. They defied the federals.

For George Washington, it was the principle of the thing too. Defiance in the West brought back unhappy memories of the revolt of Shays's men

hardly seven years before. Why had the federal government been established, if not to put down defiance of law and order? The President suspected further that local "Democratic" societies, composed of admirers of
the French Revolution and foes of Freemasonry, Alexander Hamilton, and
the Society of the Cincinnati, were inspiring resistance. In fact, events were
not marching to a plan but awaiting the inevitable incident, and this came
in the form of an eruption of gunfire, and two deaths, at the home of a local
excise collector. Disorder spread as mobs destroyed excise offices.

Federalists in Philadelphia greeted the disturbances with fear and rage,
demanding that the "white Indians" be put to the sword. Seeing an opportunity to discredit and destroy Democratic societies, Hamilton called for
immediate military action. The President concurred; if "the laws are to be
so trampled upon with impunity," he said, "and a minority, a small one
too, is to dictate to the majority, there is an end put, at one stroke, to
republican government." He called up the militia of Virginia, Maryland,
Pennsylvania, and New Jersey and was vastly relieved when thirteen thousand men responded to the order to put down their fellow citizens. The
President himself took to the field—and with him rode the original excise
man himself, target of the hatred of rebel and republican alike, Secretary
Hamilton. Washington had proceeded as far as Trappe when the good
news arrived from General Wayne.

This great show of force was mounted on the assumption of a real threat
from the whiskey rebels. Certainly there was much talk—and occasional
examples—of tarring and feathering local tax collectors, smashing the
stills of those who paid the excise, and burning the barns of particularly
obnoxious officials. But the Whiskey Rebellion was never a true rebellion.
It was oratory, mass meetings, and whiskey itself that largely kept the
rebels going. While there was talk that rebel leader David Bradford,
the popular prosecuting attorney of Washington County, might lead the
Monongahela counties to independence, the rebels were scattered, their
leadership divided. Moderates counseled moderation, and some property
holders joined the revolt mainly to deflect it from any further violence. The
strength and the involvement of the Democratic societies as a whole
proved to have been much overrated.

For there was no civil war in Pennsylvania, no fighting to speak of. Like
the Shaysites of old, Bradford and other leaders fled, leaving the rest of
the population meekly to submit to a new loyalty oath. Some rebels were
arrested, two were convicted of treason—and Washington pardoned them
both. A triumphant President wrote to a friend that the Europeans would
now see that "republicanism is not the phantom of a deluded imagination:
on the contrary, that under no form of government, will laws be better

supported, liberty and property better secured, or happiness more effectually dispensed to mankind." Order was necessary to liberty.

Washington was as angry as he was relieved. In a letter to his brother-in-law, Burgess Ball, he fulminated at the Democratic societies—could "any thing be more absurd, more arrogant, or more pernicious" than these "self-created bodies" telling a representative government what to do? In his next annual address to Congress he denounced the role of "certain self-created societies" for actions smacking almost of sedition. Republicans were indignant; they had largely followed a hands-off attitude toward the rebellion, though Jefferson had derided the campaign against it as "an armament against people at their ploughs." When Jefferson had been a member of the Cabinet, he had warned Washington that an attack on the Democratic societies would make the President appear as "the head of a party instead of the head of the nation." Now Madison saw Washington's speech to Congress as putting him "ostensibly at the head of the other party."

That was the last thing General Washington wanted. And if ever there was a case for the presidency as a symbol of unity and nonpartisanship, it was in the mid-1790s, as the European powers squared off and drew the New World into war.

DIVISIONS ABROAD AND AT HOME

In September 1792 the French revolutionaries proclaimed the French Republic. Four months later they executed their king. Ten days after that they declared war on Great Britain, Spain, and Holland. The news of these events fell like hammer blows on American opinion. Since 1789 the sons and daughters of the American Revolution had been watching the French revolutionaries with ardent hope and sympathy. Lafayette had even sent Washington the key to the Bastille. To old soldiers in taverns and hostelries, it seemed sublime that the people who had aided the American Revolution should embark on their own, and indeed they took credit for exporting the idea across the Atlantic. "Liberty," proclaimed the Boston *Gazette*, "will have another feather in her cap." Speakers broke into song and verse as they rapturized the revolutionary upsurge in Paris and the start of "freedom's glorious reign."

Jefferson was still in Paris during those early events; he even helped draft the Declaration of the Rights of Man. He was optimistic. "I have so much confidence in the good sense of man," he wrote a friend, "that I am never afraid of the issue where reason is left free to exert her force; and I will agree to be stoned as a false prophet if all does not end well in this country.

. . . Here is but the first chapter of the history of European liberty." He was not uncritical; he sent home acute observations on France's halting progress toward self-government.

John Adams had a more measured reaction. He hoped that the French Revolution, he wrote a friend, would favor "liberty, equity, and humanity. . . ." But he had "learned by awful experience to rejoice with trembling," he wrote another friend, Dr. Price. "I know that Encyclopedists and Econo-mists, Diderot and D'Alembert, Voltaire and Rousseau have contributed to this great event more than Sidney, Locke, or Hoadley, perhaps more than the American Revolution; and I own to you I know not what to make of a republic of thirty million atheists. . . ." Adams could not disguise his bias in favor of the English. Nor could Hamilton: friendship with Britain was at the heart of the Secretary's foreign policy, not least because of his admiration for English legal and economic practices.

"We think in English," Hamilton said. But the cause of France, Republi-cans said, was the cause of *man.*

Soon, however, the cause of man seemed to falter in France. The rise of the Jacobins, the execution of the king and queen, the endless devouring of new cadres of leaders, the horrifying rounds of the tumbril, produced a revulsion among some Americans. "When will these savages be satiated with blood?" John Adams demanded. Jefferson deplored the fate of the Terror's victims, but there were higher stakes—the "liberty of the whole earth was depending on the issue of the contest." Others cared not a whit about the guillotining of the king and queen—they even celebrated it. At a Philadelphia banquet the head of a pig, representing Louis XVI, was passed around while the feasters, decked out in caps of liberty, mangled it with their knives. At a tavern between Chester and Wilmington the innkeeper exhibited a sign showing a decapitated female, her dripping head lying by the side of the trunk, until the public forced him to withdraw this grim effigy of the late queen.

Thus the Terror drove a wedge between Americans, and France's war on Britain and Spain drove the wedge in deeper. The impact of the war stretched to the West Indies, to the Mississippi, to Canada, to the south-west frontier, to the posts on the northwest border still occupied by the British—areas of cardinal importance to the Americans. As American in-terests were touched and American attitudes enflamed, fierce disputes over foreign policy became linked with domestic disputes.

With dismay Washington observed the rising feeling. He had, above all, wanted to preside over a united government that could transcend "local prejudices, or attachments," and "party animosities." Before the end of his first term he was noting the "internal dissensions" that were "harrowing and tearing our vitals." To Hamilton and Jefferson he sent separate pleas for mutual forbearance and compromise. All he got for his pains was a complaint from his Secretary of State that Hamilton was intruding into foreign policy, a charge that his rival's policies were directly opposite to his own, and an indication of intent to resign; and from his Secretary of the Treasury, a response that it was he—Hamilton—who was the "deeply injured party," a charge that Jefferson's "machinations" were subverting the government, and an offer that *both* he and Jefferson resign.

If the two men acted like paranoids, at least they had real enemies in each other. Within a few weeks of assuming office Hamilton had been indulging in secret negotiations with a British diplomat, to whom he described Madison as "very little Acquainted with the world." Anglophile himself, fearful of Jefferson's Francophilism, Hamilton in effect aided the British in countering the efforts of the Secretary of State. Jefferson, on his part, fought Hamilton through political channels. He appealed to Madison: "For God's sake, my dear Sir, take up your pen, select the most striking heresies and cut him to pieces in the face of the public." Soon Madison was thwacking Hamilton hip and thigh.

Washington stood firm amid the turbulence. He kept both men in his Cabinet, and he judiciously selected from among the views of both. He rejected Hamilton's pleas that the American treaties of commerce and alliance with France be suspended. But he declared American neutrality as between France and Britain—a move that angered Republicans who could not forget France's vital aid in their own revolution.

Into this unstable equilibrium intruded the figure of Edmond Genêt. A youthful diplomat turned revolutionary, Citizen Genêt had been sent to America to shore up the cause of France, diplomatically, commercially, and militarily. Landing in Charleston in April 1793, he journeyed north to such celebration and acclaim that he arrived in Philadelphia with a head, if not crowned by a liberty cap, certainly swollen with hopes of winning a popular acclaim that would surpass even Washington's, of enlisting Americans to conduct military adventures against Louisiana and Florida and thus engaging France's old ally fully in the "cause of man." Soon he was commissioning privateers in American ports to bring in fat British prizes off the Delaware capes.

Warmly greeted by Jefferson, received even by Washington, and enthusiastically feted by Philadelphia Republicans, Genêt soon wore out his welcome with his vainglorious efforts to conduct his own foreign policy abroad. Even Jefferson cooled when Genêt renamed a captured British brigantine *Petite Democrate,* smuggled cannon and men aboard her in Philadelphia, and slipped her down the river, past Mud Island, and out to sea before Washington, visiting Mount Vernon, could take action. Soon the Hamiltonians were organizing mass meetings and adopting resolutions upholding Washington's neutrality policies and condemning Genêt. In Virginia the Madisonians retaliated through public meetings attacking the Federalist "Cabal." The result was the direct and deep involvement of large numbers of people in the making of foreign policy.

Genêt's dénouement was inglorious: Washington demanded his recall to Paris, but the Citizen, discovering that in his absence he had been converted from a radical to a reactionary in the deadly *bouleversement* of French politics, chose to stay in America, to wed Governor Clinton's daughter and retire to private life. But this tragicomedy of 1793 was a fitting prelude to the crisis of 1794. That crisis was precipitated by the collision of France and Britain over possession of the seas—and by American illusions that somehow a small nation, three thousand miles away, could remain unentangled in the struggle of the great powers.

Diplomatically, that struggle provoked the usual cynical game of sham neutrality on the high seas. Britain, possessing a mighty navy, wished to cut off the trade lines to France. France, weaker on the seas and dependent on American shipping to its home ports and to the West Indies, proclaimed its adherence to the doctrine of freedom of the seas. The United States stood on its "neutral rights." Yet even the French violated their own doctrine when, in the face of an American neutrality that for a time seemed to be favoring Britain, it seemed expedient to confiscate American ships and cargoes.

The British did not bother to be hypocritical. Hoping to starve France into submission, they proclaimed a blockade of that country, ordered the seizure of all neutral vessels transporting cargo to France, and—most threatening of all to the American merchant marine—extended their naval and seizure operations directly into the Caribbean. These decisions having been made in secret, the British Navy was able to fall on the big American trade to the Caribbean and to snare more than two hundred American ships.

As news of these depredations trickled into American ports, a wave of anti-British feeling swept through the nation. Anger mounted on reports that the English were up to other heinous acts—arming Indians on the northwest frontier, helping Barbary pirates to prey on American shipping. There were calls for war, for a second struggle for independence. Never mind that the United States had practically no army or navy; Madison suggested that the Portuguese Navy be hired. Or perhaps the British lion could be brought to its knees by commercial action. The issue cut deep into the structure of American opinion, inflaming Republican Anglophobia even further, deepening the North-South conflict, dividing even the Federalists among themselves. Deserted by some of his more martially inclined Federalist brethren, Hamilton stood staunchly against commercial retaliation against London. Britain, after all, was the main prop of his whole fiscal system.

Once again the figure of Washington—outwardly imperturbable, inwardly distressed—stood in the breach. He now lacked the official advice of Jefferson, for his Secretary of State had resigned, by prearrangement, at the end of 1793, to be succeeded by another Virginian in whom Washington had less confidence, Edmund Randolph. Moving quickly to fill the semi-vacuum, Hamilton urged the President to dispatch a minister plenipotentiary to London, and Washington agreed. The choice fell on Chief Justice John Jay. Hamilton himself drafted Jay's instructions. The move came barely in time to head off a bill passed in the House for non-intercourse with Britain; the measure failed in the Senate only on a tie-breaking negative vote cast by Vice-President Adams.

The bill had been an effort for peace, aborted if only for a time, for Republicans were skeptical of Jay's mission. A Federalist judge acting on Federalist instructions: this, they felt, would mean the path toward appeasement. Skepticism turned to indignation and wrath when copies of the treaty—two of which had to be thrown overboard from the ship carrying them when a French privateer intercepted it on the high seas—reached Philadelphia. Jay had secured admission of United States ships to British East Indian ports on a nondiscriminatory basis, as well as the opening of the West Indies trade, but only to small American ships carrying a limited number of staples. But the northeast boundary question and British and American claims and compensation questions were left open—they were referred to a joint commission to be established—and British trade with the United States was placed on a most-favored-nation basis. Nothing was settled with regard to the impressment of seamen, to the slaves "stolen" and liberated by the British, to the Indian question.

In effect, Republicans claimed, Jay had surrendered the "freedom of the seas." The opposition would appeal to the people. Soon protest meetings were held, Hamilton was hooted down when he tried to defend the treaty, and an impeachment move was launched against Jay, who was accused of selling out to British gold. The clamor against the treaty, Washington said, was "like that against a mad-dog." Jay himself remarked that he could have made his way across the country by the light of his burning effigies. And once again it was the stolid figure of Washington that calmed the political tempest. In the face of rising Republican opposition, an untimely renewal of ship seizures by the British, and his own—and Hamilton's—doubts about certain aspects of the treaty, he overrode opposition within his Cabinet from Randolph and insisted on Senate ratification. The senators complied, after striking out the tepid compromise on West Indies trade.

Washington also stood firm against Republican opposition in the House. Madison and his colleagues, exercising power over appropriations necessary to put the treaty into effect, were insisting on their right to look at presidential papers involving the treaty, but the President denied that they had that right. As the appropriations issue came to be fully debated in the House, once again the party leaders turned to the people for petitions, support at rallies, and enthusiasm. Party lines tightened in the country, and especially in the House, where voting along Federalist-Republican lines increased, and both sides met in what were the first party caucuses held in Congress. An immensely effective speech by Federalist Fisher Ames, and the defection of Republican Frederick Muhlenberg, Speaker of the House (for which defection he would shortly be stabbed by his brother-in-law, a fanatical Republican), defeated the move to withhold appropriations for the treaty.

As if argument over policy were not enough to keep the parties divided, the Administration and its opponents fought hard over power and procedure. The President's claim of sole authority to proclaim neutrality, and of his right to withhold treaty papers, his bold assertion that treaties signed by the President and ratified by the Senate were the supreme law of the land (subordinating the role of the House)—these and other presidential and congressional claims led to furious debates between Federalist and Republican. The men of '89 knew that they were creating vital precedents in resolving the ambiguous decisions of the men of '87—and the fact that many of these were the *same* men did not temper their feelings. Indeed, when Washington said that he knew what he was talking about because he had taken part in the constitutional convention, Madison and his friends retorted that that piece of parchment in itself was "nothing but a dead letter, until life and validity were breathed into it by the voice of the people" in the state ratifying conventions. The man who would come to be known as the Father of the Constitution would not accept lessons in constitutional law from the man who would become known as the Father of His Country.

Thus were Washington's hopes dashed for a foreign policy that would rise above party and sectional and group politics. Not only were Federalists and Republicans divided over the year-to-year strategy and the everyday tactics of foreign policy, they were profoundly divided over ideology, sentiment, and in their sympathies for Britain and France; over the kind of nation they were trying to build; over the kind of people Americans should become; over America's political and symbolic place in the world. Ordinarily attitudes over foreign and domestic policy are not congruent; persons combining with one another over domestic issues often split with one another over foreign. In the 1790s, however, congruence was intensifying among both Federalists and Republicans over the two sets of policies.

The result was a sharpening and hardening and deepening of attitudes separating and polarizing the Federalist and Republican groupings—a polarization that helped produce enormous popular participation in the debates over foreign policy. The further result was to lay the foundations for a powerful two-party politics, the shape of which could not be fully divined in the 1790s.

CHAPTER 4

The Trials of Liberty

In the summer of 1796 two farmers were busy improving their estates. In Quincy, Massachusetts, John Adams supervised the building of a large barn, using red cedar that he and his hands had cut from a grove in the lower township and hauled home behind a team of oxen. Every day he inspected his fields of barley and oats and rye and corn; the main problem this summer was the corn, attacked by worms. With special pleasure he rode across his once thin and stony fields, now rich from years of treatment with his special compost of salt hay, seaweed, cow dung, and horse manure, interlaid with lime.

He did not neglect his moral duties. Sundays he attended church morning and afternoon, and he reflected on the Christian teachings of love and brotherhood. Weekdays he struggled for the soul of his hired man Billings, a good worker when sober, but prone to spending days swilling brandy, wine, and cider, "a beast associating with the worst beasts in the neighborhood." Sick and dizzy, he would return to the farm, seize the hoe Adams thrust at him, and stagger from hill to hill slashing weeds and cornstalks alike. Finally Adams set about carrying enormous stones with Billings in order to sweat him out, only to provoke the man into threatening to quit, after ranting about Adams' hardness, his endless lecturing, his treating him like a hired beast. Morality won out; taken to Abigail to be paid off, Billings reconsidered, haggled a bit, and agreed to stay on at forty-five pounds a year—and to take the pledge against hard liquor.

In Monticello, Thomas Jefferson was busier than ever with the endless remodeling of his house. He had found that the interior timbers of the upper part of the house were decaying and shaky, and soon seven workmen were prying bricks loose by the thousands. Now Jefferson was planning to replace the attic with an octagonal dome that would enclose a mezzanine balcony around the interior. On the ground floor he established his own suite, with a bed alcove between his dressing room and study, which were directly connected when he drew the bed up into the recessed ceiling during the day. Outside the house two long terraces, linked by an all-weather passageway, would cover kitchen and servants' rooms on the south, and stables, carriage house, and laundry on the north. And beyond this little estate on its mountaintop stretched Jefferson's fields, the paths he called "roundabouts," and the huts that housed his 150 slaves, now mortgaged to the hilt from his heavy spending. While his home was roofless during the rebuilding, Jefferson and his family camped out under the "tent of heaven."

The two men were tending their gardens—and keeping their eyes cocked on Philadelphia, New York, and Charleston. In Philadelphia, the President had firmly decided against running for a third term and indeed was contemplating an elaborate Farewell Address. Madison and other Republican leaders were quietly preparing the way for Jefferson to run for President, though they had received little active encouragement from him. Supporters of John Adams, hoping for the united backing of their fellow Federalists, were maneuvering in the critical mid-Atlantic states. From New York, Alexander Hamilton was looking for a pliable southern Federalist who might have a chance against Adams, whom he had found unresponsive, stubborn, and occasionally weak in his Federalism.

In New York too, an ambitious, forty-year-old Republican, Aaron Burr, was hoping to win the vice-presidency—and perhaps more eventually—as Jefferson's running mate. In Charleston, Thomas Pinckney, brother of Charles Cotesworth Pinckney and second cousin of Charles Pinckney, was hoping that his recent success in gaining navigational freedom on the Mississippi from Spain would make him appear to be the kind of southern Federalist that the northern Federalists were seeking. And complicating the calculations of all the politicians was the strange presidential election system that required each elector to cast his ballot for two presidential candidates, with the man receiving the most votes winning the presidency, and the runner-up settling for the political booby prize, the vice-presidency.

The main actors were true to form. Despite his sighs for Quincy, Adams desperately wished to be President, but the custom of the day allowed him to do no campaigning, so his supporters conferred with him in Quincy and then, acting mainly on their own, organized rallies, wrote campaign pamphlets, and arranged newspaper offensives. Even less active than his rival, Jefferson told Rutledge, "I have no ambition to govern men; no passion which would lead me to delight to ride in a storm." All he wished was to plant his corn and peas "in hills or drills as I please...." While this attitude in part was a pose, Jefferson was genuinely torn between politics and plantation, and even more, between the call of public service and his right to a private life. Few would believe it, he told his son-in-law, but he "sincerely" wished to run second in the electoral college. Yet he did not discourage his backers, among whom Burr was active in mobilizing support from Tammany Republicans in New York.

Once again Hamilton was trying his hand at the game of "wastage" that was invited by the presidential election system. To win the game he must elect his kind of Federalist, which meant keeping Adams—and of course Jefferson—out of the presidency. His main card was any ambitious politician who could be tempted into running, and his main tactic was withholding votes from a front-runner so that his own man could come in. But he had to play a strong card, and his calculating eye first fell on Patrick Henry in Virginia. It seemed an unlikely choice, although Henry, now sixty, had mellowed in his opposition to the federal Constitution while hardening in his opposition to the Jefferson-Madison faction in Virginia politics. But ill and weary, he declined the honor, and Hamilton turned to Pinckney. Soon word was quietly going out to Federalist electors in the North to vote for Adams and Pinckney, and to electors in South Carolina to vote unanimously for the Charlestonian but waste a few of Adams' votes. Never mind that this maneuver might elect Jefferson, defeat the richly experienced and world-famous Adams, and disrupt the Federalist party. Hamilton played his cards coolly—but perhaps too openly or obviously, for New England Federalists, playing their own game of wastage, withheld electoral votes from Pinckney.

The result was a hairbreadth victory for Adams over Jefferson, 71 electoral votes to 68, the elevation of Jefferson to the vice-presidency—and a naked sectional split. Jefferson won not a single vote in New England, Adams only two in the South. Of the eighteen votes that Jefferson picked up north of the Potomac, fourteen came from Pennsylvania, where Republican politicians had been especially active. Most significant, twelve of the sixteen states gave their votes either wholly to Adams or wholly to Jefferson.

The close vote and the power of section reflected a rising polarization among political leaders. In his Farewell Address, Washington inveighed against quarreling over section and party. Everyone agreed and everyone kept on quarreling. The President himself was no longer a figure above the battle. The Republican editor of the Philadelphia *Aurora*, Benjamin Bache —nicknamed "Lightning Rod Junior" because he was the grandson of Benjamin Franklin and liked to apply electric shocks to Federalists— charged that Washington had deceived and debauched the nation, and had taught it that "no man may be an idol" and that "the mask of patriotism may be worn to conceal the foulest designs against the liberties of the people." Nor did Jefferson stay above the battle by distancing himself from the campaign. Indiscreet talk and letters on his part came to Washington's notice; the President, angry at Jefferson's supporters and now cooling toward his fellow Virginian, charged that every act of his administration had been tortured by the grossest misrepresentations, in terms that "could scarcely be applied to a Nero; a notorious defaulter; or even to a common pickpocket." Citizen Adet, a new "political diplomat" from France, hardly helped matters when he appealed in the press to the American people to elect Jefferson President and make friends with France again.

The election left the main contestants at odds—Adams furious over Hamilton's machinations, Jefferson none too happy about having to quit Monticello to preside over the Senate, Pinckney sorely disappointed, and Burr suspicious that he had been done in by shenanigans in Virginia.

With the coming of Inaugural Day, however, the differences were papered over, and Adams began his administration amid a glowing sense of harmony. He and Jefferson had been quoted as saying nice things about each other, and while neither believed that the other really meant them, the gestures were appreciated. Washington, profoundly happy to be returning to Mount Vernon for good, was attentive and congratulatory. Republican editors—even Bache himself—hailed Adams' Inaugural Address, perhaps with the thought that they might draw this proud and independent man, with his hostility to high Federalists like Hamilton, into the Republican camp.

They did not know their man. While he disliked the crass money-grubbers and speculators among the high Federalists, Adams detested even more the egalitarian Republicans with their "leveling" doctrines. Viewed as a conservative enslaved to rigid doctrine, and as a fussy, vain, self-pitying, pompous man, Adams in fact was a deeply emotional and even passionate person, almost as critical of himself as of his adversaries. He simply lacked the sublime—or sentimental—faith in the people found among so many of his fellow revolutionaries. Adams saw humankind as irredeemably quarrelsome, perverse, illogical. Still, they must govern themselves. The institutional solution was *balance*—balance of power among rich and poor, balance between rulers and ruled, balance between Congress and presidency, balance between order and liberty. The human solution was education, strong and selfless leadership, faith, and patience. The moral solution was private and public virtue.

Like many of his contemporaries, Adams believed in liberty, but it was a restricted brand of liberty, limited mainly to white adult males and protected against turbulent mobs, popular majorities, crass materialists, fiscal uncertainty—and the Republican "levelers."

Philadelphians: The Experimenters

By January 1797, when John Adams was laying plans for his presidency, the federal government had resided in Philadelphia for over six years. George Washington had created a government in New York City; at the end of the 1790s the capital would move to Washington, and there the government would create a city. But Adams inherited both a government and a city. For years members of Congress, federal judges, and bureaucrats had been living in hotels and boardinghouses, visiting Philadelphia's historic buildings and monuments, exploring its city life. Few could escape the influence of a city noted for its cosmopolitan urban life, its heritage of philosophical debate and practical experimentation.

Even congressmen from the great cities of New York and Boston, and from the rival city of Baltimore, could envy the spaciousness of the new federal capital. Compared with the narrow lanes and twisting alleys of other places, Philadelphia, with its broad parallel avenues and neatly laid out cross streets, was a *planned* city. Congressmen were well acquainted with the county courthouse, where they met in what was now renamed Congress Hall, and with the old city hall, taken over by the Supreme Court. They could visit again the Old State House (Independence Hall), where the new federal government had been conceived under its Liberty Bell in the previous decade. They could admire Franklin's mansion on Market Street, now completed, with its ten-foot arched passageway providing direct access from the street to the courtyard, where he had built a two-story printshop and newspaper for his grandson. And they could retire after vigorous congressional debating to the City Tavern, called by John Adams the most "genteel" tavern in America. Here, in May 1774, after Paul Revere had arrived with news that Parliament had passed a bill closing down the port of Boston, a great company of Philadelphians gathered and, after a tumultuous debate, sent word to Boston asserting Philadelphia's "firm adherence to the cause of liberty."

Congressmen from rural areas were plunged into the urban splendors and enticements of the second most populous city in America. Some, bringing their rustic spectacles with them and hobnobbing mainly with men from their own hinterlands, looked at city life with suspicious eyes. Others, more willing to explore and exploit the capital, found a city bursting with intellectual activity. Philadelphians gloried especially in the subscription libraries, and if these were increasingly open to men of all classes, they were still closed to women, who had turned to reading rooms and to circulating libraries like the one established several decades earlier by William Bradford. Men of the upper and middle classes participated in the numerous scientific societies, in the spirit of the first one founded by Benjamin Franklin and joined by a glazier, a shoemaker, and a carpenter, as well as by professional men. "The poorest labourer upon the shore of the Delaware," a minister said some years later, "thinks himself entitled to deliver his sentiments in matters of religion or politics with as much freedom as the gentleman or scholar."

Philadelphians had, indeed, long been debating a fundamental intellectual and educational issue: to what extent should students—especially poor students—be given a classical or a "practical" education? William Penn himself had complained that "we are in pain to make them scholars but not men, to talk rather than to know. . . . We press their memory too soon, and puzzle, strain, and load them with words and rules to know grammar and rhetoric, and a strange tongue or two" that would never be used, while leaving uncultivated "their natural genius to mechanical, physical, or natural knowledge." Anglican and liberal Quaker members of the city's elite had argued for a classical education along European lines. Later, Franklin worked out a compromise on the question, only to see the Latin division of the new Academy of Philadelphia exceed the English division in popularity under the leadership of teachers like Francis Alison and William Smith. Women, blacks, and the poor were taught largely by private masters, but they could also attend night schools for working people, both male and female. Philadelphia by 1790 could claim that almost complete literacy had been achieved in the city.

Philadelphians had formed societies for promoting agriculture and for "Encouraging the Manufacture of Useful Arts" only a few years before the city became the federal capital, and they founded the University of Pennsylvania two years afterwards. But the proudest boast of the city's intellectuals was still the American Philosophical Society. Modeled closely on the Royal Society of London, the APS originally was a small group of scientifically minded men like Franklin, and it was overshadowed by "The American Society for Promoting and Propagating Useful Knowledge." The two groups had competed for prestige until 1769, when they consolidated under the name of "The American Philosophical Society for Promoting Useful Knowledge." Severely restricted during Revolutionary times, the society flourished in the postwar years and had completed building its official home, Philosophical Hall, just two years before the federal government moved to Philadelphia.

The city was also famous for medical education. Its doctors had begun lecturing on anatomy and obstetrics in the absence of formal medical training, and later founded a medical college and a medical society. Dr. William Shippen, Jr., in 1767 established the first lying-in hospital in the

colonies and offered courses in prenatal care to pregnant women. The
press helped cultivate medical education; printers not only supplied information about lectures and clinical programs but published full accounts of
medical discoveries that helped dispel some of the popular suspicion of
physicians.

Congressmen from single-interest districts such as tobacco-growing
could marvel at the cultural variety and vigor of Philadelphia. Interest in
literature had grown sharply during the prosperous middle years of the
eighteenth century. English works, like those by Defoe, Swift, and Goldsmith, sold well, but magazines and newspapers eagerly printed the efforts
of local writers. The verses of William Smith and of the multi-talented
Francis Hopkinson became well known. Since the Quakers were more
interested in civic and humanitarian projects than in the fine arts, upper-
class Anglicans tended to take the leadership in patronizing painting and
sculpture.

The desire of the wealthy to preserve their images for posterity
prompted many a sign painter to turn portraitist, but later a more refined
realism both in portraiture and in landscapes replaced the clumsier efforts
of earlier days. After previous successes in London and Ireland, Gilbert
Stuart in 1794 set up a studio in Philadelphia, where he made his first two
life portraits of George Washington. Wealthy merchants also subsidized
architecture by building country houses; architects tended to ape the Georgian style of England, but at least they adapted the style to local materials,
to the stone and brick, the white pine and oak of the Philadelphia area.

Some of the cultural offerings were scarcely highbrow. Congressmen
had their choice of numerous theaters, such as the Southwark on South
Street, and traveling circuses offered pantomimes and farces. Except for
the Quakers, the churches had begun to use organs in their services, but
popular airs and folk tunes constituted the "people's music." Visiting
countrymen found ample opportunity for betting on horse racing and
cockfights. Congressmen could be sure of invitations to levees, dancing
assemblies, balls, formal dinners, card parties, and summer sojourns on
country estates. Not all of them could wholly resist the "aristocratic embrace," or wanted to.

A vigorous and partisan press mirrored the cultural vitality of the city.
During the late 1790s Philadelphia had more newspapers than any other
city in the country. Typically consisting of about four medium-sized pages,
they usually ran advertisements of merchandise and real estate on the front
and back, along with news of departure and arrival of sailing vessels,
notices of runaway slaves, stagecoach schedules, announcements of the
publication of books and pamphlets. Some newspapers covered moral and

religious news, printed poems and book reviews, and reported on scientific and medical discoveries. The inside pages usually carried letters from abroad and reports on state and congressional activities, with comments by the editor and by readers.

News was not always abundant. When the federal government moved into Philadelphia the editor of the *Aurora* complained: "As to domestic politics, no party disputes to raise the printer's drooping spirits; not a legislative sitting to furnish a few columns of debates, not even so much as a piece of private abuse to grace a paper — Zounds, people now have no spirit in them. . . . Now not even an accident, not a duel, not a suicide, not a fire, not a murder." The arrival of a President, a Cabinet, and a few dozen congressmen soon made up for some of these lacks.

On the surface, Philadelphia did indeed appear to be tranquil. In fact, the "City of Brotherly Love" was undergoing rapid change and experiencing severe tension and conflict, and these too would affect the nation's as well as the city's future.

The history of the city was shot through with contradictions. In founding the city as a "Holy Experiment" for persecuted Quakers, William Penn had made Philadelphia an open city for all believers and nonbelievers, because "no people can be truly happy, though under the greatest Enjoyment of Civil Liberties, if abridg'd of the freedom of their Consciences as to their Religious profession & Worship." This benign open-door policy inevitably helped bring a flood of immigrants—Irish, French, Dutch, and Swedish, with their various religions and sects—to the point that the Quakers were vastly outnumbered, with the result that they protected themselves by maintaining control of the Pennsylvania Assembly, with the help of a sharply limited suffrage.

On the whole, immigrant groups got along together reasonably well, but this was in part because they were considerably segregated, with the Mulberry and upper Delaware areas heavily populated by Quakers and Germans, and the southern areas, especially along the docks, by the Irish. A powerful tradition of tolerance persisted, but in 1770 a mob, inflamed by rumors that Dr. William Shippen had stolen bodies from a local cemetery for medical research, attacked his home. In the same year that the constitutional convention met in Philadelphia, a woman suspected of being a witch was killed by a city crowd.

The fundamental conflict in Philadelphia, however disguised, was economic. The brotherly city was also a class-ridden one. On the top of the social and economic pyramid sat several hundred wealthy merchants, many of whom had made their fortunes in complex triangular trading—importing and selling sugar, rum, and molasses from the slave plantations of the

Caribbean, using the profits to buy manufactured goods from Britain and France, and reselling these in the city at another profit. Often these merchants maintained dockside houses that were as unimposing as their mansions in the country were elegant. Attached to this economic elite were ministers, scholars, lawyers, and other professional men. In the middle ranks of the class pyramid stood large numbers of artisans: carpenters, shipwrights, sailmakers, millers, carriage makers, blacksmiths, harness makers, tanners, tailors, boot makers, cordwainers, and others. This stratum had its own internal class structure comprising men of differently valued skills, such as those of master craftsman and ordinary artisan, of journeymen and apprentices, who often lodged in their master's home and ate at the family table, and of women in a variety of trades and occupations. At the bottom of the pyramid were laborers, indentured servants, itinerant workers, recently arrived immigrants unable to speak English, carters, stable boys, sailors, servants, and—somewhere below but outside the pyramid—blacks.

The condition of the blacks in particular challenged fraternal shibboleths. Black people had been part of Philadelphia's history from the very start; indeed, W. E. B. Du Bois noted in his monumental study *The Philadelphia Negro* that the Dutch "had already planted slavery on the Delaware when Penn and the Quakers arrived in 1682. One of Penn's first acts was tacitly to recognize the serfdom of Negroes by a provision of the Free Society of Traders that they should serve fourteen years and then become serfs—a provision which he himself and all the others soon violated." Long divided over the issue, the Quakers finally condemned slavery in 1758 and later, on the eve of the Revolution, excluded slaveholders from fellowship in the Society of Friends. During the century before, the Pennsylvania legislature had passed harsh laws directed at blacks; one, providing for execution, castration, and whipping as punishments, and barring the meeting together of more than four blacks, was disallowed by the Queen in Council. Emancipation was restricted on the ground that "free negroes are an idle and slothful people" and tended to become public burdens, but free blacks were hardly better off than slaves, since competition for jobs brought them into conflict with white laborers. It was not until 1780, amid the liberating impulses of the Revolutionary War, that an act for "the Gradual Abolition of Slavery" was passed. The initial result, Du Bois noted, was widespread poverty and idleness.

Inequality in Philadelphia was visible, palpable, inescapable. At one glance an observer could rate the social status of hired laborers wearing linen shirts and striped trousers, mechanics with their leather aprons, skilled craftsmen with their respectable, sober attire, and rich young men decked out in the latest fashions from London. The distribution of wealth was not unlike that in other American cities: by the end of the century less than a quarter of the taxpayers owned more than three-quarters of the taxable property valued at over $50; but of a labor force of more than 10,000, over 3,000 were not taxable.

About half of Philadelphia's working class lived at or just above subsistence levels. The results were, as usual, appalling: at least a third of Philadelphia was ill housed, ill clothed, and ill nourished. The city was divided, said a contemporary observer, into several classes of company: "the cream, the new milk, the skim milk, and the canaille. . . ." This loose class structure did not produce sharp class conflict, however, in part because the working poor lacked the leadership that might have aroused them to political consciousness.

The merchants of Philadelphia were not heartless exploiters. Compared to their ilk in other American and European cities, they were in many cases unusually benevolent. This very fact, however, helped involve them in a fundamental ambiguity. They were, first of all, entrepreneurs in a city bent on enterprise and profit-making. "Under the American tradition, the first purpose of the citizen," Sam Bass Warner, Jr., said in introducing a study of Philadelphia, "is the private search for wealth; the goal of a city is to be a community of private money makers." But many merchants were also public men. They had invested large amounts of money and time in humanitarian endeavors—founding a university and medical college, subsidizing education for the poor, blacks, and women, establishing libraries, promoting the arts, easing the plight of prison inmates, improving health and sanitation, devoting themselves to cultural and philosophical matters, serving in public office. Not only the elites but the middle classes were trying to advance themselves: laborers to get better pay, apprentices to become journeymen, artisans to become master craftsmen who could control their own work, time, and future. So a deep concern for the public welfare pervaded much of Philadelphia. But where did the private man leave off, the public man begin?

This question was part of a broader, more complex one. How could a community be organized to advance the general welfare while protecting individual rights—while making the pursuit of individual rights, indeed, part of the means of achieving the general welfare? As the federal men governed in Philadelphia during the 1790s, there seemed to be less time for these questions to be decided, before events would make the decision. For change was accelerating in Philadelphia. The city was experiencing the full impact of the altered economic patterns and social relations reshaped during the War of Independence. Profits were becoming bigger and more tempting in the widening economic prosperity. The city was bursting at the seams as immigrants flooded in; the black population almost doubled in the last decade of the century.

The first question—public service versus private gain—would largely be left to the consciences of wealthy men. The second question—promoting liberty and the general welfare—occupied the best minds in Philadelphia for a century.

*   *   *

In April 1789 Benjamin Franklin, who had lived through eight-and-a-half decades of that century, lay mortally ill in the bedroom of his Market Street house. Although racked by fevers and his stone, only partly dulled by opiates, he was still philosophical; "what are the pains of a moment," he said to a friend, "in comparison with the pleasures of eternity?" Until almost the end he pursued his political inquiries; the American Philosophical Society held its meetings in his home when he could no longer even be moved into his sedan chair. And he remained the empiricist, the inquirer, the experimenter, in matters political as well as scientific. "We are, I think, in the right road of improvement," he had said the year before the constitutional convention met in his city, "for we are making experiments."

Franklin and his fellow Philadelphians had conducted the most radical of political experiments ten years before, an experiment in sharp contrast with that of 1787. Inspired by the revolutionary acts against Britain in Massachusetts and angered by the conservatism of the Pennsylvania government, a group of Philadelphians early in 1776 had used their control of the militia, the committees of correspondence and public safety, and other extralegal revolutionary organizations to overthrow the authority of the Assembly. The radicals who had engineered this coup were a very different lot from the sound and substantial men who had dominated Philadelphia's politics. Thirty-year-old Benjamin Rush led a multi-faceted life as a doctor, a professor of chemistry at the College of Philadelphia, and a sermonizer for temperance and exercise, and also as a political reformer, a millenarian who expected Christ's Second Coming, and a revolutionary Christian utopian who advocated the abolition of slavery. Forty-six-year-old Timothy Matlack was an apostate Quaker, a failed shopkeeper, a gambler, horse racer, fistfighter, bull baiter, and cockfighter whose prized bantams fought a famous match with cocks brought to Philadelphia by a New York blueblood. A habitué both of Philadelphia groggeries and of the Philosophical Society, Matlack had a remarkably wide acquaintanceship with men rich and poor, black and white. There were other notables: evangelical republicans like Christopher Marshall, artists like Charles W.

Peale, deists like Thomas Young, highly skilled artisans like Owen Biddle, and the self-taught scientist David Rittenhouse. But the political and intellectual luminary was Thomas Paine.

Born of a Quaker father and an Anglican mother in a market town seventy miles northeast of London, Tom Paine rose from apprentice to journeyman to master stay maker in only a few years, and then won a post as an excise taxer, only to be dismissed for agitating for higher pay for excisemen. Married and already separated at the age of thirty-seven, he struck out for America and a new start. Arriving in Philadelphia in 1774 with letters of introduction from Benjamin Franklin, he had intended to establish an academy for the education of young men, but was quickly swept up in the revolutionary euphoria of the city. Soon he wrote and published *Common Sense,* a sweeping attack on the Crown's interference with American trade, and a bold call to American independence. *Common Sense* scored an immediate success, running through twenty-five editions and selling well over 150,000 copies, an astonishing number for those days. This tract—the most brilliant written during the American Revolution and one of the most brilliant ever written in the English language, in Bernard Bailyn's judgment—had a quick and profound impact on public opinion.

The force of that impact was due not only to Paine's clear and blunt language, his assault on the English monarchy, his clarion call for independence; other tracts had such qualities. The impact came from his repudiation of the established thinking of centuries on the question of liberty. For most Americans, and certainly for most Philadelphians—heirs to the fine Quaker tradition of liberality and tolerance—the great issue of the 1770s was the protection and nurturing of liberty. This was also the main principle and goal of most enlightened Englishmen. The question was how to achieve this goal without sacrificing other major values such as order, stability, and virtue.

Englishmen of Whiggish persuasion were convinced that, after decades and centuries of thought and travail, the British constitution had come to represent the best way to achieve that goal. Drawing heavily from Greek and Roman thinkers who had affirmed the need of mixed government in order to achieve balance and harmony among social classes, the English had achieved such a balance of social power among king, lords, and commons that a political balance of power would be counterpoised among these powerful estates. Social equilibrium in short would produce political equilibrium, which in turn would prevent the kind of immoderate government that might interfere in men's liberties. This elaborate edifice was based on the theory that men, being naturally selfish, irrational, aggressive, greedy, and lustful, had to be not only protected in their liberty *from* government but protected from one another *by* government. The "Interest of Freedom," Marchamont Nedham had written in the mid-1650s, "is a Virgin that everyone seeks to deflower."

Paine and his fellow radicals rejected this view of human nature and the Whiggish apparatus that went with it. Perhaps the people of the Old World, divided into unequal estates and corrupted by their rulers, were prone to depravity and unreason, they granted, but Americans were different. Farmers and mechanics and all others who wore "leathern aprons," being more equal and fraternal and less grasping and competitive, were more reasonable and virtuous. Because of his faith in human nature and the perfectibility of man, as Eric Foner has said, "Paine could reject the need for governmental checks and balances."

What kind of system, then, did the radicals want? Simple, the radicals answered—a government directly representing the people, a government mirroring the wants of the people, a government that could act quickly to meet the needs of the people, a government constantly renewed by the people so that it would never become remote from them. Under a people's government the people's liberty would be secure. It was Mercy Warren's kind of polity.

How establish such a government? The Philadelphia radicals had scored a decisive coup by waging a grass-roots, populist campaign and thus gaining control of the Pennsylvania constitutional convention held in 1776 as part of the breakaway from Britain. Then they proceeded to write perhaps the most democratic, most directly representative constitution of the founding period. The new charter granted the right to vote to every white male over twenty-one. It abolished property qualifications for officeholding. It gave the state assembly control over the government of Philadelphia. And—by far the most important—it established a unicameral legislature, elected annually, with rotation in office. The new assembly would be open to the press and people, its votes published weekly, its records available to the public. In one sweep the colonial gentry had lost its political power.

The implications of the radicals' constitution were frightening to Whig and conservative alike. Any year they were so minded, a majority of the voters in Pennsylvania—perhaps a majority made up of the uneducated and the unwashed—could pass whatever laws it wished, with no power in the executive to veto or in the judiciary to void. Conservatives feared the powerful currents of egalitarianism loose in Philadelphia in this first year of independence. What if the many ganged up on the few? Did not the new constitution itself bar the imprisonment of debtors not guilty of fraud, allow people to hunt on unenclosed land, provide for schools with low fees throughout the state? What other "leveling" measures might be passed?

The radicals rejected these fears as groundless in a free society. How could any kind of republican object to putting power squarely into the hands of the directly elected representatives of the people? Indeed, the new constitution placed a limit on the number of terms a legislator could serve; that, plus annual elections, would cause legislators to be constantly refreshed by immersion in the grass roots and thus maintain their ties to the people. And if they did, the radicals contended, the Pennsylvania legislature would be a safe depository of power because it would directly reflect and embody the people's virtue, sense of good, concern for the whole public, willingness to sacrifice for the benefit of all. These public virtues grew out of people's private virtues of tolerance, understanding, benevolence, enlightenment. How could an assembly representing such virtues be harmful to the public interest?

Opponents of the new constitution flatly rejected this whole premise. They simply did not share the radicals' faith in the people's wisdom, virtue, and benevolence. So the radicals would lodge supreme power in the people? But *any* sovereign power must be guarded against; whether "that power is lodged in the hands of one or many, the danger is equally great." The new constitution presupposed "perfect equality, and equal distribution of property, wisdom and virtue, among the inhabitants of the state." The anti-radicals would not assume this. They argued that the people would deprive themselves of their own liberty, as well as others of theirs. Behind this contention was a deep fear of the people—of their leveling tendencies, their ignorance, their bumptiousness, their eternal desire for more.

None expressed these doubts better than Benjamin Rush, who soon began to have reservations about the radical constitution. "Absolute power should never be trusted to man," Rush wrote the year after adoption of the new constitution. He actually meant *men,* no matter how many, for there was no safety in numbers. "Although we understood perfectly the principles of Liberty," Rush wrote in 1787, "yet most of us were ignorant of the forms and combinations of power in republics."

Such fears led to a relentless drive against the 1776 constitution throughout the following decade. To destroy the "constitution of the people" the anti-constitutionalists went to the people themselves. Meeting in the City Tavern to plan strategy, they organized a grass-roots effort to call a new constitutional convention. The press was enlisted; one newspaper warned that Philadelphia would not be chosen as the federal capital if the state legislature remained unicameral. The anti-constitutionalists recruited candidates for the convention, organized election tickets, and won control of the convention. Soon Pennsylvania had a new constitution, replete with separation of powers and checks and balances—most notably, with a bicameral legislature and a strong, independently elected governor.

So Pennsylvania's brief experiment in popular government, in majority rule, had come to an end, as did the reign of the radicals. It would live on only as a memory that might be invoked in some future era of conflict and crisis. That rule in Pennsylvania had seen no tyranny of the majority, nor had the reign of the radicals brought radical government. Property had not been confiscated, churches leveled, merchants taxed to death. Life had gone on pretty much as before. Perhaps the radicals should have changed things more fundamentally. By the time the federal government was established in Philadelphia it was too late. Pennsylvanians lived under both state and federal governments hemmed in by checks and balances. They were doubly safe against the tyranny of the people.

But Philadelphia would be experiencing more change in the 1790s. Its population continued to expand. Craft workers started to unite in local unions. Voting participation doubled. Local political cadres began to organize grass-roots parties. For almost a decade congressmen and federal officials lived among memories of old conflicts and amid the pressures of new ones. The new conflicts challenged the Constitution of 1787, with its carefully separated powers. It remained to be seen whether a constitutional system so fragmented and inhibited could deal with rising change and conflict on a national level.

The nation would also confront formidable power abroad—and that would raise the question whether the President of the United States would need more executive authority in dealing with prime ministers and potentates.

Quasi-War Abroad

John Adams entered the presidency at a time when relationships with the French were rapidly deteriorating. Washington had sent James Monroe to Paris with the hope that he could reconcile the French to Jay's treaty, but even as good a Virginia Republican as Monroe could not placate the increasingly xenophobic and bellicose French government. Charles Cotesworth Pinckney had taken Monroe's place, but Adams had been in office only ten days when he was informed that the Directory had sent Pinckney packing too. The new President had already made clear in his Inaugural Address that the government would be in peril when a single vote could be influenced by "foreign nations, by flattery or menaces; by fraud or violence; by terror, intrigue, or venality"—an obvious thrust at the likes of Genêt and Adet. Now with the rebuff to Pinckney, and more news of French seizure of American ships in the West Indies, Adams faced a dire choice between peace and war.

He first turned to his Cabinet—a natural move, except that this was not his Cabinet but Washington's and increasingly Hamilton's. In order to unite Federalist ranks and strengthen himself with the Hamiltonian wing of the party, Adams had asked Washington's Cabinet to stay on. This meant keeping on such high Federalists as Secretary of State Timothy Pickering, a Salem lawyer and merchant as proud and haughty as the Cabots though not as rich; Secretary of the Treasury Oliver Wolcott, a Connecticut farmer and banker, who had proved himself a good administrator under Washington; and Secretary of War James McHenry of Maryland. When members of the Cabinet promptly turned to Hamilton in New York for advice on how to respond to the President, he seemed more concerned with domestic Federalist party strategy than with foreign policy. Hamilton urged his friends to press for further negotiations with Paris in order to combat Republican charges that the Federalists wanted war with France. They passed on this advice as though it were their own. Assured of backing from leaders of both parties, Adams convened a special session of Congress, which he asked to enact and fund defense measures and to approve a special mission to France.

Making up that mission was in itself an exercise in diplomacy for the new President. For the sake of weight and balance the mission should consist of three persons—but what three could undertake such a crucial and delicate assignment? It was agreed that Pinckney would be sent back, and Adams would have liked to appoint both Hamilton and Madison, but he encountered resistance to this idea. John Marshall of Virginia, an experienced lawyer and moderate Federalist, was agreed on, despite his lack of diplomatic experience. The third place Adams filled with a curious choice: Elbridge Gerry of Massachusetts. Considered by some Federalists as unreliable and even a "hidden Jacobin," but too much of a gentleman to enjoy the company of Massachusetts fishermen and rural Republicans, Gerry followed an independent course—which was the main reason Adams trusted him and turned to him for advice.

Awaiting the mission in Paris was Count Talleyrand, Minister of Foreign Affairs, a man who personified all that Americans suspected in the diplomats of the Old World. A former bishop in the Catholic Church, Talleyrand had won a reputation as a promiscuous, pleasure-loving rake, without scruples or morals—a "cloven footed Devil," a diplomat's wife had called him. He had spent two years in prudent exile in the United States and professed to know Americans well—perhaps too well, as he claimed that they pursued gold far more than liberty. On gold the French foreign minister was something of an expert, for he had amassed tens of millions of francs by shaking down European kings, dukes, and even a grand vizier.

Talleyrand did not disappoint. After being allowed to cool their heels for days, and after being informed that the Directory was outraged by Adams' Inaugural Address, Pinckney and company were approached by Talleyrand's agent, who whispered that in order to sweeten the Directory, a small *douceur* of twelve million livres or more would be necessary. The Americans rejected the proposition. Later, when the agent threatened war, Marshall replied that his country would defend itself.

"You do not speak to the point," Talleyrand's man exclaimed. "It is expected that you will offer money. . . . What is your answer?"

"It is no; no;" Pinckney said; "not a sixpence." Later a newspaperman converted this remark into a grander retort: "Millions for defense, but not one cent for Tribute."

The long months of awaiting the Pinckney mission's report had been a wretched time for John Adams. The Republicans in Congress fought almost every proposal he made, and he could not depend on Federalists or even his Cabinet, as Hamilton continued to interfere in Administration affairs from New York. Bache and other Republican editors flogged him in print as hard as they had Washington, and even though Adams pretended not to notice the scribblers, he in fact read them and was incensed by them. His relationship with Jefferson cooled again as the Vice-President, confined in Philadelphia by his Senate duties, was drawn more and more into the role of party leadership. Lacking firm congressional, party, or even cabinet backing, Adams turned for support to Abigail Adams.

He had begun his presidential days without his lady, as Washington had done without his wife, but like Washington he soon brought his wife to the capital. More outspoken than John, at least to her friends, more likely to suspect plots, even more aroused than he by the venom of Bache and the other "Jacobins," the First Lady followed events closely and conducted a wide correspondence, while managing the President's house and even the farm in Quincy from afar. There was hardly an important matter the President failed to discuss with her, though she served mainly to comfort his raveled ego and bolster his views. In their closeness they still managed to keep a little distance. On coming to his office one morning she found him reading a letter to her from Mary Cranch; she promptly lectured him on the sanctity of private correspondence.

The political doldrums in Philadelphia ended suddenly in early March 1798 with the arrival of the first dispatches from the Pinckney mission.

Reading them, Adams did not know whether to be more furious at the French or at the emissaries for their "timorous" behavior—a result, obviously, of sending amateurs abroad. The President drafted a war message to Congress that flayed French and Republicans alike, but he had second thoughts. His Cabinet urged caution, and Adams feared that publishing the mission's dispatches would overstimulate the public, and even jeopardize the lives of the three emissaries in France. In a mild final version he rebuked the French and called for stepped-up coastal defenses and protection of American shipping, including the arming of merchantmen.

Adams' action was far too little for the high Federalists, far too much for the Republican opposition. At this point the Republicans fell into a trap largely of their own making. Not satisfied with blocking some of Adams' defense measures, they demanded to see the actual dispatches from the mission in Paris, on the grounds that the saber-rattling Adams had exaggerated the hostility of Talleyrand and the Directory. While some Federalists baited the trap by joining in the call for the papers, and while some of the shrewder Republicans held back fearing a ruse, the bulk of the Republicans in the House voted through a demand for the documents. Forced to do what he had wanted to do from the start, Adams sent the dispatches to Congress after substituting the letters, X, Y, and Z for the names of Talleyrand's agents.

Publication of the documents not only raised a political storm throughout the country, it achieved the seemingly impossible—it made John Adams popular. In Philadelphia, merchants held a meeting to prepare a special letter of thanks to the President, and the French cockades that had adorned many a Republican hat suddenly disappeared. The wave of approval rolled through the sixteen states and brought to the President's house hundreds of addresses of approval from colleges, grand juries, militia companies, and meetings in small towns. The song "Adams and Liberty" was on everybody's lips. Adams, who earlier could have entered and left the theater in Philadelphia without attracting much notice, was now greeted by great shows of approval. Abigail Adams attended the theater incognito to hear a noted actor sing "The President's March," and rushed home to tell John that the audience had demanded four encores to the song and at the end broke forth in the chorus, singing and clapping so loudly that her head rang.

What could the President do with his newfound popularity? John Adams needed no lessons in the volatility of public opinion. He knew that a declaration of war while the iron was hot would be immensely popular, especially with members of his own party, but he held back. Gerry had lingered in Paris, much to the indignation of high Federalists, and Adams could not be sure whether he was softening up the French or going beyond the mission's instructions; doubtless he heard about Pickering's quip, uttered with the gallows humor of an old Salemite, that if the French would only guillotine Gerry it would be a great favor. Adams also judged that France might suddenly declare war on the United States—and the President preferred, if war must come, that the French take the initiative. So Adams contented himself with an innocuously spread-eagling message to Congress announcing that he would "never send another minister to France without assurances that he will be received, respected, and honored, as the representative of a great, free, powerful, and independent nation."

With passions unreined, events were in the saddle. A quasi-war in effect came to exist on the Atlantic and in the Caribbean as French warships continued their depredations and American sea captains, conducting their own military policy, responded on the high seas. As the war fever waxed, Congress created a Navy Department, enlarged the Army, authorized naval retaliation against French sea marauders, abrogated the 1778 and 1788 treaties with France, and finally—in July 1798—authorized naval operations on all the seas.

Still Adams paused. Marshall returned home to a hero's welcome from the Federalists, but the envoy told Adams privately that the Directory did not really want war—only to intimidate the United States into yielding. Taken aback by the American reaction, Talleyrand seemed to be having second thoughts and with his usual dexterity was sending out peace feelers through Gerry and others. The President's main concern was the Federalist wing that, still heated with war fever, was hoping to use the quasi-war as a way of conducting expeditions into the Southwest against Spain and France, and as a pretext for crushing the Republican opposition at home once and for all.

A single problem converted this whole issue into a thorn in his side. With the Army expanding, the President decided that only one man could lead it as commander in chief and hence symbolize America's unity and determination: George Washington. The old general would not come out of retirement, however, without a second-in-command who could get things done as the general wished them done—and that man was Alexander Hamilton. While Adams was urging others on Washington such as Knox and Pinckney, who had more seniority and circumspection, Pickering, McHenry, and others in his administration were conspiring with Hamilton to persuade Washington to stand fast for the New Yorker. He did, and the President, unwilling to brook the high Federalists and the ex-President, put his worst party enemy in effective command of the American Army.

The summer of 1798 had been the most gloomy of his life, Adams wrote Pickering later. He and Abigail had been able to escape the Philadelphia heat after Congress adjourned in July, but the trip north was slowed by endless dinners and addresses to the now popular President, and Abigail arrived home so ill that she was bedridden for weeks and her life for a time despaired of. The epidemic sweeping Philadelphia was claiming the lives of friend and foe alike, including that of John Fenno, the Federalist editor. Such piteous reports arrived of poor persons camped on the Philadelphia common and orphans taking refuge in almshouses that Adams sent $500 to be distributed anonymously among the poor.

Yet, in a way that few discerned at the time, this was Adams' time of greatness because of what he did not do—he refused to succumb to those demanding all-out hostilities against France. Events, to be sure, came to his aid. Naval defeats at the hands of Admiral Horatio Nelson convinced the French that they could do with fewer enemies, and American commercial interests active in the lucrative trade with the French West Indies were a force for peace. But there were long periods during which Adams could have seized on any day as "the day we went to war," to the great enthusiasm of the populace. Instead, the "day he did not go to war" stretched into weeks and months and brought the young republic to the end of its first decade in a state at least of quasi-peace.

SEMI-REPRESSION AT HOME

The panic and jingoism of early '98 left behind strange fruit—strange at least in a nation that had recently adopted a national bill of rights and seemed to worship the goddess of liberty. In one four-week period in the early summer of that year, Congress passed measures—later to be called the Alien and Sedition Acts—that threatened liberty of the press and of speech and challenged the whole conception of a legitimate or "loyal" opposition in a republic.

That men like Washington, Adams, Hamilton, and Marshall, and hundreds of other leaders who had fought for liberty as revolutionaries, could turn about only seven years after the passage of the first ten amendments and punish the kind of acts they had once committed—such as erecting a Liberty Pole—served long after as a source of surprise and dismay to later generations trying to understand the founding period. Only those able to "think their way" back into the era of the late 1790s could understand how this reversal came to pass. For this was a time when Americans were engaged in a quasi-war with France, when a full shooting war was believed imminent from day to day, when extremist Republicans were seen not only as mistaken and evil-minded but as secretly aiding and abetting the French enemy, when Republican editors in fact wrote the most scurrilous and inflammatory lies about Federalist leaders, when rumors abounded that French spies and infiltrators would attack America from within, burn down the churches, free the slaves, ravish women in the streets, and erect guillo-tines in town squares.

It was a time too of escalating domestic conflict, when pro-Constitution Republican leaders like Madison feared that the monstrous "consolidated government" they had dreaded was actually coming to pass, that John Adams was really trying to set up a monarchy or at least an aristocracy, that in taking on France the Administration was fighting the wrong war at the wrong time against the wrong nation, that the Federalists were using the war scare as an occasion for suppressing criticism and destroying the whole Republican party.

Buoyed by popular feeling, sure of their majorities in both houses, the Federalists pushed through four measures. Though innocuously entitled and phrased in dry eighteenth-century legalese, these bills laid bare the passions and conflicts of the time. An "act to establish an uniform rule of naturalization" increased the period of probationary residence for immi-grants from five to fourteen years. For years Federalists had been looking with disdain and fear on the disaffected and even "revolutionary" Scotch and Irish fleeing British oppression, and especially on the "hordes of wild Irishmen" who had come to America to disturb her tranquillity after failing to overthrow their own governments. For years Republicans had been welcoming the political support of these same immigrants—another rea-son for Federalist anger.

An act "concerning Aliens" gave the President the power to deport aliens in time of peace, and another act "respecting Alien Enemies" in time of war was passed. Because no formal war occurred, the latter act did not come into effect, but the former hung like a sword over the heads of aliens and was branded by Jefferson as a "detestable thing" that was "worthy of the 8th or 9th century."

The "act for the punishment of certain crimes against the United States" —the Sedition Act—would fine and jail those found guilty of writing, publishing, or saying anything of "a false, scandalous, and malicious" nature against either house of Congress or the President, with intent to defame them, bring them into contempt or disrepute, or excite against them "the hatred of the good people of the United States." Those prose-cuted under the act were allowed to offer evidence supporting the truth of the matter charged as libel, and a jury was empowered to decide the law and facts of the case. This measure, sweeping and harsh as it seemed, was a milder version of an earlier bill, which declared the people and government of France to be enemies of the United States and levied the death penalty on any citizen giving them aid and comfort. Since few governments or politicians have ever existed who did not feel that criticism of them was defamatory and liable to arouse hatred against them, the act was a clear declaration by the Federalists that opposition to a particular group of leaders in power was in fact opposition to the whole government and an effort to subvert the Constitution.

A new corps of leaders came to the fore in the congressional debates over these bills. Dominating the high Federalist effort in the House was a group of New Englanders, including such activists as young Harrison Gray Otis, whose ardent ambition disturbed some of the older Federalists, and Samuel Sewall, chairman of the House Defense Committee, both from Massachusetts, and Connecticut men like John Allen and Samuel Dana. An aroused group of Republicans opposed the bill in both houses; their leader in the lower chamber was Albert Gallatin. An immigrant from Switzerland, onetime Harvard instructor, frontier trader, and western Pennsylvania farmer, Gallatin had a special interest in the question of naturalization, for he had been denied a United States Senate seat to which he had been elected in 1793 because he had not been a United States citizen for nine years. Most of the voting on the Alien and Sedition bills was sharply sectional. The Sedition Act itself won the votes of only two representatives from south of the Potomac.

The "old revolutionaries" in both parties followed the efforts of the younger cohorts with mixed feelings, but mainly with approval. George Washington supported the acts in general, but made no direct defense of the Sedition Act. Alexander Hamilton opposed the earlier, harsher version of the Sedition Act but strongly approved the bill as signed. President Adams had little if any hand in framing the Sedition Bill, but he both approved it in principle and approved it in fact with his all-important signature at the bottom of the bill. Thomas Jefferson, on the other hand, thoroughly opposed the acts as steps toward tyranny, but his main objection seemed to be that this was federal rather than state control of the press.

Some waited to see the actual impact of the legislation before making up their minds. The general effect of the acts was mixed. The force of the Naturalization Act was diluted by the fact that some states had their own naturalization laws, which differed from the federal and carried their own authority. Secretary of State Pickering was put in charge of administering the Alien Act; the zealous Secretary would send Adams blank warrants to sign, but the cautious President would not delegate his authority and hence refused to comply. Still, the mere existence of the act evidently caused some French agents and a number of other persons to flee the country.

The Sedition Act had by far the most dramatic and controversial impact. Adams had no compunction about giving the indefatigable Pickering full rein to interpret the vague and sweeping law as broadly as he wished. The President felt strongly about the calumnies inflicted on him—almost as strongly as did Abigail Adams, who noted that Bache in his paper called her husband "old, querilous, Bald, blind, crippled, Toothless Adams"; the First Lady consistently favored passage of the Sedition Act, its harsh enforcement, the suppression of traitorous Republican newspapers, and the arrest of erring editors. Pickering and others moved ahead with a series of indictments and arrests. Usually the safeguards in the act—especially the prosecution's obligation to prove the malicious intent of writers and the use of truth as a defense in criminal libel—faltered in courts run by zealous Federalist judges. The fact that sixteen of the seventeen federal proceedings were set in Federalist-dominated New England and middle states indicated the importance of such judges, and of the pressure of popular attitudes in the area. Only one verdict of "not guilty" was returned in the prosecutions instituted under the Sedition Act.

Individual cases told the story of personal liberty in the America of the late 1790s. Most poignant was that of "Lightning Rod" Bache. Still in his twenties, Bache had contributed his share of vituperation and abuse to the national debate. But he had also suffered more than his share of retaliation from the powerful Federalists in Philadelphia. He had been barred from the floor of the House of Representatives, assaulted in the streets, surrounded by mobs in his home. Federalist merchants had withheld advertising, and his adversaries urged that he should be treated "as we should a TURK, A JEW, A JACOBIN, OR A DOG." When Bache's *Aurora* took advantage of a "leak" to print a conciliatory message from Talleyrand to American envoys, members of the Administration, outraged by this blow at their war policy, concocted a clumsy plot to implicate the young editor in "treasonable correspondence." The ploy failed, but in defending himself against the charge Bache made such strong statements that those statements were then seized upon by the prosecutors as the basis for bringing Bache into court on a new charge of "libelling the President & the Executive Government in a manner tending to excite sedition. . . ."

The trial was set for the October term; meantime Bache kept up his defense and wrote a brilliant editorial on liberty. In the balance of liberty and order, he wrote, the effort to protect the security of the state had gone so far as to threaten the liberty of the individual. "One of the first rights of a human is to speak or to publish his sentiments; if any government founded upon the will of the people passes any ordinance to abridge this right, it is as much a crime as if the people were, in an unconstitutional way, to curtail the government or one of the powers delegated to it."

Early in September the fever sweeping Philadelphia accomplished what the Federalists never had: the silencing of Bache. He died in the plague of '98.

A case as comical as Bache's was dolorous involved one Luther Baldwin of Newark. Old Luther, a bit tipsy already, was headed into John Burnet's dram shop in that New Jersey city just after President and Mrs. Adams had driven down Broad Street, followed by the boom of cannon fire. When another customer said to Baldwin, "There goes the President and they are firing at his a—," Baldwin replied that he didn't care if "they fired *through* his a—!" That was seditious, the dram keeper exclaimed, and turned the scoundrel over to the authorities. "Here's *Liberty* for you," a Newark newspaper gibed, and the case soon became a national joke. It was no joke for Baldwin, however, when he and his crony were tried, found guilty of "sedicious words tending to defame the President . . . ," sentenced to a total of $200 in fines, and committed to federal jail until fines and fees were paid.

A more typical case, though involving an unusual man, was that of Thomas Cooper, editor of the Northumberland (Pa.) *Gazette.* An English radical who was also a textile mill owner in Manchester and a lawyer, Cooper had escaped the oppressive English atmosphere of the mid-1790s by moving to Pennsylvania, where he practiced both law and medicine. He became good friends with another removed Englishman, the famous scientist and Unitarian minister Joseph Priestley, who had long corresponded with John Adams. Evidently finding himself with not enough to do, Cooper began to edit the *Gazette* and to imply that President Adams was a threat to liberty, popular sovereignty, and the rights of man. Reprinted in the Philadelphia *Aurora,* and distributed by Dr. Priestley in handbill form, the attack was soon denounced by the Federalists as demagogic and subversive. It was a "libel against the whole government," Adams said, "and as such ought to be prosecuted."

He would not use the Alien Act against his old friend Priestley, however, because he had simply been misled by Cooper. Indicted for sedition, Cooper had the misfortune to come before Associate Justice Samuel Chase of the Supreme Court. Widely viewed as a "hanging judge," Chase acted more as prosecutor than judge. By his rulings he largely prevented Cooper from making truth a defense; he barred admission of evidence that might have helped the defendant; and he informed the jury flatly that bad intent had been proved. Relieved of much of the burden of judging, the jury brought in its guilty verdict in twenty minutes. Chase sentenced him to six months in prison and a fine. Cooper served his time—and promptly renewed his attacks on the Administration.

These and other trials attracted national attention and aroused furious debate. That debate, however, generated more heat than light. It was conducted mainly at two levels. On the grand level of national principles and values, the Federalists simply argued that order was indispensable to liberty, that false and exaggerated attacks fomented disorder, that there was ample freedom for calm and temperate criticism of the Administration —and that, after all, there was virtually a war on. They pointed out, moreover, that the Sedition Act was far more permissive than the common law under which sedition had long been prosecuted, for under the common law truth was not a defense and malicious intent need not be proved. The Sedition Act, Federalists contended, was "remarkable for its lenity and humanity: No honest man need to dread such laws as these." Republicans, scoffing at this picture of the Sedition Act as virtually a reform law, noted its repressive features and its dependence on fair-minded judges and juries. They charged the Federalists with seeking to establish an all-powerful "consolidated" government, in which the loyal opposition would have no rights. This debate over moral principles remained unresolved.

On a second level, the debate concerned the constitutionality of the Alien and Sedition Acts. Republicans argued that in particular the Sedition Act flagrantly violated the recently adopted Bill of Rights. Federalists contended that federal courts had jurisdiction over so-called common-law offenses against the nation, by virtue of Article III of the Constitution and the Judiciary Act of 1789. Here the Federalists perhaps had the best of the argument, for at the time the First Amendment did not appear to cancel federal power over the press in all circumstances.

Between the level of passionate invocation of principle and the level of constitutional and legal exegesis, however, something was missing in what should have been the Grand Debate over the liberty of Americans. All too often the argument on both sides was couched in vast stereotypes, grandiloquent symbols, and unexceptionable goals, rather than based on systematic analysis and concrete, disciplined thought. If liberty was the supreme goal, some of the unanswered questions were: What *kind* of liberty? Liberty for *whom*? Liberty *from* whom? Liberty expressed through what kinds of channels or vehicles (press, church, assembly, or other)? Liberty in what kind of context (war or peace, a crowded street or a philosopher's study)? Liberty expressed through—or protected from— what level of government (state or national) and what branch of government (executive or legislative or judicial)? And the toughest question of all—to what degree, and in what way, should public authority be used to protect individual liberty against private power, such as that of a corporation or a tavernkeeper? Or a slaveowner?

Both the top leadership corps—the Adamses and the Jeffersons—and a second cadre of leadership—the new generation in Congress—had failed to grapple with the question of liberty in all its dimensions, complexities, and paramountcy. The question by decade's end was whether the third cadre of leadership in cities and towns and villages and hamlets throughout the nation would rise to the occasion. Their power to make a brute decision with one blow, between the Federalist and Jeffersonian approaches to liberty, lay in the approaching presidential election of 1800. But in the spring and summer of 1798 that election seemed a long way off. Would liberty in America expire in the meantime?

*   *   *

Extremism begets extremism. As they watched the Federalists seemingly bent on extinguishing liberty of speech and the press—and hence the power to oppose—some Republicans reverted to the old idea of nullification and even secession. Passions were running so high in 1798 that it seemed possible the young republic might be rent apart and the great experiment brought to an end amid disunion and even civil war. National leaders like Hamilton and Jefferson were already talking in extreme terms. All would depend on the mass of citizens and their local elected and unofficial leadership in the states and counties and towns. To an extraordinary degree, that leadership responded to crisis by recognizing its severity, but also by advocating radical but not irresponsible action.

The Alien and Sedition Acts aroused protest throughout the nation, but nowhere was the response more instant or intense than in Kentucky. Even when the House of Representatives in Philadelphia was first considering alien and sedition legislation, the Lexington *Kentucky Gazette* printed the text of an early bill, and a week later the paper was featuring a call for a mass meeting in Lexington to consider "the present critical situation of public affairs." State politicians quickly took leadership of a powerful rising feeling against the alien and sedition legislation, as the *Gazette* continued to print texts of new bills and speeches in Congress. On the Fourth of July the militia at a meeting in Lexington provocatively toasted liberty of speech and press. The protest was contagious; soon meetings were being held in other Kentucky counties.

Jefferson and Madison watched these developments somberly. The Vice-President, who could hardly expect to be protected by the Sedition Act against scurrilous Federalist attacks on *him* as a government official, pondered what action to take. His answer took the form of a series of resolutions contending that the new federal government was merely a compact among the states; that the federal government held only narrowly delegated powers; hence that "whensoever the general government assumes undelegated powers, its acts are unauthoritative, void, and of no force." Because Jefferson had close ties with a number of Kentucky politicians, his resolutions were eagerly adopted by the Kentucky legislature, but with one important tactical change—the resolutions were to be transmitted to the Kentucky delegation in Congress. Jefferson had opposed this procedure—his whole strategy now was to appeal to the states, not the national government—but the legislature preferred to follow the lead of the county politicians who favored the appeal to Congress. Thus, notes James Morton Smith, "the struggle over the alien and sedition legislation would be waged at the level of practical politics organized in national parties; political infighting rather than theoretical consideration of federal-state relations would dominate the great debate."

The Kentuckians of course hoped that other states would follow their lead. Virginia, where county and local meetings had protested the Alien and Sedition Acts, was the obvious state to pursue the battle. Jefferson as usual was in touch with Madison, who in turn worked with state politicians, especially John Taylor of Caroline, a brilliant agrarian thinker, scientific farmer, and lawyer. The Federalists were stronger in Virginia than in Kentucky, and the Virginia resolution was correspondingly milder than the Kentucky resolve. The latter would assert the right of each state to judge whether the national government had exceeded its powers; the Virginians asserted the power of the states. Even so, the Virginia resolution made a bold assertion: "In case of a deliberate, palpable and dangerous exercise of other powers not granted by the said compact, the states, who are parties thereto, have the right and are in duty bound to interpose for arresting the progress of the evil, and for maintaining within their respective limits the authorities, rights and liberties appertaining to them."

The hopes of the resolvers were now pinned to endorsement in other states, but what happened was—nothing. All the states north of the Potomac, all being Federalist-dominated, emphatically disapproved the Virginia and Kentucky resolutions by formal legislative action. The central argument of the resolutions—that the Union was simply a compact among states—was simply ignored. South of the Potomac the Republicans were strong enough to block disapproval, but they could not gain approval. Everywhere the resolutions were condemned as leading toward secession and disunion. Many of the resolutions' adversaries contended that not the states but the federal judiciary was the proper authority to pass on the constitutionality of federal laws—a hint of a major political and constitutional battle to come within five years.

It was not surprising that George Washington regretted "extremely" the resolutions, or that Abigail Adams referred to them as "mad," or that Hamilton considered them a rebellious act and suggested marching troops through Virginia. What was remarkable was that hundreds of state legislators, county officials, local editors, and other leaders should have recognized the Alien and Sedition Acts as the threat to liberty that they were, that this cadre of state and local leaders should have responded with resolutions equally extreme and dangerous, and that national, state, and local leaders, after a strenuous grass-roots debate, nullified the grand strategy of Kentucky and Virginia, as ultimately they would reject the Sedition Act. That rejection would have to await the coming political showdown of 1800.

THE VENTURES OF THE FIRST DECADE

On December 12, 1799, George Washington rode out as usual to oversee his plantations. Snow began to fall, then hail, then a "settled cold Rain," as he noted in his diary. He returned home with his head covered with snow and rain but made light of it, and went to dinner without changing. The next day was colder, and Washington, more and more hoarse as the day wore on, stayed home. In the early hours of the next morning he awoke Martha Washington to say that he was unwell. She summoned doctors, who bled him four times. He steadily became weaker. Late on the fourteenth he asked his wife to go to his desk and fetch his will, drawn up in his own hand six months before. For a time he studied the document—the watermark portrayed the goddess of agriculture with a staff topped by a liberty cap, and the text freed his slaves on his wife's death—before handing it to his wife for safekeeping.

The old general knew he was dying. During the long hours, as the doctors applied blisters and poultices to his legs and feet, and forced molasses and vinegar through his almost closed throat, he uttered no word of complaint. He seemed to wish only to go to his death with dignity, with his affairs in order, with the least bother to those around him. Coolly he monitored his own death. Toward midnight of the fourteenth he took his pulse for the last time, his fingers fell away from his wrist, and he died without a sound.

Thus passed the American leader who, perhaps more than any of his peers, viewed the new Constitution as a grand experiment that must prove itself in action. Like hundreds of others of his generation, he had lived through a series of witting or unwitting ventures in government—in the 1750s and 1760s under British monarchical and parliamentary rule, in the late 1770s under a revolutionary regime, in the 1780s in a confederation of largely independent states, in the 1790s in a strange hybrid of national and state power, of legislative and executive authority. Rarely have cadres of leadership been able to test their ideas in such spacious political laboratories.

These leaders had witnessed other experiments too. Farmers in Massachusetts and in Pennsylvania had had a fling at rebellion. Many Southerners and a few Northerners had flirted with notions of secession. Federalists had tried their hand at repression. Jefferson and Madison had proposed nullification. Rhode Islanders had tried separatism. Through all these Washington had lived, but he died as another great experiment was coming to a head—an experiment of which he heartily disapproved. He had warned in his Farewell Address against nothing more solemnly than "the baneful effects of the Spirit of Party, generally." But as the general was laid to rest in the family plot, overlooking the fields and the river he loved, the nation was on the eve of an election year—and the spirit of party was in command.

A supreme paradox lay behind that spirit. By the end of the 1790s the American people had started to build the foundations of a powerful two-party system. But: they did not fully know what they were doing. Nor did they believe in what they were doing. The strategy of 1787, that of checks and balances and the fragmenting of power, had been designed to prevent Americans from establishing parties. The received wisdom of the day—especially that of the most noted political and intellectual leaders—was absolutely hostile to political parties. And historians to this day have differed as to how these party foundations were built, despite the obstacles. But built they were.

The strategy of 1787 had been shaped first by a brilliant and masterful elite corps of leaders and then had been reshaped and ratified by a second cadre of nascent republicans and a "third cadre" of grass-roots leaders throughout the states. That strategy had been achieved in a few stunning acts—in Philadelphia in 1787, in the state ratifying conventions, in the framing of the Bill of Rights by Congress and the state legislatures. That strategy had been clear and purposeful; the Framers and their friends and opponents well knew what they were up to. The strategy of *party* emerged out of gropings and fumblings, short-run needs and narrow interests, local and state as well as national rivalries. It emerged less from national conventions and congresses than from taverns and coaching houses, local clubs and caucuses, town and state debates and elections, dram-shop rows and fisticuffs. If the constitutional strategy of the 1780s was founded on consensus, the strategy of the 1790s grew out of conflict.

The wise men of the day hated the very thought of unbridled factions and parties. "If I could not go to heaven but with a party," Jefferson said, "I would not go there at all." They had a theory of constitutions, but they had no theory of parties. To men in power, the opposition party was not a benign adversary that someday, through the ordinary rotation of "ins" and "outs," would come to power. The opposition party was at best divisive, factious, destructive, at worst illegitimate, conspiratorial, subversive, and, if allied secretly with the British or French, utterly traitorous. Federalists and Republicans alike looked on the other's activities as partisan and hence as malign, their own as transcending party and faction and hence benign. Each perceived the other, whether in Congress or state legislatures, as regimented as Prussians, itself as composed of free spirits. Typically Federalists and Republicans wanted less to compete with one another than to destroy the other, or at least absorb the other.

The Constitution had been designed to balance, fragment, and overwhelm the play of party power. Staggered elections, fragmented constituencies, the separation of powers between President and Senate and House, the division of powers between nation and states—all were intended to compel conciliation among and between parties and factions, to break the thrust of popular majorities, to submerge small conflicts in a higher consensus, to promote bargaining and compromise. George Washington marvelously symbolized and practiced the constitutional strategy of consensus.

How, then, did the Americans of the 1790s build the foundations of a party system under national leaders who feared parties, under a national Constitution designed to thwart them? Historians, speaking from different schools of thought, have offered a variety of explanations. Some see the origins of American parties in the old divisions between patriots and Tories, between foes and friends of the Constitution of 1787, between early Federalists and Republicans; other historians find the origin in the searing domestic and foreign policy issues of the 1790s; others in the state and local issues of that decade; others in the elections that pitted against one another candidates who had to find campaign allies and in the process forged factional and party links with other candidates; still others in the economic, regional, ethnic, and ideological forces that divided rich and poor, Northerner and Southerner, Congregationalist and Quaker, yeoman and slaveowner.

The question, perplexing enough in itself, has been further complicated by the tendency of historians, like blind men feeling the elephant, to confuse different aspects of the party beast with the whole. They variously perceive party as merely the existence of strong conflict over issues; or of elections and election mechanics; or of clubs or associations or movements that took on certain party forms; or of national activity such as a congressional caucus or presidential leadership of a majority; or of state and local political organizations like Tammany; or of simple contests for power between the ins and the outs. Historians have not always made clear whether they were speaking of a condition of one-party domination over a disorganized opposition, or of a two-party balance with rotation in office, or of a multi-party or multi-factional array, or of a two-party system embracing presidency, congressional majorities or minorities, state party organizations, and electoral constituencies.

Complex though they were, the origins of the American party system need not be left in a twilight zone of historical understanding. National parties seem to have originated in conflict in Congress, as Federalist and Republican factions polarized more and more around the burning questions of the day—issues between commercial and agrarian interests, between North and South, between "Anglophiles" and "Francophiles," all of which issues came to a head in the Jay treaty, with its implications for both foreign and domestic policy. As Federalists and Republicans each developed "party lines" that tied their positions on these issues together, party rivalry in Congress became heated. At the same time rudimentary state and local parties were rising out of conflict over local issues, in turn stemming from economic needs and aspirations, competition for government jobs, continuing debate over "states' rights" under the new Constitution. As national, state, and local politicians seized variously on national, state, and local issues for their political advantage, the levels of party development "hooked" in with one another. National issues debated in Congress ricocheted back into the states, enhancing party competition in the more politically advanced areas and helping mobilize latent conflict in the less advanced.

All these party growths did not amount, however, to a party system—that is, to two national-state-local integrated, hierarchical party structures, each firmly seated in mass partisan electorates, local leadership cadres, electoral organizations, governmental office, and popular understanding and acceptance of party conflict. The reasons party systems did not develop were not only intellectual; they were also social and cultural. American politics at the grass roots in the 1790s was still largely a politics of deference—family-centered, client-oriented, job-motivated. It was still mainly the politics of local elites, social status, patron-client dependency, acquiescence in the influence of local notables. The making of a party system would wait for the rise of widespread local cadres of issue-minded activists who would mediate between rulers and citizenry and who would constitute the foundations of lasting party structures.

The catalyzing force in early party development was leadership—the congressional leadership of James Madison and others, state leaders who fought their electoral battles over issues old and new, as well as the local leadership—county politicians, professional men, tavernkeepers, state legislators, business and religious activists, newspaper editors—who divided, coalesced, and redivided over issues old and new. The local leaders may have learned a vague fear of party from their intellectual elders, and certainly they had to overcome the politics of deference, but they were influenced mainly by the practical need to win the next election and seize the spoils of office.

The more zealous local leaders had their forums—the thirty or forty Democratic or Republican societies that sprang up in Pennsylvania and most of the other states during the early 1790s. Nothing could have been calculated to alarm and infuriate high Federalists more than these political clubs. Modeled on American revolutionary societies such as the Sons of Liberty, inspired by the euphoria of the French Revolution in its early stages, these societies reached out to city mechanics and country yeomen alike and drew them further into the Republican embrace, thus providing counterweight to the quieter organizational efforts of Hamilton. Even more, some of the leaders aped French revolutionary ways, addressed one another as "Citizen" and "Citizeness," and even burst into the "Marseillaise" as well as patriotic American songs. They passed countless resolutions against the Washington administration in general and Hamilton's policies in particular. Suspecting that they had helped foment the Whiskey Rebellion, Washington had left his nonpolitical perch to denounce these "self-created societies" publicly and privately and to warn that they were a "diabolical attempt" to destroy the "fabric of human government and happiness."

These political clubs soon withered, for they lacked the support of national leaders like Madison and Jefferson and were not geared into the slowly forming party machinery. The crucial political development of the mid-1790s was the shift of popular interest from mainly local issues to the rising national controversy over questions like Jay's treaty and Hamilton's bank. The retirement of Washington and the election of Adams focused the attention of state and local leaders increasingly on the nation's capital. With Jefferson still withdrawn from divisive politics, the rising national conflict was carried to the people by a host of senators, representatives, and others. Not all these were the gladiators of history. Consider the case of the "Spitting Lyon."

On the floor of the House of Representatives, Roger Griswold, Connecticut Federalist, disparaged the military record of Matthew Lyon, Vermont Republican. Lyon shot a stream of tobacco juice into Griswold's face. After the House refused to expel Lyon, Griswold strode to Lyon's desk and beat him with a cane. Lyon seized a pair of fire tongs and beat Griswold. The two men grappled and rolled on the floor until forcibly separated by other congressmen.

"Spitting Lyon" became an instant hero to Republicans, but to Federalists he was a "brute," an "unclean beast," "Ragged Mat, the Democrat." A Bostonian mourned that "the saliva of an Irishman"—Lyon had been born in the old country—"should be left upon the face of an American & he, a New Englandman." Later, not wholly by coincidence, Lyon was indicted under the Sedition Act for allegedly libelous attacks on President Adams. A Federalist justice of the Supreme Court jailed him after the jury brought in a guilty verdict. From his prison cell Lyon sent a stream of protesting articles and letters that were gleefully reprinted by the Republican press. Hailed as a martyr, the Vermonter ran again for Congress while still in jail in 1798, and won triumphant re-election.

Two years later he would enjoy the sweetest vengeance a politician could dream of; meantime, men who might not understand the philosophical differences between Jefferson and Hamilton could at least follow the case of high Federalists versus the Spitting Lyon.

By the late 1790s, thanks to Lyon and a host of other contentious politicians, conflict over issues had become nationalized. But no national party existed, except in Congress. John Adams had built a personal following within the Federalist administration, but it was not organized as a national party. Hamilton had developed a personal network reaching into the Administration and into Federalist centers throughout the states, but for party support he depended mainly on New York Federalists. James Madison had built a congressional party, organized in an informal caucus of Republican members, held together by rough party doctrine and enmity toward Federalists, and fashioned shallowly on networks of followers in congressional constituencies, but Madison retired to Virginia in 1797 just as Jefferson entered the vice-presidency.

This left Jefferson in titular command of the national Republicans, but the new Vice-President had little stomach for party leadership. The office was hardly an engine for organizing a national party, even if Jefferson had wanted to. Considering the Federalists' sponsorship of the Alien and Sedition Acts, there was a grave question whether the Adams administration would tolerate an opposition party strong enough to win the presidency. But the main obstacle to Jefferson's party leadership was not political or

even personal; it was intellectual and conceptual. He still had little understanding of the possibilities of a nationally organized party that would seek
to rally a majority of the people behind a Republican platform, win the
presidential and congressional elections, and then translate Republican
doctrines into law through control of the presidency and Senate and
House majorities. The extent of Jefferson's confusion is clear from his
leadership in promoting the Kentucky and Virginia resolutions. With their
bent toward nullification, states' rights, and even secession, those resolutions were the very antithesis of the idea of majority rule through national
party organization. They were also the antithesis of the strategy of party
opposition, which calculated that the way to overcome a bad national
administration was not to pull out of national politics and act like Chinese
warlords, but to win enough votes at the next national election to drive the
Federalists out of power.

If leaders such as Adams and Jefferson failed to understand the strategy
of national parties, could anyone else have done so? We know of only one
man who did—William Manning, a farmer and tavernkeeper in North
Billerica, Massachusetts. Around 1797 Manning wrote a tract entitled
"The Key of Libberty." To counter the organized upper-class power of
merchants, lawyers, ministers, and doctors, he called for a "Society to be
composed of all the Republicans & Labourers in the United States" and
organized on a class (educational), town, county, state, "Continental," and
even international basis. The associations would be composed of only
those who "Labour for a living." After intense political education in small
classes with access to a library and magazines, the associations would mass
their power against the elite at the polls. The "ondly Remidy" against
existing evils, he wrote, "is by improveing our Rights as freemen in elections," as long as "we ware posesed of knowledge anough to act rationally
in them." Manning concluded his tract with a constitution that spelled out
the structure and powers of the new association.

The annals of the poor. All we know about Manning is that he marched
to Concord on a famous April day but arrived too late to fight at the bridge,
that he later served two terms as a Billerica selectman, and that he wrote
one of the most prescient tracts in American history. And we know one
other thing about him—that he submitted his manuscript, with the words
formed one by one as though by a child, and with countless misspellings,
to the *Independent Chronicle,* the only pro-Jefferson newspaper in Boston.
The newspaper did not publish "The Key of Libberty," however, for the
editor about this time was arraigned for seditious libel under the Sedition
Act. The editor died before his trial came on; his brother and clerk went
to jail. By chance Manning's papers survived.

We will never know how many other village intellectuals were thinking in as radical and creative terms as Manning, while the nation's political leaders were occupied by thoughts of repression and secession. The nation would wait many years before finding another untutored thinker who would unite so brilliantly the concepts of thought and action, knowledge and power.

*   *   *

If, as Presidents and historians agreed, a dominant theme of the early republic was "the idea of America as an experiment, undertaken in defiance of history, fraught with risk, problematic in outcome," how was the experiment faring by the end of the first decade? That question had to be asked, for experimentation, no matter how unwitting or radical, must not only tolerate testing in terms of certain general criteria—it *requires* such testing. Otherwise experiments would serve only as mindless leaps into the dark. But by what criteria—by what general values, principles, purposes— could the experiment be assayed? New generations would advance new standards of judgment, but the initial criteria for the early republic had to be those of early Americans themselves.

The first was of course sheer survival, as a people, as a nation. The Declaration of Independence, in trumpeting the unalienable rights of man, listed "life" before liberty, "safety" before happiness. The Constitution was carefully framed to gain the economic and military strength of a larger republic without threatening the security of individual states. Some Americans had greeted this effort with skepticism. To convert a continent into a republic, said Patrick Henry, was "a work too great for human wisdom." It was impossible, said another doubter, "for one code of laws to suit Georgia and Massachusetts." The constitutional solution was a radical and previously untested challenge to traditional republican thought, one that, in Benjamin Barber's recent words, "turned the nation's early years into an unprecedented historical experiment," and one that could be met only by a people that, according to James Madison, had not allowed "a blind veneration for antiquity, for custom, or for names, to overrule the suggestions of their own good sense, the knowledge of their own situation, and the lessons of their own experience." For a decade, at least, the experiment in federalism had survived, despite efforts toward nullification and secession—and despite, as well, unrest and some violence at home, bloodshed along the western borders, and conflict with two great powers abroad.

National survival required economic strength. Agriculture continued to be the main American production during the 1790s, and agriculture continued to boom. Stimulated by better techniques of fertilization, crop rotation, erosion control, and other improvements, crop output skyrocketed in some places. Cotton exports from the Carolina coast rose from about 10,000 pounds a year at decade's start to 8 million pounds by decade's end. Wheat and corn production expanded in the North and West.

Commerce also grew. Exports rose strongly from an average of $20 million annually in the early 1790s to four times that by decade's end. Imports increased about fivefold during the 1790s. With population surging in the Ohio and Mississippi valleys, the sinews of continental strength were evident in the growth of manufactories, the expansion of trade especially along the big rivers, and the blossoming of ports like New Orleans. While road conditions typically ranged from fair to poor, and most rivers still had to be forded, men were building more bridges and establishing ferries. By 1800 New Yorkers were boasting of their Cayuga Bridge, more than one mile long and three lanes wide.

National strength gained from a burgeoning population. Between 1790 and 1800 the population spurted from about 3.9 million to about 5.3 million. Ohio and Mississippi were among the fastest-growing areas. Most of the rise was due to the fecundity of Americans, especially of American farm parents needing sons to help till the fields; immigration probably amounted to only about 50,000 persons for the whole decade.

Of the immigrants, those from the British Isles still predominated. But among the newcomers were people from less-known places—Oyo, Dahomey, Benin, Biafra, usually by way of Barbados and other Caribbean islands. These were African slaves. Kidnapped from their villages, sold often by other Africans to European traders for cloth or liquor or guns, herded in chains onto slave ships, they had survived the horrors of the Atlantic passage—heat, filth, stench, disease, hopeless efforts at resistance —to be herded into slave-trading ports for sale mainly to planters.

National security, individual safety, economic well-being—as these fundamental needs were to a substantial degree satisfied for much of the population, other, "higher" needs were created or enhanced. Probably the most powerful of these in the 1790s was for individual liberty. Here the record was mixed. Congress had passed, and the states had ratified, a Bill of Rights of wide scope and noble sentiments. The flush of prosperity doubtless had broadened economic opportunity and liberty of choice for many Americans. The passage and enforcement of the Alien and Sedition Laws, however, had shown how frail was the defense of these liberties. The enactment of these laws could be explained, but to explain is not to excuse. The Sedition Act lay like a blot across the luminous pages of the Bill of Rights.

Equality, like liberty, was as powerful in its appeal to early Americans as it was amorphous in meaning. "All men are created equal," proclaimed the Declaration of Independence, before even mentioning the ideal of liberty. But informed Americans had little thought that the ideal of equality required collective action to help equalize the conditions of men born in poverty, ignorance, disease, malnutrition, and despair; they would have been aghast at the notion, if indeed they could even grasp it. Rather the term meant to most Americans the idea that men were created equal only in their God-given natural rights to life, liberty, and property.

It was obvious that men in fact—much less women and children—were most unequal in their conditions at birth and that they remained unequal in intellectual and physical endowment, economic status, intelligence, appearance, and social rank, though a few fought their way out of poverty to high position, and a few of the undeserving stumbled down the primrose path to inferior rank and disgrace. As in the case of liberty, few Americans asked the tough explicit questions about the meaning of equality: What kind of equality—legal, political, economic, social? Equality to be achieved how—by the natural workings of the social and economic order, by religious teachings, by the deliberate intervention of the community, perhaps even through government? And above all, equality for whom? All men, rich and poor? Between men and women? Between adults and children? Equality for Indians, immigrants, aliens? Equality for black people?

By the 1790s, slavery had become a peculiarly southern phenomenon. Most of the northern and central states had abolished it by legislative or judicial action. Not that the freedmen enjoyed much liberty or equality; they were usually denied their political and social rights, and discriminated against. "But when we compare them to the slaves of the South," a French traveler had observed, "what a difference we find!—In the South, the Blacks are in a state of abjection difficult to describe." Nine out of ten Afro-Americans lived in the South, and almost all of these—about 96 percent—were enslaved. Accounting for over a third of the South's population, they outnumbered whites in many southern counties, though in no southern states.

Afro-Americans were better off in the upper South than the lower, under more affluent planters, in prosperous times. In a miniature class system encouraged by the masters, household workers and artisans were usually better treated than field hands, and men better than women, because often women not only worked from sunup to sundown in the fields but also were responsible for their families' cooking and parenting. Conditions on the plantations of even the "better" masters could be harsh. Washington resorted to the whip to maintain order, and a Polish poet visiting Mount

Vernon in 1798 found the "negroes' huts . . . far more miserable than the poorest of the cottages of our peasants." In general, the life of the enslaved Afro-American was nasty, poor, brutish, and often short.

But even aside from the enslaved, life under the new republic was heavily inegalitarian, even by late-eighteenth-century standards in America and Western Europe. Gross differences among men abounded in income, property, education, speech, and social status. Women lay outside the pale. Custom, men's attitudes, the English common-law heritage, and the teachings of the Protestant churches overwhelmed the efforts of the few women conscious of this inequality. Abigail Adams was one of them. "I will never consent," she wrote her sister, "to have our sex considered in an inferior point of light. Let each planet shine in their own orbit. God and nature designed it so—if man is Lord, woman is *Lordess*—that is what I contend for." It was about the same time that John Adams wrote his son Thomas: "The source of revolution, democracy, Jacobinism . . . has been a systematical dissolution of the true family authority. There can never be any regular government of a nation without a marked subordination of mothers and children to the father." But he asked Thomas to keep these words from his mother. If she heard of his views, he said, it would "infallibly raise a rebellion."

Liberté, égalité—the third great value in the revolutionary war cry of the 1790s was *fraternité*. The idea of fraternity—of a close bond based on fellowship, affection, shared goals, mutuality of interest, and loyalty—was by no means new to Americans, whether of Pilgrim or recent immigrant stock. But those who aped the latest Parisian fashion and addressed one another as "Citizen" or "Citizeness" did not always understand the true meaning of fraternity or its relationship to the two other norms in the revolutionary trinity. In fact, the three ideas could clash with one another as well as reinforce one another. "I love liberty, and I hate equality," the corrosive John Randolph of Roanoke exclaimed, and this sentiment was backed by many Americans who saw the two concepts as opposites. In practice, it is true, the three values could be mutually reinforcing, depending on their definition and application; but explicit definition of this kind of value was not in intellectual fashion in the 1790s.

Even if it were, and even though the revolutionary trinity had considerable kindling power among leaders of the new republic, the three great symbols were still not enough for many Americans. They groped for something more, for some loftier myth or purpose that would transcend the Lockean heritage of individualism and narrow equality. This myth was religious, ethical, spiritual; the purpose was to rise above self-interest and to take part in a collective effort of mutual help, fellowship, citizenship, community. The impetus was frankly religious and moralistic, even in a republic that had disestablished religion. "Of all the dispositions and habits which lead to political prosperity," Washington asserted in his Farewell Address, "Religion and morality are indispensable supports. In vain would that man claim the tribute of Patriotism who should labor to subvert these great Pillars of human happiness, these firmest props of the duties of Men and citizens. The mere Politician, equally with the pious man, ought to respect and cherish them."

Two things were necessary to create the republic of virtue, one of them obvious at the time, the other less clear. The first was education. "The Knowledge nesecary for every freeman to have is A Knowledge of Mankind," William Manning wrote in his tract, and "Larning is of the greatest importance to the seport of a free government," but the tavernkeeper added that the few were "always crying up the advantages of costly collages, national acadimyes & grammer schools, in ordir to make places for men to live without work," but were always opposed to "cheep schools and woman schools, the only or prinsaple means by which learning is spred amongue the Many." The other great requisite was leadership—the kind of leadership that, after meeting and hence extinguishing men's basic wants and needs, could raise followers to higher levels of need and value —to levels of individual self-expression and self-actualization, of collective equality, dignity, and justice, of civic virtue and ethical commitment. Such leadership was lacking in the second half of the decade of the 1790s.

These early Americans, to be sure, had enormous energy and boundless optimism. They labored, each for himself, in the vineyard of liberty. But a vineyard, in eighteenth-century usage, was also a sphere of moral activity, and the new century might tell whether these Americans were laboring only for themselves, or also for humankind.

SHOWDOWN: THE ELECTION OF 1800

On the eve of the last year of the century, American leaders were intent more on political prospects than moral. The looming national elections were tending to focus their minds. The decisive figure in this election would be Thomas Jefferson. But Jefferson hardly appeared decisive at the time. His political course during the late 1790s had mirrored the political uncertainties and party gropings of those years. Tentatively he looked for some kind of North-South combination.

"If a prospect could be once opened upon us of the penetration of truth into the eastern States; if the people there, who are unquestionably republicans, could discover that they have been duped into the support of measures calculated to sap the very foundations of republicanism, we might still hope for salvation," Jefferson had written Aaron Burr some weeks after Adams' inauguration in 1797. " . . . But will that region ever awake to the true state of things? Can the middle, Southern and Western States hold on till they awake?" He asked Burr for a "comfortable solution" to these "painful questions."

Immensely flattered, Burr requested an early meeting with the Vice-President in Philadelphia. Jefferson now became more active as party leader, working closely with Madison in Virginia and with Gallatin in the House of Representatives. Following the election setbacks to Republicans in 1798, he redoubled his efforts especially as a party propagandist. He asked every man to "lay his purpose & his pen" to the cause; coaxed local Republican leaders into writing pamphlets and letters to editors; stressed the issues of peace, liberty, and states' rights; turned his office into a kind of clearinghouse for Republican propaganda. "The engine is the press," he told Madison.

Hundreds of other men too were busy with politics, but like Jefferson earlier, in an atmosphere of uncertainty and suspense. Intellectual leaders —clergymen, editors, and others—were still preaching against the whole idea of an open, clear-cut party and election battle. Party formations were still primitive in many areas. Even fiercer than the conflict between Federalists and Republicans was the feuding between factions within the parties —especially between the Adams following and the Hamilton "cabal." Certain high Federalists were hinting at the need for armed repression of the opposition, particularly in the event of war, and Jefferson and Madison were openly pushing the Kentucky and Virginia resolutions—a strategy of nullification and even secession still in flat contradiction to the idea of two-party opposition and rotation in power. All these factors enhanced the most pressing question of all—could the American republic, could any republic, survive a decisive challenge by the "outs" to the "ins"? Or would ballots give way to bullets?

Not intellectual theorizing but heated issues, fierce political ambitions, and the practical need to win a scheduled national election compelled the political testing of 1800.

In Philadelphia, John Adams contemplated the coming test with apprehension and anger. Political and personal affairs had gone badly for him since the euphoria of '98. Abigail was ill a good part of the time, and his beloved son Charles, a bankrupt and an alcoholic, was dying in New York. As proud, captious, sensitive, and sermonizing as ever, he hated much of the day-to-day business of the presidency, and he longed to take sanctuary in Quincy; but he desperately wanted to win in 1800, to confound his enemies, to complete his work. He tried to lend some direction and unity to the Federalists, but he was handicapped by his concept of leadership as a solitary search for the morally correct course, regardless of day-to-day pressures from factions and interests. He sensed, probably correctly, that his party should take a more centrist course to win in 1800. But his own moderate positions on foreign and domestic policy left him isolated between high Federalists and moderate Republicans.

The Fries "rebellion" epitomized his difficulty. A direct federal tax on land and houses, enacted by Congress in 1798, touched off the next winter an uprising by several hundred Pennsylvanians—and especially by the women, who poured scalding water on assessors who came to measure their windows. John Fries, a traveling auctioneer, led a band of men to Bethlehem, where they forced the release of others jailed for resisting the tax. The President promptly labeled the act treasonable and ordered Fries and his band arrested. Unlucky enough to be tried before Justice Samuel Chase, the auctioneer was convicted of treason and, amid great hubbub, sentenced to die. Later the President, without consulting his Cabinet, pardoned Fries—only to arouse the fury of high Federalists. Not the least of these was Alexander Hamilton, who, his biographer says, would have preferred to load the gibbets of Pennsylvania with Friesians and viewed the pardon as one more example of Adams' petulant indecisiveness.

By the spring of 1800 Adams' wrath against the Hamiltonians in his Cabinet—especially Pickering and McHenry—was about to burst out of control. Politically the President faced a dilemma: he wished to lead the Federalists toward the center of the political spectrum, in order to head off any Republican effort to pre-empt the same ground, but he feared to alienate the high Federalists and disrupt his party when unity was desperately needed. His uncertainty and frustration only exacerbated his anger. One day, as he was talking with McHenry about routine matters, his anger boiled over. He accused the frightened McHenry to his face of being subservient to Hamilton—a man, he went on, who was the "greatest intriguant in the world—a man devoid of every moral principle—a bastard and as much a foreigner as Gallatin." Adams accepted McHenry's resignation on the spot. A few days later he demanded that Pickering quit. When the Secretary of State refused, Adams summarily sacked him. Oddly, he did not fire Secretary of the Treasury Wolcott, who was Hamilton's main conduit to the high Federalists in Adams' administration.

Thomas Jefferson, watching these events from his vice-presidential perch, had the advantage of being close to the government, if not inside it, with little of the burden of power and none of the responsibility. By early 1800 he was emerging clearly as the national leader of the Republicans.

Gone were the doubts and vacillations of earlier days. He was eager to take on the "feds," as he called them, to vanquish their whole philosophy and practice of government, to establish his party and himself in control of Congress and the presidency. He consciously assumed leadership of his party. Unable to campaign across the country—stumping was contrary to both his own nature and the custom of the day—he cast political lines into key areas through letters and friends.

His meeting with Burr paid off handsomely. The dapper little New Yorker set to work uniting New York Republicans against the divided Federalists. Then he organized his lieutenants tightly on a ward-by-ward basis; had the voters' names card-indexed, along with their political background, attitudes, and need for transportation on election day; set up committees for house-to-house canvassing for funds; pressed more affluent Republicans for bigger donations; organized rallies; converted Tammany into a campaign organization; debated Hamilton publicly; and spent ten hours straight at the polls on the last day of the three-day state election. He won a resounding victory in the election of state assemblymen—and got full credit for it from Republican leaders in Philadelphia.

The New York victory buoyed Jefferson's hopes. He recognized the critical role of the central states, and how they hung together. "If the *city* election of N York is in favor of the Republican ticket, the issue will be republican," he had instructed Madison; "if the federal ticket for the city of N York prevails, the probabilities will be in favor of a federal issue, because it would then require a republican vote both from Jersey and Pennsylva to preponderate against New York, on which we could not count with any confidence." What Jefferson called the "Political arithmetic" looked so good after the New York victory that he shrugged off the Federalist "lies" about him. He would not try to answer them, "for while I should be engaged with one, they would publich twenty new ones." He had confidence in the voters' common sense. "Thirty years of public life have enabled most of those who read newspapers to judge of one for themselves."

Doubtless Jefferson was too optimistic. The Federalists in 1800 were still a formidable party. While they were losing some of the vigorous younger men to the Republicans, they were still the party of Washington and Adams and Jay and Pinckney and Hamilton, and the vehicle of a younger generation represented by men like John Marshall and Fisher Ames. The Federalists had never been a purely mercantile or urban party; their strength lay also in rural areas and along the rivers and other avenues of commerce into the hinterland, such as the Connecticut Valley. Adams as President had immense national prestige, if not always popularity, and his "move toward the middle" broadened the party's appeal. Stung by losses in New York, the Federalists rallied their forces in other states. In New Jersey, where women were not expressly barred from voting, they "marched their wives, daughters, and other qualified 'females' to the polls," in one historian's words, and won the state's seven electoral votes.

Not only was the parties' popular support crucial, but also the manner in which that support was translated into presidential electoral votes. The selection of presidential electors was not designed for accurate translation. For one thing, state legislatures set selection of electors on a statewide basis or on a district basis, or took on the task themselves, according to a guess by the party dominating the legislature as to which system would help that party's candidate. More and more legislatures moved to choose electors themselves, rather than by popular vote. Electors were supposed to exercise some independent judgment. But more important in 1800, the electoral system was still so novel as to be open to flagrant rigging, such as changing the method of choosing electors. Broaching to John Jay such a scheme for New York, Hamilton said that "in times like these in which we live, it will not do to be over-scrupulous." It was permissible to take such a step to "prevent an atheist in religion, and a fanatic in politics, from getting possession of the helm of state." Jay was not impressed.

And so the presidential campaign proceeded, in its noisy, slightly manipulated, but nonviolent way. During the summer candidates for state legislatures toured the districts and talked to crowds where they could find them—"even at a horse race—a cock fight—or a Methodist quarterly meeting." Then a shocking event broke in on the game of politics.

*   *   *

Through the darkness and the driving rain they made their way, some on horseback but more on foot, most armed with clubs and scythes, hearth-wrought swords and crossbows, a few with guns and homemade bullets. Streaming in from all directions—some from Richmond, others from farms and plantations in the county, still others from more distant places —they gathered at a "briery spot" near a brook six miles outside the Virginia capital. These black men, perhaps a thousand strong, were fired by a common purpose: to wrest liberty from the white slavocracy. The election was as remote to them as they were remote to the politicians counting and recounting electoral odds. They were the voteless, the politically impotent, the socially outcast. But they could not be immunized against the contagious idea of liberty. A few years after the Revolution an enslaved Afro-American, using the pseudonym "Othello," had demanded:

"After a long, successful, and glorious struggle for liberty," could Americans "meanly descend to take up the scourge?"

Against the stinging whip, the "nigger boxes," the violation of their women, the disruption of their families, the black people had found little protection. They safeguarded one another in their families where their families remained intact. They formed plantation communities that were in many respects extended families or kin networks carried over from the original African culture. Black leaders organized secret associations to meet communal needs. Black preachers ministered to both the survival and the moral needs of their people. "The Preacher is the most unique personality developed by the Negro on American soil," Du Bois noted. "A leader, a politician, an orator, a 'boss,' an intriguer, an idealist." Preachers and congregations met, often secretly, to celebrate life, ease suffering, and talk of deliverance from subjection in this life or hereafter.

Black men and women found other ways of defying their masters or sealing off their own lives. They tried slowdowns and stoppages, truancy and self-injury; they pretended illness or pregnancy. They boycotted work entirely, hid out in woods or swamps, pilfered food, destroyed tools and crops, committed arson, assaulted and sometimes killed owners or overseers, fled North. But none of these worked for large numbers over time, as the slavocracy mobilized sheriffs, overseers, posses, dogs, sometimes the gibbet and usually the whip. Resistance and whipping came to be locked together in a brutal symbiosis; some masters tried to reduce their dependence on the whip, but found it essential to the system.

For black leaders there was one other way. In 1791, the same year that the Bill of Rights had been adopted—but not for the enslaved—news trickled into slave quarters about the black uprising in St. Domingue. This electrifying example of black liberation, combined with the contagious rhetoric and values of the American and French revolutions, powerfully raised the expectations and aspirations of enslaved Afro-Americans. Throughout the 1790s rumors of black plots to burn and kill kept white officials on edge in Virginia and elsewhere. Late in 1797 three black men were executed on suspicion of having conspired to set Charleston afire.

Then, early in 1800, black leaders in the Richmond area began secretly to plan their own insurrection. Most active of the group was Gabriel Prosser, a tall, twenty-four-year-old blacksmith, "a fellow of courage and intellect above his rank in life," a contemporary wrote. Other leaders were Jack Bowler, four years older and three inches taller than Gabriel and a ditcher by trade, who had been hired out to a white woman who lived about fifty miles from Richmond. In an election called by Bowler, Prosser was chosen "General" by the black rebels and Bowler "captain of light horse." Activity centered in Gabriel's family circle on the plantation of Thomas Prosser, alleged to be an unusually harsh master. Gabriel's brother Solomon, also a blacksmith, helped make swords and other crude weapons, and his wife, Nanny, and Martin, another brother and a preacher, helped organize the revolt. Moving stealthily between plantations, reconnoitering the city with the aid of forged passes, the rebels were able to reach a large number of black people in southeastern Virginia. They recruited supporters at funerals, prayer meetings, barbecues.

Powerful forces lay behind even this slender effort. An economic depression in the South had resulted in more hardship on the plantations and in extensive selling and leasing of black people. Prosser and his fellow rebels were mostly artisans and domestic workers, more removed from the field and the lash but also more marginal in their work and more likely to be uprooted. They were also more exposed to the cries of liberty and equality echoing throughout the Western world. At one meeting a rebel leader threw his arms around another and exclaimed, "We have as much right to fight for our liberty as any men." Having achieved a little status, insecure though it was, they were motivated by needs for more status, prestige, self-esteem—one reason for the hunger for military titles that were awarded to the more active recruiters. They knew their Bible, and brother Martin quoted from Scripture to prove that delay bred danger and that, as he told the leaders, God had said that "five of you shall conquer an hundred, and a hundred a thousand of our enemies."

So now the one thousand huddled near the brook, already rising fast from the downpour, and awaited the command to move across the bridge to the city. The plan was to attack the Capitol, the magazine, the penitentiary, and the governor in his house; to seize large quantities of ammunition and warehouse goods; then to set houses on fire. As the white residents tried to put out the conflagration, the rebels would fall upon them. The conquest of Richmond, the leaders expected, would ignite a chain reaction of local uprisings. Civil war would engulf the nation as free blacks, mulattoes, Catawba Indians, French troops, and even poor whites joined the cause. White women were to be spared, as were Quakers, Methodists, and French persons, for the rebels "conceived of their being friendly to liberty." French warships would land troops on the coast to help fight the slavocracy, as they had done a quarter century before to fight the British oppressors.

But none of this dream was to be. The rainstorm raged through the night, turning more ferocious by the hour, washing away the only bridge the rebels could use to get to Richmond. Neither God nor good fortune seemed on the side of the smaller battalions. Even if the bridge had remained, Governor James Monroe and his troops were ready in Richmond, for Gabriel and his men had been betrayed by a black man on the day the revolt was to happen. Quickly Monroe had fortified the Capitol with cannon, called up six hundred troops, and sent the alarm to militia commanders throughout Virginia. Retribution was swift and hard. A number of rebel leaders were quickly rounded up and executed. Gabriel escaped on a schooner but was apprehended and brought back to the capital in chains.

Monroe had vainly hoped to minimize the affair, for fear of uprisings elsewhere and of Federalist efforts to exploit the revolt in the presidential campaign. Soon a Philadelphia newspaper was proclaiming that the insurrection, which was seen as organized on *"the true French plan,"* must be decisive for Adams. Monroe turned to the Republican candidate for advice. When, he asked Jefferson, should one "arrest the hand of the Executioner?" The sage of Monticello was ambivalent. He could well understand how some would want to extend the executions. But: "Even here, where everything has been perfectly tranquil, but where a familiarity with slavery, and a possibility of danger from that quarter prepare the general mind for some severities, there is a strong sentiment that there has been hanging enough. The other states & the world at large will forever condemn us if we indulge a principle of revenge, or go one step beyond absolute necessity."

But, added the presidential candidate, "I hazard these thoughts for your own consideration only, as I should be unwilling to be quoted in the case."

Gabriel went to his death in silence, even when he was brought before the governor to explain his act; "he seemed to have made up his mind to die," Monroe said later. Another rebel did speak on facing the judge. He had nothing more to offer in defense than what George Washington would have had to offer, he said, had he been taken by the British and put to trial by them. "I have adventured my life in endeavoring to obtain the liberty of my countrymen, and am a willing sacrifice to their cause." He asked only to be led at once to execution.

*   *   *

By fall the presidential race was reaching a climax. Slander on both sides was uncontained—and the politicos of the day were masters at it. Adams was called a would-be dictator and a "monocrat" who would make the country a monarchy and his children successors to the throne. Even Adams could smile at a story that he had sent a United States frigate to England to procure mistresses for himself. The Federalists gave even better than they got. Jefferson was an infidel, a "howling" atheist, an "intellectual voluptuary" who would "destroy religion, introduce immorality, and loosen all the bonds of society" at home. The Jacobin leader was the real debauchee, Federalists whispered, having sired mulatto children at Monticello. Somehow the voters groped their way through the invective to a sense of the genuine issues. They faced a real choice. Jefferson was still silent as a candidate, but he had repeatedly made clear his stands for a frugal government, a small Navy and Army, states' rights, the Bill of Rights liberties, a small diplomatic establishment. The Federalists had made their positions clear through legislation they had passed, or tried to pass. The election would be a showdown between men, platforms, and ideologies.

Slowly the returns came in as electors met and voted in their states. The Federalists had a moment of euphoria as Adams picked up some unexpected support. By late November the two parties were running neck and neck. For a time Federalist hopes were pinned on South Carolina, on whether Charles Cotesworth Pinckney, Adams' running mate, could deliver that state's eight electoral votes. But Pinckney could not even deliver all the Pinckneys, least of all Charles Pinckney, leader of the Republican branch of the family, who through generous offers of jobs under a Republican administration, managed to persuade enough members of the state legislature to choose a pro-Jefferson slate of electors.

By late December the total vote was in. It was Jefferson over Adams, 73 to 65. But it was also Burr over Pinckney, 73 to 64, with one of Pinckney's votes diverted to John Jay.

The Republicans had won, but Jefferson had not been elected. Burr had an equal constitutional claim to the presidency. Something new and extraordinary had happened in American politics: the parties had disciplined their ranks enough to produce the same total (73) for the two Republican running mates and an almost equal tally (65 to 64) for the two Federalists. In order to prevent votes from being thrown away, each party caucus had pledged equal support to both candidates on the ticket. To do this was to run the risk that, under the Constitution, a presidential tie vote would go to the House of Representatives for decision. Both parties knowingly ran that risk. But the politics of the lower chamber would be quite different from the politics of the electoral groups meeting separately in the state capitols. The presidential race would now be focused in the nation's capitol; it would take place in a lame-duck, Federalist-dominated House of Representatives; and each state delegation in the House, whether large or small, would have a single vote.

The remarkable result was that the Federalists had lost the presidency, but in the Congress they had the power to throw the election to either Jefferson or Burr, or possibly stall indefinitely. What would they do with this exquisite consolation prize? Most of the congressional Federalists feared Jefferson the ideologue more than they hated Burr the opportunist. "They consider Burr as actuated by ordinary ambition, Jefferson by that & the pride of the Jacobinic philosophy," high Federalist George Cabot wrote Hamilton. "The former may be satisfied by power & property, the latter must see the roots of our Society pulled up & a new course of cultivation substituted." If Burr was ambitious, slippery, and even venal, well, perhaps the Federalists could make use of such qualities; "they loved Burr for his vices," John Miller has noted. Other Federalists disagreed. No matter how much they hated Jefferson, they were not going to put into the presidency a man they considered a knave and a blackguard.

The competing forces were so counterpoised that the House of Representatives went through thirty-five ballotings, all resulting in a vote of eight states for Jefferson, six for Burr, and two divided. The stalemate lasted as long as the representatives stuck to their convictions, or biases; it ended when three men—Jefferson, Burr, and Hamilton—acted out of character. Jefferson, no longer the relaxed and diffident philosopher, responded to the looming crisis with anger, but also with decisiveness and determination. He began to act like the President-elect as soon as the unofficial returns were in; thus he wrote Robert R. Livingston to ask him to serve as Secretary of the Navy—the New Yorker declined—and incidentally to discuss the bones of a mammoth that had been found near New York. He wrote Burr, congratulating him on the election results but implying ever so delicately that Jefferson expected him to serve as Vice-President. He wrote Burr again to warn that the "enemy" would try to "sow tares between us," and branding as a forgery a letter purportedly by Jefferson that criticized Burr. At the same time Jefferson subtly let out word that, while he would not make deals—he knew that Burr could outdeal him—he could be counted on to act moderately as President, to be "liberal and accommodating."

Hamilton had no time for subtleties. His clear hierarchy of animosities —he resented Adams, hated Jefferson, and despised Burr—helped him to decide early that if the choice lay between Jefferson and Burr, he would thwart the latter. While Jefferson was only a "contemptible hypocrite," crafty, unscrupulous, and dishonest, Hamilton told his Federalist friends, Burr was a "most unfit and dangerous man," a Jacobin who would overthrow the fiscal system, a rogue who would "employ the rogues of all parties to overrule the good men of all parties," and above all a Catiline who would take over the government as Napoleon had just done in France. Hamilton had little influence with the Federalist "high-flyers" (as Jefferson called them) in Congress, but his principled view that his party must not bargain with the likes of Aaron Burr carried weight with national Federalist leaders such as John Jay.

Burr played a waiting game. He assured Jefferson and his friends so convincingly that he would not deal with the enemy and balk the real will of the people that Jefferson confided to his daughter: "The Federalists were confident, at first, they could debauch Col. B from his good faith by offering him their vote to be President," but his "conduct has been honorable and decisive, and greatly embarrasses them." Burr's behavior was curious all the way through. He evidently did spurn a deal with the Federalists, but he did not take the honorable course of simply withdrawing; he never made perfectly clear that he would not serve as President if elected; he apparently allowed some of his friends to put out feelers on his behalf; and his best strategy in any event would have been inaction, since the Federalist bloc in Congress was cemented to his cause as a result of their hatred and fear of Jefferson. Still, the long-drawn-out constitutional crisis afforded Burr countless opportunities to undercut Jefferson and perhaps to win the presidency—but he remained in Albany, attending to his law practice.

Twelve weeks passed as Jefferson remained resolute, Hamilton busy, Burr inactive, and the election stalemated. There is no record of all that happened in the last confused, crisis-ridden days; in particular we know little of the role of less visible but influential politicians. John Marshall evidently angled for his own selection as President should the deadlock persist. But this much seems clear: during the final weeks the nation veered toward disunion and civil war, as Republicans threatened to bring in state militias from Pennsylvania and Virginia if the Federalists further thwarted the "popular will." The crisis revealed not merely two parties in combat but four party factions: Jeffersonians, Burrites, high Federalists mainly centered in Congress, and a group of moderate Federalists led on this occasion by Hamilton and nurtured in the nationalist, moderate leadership of George Washington.

As March 4, 1801, approached and tension mounted two developments staved off a constitutional and perhaps military debacle. Jefferson, all the while asserting that he would not "receive the government" on capitulation, that he would not go into it "with my hands tied," told a Federalist intermediary that the public credit would be safe, the Navy increased, and lesser federal jobholders left in their places. And ingenious mediators worked out an artifice that enabled Jefferson to be elected President without a single Federalist voting for him. A number of Federalists cast blank ballots, and a single congressman from Vermont now cast his state's vote for Jefferson. That congressman was "Spitting Matt" Lyon.

The crisis was over—Thomas Jefferson was elected President of the United States. Much would be made in later years of this unprecedented example of a peaceful shift from one party to another, of the avoidance of violence and bloodshed, of the example Americans had set for other constitutional republics. But it had been a close-run thing. If Jefferson had not been firm in his ambition, Hamilton not principled in his hatred, Burr not inactive; if moderates in both parties had not been in control, or if fewer politicians had respected the Constitution, the American republic probably would have lived a briefer life than many republics before and since. Perhaps most decisive in the whole episode was the willingness of state and local leaders, Federalist and Republican, to wait for the crisis to be resolved rather than break into local magazines, gather arms, and march on the Capitol. Once again "followers" had acted as leaders.

The suspense of the election quickly changed into excitement over the coming of a new President, a new party, a new government, a new program. Later Jefferson would argue that the "Revolution of 1800 was as real a revolution in the principles of our government as that of 1776 was in its form." But whether 1800 would be a real revolution—that is, a *transformation* of ideological, economic, social, and political structure—would depend on the leadership of a man who glorified revolution in theory but exercised moderation in practice.

PART II
Liberty in Arcadia

CHAPTER 5

Jeffersonian Leadership

Conrad & McMunn's Boarding House, near Capitol Hill, Washington, D.C., March 4, 1801. President-elect Thomas Jefferson, surrounded by friends and fellow lodgers, prepares to leave for his Inaugural. Virginia militiamen are parading up and down the street, and somewhere artillerymen are firing off blank salvos, but everything is low-keyed. The President-elect hardly cuts a heroic figure. A tall, lean, loosely framed man, "all ends and angles," he feels ill at ease in a crowd, even though people are attracted by his freckled, open countenance and pleasing manner. He has no wish to be a hero. No coach-and-eight is waiting to carry him to the Capitol, nor even a white horse. Rather he will walk. Shortly before nine, accompanied by a motley throng of officials, members of Congress, and Republican politicos, he sets out for the north wing of the unfinished Capitol building. . . .

Thus began an epoch in American history that would come to be known as the "Jeffersonian Era" but was felt at the time—after the anxious days of February—to be a moment of relief, triumph, and hope.

Several hundred persons had crowded into the Senate chamber to witness the shift of authority from John Adams to Thomas Jefferson. The President-elect's old Virginia adversary, Chief Justice John Marshall, stood before him to administer the oath; Vice-President-elect Aaron Burr, a man Jefferson hardly knew, waited nearby. Conspicuously absent from the proceedings was John Adams, who had quietly left Washington before dawn. After the oath-taking, Jefferson turned to the audience.

"Friends & Fellow Citizens." At this, some good Federalists in the crowd must have stirred. "Citizen"! This was the language of Paris revolutionaries.

The President proceeded in such a low, flat tone of voice that many in the audience could not have made him out if the *National Intelligencer* had not scored a beat and published the address ahead of time. In any case, the speech held few surprises. After the usual modest disclaimers and tributes to a "rising nation spread over a wide & fruitful land," he went on to lay out Republican positions: "Equal & exact justice to all men" . . . friendship with all nations, "entangling alliances with none" . . .

support for state governments as bulwarks of republicanism . . . "Economy in public expense, that labor may be lightly burdened" . . . the payment of public debts . . . "Encouragement of Agriculture, & of Commerce as it's handmaiden . . ." These principles, he said, speaking from abbreviated notes, "form ye bright constlln wch hs gone before us, & guidd our steps, thro' an age of Revoln and Reformn: The wisdom of our Sages, & blood of our Heroes, have been devoted to their attainment . . ."

Yet embedded in the address were words that doubtless stirred his audience more than did hallowed principles. These amounted to a powerful plea for conciliation.

". . . every difference of opinion, is not a difference of principle. We have called, by different names, brethren of the same principle. We are all republicans: we are all federalists.

"If there be any among us who wish to dissolve this union, or to change its republican form, let them stand undisturbed, as monuments of the safety with which error of opinion may be tolerated where reason is left free to combat it. . . .

"I know indeed that some honest men have feared that a republican government cannot be strong; that this government is not strong enough. But would the honest patriot, in the full tide of successful experiment abandon a government which has so far kept us free and firm on the theoretic & visionary fear that the government, the world's best hope may want energy to preserve itself?"

All would bear in mind, Jefferson had said earlier in the address, "the sacred principle that if the will of the Majority is in all cases to prevail, that will, to be rightful, must be reasonable: that the Minority possess their equal rights, which equal laws must protect, & to violate would be oppression.

"Let us then, fellow citizens, unite with one heart & one mind; let us restore to social intercourse that harmony & affection, without which Liberty, & even Life itself, are but dreary things. . . ."

The celebration over, President Jefferson walked back to his lodgings at Conrad's. He left behind him at the Capitol some puzzled politicians, Federalist and Republican alike. What kind of leadership did the Inaugural words portend?

Upon leaving for the Inaugural that day, John Marshall had been in the middle of a long letter to Charles Pinckney in Charleston. "Today the new political year commences, the new order of things begins," he wrote. He hoped that public prosperity and happiness would not be diminished under democratic guidance. "The democrats are divided into speculative theorists and absolute terrorists. With the latter I am not disposed to class

Mr. Jefferson. . . ." If he was a terrorist, the country faced calamity, he added, but if not, the terrorists would become his enemies and calumniators. At this point Marshall laid down his pen and left his boardinghouse to administer the oath; he had promised Jefferson that he would be punctual. Returning later to his lodgings, he picked up his pen again. He had just administered the oath to Jefferson, he told Pinckney. The speech seemed conciliatory. "It is in direct terms giving the lie to the violent party declamation which has elected him, but it is strongly characteristic of the general cast of his political theory."

The new President's political theory—this was the puzzle. The election of this amiable and diffident patrician, and of a Republican Congress, had produced Federalist invective betraying a deep fear that he would inflict some alien and despotic creed on the people. A Republican regime would mean the "ascendancy of the worthless, the dishonest, the rapacious, the vile, the merciless and the ungodly," said a letter in the *Gazette.* Fisher Ames foresaw the "loathsome steam of human victims offered in sacrifice." President Timothy Dwight of Yale prepared an oration in which he warned of a "country governed by blockheads and knaves . . . the ties of marriage . . . severed; our wives and daughters thrown into the stews." Even John Adams, in his hurt and bitterness, said, "A group of foreign liars, encouraged by a few ambitious native gentlemen, have discomfited the education, the talents, the virtues and the property of the country." His Boston homeland seemed especially outraged. A Federalist newspaper there ran an epitaph within a black border: "YESTERDAY EXPIRED Deeply regretted by MILLIONS of grateful Americans And by *all* GOOD MEN, The FEDERAL ADMINISTRATION" etc. Little old ladies in Boston, it was said, hid their Bibles under mattresses on the inauguration of the Virginia "atheist."

Those who knew Jefferson best scoffed at the Federalist portrait of him as a Jacobin dogmatist—or radical ideologue. If criticize him they must, they would have pointed to just the opposite qualities. Jefferson's mind seemed as loose and many-jointed as his big rambling frame. Although he had proudly belonged to the American Philosophical Society for many years after having helped to found it, and although he had the philosopher's bent for reflective speculation, he had never been a systematic philosopher or written a comprehensive work that could compare with—say—John Adams' *Defense of the Constitution.* His interest in nature and in science was not that of the methodical investigator but of a man fascinated by rocks, birds, flowers, trees, vegetables, crops, inventions, household contrivances, gadgets. He wrote his daughter: "Not a sprig of grass shoots uninteresting to me."

So quickly did Jefferson shift, in conversation and correspondence, from politics to farming to law to flora to seeds to literature, that it was hard to discern any focus in the man. His more superficial beliefs had to be peeled off, like the layers of an artichoke, to find the core of conviction. He was accused of being deceptive, disingenuous, even dishonest, and to a degree he was, because he tried to protect his privacy, because he feared that his personal letters would fall into the hands of his adversaries, because he adapted to the person he was talking to and the situation confronting him. Beyond all this, a central ambivalence in him was evident to some.

There seemed to be at least two Jeffersons by 1801, his fifty-eighth year. One apotheosized harmony and conciliation; viewed the small rural property holder and agriculture in general as the foundation for the good society; believed in sharply limited government, especially at the federal level; feared a consolidated national government; saw cities in general and city mobs in particular as the "panders of vice and the instruments by which the liberties of a country are generally overturned"; loathed the prospect of urbanization, industrialization, centralized finance, a landless proletariat; warned against entangling alliances abroad; ultimately embraced states' rights to such a degree that he could sponsor the Kentucky and Virginia resolutions. This was Jefferson the ideologue.

Another Jefferson, however, saw conflict among men as inevitable and called for a rebellion every generation or so; enjoyed the splendor and intellectual brilliance of big cities like Paris and Philadelphia; easily fit into Washington's administration, which began the "consolidation" and invigoration of the federal government; warned against secessionist tendencies of *Federalists;* and spent a good part of his life "entangling" America with foreign nations, especially France.

Jefferson was a practical philosopher; he was even more a philosophical practitioner, who saw the needs of the immediate situation and drew from his vast learning the ideas that were relevant to that situation. He had grown up in the Virginia tradition of public service; won a seat in the House of Burgesses at twenty-six; served none too happily as wartime governor of Virginia; represented the new nation in France; and served under the new federal government as Secretary of State, Vice-President and presiding officer in the Senate. Rarely had he allowed ideology to interfere with the practical requirements of office.

Thus the defender of revolution had, as Secretary of State, signed the proclamation against the Whiskey Rebels; the apostle of liberty had, as presiding officer of the Senate, signed the warrant for arrest of William Duane, for seditious contempt of that body. Apparent paradoxes in his views, Marshall Smelser has said, can be reconciled "by remembering that liberty was his navigating star, even though there were cloudy nights in his career when he steered in another direction." But he refused to elevate specific institutions, traditions, and practices into dogmas. All these would change, while certain principles were eternal. And now he was entering the highest office in the land, once held by his fellow Virginian George Washington, and the test again would be whether he could stand by those principles and at the same time meet the day-to-day demands of transactional leadership.

His friends had few doubts. They spent the inaugural days celebrating rather than cerebrating, although much of the festivity had a political edge. In Virginia an inaugural pageant depicted Liberty as a comely virgin, threatened by a king and a bishop and other assailants, until a trumpet sounded and a messenger proclaimed that Jefferson was President, whereupon the evil men took flight and sixteen beautiful women, one for each state, protected the virgin Liberty. Perhaps the most splendid inaugural festivity took place in Philadelphia. There sixteen horses, driven by a youth dressed in white, pulled a carriage bearing the resplendent schooner *Thomas Jefferson*. Toasts were drunk to Liberty and the Rights of Man. "Jefferson and Liberty," termed "A Patriotic Song, for the Glorious Fourth of March, 1801," and consisting of fourteen stanzas, began:

> O'er vast Columbia's varied clime;
> Her cities, forests, shores and dales,
> In shining majesty sublime,
> Immortal Liberty prevails.
> *Rejoice! Columbia's sons, rejoice!*
> *To tyrants never bend the knee*
> *But join with heart, and soul, and voice,*
> *For* JEFFERSON *and* LIBERTY.

"The Eyes of Humanity Are Fixed on Us"

His Republican friends might sing and toast and parade, but President Thomas Jefferson continued to shun grandiosity and rodomontade. Following the Inaugural, he settled back into the life of the boardinghouse, where he ate at table—and sometimes at the foot of it—with thirty or so other officials and politicos. For two weeks he transacted business in his small parlor there, before moving to the President's house, but he stayed in the big new sandstone building less than two weeks before leaving for Monticello, where he remained almost a month. But even after that, presidential affairs seemed to go slowly. There were no balls in the mansion, no parades to Capitol Hill—all part of a consciously cultivated image of republican simplicity. The President had decided to abandon Washington's and Adams's policy of addressing Congress in person; nine months passed before he sent his formal written message to the legislature.

All this was just what some of his Federalist critics expected of Jefferson —an easygoing, haphazard, aimless, even careless approach to the business of the federal government, in sad contrast to the activism and purposiveness of the two Federalist administrations. In fact, from the day of his Inaugural the new President acted according to a carefully conceived "grand political strategy" that dominated his handling of administrative, legislative, and party affairs.

In shaping this grand strategy Jefferson enjoyed the sense of writing on a clean slate. "This whole chapter in the history of man is new," he wrote his revered friend Dr. Priestley. "The great extent of our Republic is new. Its sparse habitation is new. The mighty wave of public opinion which has rolled over it is new." He continued to view the American experiment as the supreme human venture. "The storm through which we have passed," he wrote another friend, "has been tremendous indeed. The tough sides of our Argosie have been thoroughly tried. Her strength has stood the waves into which she was steered, with a view to sink her. We shall put her on her republican tack, & she will now show by the beauty of her motion the skill of her builders." Nor were they acting alone, he wrote later to a governor, "but for the whole human race. The event of our experiment is to shew whether man can be trusted with self-government. The eyes of suffering humanity are fixed on us with anxiety as their only hope."

Jefferson's grand political strategy was simple though daring in conception: to separate moderate Federalists from their "monarchical leaders"; to draw those Federalists into a new and broadened Republican majority; meanwhile to keep his own Republican following content and united through a judicious application of loaves and fishes; to forge a new party majority coalition that would sustain his policies; to kill off the high Federalists as a political power; to expect—and to try to tolerate—a new opposition rising from within the ranks of his consolidated majority party. This strategy was not simply fabricated later by Jefferson or rationalized by Republican historians *post hoc;* it was shaped by the President before he took office and was expressed time and again in communications to his friends. Thus despite his conciliatory statements in his Inaugural Address, which were cited ever after as a lofty expression of nonpartisanship, he did not design to unite all Federalists with Republicans—only those he felt he could win over to his purposes.

Noble sentiments alone did not impel Thomas Jefferson. He acted partly out of a deep and abiding anger toward the Hamiltonian and other high

Federalists. It was hard for Jefferson to hate anyone, but even after attaining the psychological and political security of the presidency, he began referring to his old enemies as a "ravenous crew," as witch burners, gross liars and slanderers, "tyrannical." Granted that Jefferson designed some of these words to gratify Republican correspondents more extreme than he; still, they reveal that he had been seared by Adamsites and Hamiltonians far more deeply than he had admitted to others, or perhaps to himself.

To a somewhat smaller circle Jefferson confided his plan to detach moderate Federalists from their "monarchical" leaders and consolidate them in a new Republican party coalition. A week before his inauguration he was noting that "patriotic" Federalists, alarmed by the specter of dissolution during the election crisis of February 1801, "separated from their congressional leaders, and came over to us." But his purpose was clear. "If we can but avoid shocking their feelings by unnecessary acts of severity against their late friends, they will in a little time cement & form one mass with us, & by these means harmony & union be restored to our country . . .," he wrote a friend three weeks after the inauguration. In midsummer he was advising a Massachusetts lieutenant that the "Essex junto, & their associate monocrats in every part of the Union" must be stripped of all the means of influence.

His determination only rose as the high Federalist chorus swelled against him. By early the next year he was telling Du Pont de Nemours that the session of Congress had indeed consolidated the "great body of well meaning citizens together, whether federal or republican, heretofore called." But, he added, "I do not mean to include royalists or priests. Their opposition is immovable. But they will be vox et preterea nihil, leaders without followers."

Did Jefferson, then, want the Federalist party to die? He not only wanted it, he expected it and planned for it. He predicted that by the end of his second year in office the "federal candidate would not get the vote of a single elector in the U.S." in a straight party fight. He even feared that the Senate would become *too* Republican in the next election, for "a respectable minority is useful as censors." He did not want this to be a Federalist opposition, "being the bitterest cup of the remains of Federalism rendered desperate and furious by despair." But it was not clear just how the new opposition would come into being.

Jefferson was as skillful and hardheaded in carrying out his grand strategy as he was brilliant and determined in conceiving it. That strategy dominated his first executive action, the choice of a Cabinet. Picking James Madison for Secretary of State was inescapable: the two men had worked together in marvelous and creative harmony for decades. Madison was pre-eminently a moderate Republican, the kind Jefferson liked; as commanding in intellect as he was unimpressive in bearing and appearance, he had an understanding of legal and constitutional nuances, and perhaps of diplomacy, that Jefferson lacked.

Apart from this Virginian, the President was determined to bring to his Cabinet Republican leaders from the middle and eastern states. The choice of Albert Gallatin for Secretary of the Treasury seemed almost as obvious as that of Madison: the Pennsylvanian had effectively marshaled Republican support in the House after Madison's departure; he took a proper Republican approach of frugality and prudence to spending and other fiscal matters; he was only forty and energetic; and the "Frenchified" aspect of the man—his Geneva birth, pronounced accent, and "Gallic features"—that provoked his enemies was no deterrent to the President. But for his other two cabinet appointments Jefferson was determined to reach into the Federalist heartland of New England, even at the expense of choosing less notable men, so that he might achieve political and geographical balance and also attract moderate Federalists to his cause. He picked Levi Lincoln of Worcester, Massachusetts, an experienced Republican politician, for Attorney General, and Henry Dearborn, an old Revolutionary soldier of Maine (still part of Massachusetts), for Secretary of War. The President had such trouble finding a Secretary of the Navy—who would want to head a navy destined for Republican shrinkage?—that the post remained unfilled for some time.

A harsher test of Jefferson's strategy of coalition and consolidation was patronage, or what he called "appointments & disappointments." As usual, the latter seemed far to outnumber the former. It was hard enough to ascertain dependably which high Federalists should be removed, which good Republicans should be hired without, as Jefferson said, *"me donn[ant] un ingrat, et cent ennemis."* The best he could do was to ask the simple questions "Is he honest? Is he capable? Is he faithful to the Constitution?" It was much harder to avoid alienating moderate Federalists whom the President wished to bring over to his party, without antagonizing Republican stalwarts hungry for loaves and fishes. Angry though he was over the near-exclusion of Republicans from office under Washington and Adams, and furious over Adams' packing Federalists into administrative and judicial offices just before leaving the presidency, he dismissed relatively few men from office, but usually waited for the slow process of death and resignation to do its work before installing Republicans. Still, he picked only Republicans.

The President's removal of a collector in New Haven roused a great furor. New Haven "was the Vatican City of New England Federalism,"

Smelser has written, "under Pope Timothy Dwight," president of Yale, whose younger brother had described respectable Republicans as "Drunkards and Whores / And rogues in scores." Answering a protest from New Haven merchants over the removal, Jefferson wrote: "This is a painful office; but it is made my duty, and I meet it as such. I proceed in the operation with deliberation & inquiry, that it may injure the best men least, and effect the purposes of justice & public utility with the least private distress; that it may be thrown, as much as possible, on delinquency, on oppression, on intolerance, on incompetence, on ante-revolutionary adherence to our enemies. . . ." The President did not exaggerate his effort; he spent endless hours corresponding about possible appointments, weighing qualifications, but always with an eye to their place in his political strategy.

Jefferson made no pretense of one-man leadership. He gave his Cabinet a central role in decision making, especially in foreign relations. He worked so closely with his Secretaries of State and of the Treasury that this *troika* provided a case study in collective leadership. Madison and Gallatin were important to him in different ways. While he consulted with Madison on almost all major political and diplomatic matters, he felt thoroughly at home in foreign policy; he saw Gallatin less often, but depended on his expertise more, for Jefferson would never have tried to serve as his own Secretary of the Treasury. Cabinet members in turn worked closely with congressional leaders and with party heads both in Washington and in the states. But no one doubted who was chief of government.

The President derided the notion that public administration had to be complex and obscure. "There are no mysteries in it," he said; when difficulties arose, "common sense and honest intentions will generally steer through them." His administrative technique appeared to be simplicity itself: canvassing of opinion outside the mansion, intensive consultation with cabinet and staff members, clear instructions couched in polite but firm language. He did not care for formality. Forms, he said, "should yield to whatever should facilitate business."

Certainly the President's mansion was more a place of business than of pomp and circumstance during these Republican years. It stood bulky and Ionic, without the porticos that later gave it more style and proportion. The great stone house was "big enough for two emperors, one pope and the grand lama in the bargain," a newspaper observed, and Jefferson, his steward, his housekeeper, several servants, and his small executive staff hardly filled it. The President worked quietly in his library at the southwest corner of the main floor, amid tables large and small, a few chairs, and a letterpress which made copies of the letters that Jefferson wrote with his own hand. For a time his main aide was Meriwether Lewis, a young army officer from Albemarle County in Virginia.

No First Lady graced the President's house, as Martha Washington had in New York, or hung her clothes out to dry in downstairs rooms, as Abigail Adams had in Philadelphia. Jefferson occupied the house for almost a year before his daughters visited him there. James and Dolley Madison stayed with him for a few weeks before setting up housekeeping on their own, and Jefferson had other guests and held some grand dinners, but most of the time the place stood cold and quiet. Federalists charged that he collected rent from his guests. Jefferson's only consolation lay in frequent visits to Monticello. Accustomed to the breezes on his mountain, he positively refused to stay in the malarial and bilious "tidewater" of Washington during the hot summer months.

Washington, Jefferson wrote a friend, "may be considered as a pleasant country-residence, with a number of neat little villages scattered around within the distance of a mile and a half, and furnishing a plain and substantially good society." He was happy to be free, he wrote his son-in-law, "from the noise, the heat, the stench and the bustle of a close built town." Few would have agreed with the President's view of either the city or the social life. One "village" consisted of the President's house and an unsightly collection of temporary government buildings and private houses extending west into Georgetown. Flanking the mansion were the brick Treasury building and the combined State and War building. A mile and a half to the east was another "village," dominated by the huge but incomplete Capitol and radiating out in a corona of avenues, most of which were still muddy trails lined by rows of stumps.

Pennsylvania Avenue, connecting the two governmental villages, was a "streak of mud newly cut through woods and alder swamps," in Irving Brant's words. In years to come that avenue would come to symbolize a large distance between the executive and legislative branches, as Pierre L'Enfant had planned in laying it out. In 1801 it symbolized the closeness of the two branches, contrary to a Constitution designed to separate them, and the legislative supremacy of a man who had long extolled the importance of checks and balances between President and Congress.

On the face of it, the legislative tasks facing Jefferson seemed far less daunting than those confronting his predecessors. Washington and Adams had needed congressional support for major fiscal programs and foreign policy initiatives. Jefferson's immediate goals were to repeal much of what had been done—to cut federal spending and the national debt, to repeal the Judiciary Act of 1801, to break away from alliances that might entangle the nation in foreign affairs, to alter Hamilton's banking program. Yet even this task of alteration and demolition would call for unity and discipline among congressional Republicans, some of whom liked particular fiscal policies, especially military spending in their own districts. The trouble was, the President complained to his friend Du Pont de Nemours, Hamilton's policies had departed from "true principles" at the very start. "We can pay off his debt in 15. years: but we can never get rid of his financial system." He would do the best he could.

Federalists warned of the Jeffersonian "phalanxes" in Congress but the Republican majorities in each house were mainly composed of fiercely independent, individualistic, and often unruly men. They had been accustomed to fighting the executive, not cooperating with him, a posture that was indeed an article of their Republican faith. Other factors encouraged disunity in Congress: "weak party organization," as Robert Johnstone says, "a high rate of turnover, divergent constituency obligations, an eighteenth-century ethos of independence from party control, rules of procedure that encouraged dissent, and 'patterned social avoidance' among men of different regions." Members of Congress were cut off from one another as a result of living in small boardinghouses scattered through the city, another scholar has pointed out, and acoustics were so bad in the House that representatives could not always hear one another when they did convene. Some time later, John Quincy Adams described the "typical" Republican legislator as "a mixture of wisdom and Quixotism. . . . His delight was the consciousness of his own independence, and he thought it heroic virtue to ask no favors. He therefore never associated with any members of the Executive and would have shuddered at the thought of going to the drawing room."

How could the new President unify a group of men so sovereign in outlook, so dependent on their state parties and local constituencies, so independent politically of *him?* Here again, Jefferson had carefully worked out his tactics: to gratify the self-esteem of legislators by deferring to the doctrine of legislative supremacy; in fact to insert himself in the life of legislators and the crucial phases of legislation and thus to become the real "chief legislator"; to do so not by seeking to influence Congress from the outside as chief executive but from inside as "chief of party" by involving himself centrally in the Republican leadership and loyalties of the two houses; and to do all this so quietly and adroitly, by working through congressional and party leaders and asking them to keep his involvement secret, that Federalists would not be aroused, nor Republicans feel threatened.

It was not hard for Jefferson to treat Congress and congressmen with exquisite courtesy and deference; it was his natural style. As a Republican long pledged to the doctrine of the legislature as the "first among equals" in the tripartite balance, he found it easy to defer to Congress in his official posture. "Guided by the wisdom and patriotism of those to whom it belongs to express the legislative will of the nation," he had said in response to the notification of his election, "I will give to that will a faithful execution." He consulted with individual legislators at length, to gain their views and information as well as to influence them, and he cleared with them letters that came to the mansion from their districts. If he had few jobs to disburse, he had another means of pleasuring congressmen far from the comforts of home—his dinners. These were superb in cuisine and especially in wines, for the President had an excellent French chef, a large collection of French and Italian recipes, and a penchant for introducing new foods from Europe. But even more, the dinners were occasions for lively talk, for Jefferson planned them that way. He brought together officials, visitors from abroad, diplomats, scientists, and senators and representatives carefully chosen from different boardinghouses to create the most fruitful blend, politically and intellectually—though he did not mix Republicans and Federalists, and invited the latter strictly by boardinghouse bloc.

Few enjoyed Jefferson's dinners more than John Quincy Adams, the increasingly independent Federalist, or made better reports of them. "I had a good deal of conversation with the President," he wrote after a dinner in 1804. "The French Minister just arrived had been this day first presented to him, and appears to have displeased him by the profusion of gold lace on his clothes. He says they must get him down to a plain frock coat, or the boys in the street will run after him as a sight." Three years later Adams reported on "one of the *agreeable* dinners I have had at Mr. Jefferson's," among a company chiefly of congressmen. The talk ran from wines to philosophy to Fulton's steamboat and torpedoes to "oils, grasses, beasts, birds, petrifactions, and incrustations." "Mr. Jefferson said that the *Epicurean* philosophy came nearest to the truth, in his opinion, of any ancient system of philosophy, but that it had been misunderstood and misrepresented. He wished the work of Gassendi concerning it had been translated. . . . I mentioned Lucretius. He said that was only a part—only the *natural* philosophy. But the *moral* philosophy was only to be found in Gassendi."

The President's involvement in congressional policy making was continuous and pervasive. He and his officials provided congressmen with "material" ranging from information to actual drafts of bills. Department heads testified before congressional committees and remained to help draft bills in executive sessions. And of course the President always had the right to veto legislation, but the practice of a veto on purely policy grounds was not yet established, and Jefferson did not exercise it or—evidently—threaten to exercise it. More important, he worked closely with congressional and party leaders on the Hill, calling them into frequent conferences, helping them deal with obstacles, talking with other politicians who might help the congressional leaders and hence him. The President encouraged likely Republicans to run for Congress and to try for leadership positions. By no means did things always go smoothly, especially in the first year or two. But he achieved unsurpassed cooperation in Congress by throwing into the balance every ounce of his political skill, his personal charm, and his moral authority—authority all the greater because this was *Jefferson* who was asking for support.

The President covered his political hand by planning on secrecy and by insisting on it. His obsession with secrecy might have been considered pathological if he had not experienced serious political setbacks in earlier days when letters of his had been intercepted and exposed. Repeatedly he asked his political lieutenants not to trust the confidentiality of the post office and to keep his letters to themselves, or share them only with trusted persons. He concealed his interference in Congress mainly, however, by intervening indirectly through his leaders there. And those leaders well knew, from correspondence and conversations, what the President wanted.

To conclude that Jefferson dominated the legislative process largely because he dominated the Republican party in Congress—that he was chief legislator mainly because he was party chief—is to assume that the Republican party itself was strong and united in both House and Senate. Historians have long debated this question. In the last century, influenced by Federalist politicians and journalists who suspected that the President was marshaling his legislative troops like a Prussian drillmaster, chroniclers saw a powerful party caucus at work. More recent and more sophisticated analysis has challenged this conclusion, but may have overreacted to the previous Federalist bias. Certainly the party systems both in the nation and in Congress were primitive affairs compared to those that emerged later. The congressional party did not openly elect leaders and whips and other officials, or impose formal discipline, or choose policy or steering committees. But an informal congressional party has been identified, comprising Republican senators and representatives powerfully committed to certain values and policies, a group of congressional leaders in close touch with the rank and file in both houses and with the President, and a rudimentary but influential caucus system. Those caucuses were so informal, and they met so secretly because of the bias against "party machinations," that evidence of their existence has been elusive and scattered. But some kind of meeting was held—serving the function of a caucus without being labeled by that name—to unify the positions of Republican lawmakers before major legislative actions on the Hill. A formal flow chart is not necessary, as Johnstone says, for a group of persons to act as a cohesive and effective force. It was largely through this loosely organized but zealous and well-led majority of Republican senators and representatives that Jefferson exerted his legislative leadership. He was chief executive and chief legislator among a collective of executive and legislative chiefs.

To Louisiana and Beyond

Europe savored a moment of peace at the start of the new century. During the lull France and England, the great mobiles of European politics, swung in uneasy balance with each other. Surrounding these central mobiles were lesser ones, Spain, Holland, Naples, Prussia—suspended in arrays of alliances and animosities.

Each mobile was a cluster of satellite mobiles, a quivering balance of domestic politics embracing royal pride and ambition, party and leadership rivalries, military chieftains, religious establishments, parliamentary combat, economic interests. Conflict within satellite mobiles often set the parent mobile to trembling and pulsating, causing disturbances throughout the system. Usually the arching balances of the whole system righted themselves, but there was always the threat that the tempest of war would leave the balance of mobiles shattered.

A far-off mobile in this precarious array of balances was the land called Louisiana. In the very different perspective of Americans, Louisiana was their western borderland, nearby but mysterious, filled with endless forests and swamps, peopled by roving Indian tribes, and rich in fertile land for settlers moving west. Fronting this area was the legendary Mississippi, rising somewhere in the far north, swelling miles-wide and shallow as it approached the Gulf of Mexico, and providing a boulevard to the world for husbandmen and flatboatmen throughout the area. To Westerners, Madison said, the Mississippi was everything—"the Hudson, the Delaware, the Potomac, and all the navigable rivers of the Atlantic States, formed into one stream." And at the foot of the Mississippi lay New Orleans, a place of exotic peoples and erotic temptations, a commercial center vitally necessary to American traders for depositing their goods for transshipment abroad—and a city owned by the Spanish and ruled over by a formidable Spanish *intendant*.

The vast area both to the east and the west of the Mississippi was

"Republican country." As Virginia landowners bought and sold "Western" acres by the tens of thousands, as Virginia frontiersmen and settlers moved down the long valleys into Kentucky and Tennessee and western Georgia, Republican ideas and politics had moved with them. Virginia politicians had cultivated ties with the Kentuckians who were seeking political self-government and economic development. Jefferson had always had a "peculiar confidence in the men from the western side of the mountains," in his words, as they had had in him. Kentucky had become a state in 1792, and Tennessee in 1796, but western Georgia was far behind. Not until 1802 would Georgia cede to the nation the whole region between its present western border and the Mississippi, thus creating most of the states of Alabama and Mississippi.

Virginia Republicans in 1801 were watching with hope the rising new empire to the west, watching with scorn the quarrelsome old empires to the east. But sometimes to see west they had to look east. In his Inaugural Address, Jefferson had expanded complacently on America's favored situation: "Kindly separated by nature, and a wide ocean, from the exterminating havoc of one quarter of the globe. . . . Possessing a chosen country, with room enough for all descendants to the 100th & 1000th generation. . . ." Within three weeks he was writing a friend, "It ought to be the very first object of our pursuits to have nothing to do with the European interests and politics. . . . we have nothing to fear from them in any form." Within a few weeks the President was reading reports that Spain was ceding Louisiana and the Floridas to the French. Napoleon on our rear borders! The Atlantic suddenly did not seem so wide.

"It is a policy very unwise in both, and very ominous to us," the President wrote Governor Monroe. A French reacquisition of Louisiana would make the area a pawn of the fiercest rivalry in the West—that between France and England. It would place French armies athwart America's western frontier—French armies now under the control of a man Jefferson increasingly detested, Napoleon Bonaparte. It would enable the French to choke off American commerce in New Orleans or farther north.

Jefferson already had reason to fear Bonaparte's imperial ambitions. The First Consul was organizing an expedition to Saint Domingue in order to overthrow the regime of General Toussaint L'Ouverture, the black leader who had seized power after a bloody slave rebellion. Jefferson did not object to the attempt to suppress Toussaint—he feared the implications of an independent black republic—but would Bonaparte stop there? If the French ruler could send 20,000 soldiers to the West Indies, could he not dispatch other armies to Louisiana, a far greater temptation? And if France regained Louisiana, would there be no reaction from England, which had driven them out of the area years before and which still commanded the seas?

Federalists demanded that the President take aggressive action to forestall French and English imperial ambitions on the western frontier, but Jefferson preferred the methods of diplomacy. He had dispatched the seasoned New York Republican leader and diplomat Robert Livingston to Paris as Minister to France, with instructions to dissuade the French from acquiring Louisiana if the deal with Spain had not already gone through, or, if it had, to look into the possibility of American acquisition of Spanish Florida. Livingston found Talleyrand elusive and evasive. By April 1802, when the cession of Louisiana to France seemed definite, Jefferson instructed Livingston to warn the French government that the "day that France takes possession of N. Orleans" is "the moment we must marry ourselves to the British fleet and nation." The President now was practicing diplomacy with a mailed fist. Never wholly captive to his pacifist yearnings, he was during this period quietly strengthening American outposts along the western borders.

Even so, Jefferson was hardly reckoning with the imperial ambitions of Napoleon Bonaparte. Frustrated by the British in the east, the First Consul was turning west to redeem French territory lost by the Bourbons and not recovered by the bellicose revolutionaries of the 1790s. His expedition to Saint Domingue had met with initial success; even Toussaint was now in French hands, albeit as the result of trickery. With that island and other parts of the West Indies back under French control, Napoleon's "New France would extend its sheltering arms round the whole Gulf of Mexico and the Caribbean, taking in not only the islands but also Louisiana and the Floridas," in Oscar Handlin's summation. "Resting on a fulcrum at New Orleans, the two great areas of the empire could balance one another." During the summer of 1802 Napoleon organized in Holland an armada to carry a huge army and his ambitions into Louisiana. He was delayed, however, by machinations within the Spanish court; only after Napoleon had promised Italian lands to the Queen's brother was Louisiana ceded by Spain and the expeditionary force told to prepare to depart.

In the autumn of 1802, while this fleet was mobilizing, word reached Washington of an event in New Orleans that catalyzed American fears about the future of Louisiana. The Spanish *intendant* there had suddenly revoked the right to deposit goods in the city while awaiting their sale or shipment. It could be a potentially fatal blow to American exports. Mississippi traders and boatmen were wrathful, and Washington politicians indignant—and curious. Why had the *intendant* acted at this moment? Obviously, it must be part of the French plot. Later it was learned that the *intendant* was acting on orders from Spain. According to one theory, Napoleon was stalling on his promises to the Spanish court, offering the Queen not the province she wanted but other Italian lands, and to be turned over not to her brother but to her nephew; and the Queen was happy to find a way to complicate Napoleon's future in Louisiana. Another view is simpler: the *intendant* was furious at American smugglers. But such reasonable views had little standing at the time. If Napoleon was organizing an expedition in Holland, he certainly would not be above provocations in the territory he hoped soon to occupy.

Jefferson and Madison stepped up their diplomatic counteroffensive by dispatching James Monroe to Paris to bolster Livingston's efforts. This move would also placate some of the western firebrands, for Monroe, who was just ending his term as governor, had big landholdings in Kentucky, many friends and allies there and farther south and west, and a reputation as a spokesman for Westerners. The Federalists were already exploiting the situation by demanding action, so the President's move could head them off as well. Monroe was about to leave for Kentucky to look after his interests there when the urgent presidential summons arrived:

Washington, Jan. 10, 1803

DEAR SIR,—I have but a moment to inform you that the fever into which the western mind is thrown by the affair at N. Orleans stimulated by the mercantile, and generally the federal interest threatens to overbear our peace. In this situation we are obliged to call on you for a temporary sacrifice of yourself, to prevent this greatest of evils in the present prosperous tide of our affairs. I shall to-morrow nominate you to the Senate for an extraordinary mission to France, and the circumstances are such as to render it impossible to decline; because the whole public hope will be rested on you. . . .

No Virginian could resist such a call, least of all Monroe. Soon he was receiving instructions—formal from Madison, informal but authoritative from the President. When Monroe, after waiting several weeks for Congress to authorize and finance the mission, finally sailed from New York early in March 1803, he carried with him instructions to offer almost $10 million for New Orleans, if need be, or at least to regain some advantages for American traders on the Mississippi.

On reaching Paris, however, the envoy extraordinary found the situation remarkably changed. Livingston had been patiently working on the French with offers and veiled threats, but with little effect; suddenly, to his astonishment, Talleyrand was sounding him out as to what the American government would pay for the entire colony. Napoleon had received two pieces of staggering news: his fleet had become icebound in Holland just as it was to sail for the occupation of Louisiana; and his army in Saint Domingue had been almost annihilated by yellow fever. With his hopes for a western empire vanishing, Napoleon was turning back to his main enemy, England. In one blow he could diminish the possibility of an Anglo-American alliance, perhaps gain a potential ally against Britain, and in any event pick up some much-needed cash.

Quickly Livingston and Monroe arranged terms with Napoleon's Finance Minister: $11,250,000 for all of Louisiana, the United States to set aside $3,750,000 to pay for American claims against France; protection for Indian rights and for some commercial privileges for French traders. These terms—indeed, buying Louisiana at all—greatly exceeded the envoys' instructions, but they had no doubt of Jefferson's and the nation's approbation. The Republican *National Intelligencer,* getting the news just before Independence Day, declared that this Fourth of July was a proud day for the President, not simply because of gaining vast and rich lands, but because "We have secured our rights by pacific means: truth and reason have been more powerful than the sword."

This was Jefferson's proudest boast too; "Peace is our passion," he wrote an English friend. Federalists were skeptical and suspicious. "We are to give money of which we have too little for land of which we already have too much," "Fabricus" wrote the Boston *Columbian Centinel.* This "great waste, a wilderness unpeopled with any beings except wolves and wandering Indians," would be cut up into numberless states, so that Virginia could continue to lord it over all the other states—and all that cheap and fertile land would further depress land values in New England.

A "great waste," unpeopled by whites—just where and what was Louisiana anyway? No one knew for sure. The tract lay between the Mississippi and the Rockies; it comprised over 800,000 square miles, and it would double the size of the United States. But the legal boundaries were those of whatever the French had ceded to Spain forty years before, and neither the French nor the Spanish could be, or would be, very precise. It was not clear at all whether the cession included West Florida and Texas. But for the moment Americans did not fuss over details; they celebrated one of the biggest real estate transactions in history with festivals and feasts, toasts and songs.

Jefferson's brilliant success left him with a political boon and a constitutional dilemma. The Constitution contained no grant of authority to acquire territory, or to admit a territory to the Union and its inhabitants to citizenship. And Jefferson headed the party of strict and narrow construction of the Constitution. As usual, the President consulted widely on the matter, but his Cabinet was divided, Attorney General Lincoln doubting the power to acquire and Treasury Secretary Gallatin affirming an "inherent right" to do so. His friend Tom Paine took a view Jefferson might have expected from a man of eminent common sense: "The cession makes no alteration in the Constitution; it only extends the principles of it over a larger territory, and this certainly is within the morality of the Constitution. . . ."

Jefferson did not agonize long about the right to acquire; the need to act was vital and palpable. "A strict observance of the written laws," he wrote some time later, "is doubtless *one* of the high duties of a good citizen, but it is not *the highest.* The laws of necessity, of self-preservation, of saving our country when in danger are of higher obligation. To lose our country by a scrupulous adherence to written law, would be to lose the law itself, with life, liberty, property and all those who are enjoying them with us; thus absurdly sacrificing the end to the means. . . ."

The constitutional question of citizenship and statehood was harder to settle, especially now that the Federalists, originally the party of broad construction, were taking a narrow view, while many Republicans were switching to the opposite side. Jefferson drafted some proposed amendments, one of which read simply, "Louisiana as ceded by France to the U.S. is made a part of the U.S. Its white inhabitants shall be citizens, and stand, as to their rights & obligations, on the same footing with other citizens of the U.S. in analogous situations." Slowly he swung away from the idea of a constitutional amendment as he faced several imperative facts. Livingston warned that Napoleon—who had the dictator's luxurious power of being able to shift his nation's strategy from east to west almost overnight —was growing impatient with delay. The amending process laid out in the Constitution was long and tricky. Few seemed deeply concerned about the constitutional problem—even the Federalists were moving to different grounds—and his party was pressing for action. With a final bow to constitutional scruples, the President said he was prepared, "if our friends think differently," to "acquiesce with satisfaction, confident that the good sense of our country will correct the evil of construction when it shall produce ill effects."

Congress was eager to act. The Senate, after four days' debate, approved the treaty by a vote of 24 to 7. Both houses of Congress shortly passed, by heavy majorities, a measure authorizing the President to take possession of the Louisiana territory. But now Jefferson too, with the formalities over, was eager to move ahead. And he was consumed with curiosity about the new land—its soil, appearance, vegetables, animals, mountains, climate, Indian population, minerals, *everything*. The nation had bought Louisiana; now someone would have to find out just what had been acquired.

* * *

It was a lackluster start for an expedition destined to become an epic. Three workaday boats bobbed gently on the Missouri: a fifty-five-foot keelboat, carrying one square sail and twenty-two oars, and decked over at the bow, with a cabin astern; and two low, open boats called pirogues, one of seven oars and the other of six. During the day a gang of American soldiers and French rivermen finished packing the boats with 14 bales of presents for Indians, arms and ammunition, 28 bushels of "parch meal," 20 barrels of flour, seven barrels of salt, 50 kegs of pork, 50 bushels of meal, drugs and medicine, tools and scientific instruments. The co-leader of the expedition, Captain Meriwether Lewis, was not even there; he had gone to St. Louis on official business and, it was said, to dally with the girls in a final fling. But "Captain" William Clark—he was actually a lieutenant —was very much there, closely directing operations. Also present were Clark's slave York, a handsome man colored a deep ebony, Private Cruzat and his violin, one sergeant, one corporal, 27 men, "7 French," and Clark's dog Scannon, a Newfoundland.

The expedition did not get under way until late afternoon of this day, May 14, 1804, and even with the help of a "jentle brease" moved upstream only four miles. That night it rained, leaving all fires extinguished, and "Some Provisions on the top of the Perogus wet," as Clark wrote in his journal. The army landlubbers had loaded the boats heavily in the stern, so that the bow stuck up and ran up on logs and other snags in the river. But soon the weather turned fair, the boats were reloaded, Lewis rode overland to join the company, and the craft were passing between high bluffs and forested banks, all of which Lewis and Clark duly noted.

At last the dream was being realized—the dream of countless Frenchmen, Englishmen, and Spaniards, the dream of striking west from the northern reaches of the Missouri to the distant and mysterious alps, conquering these heights, and then moving down the coastal rivers to the Pacific. Rivermen, soldiers, trappers, and traders had penetrated the prairie lands, and Indians already lived there, but no one had broken through to the Pacific and brought back a record of the trip. For years Jefferson too had dreamed the dream, and now that he was President, and the issue of Louisiana and the western lands was coming to a head, he could act. Months before the purchase of Louisiana became a real possibility, he asked Congress for an appropriation of $2,500 "for the purpose of extending the external commerce of the United States." His purpose rather was multifold: he wished to gain for America the English and French trade in "furs and peltry" but he was interested also in the political and military uses of an expedition, and as a naturalist he was eager to know more about the vast territory and to share his findings with other members of the American Philosophical Society.

Only resourceful and skillful men could lead such an expedition, and Jefferson felt he had found the ideal combination in Lewis and Clark. Both were young and vigorous Virginians, and experienced woodsmen, and both were good Republicans—Lewis ardently so. Of Lewis the President wrote long after that he was of "courage undaunted; possessing a firmness and perseverance of purpose . . . ; careful as a father of those committed to his charge, yet steady in the maintenance of order and discipline; inti-mate with the Indian character, customs, and principles; habituated to the hunting life . . . honest, disinterested, liberal, of sound understanding, and a fidelity to truth. . . ." Jefferson could speak almost as warmly of Clark, whose family he knew well. They were men the President could guide, and he issued elaborate instructions for the expedition.

"The object of your mission," he wrote Lewis on June 20, 1803, "is to explore the Missouri river, & such principal stream of it, as, by it's course & communication with the water of the Pacific Ocean may offer the most direct & practicable water communication across the continent, for the purposes of commerce." The mission, Jefferson said, had been com-municated to the ministers in Washington from Spain, Britain, and France, the new owner of Louisiana. Beginning at the mouth of the Missouri, the explorers were to note the details of geography and river transportation; of the inhabitants' possessions, languages, traditions, monuments, occupa-tions, food, clothing, diseases and remedies, physical circumstances, reli-gion, and morality; of the soil, produce, animals, minerals, climate, "the dates at which particular plants put forth or lose their flowers, or leaf, times of appearance of particular birds, reptiles, or insects." The expedition was to be entirely pacific; Lewis was to "err on the side of your safety" in case of confrontation with superior forces, and to bring back his party safely, even if it be with less information.

Lewis spent months preparing for the expedition. He bought scientific instruments and medicine in Philadelphia, even consulting the famous Dr. Rush, had an iron boat built at the arsenal of Harpers Ferry, bought some dubious "portable soup," and amassed hundreds of brooches, rings, ear-rings, beads, looking glasses, and even scalping knives as presents to Indians. He also acquired an air gun, an English import that, after being pumped up with air, could eject bullets more quickly than a Kentucky rifle

could be loaded, wadded, and primed, but with power more to stun than
to kill. From everyone he met he collected information on the western country. From frontier army posts he handpicked his men, most notably his co-
commander William Clark, an old friend who had probably talked with Daniel Boone himself. Boating down the Ohio River from Pittsburgh, he
gathered up more men, including Clark at Louisville, and then turned out of
the Ohio and up the Mississippi to the St. Louis area, where the party spent
the winter of 1803–04 building boats.

And now, in the spring of 1804, they were pushing their way west against
the current of the mighty Missouri. It was hard going. Boats continued to
snag on invisible obstacles. Tow ropes parted. A mast broke. Mosquitoes
drew blood. Stomachs upheaved and boils broke out. Shore parties fought
their way through dense forests and thickets as they hunted game and
botanical specimens and herded the expedition's horses. At night the party
usually camped in tents by the river, after trading and dickering with
friendly Indians. It was not a company of saints or heroes. Men returned
to camp drunk from nearby forays, spoke "disrespectfully" to their commanders, went about without leave, slept on guard duty, stole whiskey
from the company keg, even deserted. But this was an army unit and
discipline was swift and sure. After courts-martial, men were lashed with
switches 25 to 100 times on their bare backs. And painfully, steadily,
determinedly, they moved upstream through the Dakotas.

The expedition stopped repeatedly for long powwows with Indian
chiefs. Lewis had clear instructions from Jefferson about dealing with the
natives: to "treat them in the most friendly & conciliatory manner which
their own conduct will admit; allay all jealousies as to the object of your
journey, satisfy them of it's innocence, make them acquainted with the
position, extent, character, peaceable & commercial dispositions of the
U.S., of our wish to be neighborly, friendly & useful to them, & of our
dispositions to a commercial intercourse with them." A chief wishing to
visit Washington would be conveyed there at public expense. If any of the
chiefs "should wish to have some of their young people brought up with
us, & taught such arts as may be useful to them, we will receive, instruct
& take care of them." Visits of chiefs or young people "would give some
security to your own party," Jefferson added.

In fact, the explorers found the Indians on the whole friendly but most
perplexing. Otos, Omahas, Missouris, Sioux, Pawnees, Poncas, Arikaras
. . . the tribes seemed of endless number and variety, and many were
divided into complex subgroups. The tribes along the river seemed to
coexist in near-anarchy; Sioux chiefs thought they were at war with twenty
tribes and at peace with eight, but they were not sure. To the unknowing

Americans, Indian behavior seemed erratic and unpredictable. Some of the natives were friendly, some hostile; some thieving and some honest; some abstemious, some sottish; some communicative, some not. At best communication was poor, in part because of the numberless dialects. Lewis had a set technique for dealing with the natives: to announce at a parley that he had been sent by the great white father to assert American sovereignty and to receive the fealty of the red children; then to distribute American medals and flags and lavish gifts of beads, cloth, trinkets, and badges.

But two cultures were meeting along the banks of the Missouri, and they often clashed. The whites were appalled by the natives' craving for the more putrid meat, even the intestines and offal of long-decaying animals; appalled and delighted by their definition of hospitality as providing guests with food, presents, and "temporary wives," most often the sisters or spouses of their hosts; amazed by their ability to play, stark naked, lacrosse on ice at 25 degrees below zero. The Indians for their part gaped at these creatures with white skins and hair all over their faces; and gaped even more at the black man York. In village after village natives crowded around the slave; some would wet their fingers and try to rub away his blackness to find the "natural" color underneath. The Indians were dismayed by some of the whites' behavior. An Arikara chief said, after watching a flogging, that it was wrong to humiliate persons like that; the chief said that in his nation, according to Clark's report, they "never whiped even their Children from their burth." In such cases, the chief added, they would simply put the man to death.

After wintering in well-fortified huts at the great bend of the Missouri in (present) North Dakota, the Americans struck out in the spring of 1805 toward the western mountains. The going became more and more arduous and perilous as the river narrowed. The big pirogue had to be abandoned, as the men continued in canoes and keelboats. They coped with fearsome grizzlies, rattlesnakes, exhausting portages around falls, overturned boats, deep-biting mosquitoes, scanty game and hence inadequate food. They were now in almost unknown country, and desperately anxious to find the best route to avoid being caught in the high mountains in the winter. They were guided by long reconnoiters of Missouri tributaries and also by a new member of the party, Sacagawea, the very young wife of a Frenchman who also joined the expedition. Captured by the Minnetarees a few years earlier and traded from warrior to warrior and finally to the white trader, the squaw-wife vaguely remembered some of the territory of the upper reaches of the Missouri. Pregnant at the time, she bore her baby stoically on the trip and carried him until the end.

Toiling up through the mountain valleys, desperately making friends with Indian tribes to gain information on passages west, the explorers in a final convulsive effort made their way through the mountain passes of the continental divide, and groped for and found the tributaries of the Columbia River. Boating down the roaring Columbia was perilous but at least comparatively rapid, and by late fall the party reached the coast and stared, elated, at the Pacific. After enduring a wet and depressing Oregon winter, they headed back east over the Rockies and then split in two, as Lewis followed the Missouri back and Clark led a party along the Yellowstone, all in an attempt to bring back to Mr. Jefferson as many observations and specimens as possible. Hardly a day on the return trip, as on the outward one, was free of troubles—illness, skirmishes with Indians, lost or stolen horses, encounters with animals, bad falls from horses or cliffs—but the two parties reunited on the Missouri and then moved rapidly down the muddy river to St. Louis, and home.

The expedition had been extraordinarily successful, an almost unbelievable combination of planning, skill, resourcefulness, courage, persistence, faith, and colossal luck. Despite the endless perils, ranging from grizzly bears to venereal disease, not a man had been lost, save for a victim of what was apparently appendicitis. The trip was a rare act of leadership on the part of Lewis and Clark, the kind of leadership that challenges, inspires, goads, and finally elevates followers, until they too become leaders. The two men, operating in remarkable harmony as coequals, turned out to be near-perfect choices to head the expedition, but success lay too with "ordinary" men who could make their own boats and shelter and moccasins and clothes and ammunition, with a slave who could cook, with a young Indian squaw who could help guide and translate. The journey was a monument to the potentials of the common people whom Jefferson idealized.

In St. Louis, early on the day after arriving, Lewis tore some blank sheets from his journal and wrote to the President:

"In obedience to your orders we have penetrated the Continent of North America to the Pacific Ocean and suficiently explored the interior of the country to affirm that we have discovered the most practicable communication which dose exist across the continent." Lewis had journeyed east, to Charlottesville, before he received Jefferson's reply:

"I received, my dear sir, with unspeakable joy your letter of Sep. 23 announcing the return of yourself, Capt. Clarke & your party in good health to St. Louis. The unknown scenes in which you were engaged, & the length of time without hearing of you had begun to be felt awfully. . . ." The President did not exaggerate. As the months had passed and fears mounted that the whole expedition had been lost to cold or starvation or

Indians, he had grieved over his responsibility for the probable fate of these young men. Now they were back—and with all those specimens!

CHECKMATE: THE FEDERALIST BASTION STANDS

As good Virginia Republicans, Meriwether Lewis and William Clark were pleased to find on returning home in 1806 that their party and their patron had prospered. The Republican party was dominant in the presidency, in Congress, and in most of the state executive offices and legislatures. Unanimously renominated by the Republican congressional caucus early in 1804, Jefferson had gone on to defeat Charles Cotesworth Pinckney by the lopsided vote of 162 to 14. The Federalist candidate had lost his own state and all of New England save for Connecticut. Yet if most of the old Federalist strongholds were in ruins, a most powerful bastion of a different kind remained for the party of Washington and Adams and Pinckney. There the President had sustained a defeat, the magnitude of which was hardly recognizable even to Jefferson himself.

That defeat had begun with an incident during the days of transition between Presidents Adams and Jefferson. In his famous "midnight appointments," Adams stayed up late—probably to about 10 P.M.—on the eve of Jefferson's Inaugural, busily signing commissions that would provide jobs for a host of deserving Federalists. The next day, after John Marshall swore Jefferson into the presidency, the Chief Justice at the request of the new President stayed on briefly as Secretary of State until James Madison could take over. And so it happened that a good Federalist still was running the State Department when John Adams' "midnight" commissions came over to the department to be duly sent out to the waiting appointees. But Marshall had never been wholly attentive to detail, and there was much on his mind that day, since he was in the remarkable situation of serving as both Chief Justice and chief cabinet member. He neglected to send out a number of the commissions, and some time later Jefferson, who happened to be at the State Department, found the commissions there, still lying on a table.

With elation the President realized what he held in his hands. He was already angry at Adams' last-minute effort to pack the government with Federalists—the "one act of Mr. Adams's," he later wrote Abigail Adams, which "ever gave me a moment's personal displeasure." He was also provoked by the fact that neither Washington nor Adams had appointed a single Republican to the entire federal judiciary, and by the Judiciary Act of 1801, which the Federalists had rushed through Congress just before Adams left office and the Federalists lost control of the legislature. That act had relieved the justices of circuit court duty, created sixteen new circuit court judges, and reduced the number of Supreme Court justices from six to five at the next vacancy—which meant that the new President would be delayed indefinitely in making his first high court appointment. What to do about this kind of court packing? Jefferson resolved to have the Judiciary Act repealed as soon as possible. He would make a few recess appointments of his own. And he would issue pardons to persons punished under the Alien and Sedition Acts.

Meantime, here were these undelivered commissions. Why deliver them? He instructed Secretary of State Madison not to. Of all Jefferson's countermoves against his foes' judiciary packing, this seemed the easiest and most innocuous. It turned out to be the most consequential.

At this point Republican leadership suspected that the high Federalists, beaten at the polls, were already plotting under Marshall to entrench themselves in the judiciary. The Republicans were quite right, except that this was no secret plot but rather an open, deliberate, carefully worked out strategy. And certainly Marshall was the leader. Even apart from his hostility to Republicans—especially Republicans in his own state of Virginia— he had long hoped that the federal judiciary would take its rightful place as one of three coordinate but independent branches of the new government. Somehow that had not happened. The first Chief Justice, John Jay, was an illustrious Federalist leader who had felt that serving as United States Minister to the Court of St. James's and even campaigning (successfully) for governor of New York were wholly compatible with holding his high judicial office. His successor, Oliver Ellsworth, had also been Minister to France. No harm had seemed to result, since the court heard few cases and rarely sought to exercise much influence. But Marshall was resolved to change all this. And now he had tenfold reason to do so, for the fanatical Republicans had taken over both the executive and legislative branches, and as his fellow Federalist Gouverneur Morris admitted, in "a heavy gale of adverse wind" they could hardly "be blamed for casting many anchors to hold their ship through the storm." The biggest anchor would lie in the Supreme Court, until the Federalists could regain control of both presidency and Congress.

Thus the scene was laid for a collision between Marshall and Jefferson. People marveled that two men so alike—both lawyers, Virginians, ex-revolutionaries, politicians, and blood cousins to boot—could so dislike each other. But political ambition and ideology can be thicker than blood. As a nationalist and conservative Marshall had been drawn steadily into the Federalists' orbit, while Jefferson had clung to the party of states' rights and popular sovereignty. Determined though he was to assert judicial independence, however, the Chief Justice knew that he had to move with care. Unlike the President, he had no troops, no arms. Unlike Congress, he and his brethren were not chosen by the voters.

At least he could take comfort from the justices, stout Federalists all, who flanked him on the high court. The most senior associate justice, William Cushing of Massachusetts, had faced down Shays's rioters years before and was one of the few American judges still to wear a wig, English style. William Paterson of New Jersey, main author of the famous compromise between the large and small states in the 1787 constitutional convention, was a former governor of his state. Samuel Chase of Maryland, a "high Federalist" if there ever was one, a former Son of Liberty, long a nationalist, was a brilliant ideologue who had already mapped out the frontiers of national power in court decisions. Alfred Moore of North Carolina was a soldier and lawyer. Bushrod Washington was the first President's nephew and an old and close friend of Marshall's.

The Chief Justice could marshal and mobilize his brethren; he could not manipulate them. Like any leader of a political collectivity, he had to pick his way between the wings of his court. Chase, the judicial firebrand, warned him that his conscience had to be satisfied on the question of judicial power, even though "my ruin should be the certain consequence," while the moderates on the court urged him to be cautious in antagonizing the political branches. Carefully the Chief Justice analyzed the way in which he could establish the dignity and power of the high court. Dignity was hard to come by, for the brethren convened in a drab room, with a small fireplace, in the Senate wing of the Capitol. But Marshall would bide his time and pick his judicial ground, however insignificant the particular case might be, for establishing the power of the court against the political branches.

Jefferson's political position somewhat resembled Marshall's. He too sought to mobilize the power of his party in the two political branches, but he also had to pick his way between the wings of his party in and outside Congress. Exhorting him to take on the Federalist judicial stronghold in direct political combat were a group of "sweeping Republicans" centered especially in the House. One of the most militant leaders, William Branch Giles of Virginia, warned that the great revolution was "incomplete, so long as that strong fortress is in possession of the enemy." Judicial—and hence Federalist—power must be extirpated root and branch. Then too, party loyalists were demanding jobs, and nothing was more enticing than a lifelong judicial appointment.

On the other hand, moderate Republicans were loath to assault the judiciary, in part because they respected a measure of judicial independence, in part because they had little stomach for confronting John Marshall. Jefferson, moreover, was still intent on winning over and retaining the support of moderate Federalists, and nothing would drive them back into the hands of the Federalist party faster than a determined attack on the Supreme Court.

Typically, the President faced this problem by taking one step at a time. The first was obviously to repeal the partisan Federalist Judiciary Act of 1801. When Senator John Breckinridge of Kentucky, an old ally of Jefferson's from the days of the Virginia and Kentucky resolutions, introduced a repeal bill in January 1802, a furious battle broke out, as the Federalists accused their adversaries of seeking to destroy the independence of the judiciary. Clearly the Federalists would defend their bastion to the last man, but in the Senate voting the Republicans had the last man on the floor, as the bill passed 16 to 15. Giles and Randolph mobilized a strong vote for the bill in the House. Republicans in Congress relied not only on traditional arguments against "judicial tyranny" but on the fact of Jefferson's clear support for the measure; this was the *President*'s bill.

The Republicans' next step was even more controversial—a bill that by manipulating the scheduling of Supreme Court terms would in effect delay the next session of the high court for over a year, until February 1803. This maneuver would thwart any effort by the court to invalidate the repeal act before it could take effect. This bill passed too. Incensed and indignant, the justices considered the extreme step of refusing again to ride circuit and thus declaring the act unconstitutional. Chase in particular wanted to fight back, on the ground that this kind of meddling by President and Congress in the internal functions of the court would cripple it. Marshall was tempted to follow the strategy of defiance, but other members of the court took a more conciliatory position, he needed a united bench behind him, and he had to be sure of his ground. He waited for a better opportunity to strike back.

That opportunity was already developing in the form of a routine plea by a Washington Federalist named William Marbury. An applicant for the position of justice of the peace, Marbury had had the misfortune to be one of Adams' midnight appointments, the commission for which had fallen into Jefferson's hands. What could be more natural for Marbury than to turn for relief to the court headed by the very man, John Marshall, who had neglected to deliver him his commission? Marbury went directly to the high court with a plea that the court order the Secretary of State—now James Madison—to deliver him his commission, on the ground that the original Judiciary Act of 1789 authorized the court, in situations when federal officials were not carrying out required "ministerial" acts, to issue writs of mandamus requiring those officials to perform the said duties.

Marshall pondered his dilemma. If he granted Marbury's plea and issued the mandamus, Jefferson and Madison could ignore or reject it, on the grounds that the judicial branch was now interfering in the executive's internal affairs. The court would then be powerless—no court official could make Madison deliver up a commission—and the federal judiciary would appear more impotent than ever. But if the court refused to issue the writ of mandamus, it would seem even more impotent, unable to perform one of its most elementary functions. What could Marshall do? Only a supreme judicial strategist could snatch victory from such a weak position.

On February 24, 1803, the members of the high court took their seats in the dingy basement chamber. "Oyez, oyez, oyez!" cried the clerk, as he admonished all gentlemen having business with the court to draw near and give attention. The clerk concluded sonorously: "God save the United States and this Honorable Court." Marshall was about to do the latter. The Chief Justice was hardly a striking presence, with his tall, meager frame, sober dress, and hard, dry voice, but to many his logic seemed commanding. He began to read.

After a perfunctory start he reviewed the facts of the case. Then he posed three questions: Did Marbury have a right to the commission? If he had such a right, did he have a remedy under law against Madison's denial? And if he had such a remedy, was it a mandamus from the Supreme Court? Marshall's answer to the first two questions came in an hour-long lecture in which, using judicial language, he scolded the President and the Secretary of State for failing to conform to the law. Withholding of Marbury's commission was an act "not warranted by law," the Chief Justice stated flatly, "but violative of a vested legal right." And certainly Marbury had a remedy. "The very essence of civil liberty" consisted in the "right of every individual to claim the protection of the laws, whenever he receives an injury," Marshall intoned. Presidents and Secretaries of State, in short, had to obey the law just like anyone else. That raised the third question: Could the Supreme Court properly demand that Madison turn over the commission to Marbury?

The answer obviously seemed yes, and the moment seemed to have come for a dramatic confrontation between Jefferson and Marshall, between Republicans and Federalists, between the elected branches of the government and the appointed. But no; Marshall appeared to be off on another tack. Marbury had brought his case under an article of the 1789 Judiciary Act giving the Supreme Court original jurisdiction in certain cases. The Constitution, however, granted original jurisdiction to the court only in very limited kinds of cases and this, said Marshall, was not one of them. If the court followed the act, he said, it had jurisdiction, but if the court followed the Constitution, it did not have jurisdiction. Then the Chief Justice proceeded to what struck his Republican auditors as a patriotic stump speech, filled with self-evident statements and self-answering questions, all of which served his political purposes.

The people, he said, had "an original right to establish, for their future government, such principles as, in their opinion, shall most conduce to their own happiness." In short, the people had a right to draw up a constitution. "The powers of the legislature are defined and limited; and that those limits may not be mistaken, or forgotten, the constitution is written." No one had doubted this. In a series of positive and sweeping sentences, the Chief Justice argued the obvious—that the law must give way to the Constitution—and he largely assumed the far less obvious—that it was up to the *courts* to rule whether another branch of the government had exceeded the Constitution. As J. W. Peltason has written, in typical fashion Marshall stated the question in such a way that the answer was obvious. Should the Supreme Court enforce an unconstitutional law? *Of course not.* Should the Supreme Court decide when Congress or President had violated the Constitution? *Of course.* So: Congress in the Judiciary Act of 1789 had sought to grant the court a power prohibited by the Constitution; that section of the act was unconstitutional; thus the court had no power to act in this situation, even though Madison had acted improperly; case dismissed.

There were two immediate and sharp reactions to the opinion. One was Marbury's; the poor wretch had been denied his commission once because of Marshall's evident negligence; now he was being denied his commission again, even though Marshall said he had a right to have it. The other was that of Republican leaders, and it was pure indignation. Jefferson and Madison could hardly be oblivious to their young rival who, from the sanctity of the bench, was lecturing them as to how they should conduct their executive department. The sharpest reaction came from the Republican press, which also saw Marshall's opinion simply as a Federalist attack on the two Republican-controlled branches.

"The efforts of *federalism* to exalt the Judiciary over the Executive and Legislature," said the Boston *Independent Chronicle,* "and to give that favorite department a political character & influence, may operate for a time to come, as it has already, to the promotion of one party and the depression of the other, but will probably terminate in degradation and the disgrace of the Judiciary. . . . The *attempt* of the Supreme Court of the United States, by a mandamus, to control the Executive functions, is a new experiment. It seems to be no less than a commencement of war between the constituted departments. The Court must be defeated and retreat from the attack; or march on, till they incur an impeachment and removal from office."

But the *Chronicle,* and most Republicans, had missed the point. The court had not invaded the executive, only upbraided it. Indeed, it had invalidated the congressional act granting power to the court to take original jurisdiction in certain matters. What the Chief Justice had done was far more important, and its significance dawned only slowly on many Republicans. Marshall, in voiding an act of Congress signed by the President that gave the court a small power, was creating the great precedent of judicial invalidation of congressional action, and—the supreme strategic triumph for Marshall—was doing so in a way that the executive could not thwart. If Marshall had demanded that the executive take certain action, such as giving that commission to Marbury, Jefferson and Madison could have— and probably would have—coolly refused. But how could Jefferson & Co. stop the court from *declining* to exert power? The Republicans were helpless. To add salt to their wounds, the action of the court in reviewing one of its own alleged powers even comported with Jefferson's notion of coordinate constitutionality by each branch in its sphere.

Of course, *Marbury* was only a weak precedent for judicial invalidation of laws passed by Congress and signed by the President. But that precedent was destined to become a time bomb, ticking away for half a century, until it would explode amid the most grievous crisis in American history.

*   *   *

It was ironic that it was Jefferson who should have failed to overcome the judicial bastion, for otherwise he was displaying a brilliance of political leadership that would hardly be matched in two hundred years of nationhood. If that brilliance blinded some Republicans to potential weaknesses in his leadership, its full import would not be evident for some years.

Jefferson led, first of all, as chief executive. Those who feared—or hoped —that the relaxed, ruminating, casual Virginia aristocrat would let others run his administration could hardly recognize the decisive figure in the White House. Jefferson did not need to bestride a white charger or bark out orders to assume the role of chief executive. He had a quiet air of authority, a steadfastness of purpose, a superb sense of timing, and the capacity to look ahead. His historic actions, such as the purchase of Louisiana, turned on many smaller decisions. Thus in sending Monroe abroad he did not waste time asking his friend whether he would like to go; knowing of Monroe's public-spiritedness, he informed the retiring Virginia governor that public necessity demanded he go, that he was putting his nomination through the Senate, and that he expected to see him in Washington promptly. In moving quickly to dispatch Lewis and Clark to an area beset by imperial ambitions, he was risking heavy censure if the explorers met some disaster, but the luck of the audacious was with the President as well as with the expedition.

He defended executive independence and executive prerogative—withholding certain presidential papers, for example—as compatible with the system of checks and balances, and indeed as required by it. Only the President could command the necessary overview of the government, he felt; the President alone provided a "regulating power which would keep the machine in steady movement." He demanded unity within the executive. He asked understanding from those who did not, like the chief executive, "command a view of the whole ground." No Hamiltonian, he held as firm a conception of executive leadership as did Hamilton.

Still, this was collective executive leadership, with the President soliciting and responding to the advice of his Cabinet. Years later he boasted that his Cabinet of six persons had presented an example of harmony without parallel in history. "There never arose, during the whole time, an instance of an unpleasant thought or word between the members." Harmony was produced by a modifying of one another's ideas. "But the power of decision in the President left no object for internal dissension, and external intrigue was stifled in embryo by the knowledge which incendiaries possessed, that no division they could foment would change the course of the executive power."

The leadership of the legislative branch that Jefferson had so indirectly but firmly exerted during his first two years in office carried on through the rest of his term. The basis of that leadership continued to be party solidarity, and the role of party was expanded after the Republicans gained strength in the "off-year" elections midway through the term. Party membership was still a bit ambiguous, but Jefferson estimated that Republicans outnumbered Federalists 103 to 39 in the House and 25 to 9 in the Senate. He continued to exert party influence more by persuasion than dictation, far more by skillful use of patronage and the party press than by public efforts to impose his ideas. He picked his way through the minefields of schismatic state politics by tolerating differences. "His ability to hold the Republican party together nationally when it was rocked by state party divisions and to retain the attachments of virtually all sides involved in the internal divisions of state politics," Noble Cunningham concludes, "was an accomplishment that only a superb politician could achieve."

The Jeffersonians' party strategy continued to be the pre-emption of the middle ground, where all but "sweeping" Republicans and the highest of "high Federalists" could meet and join hands. The President carefully doled out appointments to Republican moderates, while leaving Federalist moderates in office where feasible. But Jefferson's appeal transcended party. His ultimate political strategy was to turn to the people—or at least the active citizens among them—because he respected them and believed in them and expected much from them. He was one of those rare leaders who, in responding to people's fundamental wants and needs, aspirations and expectations, and in pursuing some powerful vision or goal, transcend the passing eddies of public opinion, and even more, educate the popular will, sensing authentic but unexpressed wants and needs in the people. That is the ultimate engagement between leader and led, and that kind of leadership Jefferson demonstrated in his program, his methods, and his *persona*.

Yet, the very success of the Jeffersonian leadership carried the seeds of new crisis. Great leadership is forged in the crucible of conflict, as the careers of Jefferson, Hamilton, and Adams had so amply demonstrated. What happens, then, when leadership succeeds so well, by mobilizing the support of so many of the people, that conflict either dwindles or is displaced into extra-constitutional, even violent arenas? What happens, in the Jeffersonians' case, when leadership draws such wide support across the party spectrum that opposition shrinks and threatens to crumble, and conflict exists only between the great mass of moderates and the extreme or the desperate?

Jefferson's answer to this question was that once the moderate Federalists were won over and the high Federalists crushed, the ballooning Republican party would split into two moderate, responsible, competitive parties. "We shall now be so strong," the President wrote a friend in May 1802, "that we shall certainly split again; for freemen thinking differently and speaking and acting as they think, will form into classes of sentiment, but it must be under another name, that of federalism is to become so scouted that no party can rise under it. . . . the division will substantially be into whig and tory, as in England, formerly. . . ." But Jefferson had to admit that no "symptoms" of a new party split had shown themselves, nor would they until after the midterm election. And the President developed a disturbing tendency to equate the Republican party with the whole nation.

As Federalist strength declined at midterm and still more in the 1804 presidential election, no significant division developed in the Republican party. Perhaps Jefferson was too skillful a conciliator. Was the new young republic becoming a one-party state?

A startling event made this question more urgent. One man Jefferson had not conciliated—and intensely distrusted—was Vice-President Aaron Burr. Rumors abounded among the Jeffersonians about Burr's striving for the presidency during the crisis of February 1801, just as Burr and his friends suspected that Jefferson had finally won out through a secret deal. The President had virtually ignored Burr on patronage matters and instead dealt with the latter's adversaries in New York, the Livingston and Clinton factions. Although Jeffersonians suspected that Burr would work out a coalition with the Federalists, the Vice-President was still a mortal enemy of the titular leader of that party, Alexander Hamilton. When Burr, weary of his frustrating job as Vice-President, decided to run for governor of New York, Hamilton was furious at the notion that some of his more opportunistic fellow Federalists would support this ambitious little man. He so attacked Burr's character that the duelists' code required a confrontation. It occurred on July 11, 1804, at a secluded spot across the Hudson River in New Jersey. Hamilton, it is thought, intended to miss in the hope that Burr intended likewise. Burr sought to kill. Hamilton died of a bullet in his vertebrae, after hours of intense suffering. The remaining great hope of the Federalist party was gone, along with any hope that Burr could draw the Federalists into a new alliance.

Thus Jefferson was left as head of a burgeoning party, confronting an opposition dwindling both in Congress and in elections. He was the leader of an organized majority. He was a firm believer in majority rule as the practical expression of government by the people, but he also recognized that majority rule must not mean extremist rule. "All, too, will bear in mind this sacred principle," he had said in his Inaugural Address, "that though the will of the majority is in all cases to prevail, that will, to be rightful, must be reasonable: that the Minority possess their equal rights, which equal laws must protect, & to violate would be oppression." Implicit in this doctrine of majority rule were certain assumptions. One was that the majority would necessarily embrace so many diverse interests, sections, and attitudes, in a pluralistic nation, that the majority would pursue a moderate and balanced program; a second was that the majority would represent the great mass of people. Both these assumptions could be questioned: under certain conditions a majority could become as oppressive and fanatical as a minority; and Jefferson's majority even at best encompassed only free, male, and largely property-owning Americans. Crucial to Jefferson's belief in majority rule was his belief in the minority's "equal rights," but what politically would guarantee those rights? A strong opposition party, but Jefferson lacked a firm understanding of the role of party opposition.

It was precisely here that Jeffersonian theory left an intellectual gap—

a gap that Marshall's judicial theory brilliantly filled. For if there was inadequate political check on the majority—that is, on the government— there must be an adequate constitutional check institutionalized within the governmental structure. And clearly that vital check on the popular majority must be the judiciary, itself protected against the immediate power of the electorate.

Aaron Burr's bullet, it was said, had blown the brains out of the Federalist party. This was a half-truth at best; Federalist brains remained very much intact in the heads of John Marshall and his brethren entrenched in the federal judiciary. Marshall, in particular, had a better grasp than Jefferson of the constitutional scope and political implications of various kinds of judicial review. The most minimal kind of judicial review—and one that Jefferson respected because he believed that each branch of government should be independent—was the power of the courts to protect their own existence and manage their own internal affairs. A somewhat higher form of judicial review was that of state legislation, and most Americans at the turn of the century agreed that the federal courts must exercise this power in order that there be an "umpire of federalism." A still broader form of judicial review was that of presidential action; for centuries Englishmen and Americans oppressed by kings or royal governors had been turning to the courts for relief. The fullest form of judicial review was that of congressional action—the awesome authority to invalidate laws passed by the elected representatives of the people. This was an enormous power, and an anomalous one in a "government by the people."

Seizing on Marbury's complaint, Marshall had used that most minimal form of judicial review in order to create the vital precedent for the largest form. Practically, there was nothing Jefferson could do about this, but it is doubtful that intellectually he grasped the enormous implications of what Marshall was about. Ostensibly the Chief Justice was simply protecting the independence of the federal judiciary, at the same time that he was refraining from interfering in the executive's domain; in fact, he was actually denying a power granted to the Supreme Court by the Congress. Rarely has such potentially vast power been so nicely disguised.

If Marshall had placed a check on the Republican President and Congress, he had established a potential checkmate on popular majorities for years to come. But would that checkmate, in a nation destined to pass through ceaseless social change and violent political conflict, in a nation still encircled north and south and on the oceans by foreign powers, turn out to be that most dangerous condition for a democracy: stalemate?

CHAPTER 6

The American Way of War

The Cathedral of Notre Dame, Paris, December 2, 1804. Before a dazzling array of marshals, ecclesiastics, and *nouveaux princesses,* Napoleon Bonaparte places a fake Carolingian crown on his head and proclaims himself Emperor of France. Behind him sits a glum Pius VII, who has joined Napoleon and Josephine in wedlock only the night before—the couple had neglected to be married in church—in order to legitimate the coronation. At the ceremony Napoleon does not prostrate himself before the Pope, nor will he take communion. The Corsican will bow to no authority, except that of the people, who in a plebiscite hardly a week before have "elected" him emperor by a vote of 3,500,000 to 2,500. He is the new Caesar, the new Charlemagne. . . .

Three days later the Emperor presented his colonels with their new battle standards: imperial eagles that would symbolize his leadership in creating a new Roman Empire, though hardly a Holy one. By spring his Grand Army was pressing east, while England desperately organized a defensive alliance of Russians, Prussians, and Austrians. In October 1805 Napoleon's spirited troops routed the Austrians at Ulm and the Emperor was soon sleeping in the palace of Schönbrunn in Vienna. Six weeks later, at Austerlitz, in a classic maneuvering of massed but mobile troops, Napoleon outgeneraled the combined forces of Alexander of Russia and Francis of Austria, cut the enemy in two, killed or wounded 26,000 men, and sent the rival emperors into headlong retreat. It was at this battle that Andrei Bolkonsky, in Tolstoi's *War and Peace,* lying wounded on his back, reflected on the nature of war, leadership, and history.

In London, an aging monarch contrasted drably with the military hero of France. "Mad" George III reigned in the forty-fifth year of his kingship. Not insane but afflicted with porphyria, he was at times so wild and delirious that his doctors, applying the standard treatment of the day, tied His Majesty to his bed or even strapped him into a "waistjacket." For months his subjects had stood on the alert while Napoleon built flotillas of flat-bottomed boats big enough to carry infantry, field pieces, and horses into the coves and beaches of southern England. But the Royal Navy stood in the way, and Napoleon turned back to his land conquests.

Londoners had hardly received the bleak news from Ulm when an electrifying report arrived from the Navy. Admiral Horatio Nelson, victor over Napoleon's fleet in the Battle of the Nile some years earlier, had decoyed the combined French and Spanish armada out into Atlantic waters off the Cape of Trafalgar, broken the heavily gunned allied line, and routed the enemy. Englishmen thrilled to the news that Nelson had signaled from his flagship, "England expects every man to do his duty," then grieved over the report that Nelson had fallen before a musket ball. When Napoleon triumphed at Austerlitz a few weeks later, the shape of the military chessboard in the West was set for almost a decade: France was master of the Continent, England mistress of the seas.

In Washington, Jefferson and Madison followed these events with a sense of both involvement and detachment. They suspected the intentions of both the major powers and saw no need to take sides; the revolutionary France that Jefferson had welcomed had now been compromised and betrayed by a man whose militaristic flamboyance and Machiavellian statecraft he detested. But the President knew too that, however much he and the other Republican leaders wished to maintain strict neutrality, decisions in London and Paris, and at other points in the swaying mobiles of global politics, would closely touch Americans on the high seas and indeed in their ports and farms and factories. The Jeffersonians had reason to fear involvement: a republican disdain for the machinations of the courts of Europe; the vulnerability of a secondary power to the fleets and armies of a major, coupled with the military unpreparedness of the young nation. The President also feared involvements that would allow events to be controlled more by accident than by leaders, more "by chance than by design."

Jefferson also had some sense of insecurity about dealing with the veteran diplomats of Paris and London. "An American contending by stratagem against those exercised in it from their cradle would undoubtedly be outwitted by them," he observed to Madison; the President was referring to Minister Robert Livingston but knew that he himself was widely charged with gullibility in diplomacy. Jefferson had had extensive diplomatic experience, of course; his main handicap was his hope to apply morality to foreign relations. Talleyrand suffered no such encumbrance.

The President had learned early in his first term that, no matter how eager he might be to follow an independent course, the affairs of the New World would be entangled with the Old as long as American ships sailed the seas. That reminder had come from the rulers of Algiers, Morocco, Tunis, and Tripoli, the "Barbary pirates" who had been seizing American ships and their "infidel" crews. American rulers had preferred to pay tribute rather than build a navy big enough for a transatlantic expeditionary force against the pashas' ships and moated fortresses. When Barbary avarice and truculence seemed to mount at the turn of the century, Jefferson dispatched the *Constitution* and a few other vessels to bring the pirates to book.

The results were a comic-opera combination of disaster—the *Philadelphia* ran aground chasing pirates and was taken by the buccaneers—and some heroic actions, exemplified by young Lieutenant Stephen Decatur, who boldly piloted a captured ship into Tripoli harbor and put the torch to the *Philadelphia.* Unable to take Tripoli by sea, the Americans now attacked by land. A small band of Arabs, Greek soldiers, and seven Marines marched for an arduous month from Alexandria through the desert, stormed Derna in a brief action, and jolted Pasha Yusuf into making peace, at the additional cost of a $60,000 sweetener for his court. The whole Barbary adventure ended with a few gains: at least temporary peace with Yusuf and the other pashas; training in seamanship, especially with the cheap, shallow gunboats that parsimonious Republicans preferred; and a fine line in a grand Marine song.

If this was a lesson in Old World involvement from the east, events to the west showed that the most sensitive domestic rivalries could become entangled with foreign relations.

The event makers were two remarkable men who had lived half inside, half outside, the young nation's political and military leadership. One was Aaron Burr, who at the conclusion of his vice-presidency in 1805 was still an object of excitement, distrust, and mystery. A descendant of rigorous Presbyterians, including the great scholar-moralist Jonathan Edwards, he had come to reject the moral and political codes of his day. Short, balding, "persuasive" of eye and tongue, he pursued women so indefatigably and successfully as to qualify him for the title of an American Casanova. An able officer in the Revolution and a brilliant political organizer, he seemed to discipline all except himself. Yet if Burr was prepared in 1805 to betray his nation, he felt betrayed by the established leaders—by the Republicans, who had failed to re-elect him as governor of New York in 1799 and closed ranks against him in the presidential competition of 1801, and by the Federalists, who would never forgive him for killing Hamilton on that dubious field of honor, the dueling ground. Even before he left the vice-presidency Burr was conspiring to undertake his fantastic venture: to invade Mexico, a colony of Spain, seize western territories of the United States, and create a new nation headed, presumably, by himself.

James Wilkinson, the man Burr conspired with, was an even stranger combination of opposites. At the age of twenty a brevetted brigadier general in the War of Independence, he was implicated in a move to unseat Washington as commander in chief. He nevertheless rose to the top of the American military establishment, winning appointment as military governor of Louisiana in 1803. He was also a paid secret agent of Spain—the "most consummate artist in treason," Frederick Jackson Turner called him, "that the nation ever possessed." If Burr's weakness was women, Wilkinson's was gold, gold from any source, English, Spanish, or American. He was also a faithless ally. At the climactic moment, after Burr had organized men and boats all along the Ohio River for a rendezvous in New Orleans and the presumed attack on Mexico, Wilkinson decided to sell Burr out in order to maintain his own standing with both the American and Spanish governments.

Burr had talked with so many persons—politicians, soldiers, rivermen, adventurers—that Jefferson had long known he was up to something—but what? Only on receiving from Wilkinson a report filled with horrendous portents and alarums did the President issue a proclamation warning of a "military expedition or enterprise against the dominions of Spain," though saying nothing of secession. He issued a blanket order to federal and state officials to search out and apprehend the villains. A few weeks later Burr arrived in Natchez with a ragtail collection of men and boats, only to learn that Wilkinson had denounced him and ordered his arrest. Burr surrendered, then jumped bail and raced toward Spanish Florida, but was intercepted and taken to Richmond, there to await trial on a charge of treason.

Burr had tried to draw scores of western politicos—Ohioans, Kentuckians, Tennesseeans, Louisianans—into his conspiracy. The fact that so few had responded—indeed, state and local officials had tried to thwart his boat-collecting efforts and to indict Burr himself—showed the durability of a young republic in the face of the kind of adventure that had brought earlier republics to ruin. Burr had also tried to lure Englishmen, Frenchmen, and Spaniards into his web. If he had attacked Mexico, Washington's relations with Paris and London, as well as Madrid, would have been affected. The mobiles were separate but interdependent. But by now the Jeffersonians were in far more direct confrontation with the colossi of Europe.

"THE HURRICANE . . . NOW BLASTING THE WORLD"

By 1806 Britain and France were locked in deadly embrace, but they could not find a place to fight. After Trafalgar the French crocodile could not venture into the water; after Austerlitz the English sea lion could not venture out of it. For a time the two powers fought a mainly economic war. British naval might had swept much of France's shipping off the high seas, while Napoleon tried every means of stopping neutral trade into England. The French allowed American shippers to trade with the West Indies, while Britain sought to cut off the economic lifelines between the islands and France. Yankee skippers battened on this arrangement by bringing cargos from the French West Indies into American ports, "Americanizing" the cargo by landing it and paying duties on it, and then reloading it and carrying it to ports still under French control.

For a time, the English tolerated this subterfuge of the "broken voyage." But, as pressure mounted from British shippers furious over the fast-rising profits and trade monopolizing of the rapacious Yankees, and as the English economic war against the French faltered, a London admiralty judge conveniently ruled that the non-continuous voyages were actually continuous; shortly British warships seized scores of American merchantmen, especially in the West Indian trade. The British sought to settle another grievance. For hundreds of years the Royal Navy had manned its "floating hells" by sending out press gangs to snatch able-bodied young men out of grog shops and off the streets. British seamen fled from their vile living conditions and the cat-o'-nine-tails by shipping in the American naval or merchant services. At times His Majesty's ships could not leave port because of desertions. Ordered to fetch the fugitives, English sea captains hung off Atlantic ports, boarded American ships, and searched for English deserters. Quarterdeck justice was often harsh, as officers ruled that some seaman pronouncing "peas" as "paise" was an Irishman and hence a British subject, while if he talked through his nose he was probably a Yankee.

Inevitably, these incidents set off explosions of rage in American ports. When a British warship fired a careless shot across the bow of an American sloop and splintered the main boom instead, killing the mate, the victim's mangled body was carried to New York and paraded through the streets on a raised platform. Washington and London exchanged protests, but the English public was so angered by the Yankees "stealing" both trade and sailors, and the Royal Navy was concentrating so single-mindedly on its economic war against France, that no basis of compromise could be found. James Monroe, resident minister in London, backed up by William Pinkney, a Maryland lawyer, extracted a treaty from the Foreign Office that was so weak on the question of impressment that Jefferson refused to submit it to the Senate.

Slowly Britain and France tightened their economic nooses on each other. When London declared a blockade of the European coast from

Brest to the river Elbe, Napoleon counterattacked by establishing, under the so-called Berlin Decree, a complete blockade of the British Isles. As decree followed decree, zealous English captains pressed their efforts against American commerce and English "deserters."

Then occurred *the* incident. When on July 2, 1807, the American frigate *Chesapeake* was hailed off the Virginia coast by the British frigate *Leopard*, the American commander, assuming the *Leopard* was bent on an innocent errand, allowed her to draw near without piping his own men to quarters or bothering to have the loggerheads heated red-hot for firing his guns. The English captain requested permission to board and search the *Chesapeake*, but its commander refused—the English were allowed to search merchantmen, not warships. The *Leopard* promptly poured three broadsides into the defenseless *Chesapeake*, hulling her twenty-two times and killing or wounding twenty-one seamen. The search party found only one genuine deserter, who was court-martialed and hanged from the yardarm. Three other sailors, two of them black and all three American citizens, were seized and held by the British.

Anger swept the Atlantic coast after the *Chesapeake* labored into Norfolk. British stores were destroyed and seamen roughed up, as editors and mass meetings declared war on the enemy. The *Chesapeake* seemed to symbolize innocent, defenseless America. Not since the battle of Lexington, Jefferson said, had he seen the country in such a state of exasperation. "The British had often enough, God knows, given us cause of war before; but it has been on points which would not have united the nation," he wrote William Duane. "But now they have touched a chord which vibrates in every heart." But what to do?

For a while the President temporized, hoping that London would offer some concessions on impressment in the wake of the *Chesapeake*. But by the end of 1807 he knew he must act. Many still called for war, but Jefferson quailed at the prospect. While no pacifist, he dreaded the bloodshed and waste inevitable in a war against Britain, the financial cost for the government, the divisions it would cause between Anglophiles and Francophiles. Another alternative was arming American warships or merchantmen, or both, to protect trade. But these half-measures would have mixed results and might precipitate a war in any event. The only other course was an embargo on all trade with Britain, thus putting the English on short rations. By December the President had concluded that the choice lay among "War, Embargo, or Nothing."

In mid-December the President asked Congress for an embargo act, and both House and Senate responded quickly and enthusiastically. The Embargo Act prohibited virtually all land and seaborne trade with foreign nations. American vessels were forbidden to leave for foreign ports; coasters were required to post a huge bond as guarantee that cargos would not be shipped abroad. Foreign vessels could not carry goods out of American ports. It was a desperate, sweeping measure—but even more remarkable was Jefferson's almost fanatical effort to make the act work. When widespread smuggling and other evasions and violations occurred along the thousands of miles of Canadian border and Atlantic coast, the President's response was to tighten the act and to strengthen executive control to the degree that he was wielding unprecedented presidential power.

The Embargo Act was designed to cut and batter the British economy but to be tolerable to the American. It had virtually the reverse effect. The impact on Atlantic ports was immediate and severe, as hundreds of ships and thousands of seamen were idled. "Ships rotted at the wharves; forests of bare masts were silhouetted in the harbors; grass grew on hitherto humming wharves; bankruptcies, suicides, and crimes increased; soup kitchens were established," Thomas Bailey noted. Ironically, many Yankee sailors sought employment in the British merchant marine, thus easing the need for impressment. The political effects were also emphatic, as the coastal cities in particular rallied against the "dambargo." Sang a New Hampshire poet in Dover:

> Our ships all in motion,
> Once whiten'd the ocean
>   They sail'd and return'd with a Cargo;
> Now doom'd to decay
>   They are fallen a prey,
>   To Jefferson, worms, and EMBARGO.

The sluggish Federalist party came to life in protest against Jefferson's "Quaker-gun diplomacy." Even high Federalists could now appear to be friends of jobless sailors and other workers.

The strategy of the embargo was that the hurting English economy would cause public opinion to pressure the ministry into compromises. But the persons most affected—workers reduced to pauperism in the English textile industry dependent on American cotton, and people suffering privation in Newfoundland and the West Indies—were the ones with least influence on British policy. The military and business establishments, intent on challenging America's rising mercantile power, pressed the ministry to stand firm.

Jefferson had uncharacteristically launched the embargo without full support from his colleagues; Gallatin, for one, preferred war to a permanent embargo. Republican state leaders, especially in the Northeast, were thrown on the defensive. Yet the President pursued his policy with relent-less determination, and at cost to some of his basic principles of govern-ment. As evasions mounted, he received power to employ the militia freely in enforcing the law. Authority to call out the regular army and navy was granted to collectors, who were placed under the President's direct policy control. Under the pressure, something of the spirit of "Jeffersonianism" seemed to escape from Jefferson himself, as he verged on embracing guilt by association, condemning whole communities instead of individual viola-tors, and, on one occasion, supporting an effort to indict some embargo violators on the charge of treason; the case was thrown out of court by a Jeffersonian judge.

An impervious Britain, a stubborn President, a restive party and Con-gress, a mounting opposition—something had to give. The tightened em-bargo rules set off new paroxysms of rage in New England. The Massachusetts legislature threatened to disobey the law, amid talk of seces-sion. The President was pictured as both arbitrary and weak. In Massachu-setts a budding thirteen-year-old poet, William Cullen Bryant, touched on all of Jefferson's vulnerabilities, including his alleged black mistress:

> When shall this land, some courteous angel say,
> Throw off a weak, and erring ruler's sway? . . .
> Oh wrest, sole refuge of a sinking land,
> The sceptre from the slave's imbecile hand! . . .
> Go, wretch, resign the presidential chair,
> Disclose thy secret measures foul or fair . . .
> Or where Ohio rolls his turbid stream,
> Dig for huge bones, thy glory and thy theme,
> Go scan, Philosophist; thy ****** charms,
> And sink supinely in her sable arms. . . .

A group of Republicans unexpectedly broke the impasse by a vote to repeal the embargo. A "sudden and unaccountable revolution of opinion took place the last week, chiefly among the New England and New York members," the President wrote his son-in-law early in February 1809. The defectors set the date of repeal on the day of Jefferson's retirement. Thus was a deeper quagmire averted. The President was bitter about the deser-tions. The "hurricane which is now blasting the world, physical and moral," he wrote a friend "has prostrated all the mounds of reason as well as right." But he made no great effort to save the embargo. He too seemed to feel the game was played out. Certainly *he* felt played out; sixty-five years old in his last year in office, he was desperately eager to return to Mon-ticello for good.

Jefferson had staked so much on the success of the embargo that he seemed to leave office a defeated man. Some said that he had "fled" Washington. This was the view of many contemporaries. As years passed, it became clear that in most respects his presidential leadership had been as effective in his second term as in his first. Save for the embargo, he had continued to demonstrate, in his close collaboration with Madison, Gallatin, and other administration officials, that collective executive leadership was possible under the Constitution. Again save for the embargo, he had exercised firm, though unobtrusive, direction of the Republicans in Congress and, to a lesser extent, of the Republican party through the nation. While he had seen no need to present Congress with a comprehensive program of proposed legislation, the measures he did support usually passed smoothly through the two houses. Often the President had to draw on the resources of his personal leadership—especially on the infinite respect and love Republican leaders had for him—in order to mediate factional disputes among Republicans.

Still, even this benign and potent leader came up against constraints on presidential power. The impeachment of Justice Samuel Chase suggested one of those constraints—the independence of the judiciary. A hard-line Federalist, Chase had turned his courtroom into a forum for intemperate attacks on the President and the Republican party. It was one thing when he lambasted the administration as weak and incompetent, something else when he condemned the repeal of the Judiciary Act of 1801—an act validated by Chase's own court—as a blow for "mobocracy." Jefferson indirectly, and the Republican leadership in Congress directly, organized impeachment proceedings against Chase, but they could not mobilize the necessary two-thirds vote in the Senate, and the justice was acquitted, amid the huzzas of high Federalists.

Chase was small game compared to Jefferson's real bête noire in the judiciary. Mustering majorities on critical issues, using his superb judicial and political mind to influence his brethren, the unassailable John Marshall continued to preside magisterially over the Supreme Court. The looming treason trial of Aaron Burr brought the two Virginians again into direct confrontation. Deeply disturbed over the "conspiracy," Jefferson threw himself into the investigation and proceedings in the case. But the Chief Justice's zeal for Burr's punishment did not match the President's. Marshall released two of Burr's accomplices for lack of evidence of treason, claimed (but did not try to enforce) the right to subpoena the President to appear in court, and sharply narrowed the definition of treason. Burr was acquitted; when the New Yorker was presented with a new treason charge, Marshall allowed bail. Jefferson, who in his zeal had openly pre-

judged Burr's guilt, was appalled—and helpless. He could find some vindication but little comfort when Burr jumped bail, fled to France, and tried
to interest Napoleon in making peace with England in order to organize
an Anglo-French invasion of the United States.

Jefferson's preoccupation with the prosecution of Burr and the latter's
acquittal clouded the final year or two of his presidency. But he was even
more preoccupied with the embargo, and though this failed too, he was
satisfied with his stewardship. Indeed, he felt that he had protected the
nation's internal security by his vigilant reaction to Burr's adventurism,
just as his economic war against Britain had saved the nation from both
war and humiliation. He had served the people's most basic need—security
—and had done so without war. In March 1809 he left the presidency as
he came in, a man of peace.

* * *

The final test of Jefferson's power and leadership lay in the choice of his
successor. Few in the Republican establishment doubted that this would
be James Madison. For more than three decades the two men had worked
so closely together that their adversaries could attack Madison for being
Jefferson's cat's-paw or Jefferson's mastermind with equal plausibility. A
battle for the Republican party nomination loomed when James Monroe
returned from England still smarting over Jefferson and Madison's repudiation of the agreement he had signed with the British. With dismay the
President saw a fight break out in his own party as John Randolph and
other anti-Administration Republicans turned to Monroe in an attempt to
head off Madison. "I see with infinite grief a contest arising between
yourself and another, who have been very dear to each other, and equally
so to me," Jefferson wrote Monroe. ". . . I have ever viewed Mr. Madison
and yourself as two principal pillars of my happiness." He knew that the
behavior of his two friends would be "chaste," but he warned Monroe
against letting "your friends" exacerbate passion and acrimony. In vain;
while the rivals did not campaign, their friends fought a vitriolic battle in
pamphlets and newspaper columns.

The President gave quiet but powerful support to his Secretary of State.
When Madison's conduct of foreign affairs was attacked, Jefferson released
hundreds of documents attesting to Madison's patriotic firmness with Britain and France. Election polemics turned mainly on foreign policy, especially the embargo; no one contended that "politics stops at the water's
edge." The contest was further enlivened when the Federalists again chose
a ticket of Charles Cotesworth Pinckney of South Carolina and Rufus King
of Massachusetts and New York, and when the aging Vice-President,

George Clinton, simultaneously ran for President and Vice-President. In the end, Jefferson's and Madison's long years of leadership paid off. Madison bested Monroe handily both in Virginia and in the congressional caucus, and went on to defeat Pinckney in the electoral college, 122 to 47. Clinton won only six votes—all from New York—but hung on to his vice-presidency.

The man who entered the President's mansion in March 1809 had stood so long in Jefferson's shadow that for a time even his friends found it hard to accept him as chief executive. As unawesome as ever in appearance and demeanor, Madison was as poor a speaker as Jefferson and also lacked his intellectual versatility and spacious imagination. What he did bring to the presidency was a penetrating understanding of both the theory and practice of American government, a thorough grasp of Republican doctrine, a mastery of party and legislative mechanics, and long experience in the conduct of foreign relations, though he was criticized for never having served abroad. And if he was also faulted for his stiff and sometimes frigid manner, he had—Dolley.

Raised as a Quaker, widowed by a young lawyer who died of the plague, Dolley Payne Todd had grown into a woman of great charm and striking figure when she married James Madison, then forty-three and already famous. In the White House, as the mansion was just coming to be called, she was soon holding spirited levees and refurbishing the drab interior with the help of the queenly sum of $26,000 granted by Congress.

THE IRRESISTIBLE WAR

The new First Lady displayed her sense of diplomacy at the very start, when at dinner before the Inaugural Ball in Long's Hotel she maneuvered her full and exuberant self between the English and French plenipotentiaries, thus fending off unpleasantness. Her action was symbolic as well as skillful. Her husband had entered office at a time when the struggle between Britain and France was engulfing more and more Europeans, with the United States now set on a relentless march toward war. It would be a poor war, and a poorly understood one. It was a war that Americans did not win—a fact ignored by latter-day patriots claiming that America had never lost a war or won a peace conference. Mislabeled as the War of 1812, it was actually the War of 1812–15. Misjudged in history as the outcome of drift and indecision and bungling and chance, it was rather an irresistible war—irresistible because Americans were caught up in ineluctable circumstances, irresistible because some Americans did not want to resist it.

The central circumstance towered over Madison's first term as it had over Jefferson's second: America was a third-rate power caught in the jaws of Great Power conflict because of her desire to sail on the high seas and to trade in foreign ports. Conflict was not a result of Washington misjudging the positions of London and Paris. It was clear to all that Britain continued to view her maritime supremacy, including the right of impressing her subjects on foreign ships, as absolutely vital to her national security and to the immediate purpose of fighting France. Napoleon was just as intent on excluding neutral ships from trading with Britain. After the failure of the embargo, the United States was insistent on its right to trade. Aside from the delays of several weeks in transatlantic messages, the diplomats of the three nations had no serious problem of communication. Literally thousands of hours were consumed in lengthy correspondence and face-to-face discussions. The nations were in conflict not because of ignorance but because they had conflicting interests.

Even if there had been some decisive way out of the impasse, Madison might have lacked the power to take advantage of it. He was not destined to be a strong President. At the very start he was denied the right to choose his own Cabinet. Having worked long and fruitfully with Secretary of the Treasury Gallatin, the new President wanted to promote the Pennsylvanian to Secretary of State. When a group of anti-Gallatin senators headed by Samuel Smith of Maryland warned Madison against this step, the President capitulated by shifting Smith's brother Robert from the Navy Secretaryship to the top cabinet position. Gallatin nobly stayed on at Treasury.

Factionalism was rife in the Republican party as Jefferson's harmonizing hand fell away. John Randolph, who had broken with Jefferson years before but muted his attacks on him, now turned on Madison in cold fury. Descended from a family long noted for its idiots, geniuses, neurotics, and eccentrics, Randolph lived alone on his plantation named Bizarre, excluded women from his intimate life, enjoyed bringing his hunting dogs onto the House floor—and was probably the most brilliant and ferocious orator in Congress. By this time Randolph headed a small but active band of "old Republicans" who came to be known as the "Quids."

With his party divided between numerous Francophiles and a few Anglophiles such as Randolph, Madison groped for a foreign policy that would defend his nation's rights and honor without embroiling it in a shooting war with Britain or France or both. The Non-Intercourse Act, which replaced the Embargo Act in March 1809, forbade trade with the two powers until they ceased violating neutral rights. This act seemed only to provoke the French into more ship seizures and the British into more impress-ments. In May 1810 Madison and the Republicans tried a new tack—a measure authorizing the President to reopen trade with Britain and France, with the remarkable proviso that if either nation ceased violating America's neutral rights, the President could prohibit trade with the other.

The Administration and Congress clearly were looking for the first sincere bidder, but this was a situation made to order for the Machiavellian ruler of France. Napoleon promised ambiguously to revoke his decrees against American shipping on condition that Washington would break off trade with Britain unless London ceased its interference with American ships. The President, eager for some way out of the impasse, seized this bait. On the understanding that Napoleon actually had canceled his earlier decrees, Madison prematurely issued a proclamation reopening trade with France and halting commerce with Britain. The Emperor in fact had not changed his policy, and at times there seemed to be a nightmarish possibility that the United States, France, and Great Britain might be engaged in a unique three-cornered war of all against all.

For a time the mobiles stayed in unsteady equipoise as Paris contended that it had in effect revoked its restrictive decrees, London claimed that the French had not, and Madison was left in an anti-British position because of his impetuous proclamation. Early in 1811 the President, convinced that his Secretary of State, Robert Smith, was both indiscreet and disloyal as well as incompetent, decided to strengthen his administration by appointing James Monroe in his place. The appointment had to be handled delicately, for Monroe had so deeply resented Madison's earlier rejection of his treaty—and the "succession politics" of 1808—that he had broken off his relationship with his old friend. With the quiet help of Jefferson, communication between the two men was restored; it had not escaped the ambitious Monroe that both Presidents Jefferson and Madison had served earlier stints as Secretary of State. More Anglophilic than most Republicans, Monroe hoped to ease relations with Britain, but he found London to be intransigent.

By the fall of 1811 Washington seemed pinioned diplomatically between France and Britain, politically between Federalists opposing war with Britain and Republicans ready for it, or at least resigned to it. What could tip the balance? The answer came from the West. Some Easterners doubted that the settlers in the distant hinterland, in those obscure regions along the Ohio and the Mississippi, would feel much involved in a conflict over ships and men on the high seas.

"We, whose soil was the hotbed and whose ships were the nursery of Sailors," the Boston *Columbian Centinel* protested later, "are insulted with the hypocrisy of a devotedness to Sailors' rights ... by those whose country furnishes no navigation beyond the size of a ferryboat or an Indian canoe." In fact those ships often carried western produce, those impressed sailors might hail from Ohio or Kentucky or Louisiana, and men used to protecting themselves with guns on the lawless frontier argued that the nation should do the same on the high seas. The Westerners had more proximate concerns. On the southwest lay West Florida, stretching west from the Mississippi to the Perdido River, a Spanish dominion that had been seized by southern adventurers in 1810 and later claimed by Madison on the grounds that West Florida had been included in the Louisiana Purchase. Spain was not strong enough to defend this strategic territory, with its navigable rivers reaching up into American territory, but Westerners feared that it might be seized by Spain's ally, Britain.

To the northwest lay an even more vulnerable territory, in Westerners' eyes. As more and more hunters, trappers, and land-hungry settlers moved into Michigan, Indiana, and Illinois, they encroached onto the living space of tens of thousands of Indians who, the settlers suspected, were being supplied with guns and ammunition by the English. For the most part, the Indians had been passive in the face of white intrusion, as some of their chiefs bartered away land rights for liquor, baubles, and pensions. But out of tribal demoralization had risen a new leader, the Shawnee chief Tecumseh, who, with his brother the "Prophet," began to organize a broad tribal confederacy against the westward sweep of the white man. The two leaders established their capital in Prophet's Town, Indiana, at the juncture of the Tippecanoe and Wabash rivers. In the fall of 1811 the governor of Indiana Territory, General William Henry Harrison, marched about a thousand men to the Tippecanoe and provocatively encamped about a mile from the Indian capital. Tecumseh and his warriors attacked the encampment at dawn; Harrison's troops beat them off, at a heavy price in casualties, destroyed their food supplies, and then fired the settlement. As a wave of indignation passed through the Northwest, the cry arose that the English were behind the "Indian troubles" and must be driven out of Canada.

No voice expressed western feeling more eloquently than that of a thirty-four-year-old Kentuckian, Henry Clay. Born in Virginia and admitted to the bar there, he had traveled west through the Cumberland Gap to Lexington, where he soon prospered among the gambling, hard-drinking, land-speculating gentry of the bluegrass region. After serving two unexpired terms in the United States Senate—the first when he was barely thirty—he was elected a member of Congress in the summer of 1811 and chosen Speaker the very day he showed up in the House. As a senator he had become the leader of a young, militant, even martial group of legislators who were eager for a war against England. In their anger Westerners had turned to him. "Will Congress give us war this winter?" Thomas Hart Benton had written Clay from Tennessee. "Or, will the majority . . . wait for chance or destiny to mend our condition?" And in contrast to the cautious Madison, Clay took the kind of cocky, pugnacious stance they liked.

"The conquest of Canada is in your power," Clay had told the Senate. "I trust I shall not be deemed presumptuous when I state, what I verily believe, that the militia of Kentucky are alone competent to place Montreal and Upper Canada at your feet. . . ." As Speaker, Clay renewed his pressure on the Administration to go to war.

But war against whom? Britain was the wrong enemy, Federalists were asserting; the French were preying on American commerce—especially ships bound for eastern ports of Europe with lucrative cargos of grain. Members of Congress were attacking both governments. "The Devil himself could not tell, which government, England or France, is the most wicked," Nathaniel Macon exclaimed. For a time the Administration actually contemplated a triangular war. The whole "business is become more than ever puzzling," Madison wrote Jefferson late in May 1812. "To go to war with Eng^d and not with France arms the federalists with new matter, and divides the Republicans some of whom with the Quids make a display of impartiality. To go to war ag^st both, presents a thousand difficulties, above all, that of shutting all the ports of the Continent of Europe ag^st our Cruisers who can do little without the use of them." The Federalists, he feared, would exploit such difficulties. The only argument for "this triangular war as it is called" was that it might hasten a settlement with one of the two nations. But Madison was doubtful even of this. Jefferson and other cooler heads could hardly imagine war with both powers. Britain had been by far the more provocative, and the more recently provocative. And Britain was an old enemy, France an old ally.

So it would be war with Britain, and Britain alone. Madison was determined to act, and he was strongly backed by the Secretary of State. "Our wrongs have been great; our cause is just. . . . Let war therefore be forthwith proclaimed against England," Monroe wrote anonymously in the Republican party's newspaper, the Washington *National Intelligencer.* But Madison and Monroe knew that for such a drastic step the Administration must have the united support of Congress, and the Federalists were waiting for a ship to arrive from England with London's final answer to America's protests. But when H.M.S. *Hornet* sailed into New York Harbor, she brought few signs of British conciliation.

On June 1 Madison sent his war message to Congress. After a long statement of trade and impressment grievances he concluded: "Such is the spectacle of injuries and indignities which have been heaped on our country, and such the crisis which its unexampled forbearance and conciliatory efforts have not been able to avert." Madison had prudently canvassed the Congress to be sure of a war measure, and young "war hawks" such as Clay and John C. Calhoun, the South Carolinian who headed the House Foreign Affairs Committee, guided the measure through Congress. Even so, the results betrayed deep division in the Congress, as the House voted for the war bill 79 to 49, and the Senate, after several days' intensive debate, by only 19 to 13. The tally was strongly partisan, as about three-quarters of the Republicans present in the House voted for war, and the Federalists there voted against. The result had a sectional cast too, as Westerners voted almost solidly for the war bill, Southerners did so strongly, aside from John Randolph and a half dozen mountain Virginians and North Carolinians, and the central Atlantic states voted heavily for the bill. But the northern states—even the northern seaboard—were not solidly against the measure. Indeed, so many economic, xenophobic, expansionist, geographical, and particularist (land hunger, hostility toward Indians) factors seemed to be interwoven in the congressional vote that the pundits of the day, and historians ever since, have debated the causal forces.

Cutting through all these forces, and possibly the most powerful but certainly the least measurable of them all, was ideology. Almost all Americans were deeply angered by Britain's maritime policies, and especially by impressment, and they were angered by impressment because it struck blatantly at the heart of a most solemn credo. Two astute observers of the day understood this. Said John Quincy Adams: "The State, by the social compact is bound to *protect* every one of its Citizens. . . . The principle for which we are now struggling is of a higher and more sacred nature than any question about taxation can involve. It is the principle of personal liberty, and of every social right." Said John C. Calhoun: "This is the second struggle for our liberty." Individual liberty from the slavery of impressment, and national honor and independence from Britain—these were fused in the public mind. A Fourth of July toast in Boston captured this feeling best: "The War—The second and last struggle for national freedom—A final effort to rescue from the deep the drowning honor of our country."

*　　*　　*

By the summer of 1812 James Madison not only had a military struggle on his hands; he also had a political one. This was a presidential election year, and Madison, like his three predecessors, was running for a second term. In May, at the height of the fever for war, he had been unanimously nominated by the congressional caucus, composed of Republican members of Congress. But later that month, New York Republican legislators, rebelling against the Virginia dynasty in their party, nominated De Witt Clinton for president. Nephew of Vice-President George Clinton, who had just died in office, De Witt was typical of the new breed of young, opportunistic politicos who were challenging Republicans and Federalists of the old school.

Clinton's nomination put the Federalists into a dilemma. If they chose a true-blood Federalist of the John Marshall caliber—and Marshall was sounded out—they still could not hope to defeat an incumbent President at the polls (Marshall declined to swap a chief-justiceship in hand for a presidency in the bush). At a party convention in New York—the first "grass roots" nominating convention in America—the Federalists, amid much misgiving, left the way open for state Federalist parties to support Clinton. Soon Clinton's supporters were appealing to antiwar New Englanders with such slogans as "Madison and War! or Clinton and Peace!" while promising voters farther south that the New Yorker as President would prosecute the war with vigor. Since electors would be chosen during the summer and fall, Madison was under constant pressure to provide military victories.

Rarely, however, have military pretensions and military resources diverged more sharply. The Administration's strategy was aggressive: to strike north into Canada, to join hands with Canadians believed to be eager to throw off the British yoke, and to seize Montreal after isolating it from the west. To accomplish these aims, Madison could muster an assortment of army officers who had never commanded men under fire but who had won posts through connections in Washington or through election by troops in the field; a regular army of about 12,000 men scattered in outposts around the nation's borders; a potentially large militia, but currently under state control and unavailable in most of New England because of hostility there to the war; a small but professional navy; all too few engineers and other experts; and an almost nonexistent command structure, so that each ship and every army in the field would have to operate virtually on its own. During the long months and years of deteriorating relations with Britain and France, Congress had never faced up to the need for a major defense program. Canada's forces were small and scattered too, but they were well trained, with experienced officers.

Amid great expectations General William Hull led several regiments of regulars and volunteers north from Dayton through Ohio swamps and wilderness to Detroit. From Detroit he dispatched troops across the frontier into Canada, then issued a proclamation advising Canadians either to come over to the American side or to stay at home; white men found fighting with Indians, he added, would not be taken prisoner but shot. Facing Hull on the Niagara frontier were Canadian troops and "Tecumseh's revenge." Biding his time after Tippecanoe, the Indian chief had mobilized over a thousand warriors to support the Canadians.

Tecumseh was to prove Hull's undoing both militarily and psychologically. While the American dawdled, fast-moving Indian braves harassed his long communication line to the south. The British commander, having intercepted American dispatches, adroitly played on Hull's mounting fear that he and his men would be cut off and turned over to the mercy of the redskins. More and more distraught over the plight of the civilians, who included his daughter and grandchildren, Hull lost his nerve. He surrendered without firing a shot. He was later court-martialed, sentenced to death for cowardice, and pardoned by Madison for earlier bravery.

A hard-riding horseman brought the shocking news to the President while he was en route to Montpelier for relief from the Washington heat. Madison immediately turned back to the capital and summoned a cabinet meeting. More bad news was arriving from the north. Hull had sent a young captain to Fort Dearborn (on the present site of Chicago) to evacuate the post. Several hundred Potawatomies fell upon the small band of soldiers and civilians and massacred over half of them. The Indians beheaded the youthful commander, cut out his heart, and ate it.

Gloom in Washington was relieved only by news from Boston. About 750 miles off the coast, the *Constitution,* under Captain Isaac Hull (a nephew of the disgraced general), had caught up with H.M.S. *Guerrière,* closed with her, poured in heavy broadsides of round and grape, and reduced her to such a gaping hulk that the British surrendered and the *Guerrière,* useless even as a prize, was put to the torch. This small but electrifying victory at sea, and the repulses all along the Canadian frontier, epitomized the course of the war during its first year.

Now under heavy criticism from Federalists and antiwar Republicans, Madison and his Cabinet laid their plans for 1813. A heavier effort would be mounted both in the North and on the Atlantic. Congress boosted soldiers' pay, expanded the regular army, and authorized more warships. Madison decided to sack his Secretary of War, William Eustis, a Massachusetts physician and Republican politico with little war experience, as well as his Secretary of the Navy, who was reported often to be in his cups by midday. New secretaries, Madison hoped, would weed out the incompetents among the high command.

Would the commander in chief himself be sacked? By fall Madison's foes were seizing on every blunder and mishap to fortify their arguments about unpreparedness and Washington fumbling. They made much too of the congressional caucus as undemocratic, even aristocratic. "The current Elections," Madison wrote Jefferson, "bring the popularity of the War or of the Administration, or both, to the Experimentum crucis." With New England leaning toward Clinton and the South and West toward Madison, New York and Pennsylvania were the swing states. In New York, where electors were chosen by the state legislature, the Federalist floor manager, a young and inexperienced state senator from Kinderhook named Martin Van Buren, so brilliantly outmaneuvered the Republicans that he won a clear majority in the legislature—and hence all of New York's 29 electoral votes—for Clinton. In Pennsylvania's popular balloting for presidential electors, the Clinton men capitalized on dissatisfaction over the war effort in the western mountain country, but Madison swept the more populous areas. Pennsylvania's 25 electoral votes for the President were decisive in the electoral college, which Madison carried by only 128 to 89. The President began his second term—and his stepped-up war effort—with a dubious vote of confidence.

The Administration planned to make 1813 a year of decision in the North by building up its land, water, and amphibious forces across the long frontier stretching from Detroit along Lakes Erie and Ontario and up the St. Lawrence to Montreal. Madison now had a new War Secretary in John Armstrong, a New York politician and diplomat, and a new Navy Secretary in William Jones, a Philadelphia merchant-politician, but his key appointment was General William Henry Harrison, of Tippecanoe fame, as senior officer in the Northwest. Harrison's early efforts to retake Detroit, however, ended in one bloody defeat and one ambush by his old adversary, Tecumseh. Harrison prudently went on the defensive while Commodore Isaac Chauncey built warships on Lake Erie to control this crucial waterway. Chauncey had the help of a twenty-eight-year-old naval officer, Captain Oliver Hazard Perry, a Rhode Islander who had gone to sea at eleven and had already fought the Barbary pirates. The British too were feverishly building up their fleet strength on the lakes, but vital supplies were slow in coming from a far-off motherland now in mortal conflict with France.

By summer's end Perry's ships were strong enough to risk engagement with the Royal Navy. The small fleets met off the island of Put-in-Bay in the bloodiest naval fight of the war. Earlier in the year, after the British frigate *Shannon* had crippled the *Chesapeake* off Boston, the dying American captain had murmured, "Don't give up the ship." Perry had this last order inscribed on the colors of his flagship, the *Lawrence,* but after the *Lawrence* was smashed almost to pieces, with 80 percent of her men casualties, Perry coolly shifted his flag to another ship and directed the demolition of the

British fleet. Then he sent to Harrison another memorable war cry, "We have met the enemy and they are ours."

Otherwise, 1813 did not turn out to be very decisive in the north. To be sure, Perry's triumph allowed Harrison to move 4,500 men across Lake Erie to Fort Malden, south of Detroit, and to force the British, over Tecumseh's protest, to evacuate Detroit, and move east, where Harrison caught up with the British force on the north bank of the Thames, taking almost 500 prisoners and killing Tecumseh. But the crucial drive northeast to Montreal faltered in the face of powerful resistance. The Americans occupied York (Toronto), the capital of Upper Canada, and burned the Assembly houses and other public buildings, but this proved a Pyrrhic victory.

*   *   *

For two years the adversaries had looked like a couple of roustabouts fighting in a barnyard, each throwing wild haymakers at the other, drawing much blood but not coming close to knocking the other out. Would the third year be any different? The global balance of mobiles was swaying as Napoleon, after repeated defeats at the hands of the Prussian and Austrian and Russian troops he had once beaten so decisively, abdicated his throne and departed for Elba. For Americans this meant that crack British regiments would soon be shipping out of Bordeaux and other French ports for America. But the American Army was becoming more professionally led too, as Madison and Armstrong replaced older generals with men like Jacob Brown, George Izard, Andrew Jackson, and Winfield Scott. During 1814 combat in the north focused on the Niagara area between Lakes Erie and Ontario; fighting to the west dwindled into raids and skirmishes. Scott led well-drilled troops to a victory over the British at Chippewa, an engagement treasured ever since by West Pointers because of the English commander's surprised cry: "Those are Regulars, by God!" Three weeks later, in the heaviest ground action of the war, Scott's and Brown's men were so badly mauled in the Battle of Lundy's Lane that they fell back on Fort Erie, which the British promptly put under an unsuccessful siege.

Frustration and stalemate also characterized the action much farther east, on Lake Champlain. In a combined land-sea offensive for which they were becoming famous, British troops drove down the western shore of the lake, in coordination with a large fleet headed toward American warships and troops concentrated at Plattsburgh. Captain Thomas Macdonough was ready for the attack and after a furious engagement destroyed all the enemy vessels except for several gunboats. Their dream of an advance south along the Hudson shattered, the British pulled back to Canada.

For the Americans, sadder events were at hand to the south. Powerful British fleet units had been ranging for months up and down the Atlantic coast, blockading major ports, putting in landing parties to raid and burn small ports, bottling up a good part of the American fleet in well-protected harbors. Single American warships and privateers, cruising far across the Atlantic and even into the Pacific, won some glorious victories, but these were hardly more than pinpricks to the Royal Navy, augmented after Elba by reinforcements from European waters. During the early summer of 1814, rumors reached Washington that the Royal Navy planned a massive attack up the Chesapeake. Madison and his generals, doubting that enemy assault troops would move very far from their warships, and not sure just where the British would strike, took disorganized half-measures for defense.

In mid-August, news arrived that a mighty British armada of warships and transports had suddenly appeared at the mouth of the Patuxent River. Then came reports that several thousand enemy troops were marching toward Washington. In a nightmare of misjudgments as to enemy plans, poor communication among state militias intent mainly on protecting their own turf, and mediocre generalship, a large but separated collection of American defense forces was overcome one by one. The British assault at Bladensburg, a few miles east of Washington, sent the militias streaming back toward the capital. The President, who with Monroe had been closely reconnoitering the defense of Washington, escaped into the Virginia countryside. There he met up with Mrs. Madison, who had managed to send off documents, plate, and the Gilbert Stuart portrait of George Washington, hastily torn out of its frame, before she fled from the White House with dinner still set on the table. When the President and his party returned to Washington after the British withdrew, they found the White House and the Capitol building in smoking ruins. The British also had run a few warships up the Potomac and exacted a king's ransom of vital military stores from the merchants of Alexandria as the price of leaving the city unburned.

Washington burned—the first family sent scurrying to safety—Alexandria humiliated: a wave of mortification and anger swept through the country, even into New England. Nonetheless, the British raid on Washington turned out to be more important psychologically than militarily. The American war effort by the end of 1814 was still so decentralized that the head could be cut off for a time without harming local efforts by mainly state militias. Indeed, when the British amphibious army moved on up the Chesapeake to Baltimore, it was bloodily repulsed by the militia. But these events in the heart of the country excited a patriotic nerve, and it was perhaps this nerve that was touched when Francis Scott Key, after watching the bombardment of Baltimore forts through the night, strained to see whether the flag was still there—and, assured that it was, wrote a star-spangled anthem.

But this was also a time of disillusion and disenthrallment for the Americans. By the end of 1814 military prospects looked so bleak that the Administration was willing to settle for the status quo ante as the basis of a peace negotiation with Britain. In purely strategic terms, the war was a standoff at this time, but if one measures war achievements by war aims, the United States had lost, for there was little sign that Britain was prepared to yield any of its "rights."

If American military aspirations were deflated, however, the American way of war was even more directly challenged. American leaders had not been pacifists; Washington and Adams, Jefferson and Madison, were naïve neither about the bellicose tendencies of humankind nor about the likelihood of clashes among nations in a world of independent sovereign states. They recognized that national security was a prime responsibility of government. The Constitution listed the "common Defense" even before the "general welfare" as the power and duty of Congress; and in the *Federalist* John Jay wrote that, of all the people's needs, "providing for their *safety* seems to be the first."

The problem, especially in a republic, was how to maintain a military establishment strong enough to protect the people's safety but controlled enough not to invade their liberties—in short, how to harness the war beast. No easy solution was possible in a world of shifting mobiles and in a young nation led by men who could not agree even on the definition of liberty, as the Alien and Sedition Acts had demonstrated. This dilemma left the nation ambivalent over both the theory and the practice of war. Ideologically, most Americans opposed heavy defense expenditures, large standing armies, centralized military decision making and administration, military professionalism in the form of a permanent officer class. In practice they knew the need for protection from predator nations on their borders. The upshot was reliance on defensive measures such as coastal fortifications, scatteration of the federal troops among many ports and posts, heavy dependence on state militias, the building of gunboats as the prime naval weapon, and acceptance of a small but professional navy as "safer" than a professional army. Such half-measures proved woefully inadequate in the War of 1812. Typically the state militias lacked—at least until they were well blooded—adequate discipline, professionalism, and soldierly skills; and commanders lacked the necessary generalship. The United States Military Academy had been founded at West Point in 1802, but the nation still had no considered strategic doctrine or even a native military literature. The Royal Navy proved to be skillful in evading the coastal defenses, and the scores of gunboats, while occasionally useful in shallow water, could not begin to cope with the great British ships of the line. The nation did have a strong potential of military arms. During the 1790s Rhode Island and Maryland "furnaces" had begun casting and boring cannon for fortresses and frigates, and by the turn of the century the Springfield Armory, established by the government, could produce over 5,000 muskets a year. It was the government's need for quantities of guns that enabled Eli Whitney in New Haven to finance and organize mass production through development of power tools, interchangeability of parts, and mass assembly.

Even so, the fact that the United States was a third-rate military power centrally affected its pretensions, whether in peace or war. While General Hull marched on Canada with 900 men, Napoleon was invading Russia with an army of half a million. Fourteen hundred sailors fought in the decisive battle for Lake Champlain, a mere tenth of the number present at Trafalgar. Napoleon's taking of Moscow and his bitter, death-ridden retreat had far more to do with the future security of the United States than the British capture of Washington. Once Napoleon was defeated, the United States had little chance of victory.

The greatest lack in the American way of war was a leadership that could define and pursue a set of national ends that had some relation to the needs and aspirations of the people and the political and military capabilities of the nation. American involvements and interests abroad—most notably a world trade that brought American ships and sailors into dangerous waters —far outran American commitments and capabilities. The men who organized the governmental system so brilliantly for the effective but prudent conduct of domestic affairs did not shape an equivalent strategy for the conduct of military and other foreign affairs. Indeed, the genius of the former strategy—the dispersion of power—ran counter to the commanding military need for concentration of power and speed of deployment. And the military failure lay largely in the ideology of peace.

If Americans had been abjectly defeated in the War of 1812, out of desperation they might have shaped a new strategy of war, as other vanquished nations had done. But they were not so defeated. And then, in January 1815, came stunning news that left Americans in euphoria and put the whole war in a happier light. For some months a major general of the Tennessee militia, Andrew Jackson, had been warring against the Creek Indians—who earlier had been aroused by a visit from Tecumseh, encouraged by the British, and armed by the Spanish. After wiping out a Creek force of 900 braves at the Battle of Horseshoe Bend, Jackson turned to the defense of New Orleans, which the British were planning to capture in order to control the Mississippi. Jackson was ready for the redcoats when they marched against his breastworks on January 8. Within an hour American cannon and rustic sharpshooters cut down over 2,000 men. American casualties were reported to be twenty-one. The British retreated to their ships.

The Battle of New Orleans came too late to affect the terms of a treaty of peace that was being completed in far-off Europe even as the British advanced on Jackson's redoubts. That treaty reflected the nation's low military estate before Jackson's victory. It also reflected the shifting balance of political forces in Britain and America—especially the rising opposition of English trading and manufacturing interests to the war, and the continuing criticism and foot dragging of a declining but still potent group of antiwar Federalists, mainly along the New England coast.

WATERSIDE YANKEES: THE FEDERALISTS AT EBB TIDE

In mid-December 1815 a small group of genteel, prosperous-looking men filed into the tall and spacious council chamber of the Connecticut State House, a majestic building designed by Charles Bulfinch and located not far from the Connecticut River. This was a group of potential rebels, meeting amid great excitement. Angry over the British occupation of part of Maine, fearful that Washington would not protect the New England coast against the British, and resentful above all toward the Virginia dynasty and its embargoes and other interferences with New England commerce, this company of New England Federalists was meeting to consider drastic, though nonviolent, action against Washington. Federalist newspapers in Boston, including the respectable *Columbian Centinel*, were calling for actions that bordered on secession. In Washington, Secretary of War Monroe was concerned enough to send to Hartford a confidential agent, in the guise of an army recruiting officer, to report back intelligence on this dangerous group, but the officer was not able to get into the secret sessions. Monroe was alarmed enough to authorize federal troops in New York to take prompt action in the event of an uprising.

Monroe need not have worried. What was happening in Hartford was not a lunge for power by a fearsome party cabal. It was something far less portentous and far more poignant—a final convulsive effort, half protest, half death cry, of a movement slowly passing out of existence. The plight of the Federalists was doubly ironic. A political force that had been organized by men who were militantly anti-British and anti-Tory was now dying in part because its leaders were considered American Tories and pro-British. And its leaders, seemingly reluctant to demand freedom of the seas for American shipping, were the political descendants of an earlier generation of men who had emerged from the port cities of America to assert their maritime rights against the British navy.

The waterside Yankees who survived as political forces after the Revolution had been a formidable crowd, even in their second ranks. George Cabot—born of a North Shore merchant, dropped from Harvard in his freshman year for rebelliousness and neglect of studies, and soon thereafter the master of a schooner in the transatlantic trade—believed in an ordered, hierarchical, deferential, inegalitarian society run by the best people, like himself. Timothy Pickering, born in Salem, was a cantankerous, outspoken elitist, so politically outrageous and personally unpopular that Federalist party leaders kept their distance from him. Theophilus Parsons, born in Byfield, a few miles southwest of Newburyport, practiced law in the latter city and then in Boston, opined that the whole government, not just the Senate, should be under elitist control, and later became chief justice of the Massachusetts Supreme Court, where he was dubbed "The awfullest Parsons" by young lawyers. Samuel Sewall, born in Boston, practiced law in Marblehead before moving to Maine, and later succeeded Parsons as chief justice. Stephen Higginson, born in Salem, later an import merchant in Boston and a naval officer, took an openly elitist position in his writings and frowned on the politicking of younger Federalists.

Some Federalists of the old school stood a bit apart from these men. Fisher Ames, born in Dedham, was so egregiously alarmist and pessimistic about the dangers of democracy, indeed so "lethargic, raving, sanguine and despondent," as he described himself, as to embarrass other Federalists. And Harrison Gray Otis, born of an eminent Boston family, combined his elitist views with such elegance of bearing and moderation of political tactics as to give him a special role in linking old-school and new-school Federalists.

The Federalists meeting in the port city of Hartford were the financial and political heirs of merchant shippers, whalers, shipbuilders, fishermen, sailmakers, and hosts of others engaged for over a century in trading and shipping out of the ports of the northeastern seaboard. Some of these men operated out of inland towns, such as Hartford and Poughkeepsie, that could be reached by oceangoing vessels tacking back and forth up wide rivers. But most presided over their offices, countinghouses, wharves, and shipping fleets in the string of coastal ports stretching from Portsmouth to New York City and points south. And what a coastline this was—gnarled and wrinkled and scoured by sea and ice, battered by suddenly gathering summer storms and winter tempests, and broken by small rivers that invited a wharf to be built along the low banks and flatlands where they joined the Atlantic.

To a returning sea captain most of the port towns presented familiar sights. He would emerge from a forest of ship's masts and furled sails to pick his way through a maze of bags and boxes, barrels and chests alongside warehouses, sail lofts, mast yards, and rope walks, until he came to the closely packed houses of artisans, small merchants, and single or widowed women shopkeepers. He would walk along the streets here, where ground-floor shops opened up on the sidewalks and living quarters nestled in the overhanging upper stories, with their peaked gables, tiny-paned windows, and hand-split clapboards darkened by a century of salt and rain. Heading farther into town, he would come onto High Street, flanked by three-story square-built brick homes of the wealthier merchants. When he entered one of these houses to report on his voyage, the captain would find objects imported from previous voyages: china from the Far East, furniture from England and France, hangings from Spain, souvenirs from West Africa. And climbing to the widow's walk, captain and merchant could scan a wide panorama from the busy harbor below to the fields and blue hills disappearing into a summer haze to the west.

These ports had their distinctive features too. In the Massachusetts crescent stretching from Cape Ann to Cape Cod, Salem was the largest, grandest city to the north, the sixth city in the United States in 1790. No one has pictured the Salem of that year better than Samuel Eliot Morison: "Her appearance was more antique even than that of Boston, and her reek of the salt water, that almost surrounded her, yet more pronounced. For half a mile along the harbor front, subtended by the long finger of Derby Wharf, ran Derby Street, the residential and business center of the town. On one side were the houses of the gentry, Derbys and Princes and Crowninshields, goodly gambrel or hip-roofed brick and wooden mansions dating from the middle of the century, standing well back with tidy gardens in front. Opposite were the wharves, separated from the street by counting-rooms, warehouses, ship-chandlers' stores, pump-makers' shops, sail-makers' lofts; all against a background of spars, rigging, and furled or brailed-up sails. . . ."

Close by Salem—and long viewed by Salemites as the town of people who were "rude, swearing, drunken, and fighting" and, worst of all, poor —lay Marblehead, the leader in the Yankees' great cod-fishing industry. Long before the Revolution, Marblehead had a fleet of 120 fishing schooners sailed by more than a thousand hands. Sloops or schooners with seven or eight men could make four or five round trips a year to fine fishing grounds such as Georges Bank off Cape Cod, and a fisherman kept an eye cocked for mackerel and herring as well. A string of fishing towns to the south of Boston—Cohasset, Plymouth, Cape villages, reaching around to Nantucket and New Bedford—kept hundreds of ships in the fishing trade. Plymouth soon would become less noted for her fishing, or even as the Pilgrims' landing place, than as a center for rope making.

In the center of the Massachusetts crescent, and at its heart, lay Federalist Boston. With its total tonnage several times larger than that of any rival, Boston was not only the great port of the Commonwealth but its financial, intellectual, political, and cultural center. It was pre-eminently a city of the sea, drawing much of its wealth and its sustenance from Atlantic waters, by which it was virtually isolated when the spring tides reached far inland on the flats west of Beacon Hill. As one approached the city by the Charles River Bridge, Boston seemed "almost to stand in the water, at least to be surrounded by it, and the shipping, with the houses, trees, and churches, having a charming effect." Boston boasted of its fine buildings, and especially of the man who designed many of them, Charles Bulfinch, but not of its maze of streets, which were reputed to be almost as muddy and rutted as the original cow paths, and just as narrow and tortuous. Outside the harbor stood probably the most famous lighthouse in America, "Boston Light," founded almost a century before, repeatedly devastated by fire, destroyed in turn by each side during the Revolution, but always rebuilt.

Boston was the financial hub of New England and of much of the Northeast, as well as of her own state. Providence, along with such Connecticut ports as New Haven and New London, had harbors deep enough to ship goods directly across the Atlantic, but Hartford and other, shallower ports dispatched their goods to Boston for transshipment overseas. Produce from Springfield, Northampton, and other towns north of the rapids above Hartford had to be sent down the Connecticut River on barges to Hartford, for transferal to deep-water harbors. Logs from the Vermont and New Hampshire banks of the river were floated down to shipbuilders perched along the lower reaches of the Connecticut.

Boston also transshipped goods from north of Cape Ann—from the old docks of Newburyport and Portsmouth and Portland. The execrable roads inland made it easier for some of these ports to trade by sea with Boston than by land with towns not far inland. Boston merchants had long enjoyed close commercial relationships with their northern neighbors "down east"; Boston indeed was the capital of Maine for many years. But the northern Yankees valued above all their independence from London *or* Boston. When Portland refused to ship her highly prized masts for use of the British fleet during the first year of the Revolution, the Royal Navy bombarded the city and burned much of it to the ground. Established societies in Bangor and Portsmouth enjoyed looking down on the vulgar nouveaux riches of Boston.

*   *   *

Yankee merchants were profit takers. They made money—and lost it—by buying, swapping, shipping, and selling goods in whatever way seemed most profitable. For this purpose they bought, built, used, and sold not only merchant ships but fishing boats, coasters, whalers, privateers, and smaller craft. They traded in whatever commodity would turn a likely profit: fish, bricks, butter, timber, hay, brooms, buckets, molasses, in exchange for mahogany, coffee, sugar, cocoa, tea, spices, nails, machinery, fashions, silks—hundreds of things from scores of ports around the world. Sometimes they dealt also in rum, opium, and human flesh. "Commerce occupies all their thought," a foreign observer wrote in 1788, "turns all their heads, and absorbs all their speculations." When they felt that conditions permitted or required it, the Yankees smuggled goods and sent out privateers to prey on "enemy" ships.

To take profits the merchants took risks. Their ships were sunk off Cape Hatteras or Cape Horn, burned by accident, captured or destroyed by French or British men-o'-war, seized by pirates off Morocco. Seamen took much greater risks—of life itself—with little profit. "A mariner's life was the most dangerous calling a man could choose during the age of sail," according to three historians of the period. ". . . Sunken ledges and sandy shoals reached out from the scenic New England coast to impale hundreds of hapless ships driven before a winter gale or lost in a thick summer fog." Of Salem's four hundred widows in 1783, most had finally waited in vain on the widow's walks atop their mansions, or in a dwelling down by the wharf.

Merchants were the social and political, as well as economic, leaders of their ports. They presided over a pervasive class system of merchants, veteran sea captains, and professional men at the top, master artisans and clerks in the middle, and dock laborers and seamen at the bottom. The merchants sent their sons to Harvard or out to sea eventually to become sea captains, imported the finest silver and linens from abroad, had their wives and daughters painted by Copley and adorned in the latest London fashions, maintained mansions both near their businesses and out in country seats. The lower classes did none of these things. The merchants set themselves off by their manner of dress—perhaps a scarlet broadcloth coat, fancy ruffles, and sword—and by their demand for deference from their inferiors, in the form of a finger to the brow or the tipping of a hat.

A deferential society, and also a deferential politics—at least for a time. Before the Revolution the "best people" in Salem and Newburyport and other ports ran community affairs; voting participation was low, and dominated by the elite. Political conflict tended to be factional, personal, local, and subdued. New England merchants turned to political action less in defense of their theoretical than their economic rights. They led the Revolution—or at least financed it—not out of political or social radicalism but because Britain was threatening their maritime interests. But revolution drew in other elements—men who called themselves Sons of Liberty, mobs that seemed to have little regard for property, editors none too respectful of the gentility. Although the Yankee merchants survived the war with their social and political system largely intact, the ranks of the economic elite had been breached. At the end of the century in Newburyport, for example, an ex-cordwainer, an ex-chaise maker, and an ex-leather dresser had risen to the economic top. How would the conservative Yankees of the New England ports make out in the new, extended republic?

If the Yankee ports were economically adventurous and cosmopolitan, politically and intellectually they tended to be conservative and even stagnant. While Portland and Salem and Hartford doubtless were too small to support lively and innovative cultures, Boston and Cambridge together comprised almost a metropolis, but most of the ruling Bostonians and Cantabrigians were rich, Whiggish, status-minded, and dignified. Some knew how to live in magnificent style, Van Wyck Brooks noted: "The Cushing house in Summer Street was surrounded with a wall of Chinese porcelain. Peacocks strutted about the garden. The Chinese servants wore their native dress. The older folk, sedate, a little complacent, dwelling in the solid garden-houses that stood about the Common, each with its flagged walk and spacious courtyard, filled with fragrant shrubs, shaded by its over-arching elms, were genial and pleasure-loving, as a rule. Harrison Gray Otis, at the age of eighty, after forty years of gout, breakfasted every morning on pâté de fois gras."

Although these cosmopolitans liked to call their town the Athens of America if not indeed the hub of the universe, their intellectual life, Brooks observed, was timid, cautious, and highly derivative from English culture. Things were no better in Cambridge, despite the dominant intellectual role of Harvard College. Indeed, Harvard too was parochial, complacent, more tolerant of eccentricity than innovation. It could boast a few remarkable professors, such as Levi Hedge, who had devoted fourteen years of his own and drafted adult members of his family to completing his *Elements of Logic,* and Dr. Henry Ware of Divinity, who had nineteen children; but classes were usually dull recitations, and the standard of learning at Harvard was not high.

Still, one could detect cultural stirrings in these port towns. Even the smaller had their literary societies and historical associations. Religious and political disputes were often more heated than ever. Exciting young men were coming to Harvard to teach. But only the most doting parent or perspicacious teacher could have detected the potential genius of the chubby Emerson boy in Boston, the solitary, fatherless young Nathaniel Hawthorne of Salem, the frail farm youth, John Greenleaf Whittier, in Haverhill reading the poems of Robert Burns, the little orphan Edgar Allan Poe, born in Boston, precocious young Henry Wadsworth Longfellow of Portland.

* * *

Jeffersonian Republicans held dark suspicions about the New England Federalists—even more the Boston brand, and above all the Essex Federalists, who were reported to be the aggressive and conspiratorial heart of Federalism. Federalists were indeed loosely organized in the "Essex Junto." Lying north of Boston between the promontory of Cape Ann and the farmlands of Peabody, bounded on the north by Newburyport, on the east by Gloucester, and the south by Salem, Essex County was the heartland of fashionable waterside society. If foreigners called all Americans Yankees, and if Southerners called all Northerners Yankees, and if New Englanders called eastern Massachusetts men Yankees, then the true heartland of Yankeedom lay in this country "north of Boston." Old-school Federalists were aided by two other forces. One was the party leadership in the cities and towns along the Connecticut from southern Vermont and New Hampshire to the Atlantic; often these Federalists were more papal than the Pope. The other was the Congregationalist leadership of New England, and the Federalist press in the seaports, which week after week followed a high Federalist line and provided powerful ideological buttressing to the views of the old school.

But despite the suspicion of powerful juntas meeting secretly to spin out their diabolical plots against innocent victims, the Essexmen had little political influence, at least after the turn of the century. They constituted a tiny minority of the Federalist party, which kept its distance from them when elections had to be won or legislation passed. Their strength lay chiefly in their absolute ideological commitment to reaction; the "Essexmen," according to David Fischer, "were conservative in the double sense that they resisted change and sought to restrict the power of the people;

their conservatism was ideological, for they defended not merely a fixed position but fixed principles." Those principles were the fundamental inequality of men and especially women, the sanctity of property and of contracts, social deference, the necessity of upper-class leadership, the danger of popular rule and of devices that would facilitate popular rule. All these principles were anathema not only to the rising body of Jeffersonian Republicans but to moderate Federalists as well.

So ideologically committed were the Essexmen, and so socially prestigious, that their pronunciamentos, amplified by press and pulpit, loomed like a small but ever-threatening thundercloud over the turn-of-the-century political scene. By taking a position so far to the right, the Essexmen moved the political spectrum in their direction. Still, their influence was sharply limited. For one thing, few Essexmen were willing to plunge into the political arena that they disdained, or saw the need to. But even more, their ideology, as they applied it, had a hypocritical ring to it. Much as they prated about public service, self-sacrifice, the public good, and the like, most Essexmen were ultimately committed to protecting their own commercial interests. They were too devoted to "personal and selfish views," John Quincy Adams said. And the occasions when the Essexmen fought hardest in politics were times when the national government took actions that seemed to hurt their maritime and commercial interests, although they were astute enough to flesh out the proclamation of their position with ardent denunciations of "mobocrats" and Francophiles.

Buffeted by the winds of revolution, tempered in the stresses of the founding period, the elitist and capitalistic ideas of the Yankee merchants flowed into three great currents of Federalist thought and action at the turn of the century. One of these currents brought an authentic expression of Anglo-American conservatism. Another contributed indirectly to the evolution of an enduring party system. The third led to Hartford.

No one in America embodied and practiced the first brand of conservatism more zealously than John Adams. Born and brought up amid the Massachusetts maritime economy, educated in the lecture halls of Harvard and the courtrooms of Boston, steeped in the New England heritage of Calvinistic Puritanism combined with a Unitarian faith in reason as a means of finding the true meaning of God, Adams stood by those conservative ideas as tenaciously as any man could who lived for—and off—appointment and election to high office for most of his working life. The power of his philosophy lay in the way in which his theories of the ineluctable nature of man linked with his views on the proper ends of man, and both of these undergirded his ideas as to the proper organization of government. "Aim at an exact Knowledge of the Nature, End, and Means of

Government," he instructed himself early in his career. "Compare the different forms of it with each other and each of them with their Effects on public and private Happiness. Study Seneca, Cicero, and all other good moral Writers. Study Montesque, Bolinbroke. . . ." Study them he did, and any other work he could get his hands on.

He grimly, yet happily, rejected all notions of the natural goodness of man. Neither totally depraved nor totally innocent, men had natural tendencies toward corruption, pride, faction, folly, and ambition. Men would constantly be tested, and must resist temptation. By no means did he exempt himself from this internal struggle.

"Which, dear Youth, will you prefer?" he addressed himself—a life of "Effeminacy, Indolence and obscurity, or a life of Industry, Temperance, and Honour? . . . Let no . . . Girl, no Gun, no Cards, no flutes, no Violins, no Dress, no Tobacco, no Laziness, decoy you from your Books. . . ." He chastised himself for waking up late, so that by ten in the morning his "Passion for knowledge, fame, fortune or any good" was too languid for him to apply with spirit to his books.

The existence of evil tendencies in men made all the more necessary a spirit of moral reform, of public virtue in the community. "There must be a positive passion for the public good, the public interest, honor, power and glory, established in the minds of the people, or there can be no republican government, nor any real liberty. . . ." The enemy of public virtue was individual self-interest. Americans respected the "rights of society" over "private pleasures, passions and interests" as much as any other people, but even in New England he had "seen all my life such selfishness and littleness." The "spirit of commerce" above all corrupted "the morals of families" and threatened the purity and nobility necessary in a great republic. Virtue in a people was necessary but not adequate.

What, then, could safeguard and express virtue, could suppress the evils of ambition, faction, selfishness, corruption, self-indulgence? The solution lay in a properly designed government—a government carefully balanced among popular, aristocratic, and monarchical elements through an institutionalized equilibrium of executive, upper legislative chamber, lower chamber. Left alone, each of these elements "ran headlong into perversion in the eager search by the rulers, whether one, few, or many, for more power," Gordon Wood has summarized this view. "Monarchy lunged toward its extremity and ended in a cruel despotism. Aristocracy, located midway on the band of power, pulled in both directions and created 'faction and multiplied usurpation.' Democracy, seeking more power in the hands of the people, degenerated into anarchy and tumult. The mixed or balanced polity was designed to prevent these perversions."

Adams wished above all to protect the power of the executive in such a balanced system. Legislatures, representing both popular and aristocratic forces, tended to outbalance the executive—a tendency dramatically manifested in the state constitutions adopted during the Revolution. The American President, he felt, should hold absolute power of making federal appointments, framing treaties, and even declaring war. "You are afraid of the one—I of the few," he wrote Jefferson a few months after the Constitution was framed.

No wonder that Adams was appalled by the Pennsylvania constitution of 1776: A unicameral legislature; a weak, practically nonexistent executive; annual rotation in office; But what else would one expect from the likes of Franklin and Paine?

The animating force behind all Adams' ideas was his belief in liberty and his abhorrence of equality. It was a love of universal liberty, he said, that had "projected, conducted, and accomplished the settlement of America." But there preyed on his mind the constant fear that liberty would degenerate into licentiousness and anarchy. And here Adams' fear of equality sapped his love of liberty. He loathed the very thought of "leveling," of mob action, of the rabble taking over. Extend the vote in Massachusetts, he warned, and "new claims will arise; women will demand a vote; lads from twelve to twenty-one will think their rights not closely enough attended to; and every man who has not a farthing will demand an equal voice with any other, in all acts of state."

Under the press of events Adams' defense of liberty often was reduced to that of property. "Property," he said, "is surely a right of mankind as really as liberty." He drew lurid pictures of a majority of the poor attacking the rich, abolishing debts, dividing all property among them, and all this ending in idleness and debauchery. The idea of property as liberty was shared by many of Adams' fellow citizens, even by good republicans, but Adams never made clear where personal or private liberty in property left off, and commercial or corporate liberty of property began. In the end— as most cruelly demonstrated by the Alien and Sedition Acts—he was willing to sacrifice liberty of speech before he would give up the right of property.

It is not granted to many leaders to carry out in practice what they had conceived in theory. Adams had that privilege—and that misfortune. A popularly elected House to represent the people, an indirectly chosen Senate to protect property, a strong executive to make appointments and conduct foreign relations, an expansion of national over state power, all expressed in a stable, respectable, high-toned federal government— Adams rose with this kind of government as Vice-President and President, and fell with it when the Republicans swept to electoral victory in 1800. But intellectually the ultimate victory was his, for he left a bequest of thought and action on which American leaders long would draw.

FEDERALISTS: THE TIDE RUNS OUT

Almost two hundred years later the fall of the Federalist party is still something of a mystery. The Federalists assumed power so readily and exercised it so effectively during the 1790s that one might have expected a long one-party rule like those in many other post-revolutionary regimes. In Washington, Adams, and Hamilton the party possessed unsurpassed political leadership, and this trio was backed up by scores of brilliant congressional and state leaders. Whatever their day-to-day blunders and miscalculations, the Federalists worked out in that decade a strategy of government and policy that seemed well attuned to the long-term needs of the American people.

Yet at century's turn Washington was dead, Adams defeated, Hamilton compromised, the party repudiated. These misfortunes and setbacks need not have been fatal, but in fact the party never again won the presidency or lasting majorities in Congress and finally it died. Why? Not because it had become—in 1800—a merely sectional party, shrunken to its New England enclaves; the Federalists still had large constituencies in New York, Maryland, Virginia, the Carolinas. Not because it stagnated organizationally; the Federalists experimented with party machinery that served as models for the party systems that developed later. Not because its leadership died away; in the void left by the defeat of the party in 1800, a host of new, young, vigorous, practical leaders came forward to rejuvenate the party—and to constitute another major current of Federalism.

Despite all this, the party could not re-establish itself in the new century. The Federalists scored some signal successes in various states over the next decade and a half, and they maintained their opposition role in Congress for a time, but in the electoral college, even allowing for its artificial inflations of majorities, their string of defeats was awesome: 1804—Jefferson 162 to Charles Cotesworth Pinckney 14; 1808—Madison 122 to Pinckney 47; 1812—Madison 128 to (Federalist-supported) De Witt Clinton 89; 1816—Monroe 183 to Rufus King 34. It is not easy to kill off a great political party, as later political history has attested; how did the Federalists accomplish such a convincing demise?

The problem was partly one of leadership. The Federalists had always been peculiarly dependent on elevated leadership; Washington, Hamilton, and the rest helped compensate for the Federalist lack of grass-roots organization. Yet high Federalists had an anomalous relationship with the men who had to build coalitions and win votes. John Adams' "curious relationship" with the "gentlemen of the old school," in David Fischer's words, illustrated the problem. Not only did Adams scorn the Boston merchants' preoccupation with moneymaking, and warn against diverting people "from the cultivation of the earth to adventures upon the sea." As a vote-seeking politician Adams was difficult for the high Federalists to figure out. "With regard to Mr. A.," wrote an Amherst Federalist, "it is impossible to calculate upon him. It would puzzle the angels to develop the motives of his conduct." Angered by old Federalists' hostility, Adams accused them of "stiff-rumped stupidity."

As with father, so with son. The mentality of the Essex Junto was manifested in the apostasy of John Quincy Adams. With John Adams safely retired to Quincy and somewhat protected against the slings and arrows of outraged Federalists, his son proceeded to make himself equally unpopular by his posture of being above party politics. Adams had openly supported some of Jefferson's policies and he differed with the pro-British stance of the Essex Junto. Aroused by the *Chesapeake* affair, young Adams, although a United States senator ostensibly elected as a Federalist, met openly with Republican leaders to plan strategy against British depredations. The Essexmen were angry when Adams supported the embargo, and furious when he attended a Republican congressional caucus for the presidential nomination for 1808. Federalists moved smoothly to the task of party discipline. Six months before the normal time for choosing senators, they replaced John Quincy Adams with one of their own. Instructed also to oppose the embargo, he promptly resigned. Following the old Massachusetts political admonition of "Don't get mad, get even," he used his new Republican party affiliation to counterattack Federalism and win the presidency a generation later.

A major reason for Federalist party decline lay in their hallowed but increasingly anachronistic beliefs in the stewardship of gentlemen of learning and virtue, in the need to protect the rights of property, in order as a prerequisite to liberty, in the natural hierarchical order among citizens, in the need for balance and harmony among classes and interests. These ideas were becoming increasingly incompatible with the expanding market society, the growing materialism and acquisitiveness of Americans, the scuffle of persons and interests for self-advantage. Their ideas were not necessarily wrong, but rather mean and elitist and outdated at the time of rising democratic sentiment. The high Federalists' crabbed view of liberty contrasted with the broader Jeffersonian concept. Thus Federalist judge Samuel Chase: "liberty . . . did not consist in the possession of equal rights, but in the protection by the law of the person and property of every member of society, however various the grade in society he filled." Samuel Lyman, Massachusetts congressman: "a higher degree of liberty cannot exist without endangering the whole . . . nothing is so unequal as equality." Samuel Sewall, Massachusetts judge: "Liberty is security, destroy security, therefore, and you destroy liberty."

Fisher Ames could even joke about the matter. "I derive much entertainment from the squabbles in Madam Liberty's family," he wrote. "After so many liberties have been taken with her, she is no longer a *miss* and a virgin, though she still may be a goddess."

The younger generation of Federalist leaders, however, put modern organization ahead of old ideas. The Federalists had ended the century a disorganized as well as a defeated party. "The Federalists hardly deserve the name of a party," Fisher Ames complained. "Their association is a loose one, formed by accident, and shaken by every prospect of labor or hazard." For a time Federalists mocked the organizational efforts of their Republican foes. A Federalist satire, "The Grand Caucus," presented four Jeffersonians—"Will Sneakup, Esq., Obedumb Bragwell, Esq., Squire Quorom, Esq., and Lord Cockedoodledoo"—constituted as a "self-created convention" which after various shenanigans came up with that very same foursome as its candidates for office.

But nothing succeeds like failure. As the Federalists suffered defeat after defeat, they imitated the Republicans' organizational efforts and innovated on their own. They experimented with state legislative caucuses, some of which became increasingly open, with panoplies of state, county, city, ward, and town caucuses, committees, and committees of correspondence. These grass-roots organizations raised money, published pamphlets and broadsides, and above all—their distinguishing feature as a party mechanism—nominated candidates for office. Some of the old-school Federalists were appalled by such political organizing, with all its implications for popular appeal and politicking. Jeremiah Smith frowned on the picture of "half a score of red hot feds well stuffed with brandy and conceit all talking together. . . ."

All these were state efforts. Could the Federalists build a national party? The incentive was enormous, since the Republicans' control of the presidency and Congress cast shadows over the whole political scene. The Federalists were assisted by national developments—most notably the ratification of the Twelfth Amendment, which changed the procedure in the electoral college so that each elector, instead of voting for two candidates without indicating which he wanted for President, would cast separate votes for President and Vice-President. This was the Republicans' retroactive solution to the Jefferson-Burr impasse of 1800, but it meant that the Federalists would not encounter a similar crisis erupting between two leaders or factions of their party. Federalists also experimented with rudimentary "conventions," as they called them, comprised of delegates from a number of states who "nominated" a presidential candidate—a nomination that was not binding, but had some credibility and impact.

Given time, the younger Federalists might have built a national organization strong enough to overcome its twin problems of leadership and credo—the former by supplying stable grass-roots support for national candidates and officials, the latter by recruiting a far greater variety and number of third-cadre activists through local caucuses and other party machinery. But history did not allow the Federalists time. Not only were the Republicans moving ahead with their own remarkable leadership, improved organization, and popular appeal, but the Federalists also found themselves on the unpopular side of foreign-policy issues. Inflamed by Jefferson's "Frenchified" foreign policy as well as by the Louisiana Purchase, Senator Timothy Pickering played with the notion of a Northern Confederacy including the five New England states, New York, and New Jersey. Secession! The idea appealed to some of the Essexmen who had already given up on the new nation, but it outraged others—including leaders of the Junto itself—who had not worked so hard for Union to see it dissolve within twenty years. The "plot" got nowhere—but a few high Federalists talking about it tainted the image of the whole party.

As the iniquitous Republicans kept their grip on the presidency and Congress during the Jefferson and Madison years, waterside Yankees of the Essex Junto credo and temperament grew desperate about the public interest and security and their own. Feeling had risen to a pitch when ships and sailors stood idle on the heels of Jefferson's embargo of late 1807. If they could not control or measurably influence the Washington government, what alternatives were there for high Federalists but submission or defiance? Yankee merchants had not grown powerful and prosperous through submission, but whom or what could they defy? A grand precedent stared them in the face—the effort of the Jeffersonians themselves to challenge the legitimacy of the Alien and Sedition Acts. There was more talk of secession on the part of some Essexmen—to the tune of patriotic denunciations by Republicans. Fearing divisive action by the old guard, moderate Federalists diverted much of this feeling into the presidential politics of 1808. Then the War of 1812 brought a far more serious crisis —the Maine coastline occupied, Madison's war effort faltering, New England ships and commerce devastated.

Now—at last—the high Federalists acted. Pressured by the waterside

Yankees and by their commercial, legal, and political allies along the Connecticut River and its reaches, the Massachusetts legislature invited the New England states to send delegates to a convention in Hartford. The maritime states of Rhode Island and Connecticut supplied members; from New Hampshire and Vermont came only delegates of southern counties bordering the Connecticut. A climactic political event seemed at hand—and the testing of a third, and politically dangerous, brand of Federalism.

What followed illustrated the crucial difference in politics and history between what politicians do and what people perceive them as doing. In fact moderates were in control of the convention process from start to finish. Not Pickering or Sedgwick and the other extremists, but sober and responsible men such as George Cabot and Nathan Dane and, above all, the pleasantly soothing Harrison Gray Otis attended. Of the twenty-six delegates at Hartford, twenty-one were lawyers, five merchants. While the convention did call for state interposition "in cases of deliberate, dangerous and palpable infractions of the Constitution, affecting the sovereignty. of a State and liberties of the people"—shades of the Kentucky and Virginia resolutions!—no fiery proclamations or threats of secession emerged from the secret meetings; on the contrary, such safe outcomes as denunciations of Republican rule and calls for constitutional amendments to limit commercial embargoes, trade restrictions, and presidential power in general. The convention "recommended" adoption of such amendments by state legislatures or by conventions of the people.

The popular image of the proceedings was quite different. Highly embroidered by a gleeful Republican press, a picture emerged of a small cabal of New England arch-conservatives meeting in secret in a Federalist town to plot secession and the disruption if not the overthrow of the republic. Opposition to the rising egalitarianism of the day, a devotion to their selfish interests over the public welfare, and, worst of all, friendship for the British—all this put the Federalists in the worst possible political posture. The Republican leadership, however, was genuinely concerned about the meeting. Madison was found by a visitor to look "heartbroken," his mind full of the "New England sedition," and Jefferson was stirred enough in his retirement to demand that the "Essex Junto" be stripped of power.

Things could hardly have ended worse for the Hartford Federalists. News of the Treaty of Ghent and of Jackson's victory at New Orleans left the conventioneers looking both foolish and defeatist. It became easy to caricature them as traitors and subversives who put "blue lights" up off the Connecticut shore to signal British privateers. The impression of selfishness, reaction, and subversion was too heavy a load for the Federalists, as they began their protracted death watch.

CHAPTER 7

The American Way of Peace

I N the sleepy Flanders town of Ghent, in the late summer and fall of 1814, five Americans met, quarreled with one another, parleyed with the enemy—and wrote a treaty that helped keep Americans and British at peace with each other for a century, and in close alliance for decades after that.

The Americans in Ghent made up a prodigious quintet. The most senior, though still in his early fifties, was Albert Gallatin, happy to be free of his long tour as Secretary of the Treasury, as sagacious, tactful, and reasonable as ever. The most famous was the young Speaker of the House of Representatives, Henry Clay, the Kentucky "war hawk," as pacific now as he had been bellicose, but no less a spokesman of the West. There were two experienced diplomats, James Bayard of Delaware, still remembered for having helped Jefferson win the presidency in the crisis of February 1801, and Jonathan Russell, a New Englander. And there was the formal head of the delegation, John Quincy Adams.

Gallatin was the real leader of the delegation, and it took all his diplomacy to keep the diplomats together. The five men lodged in bachelor quarters in a genteel residence. They usually ate together, save for Adams, who arose early, dined at one, and morosely noted that the others did not fall to until four. "They sit after dinner and drink bad wine and smoke cigars, which neither suits my habits nor my health, and absorbs time which I cannot spare." Finally Gallatin persuaded him to dine with the others. Sometimes Adams would be rising just as Clay came in from a night of drinking and card playing. The fact that Clay spoke for western interests, and Adams for New Englanders such as fishermen, while both had their eyes on the presidency, did not make for harmony, but Gallatin smoothed matters over with his plea, "Gentlemen, gentlemen, we must remain united or we will fail. . . ."

The Americans faced daunting circumstances. Britain, Russia, Prussia, and Austria were planning a Quadruple Alliance to protect the victorious allies against a resurgent France, which was described to Clay by the American minister in Paris as "a political volcano, ready to explode whenever the match shall be applied." Napoleon had been packed off to Elba.

The Royal Navy now ruled the seas, the Duke of Wellington bestrode Europe. His crack troops were already shipping out of Bordeaux and sailing toward America, where they could join the drives down the Hudson or into the mouth of the Mississippi. The confident English had allowed Adams & Co. to cool their heels for weeks before dispatching their delegation, which on arrival struck the Americans as a collection of nonentities. Even meeting in Ghent was on British sufferance, for the area was occupied by redcoats. "What think you of our being surrounded by a British garrison?" Clay wrote a friend.

Hardly deigning to conceal their sense of mastery, the British negotiators presented the Americans with stiff demands: the United States to be forbidden fortifications and armed vessels on the Great Lakes; a vast territory south of the lakes to be created for England's Indian allies, and as a buffer against American expansion; the United States to cede lands in eastern Maine, northern New York, and west of Lake Superior. The Americans were staggered by these proposals, but especially by the notion that they should surrender the whole of the Northwest Territory, comprising the (present) states of Michigan, Wisconsin, and Illinois, and much of Indiana and Ohio, according to the calculations of Gallatin's son James.

"Father mildly suggested that there were more than a hundred thousand American citizens settled in these States and territories," son James noted in his diary. "The answer was: 'They must look after themselves.'"

The Americans—all but the poker-playing Clay, who felt he knew a bluff when he saw one—prepared to pack their bags. But the parley did not end, for neither side was wholly happy with this ignominious war. Negotiations for peace had actually started within a few weeks of the commencement of the war, and had continued in various guises until Ghent. What each nation expected of a peace treaty had been closely affected by the turns of fortune on the battlefields.

Early in October news reached Ghent that Washington had been sacked, but then came the report of Macdonough's brilliant victory on Lake Champlain. This repulse of the British thrust toward the Hudson, combined with Perry's and other earlier naval victories, critically influenced the thinking of the pre-eminent English military leader, Wellington. Offered the command in Canada, the Iron Duke bluntly informed his political superiors that he could not promise much in the light of American naval power on the Lakes, and what's more, they were in no position to demand territorial concessions from America. No ministry could ignore such advice from the hero of Waterloo.

Both sides at Ghent accordingly modified their proposals. The Americans long since had given up their key demand for the end of impressment, but this was made easier by the knowledge that the defeat of France made impressment no longer vital to the Royal Navy. The British dropped their claim of a huge buffer land—their Indian "allies" could hardly press them on this matter as much as their Canadian brothers could on others—and modified their call for territorial concessions. A last-minute hitch loomed when the British suddenly challenged long-held American fishing rights off Newfoundland. If New England mariners wanted to fish in Canadian waters, Englishmen should have the right to navigate the Mississippi. Clay was furious when Gallatin and Adams supported such a deal. He would sign no treaty, he proclaimed, that granted Mississippi navigation rights to the enemy.

"A dreadful day," young Gallatin wrote in his diary. "Angry disputes on the *contre-project.*" His father and Adams wanted the deal. "Mr. Clay would not hear of it. . . . Nothing arrived at." By now, however, Gallatin knew that peace was likely, for he had received, according to his son, a private note from Wellington assuring him of the Duke's good offices. When young James started to copy this note, his father snatched it from him and burned it.

By the day before Christmas 1814, all issues had been agreed on, or postponed. Essentially the parties settled for the status quo ante. It was, as Thomas Bailey later judged, a truce of exhaustion rather than of persuasion, with important boundary issues left for later arbitral commissions. The treaty was signed December 24, 1814. The Americans invited their late adversaries to a dinner at which Adams toasted "His Majesty the King of England!" The British did the honors on Christmas Day, inviting the Americans to a dinner that included roast beef and plum pudding straight from England. The band, young Gallatin recorded, first played "God Save the King," followed by a toast to the King, and "Yankee Doodle," with a toast to the President.

Good Feelings and Ill

Three thousand miles away that President anxiously awaited word of the terms of peace. Madison need not have worried. News of the Treaty of Ghent arrived about the same time as reports of the triumph of New Orleans. The two events seemed to become mixed together in the popular mind. "GLORIOUS NEWS!" proclaimed *Niles' Weekly Register. "Orleans saved and peace concluded."* Bells were rung, guns fired, holidays proclaimed, pupils liberated from school. The public feeling of joy and happiness, reported the New York *Evening Post,* showed how "really sick at heart" people of "all ranks and degrees" were of the war. "Broadway and other streets were illuminated by lighted candles," the newspaper reported; "the city resounded in all parts with the joyful cry of a peace! a peace!" Boston was reported to be in a "perfect uproar of joy." Amid the euphoria the Senate ratified the treaty without a dissenting vote—one of the most popular ever negotiated by the United States.

But there was some ill feeling too. Bellicose Americans still wanted to attack Canada, especially after General Jackson had shown what could be done on the Mississippi. Some Federalists argued that the war should not have been fought in the first place. Many Canadians felt deserted by the English. And many Britishers felt sold out by their government; their sentiments found a voice in the *Times* of London, which saw the British as retiring from the combat with "the stripes yet bleeding on our backs," and lamented that the treaty "betrays a deadness to the feelings of honour."

Like all wars, that of 1812–15 extinguished some problems and heated up others. One of the latter was the border with Canada, which remained to be negotiated with London. The Great Lakes, where costly naval battles had been fought, were the critical area. For years American leaders— notably John Adams in Paris and John Jay in London—had dreamed of a permanent disarmament of the Lakes. Now the opportunity had come. The House of Representatives led the way, though partly out of reasons of economy, by authorizing the President to have the fresh-water navy laid up or sold, after first preserving their "armament, tackle, and furniture." Would Britain follow suit? John Quincy Adams, now minister in London, sent word that the Cabinet was determined not only to maintain but to increase their naval power on the Lakes. Monroe instructed him to propose a mutual limitation of armed vessels.

With negotiations well under way, Madison could turn to pressing domestic problems. At war's end, he had only two more years to serve. His annual message to Congress in December 1815 was the first he was able to devote mainly to domestic issues. It was a paradoxical occasion. Congress was ignominiously meeting in the Patent Office, the only major federal building spared by the British, but its leadership had never been more lustrous: Calhoun, Webster, Pickering, Clay. The Kentuckian had been re-elected to the Speakership the first day he returned to the House after his year and a half abroad as a peace commissioner. The secondary leadership was hardly less impressive: Richard M. Johnson of Kentucky, William Lowndes of South Carolina, Samuel D. Ingham of Pennsylvania, all Republicans, and a small band of articulate Federalists. But most remarkable was Madison's message.

It started out by claiming victory—not over the British, but over Algiers, where Captain Stephen Decatur had recently exacted a peace agreement from the Dey after a brilliant attack and had gone on to gain similar guarantees from Tunis and Tripoli. If this pleased the members of Congress, the mood swiftly changed as the President came to his proposals. He called for expanded defense, "both fixed and floating," and for more skilled and disciplined state militias. He asked for tariff protection for young manufacturing establishments. He talked about the need for the "General Government" to build roads and canals, and to make rivers more navigable, provided that such steps were—or could be made—constitutional. And he said, in words that were as startling in substance as mild in form, "If the operation of the State banks cannot produce this result"—a uniform national currency—"the probable operation of a national bank will merit consideration."

Stepped-up defense in peacetime? Tariffs? Internal improvements? A national bank? What heretical doctrine was this? And from the pen of James Madison, second only to Jefferson among Republican founding fathers? Then and later the "old Republicans" brought out their sacred texts. "The evil of the times is a spirit engendered in this republic, fatal to Republican principles; fatal to Republican virtue;", cried John Randolph, "a spirit to live by any means but those of honest industry; a spirit of profusion; . . . a spirit of expediency not only in public but in private life. . . . There are very few who dare to speak truth to this mammoth. The banks are so linked together with the business of the world that there are very few men exempt from their influence."

Only a few congressmen realized that they were witnessing a profound shift in the Republican party—a shift that would alter the nation's politics for decades to come. In its many rooms, the mansion of Republicanism had always had a place for activist, mercantilist policies of government support for economic development. Gallatin, in a series of masterly reports in the last year of Jefferson's presidency, had called for a national transportation and communications network as part of a ten-year plan that, William Appleman Williams has commented, "made Hamilton appear a fumbling amateur." Then had come war, always the forcing house of economic change. The federal government had become deeply involved in raising and spending money, promoting industry such as iron foundries and ship manufacture.

Younger, more entrepreneurial Republicans like Henry Clay shucked off the old Republican bias against federal economic action. Madison himself, under the pressure of war, shifted his ground. "Altho' I approve the policy of leaving to the sagacity of individuals, and to the impulse of private interest, the application of industry & capital," he wrote a correspondent a few months after leaving the White House, "I am equally persuaded, that in this as in other cases, there are exceptions to the general rule, which do not impair the principle of it. Among these exceptions, is the policy of encouraging domestic manufacturers, within certain limits, and in reference to certain articles."

Out of the old Republican party a new political force was arising, more nationalist, more entrepreneurial, more interventionist than the old. Politicians were switching sides. Madison, who had vetoed a bank bill in January 1815, signed, hardly fifteen months later, a measure creating the Second Bank of the United States, capitalized with the huge sum of $35 million. Calhoun had introduced the bill; Clay, who five years before had argued that such a bill was unconstitutional, left the Speaker's chair to explain why he had changed his mind; and Federalists, advocates of the first United States bank only two decades before, largely voted against it. So many "old" Republicans joined Federalists against the bill as almost to defeat the measure in the House. The bank began operating at the start of 1817.

More was involved in all this than economic and political change. The very spirit and character of the nation seemed altered after the war. In part this was a matter of self-satisfaction and celebration. "I can indulge the proud reflection that the American people have reached in safety and success their fortieth year as an independent nation," Madison said in his last message to Congress, in December 1816; "that for nearly an entire generation they have had experience of their present Constitution," and "have found it to bear the trials of adverse as well as prosperous circumstances; to contain in its combination of the federate and elective principles a reconcilement of public strength with individual liberty, of national power for the defense of national rights with a security against wars of injustice. . . ."

The "reconcilement of public strength" and "individual liberty"—this was the essence of the political achievement. But the spirit of 1816 and 1817 went beyond this. It was a feeling of self-confidence, of having won —or so it was thought—America's "second war of independence." It was the boast that America now had established herself in the family of nations as a power that must be respected. It was the notion that at last Americans had achieved a sense of self-identity, of spirit, of earned esteem and hence of self-esteem. "A great object of the war has been attained in the firm establishment of the national character," Clay told officials of the city of Washington on returning from Europe in September 1815.

Few Americans embodied this spirit more visibly than James Monroe, the heir apparent to the presidency. "The experiment" of war, he said, "was made under circumstances the most unfavorable to the United States, and the most favorable to the very powerful nation with whom we were engaged. The demonstration is satisfactory that our Union has gained strength, our troops honor, and the nation character, by the contest." Now in his late fifties, Monroe, with his big strapping frame, erect bearing, and plain, deep-lined face, looked more like a leader of the Virginia gentry than of the "Virginia dynasty." Less reflective, philosophical, or profound than his mentors Jefferson and Madison, he was known as a man of common sense, good judgment, and courage. He was deeply experienced, as Revolutionary officer, Continental Congressman, United States senator, diplomat, governor of Virginia, and Secretary of State doubling as Secretary of War during the final critical months of the war. Monroe's thinking had changed considerably since the days when he opposed the Constitution because it vested too much power in the chief executive. Now he looked forward to being a strong President of a strong nation.

Not all supported this ambition. Even in Virginia, the foundation of Monroe's support, "old Republicans" were hostile to his candidacy. Once again the party's nomination would be decided by "King Caucus," the traditional meeting of Republican members of Congress, but here Monroe faced formidable opposition in Treasury Secretary William H. Crawford. In turn senator from Georgia, Minister to France, and Secretary of War, before taking over Treasury, Crawford was almost as experienced as Monroe; even more, the tall, ruddy-faced Georgian was the kind of orator, superb storyteller, and genial handshaker that endeared a leader to politicians in both houses. He also benefited from a widespread feeling that it was time to curb the Virginia dynasty and Virginia influence. This feeling was strongest in the Empire State, which had provided the nation with neither President nor emperor, but New Yorkers were divided between supporters of the politico and reformer De Witt Clinton and of the rising young state politician Martin Van Buren.

The machinations of 1816 are still not wholly clear, but it probably was the Crawfordites who posted an anonymous notice calling Republican senators and representatives to a nominating session. Monroe's supporters boycotted this rump caucus, which attracted so embarrassingly few members that it could only summon a second caucus. At this point Crawford seems to have experienced a failure of nerve. It was not easy to take on the senior member of the Cabinet; moreover, at the age of forty-four, the Georgian felt he could wait a presidential term or two and run again in 1824 at the latest. At the second caucus Monroe beat him by the unimpressive margin of 65 to 54.

The Federalist party was so weak in 1816 that Monroe's nomination was tantamount to election. The party of Washington and Hamilton chose the veteran New York politician Rufus King, and then failed to unite its thin support even behind him. Monroe vanquished him in the electoral college, 183–34, with the shrunken Federalists monotonously clinging to their majorities in Massachusetts, Connecticut, and Delaware. The Virginia dynasty stood fast.

*   *   *

"The American people," President James Monroe said in his Inaugural Address, ". . . constitute one great family with a common interest." The government had been in the hands of the People. The People had built and sustained the Union. Only when "the People become ignorant and corrupt" did they become the "willing instruments of their own debasement and ruin." Hence: "Let us, by all wise and constitutional measures, promote intelligence among the People, as the best means of preserving our liberties."

To many, this paean to the People was so much Republican oratory. But Monroe was not just indulging in cant. He had a plan based on a hypothesis that, as he wrote Andrew Jackson, "the existence of parties is not necessary to free government. . . ." His plan was no less than to rid the nation of party rivalry. Inheriting Jefferson's theoretical dislike (though actual utilization) of party, Monroe would go far beyond him. Whereas Jefferson proposed to win over moderate Federalists, isolate "monarchical" types, and build a new party, Monroe proposed to offer the Federalists the chance to "get back in the great family of the union," thus to broaden the Republican ranks, and then to govern on behalf of the whole People, the American Family, the national consensus.

"The nation has become tired of the follies of faction," Nicholas Biddle said after the election.

To raise his administration above party rivalry, to speak for the American family, to act on the national consensus, Monroe resolved on a glittering ministry, a Cabinet of all the talents, a leadership from all the sections. From the East, for Secretary of State, John Quincy Adams. From the West, for Secretary of War, Henry Clay. From the South, for Secretary of the Treasury, William H. Crawford. But not all the leaders were willing to crowd into the new President's tent. In particular Henry Clay, sorely disappointed that he had not been proffered State, declined War. Unable to find for this post another Westerner of sufficient stature or caliber, Monroe appointed the brilliant young Southerner John Calhoun, who was rising to an eminence that would rival Clay's. All these men were Republicans.

Where were the Federalists in this non-party administration? Monroe said he wanted to give the opposition a chance for reconciliation but he appointed few Federalists, mainly out of fear of alienating Republicans. Federalists did not protest unduly. They could forgo Republican *patronage,* they calculated, as long as Monroe seemed to embrace Federalist *policies.*

If Americans were now to be one family with the President as their father, a grand tour seemed a fine way to demonstrate popular support for the new leader. Three months after his inauguration, Monroe, accompanied by a small party, set off for New England. He was greeted by friendly crowds and subjected to parades, reviews, and tours all the way up the eastern seaboard, but enthusiasm rose to a pitch in Boston. Was the old city making up for its long coolness to Virginia dynasts? Forty thousand persons, it was estimated, lined the streets and filled every window as the presidential party moved through the streets to Boston Common. Over the next few days Monroe inspected defenses, greeted delegations, reviewed troops, toured the Watertown arsenal and a Waltham cotton factory, heard Edward Channing orate in Faneuil Hall and William Ellery Channing preach a Unitarian sermon, visited Bunker Hill and "Old Ironsides," and drove to Harvard, where he received an honorary Doctor of Laws degree amid much pomp and circumstance. Just as he hoped, Federalists—including even his old foe Timothy Pickering—greeted him warmly. Indeed, the main political problem was the unseemly jockeying between Republican and Federalist leaders to honor the President; even this kind of party rivalry disturbed the grand harmonizer.

So Monroe could reign; could he rule? Madison had bequeathed him some issues that did not admit of easy conciliation. One was the bank, which actually began operations only a few weeks before Monroe took office and generated controversy by its mere existence. Another was federally subsidized internal improvements, especially roads.

Westerners in particular had been clamoring for better connections with the market centers of the eastern seaboard. The typical inland road of the time was still a rough and meandering strip of rutted earth that often might turn into a bog that could swallow carriage wheels, or into a streambed that could break them. In his last annual message to Congress, Madison had favored a federally financed network of roads and canals, but he believed that a constitutional amendment was necessary before the federal government could undertake such a project. Calhoun, arguing that internal improvements were sanctioned by the general welfare clause of the Constitution, had helped push a bill through a closely divided House and Senate, only to see Madison veto it the day before he left the White House.

Early in Monroe's presidency George Tucker of Virginia presented a report by the House Committee on Internal Improvements affirming the power of Congress to construct roads and canals. Monroe anxiously consulted with ex-President Madison.

This time it was Henry Clay of Kentucky who took on a foot-dragging Virginia President. Rarely had "Harry of the West" so brilliantly commanded the floor of the House. Treating his foes with exquisite courtesy, mixing heavy constitutional arguments with stiletto thrusts, he touched on Monroe's regal tour, with his loyal subjects rising to salute the "entrance of the sovereign," and he sarcastically exploited Monroe's inconsistencies and the inadequacies of his constitutional arguments. The President, he said, had given the House only "an historical account of the operations of his own mind." Friends of the Administration rose to rebut him, but he brushed them off like so many flies. His constitutional arguments were hardly new; they were the Hamiltonian case for federal power. But Hamilton, the proponent of executive power, would hardly have accepted Clay's attack on Monroe's supporters for ascribing "imperial powers" to their chief.

Clay bluntly attacked Monroe's idea of rising above party. "We are told," the Speaker said acidly, "that in these halcyon days there is no such thing as party spirit; that the factions by which the country has been divided, are reduced to their primitive elements, and that this whole society is united by brotherly love and friendship. . . . Sir, I do not believe in this harmony, this extinction of party spirit, which is spoken of; I do not believe that men have ceased to be men, or that they have abandoned those principles on which they have always acted hitherto."

The President hardly needed Clay to remind him of the difficulties of partyless government. It was soon clear that if men did not divide into two parties, they would divide into countless factions within parties. To govern without party support, moreover, meant that the President lacked allies when he needed them. And he needed them most when the going was rough—most notably after the Panic of 1819.

The causes of that panic were manifold—worldwide readjustments after the Napoleonic wars, overexpansion of credit, low prices of imports from Europe—but the debtors of Kentucky and South Carolina and other western and southern states did not look for remote sources of their troubles when their loans were called in or their mortgages were foreclosed. Nor did the tradespeople and laborers who lost their jobs. The culprit was tangible and visible—the United States Bank. Though the bank's desperate efforts to save itself were a sign more of weakness than of strength, this

was a time for hyperbole. "All the flourishing cities of the West are mortgaged to this money power," said Senator Thomas Hart Benton of Missouri later. "They may be devoured by it at any moment. They are in the
jaws of the monster!" Someone else said: "The Bank was saved, and the
people were ruined."

An even harsher challenge to the "era of good feelings" came shortly
—a flare-up over slavery. This issue, it was true, had not yet achieved
formidable proportions, and even now it did not rise as an issue in itself,
but was suddenly projected into Washington politics when the Missouri
Territorial Assembly petitioned Congress for statehood. At this time the
twenty-two states in the Union were equally divided between slave states
and free. This was no coincidence, since the respective political weight of
North and South had been carefully balanced by the alternate admission
of free and slave states. Despite the three-fifths rule, the free states had 105
votes in the House, the slave states 81. But the Southerners counted on
the equal vote in the Senate to sustain the political balance.

Maintaining that balance was the central thrust of the political efforts of
1820 that later came to be known as the Missouri Compromise. The legislative path to compromise was long and tortuous, as northern legislators
tried to limit slavery in Missouri and to the west, and were beaten back by
southern lawmakers. Representative James Tallmadge of New York sought
to amend the Missouri statehood legislation by prohibiting the further
introduction of slaves into the state and requiring that all children born of
slaves in Missouri be freed at the age of twenty-five. The House passed this
amendment; the Senate killed it. When the organization of Arkansas Territory came before Congress, John W. Taylor of Saratoga County, another
New York congressman who shared Tallmadge's moral objection to the
extension of slavery, moved to prohibit its further expansion. This was
defeated, and Congress admitted Arkansas with no curb on slavery. After
Maine had freed itself of Massachusetts and petitioned for admission,
Maine was used as a counter to Missouri. When the Senate coupled the
admission of Maine and Missouri, Senator Jesse B. Thomas of Illinois
proposed an amendment providing that Missouri be admitted as a slave
state but that, in the rest of the Louisiana Purchase, slavery be barred north
of latitude 36°30'. This amendment the Senate passed, but the House
balked. After considerable attitudinizing, confronting, foot dragging, and
dickering, Maine was admitted as a free state, Missouri as a slave state, and
the northern boundary of slavery was fixed at 36°30'.

This was the "Missouri Compromise," but the compromising was not
over. Missourians soon met in convention in St. Louis and adopted a

constitution empowering the legislature to exclude free Negroes and mulattoes from the state. Feeling betrayed, the compromisers for the North, with the powerful help of Henry Clay, arranged the "Second Missouri Compromise," stipulating that Missouri would not finally be admitted until the legislature promised that nothing in her constitution could be interpreted as sanctioning the abridgment of the privileges and immunities of United States citizens. On that basis Missouri was admitted. Later, the state repudiated this undertaking.

This trading and brokering took place amid a curious vacuum. Despite much editorializing, the country was not deeply aroused. Northern feeling against slavery had not developed strongly, nor did the slaveholders yet feel mortally threatened. Congress was less a scene of grand confrontation between the two sides than an arena for guerrilla warfare, as small factions clung to protected positions on the ideological battlefield. The compromise was not so much a solemn compact between North and South, as Glover Moore said, as "merely an agreement between a small majority of the Southern members of Congress and a small minority of the Northern ones." Aside from a sweeping attack by Rufus King on the whole moral and philosophical case for slavery, debate was mainly legalistic. Any transcending moral issues fed into the fragmented machinery of Congress were divested of their ethical content by endless constitutional logic-chopping, then quietly enervated in the backstairs trading and brokering that produced the compromise.

The debate aroused no great confrontation between the two parties, because there were no longer two parties, only a bloated conglomeration of Republicans and a dying band of Federalists. The debates aroused no dramatic encounter between President and opposition party leader, for the latter did not exist and the former wanted things as they were. Monroe was essentially passive throughout the long course of the debates. He feared that the issue might get out of hand and intrude into his re-election campaign in 1820, but he won a second term with only a single elector in opposition, and some wondered whether he might have expended more of his political capital on such a major issue.

To Jefferson the debates came "like a fire bell in the night." But the fire bell seemed to awaken few outside the politicians and the press, in part because the politicians mainly wanted it that way. Perhaps the fire bell aroused the Virginia conscience, but Jefferson used a more apt figure when he said, in noting the lack of considered measures for dealing with slavery, "We have the wolf by the ears, and we can neither hold him, nor safely let him go."

ADAMS' DIPLOMACY AND MONROE'S DICTUM

Stretching two thousand miles to the west of the United States at the end of the War of 1812–15, and five or six thousand miles to the south, lay the vast possessions of Spain and Portugal. Rooted in the culture and heritage of Britain and northern Europe, most Americans had a poor and contorted understanding of the empire that flanked them from California along the Pacific shores of Mexico through the Caribbean, to the long shoulder of Brazil jutting far out into the Atlantic. Of heroic stories of Columbus and Cortes and Pizarro, North Americans learned in their infancy. Sailors and traders brought back tales of exotic and erotic adventures in great ports such as Havana, San Juan, Rio de Janeiro, Montevideo, of frightful tempests and endless storms off Cape Horn, of pleasant trading places like Acapulco and San Francisco. But little was known, outside the ranks of diplomats and a few scholars, of the Latin cultures that had begun to flourish in Central and South America during the sixteenth century while North America was peopled by native Indians and a few white settlers.

North Americans knew little of the glories of a Spanish America that was enjoying a kind of Indian summer in the early nineteenth century—of the creative patronage of the arts, of the brilliant circles of learning, of the astronomical observatory in Bogotá, of the already ancient university in Santo Domingo, of the school of mines in Mexico City. Most *yanquis* comprehended only dimly a polity of Spanish state rule from the Crown in Madrid through a great pyramid of viceroyalties, such as New Granada, Peru, New Spain (Mexico), down through presidencies, captain-generalcies, and *audiencias.* And even less did they understand or appreciate the Church that, now stern and now benign, spread its spiritual arms over Spanish and Indian alike and often, to a far greater extent than northern missionaries, made an effort not merely to convert the Indians but to understand and accommodate their language, customs, and needs. Nor did most Latin Americans know or care much about the small republic to the north, with its Protestant culture and often bumptious diplomacy.

The two cultures confronted each other along a hazy boundary from the northern reaches of the Floridas to Louisiana and then across the southwestern desert. The Administration ended the war with a good deal of ill feeling toward the Spanish. He had been looking at some official Spanish documents, President Madison told the chief clerk of the State Department, and they backed up all the earlier accounts "of the extreme jealousy & hatred of us prevailing in the Spanish Court, and prove that after the fall of Napoleon, there was a project entertained, for taking advantage of our war with England, and the expected succour of the latter to Spain, to settle all territorial matters with the U.S. according to Spanish wishes." For years the Floridas had lain like a pistol aimed at the Mississippi, the central artery of American commerce, with East Florida the butt and West Florida the barrel, Samuel Flagg Bemis noted; now, with sections sliced off earlier by the United States, the pistol looked more truncated. But it was still dangerous, and must be muzzled.

Who would do the muzzling, and how? The military action was undertaken by Andrew Jackson, but the guiding hands were those of James Monroe, and especially of John Quincy Adams, in a brilliant display of American *Realpolitik.*

While Monroe was still Secretary of State, and Adams Minister to Britain, Adams in London had confronted the British Foreign Minister, Lord Castlereagh, with Washington's suspicions that Spain had secretly ceded Florida to Britain.

"As to that," Castlereagh said, "I can set you at ease at once. There is not and never has been the slightest foundation for it whatsoever. It never has been even mentioned."

"I am sure the American government will receive with much pleasure the assurance given me by your Lordship that no such cession has been made," Adams said.

"None whatever," Castlereagh continued. "It has never been mentioned, and, if it had, it would have been decisively declined by us. Military positions may have been taken by us during the war, of places which you had taken from Spain, but we never intended to keep them. *Do you also observe the same moderation.* If we should find you hereafter pursuing a system of encroachment upon your neighbors, what we might do defensively is another consideration."

"I do not precisely understand what your Lordship intends by this advice of moderation," Adams said smoothly. "The United States have no design of encroachment upon their neighbors, or of exercising any injustice toward Spain."

Castlereagh's warning did not deter Monroe and Adams from taking a strong line toward Spain on Florida when they became President and Secretary of State in 1817. The United States held certain advantages. The Louisiana treaty had left quite vague the boundary west of the Mississippi. Spain's military grip on Florida had weakened as she siphoned off troops to fight insurgents in South America. Florida had become a haven for privateers and runaway slaves; even more, Seminole Indians, harboring resentments against the Americans, had thrust across the border to "pillage, burn, and murder." For its part, Madrid was less interested in keeping the disorderly settlements and treacherous swamps of Florida than in securing its holdings to the west. The Spanish minister in Washington, Don Luiz de Onís y Gonzales, was instructed to defer any cessions of the Floridas until Washington compromised on Texas. Onís was happy to drag his heels, but events would not permit this, for Americans in lower Georgia were clamoring for a punitive expedition into Florida against both the Seminoles and the Spanish.

Who could do the job better than Andrew Jackson, long a frontier nationalist and harrier of Indians and Spaniards, and already in place as commander of the Southern Division? All that was needed was an incident, and this had been conveniently provided when, in November 1817, American troops burned a Seminole border village and the Indians in retaliation ambushed an American hospital ship and killed forty-five soldiers, women, and children. Jackson urged on Monroe that the "whole of East Florida be seized and held as indemnity for the outrages of Spain upon the property of our Citizens." The government need not be implicated, the general added. "Let it be signified to me through any channel . . . that the possession of the Floridas would be desirable to the United States, and in sixty days it will be accomplished." Jackson received no direct reply to this letter; all he did receive was murky instructions from Washington that left him just where he liked to be: on his own.

Early in March 1818, Jackson crossed the border with about two thousand men. Acting with his usual dash and élan, in a few weeks' time he chased Indians, seized Pensacola and other key Spanish posts in Florida, confiscated the royal archives, court-martialed and executed two British subjects suspected of aiding the enemy, deposed the Spanish governor, and declared in force the revenue laws of the United States. After howls of indignation in London and Madrid, he expressed regret only for failing to hang the Spanish governor.

Patriotic Englishmen reacted with predictable wrath to the "murder" of their fellow countrymen. The press, exhibiting Jackson in their street placards, denounced him as a tyrant, ruffian, and murderer, United States minister Richard Rush reported from London. There was even talk of war. Patriotic Americans responded to Jackson's incursion with predictable delight. Public dinners offered toasts to the man who had vanquished Spanish, Indians, and British all in one stroke, and gained real estate to boot. *Niles' Weekly Register* reported that the general's popularity in the West was unbounded—at his call 50,000 warriors "would rise, armed, and ready for any enemy." Tammany Hall resolved that the "manly" general was justified by the "law of nations" and approved of his teaching "foreign emissaries that the United States was not to be outraged by spies, traitors, and lawless adventurers." New York awarded the hero the freedom of the city—in a golden box. In Washington, Onís demanded an explanation, while Congress, after wrangling over Jackson's actions in a month-long debate, during which the galleries were crowded almost to suffocation and cuspidors overturned in the rush for seats, decisively defeated resolutions condemning the hero's conduct.

The crucial move lay with President Monroe and his Cabinet. All seemed to agree that the general had exceeded his orders. Secretary of War Calhoun, stung by what he saw as Jackson's defiance of his own orders not to challenge the Spaniards, wanted him court-martialed. Secretary of the Treasury Crawford joined in the condemnation. Both men had their eyes on the next election—and on Henry Clay, who was making capital against both Jackson and the Administration. The President as usual looked for a consensus, and he might have had one, except for his Secretary of State.

John Quincy Adams did not like Andrew Jackson; the Tennesseean was not his kind of man. Nor did he approve of the general's excesses in Florida. But Adams saw an opportunity that transcended personalities, an opportunity to exercise American statecraft, to advance his dream of a transcontinental nation, and to promote his rising hopes of a second Adams presidency. Instead of allowing the Jackson incursion to be elevated to a moral issue forcing the United States on the defensive, he treated it as a fait accompli that put Washington in a stronger position in dealing with Madrid over the whole transcontinental border. "On the receipt of Genl. Jackson's report of his proceedings there," Monroe wrote ex-President Madison a few weeks after, "we had three great objects in view, first to secure the constitution from any breach, second to deprive Spain and the allies of any just cause of war, and third to turn it to the best account of the country." The third responsibility was peculiarly Adams'. In his instructions to the United States minister in Madrid, Adams took the offensive. He charged Spain with having failed to restrain her Indians and in fact with encouraging them; he defended the execution of the two Britons; he demanded the punishment of the guilty Spanish officers and —audacity of audacities—he laid claim to an indemnity for the cost to the Americans of pursuing the Indians.

Having established a strong bargaining position, Adams proceeded to negotiate with Onís in Washington. They had long been discussing the western boundary; now they sought a total settlement. As a sweetener, Spain's posts seized by Jackson were returned to her, though her demand that Jackson be punished was rejected. Week after week, Adams and Onís shuffled maps and haggled over territory, as large tracts of land hung on day-to-day agreements over tentative boundaries based often on vague information about the location of mountain ranges or the configuration of rivers.

Onís was no equal to Adams as a negotiator, in part because of inferior ability, in part because his king, the repellent Ferdinand VII, had a reputation for exiling his envoys to distant monasteries for exercising too much latitude in bargaining. In the end, after Monroe delivered a near-ultimatum to the foot-dragging Onís, the Adams-Onís treaty was signed in February 1819. Spain renounced all her claims to West Florida and ceded East Florida to the United States; the United States repudiated its claims to Texas; the western boundary was defined as running from the mouth of the Sabine River, then northwest along the Red and Arkansas rivers and the 42nd parallel, from which it proceeded due west to the Pacific. In essence, the Spanish claims to the Pacific Northwest were surrendered to the United States in exchange for the equally immense territory in the Southwest.

On February 22, 1819, Adams and Onís affixed their signatures to the treaty. "It was, perhaps, the most important day of my life," Adams wrote in his diary. He had secured Florida. But he forbade exultation—it was the "work of an intelligent and all-embracing Cause." Two days later, the Senate unanimously advised and consented to the treaty. Spain's pistol to the south had been removed. Few asked whether its cannon had been entrenched two thousand miles to the west.

*   *   *

Even while Adams was negotiating with Spain, the old mobiles of international politics were beginning to shudder before the gusts of powerful forces that were bringing new groups to power in Latin America. By some common alchemy of the human spirit, people across the long reach of the Latin world were seeking to transform their lives by rebelling against autocratic rulers and ancient laws. The Holy Alliance, formed in part to put down the revolutionary spirit, suddenly confronted rebellions in Naples, Spain, Portugal, and Greece. Long-fermenting unrest in Latin America swelled into liberation movements led by the spirited young Venezuelan Simón Bolívar, by the Mexican priest and patriot Miguel Hidalgo, by the Argentinian general José de San Martín, and many others. Two years before Adams signed the treaty with the old regime in Madrid, San Martín crossed the Andes to defeat the Spanish at the Battle of Chacabuco and thus helped bring about the liberation of Chile. Two years after that treaty, Bolívar won the last major battle of the war in Venezuela, and Mexico gained its independence; a year after that, the Brazilian Empire was declared independent under Pedro I.

Americans watched admiringly as patriots came to power who used the Declaration of Independence as sacred writ and George Washington as a model. Americans watched apprehensively as the Holy Allies agreed to mandate Austria to put down the republican revolution in Naples and in the Piedmont, as the allies approved French military intervention in Spain to suppress the new constitutional government there. The European leaders invited Britain to share these sacred responsibilities, but by now Castlereagh was frustrated by his involvement in the alliance. The servant of a dynasty that owed its throne to the Glorious Revolution of 1688, he could hardly embrace with passion an anti-revolutionary entente. Moreover, influential English opinion was turning away from the embrace of reactionary, absolutist regimes toward flirtation, at least, with political liberalism and a freer commerce. Beset by these and other pressures, Castlereagh went mad, cut his throat with a penknife, and thus made possible the succession to the Foreign Ministry of his fierce rival, George Canning, who also feared the reactionary power of the Holy Allies and sought to build a balance of power against them.

Why should not the "two chief commercial and maritime states of both worlds," as Canning described Britain and the United States, be part of that counterbalance? Thus the swaying mobiles of the Western world could be brought back to an equilibrium. Canning broached the idea to Minister Rush, who passed it on to Washington. President Monroe treated the question as one of the gravest of his career. Would this be a departure from the doctrine of non-involvement in European affairs—a doctrine sanctified by Washington and engraved in his Farewell Address? Typically ambivalent in his own reaction, eager for a collective judgment, Monroe turned first to the bearers of the Virginia tradition. Both Jefferson and Madison counseled cooperation with Britain in what Madison called the "great struggle of the Epoch between liberty and despotism." Reassured, Monroe called a meeting of his Cabinet. By the time it convened, the Russian minister had advised that the Tsar would not receive agents from any of the rebellious governments in America and congratulated Washington on its neutral attitude toward those governments. Were the Holy Allies planning some effort to restore his former colonies to Ferdinand?

At first, the Cabinet seemed to favor a joint declaration with Canning against interference in the Americas by the Holy Alliance, even if it should commit the United States never to take Cuba—long coveted by none other than Jefferson—or Texas. Britain had the power to seize both Cuba and

Texas, Calhoun observed, and thus would be pledged equally with the United States against such action. Adams demurred. He wanted no action that would bind the Administration's hands if Texas or Cuba wished to join the Union, or in case of emergency. He was averse, the President replied, to any course that would appear subordinate to that of Britain. Adams wanted to take advantage of the Russian note.

"It affords a very suitable and convenient opportunity," he told the Cabinet, as he remembered the discussion, "for us to take our stand against the Holy Alliance and at the same time to decline the overture of Great Britain. It would be more candid, as well as more dignified, to avow our principles directly to Russia and France, than to come in as a cock-boat in the wake of the British man-of-war." All seemed to agree. As the meeting broke up, Adams cornered the President. The answers to the British, the Russians, and the French "must all be parts of a *combined system of policy and adapted to each other.*"

In meetings that followed, the Cabinet hammered out a policy, with Monroe and Adams taking the lead. The policy was the dual one of disclaiming any interference in the political affairs of Europe and declaring an "expectation that the European powers would equally abstain from seeking to spread their ideas in the American hemisphere," or to take any part of it by force. The United States had already said "Hands Off" to further colonization of the New World; now it would say the same to further conquest or intervention.

It was an enormous step forward from non-colonization to non-intervention, but Adams was ready to accept the restraints required by this position. When Monroe proposed a message to Congress that would state these policies but would go on to reprove France for invading Spain and acknowledge the rebelling Greeks as an independent nation, Adams objected. This suggested entanglement in European affairs—why defy the powers? He finally brought the President around, but it was Monroe who decided to enunciate the doctrine in a message to Congress rather than in diplomatic communications to other capitals. Even so, he did not dramatize his message but rather embedded it in widely separated places in his message of December 2, 1823:

The "occasion has been judged proper for asserting . . . that the American continents, by the free and independent condition which they have assumed and maintain, *are henceforth not to be considered as subjects for future colonization by any European powers.* . . .

"We owe it . . . to candor and to the amicable relations existing between the United States and those powers to declare that *we should consider any attempt on their part to extend their system to any portion of this hemisphere as dangerous to our peace and safety.* With the *existing* colonies or dependencies of any European power we have not interfered and *shall not interfere. . . .*

"Our policy in regard to Europe, which was adopted at an early stage of the wars which have so long agitated that quarter of the globe, nevertheless remains the same, which is, *not to interfere in the internal concerns of any of its powers. . . .*"

Monroe's doctrine hardly fell as a bombshell on Capitol Hill, but there was widespread satisfaction with it inside Congress and among the press and public outside. British and European conservatives generally were outraged. "Blustering"—"arrogant"—"monstrous"—were some of the words used. It merited only "the most profound contempt," according to the tsarist government. Chancellor Metternich dismissed it as "indecent." Liberal Europe was pleased. The aged Lafayette congratulated Monroe on his "manly message" and his bold stand against the "Hellish Alliance." Across the South Atlantic, Latin Americans, including the great Bolívar himself, generally applauded Monroe. But they were not sure just what he meant, or just how the United States would carry it out. Would European imperialism simply be replaced by North American?

Or would both be replaced by an ascendant capitalism? After the dislocations of the Napoleonic wars and the postwar readjustments, the 1820s were bringing an enormous expansion of trade and manufacture in both the United States and Britain. Fundamental to Canning's desire for Anglo-American political cooperation was his awareness of the need of British manufacturing interests for access to the growing American market. Free trade pressure in Britain was bursting the bonds of the old mercantilist system. Why quarrel with a huge source of customers? It was this need for commercial reciprocity with Washington that explains London's refusal to respond aggressively to Monroe's dictum. The United States in turn needed good trade relations with Britain because of the markets it controlled—and the great navy London could deploy along the trade routes of the world. And Washington's interest in the new nations of Latin America was a commercial as well as a political and moral one.

In due course, Monroe's dictum would be sanctified and converted into the Monroe Doctrine. Some Americans had reservations. The message was flamboyantly unilateral. Having cold-shouldered Canning, the President was not inviting any other nation to share the burden of preventing the hemisphere from being further tainted by Europe. No consultations were held with Latin American governments. Indeed, the doctrine called for self-restraint on the part of the United States, but in Europe, not in Latin America; presumably the *yanqui* could intervene to the south as much as he wished. Efforts by some Latin American representatives to convert the doctrine into a defensive alliance for American security were rebuffed in Washington. Facing Europe, the doctrine was isolationist; facing south, it could be deeply interventionist, allowing Washington to act against European intervention—and Latin American revolutions?—at will. It became apparent later that the Holy Allies lacked the means, and perhaps even the necessary will, to intervene effectively against Latin American revolutionaries.

In many ways the doctrine was simply a reassertion of old policies, such as Washington's warning against "entangling alliances," and the No-Transfer principle, which had forbidden the transfer, by one European power to another, of any possession in the New World. Yet it embraced new and even revolutionary potentials, both generous and ominous, especially in a revolutionary age, for it contained the seeds of future pan-Americanism and the recognition of the rights of revolutionaries. Much would depend on Washington's interpretation, evolution, application, and enforcement of the doctrine. None could foretell all this, but it might at least have been possible for a Latin American critic to say in the 1820s what Salvador de Madariaga wrote in 1962: "I conclude that the Monroe Doctrine is not a doctrine but a dogma . . . not one dogma but two, to wit: the dogma of the infallibility of the American President and the dogma of the immaculate conception of American foreign policy."

John Quincy Adams, of course, would have agreed with neither proposition. For him, foreign policy emerged not out of pure, ethical considerations, but out of the most hardheaded analysis of a nation's true self-interest. And foreign policy making was not merely a presidential effort, but the product of intensive discussion and collaboration among cabinet members, congressmen, and diplomats—the product of collective leadership.

Even these precepts, however, were not enough to define the American way of peace in the 1820s. The founders of the American republic during the half century after the start of the Revolution had shouldered the double burden of organizing the constitutional foundations of a lasting republic and of developing a strategy for protecting the existence and future expansion of that republic in a predatory world. The first effort resulted in a written constitution, the second in a series of precedents, actions, laws, speeches, understandings, and diplomatic notes. By the 1820s these constituted a body of thought and action embracing the principles and practices of sovereign independence to protect the liberties of free peoples, abstention from the everyday alliances and collisions of European affairs, freedom of commerce and navigation on the high seas, self-determination of peoples, especially in Latin America, and non-intervention and other ideas contained in Monroe's dictum. But leaders of American opinion—teachers, theologians, ministers, scholars, editorialists, assorted reformers and humanitarians, including some men in government—believed also in certain moral precepts, such as international arbitration, pan-Americanism, globalism, anti-imperialism, suppression of the international trade in slaves, and, above all, aid to people seeking liberation from tyranny.

The political dilemma for American policy makers was not in choosing between a hardheaded, "practical" strategy and a moralistic or idealistic one; it was all too easy for them to pursue policies of narrow national self-interest and clothe them in the rhetoric of benevolence and altruism, as Western leaders had done for centuries. Rather, the dilemma lay in how to follow narrow policies of self-protection when large sections of public opinion wanted not only to protect their nation but also to help other peoples—especially people apparently struggling for liberty—mainly out of altruism but also on the theory that in the long run such help might serve their own nation's paramount interests. Jefferson was the very model of a President who spoke in moral terms, but he *acted* often on the basis of the most *Realpolitik* if not ruthless conception of national self-interest. Alexander Hamilton won an early and deserved reputation as a theorist and practitioner of *Realpolitik,* but even Hamilton had to allow for consideration of Americans' values. Thus, in rebutting those who wanted to help revolutionary France against England because they felt that America should be faithful to treaty obligations, grateful to a country that had helped Americans gain independence, and helpful to French republicans and revolutionaries, Hamilton argued that nations help other nations mainly out of self-interest, that the rule of morality between nations was different from that between individuals, that nations should indulge the "emotions of generosity and benevolence" only within strict bounds. But even Hamilton had to grapple with the issue of "how far *regard to the cause of Liberty* ought to induce the United States to take part with France in the present war"—which he did by questioning whether the cause of France was truly the cause of liberty, and whether the liberty of Americans would truly be at stake in the event of the fall of France. Thus, the issue was not the value of national safety versus the value of liberty, but establishing priorities, institutions, mechanisms, and rationales in serving both the value of safety and the value of liberty.

It was the genius of John Quincy Adams, and to a lesser extent James Monroe, to know just where they stood on this issue. Adams' great accomplishment lay not so much in shaping the essentials of what would become known as the Monroe Doctrine, for those essentials grew out of earlier American doctrine and practice, but in drawing the line between protecting the immediate national interest and intervening, if only rhetorically, in European affairs in defense of Greek, Spanish, and Italian rebels and liberationists. In Adams, as Hans Morgenthau later wrote, we are "in the presence of a statesman who had been reared in the realist tradition of the first period of American foreign policy, who had done the better part of his work of statecraft in an atmosphere saturated with Jeffersonian principles, and who had achieved the merger of these two elements of his experience into a harmonious whole."

Still, Adams could resolve the apparent dilemma of realism versus moralism in part because he had a somewhat shrunken and attenuated concept of liberty; as Morgenthau said, between his "moral principles and the traditional interest of the United States there was hardly ever a conflict." How would the American way of peace fare when men in power had a more generous view of the necessary dimensions of liberty, when continental and global expansion would bring the nation into closer involvement with the self-interest of other nations and the wants and needs and aspirations of other peoples, when the nation's self-interest and self-esteem would become—not least in the eyes of leaders including Adams himself—entangled with the burning issue of the slave trade, and when many Americans sought, even under new conditions, to return to the "old" Virginians' ample view of America as primarily the vineyard of liberty, as a decisive experiment for mankind?

VIRGINIANS: THE LAST OF THE GENTLEMEN POLITICIANS

James Monroe's own venture in a government of harmony, far above the din of party combat, ended badly. Not only did the Republican party dissolve into numberless factions fiercely contending for power and pelf in the presidential elections of 1824; Monroe could not even keep the peace in his own official family. During his last weeks in office he had a visit from Treasury Secretary Crawford. Long ailing, and now bitter over his frustrated presidential hopes, the Georgian pressed Monroe hard over some customs officials Crawford wanted appointed in northern ports. Why was the President procrastinating? he demanded. When Monroe explained that members of Congress had asked for a delay in order to supply some information, Crawford erupted in accusations of presidential dilly-dallying and indecisiveness. The President heatedly demanded that Crawford treat him with respect. Crawford raised his cane as if to strike the President, crying out, "You damned infernal old scoundrel!"

Monroe seized tongs from the fireplace, holding Crawford at bay and threatening to have him turned out. The Secretary suddenly backed down, made his apologies, and departed. The two left office on March 4, 1825, without having spoken to each other again.

Evidently his Virginia birth had not made Crawford into a Virginia gentleman, but in any event the Virginia presidential dynasty ended that March day when Monroe left office. A few months later the pilgrimage to Monticello of General Lafayette, the Guest of the Nation, brought a final and poignant rallying of the dynasty. Jefferson and Madison were there. Never having really retired, both had been feverishly involved in collecting a small but illustrious faculty for the new university in Charlottesville. Planning the architecture and pedagogy of the university had given Jefferson a brief golden autumn in his life. "He is now eighty-two years old, very little altered from what he was ten years ago, very active, lively, and happy, riding from ten to fifteen miles every day, and talking without the least restraint, very pleasantly, upon all subjects," wrote a visitor, a young Harvard professor. Jefferson had become much feebler a few months later when he greeted Lafayette, Madison, and Monroe at Monticello, in the stifling Virginia heat of August, but the talk of American and French life and politics ran until late at night.

Perhaps the three Virginia ex-Presidents sensed that this was the last time they would meet, but they could hardly have known that the Virginia dynasty was at an end. For half a century or more, the Old Dominion had supplied cadre after cadre of luminous national leadership—from the earlier generation of Washington, George Mason, Patrick Henry, George Wythe to the last one of James Monroe and his contemporaries. During that half century the commonwealth had incubated not only four Presidents for a total of thirty-two years, and a Chief Justice who would last thirty years, but a host of secondary leaders—cabinet members, congressional luminaries, diplomats, scientists, generals, explorers, judges, political theorists, envoys—who expressed, politically and intellectually and culturally, the collective genius of Virginia both in the commonwealth and in the country. And undergirding this elite were, as Richard Beale Davis found, "at least several hundred" persons who developed "the political mind through which Virginia made herself felt."

Suddenly this rich vein of creative genius came to an end. Never since, during the past century and a half and more, has a Virginia leader been elected President. Men from other states made up the new cadres of governance. How explain the Old Dominion's sunburst of leadership during the nation's founding years?

Intellectual leadership may flourish in cultures where at least a few persons enjoy enough leisure and enough security from economic harassment to allow the fruitful reading, conversing, corresponding, writing, and reflecting necessary for disciplined and creative thought. The plantation life of Virginia provided such a culture for the masters. Neither the long trips by horseback or jolting carriage nor the slowness of the post stopped the elite from exchanging ideas by mail or in meetings, or from striking sparks off one another. Intellectual leadership in Virginia was a collective enterprise. Not only the Jeffersons and Madisons but the run-of-the-plantation Virginia gentlemen took pains to be well educated and informed. Robert Carter III subscribed to British and American journals and built a library of 1,500 volumes, ranging in subject from music to religion to politics; he read avidly and lent his books to his friends. John Bernard, visiting the young republic in 1797, had found men "leading secluded lives in the woods of Virginia perfectly *au fait* as to the literary, dramatic, and personal gossip of London and Paris." Wrote one planter to an English friend, better "never born than ill bred."

The country lives of these gentlemen embraced a "curious contradiction," as Louis Morton observed. Carter and his friends thoroughly enjoyed the rich offerings of Virginia's rural life—hunting, racing, fishing, riding, drinking, gambling, cockfighting. But Carter's Nomini Hall overflowed with the sounds of learned discussions and lively music, of polite socializing and stately dancing. There was a deeper contradiction. The sons of the Virginia elite grew up in gracious homes, accustomed to the services of slaves and to the finest imports: Irish and Scotch linens, Madeira wine, German beer, French silks, shoes, and hats. But tobacco, the underpinning of much of this wealth, was notoriously unstable in price and unpredictable in yield. Some planters relied on their Scottish stewards— "factors"—to handle their business affairs, but many others employed their own intellectual resources to meet the challenge. Tales of Jefferson's scientific farming are commonplace—but Jefferson himself regarded Madison as Virginia's best farmer. Robert Carter devoted long months to personal supervision of his sprawling estates, as did John Randolph, one of the few planters ever to clear himself of debt.

Perhaps the contradiction itself—the interest in intellectual pursuits and the need to master prosaic business matters—helps explain the full flowering of the cultural life and the political genius of the Virginia elites. The conflict between the two ways of life helped produce a brilliant hybrid, enabling the scientific minds and philosophical pens of Randolphs and Jeffersons and a host of less-known men to turn out treatises on animal husbandry and crop rotation, as well as on literature, government, and public affairs.

It took powerful feelings of duty, moral and religious responsibility, and self-efficacy and purposefulness to draw youths away from the diverse and diverting life style of the Old Dominion. Here their education often played a key role. These Virginians, said Henry Adams in an unusual tribute from the hub of the intellectual universe, "were inferior to no class of Americans in the sort of education then supposed to make refinement. . . . Those whom Liancourt called 'men of the first class' were equal to any standard of excellence known to history." Colonial gentlemen believed in rigorously educating their sons in mathematics, classics, modern languages, perhaps some history and philosophy. The Virginia scion was favored with much individual attention; it was common, Edmund S. Morgan observed, for students to be educated up to the level of their particular needs and abilities. Sometimes planters would send their sons to small private schools—there were no public ones. Others would hire a young tutor to live in, sharing the family's meals and social activities, and occupying an ambiguous position between social equal and mere employee. Some sons went abroad to study at Cambridge or Oxford; more often they went off to Harvard or Yale or Princeton, or to William and Mary, which gave its students considerable choice in their plan of study and rightfully boasted of its diverse and brilliant faculty. In the South as in the North, women had little share in such educational opportunity.

Perhaps the best school for young Virginians was the commonwealth itself. If great leadership emerges out of pervasive social and political conflict, Virginia was an ideal breeding ground for future Presidents and congressmen. Fierce battles had raged between burgesses and royal governors over local autonomy, but the conflict dividing most Virginians most sharply during the late eighteenth century was the status of the Anglican establishment and, after it was disestablished, that of its successor, the Protestant Episcopal Church. Following years of struggle and frustration the dissenters managed to get lands given to the Episcopalians reclaimed —others said confiscated—by the state. But the dissenters were by no means united, except against the common "Anglican" enemy. Old-line Presbyterians, Methodists, and Baptists genteelly proselytized unbelievers and competed for constituents. New-Light Presbyterians and Separate Baptists, opposing the "establishments" in their own denominations, ranged the valleys seeking to restore Christians to the literal reading of the Bible. Regional conflicts—especially between piedmont and tidewater— variously sharpened and cut cross the religious ones. Polemical and partisan newspapers amplified these and other voices of dissent. And a generation after the War of Independence echoes of the fierce Revolutionary disputes in Virginia had not wholly died away.

Exposed to an environment of conflict, these proud, educated, opinionated, and articulate men did not fit easily into two political and intellectual camps called Republican and Federalist. They divided, intersected, and overlapped to the degree that almost every Virginian politician-intellectual made up a party of one. But a rough four-party pattern emerged out of the bi-factional divisions within each party. The followers of Jefferson and Madison and Monroe dominated Republican politics and maintained a powerful base there for half a century, but this presidential and congressional leadership, modifying its ancient principles to meet day-to-day exigencies, faced mounting opposition from the "pure" Republicans headed by John Randolph, John Taylor, William Branch Giles, and many others. They felt pure because they had stuck to the ancient faith of minimal government as *the* means of protecting liberty, of strict construction of the Constitution, of states' rights, of legislative supremacy over both executive and judicial branches and state militias over standing armies, all embedded in agrarianism as a way of life and anti-mercantilism as a way of thought. The Republican establishment in Virginia often feared the polemics of these adversaries, variously called the old Republicans, radicals, or the Quids or Tertium Quids, more than that of the Federalists.

Leader of the Quids was one of the most extraordinary figures in American politics, John Randolph of Roanoke. Having survived at nineteen a mysterious illness that left him impotent and beardless, with a rich soprano voice, he seemed to compensate with clothes of Revolutionary buff and blue, his superb aplomb as he swaggered through the halls of Congress booted and spurred and whip in hand, and above all his devastating oratory. "For hours on end his shrill but flute-like voice irritated and fascinated," Dumas Malone wrote, "pouring upon his audience shafts of biting wit, literary allusions, epigrams, parables, and figures of speech redolent of the countryside." His meteoric rise in the House of Representatives had been matched by a hard fall, as he turned against the Jefferson circle and later lost his seat to Jefferson's nephew, John W. Eppes. Randolph was a man of contradictions: scion of a great aristocratic family but dwelling in a rather shabby house, possessor of several hundred slaves on 8,000 acres but knowing in his heart that slavery was wrong, yearning for the land and home he loved but often lonely and miserable there, and sodden with drink. But on one matter Randolph was consistent: he took and clung to the most extreme view of liberty as personal independence and autonomy, as a jewel to be protected against power and corruption and the temptations of office, as a sacred right to be free of "all encroachment, State or Federal . . ." He summed up his philosophy in six words: "I love liberty, I hate equality."

At the opposite end of the Virginia spectrum sat John Marshall, in the middle of the high bench. During the years after *Marbury* the Chief Justice assumed just the judicial posture that his Federalist mentors would have hoped for. Where Randolph virtually equated liberty with states' rights, Marshall took a broadly expansive view of national power. In a long series of decisions he led the court to a broad construction of the Constitution. In *M'Culloch* v. *Maryland* in 1819, he not only struck down a Maryland law that taxed the Baltimore branch of the Second United States Bank; he proclaimed that the powers of the national government were derived from the people and were directly exercised on them, that the powers of the national government were supreme within the orbit assigned to it, and opined—echoing Hamilton years earlier—"Let the end be legitimate, let it be within the scope of the constitution, and all means which are appropriate, which are plainly adapted to that end, which are not prohibited, but consist with the letter and spirit of the constitution, are constitutional." In *Gibbons* v. *Ogden* five years later, Marshall and his court voided a monopoly granted by New York for operation of steamboats between New York and New Jersey and broadly interpreted the nature and scope of congressional power under the commerce clause. That power, he said, "does not stop at the jurisdictional lines of the several states." For Randolph and his fellow Quids the worst of it was that, while they had to throw themselves on the mercy of the voters every two years or so, John Marshall sat there blandly issuing these nationalistic decisions—and could do so for life.

On the whirling merry-go-round of American politics, sometimes a congressman could strike back at a President, only to be countered in turn by a Chief Justice. Such was the case with Randolph, Marshall, and Jefferson in the seamy affair of the Yazoo land fraud. In 1796 the Georgia legislature had revoked a grant of 35 million acres in its unorganized western territories along the Yazoo River, charging that the land companies receiving the land had bribed legislators into voting for it. After Georgia ceded the territories to the federal government, the Yazoo claims fell to President Jefferson and Secretary of State Madison. The two Virginians preferred to settle with the politically powerful New England land companies that had bought the disputed titles; in the House, however, John Randolph rose in his wrath. Denouncing the pro-Yazooists as "unblushing advocates of unblushing corruption"—and privately relishing the slap he administered to Madison and, indirectly, to Jefferson—Randolph stopped bills to compensate the claimants in three sessions of Congress.

In desperation, the Yazooists turned to the third branch of the government. One of the claimants brought against another a suit so contrived as to test all the questions involved in Georgia's repeal of the grant. A stellar lineup of Federalists argued this case of *Fletcher* v. *Peck* before the high Federalist Chief Justice Marshall. John Quincy Adams, Robert Goodloe

Harper, and Joseph Story presented the Yazooist arguments; Luther Martin, tacitly in sympathy with his opponents, made a weak case for Georgia —and was so drunk, to boot, that the court had to be adjourned until he sobered up. But for all the atmosphere of contrivance and force, John Marshall handed down a marble-sheathed decision. The land grants were contracts between Georgia and the land companies, he ruled, and the legislature had reneged on its part of the bargain. As a "member of the American Union," Georgia was bound by Article I, section 10, of the Constitution, which forbids the passage of laws impairing the right of contract. Georgia could not legally rescind the grants once they were made; the federal government would have to compensate the claimants. Defeated, Randolph could only rage—while Marshall, in ruling that states were bound by the contract clause of the national Constitution, erected another pillar of federal power in the temple of American law.

Standing at the extremes of Virginia's political and ideological continuum, Randolph and Marshall had only small followings of their own. The tiny faction of disaffected men around Randolph shrank to an impotent remnant after their brief threat to party unity. John Marshall towered over his Federalist colleagues, who were successful mainly at winning minor offices when they won them at all. Far more potent in day-to-day Virginia politics were Jefferson and Madison's combined followings, and the "Richmond Junto," numbering such state and local leaders as William Wirt, Spencer Roane, Cary Nicholas, and Thomas Ritchie of the influential Richmond *Enquirer*. But the powerful appeals of Marshall and Randolph lived on far beyond them, and for generations constituted the heart of the debate about state versus national power.

*   *   *

The Virginia planter-politicians—much more than the activists in any other state—had taken a clear lead nationally in conceiving, framing, establishing, and inaugurating a radically new political system. They had tried an experiment in popular self-government, in "government by the people," in republicanism—an experiment that inevitably turned into a series of particular experiments as new leaders took command in legislature, executive, and judiciary, and at various levels of governments. George Washington's experiment in magisterial, consensual government, combined with executive leadership by an activist Cabinet, had been followed by John Adams' venture in a government of presidential initiatives balanced by a gathering party opposition. Jefferson's experiment in combined executive, legislative, and party leadership had given way to Madison's frustrating experience with governmental and political checks and balances—an experience he had anticipated in his *Federalist* papers. Monroe had tried a strategy of subordinating party spirit, only to be swallowed up in the bitter politics of a divisive factionalism. The states had been trying out new constitutions of their own.

Convinced that scientific inquiry could be applied to politics just as much as to physics or astronomy, political leaders in Virginia and other states closely monitored the governmental experiments taking place in the numerous laboratories of American politics. After fifty years of experience with revolution and revolutionary governments, including a period of weak national government and then the adoption and implementation of a new federal Constitution and a dozen or so state constitutions, the time might have seemed appropriate for an assessment of this experience. Indeed, such a reassessment might have been deemed urgent because, on the eve of the nation's fiftieth birthday, constitutional and political questions of profound importance remained unresolved.

The most obvious of these questions was the central one around which the convention of 1787 had revolved—state versus federal power. On several occasions powerful regional groups—most notably Virginians and Kentuckians in 1798 and waterside Yankees in 1814–15—had challenged federal authority in a dramatic, even menacing fashion, but the political issues had been mediated by moderate men without any resolution of the burning question of whether states could ultimately challenge the moral and constitutional authority of the central government. The Constitution had proved flexible enough to accommodate some broadening of federal power—as in the establishment of a national bank—at least as the Supreme Court had interpreted that charter. But the actual division between federal and state power remained clouded. Few doubted that the usual economic and sectional issues would continue to be worked out by the ordinary processes of bargain and compromise. But what if issues of unusual intensity arose, requiring extraordinary leadership and decision? Already South Carolinians were beginning to be restive enough about past and prospective tariff policy to question federal authority and even to raise the specter of secession and disunion. A few warned that slavery itself might become such an issue.

The other key question that the Framers had faced in 1787—the distribution of power among separated departments of government—was in an equivalent state of indeterminacy after fifty years of experience. Once again the Constitution had shown itself marvelously adaptable to the shifting patterns of congressional and executive influence and interaction, from the executive leadership of Washington and Adams to the party leadership of Jefferson and Madison and the non-party rule of Monroe.

Certain constitutional provisions had been defined enough and agreed on enough to be foreclosed—for example, the absolute veto of the House and Senate over each other, and the power of the Supreme Court to invalidate congressional enactments signed by the President, as well as state legislation deemed unconstitutional.

But crucial questions remained open. The President's veto power had hardly been used; was this to remain a weapon-in-waiting, to be employed only when the President's own constitutional authority was threatened? The Supreme Court had long ago in *Marbury* vetoed an act of Congress and had got away with establishing this mighty precedent because the vetoed act gave minor power *to* the court; what would happen if the Supreme Court voided a major congressional act closely touching intensely flammable regional, economic, social, or political interests? Grave issues of checks and balances, moreover, often interacted closely with issues of states' rights. What would happen, for example, if the power and prerogatives of a branch of the federal government, such as the Senate, were closely attached to the pride and interest of a major region?

Such issues had mainly been ignored. If the immediate reason for this evasion was political—the ability of politicians to defuse potentially explosive moral and constitutional issues by converting them into political and legal issues amenable to brokerage—the deeper reason was intellectual. The heirs of the 1820s to the creative political and constitutional leaders of the 1770s and 1780s were failing to live up to the intellectual vision of the founding fathers.

The main failure lay in the Jeffersonians' reluctance to exploit the experience in actually running a republican government, in reassessing the theoretical and practical problem that had occupied them in framing the 1787 Constitution. That problem was the prevention of tyranny on the part of the rulers from within government and on the part of the people outside. "The accumulation of all powers, legislative, executive, and judiciary, in the same hands, whether of one, a few, or many, and whether hereditary, self-appointed, or elective," Madison had written in *Federalist* 47, "may justly be pronounced the very definition of tyranny." He saw each problem as having a solution. Tyranny within the government could be curbed through putting pieces of governmental power—legislative, executive, and judicial—into separate hands: into Congress, the presidency, and the courts. Tyranny from outside the government—from aroused popular minorities or majorities—could be blocked by the social checks and balances resulting from "extending the republic" to cover a multiplicity of interests.

Under Jefferson the Republicans themselves had run an experiment that might well have resolved Madisonian fears of government and majority tyranny. For six years Jefferson had largely held legislative and executive leadership in his own hands; for six years a rough, inchoate popular majority had governed itself through that leadership. The constitutional heavens had not fallen; Jefferson, Madison & Co. had not indulged in tyranny within the government, nor had the popular majority used its control of government to suppress the liberty of minorities or individuals. John Adams' Alien and Sedition Acts were indeed a reminder that no government, even with checks and balances, was wholly safe. But the main lesson of the first fifty years was that government in an authentic republic need *not* be tyrannical. Pennsylvanians had even tried in their state an experiment in popular rule unbridled by checks and balances, with no apparent danger to their lives or fortunes.

The main lesson of those years, on the contrary, was quite different—that government could not long continue to be unresponsive to the basic needs of the great number of people—of white males, even aside from women, slaves, Indians, and the poor. But the thinkers of Virginia and other enlightened states could not see this because of their narrow and negative definition of liberty, and here lay the real—the ultimately *moral*—failure of the Virginians. American thinkers were still imprisoned in the old Lockean conception of liberty as an individual "natural right" to be protected against government—that is, against collective action by fellow human beings—rather than as an opportunity for mutual help in self-enhancement and self-fulfillment. The tragedy of the Virginians was that in their treatment of black people—and to a lesser extent white women—they violated even their own narrow conception of liberty.

The intellectual leadership cadre of the 1820s took an equally stunted view of the other great moral value of the era, equality, affirming abstractly the equal rights of all Americans, except slaves and perhaps women, to liberty and property without grappling with the questions of how, concretely, institutions could be devised in a republic, and measures passed, to help persons realize genuine social and economic and psychological equality, without putting undue strain on the republic. Expecting the second generation of thinkers to solve such problems, which still largely elude us today, would, of course, be unrealistic; but it was precisely the genius of the earlier generation of thinkers at least in conceptualizing moral and constitutional issues, and in shaping institutions to try to deal with such issues, that marked the difference between the 1780s and the 1820s.

If Virginia had led that earlier generation, it seemed most impoverished by the time of the second. Perhaps the end of the dynasty of the thinking gentlemen politicians of Virginia reflected underlying social and economic changes—the decline of the tobacco economy, the failure of Virginia to develop economically compared with the other middle states, the drift of potential leaders over the mountains to the West. Or perhaps that decline had long been fated. The incandescent glow of the Virginians had always been shadowed by their defense of the persisting system of social deference and hierarchy, the genteel subordination of women, the unavailability of schooling for great numbers of black and white children, and above all the blight of slavery. In these subordinate ranks lay concealed much of the potential social and moral and political grass-roots leadership of the Virginia of the next generation but that potential was left immobilized, and never to be realized, on the blind side of the leaders of the Old Dominion.

THE CHECKING AND BALANCING OF JOHN QUINCY ADAMS

It had been clear for months, even years, that 1824 would bring no ordinary election. Monroe's campaign effort in the previous presidential election had been such a tepid enterprise—fewer than 1 percent of the whites in his own state of Virginia bothered to go to the polls—that even at that time politicians were less excited by the current "race" than by the battle royal in prospect four years hence. The one elector who had voted against Monroe in 1820—William Plumer, of New Hampshire—had cast his ballot for John Quincy Adams as a way of publicizing Adams' availability four years later. Monroe's administration was hardly under way when Adams and the congressional politicians were busy electioneering.

Eagerly the press looked forward to the battle of the titans. Treasury Secretary William H. Crawford, widely considered the heir to the Virginia dynasty even though he was a Georgian, seemed an early front-runner, but for just that reason he attracted opposition from his rivals. Secretary of State Adams had reason to feel that he had rights of succession by virtue of holding the office that Madison and Monroe had used as a springboard to the White House. A "worm preying upon the vitals of the Administration within its own body," was Adams' reasoned view of Crawford's role in the Monroe Cabinet. Henry Clay had quit the House of Representatives in order to concentrate on his lucrative law practice; he returned to the House in 1823, immediately won re-election as Speaker, and let his friends organize support for him in the states. As impressive as ever for his quick intelligence, compelling personality, and baffling combination of political daring and compromise, Clay calculated that he could win enough electoral votes to place among the top three candidates and then win election in Congress. John Calhoun was demonstrating, as Monroe's Secretary of War, that his executive skills matched his parliamentary talents. Still at this point a nationalist who favored protectionism and internal improvements, Calhoun hoped that his support in the North, however spotty, combined with southern backing, would at least gain him the magic circle of three. And Senator Andrew Jackson, an outsider temporarily inside, reckoned that his reputation as router of redcoats and redskins guaranteed him a personal popularity that could be converted into an electoral college majority.

None of these four men liked Adams, and the feeling was more than mutual. Adams feared his opponents too, to the point where he urged Monroe to give them diplomatic appointments that would take them out of the country—Clay to Colombia (or Chile, or Argentina), Jackson to Mexico, and De Witt Clinton, another possible rival, to wherever. All declined.

Soon the election race became a surly free-for-all, a far-flung game of King of the Rock—and a strident and ironic cacophony during the "era of good feelings." Candidates' followers spread spiteful whispers about their opponents. No candidate or party put out a program, or saw the need to. Every candidate ran on his record, though most voters were hardly aware of that record, save in the case of Adams and perhaps Clay. Each candidate organized, or at least attracted, a personal following that carried his message to state and local political leaders. Each candidate coped with the mélange of state or local party conventions, legislative caucuses, mass meetings, and of course the congressional caucus, and each argued for the special legitimacy of that portion of the electoral process that favored his own candidacy.

And that electoral process was slowly changing. The congressional caucus had come into increasing disrepute; those who took part usually had been elected at least two years earlier, and the states and districts not represented by a party in Congress perforce were not represented in its caucus. King Caucus was giving way to the mixed caucus, which did seek to be more representative, and then to party conventions designed to mirror the party constituency. And more and more persons were voting in party and state elections as the suffrage was slowly broadened.

Crawford fell victim to these changes when his supporters convened the congressional caucus and only sixty-six members showed up. Burdened also by ill health, Crawford slowly lost ground. Earlier, Calhoun had quit the presidential sweepstakes, and nimbly joined the vice-presidential, after he was beaten by Jackson forces in the Republican state convention in Harrisburg. The followers of Adams, Clay, and Jackson redoubled their efforts, especially in state legislative caucuses. Maintaining their posture of being above the battle, the candidates acted through their newspapers and circulars, committees of correspondence, and key state and party leaders to mobilize support. Soon it became evident that the more "popular" the selection process, the more evident was Jackson's grass-roots support. Rivermen, miners, farmers, and mechanics endorsed Jackson in a Harrisburg mass meeting and sent their "nomination" in a letter penned by a local barkeep. A schoolteacher wrote from Cincinnati: "Strange! Wild! Infatuated! All for Jackson! . . ." It was like the "influenza," and "I regard Mr. J. as the most independent of the southern gentry, one on whom they will be least likely to unite. . . ." If the influenza passed off soon, "the patients will vote coolly and dispassionately for the best man—Mr. Adams."

The combat between Clay and Jackson was especially intense. Both "Harry of the West" and the Hero of the West protected their state turfs while eyeing each other's. Jackson flared up when he heard that the governor of his own state of Tennessee was conniving with Clay. Conceding New England to Adams, the Speaker and the general fought for support in the middle states. Inevitably they were entangled in the local rivalries of politicians who were more intent on controlling state patronage than the national presidency. In the imperial politics of New York State, Martin Van Buren and other chieftains of the Regency led "Bucktails" against De Witt Clinton. The Regency supported Crawford, but as the Georgian's prospects declined, other candidates looked to the Empire State for support. Elsewhere the Republicans were even more fragmented, as followers mobilized around a congeries of state as well as presidential candidates. Federalists, with little to divide over, were hardly heard from; their party as an organization was defunct.

The electoral college results nicely mirrored the fragmentation of Republicanism: Jackson 99, Adams 84, Crawford 41, Clay 37. Jackson's popular vote of about 153,000 almost equaled the combined vote for Adams and Crawford. Adams won all of New England's electoral votes, most of New York's, and a surprising degree of support in the South. Jackson picked up Pennsylvania's solid block of 28 votes, plus an expected good share of the South. Crawford drew his strength mainly from the South, including Virginia, and Clay from the West. Once again the faulty presidential electoral system was to bedevil American politics, as the election was thrown into Congress, where each delegation, whether as large as New York's (36) or as small as Illinois' or Delaware's (3), had the same single vote. And Henry Clay, the trailer in the electoral college, looked like a winner in the Congress, for he could now do some shopping about.

And that is evidently what he did. "The friends of Jackson, Adams, and Crawford watched him in dismay as—gay, insouciant, and somehow menacing—he wandered from boardinghouse to boardinghouse, from banquet to banquet, not a candidate but a kingmaker," according to George Dangerfield. But Adams, if less mobile, was no less political. He neglected not a single opportunity to win over a state to his support, Bemis concludes. Jackson's and Crawford's supporters were also on the move. Who would make the winning deal with whom? In mid-December, Robert P. Letcher, a Kentucky congressman and intimate friend of Clay, had several talks with Adams. Long used to such negotiations, the Secretary of State offered some conciliatory remarks about the Speaker. But what Clay's friends wanted to know was whether Adams would assure Clay of a central role in his administration. Adams gave the necessary assurances. Later he and Clay met for hours and talked about the future, on the premise of those assurances. Clay was satisfied.

No outright deal was made. No definite promise was given or contract signed. The two men traded in the soft currency of subtle implications and raised expectations, knowing that this currency was backed up by the hard political cash of agreed-on perceptions of shared interests. The effect on Clay's thinking was magical. Having written to one friend on December 13, 1824, that he was not sure whether he would swing his support to Jackson or Adams—"And what an alternative that is!"—Clay was writing on December 28 to another friend that he had definitely decided for Adams.

"What I would ask," Clay wrote, "should be the distinguishing characteristic of an American statesman? Should it not be a devotion to civil liberty?" He could not, he added, on principle support a military man.

On February 9, 1825, the House of Representatives, voting by states, elected John Quincy Adams President of the United States. He had done his work well. He won not only Clay's three states (in the electoral college) of Kentucky, Ohio, and Missouri, but also Jackson's states of Louisiana, Maryland, and Illinois. He won New York too when the longtime Federalist Stephen Van Rensselaer cast the delegation's decisive vote either because Adams had promised him understanding treatment of Federalists, through the mediation of Daniel Webster, or because, as Van Rensselaer said later, he bowed his head in prayer when his turn came to vote and saw an Adams ballot on the floor.

Said John Randolph: "It was impossible to win the game, gentlemen; the cards were packed."

Within two days President-elect Adams offered Clay the Secretaryship of State. "So you see," Andrew Jackson wrote, "the *Judas* of the West has closed the contract and will receive the thirty pieces of silver."

Far north, the town of Quincy still awaited the election news. When the patriarch John Adams was awakened with a horseman's report, his heart swelled with pride. He was sad only that Abigail had not lived to see her firstborn become "guardian of his country's laws and liberties." The father seemed far happier than the son. When Daniel Webster came to Adams' F Street house and formally notified him of his election, it was said that Adams stood shaking, sweat pouring down his face, as if considering the specter of all the un-Adams-like deals and compromises he had made to get to the top of the greasy pole.

*   *   *

Well might Adams shake and sweat. Rarely has the character of a presidential election had such a direct impact on the presidency that followed —and perhaps on the President himself—as that of 1824.

His hopes and goals he deeply felt. Rising above party and faction, he would serve as the steward of the people in an effort to enact and administer a program carefully designed to bring economic progress and political and social unity to the nation. His goals were founded squarely on his moral and political principle of personal liberty and property to be protected not merely from government but through government. This government would include the federal government, which Adams did not fear and which he liked to term the National government, always with a capital *N.* Echoing some of Hamilton's ideas, his program was an extension of Monroe's and Clay's—internal improvements, wise use of federal lands in order to pay for those improvements, the fostering of science and education, "cautious" tariff protection of industry as a means of safeguarding the nation's independence. After winning the reluctant support of his Cabinet for this program, the President wrote in his diary that the "perilous experiment must be made."

Perilous it was, largely because Adams lacked the political resources for a positive program. Amid heavy pressures from all sides he tried to create a broad-based Cabinet, but Gallatin would not return to Treasury because he preferred State, Jackson would not accept the War Department, and the new Vice-President, John Calhoun, attacked the new Cabinet as not sufficiently representing the South. Highly dependent on congressional support, Adams was pleased that his supporter John W. Taylor of New York was elected Speaker to succeed Clay, but in the Senate Calhoun gained influence over key committees and busied himself jockeying for a future Calhoun presidency rather than the existing Adams administration. Then, at mid-term, Taylor lost the Speakership to Andrew Stevenson, a Virginian unfriendly to the President. A negative and ungainly leadership coalition of Calhoun, Van Buren, Jackson, and others, united only by their distaste for Adams and eagerness to succeed him, dominated Washington's politics.

It soon became apparent that Adams had only the intentions of a good steward, not the qualities of a great leader. He was, for one thing, a true son of Puritan Boston—and of John Adams—when it came to political pleasantries. It was hard to make conversation with him as he presided at a White House dinner, and he had a genius for putting politicians off—and his foot in his mouth—on his brief trips into the country. He was inept at communicating his hopes and proposals to Cabinet and Congress, much less the voting public. But his personal failings were the lesser problem. Like Monroe, he lacked the foundation of party leadership and followership that might have helped him at crucial moments, and Adams possessed neither the desire nor the means of strengthening his party. Indeed, he was so profoundly anti-party that he refused even to use patronage to strengthen his position. And he had not developed the personal backing of party leaders throughout the country—the kind of leaders that Madison and Jefferson had converted into a new and powerful political organization. Rather, a new party was forming against him. Adams was also defeated by his theory of government. He knew that leadership must be a collective enterprise, but he also believed in the constitutional checks and balances designed to thwart such leadership. Never a transforming leader, neither was he skillful as a transactional one.

All Adams' difficulties came to a head during the last two years of his term, in the congressional effort to enact tariff legislation. A moderate measure had been passed in the final year of Monroe's administration; now the protectionists were back, eager to boost levies on iron, hemp, flax, and other commodities. Meetings of wool growers and manufacturers in Harrisburg, Poughkeepsie, and elsewhere reflected rising protectionist feeling in the country. Adams was so apprehensive about tariffs—"Beware of Trap doors," he said of them to a son taking a seat in the Massachusetts legislature—that he gave his Secretary of the Treasury, Richard Rush, the job of defending them. But even the suspicious Adams could hardly anticipate what lay ahead. Van Buren and the group of Jacksonians who dominated the House Committee on Manufactures concocted a tariff bill full of provisions that favored the agrarian Northwest and Middle States, while giving short shrift to the manufacturing interests of New England. If Adams signed it, he would alienate the South and strain his own credibility, and if he vetoed it, he would antagonize both agrarian and manufacturing interests in the rest of the country. Either way, the crucial Middle States would be drawn into the Jacksonians' camp.

With shrewd bargaining by Van Buren, the bill passed Congress, as New Englanders like Webster salvaged what they could for industrial interests, and Adams signed the "abominated" tariff, though he knew full well that he was jeopardizing his southern support. He detested the squalid legislative deals that produced such a bill, but could he object to such cynical brokerage when he had made his own political deals to win the White House?

So the administration of the lofty John Quincy Adams came to an end in the wake of a wild free-for-all, a scramble for special advantages, a legislative battle whose main relevance to manufacture, as John Randolph said, was the "manufacture of a President of the United States." This "democratic" nationalism of popular interests was a far cry from Adams' planned, rational, centralized, collective, "economic" nationalism. "Nothing could be less in keeping with the custodial philosophy of President Adams," Dangerfield said, "or less adjusted to the centralizing system of Henry Clay" than the "Tariff of Abominations." Still, he signed it.

He signed it because, by early 1828, the tariff, and Adams' own political fortunes, had been swallowed up in the gathering battle over the presidency. He signed it, knowing that the South would denounce it to the point of murmuring about seceding. His "perilous experiment" of presidential stewardship and collective national effort had given way to the haphazard, competitive play of economic and sectional interests. And these interests in turn both reflected and generated powerful economic forces changing the face of America in the 1820s and 1830s—forces that one day would hold many a politician in their iron grip.

JUBILEE 1826: THE PASSING OF THE HEROES

"Ye shall hallow the fiftieth year, and proclaim liberty throughout the land to all the inhabitants thereof; it shall be a jubilee unto you." Americans were happy to obey the biblical admonition in celebrating the half century of the Declaration of Independence. As he entered his second year in office, John Quincy Adams had taken pleasure in plans for a celebration in Washington—and even more for a jubilee in Boston, to which his father would be invited. And it was hoped that another signer of the Declaration —indeed, the drafter of it—could journey from Monticello to the festivities in the nation's capital.

For John Adams and Thomas Jefferson still lived, the one in his ninety-first year, the other in his eighty-third. A few years earlier Jefferson had broken his arm and wrist in a fall at Monticello, and a stiffened hand combined with other ills of old age left him in severe pain for months on end, but he had recovered enough to ride several miles a day. Adams was failing. "I am certainly very near the end of my life," he wrote in January 1826. Whether death would simply mean the end, which he did not believe, or transit to life under a constitution of the Universe, "I contemplate it without terror or dismay."

Adams had shared these private thoughts with his old adversary. For fourteen years the two heroes of the Revolution had been writing each other in what turned out to be a magnificent correspondence. Before that the two men had been politically so estranged that it took the best diplomatic efforts of intermediaries to persuade each that the other wished to restore the friendship of Revolutionary days. The correspondence had started awkwardly when Adams wrote Jefferson that he was sending him separately a packet containing "two Pieces of Homespun," since the Virginian was a "Friend of American Manufactures." Jefferson responded with a long letter about the relative lack of machinery in Virginia, except for the "Spinning Jenny and loom with the flying shuttle" that could be managed in the family. When the "homespun" arrived, it turned out to be a copy of John Quincy Adams' lectures on "Rhetoric and Oratory" while he was a Harvard professor. Jefferson found them a "mine of learning and taste," he wrote the proud father.

From there the correspondence took off, ranging across religion, history, Indians, the essence of aristocracy, Napoleon's character, the influence of women, the perfectibility of human nature, and soaring into the realms of philosophy and theology. The two men refought old battles, straightening out history, each to his own satisfaction. Jefferson did not take sharp issue with Adams, however, and he was wise in this, for the latter was extremely defensive about his place in history. Years before, when Mercy Warren published her account of the Revolution, Adams had been outraged by her conclusion that his revolutionary principles had been corrupted by his long stay in London, and that he leaned toward monarchy and was inordinately proud and ambitious. Angry exchanges had followed for weeks, terminated only by the intervention of Elbridge Gerry and the exchange of loving letters and locks of hair. Adams still had the last word, observing to Gerry, "History is not the province of the ladies."

But now John Adams had mellowed, and he professed his affection for Jefferson even while debating him. There was much talk of family and friends—especially of old comrades dead or dying. Adams was inordinately proud of his numerous progeny, even though he granted that children have "cost us Grief, Anxiety, often Vexation and sometimes humiliation." Abigail Adams occasionally added a friendly line, until she died of typhoid fever in her seventy-fourth year. Words were in vain,

Jefferson wrote the inconsolable Adams, but they both could look forward to "an ecstatic meeting with the friends we have loved and lost and whom we shall still love and never lose again."

And so the two men, constantly professing their friendship, wept and sparred and totted up historical accounts together, Adams with his palsy hardly able to write, Jefferson laboriously penning his gracious but spirited letters. Nothing lay outside the play of their minds. Adams was still unyielding on matters of prime importance—and to him this included how governments were constituted. His experience with the Constitution had not changed his old views of the arrangement of powers. "Checks and Ballances, Jefferson, however you and your Party may have ridiculed them, are our only Security, for the progress of mind, as well as the Security of Body." There had always been party differences, Jefferson argued, and there always would be, for "every one takes his side in favor of the many, or of the few, according to his constitution, and the circumstances in which he is placed. . . ." Yes, replied Adams, it was precisely because parties had always existed and fought each other with ridicule and persecution that the Science of Government was the least advanced of all the sciences.

They argued briefly about the nature of liberty, but with no more acuteness or imagination than their fellow Americans. The principles of liberty were unalterable, Adams said. Then later he wondered, "Is liberty a word void of sense?" If it was, there could be no reward or punishment. Perhaps at "the bottom of the gulph of liberty and necessity" there might be the key to unlock the universe, but only God held the key. One thing was clear, though: without virtue there could be no political liberty. Jefferson was discreetly reserved on questions of liberty and equality, so enkindling were they to his friend.

The correspondence faltered as the Jubilee year neared. In June 1826 a committee of Bostonians waited on John Adams to invite his honored attendance at the celebration, but he was too weak to make the carriage ride. Instead, he wrote a letter in tribute to the Declaration of Independence, adding that despite man's folly and vanity he could see hope for improving the condition of the human race. Though Jefferson was eager to go to Washington, he knew he could not; he wrote that the Declaration would be "the signal of arousing men to burst the chains under which monkish ignorance and superstition had persuaded them to bind themselves, and to assume the blessings and security of self-government . . . the free right to the unbounded exercise of reason and freedom of opinion. . . ."

In Washington, on the Fourth of July 1826, President John Quincy Adams and Vice-President John Calhoun rode in their carriage amid a grand parade along Pennsylvania Avenue to the Capitol. There a Revolutionary War veteran read the noble words of the Declaration. A plea was made to subscribe money to keep Monticello from being put up for sale. In New York, Governor Clinton put on a feast of roast oxen and ale for ten thousand guests. Bostonians so crowded into Old South Church that they were "squeezed to a hot jelly," except in the galleries reserved for women. Philadelphia, where it had all happened, contented itself with a parade and a program in Independence Hall. In Charlottesville a student at the University of Virginia read the Declaration of Independence.

Its author was not there. On his hilltop nearby, he had awakened from a long sleep the night before to ask only, "This is the Fourth?" and he died around midday, as the celebrations were under way. About this time in Quincy, John Adams awoke as from a coma, muttered "Thomas Jefferson survives," and died before the setting of the sun.

CHAPTER 8

The Birth of the Machines

LOUNGERS on a lower Manhattan pier in the fall of 1792 might have noticed a well-dressed, elegantly spoken young man board a sailing vessel for Georgia. This was Eli Whitney. A Yankee tinkerer, inventor, and jack of all trades, Whitney had learned mechanical skills growing up on a Massachusetts farm. In this, his first trip South, he found himself in the company of Catherine Greene, the young widow of the Revolutionary War general Nathanael Greene. She was traveling to her rice plantation, Mulberry Grove, twelve miles outside of Savannah, Georgia, while Whitney was drifting into his first job as a tutor to children on a neighboring plantation. Reserved, serious, churchgoing, young Whitney was dazzled on the long trip by the flirtatious Mrs. Greene; when she invited him to visit Mulberry Grove, he accepted. Her world of carefree parties and gay entertainments was beyond his understanding and experience. The "moral world," he said, "does not extend so far south."

He heard serious discussion of only one topic from the planters who gathered at Mulberry Grove to sip port and Madeira: their need for a machine to clean the seeds from short-staple inland cotton. Whitney determined to meet this need. Planters were seeking a staple to lift agriculture out of depression. The main crop south of the Mason-Dixon Line in 1800, tobacco, had brought low prices on the international market for a decade and was exhausting the soil. Rice and indigo sales were realizing only small profits, thus threatening the large capital investments in slaves in the rice districts of Georgia and South Carolina and the tidewater of Virginia and Maryland. With an almost static population, the South was attracting few new settlers from the North or from overseas. Most farmers worked their small subsistence farms of from 100 to 300 acres with their families as the only labor. Planter and small farmer alike were looking for a cash crop to reap larger profits.

Eli Whitney had never seen a cotton boll. When he examined one, he found the fiber intertwined with seeds covered "with a kind of green coat resembling velvet." Whitney later wrote his father that he "involuntarily happened to be thinking on the subject and struck out a plan of a Machine in my mind." Spurning an offer of 100 guineas for his "little model," he decided to quit school and perfect an engine to clean cotton of its seeds. For six months Whitney labored behind locked doors in a basement room of the plantation house. By April 1793, he had designed a gin (short for engine) that used rotating wires in a cylinder to pull the lint through holes too small to pass the seed. Brushes revolving in an opposite direction cleaned the cotton from the wires. One man, using a hand crank, could produce fifty pounds of cleaned cotton a day.

Granted a patent in February 1793, Whitney formed a partnership with Phineas Miller, the manager of Mulberry Grove, to exploit the gin. They offered to clean any quantity of cotton at sites throughout the South for the price of one pound of clean cotton for every five pounds delivered with seed. By mortgaging the Greene estate, the partners secured enough money for Whitney to equip and man a workshop in New Haven to manufacture the gins. But the cotton gin was so simple that any competent mechanic could duplicate it; and many did. Whitney had to spend his small earnings fighting infringements on his patent. He never profited in proportion to the cotton gin's impact on the national economy.

The most consequential innovation of the day, Eli Whitney's cotton gin removed a bottleneck between the planting of cotton and exporting it to the voracious factories of Britain. Expanding sixtyfold from 1790 to 1815, the cotton trade caused an economic revival in the Old South and hastened settlement of the Southwest. Cotton was to replace all other crops in profitability. Supply did not catch up with British demand for years, and the price of cotton reflected the demand, staying at ten cents a pound except for 1811 and 1812, years of tension and then war between the United States and Britain.

Some sensed that a different kind of price might have to be paid. The "inventions of the cotton-gin, the carding machine, the spinning-jenny, and the steam-engine," a southern journal noted, "combined to weave that net-work of cotton which formed an indissoluble cord, binding the black, who was threatened to be cast off, to human progress."

Merchants in northern port cities began to share in cotton profits and in the general trade prosperity. With Britain and France at war, American merchant-shippers sold both countries produce of northern farms close to the coast—wheat, rice, flour, barreled beef and pork, and rum. Wagons brought farm products into New York City, soon to lead all other ports in trade owing to its auction sales of British manufactures; its regularly scheduled shipping service; and later its resident agents with branch offices in all the major cotton ports to supply credit, shipping, and maritime insurance to the cotton planter. Oxcarts laden with produce rolled into Philadelphia, located on two waterways with an outlet to the sea, and into

Boston, leader in the China trade, with a large harbor where five hundred ships could dock, load, and sail for world ports. By the turn of the century Yankee ships had become familiar in harbors the globe over.

It was a grand period for innovators and entrepreneurs. A merchant prince of Boston, Francis Cabot Lowell, profited first in the European trade by entering business with his wealthy merchant uncle, William Cabot. Willing to assume heavy risks, Lowell took charge of valuable cargo on his uncle's ships. In 1795 British sailors boarded his ship to search for goods destined for France; they found no evidence of blockade running —but Lowell's cargo found its way to France. The adventurous Lowell sent out eight ships to vie for world trade.

Lowell was typical of many merchant-shippers in Boston and New York. Their agents maintained contacts with village storekeepers who dickered for the produce of outlying northern farms. City merchants with their warehouses, overseas contacts, and easy access to credit could ship, insure, and sell northern farm produce or the tobacco and cotton of the southern planter, and planters boosted their profits by consigning their crop to an agent who would hold it, watch prices, and sell it at a favorable time. The merchant or his agent could advance credit to the large planter until the next crop came. It was a barter economy with scarce money. Credit in goods was extended to carry farmers from crop to crop by the storekeeper or merchant.

Lowell's interests were wide-ranging—cotton trading, banking, and real estate with his building of India Wharf in Boston Harbor in 1808. Nervous, high-strung, inclined to overwork, he was known as a hardheaded businessman with family connections through intermarriage to the wealthiest and most prominent merchant families of Boston. He was also an economic leader who turned the merchant wealth of Boston from overseas shipping into cotton textile manufacture after the embargo in 1807–08 cut off trading ventures with Britain and France and after exports of agricultural products fell sharply. Merchants soon began to look for other profitable enterprises. Sensing that one day industry would rank as high as trade, Lowell led other Boston merchants to shift from overseas trade to the manufacture of textiles.

Moving crops to merchants in the cities was a central problem of the agricultural economy of America in 1800, especially in the North. In the South, planters could ship cotton and other products to port on numerous waterways, while in the North highways radiated from the principal eastern cities. Oxcarts from Concord, only twenty miles from the sea, could travel to Boston from the backcountry to supply city dwellers as well as to load ships bound for foreign ports. But farther inland, only a few roads might run from the interior to a waterway. With construction and maintenance of roads in the hands of local officials, a basic road in 1800 was a cleared path through the trees, an improved one was crowned high with dirt and edged by a gutter. Farmers could profitably haul freight only very short distances. One wagonload of goods sent from Augusta, Maine, to Savannah, Georgia, took almost four months, at a cost of $1,000. The northern farmer who was not close to a market or a river exchanged his surplus crops for necessities for his family in the village store. He did not try to expand production; there was no market in which to sell.

Once again, it took some innovators and tinkerers to see the potential of steam as a source of power. Since that day during the Philadelphia convention when John Fitch had experimented with his boat *Perseverance,* traveling at a snail's pace on the Delaware River, James Rumsey had also launched a steamboat on the Potomac River in 1787, and John Stevens of Hoboken, New Jersey, took the lead farther north. Toward the close of the eighteenth century, "a sort of mania began to prevail . . . for impelling boats by steam-engines."

Two decades passed before steamboats began to operate on western waters; by then leadership in steamboat building and operating had passed to two men who brilliantly solved the problems of boat construction, business security, and profits. The resources and organizational talents of both Robert R. Livingston, New York manorial farmer, and Robert Fulton, mechanical genius, would make the steamboat a reality on the western waters of America.

By facilitating upstream travel on the Ohio and Mississippi rivers, the steamboat opened up the fertile country of the Northwest Territory stretching from the Appalachian Mountains to the Mississippi River. Settlers who homesteaded in the West after the War of 1812 could market their surpluses. Interregional trade changed local, self-sufficient economies to one commercial economy with each region producing its specialties for the national market—foodstuffs in the Northwest, cotton in the South, and capital, ships, and manufactured goods in the East. A traveler who knew the Northwest Territory wrote in 1817.*"The center of population and wealth is rapidly inclining *westward; and within a very few years hence it will 'cross the mountains'.* . . . I look forward to the time, as at no great distance, when the great western rivers and lakes shall be covered with hundreds of steam boats, performing regular voyages between New Orleans and the numerous ports on the Mississippi and its great tributaries. . . ."

FARMS: THE JACKS-OF-ALL-TRADES

It was sheep-shearing time on Chancellor Robert Livingston's estate, in the spring of 1810, and he had invited friends to drive over and admire his fine merinos. Elegant phaetons wound their way up a long avenue bordered by feathery locust trees and deposited the guests at the manor house. Outside the visitors could admire the breathtaking view of the jagged Catskills across the Hudson River; inside, the tapestry, silver, and fashionable French furnishings that the chancellor had collected when he had been Jefferson's Minister to France. After a lavish dinner in the greenhouse, among large ornamental plants, the guests strolled along grassy lawns and orchards to a park devoted to the care and feeding of merino sheep. Then they watched while fleece was cut from the merinos in great fluffy swaths. Some of the sheep were sold, at prices ranging from $40 to $1,000 a head.

The chancellor was a prime leader of the New York Society for the Promotion of Agriculture, Arts, and Manufactures, organized in the early 1790s by seventy-two farmers who had large holdings, time to keep abreast of writings on farming, and funds to experiment with promising agricultural methods. Descended from a family that owned over 300,000 acres originally granted by the Dutch, Livingston pursued his experiments on lands that bordered the Hudson for twelve miles and stretched east toward Massachusetts. One of the first scientific agriculturalists to urge the use of gypsum as a fertilizer, he built a mill to grind the substance. Writing in the society's *Transactions* on soil conservation, he showed how sowing grass and clover on worn-out fields could restore fertility. But his passion was merino sheep, which he had discovered in France and imported to his own country. His first tiny flock—two merino rams and two ewes—were dirty brown in color, their wool greasy and closely curled, but after cleaning the wool seemed whiter and softer than any other. The society proudly circulated 1,000 copies of Livingston's "Essay on Sheep." After the trade embargo of 1808 helped produce a kind of merino sheep craze, Livingston and other gentlemen farmers expanded their flocks and built several woolen mills, to their further profit.

Livingston and his friends wanted to do more than improve their own knowledge, however; they sought to improve the farm practices of their tenants. But the gulf was too deep. Most of their tenants could not read, and those who could would hardly have studied the *Transactions*. The tenants on the feudal estates of the large New York landowners were even less productive and more slovenly in their farming practices than many freehold farmers. They tried to extract everything they could from the land at the moment. The average farm on the Clermont estate comprised about 70 acres of leased land, with usually about one-third of the acreage under cultivation. Rent for the land was twenty-five bushels of winter wheat, four hens, and one day's "riding" for the landlord with a team of horses or oxen. The chancellor possessed all milling and mining rights to the land and exacted a "quarter-sale"—one-third of the selling price—if the tenant tried to sell his improved farm to another. Though many of the chancellor's acres were vacant, he hoped the lands would fill up, values would increase, and he could sell at a large profit. But very often new settlers bypassed New York and went on to the western states where land was open for settlement and a farmer could buy cheaply from the government.

Farther north, life for the farm owner could be less benign. Thomas Coffin battled nature in 1825 to wrest a living from New England's rocky soils. Summers could bring temperatures of 90 degrees and drenching rains that would rot ripening crops in the fields of his farm in Boscawen, New Hampshire. Winter was worse with temperatures as low as 20 to 30 degrees below zero and snows of two feet deep, forcing Coffin and his neighbors to break out roads to haul wood for his fifty-year-old frame house on Water Street. For heat northern farmers needed large quantities of wood—fifteen cords a year, on the average—so that constant cutting of wood, along with threshing and winnowing the wheat crop in the barn and washing the yearlings with soap, kept Coffin working all winter long.

Springtime brought plowing, using the common New England wooden plow with an iron colter to cut the sod. With this plow and strong oxen an acre was a good day's work, given the rough, rocky soils of the farm. Coffin and his sons then harrowed the ground to break up roots. The next task was to sow seeds of barley, oats, and peas, followed by a brushing to cover the scattered seed. Coffin's sons dropped corn and potato seeds by hand into small holes they had dug. Potatoes were an important part of the agricultural economy of the North. Thomas Coffin could produce 500 bushels of potatoes a year—enough for his family plus seed for next year and a surplus to sell or trade in Boscawen.

Coffin's was a prosperous northern farm like many others of about 100 to 200 acres worked by the owner's family. Farmers knew little about seed selection, soil composition, or fertilizers; waste was taken for granted; and land was plentiful; so most farmers would rather do as their fathers had always done rather than farm "by the book." Typically, they planted only a small amount in crops, perhaps six out of one hundred acres. A little more land would be in meadow and about the same in weeds, brush, or woodland range. The rest of the farm lay fallow until the farmer had exhausted his tilled acreage and had to cultivate a new section. He then let the exhausted land return to weeds and brush, which would supposedly bring it to fertility once again.

Tools were simple, yet ingenious. In summer Coffin and his sons hoed crops by hand, pulled weeds, mowed and raked hay and brought it under cover. They reaped rye with a smooth-bladed reaping hook or a long, narrow-bladed sickle, cradled oats, and mowed wheat and barley with a scythe. Shortage of labor for harvesting wheat was a crucial problem for northern farmers. Thomas Jefferson noted in 1793 that "every laborer will manage ten acres of wheat, except at harvest." The farmer sowed only as much in the spring as he could harvest in late summer with the cradle, the long scythe blade paralleled by a rack of wooden fingers. An expert cradler could earn a dollar a day at harvest. If a man with a sickle could cut one-half to three-quarters of an acre a day, a man with a cradle could cut two to three acres a day. Only the later invention of the reaper removed the bottleneck on wheat growing.

Coffin fed livestock all winter long with hay cut and cured in summer. Cutting was by scythe, followed by raking, drying, and loading into wagons hauled by oxen to the haymow of the barn. It took tremendous energy and muscle to swing the scythe for hours. Coffin wrote in his diary one July day: "uncommon warm for three days, we mowed, raked, got in three small jags [loads], we are almost sick." Although Coffin sometimes hired extra hands at from six to nine dollars a month to help him bring hay under cover before rain, the average northern farmer with poor or uncleared land could not afford permanent help. Shortage of farm labor, according to Timothy Dwight, contributed to neglect of the soil, failure to rotate crops, and inattention to fertilizers or other soil-improving minerals.

Harvest was the time to hunt up the cattle in the summer pasture. The average farm had ten to twenty sheep, fifteen head of cattle, including five dairy cows. It also had fifteen pigs which often ran wild in the woods, fed only just before slaughter. One English agriculturist reported in 1798: "The real American hog is what is termed the wood-hog . . . they are long in the leg. . . . You may as well think of stopping a crow as those hogs. They will go a distance from a fence, take a run, and leap through the rails, three or four feet from the ground, turning themselves sidewise. These hogs suffer such hardships as no other animal could endure."

New England farms differed from fertile Pennsylvania and New York farms in that much of the soil was thin and stony and the growing season shorter. The Connecticut Valley and the Champlain area of Vermont were exceptional areas in New England for farming. Maize was the largest crop on the mixed farms owned by most of the New England farming popula-

tion. Thomas Coffin could support his family with the products of his farm
—flax and wool for clothing; barley and wheat for his livestock; peas,
potatoes, corn, and vegetables for his table; plus milk, dairy products, veal,
beef, pork, lamb, and mutton—all raised on his self-sufficient farm.

Coffin marketed surplus pork, veal, cider, and cheese in Boscawen, but
his home and farm had been in his family for generations, so he did not
need to buy on credit to clear or maintain his farm. Coffin could also sell
trees on his farm. New England farmers hauled logs on great sleds to a
"brow," a landing place by the river. In the spring, upon ice-out, the logs
on the brow would float off to a mill. To the nearby Merrimack River Coffin
brought logs that would be used in building Manchester factories. "If by
hard labour and frugal economy," one observer noted, "the common
independent Yankee farmer, such as the traveller meets with anywhere in
New England, lays up annually from four to seven hundred dollars, he is
a thriving man and 'getting rich.' "

Like most New England farmers, Coffin had to be a jack-of-all-trades. He
was a carpenter, mechanic, wheelwright, cooper, well digger, woodcutter,
cider maker, maple-tree tapper, fence builder, drover, paperhanger, rudimentary blacksmith, harness maker. (He was also a diarist, to history's
benefit.) He not only repaired tools; he sometimes made them, or adapted
them to his own purposes. Coffin was not equally skillful at all these tasks;
but few farmers were more versatile than this Boscawen husbandman. No
wonder he was a "thriving man."

Mixed farming in New England was a year-round, time-consuming occupation absorbing all the energies of Coffin and his wife, Hannah, who
washed, cooked, sewed, and cleaned while rearing six children. Large
families of from six to eight children were the rule on New England farms.
Farm women spun and wove all the family's clothing out of flax or wool,
and they made soap and candles. The period between 1775 and 1815 was
the high point of home industry.

If close to a market in a village or city, farm women wove textiles or
produced shoes to sell. Daughters entering the new textile mills then rising
in New England and Pennsylvania often returned part of their earnings to
needy parents, who tried to finance the migration of some of their children
to the West while keeping their farm intact. The surplus property, livestock, and equipment were rarely enough for families on even good-sized
northern farms to give each child a farm. Only in the 1830s did farm
families start limiting the number of children they had, thus providing
fewer offspring with more land. Farm land values in New England were
generally high, owing to the large population and numerous towns; a good

spread in Connecticut in 1807–08 brought between $40 and $50 an acre. These high land values encouraged landless young families to emigrate to the West.

Down South, population was also shifting westward, especially after the War of 1812. Farmers and planters had turned to raising cotton, which had a high value in relation to its weight, and with the invention of the gin, planters could profitably raise and process cotton for the market. New machines and processes lowered costs of cotton textiles, encouraging their substitution for woolens and linen. After the embargo and the War of 1812, England needed cotton to supply its textile mills and prices soared. Not until 1827 did supply begin to overtake demand, with the price of cotton in the New York market dropping back from thirty cents a pound to nine. At the same time the price of slaves rose, and cotton planters, dependent on the North and West for foodstuffs and manufactured goods, found they needed more working capital as the yield of their worn-out tobacco and wheat lands declined. Large planter and small farmer alike began the trek toward more promising lands of the Southwest. Between 1816 and 1820 the combined population of Alabama and Mississippi leaped from 75,000 to 200,000. Other states with cotton lands experienced similar growth. Louisiana had 76,000 settlers in 1810, 143,000 in 1820, and 215,000 by 1830.

Thomas Smith Gregory Dabney was one of the men who moved west. Lured by the rich profits to be made in cotton, he left his model plantation, Elmington, in Virginia to lead his family and slaves to 4,000 acres of prime cotton land he bought from several small farmers in western Mississippi. When wealthy planters like Dabney migrated, they purchased the best cotton lands for low prices in the rich soil of Alabama and Mississippi. The small farmer found he could not compete with the large planter and was usually willing to sell out if the planter made him an attractive offer. Good cotton land sold for five to ten dollars an acre; clearing cost eight to fifteen dollars an acre; fencing, three to six. Small farmers could not meet these expenses, build the necessary home, and subsist until returns from the cotton crop came in, so many sold out and migrated farther west. Dabney had capital. With a labor force of 500 slaves, he brought his new land into production at the rate of 100 acres a year.

During the mild southern winters slaves cleared land, chopped logs, and rolled them for new fences. Plowing of new land began in February; soon field hands would be keeping the plows constantly in action "listing up" new ground. In April slaves began planting cotton. A narrow plow pulled by a single horse opened a ridge; the sower then followed with a sack from which he threw the cotton seed, scattering twenty grains for every stalk that would grow. A field hand with a harrow followed the sower, covering the seeds lightly. Each set of three hands—plower, sower, and harrower—planted ten to fifteen acres a day between early April and the middle of May.

After the plants sprouted, thinning out or "scraping" began, and every hand came into the field with a hoe. A plow first ran a light furrow on each side of the row of cotton plants, and the hands "scraped" or thinned out the extra plants in the rows. Slaves then cultivated the ground around the plants all summer.

Cotton picking began in late August and might continue until the end of December. At dawn bells awakened slaves, men and women alike, so they could be in the fields by first light, and they would remain there until dark. Each slave, wet from the cold dew, brought a large basket and two coarse cotton bags strapped to the neck. The slave left the basket at the end of the row and proceeded to pick; when her two bags were full, she went back to her basket and dumped the cotton into it. At nightfall, she took the basket on her head to the scaffold yard for weighing. The overseer met all hands at the scales with lamp, slate, and whip. He then weighed each basket and entered the weight beside the slave's name on his slate. A slave might not know beforehand if she had met the quota. According to one observer acquainted with the labor practices of overseers, on some plantations "those who are found to have brought in less than their usual quantity" received ten, twenty, or fifty stripes with the whip.

Overseers usually came from the small-farmer or landless classes of the region. Responsible to many absentee planters, they knew that their jobs and reputation rested on one thing only—how many bales of cotton they could produce from each acre of the planter's land. It was usually of little concern to the owner how the overseer secured a large crop, although the planter did want his investment in workers maintained in efficient operating condition.

Cold and haughty in appearance, Dabney himself supervised the 200 slaves at Burleigh, his plantation, wearing gloves as he rode horseback through the fields. The other three sections of his estate Dabney regularly assigned to overseers. Field slaves on the Burleigh plantation picked cotton on a piece-rate system, with 400 pounds considered a good day's output, although many picked 500 pounds according to the memory of Dabney's daughter, who wrote about Burleigh several years later. One Southerner said in 1825 that to pick 400 or 500 pounds a day "requires such brisk and incessant motion that it could not be done two days in succession without danger of life or health; and is only attempted for a wager or such like reason." He maintained that the average weight picked by all hands on a place, including children, was 150 to 160 pounds a day. Each hand could produce five or six 400-pound bales a year. Dabney's overseers weighed each slave's output three times a day and entered the number of pounds picked by field hands opposite their names on a slate.

To maintain his slaves in their most efficient working condition, Dabney provided them food, clothing, medical care and supervision; two woolen suits in winter and two in summer made by household servants on the plantation; and about five pounds of pork and other rations each week. Dabney felt his slaves worked harder if they received half of Saturday and all of Sunday off from field work.

Like other planters, Dabney tried to make his estate as self-sufficient as possible. He required twenty-seven servants to wait upon his family in the plantation house as well as other trained slaves to conduct plantation operations—carpenters, blacksmiths, millers, seamstresses, laundresses, and cooks. Dabney raised sheep, pigs, horses, and mules on the plantation and butchered from 150 to 175 pigs each year, since pork was the mainstay of his slaves' diet. He cured his own hams and kept a herd of forty cows for dairy products for the household. But the alluvial lands of the Mississippi delta did not favor corn, so most planters imported large quantities of corn and pork from northwestern farmers.

Like Livingston, Dabney tried to improve the yields from his land. He studied better farming practices, published numerous articles in the *Mississippi Farmer,* and served as president of the State Agricultural Society. Versatile in his way, he investigated the new agricultural implements such as better plows and advocated their use. But he was working his land with forced labor, which often quietly resisted his best management efforts. Slaves were not interested in diversifying crops, improving livestock, or developing new techniques and machinery to enrich the master. They had little incentive to use better tools and at times deliberately broke or lost them. They had their own ways of evading the overseer. One observer wrote of the weighing of cotton picked by slaves, "It is not an uncommon occurrence for an overseer, who is even vigilant, amid the crowd of negroes and baskets, with only one lamp, held close to the scales and slate, to weigh some of the heavier baskets several times, their exact weight being changed by taking out, or putting in a few pounds; while the lighter ones pass entirely unnoticed."

A technological backwardness pervaded the region. Investment in agriculture for large planter and small farmer alike meant investment in slaves. Even small farmers moving west usually invested in slaves rather than in improved implements or techniques. One northern journalist, Joseph Ingraham, observing some small farmers in 1833 at the port of Natchez,

Mississippi, wrote: "Seated in a circle around their bread and cheese were half a dozen as rough, rude, honest-looking countrymen from the back part of the state as you could find in the nursery of New England's yeomanry. They are small farmers—own a few negroes—cultivate a small tract of land, and raise a few bales of cotton, which they bring to market themselves. Their carts are drawn around them forming a barricade to their camp, for here, as is customary among them, instead of putting up at taverns, they have encamped since their arrival. Between them and their carts are their negroes. . . ."

These small farmers worked isolated, hilly regions and lived a backward, self-sufficient way of life. Lacking capital, they could not buy industrial products, nor could they easily move their surplus crops to market without a transportation system. In turn, manufactures in the southern states declined after 1810, owing to a lack of good transportation, a rural market, and free labor not tied to the land.

Many of the planters of the time were absentee owners. Dabney spent the long, hot summer months on the Gulf coast away from his plantation. In the fall he supervised the picking and the ginning on his plantation. Field hands could gin about three to four bales of cotton a day and press about ten to twelve bales a day with a steam press. Dabney accompanied the cotton to market, riding with the wagons to the shipping point about sixty miles away. New Orleans and Mobile were major ports for shipping cotton to the Northeast and to England. In 1822, New Orleans received 161,000 bales; in 1830, 428,000 bales. Sugar shipments rose from 30,000 hogsheads in 1823 to 186,000 in 1845. By 1830 leadership in cotton production had passed from the Atlantic states to the Gulf states.

Planters sold their cotton directly to resident New York factors who, as agents of New York banks, could advance them long-term credit to buy more land and slaves. "The system of credit in this country is peculiar," a New England journalist observed. "From new-year's to new-year's is the customary extension of this accommodation, and the first of January, as planters have then usually disposed of their crops, is a season for a general settlement throughout every branch of business. The planters have their commission merchants in New Orleans and Natchez, who receive and ship their cotton for them, and make advances, if required, upon succeeding crops. Some planters export direct to Liverpool and other ports, though generally they sell or consign to the commission merchants in Natchez, who turn cotton into gold so readily, that one verily would be inclined to think that the philosopher's stone might be concealed within the bales."

The system fostered careless business methods. The planter, having sold his crop at the port, did not have to check on shipping, the price of imported goods, insurance, or freight. He left these concerns to New Yorkers, who dominated the financial life of the South. Planters even developed a certain disdain for business and for the labor that maintained it. Factors made loans to keep them in funds until the next crop, at an interest rate of 8 to 12 percent, to which they added a brokerage fee of 1 to 2.5 percent. Cotton profits flowed to the Northeast for services and manufactured goods and to the West for food, leaving little investment capital in the South. Southern banks, which were usually controlled by powerful planters, largely financed the extension of the slavery system, as did Britons who invested in the Southwest to increase the cotton trade.

The southern agricultural system was inherently wasteful. Large amounts of land were controlled by absentee planters and worked by forced, unwilling slaves driven by overseers intent on extracting as much as possible from the worker and the land. Instead of crop rotation or fertilization, planters abandoned worn-out land to weeds and cleared more until it too was sterile. Overseers made few efforts to restore fertility to the soil by plowing clover or peas; instead they plowed up and down on slopes for cotton rows and cultivated them, leading to serious soil erosion. By 1839, one writer in Georgia observed that thousands of acres of Georgia land were nothing but "sterile red clay, full of gullies." Cotton growing rested on exploitation—of both soil and slaves.

No transportation system went into the interior, where yeomen farmers remained isolated, self-sufficient, and backward. Canals, turnpikes, and local roads would transform northern agriculture from subsistence to commercial farming. In the South, where planters dominated the state legislatures as well as the banks, expanding income had little multiplier effect. It flowed instead to the North and West for services, manufactures, and foodstuffs.

By 1830, American agriculture had not changed significantly from what it was in 1800. Heavy farm machinery, university agricultural schools, and experiment stations would come later in the century. But improvements were taking place almost daily under the leadership of gentlemen farmers like Livingston who had the capital and the time to diversify crop production, experiment with fertilizers, improve livestock through better breeding, and import new stock such as the merino sheep. In the North, the iron plow of Jethro Wood came into widespread use through the leadership of the gentlemen farmers. Wood perfected a plow in 1819 with both wooden and cast-iron parts, and sold it for a modest price. The iron plow, according to one historian, reduced the labor required in plowing by about half. In 1844, a Southerner visiting the New York State Agricultural Fair wrote that "the best models of the plow, perhaps in the world," were there, enabling northern farmers to plow more deeply and raise crops in "greater abundance . . . in comparison with ours."

In the South, improvements in processing took place largely through applying horsepower and later steam power to cotton gins on large plantations. Steam presses also increased the amount of cotton made into bales on plantations. Once settlers had migrated over the mountains into the Southwest to raise cotton, demand for farm products increased, while laborers moving into the factories of the cities also expanded the market for farm products.

The general rise in demand, coming after long decades of nearly constant markets, stimulated the research and experimentation that eventually bore fruit in the agricultural inventions of the 1840s and 1850s. As improved transportation began to link the nation's sections, farmers had an incentive to produce for a growing national market.

FACTORIES: THE LOOMS OF LOWELL

Eli Whitney's financial losses in 1796 with the cotton gin were a heavy blow. He was still looking, at thirty-one years of age, for a way to make a good living. "Bankruptcy & ruin were constantly staring me in the face & disappointment trip'd me up every step I attempted to take. . . . Loaded with a Debt of 3 or 4000 Dollars, without resources and without any business that would ever furnish me a support, I knew not which way to turn." Troubles multiplied. His workshop in New Haven where he was making cotton gins had burned to the ground. And all the while, the image of Catherine Greene "so possessed him" that "he was unable to give himself to another woman." She was remarried in 1796—to Whitney's partner in the cotton gin manufacture, Phineas Miller. It would be twenty years—Whitney would be fifty-one and Catherine in her grave—before he could bring himself to marry another woman.

But Whitney's tenacity never lessened, nor did his initiative and enterprise. After analyzing his financial problems he turned from Mulberry Grove to the federal government, from making cotton gins to manufacturing small arms. He had no experience in producing guns and no gun factory, but no matter. He knew that he could solve his financial problems if the Treasury would pay for his workshop. He also knew that the outbreak of war in Europe in the 1790s made it essential for the American government to acquire guns for defense.

Whitney sent Secretary of the Treasury Wolcott a bold proposal to manufacture on a "new principle" 10,000 muskets—a fantastic number in those days—to be delivered to Washington within twenty-eight months.

Granted a contract for $134,000, Whitney used an advance of $10,000 to start building an armory. He already had the workers, having recruited them from Massachusetts to make cotton gins. After buying a suitable water-power site on the Mill River outside New Haven, consisting of two hundred acres with three old houses, he added a new barn, five stone dwellings for workmen, a stone store, plus a dam and bridge. Since mills and armories had to rely on water for power, Whitney like other early industrialists located his mill in a rural area and purchased a "mill privilege"—the right to control all or part of the available power.

Whitney worked closely with his men, who in turn were dependent on him for their jobs and houses. Somewhat isolated in their environments, workers generally found it hard to move away when employers like the ironmasters in Pennsylvania and the mill operators of Rhode Island paid wages not in cash but in credit at the company store. "My intention is to employ steady, sober people and learn them the business," Whitney wrote. "I shall make it a point to employ persons who have family connections and perhaps some little property to fix them to the place."

Westward settlement was already tightening the scarce labor supply of the northeastern states. From the rugged hill farms of western New England, the abundance of western land drew away many potential workers who might otherwise have migrated into the towns or cities to form a more abundant labor force. Whitney had gone for his labor supply to his home area of western Massachusetts, the area of southern New England called "the northern hive," from which youngest sons and then whole families migrated to western New York and Pennsylvania. Manufacturing had to attract labor from the farming frontier or else draw new hands such as women and children into the labor market.

Whitney sought young, unskilled workers for training but he found that he must "be present during the formation of every Pattern, Model, Mold, etc.," as he wrote to explain why he could not fulfill the government contract for guns in the specified time. To mechanize the manufacturing process, Whitney had to invent an elaborate system of guides, patterns, templates, gauges, and jigs so that his unskilled workers could produce, in large numbers, a musket from a model that skilled craftsmen had previously made. It took him ten years to deliver 10,000 arms.

Armorers averaged thirty-two dollars a month, the skilled iron workers in Pennsylvania, twenty to twenty-four dollars. Unskilled workers such as the coal miners of Pennsylvania made five to ten dollars a week, whereas laborers working in construction work, woodcutting, and road building, where the demand for unskilled labor was low, earned from sixty to ninety cents a day. Work in the mines or on construction was intermittent, however, so unskilled laborers seldom earned a full month's wages. Arms making generally paid armorers by piece rates according to the skill required by the job.

A man's working day depended on the speed he could apply to his individual task. At the Harpers Ferry Armory in Virginia, many diversions interrupted the working day. Armorers quit work to share a cup of whiskey, or they might move to the armory yard to watch dogfights, cockfights, and bloody matches between co-workers, usually placing bets on the outcome. Evangelists, orators, and peddlers drew armorers away from work, as did holidays, barbecues, and celebrations.

The craft ethic caused many armorers to resist mechanization of the industry, on the grounds that an armorer's task was to make a complete product—lock, stock, and barrel. To learn the craft, a son worked with his father or an apprentice with his master for at least five years to learn such arts as barrel making, lock forging, or filing, stocking, and finishing a musket. The center of the craft tradition in arms making was Philadelphia, where German-born craftsmen served apprenticeships in Pennsylvania gun shops, often migrating to Harpers Ferry at later times. The push for interchangeable parts came not only from gifted arms contractors like Whitney who were eager to cut costs and replace craft skills with machinery, but also from the government, which wanted soldiers to be able to replace broken parts of a musket in the field. Whitney never mastered complete interchangeability before his death, but his methods were adopted and improved upon by other independent arms makers such as John Hall at Harpers Ferry and Simeon North, who were able to assemble rifle components in a case-hardened state as early as 1824.

The system of interchangeable parts manufacture begun by Whitney and others in the small-arms industry changed the life and work of many craftsmen, such as Johann Ludwig Eberhardt, a clockmaker of Salem, North Carolina. Members of the Moravian Church migrating from Germany had settled first in Pennsylvania and then, after receiving a grant of 100,000 acres in 1766 in the North Carolina piedmont, moved on to the area to be called Salem. Their settlement was never to be a frontier farming settlement but a center for trades and crafts. They drew up plans for a gristmill and sawmill, brewery and distillery, a store, apothecary shop, tanyard, pottery, gunsmith, blacksmith, gunstock maker, tailor shop, shoemaker, linen weaver, saddlery, bakery and carpenter, joiners, masons, and a tavern. The people of Salem, a town of two hundred people, also needed a clockmaker, and on November 29, 1799, the community imported Johann Ludwig Eberhardt, a strong-willed, impetuous, impatient forty-one-year-old clockmaker from Germany.

In Salem, all admitted had to conform with rules about morals, religion, and behavior established by the Board of Elders. The Elders objected to Eberhardt's excessive indulgence "in the use of spiritous drink," but he had come to Salem to settle down and at age forty-one approached the Elders for permission to marry. The Elders Conference rejected the first woman Eberhardt proposed to; his second choice was put to the Lot, a small wooden bowl containing three paper cartridges: "Ja" or "Nein" or a blank, which meant the question required further consideration. The Lot said "Nein" to Eberhardt's second choice, requiring him to choose a third woman, favored at last by the Elders Conference and the Lot.

A supervisory committee exercised as much control over business and property as did the Elders Conference over morals. The committee decided which crafts and trades should function, how many craftsmen could do business in each, what prices should be charged, what wages paid. Eberhardt had to ask permission to buy a house for his residence and his shop, and the committee assigned him other duties such as winding and tending the town clocks in the church, ringing the noon bell, and repairing broken clocks. Eberhardt's business was typical of clock shops of the early nineteenth century, requiring a variety of other skills such as working in metals, smithing, and casting. After importing most parts from England via Philadelphia, Eberhardt filed, scraped, and polished plates and wheel blanks for his clocks, assembling the final individual, handcrafted clock. He made an average of eight clocks per year, charging forty to sixty dollars apiece. His business was an exacting, one-man operation. Though he had apprentices, he could not get along with them and eventually let all of them go.

Eberhardt's death in 1839 marked the end of an era of craftsmanship. He was the last clockmaker in Salem. Handmade clocks gave way to Eli Terry's and Seth Thomas' machine-made versions. Like Whitney, Terry began to use guides, patterns, templates, gauges, and jigs in the making of his wooden clocks in the Connecticut Valley. With the installation of machinery he was able to turn out clocks in lots of one to two hundred which he peddled about the countryside on horseback for fifteen dollars a clock. His thirty-hour shelf clock, patented in 1816, changed the business. By 1852, the year of his death, he was producing 10,000 to 12,000 metal clocks a year which sold for five dollars apiece.

Industrialists Eli Terry, Eli Whitney, Samuel Colt, and Simeon North tirelessly experimented with machines to cut metal into precise shapes and produce interchangeable parts in clocks and small arms. The problems confronted by these manufacturers were similar technologically to those in a number of other industries, such as sewing machines and agricultural implements. Unlike Eberhardt, who looked upon himself as responsible for a complete, one-of-a-kind product, the industrialists were flexible and experimental tinkerers who improved the manufacturing process by mechanizing it step by step. Their incentive to adopt labor-saving techniques to cut costs was heightened in an expanding economy and population. Farmers with land and a transportation network to market farm products could do well, but in spite of the scarcity of skilled and unskilled labor, workers, whether craftsmen, skilled workers, or common laborers, did not share in the profits of industrialization to the extent the manufacturer did.

With a new war starting in 1812, Whitney signed a bigger contract with the government to deliver 15,000 muskets. He was able to complete the contract in two years owing to his use of filing jigs, milling machines, and other devices. Little was new in the process. Interchangeable parts manufacture developed much earlier in Europe, but men like Whitney applied machines and methods to manufacture products in a nation where demand for machine-made goods and ability to buy were greater than in many countries in Europe. Whitney died a rich man, leaving an estate of more than $130,000 in savings and personal notes held by him. At this time a skilled millwright or carpenter earned eight dollars a week and a canal laborer four dollars a week, often paid partly in board.

* * *

The leader in industrial expansion between 1815 and 1860 was the cotton textile industry, and the leader in cotton textiles was the man who set up the first integrated cotton textile factory, Francis Cabot Lowell. Merchants in the carrying trade had grown rich, with profits during good times averaging $50 to $70 million dollars annually. But the carrying trade dwindled within a few years because of the Embargo Act of 1807 and the Non-Intercourse Act of 1809, as the United States struck back at French and British attacks on American sea commerce. Some merchants began to look for more secure areas to invest their profits. The cotton gin had helped boost American consumption of cotton from 1,000 to 90,000 bales a year, as merchants with warehouses, easy access to credit, resources to purchase raw material in large lots, and experience in merchandising turned to cotton textile manufacture as a way of making large and steady profits.

Fifteen of Samuel Slater's cotton mills had started up by 1807 in Rhode Island. Slater had been an apprentice in England to a partner of Richard Arkwright, an early inventor of cotton textile machinery. In his head Slater had carried the plans of the Arkwright machinery to New York in 1789; this memory feat, his friends claimed, outfoxed English customs officials enforcing the law forbidding the export of machinery plans or apprentices. Slater came to Pawtucket, Rhode Island, at the invitation of the wealthy Providence merchant Moses Brown to build a cotton spinning frame of twenty-four spindles. Textile production took two steps—spinning, in which the spindle stretches and twists fibers into yarns, and weaving, by which fabric is made by the interlacement of groups of yarns at right angles to each other. Slater's mills did only the first stage—spinning. The yarn from the mills went to hand weavers who wove the yarns into cloth in their farm homes.

Lowell, unlike Slater, saw the possibilities for profit in bringing the whole process for making cloth into the factory, where unskilled workers could produce by machinery. This would lower costs, for hand weaving was expensive. In 1810, overworked, ill, and exhausted from his ventures in real estate and commerce, he sailed for Edinburgh for a rest cure with his wife, Hannah Jackson Lowell, and his sons. Patrick Tracy Jackson, Lowell's brother-in-law, managed his affairs and the trading fortune during his absence. Never able to stay idle long, Lowell toured the factory of a large iron manufacturer and then visited the Manchester, England, cotton mills for several weeks. There he observed the Horrocks and Johnson power loom, which incorporated a machine for "dressing" the warp with a starch coating to make it strong enough for power weaving.

Returning to Boston in 1812, Lowell sought the help of an Amesbury mechanic, Paul Moody, to construct a power loom. Together they fashioned a successful one operated by a camshaft. There was nothing remarkable in their power loom—other manufacturers were close to building one as efficient as Lowell's and later even superior to it; but none of the small partnership and family-owned enterprises of southern New England could match Lowell's command of investment capital to establish new factories, power systems, and machines on a big scale.

Lowell persuaded Jackson and Nathan Appleton, a wealthy Boston merchant, to join him in raising $400,000 for the venture, including purchase of the power rights on the Charles River in Waltham, with its ten-foot waterfall. An elbow of land jutting into the Charles River and linked by the Great Sudbury Road to Boston provided an excellent factory site. The Boston Associates, as they were called, eventually included the most prominent merchant families in the city—Jackson, Appleton, Lawrence, Cabot, Dwight, Amory, Lyman, and Lowell, all linked by marriage. Lowell designed the buildings for the Waltham mill, including a machine shop where the spinning, carding, and weaving machinery would be made, a small mill with about 2,000 spindles in operation by 1816 and a larger one of 3,500 spindles in operation a few years later.

It was easier to buy machinery than to hire workers, but Lowell had the foresight to attract a new factory labor force of young women from the large New England farm families whose hilly land could not support all its young people. The Waltham system was to be different from the poverty and misery of the English system of labor, different also from the Slater mills that employed large families and put small children into the mills. Too complicated for children to operate, the power looms did not require strength so much as dexterity, and some women knew weaving from work at home. When young men became agricultural laborers, tenant farmers, or moved west, young farm women often went into the factories. Nowhere else could they make as much money. The "mill girls," as they called themselves, were a temporary labor force. Expecting to work for three or four years and return to the farms or get married, they were not at first eager to demand better working rules.

By 1826 the Waltham mills employed five hundred operatives, who were paid from two to four dollars a week, from which $1.25 for room and board was deducted. The power loom saved considerable labor cost over the hand-loom weaving method. In the machine shops, skilled machinists received fifty cents to two dollars a day, while the superintendent earned two dollars a day. One of the chief attractions of the Waltham mills was that they paid their workers in cash.

The venture was an immediate financial success, paying dividends of from 8 to 13 percent on investments. Lowell and his associates were experienced merchandisers, having already shipped British and Indian cloth, and when the British dumped cotton goods in the United States after the War of 1812, the fine English cotton textiles did not drive out the coarse cotton products of Waltham. In 1816, Lowell had gone to Washington to lobby for a new tariff of 6¼ cents a square yard which would protect the Waltham product against cheap cotton goods from India but would not protect Rhode Island manufacturers of hand-woven calico from imports of fine English cottons.

New England offered a more advantageous environment for factory development, for it had few craftsmen and skilled weavers to resist the machines turning out coarse, unbleached sheeting. With its big water supply and the ample labor force from the poor hill farms of Massachusetts, Waltham was an excellent site for the complete cotton factory. The only comparable locality for cotton mills was Philadelphia, the city to which skilled spinners and weavers had migrated during the colonial period, but unskilled workers were not plentiful there, as the farms of eastern Pennsylvania were fertile and migration to the West was easy.

By 1820 Moody had harnessed the power of the Charles River, so the

Boston Associates looked elsewhere for a new supply of power to build mills from the profits of Waltham. Appleton, Jackson, and Moody selected the community of East Chelmsford, where the Concord and Merrimack rivers came together at Pawtucket Falls—a falls of thirty-two feet from a large watershed that could provide over 3,000 potential horsepower, enough for fifty mills like the two in Waltham. Agents quickly bought four hundred acres from unsuspecting farmers in 1821 and gained control over the entire power of the Merrimack. The community was named Lowell in honor of the financial leader, who had died in 1817 at only forty-two. By 1839, nine textile companies were in operation. The population of Lowell expanded from 200 in 1820 to 30,000 by 1845.

Women made up by far the larger part of this population explosion. A long, low black wagon, called a "slaver," cruised along Vermont and New Hampshire farm roads in charge of a "commander" who received a dollar a head for any girl he could "bring to the market." Lowell and the other mill towns made factory work respectable by providing strictly chaperoned boardinghouses and requiring church attendance on Sunday. Female labor constituted over two-thirds of the factory labor force.

The mills of the paternalistic Boston Associates instituted a set of regulations to protect the young women and ensure discipline and compliance. An employee had to remain with the company for at least twelve months once she began work, and to give the company at least two weeks' notice before she could quit, or her name would go on a blacklist. She was to work fourteen hours a day, six days a week. While she could attend the church of her choice in Lowell, Sunday school was often taught by her overseers.

Lucy Larcom, one of five thousand Lowell girls, began work in 1835, changing the bobbins on the spinning frames when she was eleven years old. After her mother had been widowed and left alone with nine children, she too came to Lowell to work as a boardinghouse matron. During or after work, it was a life without privacy. In the boardinghouses the girls ate in a large communal dining room and slept six to a room, two to a bed. The inmates were locked in their boardinghouses at ten o'clock. In the factory Lucy worked from five in the morning to seven at night, with thirty minutes allowed for lunch and for dinner. Lucy found the work tedious, but there were moments of relief. While the girls could not read on company time —literature in the mills was strictly forbidden—they enjoyed a good deal of camaraderie. And an overseer allowed Lucy to sit in the window and watch the flow of the Merrimack River.

The mill owners were proud of their productive mills, constantly improved machinery, efficient labor force. They conceived of Lowell as a social experiment "that would be a shining example of those ultimate

Yankee ideals: profit and virtue, doing good and doing well." Visitors were impressed by the boardinghouse system, the chattering, vivacious mill girls, and especially by the educational opportunities of Lowell—by the Lowell Library, begun in 1825 with five hundred dollars from the company, and the Lyceum, also built by the company, which offered twenty-five lectures a year for fifty cents each, as well as night courses. Visitors wrote glowing—and often misleading—reports of busy mills and happy mill girls.

As the success of the Lowell and Waltham mills attracted new investors, the Boston Associates built mills on eight of New England's best water-power sites—Chicopee, Holyoke, and Lawrence in Massachusetts; Dover, Manchester, and Nashua in New Hampshire; Biddeford and Saco in Maine —eventually comprising one-fifth of America's cotton textile industry, all centrally controlled with other ventures in finance, insurance, and rail-roads. The protective tariff of 1816 allowed American industrialists to monopolize the market for the mass-produced, inexpensive, low-grade cotton cloth so much in demand by western settlers. The gin had lowered the price of cotton far below that of flax or wool, so the industrialist could buy cheap raw cotton, manufacture it into cloth, and sell it in a rapidly expanding internal market. The American standard of living was rising faster in this period than that of any other nation in the world.

Other industries such as firearms, woolens, iron, agricultural machinery, shoes and leather products expanded also, but no other industry rose so fast in the early years of 1816 through 1830 as did the cotton textile industry. The total number of factory spindles reached 1,750,000 by 1835. By 1840 mills employed 100,000 people, compared with 5,000 in 1816. The pioneering methods of the cotton textile industry influenced the methods of other industries. Men employed in developing machinery for the cotton textile industry supplied the skills and know-how for other mechanizing industries.

The innovating leaders needed more than machines and manpower; they needed money. Lack of capital was the principal problem of business-men in the early nineteenth century. As the Napoleonic wars made the United States the major neutral carrier with a corresponding rise in mer-cantile fortunes, northeastern states with competing seaports promoted their cities and tried to attract capital in various ways, such as awarding charters to businesses to incorporate. Savings banks arose rapidly in the northern and middle states and became capital suppliers to commercial banks either by redepositing deposits or by stock investments and loans to rising industries.

States had no requirements for reserves, so clearinghouses for interbank claims were developed through the leadership of the Boston Associates.

They were the directors of the Suffolk Bank of Boston, which in 1822 began to clear notes from country banks for the city banks of Boston, requiring country banks to maintain a five-thousand-dollar deposit in the Suffolk Bank and enough besides to redeem each of its notes. Lowell had received a corporate charter from the Massachusetts legislature and was able to draw on the profits of the Boston mercantile community. These merchants, with profits from the overseas trade, were people to look to for capital when banks would not take the risk.

Many of his friends and relatives had thought the plan of Francis Cabot Lowell for a cotton textile mill "a visionary and dangerous scheme." Lowell's leadership had convinced them otherwise.

FREIGHT: THE BIG DITCHES

The August day was hot and sultry when the extraordinary contraption, appearing to be a raft topped by a furnace, fired up in the Hudson River at New York City. On board were forty passengers—all members of the Livingston clan—who huddled together trying to avoid sparks and soot from the steamboat's engine. Undercurrents of "I told you so; it is a foolish scheme; I wish we were well out of it," grew louder. The steamboat's inventor, Robert Fulton, later wrote, "There were not perhaps thirty persons in the city who believed that the boat would ever move one mile an hour. . . ." Two men had no doubts: Chancellor Robert R. Livingston, an avid student of steam navigation, Fulton's mentor and financier, and Fulton himself, mechanical genius and inventor.

Fulton had no time for talk, being too busy trying to find out why his steamboat was steaming but not moving. Soon he solved the problem, and the boat left New York City bound for the chancellor's Clermont estate. As news of the boat's voyage moved up the Hudson faster than its speed of five miles per hour, people lined the shore to gape at the clanking, splashing craft, shooting a fiery shower of sparks as it panted its way. It was a frightening spectacle to some who watched from shore—the coming of the end. A few ran to their homes and locked the doors in fright, but the North River Steamboat of Clermont, later known as just the *Clermont*, roared on to Livingston's Hudson River estate, finishing the distance of 110 miles in twenty-four hours. The steamboat traveled forty miles to Albany on the following day.

"The power of propelling boats by steam is now fully proved," the elated inventor wrote of his triumph. ". . . It will give a cheap and quick conveyance to the merchandise on the Mississippi, Missouri, and other great rivers, which are now laying open the treasures to the enterprise of our countrymen." Fulton intended to use his steamboat on western waters and make upstream navigation possible on the Mississippi. His experiment was but one in a long string of successes. Tall, handsome, and forty-one, with curly black hair and dark eyes, he looked like an English gentleman who had married into the Livingston clan and been accepted, as indeed he had. Nothing if not confident, Fulton had a talent for persuading wealthy investors to finance his imaginative adventures. His first patron, Joel Barlow, a radical and cosmopolitan poet living in France, had introduced him to Livingston.

Fulton had traveled to Europe in 1787 to study miniature painting and did not return to the United States for twenty years. In Europe he came to be fascinated by transportation and the building of steamboats. Soon he was corresponding with Boulton and Watt in England about the purchase of a suitable steam engine for boat propulsion. A voracious reader of studies about steam navigation—especially the work of John Fitch, John Stevens, and Oliver Evans, all of whom had launched workable steamboats —as well as theoretical works on hull design, Fulton wrote a treatise of his own on the improvement of canal navigation. He moved to France in 1799 to confer with the French Directory about another dream of his, submarines. Encouraged by the French government, at war with England, Fulton perfected a submersible in which he and a crew of three, aided by a compressed-air tank, could submerge as deep as twenty-five feet and stay under for four and one-half hours. The French government agreed to reward him handsomely if he destroyed one of the British warships blockading the French coast, but Fulton never engaged a British ship. The French lost interest, and Fulton turned to his other pursuits.

Fulton became acquainted with Livingston while in France. The improvement of transportation through steam-powered vessels was a lifelong obsession of Livingston, as it was with other landowners of the period. In 1798, the Hudson grandee had a bill presented to the New York Assembly repealing an act of 1787 that gave John Fitch the sole right to use steamboats on the Hudson River and now awarding Livingston the privilege for twenty years, provided he could build within a year a boat of twenty tons and propel it by steam at the rate of four miles an hour.

Financed by Livingston, Fulton set to work late in 1802 to build an experimental boat to navigate on the Seine River of France. Since the inland navigation of American waters was their purpose, however, they both agreed to shift the experiments to the United States. After buying and shipping home a steam engine and boiler made by Boulton and Watt of

England, Fulton designed a vessel for it in the shipyards at Paulus Hook Ferry. It was a long and narrow boat—150 feet by 13 feet—with a flat deck and open machinery, planned for eventual use on the Ohio and Mississippi rivers.

Since a steamboat, in comparison with a textile factory, required little capital to build—$900 to $1,200 for the smaller boats and later $5,000 to $40,000 for the ferries—competition was stiff. Rivals sought advantages in state monopoly grants and expensive patent suits. Livingston won a second and third extension of the New York state monopoly, thus gaining the exclusive privilege to operate steamboats in New York waters and to have the privilege extended by five years for each additional boat built—the whole time not to exceed thirty years. Livingston felt he had every right to the monopoly since he had supplied leadership and capital, through the sale of some of his lands, to a project which would eventually benefit the nation as a whole. He supplied the inventor with a state monopoly and commercial advantage, for Livingston brought the steamboat to the attention of his merchant friends in New York City who would want to use a steamboat service. Livingston also brought stability and direction to the partnership, constantly summoning Fulton back from his other canal and submarine interests to the completion of the steamboat in 1807. "Mechanicks is my hobby horse," he wrote.

Fulton, in turn, gave his engineering talents and inventiveness to the partnership. The North River Steamboat was by no means original, for many others had built workable steam vessels (though none had lasted). Fulton approached the problem by studying the errors and successes of others, keeping careful records of his readings and experiments, and constructing trial models before going full-scale. Although his European training had taught him to study all aspects of a subject scientifically rather than tinkering, he wanted a practical and commercial success more than he wanted the claim of originality. Expanding his factory at Paulus Hook Ferry, he built another steamboat in 1810 and was offering ferry service from New York to Albany twice a week. He also turned to the area which had always been his object—the Mississippi River. Here the steamboat would transform the inland transportation system of the United States.

* * *

Walled off by the Appalachian Mountains, the Northwest was not easily accessible to manufactured goods from Europe and the Northeast, and the Northwest in turn could not profitably export to the East because of the high cost of wagon transport. As migrants poured over the Appalachians after the War of 1812 to settle and farm, they began to produce a surplus of heavy staples—grain, meat, whiskey, lumber, and livestock. How to market and transport this surplus? Heavy farm items such as wheat and flour could not absorb the freight charge of thirteen dollars a barrel to move from Pittsburgh to Philadelphia when the flour itself sold for ten dollars. Horses could draw loaded wagons about twenty miles a day, or two miles an hour.

Highways were still primitive, even though states had awarded monopolies to turnpike builders to encourage the construction of better roads. The national government itself built a highway partially from the sale of Ohio public lands to connect Ohio with the Atlantic. In 1818 this "National Road" opened for traffic from Cumberland on the Potomac River through the lower western corner of Pennsylvania to Wheeling. Although the new highway boasted a fine-stone surface and heavy bridges, traffic was so heavy as to wear it out in places. Maintained for the most part by local authorities, state roads were poor; only the best were comparable to the improved backcountry roads of today. The traveler could expect anything on local ways, even the building of fences across them. As late as 1841 one traveler found that a settler needing clay for his house chimney had dug a big hole in the middle of an Illinois state road used by the mail stage. The few improved highways such as the Pennsylvania Turnpike and the National Road did not lower the cost of freight transportation, which, to be at all profitable, had to go by water.

With his usual shrewdness Fulton sized up the steamboat possibilities of the Mississippi. Carrying freight by flatboat or keelboat was essentially one-way, time-consuming, and expensive. Farmers floated their products downstream to New Orleans on flatboats, sold off their boats for a pittance, and then usually had to walk home to Pennsylvania, Ohio, and Indiana over the Natchez Trail to Nashville and points north. The miracle of steam would enable boatmen to breast the current and convert the Mississippi into a huge two-way traffic link. With Livingston and Nicholas Roosevelt, Fulton organized the Mississippi Steamboat Company in 1809 to navigate the Mississippi River from New Orleans to Natchez.

Fulton and Livingston sent Nicholas Roosevelt west in the same year to study navigation opportunities on the Ohio and Mississippi rivers and then build a steamboat at Pittsburgh. In April 1811, their company persuaded the territorial legislature of Louisiana to grant them the exclusive use of the lower Mississippi River for steamboats. Once again Livingston's influence helped secure a steamboat monopoly—in this case because of his key role in negotiating the Louisiana Purchase of 1803. The partners awarded Roosevelt a contract to build the Mississippi steamboat. Construction began in 1811 on the Monongahela River in Pittsburgh amid endless difficulties. Fifty mechanics had to be imported from New York City, materials were in short supply, and the Boulton and Watt engine did not arrive, forcing substitution of an earlier engine.

The adventurous Roosevelt and his pregnant wife, Lydia, decided to make the first trip with no passengers. A crowd assembled as the *New Orleans* hissed and clanked down the Monongahela River, reaching Cincinnati by the second day. Bystanders lined the wharves of the Ohio River as the boat pushed its way behind the gentle current. By the fourth day, the *New Orleans* reached Louisville, where the boat docked because the falls on the Ohio River were too shallow for passage. The indomitable Lydia used this interval to have her baby. Then the couple renewed their journey; as if the baby were not enough, they had also taken on a Newfoundland dog. The steamboat tied up to shore at regular intervals to allow the crew to chop wood for the boiler. By the time the boat reached Natchez, thousands were lining the shore to see it, but the steamboat pushed on to New Orleans, reaching there by mid-January with wife, baby, dog, and husband still intact.

The denouement was anticlimactic. Fulton kept the *New Orleans* in service only between New Orleans and Natchez, never going back upriver. Two years later, the *New Orleans* hit a snag and sank.

Other steamboats quickly replaced it in the river trade. These vessels for the western waters had to be lighter in order to navigate through greater hazards of low water, falls, and floods, compared with steamboats on the protected northeastern waterways. Mississippi boats used high-pressure steam, which brought on more explosions and other accidents. The average life of western steamboats was four years, whereas boats using low-pressure steam in the Northeast lasted seven. Shifting sandbars and snags, rupturing boilers, and obstacles caused numerous casualties. More intense competition and higher operating expenses owing to heavier depreciation and costs seemed to be the lot of Mississippi steamboats.

The steamboatmen were undaunted. Four years after the maiden voyage of the *New Orleans,* the *Washington,* piloted by Henry M. Shreve, a veteran keelboat captain, did make the return trip upstream to Louisville. A keelboat with a cargo of from ten to forty tons and a crew of eight to twenty men had done well to pole six miles a day upstream, taking three to four months to reach Louisville from New Orleans. Shreve made the upstream trip to Louisville in twenty-five days. By 1817 seventeen steamboats, averaging about 190 tons each, were operating on western rivers; three years later there were sixty-nine. Fulton's audacity and practicality had paid off.

Despite all their theatrics, steamboats were slow to affect transportation as a whole. The early vessels were unreliable, dependent on the stage of the river, and too expensive to transport low-value heavy freight such as coal, lumber, and iron, which continued to go on keelboats until the middle 1830s. With more and better vessels, the value of goods received at New Orleans rose from $10 million in 1816 to $17 million by 1819, but the difference was not all due to steamboats, since the number of flatboats and the amount of freight they carried also rose. A dramatic effect of the steamboat, however, was on the lives of flatboatmen. Instead of one trip a year, midwestern farmers could now make four.

One of them, a nineteen-year-old Indiana boy named Abe Lincoln, contracted with a farmer in April 1828 to take a flatboat full of farm produce to New Orleans. With another youth Lincoln left Rockport, Indiana, and floated down the Ohio and the Mississippi trying to avoid snags and sandbars along the 1,200-mile journey. Seven slaves set upon their flatboat as it lay at anchor near a river plantation outside Baton Rouge, where they had stopped to trade part of their produce for sugar, cotton, and tobacco. The youths were barely able to fight off their attackers and pull anchor. When Lincoln reached New Orleans, he gaped at the crowded wharves where over a thousand flatboats were tied up while farmers and slaves unloaded produce which would be reloaded on sailing ships bound for northeastern cities and for Europe. Returning home by steamboat, Lincoln landed in Rockport with twenty-five dollars in his pocket for three months' labor.

Steamboats also lowered passenger rates for upstream travel, from about one hundred dollars from New Orleans to Pittsburgh to less than half of that. Some farmers saved even this fare by working their way home. The drop in rates made it more profitable for northwestern farmers to raise and sell their produce at New Orleans since now this produce could pay for more eastern manufactures. Farmers had an incentive to expand production for the market; and settlement in the Midwest increased. Before the steamboat, it cost seven to ten dollars per hundred pounds to ship manufactures to Cincinnati or Pittsburgh; the steamboats carried freight for two or three dollars and then as low as one dollar per hundred pounds.

As competition increased in western waters, the Fulton-Livingston monopoly, with no means to enforce it, collapsed by 1817. Their monopoly of New York State waters was also challenged. In 1824, John Marshall's Supreme Court declared the New York grant an unconstitutional invasion of the right of the federal government to regulate interstate commerce. Steamboats on the Hudson River carried passengers and expensive freight, and after the opening of the Erie Canal, they pulled barges slowly along the canal as rates fell.

As internal commerce expanded, each region of the country specialized

—the South in cotton; the Northwest in foodstuffs; the Northeast in manufactures—with a growth of the internal market and diminishing dependence on Europe. Steamboats on western waters solved one bottleneck to the development of the Northwest—lack of markets for western farm products. Southwestern planters specializing in cotton production for national and international markets needed foodstuffs, and an important river trade, stimulated by steamboats, developed between the two regions. The southwestern planter found it more profitable to devote his slave labor to cotton; and the small farmer of the Northwest supplied the planter with the corn and pork he needed to feed his labor force. A host of cities were springing into existence—Pittsburgh, Cincinnati, and Louisville on the Ohio; Memphis, Vicksburg, Natchez, and New Orleans; St. Louis, Clinton, Dubuque, and St. Paul on the Mississippi.

*   *   *

By the 1820s the newest form of transportation—steamboats on inland waterways—was coming into competition and combination with one of the oldest forms—canalboats pulled by horses or mules. While steamboats on the Mississippi and other western rivers were binding the South and West together in trade, the Northeast had lain isolated from the Northwest, locked behind the broad Appalachian range. Then, in a daring act of imagination, planning, and execution, some resourceful New Yorkers created a new waterway to the West that would transform the northern transportation system and alter the whole pattern of American economic and social development.

For years New Yorkers had dreamed of an opening to the West, centered on the Mohawk-Oswego water route running through a fifty-mile break in the Appalachian chain. It took men of vision—dreamers, even—just to conceive of a huge ditch that would run 360 miles from the Hudson to Buffalo, a ditch that would have to be cut through swamps, solid rock, dense forest; that would have to scour out some rivers and bridge others; that would have to climb hills and descend dales; that would need tens of thousands of men to build and thousands to maintain; and that would cost millions of dollars.

Such a visionary was Elkanah Watson. Born in Plymouth, indentured as a servant to the wealthy Brown family in Providence, young Watson had later been entrusted with messages and money from the colonies to Benjamin Franklin in Paris during the Revolution. Fascinated by the Dutch canal system, Watson returned home, settled in New York, and organized the Bank of Albany. After persuading several leading businessmen and landowners to tour central New York with him in 1788, he helped win from the

New York legislature a canal law authorizing the surveying of the Mohawk route. Watson was a director of two canal companies that improved that route, but it became evident that private enterprise could not alone build the big canal. Either the state or federal government must handle the job, but Jefferson and Madison were not interested in spending money on a prodigal northern ditch.

A politician picked up the failing standard. De Witt Clinton was a man of parts—a patron of schools, charities, and the arts, a founder of the New-York Historical Society, an amateur scientist and horticulturalist. A commanding figure and orator, dubbed "Magnus Apollo," he was also a politician who wanted to realize dreams. As mayor of New York City, canal commissioner, and later governor, he drove the canal measure through the legislature and into realization over the opposition of local interests favoring different routes, Tammany parochialism, and assorted naysayers.

Every step of the authorizing, financing, planning, and building of the canal came hard and dearly. New York lacked trained engineers for such a project, so men like James Geddes and Benjamin Wright and unstoried experimenters and tinkerers had to learn on the job. Canal builders lacked excavating machinery, so ditches were dug by crowds of men with shovels and crude derricks. Hundreds of "Irish bogtrotters" and other untrained laborers were kept at work for long hours amid the muck, and at peace among themselves. Yet the engineering and craftsmanship had to be of the first order. Canal walls and bottoms must be sealed against muskrats and boat wash; this was done by using local muck that was found to set "as hard as stone." Scores of locks, with their long, stone-lined channels and huge wooden gates, must be built in places with water plentiful enough to fill and empty a basin scores of times a day. Bridges and aqueducts had to be erected high over rivers and impossible terrain, and strong enough to support boat, crew, and cargo. Some of the aqueducts were architectural glories.

Finally the job was done—a canal 363 miles long, 4 feet deep, 28 feet wide at the bottom and 40 at the top, with 83 locks lifting boats to a height of almost 600 feet, and costing over $7 million. Such a feat called for celebration, and the New Yorkers did not fail the occasion. On a morning late in October 1825 the canalboat *Seneca Chief* nosed into the canal at Buffalo carrying two kegs of the "pure water of Lake Erie," Governor Clinton and other dignitaries, and a giant portrait of Clinton in Roman toga. The *Seneca Chief* and its escorting canalboats—one of which carried two Indian youths, two bears, two fawns, two birds, etc., and of course was named *Noah's Ark*—traveled east, reaching Rochester the following afternoon, Syracuse two days later, Utica the next day (where the passengers stopped for church), Schenectady on Tuesday, and Albany the next day, just a week after departure.

Gun salutes, speeches, parades, and official banquets greeted the little fleet at these stops, but the climax came in New York City. Scores of decorated vessels put on a "Grand Aquatic Display," followed by the "wedding of the waters" consummated when Governor Clinton poured a keg of Lake Erie water into the Atlantic. A huge parade in Manhattan featured a solid mile and a half of bands, military units, trade guilds, and floats representing butchers, tanners, cordwainers, and even a working press mounted on a high wagon and turning out leaflets with verses:

> 'Tis done, 'tis done! The mighty chain
> Which joins bright Erie to the Main
> For ages shall perpetuate
> The glories of our native State.

Philadelphians had followed the progress of the Erie Canal with feelings of admiration, envy, and commercial competitiveness. If the New Yorkers could overcome hundreds of miles of wilderness and inclines, why could not Pennsylvanians conquer the towering mountains to the west? Merchants, bankers, and promoters persuaded the state legislature in 1826 to authorize a canal between Philadelphia and Pittsburgh. Living up to the heritage of Franklin and Gallatin, the Pennsylvanians built a railroad from Philadelphia to Columbia on the Susquehanna; then, to cross the 2,291-foot-high Allegheny ridge, they fashioned the remarkable Allegheny Portage Railroad. Canalboats were floated onto cradles, which were then pulled out of the water and up a series of five inclined planes by stationary engines; at the top of each plane horses pulled the cradle onto a level stretch. Once over the top, the cradles were eased down inclined planes on the other side by horses, and deposited into a river and canal system headed west to Pittsburgh.

Brilliantly successful engineering—but faulty economics. Canalboatmen on the Pennsylvania found the route slower and more expensive than the Erie. The former had twice the number of locks as the latter, and a complex system of railroad and canal technology, depots, and agents had to be maintained. Virginia canal builders were unable even to overcome the western heights. Promoters of the Potomac and James routes to the West ran into too many problems of local scrambles for canal routes, lack of capital, and inadequate technology to span the Alleghenies and marry with the Ohio.

Still, the success of the big Erie ditch had touched off a kind of canal mania. By 1840 the states had built a total of over 3,000 miles of canals, at a cost of around $125 million, but the credit systems of three states were almost bankrupted. Canal builders had to be gamblers. When the Indiana legislature in the mid-1830s authorized construction of more than 1,200 miles of canals, the state bonded itself for $10 million, a debt of twenty dollars for every inhabitant. The construction led to near-disasters. Laborers on the canals were mainly Irish, half from northern Ireland and half from the southern counties. In Indiana's own "Irish war," fighting broke out near the present city of Wabash, and the state militia had to be called. Despite floods, cholera, and numerous other difficulties, Indiana's canal reached the Ohio, but the tolls failed to pay even for its maintenance.

By the 1840s the United States had a canal system—three systems, actually, comprising short tidewater canals along the coast from New England to South Carolina; "trunk line" canals that reached into the mountains and in two cases—the Erie and Pennsylvania—crossed them; and interior canals branching out from the Ohio and from Lakes Michigan and Erie. By the end of the 1830s canal and river boats were the kings of American transportation, but their reign was to be short. Canal transport was slow and cumbersome. At four cents per ton per mile, freight was not cheap. In the North, the waters lay frozen several months a year. Yet the canal system was far more developed in the North than in the South, leading to a regional imbalance. As economic connections developed among the Northeast, the Great Lakes, the Ohio, the Mississippi cities, and New Orleans, the southeastern states were bypassed.

And at its height, the reign of water transport was threatened by a new noisy monster, one that might invade the most sylvan scene—the steam engine on rails. But not for another decade or two would this monster become king.

THE INNOVATING LEADERS

Early in 1808 Joshua Forman, a New York State assemblyman and Erie Canal enthusiast, heard that Treasury Secretary Albert Gallatin had just issued a report calling for a national system of roads and canals, including some kind of canal connecting the Hudson and Lake Erie. Gallatin had even proposed three millions of federal dollars for the Erie project. Elated, Forman journeyed to Washington and, through the good offices of a New York congressman, gained an interview with President Jefferson. To his dismay he found the President rather cool, even surprised that Forman would be trying to tap the federal treasury so quickly. And for once Jefferson's mind was on more parochial matters.

"Why, sir," Jefferson said to Forman, "here is a canal for a few miles, projected by George Washington, which if completed would render this [Washington] a fine commercial city, which has languished for many years because the small sum of 200,000 dollars necessary to complete it, cannot be obtained from the general government, the state government, or from individuals—and you talk of making a canal 350 miles through the wilderness—it is little short of madness to think of it at this day."

Madness! But the crazy New Yorkers pushed that canal through the wilderness, and afterwards De Witt Clinton could not resist twitting Jefferson about that conversation with Forman. The old man confirmed the conversation, adding, "Many, I dare say, still think with me that New-York has anticipated, by a full century, the ordinary progress of improvement." Jefferson mused further:

"This great work suggests a question, both curious and difficult, as to the comparative capability of nations to execute great enterprises." Did New York, he wondered, have an economic advantage? "This may be;—or is it a moral superiority? a sounder calculating mind, as to the most profitable employment of surplus, by improvement of capital, instead of useless consumption. I should lean to the latter hypothesis, were I disposed to puzzle myself with such investigations; but at the age of 80, it would be an idle labour, which I leave to the generation which is to see and feel its effects."

Others wondered at the time, and have questioned since, how a small nation with a rudimentary economic system could have embarked on such bold and costly efforts, whether successful as in the case of the Erie, or less so as with the Pennsylvania project, but always difficult, expensive, and risky. The ultimate source of the economic changes lay in material needs for better and cheaper food, clothes, and homes, and in requirements for psychic and material security. But we lack the data to measure those needs in the early nineteenth century, and can only assume that they existed among the Americans of that day as they do among all peoples, in various combinations and degrees. How did such needs become translated into economic change and progress in an isolated, mainly rural nation, lacking capital, organized technical training and expertise, and experience in the management of big enterprises?

Perhaps the most striking aspect of economic change during this period was the extent to which innovating leaders with "sounder calculating minds," in Jefferson's phrase, stepped forward to experiment, invent, organize, and manage. The exploits of lone, daring men have come down through history. Certainly the tenacity of a Whitney, the creative daring of a Francis Lowell, the imaginative patronage of a Livingston played a major part in technological change and progress. Certainly, too, the involvement of men of affairs like De Witt Clinton, and of republican aristocrats like Livingston, was crucial in particular moments. But innovating leadership was essentially a collective effort. For one thing, the seemingly solitary innovators were often members of large and influential families, such as the Browns of Providence and the Dwights of Chicopee, that collectively involved themselves in new ventures. Francis Cabot Lowell's father, John, had married in turn a Higginson, a Cabot, and a Russell, and had sired offspring by all three, so it was not surprising that Francis' efforts were aided and abetted, and occasionally impeded, by a plethora of in-laws and other members of an extended family that helped form a local and regional community which, in Robert K. Lamb's words, closely affected "the processes by which certain decision-makers at strategic points in the social structure contribute to economic, political, and social change."

But even more, innovating leaders emerged from a variety of groups and situations. Many farmers were as much inventors as husbandmen, eternally tinkering, patching up, imitating others, swapping tales of their experiments and experiences. Homely contrivances and techniques were handed down from father to son. Untrained mechanics improved methods of spinning and weaving, of running steam engines and railroad portages and canal locks. In building the Erie Canal the diggers improvised on the spot. European canal experience had left no manuals for dealing with stretches of swamp near Syracuse that, with their snarled and matted roots, were harder to cut through than rock, where at least hand drills and gunpowder could be used. "Sharp plows were devised for cutting the tangled roots," according to Broadus and Louise Pearson Mitchell. "Horse-drawn scoops were substituted for shovels. A cable, a wheel, and an endless screw permitted a man, aided by the power of one horse, to pull over the largest trees." Stumps were twisted and torn out of the ground by an ungainly contraption—a cable pulled by a horse and attached to a great wooden wheel, inside of which was fastened a smaller drum wound about by a cable attached to the stump.

These collective acts of innovators were spurred by the most influential leadership collectives in America during the 1820s and after—the state governments. With power to intervene in and regulate economic life left largely to the states under the federal Constitution, legislators and governors became the target of promoters seeking legislation, subsidies, and other kinds of help and sponsorship—and often the promoters were as much inside the government as outside. The granting and withholding of monopolistic rights and other privileges, the subscription to the stock of new corporations, the regulation of enterprises through charters issued by the state, the subsidy of private ventures but again with strings attached,

the direct establishment and financing of public enterprise by the state—
all these brought the collective action of the states directly into the economic life of Americans. This was especially true of transportation: the
states played the main role in initiating, planning, and financing most of
the canals and many of the roads and turnpikes.

Innovating leadership thus proceeded from the most variegated sources
—from state governments, from European experience and manuals, from
the studies and experiments of innovators with wealth and status like
Livingston, from fathers and mothers, from the exchanges of ideas in
professional societies and local groups, from fellow tinkerers and improvisers on the job, often under the lash of dire necessity. To be sure, much
of this innovation was contained within class lines; poor farmers, mill girls
in Lowell, and Irish bogtrotters along the canals were victims of existing
technology rather than agents for changing it. But among the more educated, mobile, skilled, and affluent classes, innovations in one place soon
fertilized developments elsewhere. Elkanah Watson, a gentleman farmer
in Albany and member of the New York Society for the Promotion of
Agriculture, Arts, and Manufactures, modeled his farming practices on
Livingston's. After purchasing 250 acres near Pittsfield, Massachusetts,
Watson bought a pair of merino sheep from the chancellor and put them
on exhibition in the Pittsfield town square. Farmers flocked to the scene.
"Even women," wrote Watson, "were excited by curiosity to attend this
first novel, and humble exhibition." Watson became the first president of
the Berkshire County Agriculture Society, which held an annual fair.
County fairs became an easy means for farmers to learn about, and display,
the latest agricultural practices and to put their prize stock on sale.

*   *   *

The rapid spread of innovations and inventions seemed inexorable in
retrospect but most of these changes were charged with conflict. Many
Americans had aesthetic and even philosophical objections to the invasion
of machines into quiet farmyards and waterways. Many farmers shunned
innovation because they liked the old ways of doing things, or simply
feared change. The innovators themselves had to overcome obstacles at
every turn. The small profits Whitney made from his cotton gin he had to
use in fighting infringements on his patent. For years Fulton kept up a running quarrel with rivals who impugned the novelty of his own steamboat
innovations.

But the political conflict transcended the personal. The extent to which
government—federal, state, or even local—promoted innovation and development was a matter of fierce partisan and regional debate. If Pennsyl-

vanians competed with New Yorkers in digging their way west, cities within the states fought with one another about the location of turnpikes and canals. Furious debates broke out among engineers and laymen as to the relative advantages of turnpikes, riverways, canals, and (later) railroads. The use of taxpayers' money as against private investors' was another bone of contention, though it came to be widely recognized that only the federal or state governments could finance vast projects like the Erie Canal.

Conflict over such matters produced a higher consciousness of ways and means, methods and goals. Sometimes conflict aroused direct mobilization of the populace, producing grass-roots leaders who further aroused the people to political consciousness. When Clinton was removed from the New York City mayoralty by pressure from Tammany Hall, and Erie Canal prospects seemed doomed, this energetic New Yorker fought back. Working closely with a few associates, he decided to "go to the people" in a final effort to mobilize support for the canal. First he held a meeting of a hundred prominent men in New York City; then he sent material from this meeting throughout the state; then rallies were held in scores of cities and villages along the proposed route; finally, petitions with over 100,000 signatures were sent to the legislature.

It was a superb political operation, directed squarely at the key economic interests. "Wealthy Federalists—large landholders in the west and great merchants in the cities—as well as western farmers were attracted to Clinton's banner," Julius Rubin wrote. "The Irish, whose numbers had recently increased greatly, rallied to Clinton because of past favors and in reaction to Tammany's nativist policy. . . . Large merchants and western farmers, aristocratic landholders and poverty-stricken immigrants—all united behind Clinton and his great canal project." The Erie, like most great projects, was conceived not in benign consensus but aroused consciousness that enabled men to fight—and win—the political battle.

The changes in farming, manufacturing, and transportation accelerated in the 1820s and later produced a quickening of commerce in the cities and along the roads and waterways of America. A territorial division of labor developed among the three great regions of the Union, with the South producing plantation staples for the foreign markets, the East increasingly engaged in making goods and capital and selling both to the South and West, and the West growing grain and livestock that supplied the rising needs of the South and East. The old-time triangular maritime commerce before the Revolution had given way by 1830 to a new triangle, creating an "intersectional indebtedness," in Louis Schmidt's words, "the West paying for its manufactures from the East with its sales to the South in somewhat the same manner that New England paid for its manufactures from the mother-country during the Colonial period by the sale of its commodities to the West Indies." The huge, lopsided commerce, moving south down the Mississippi to New Orleans, eastward and northward along the Gulf and Atlantic seaboards to the northern seaports, and westerly toward the Ohio Valley and Great Lakes area, would help produce a political imbalance as well.

To a large extent these changes in the pattern of economic growth were the product of millions of tiny decisions by farmers, manufacturers, traders, and transporters who had little knowledge about, interest in, or control of the gigantic economic forces that would come to grip the nation before the end of the century. These persons were intent on immediate gain, perhaps even sheer financial survival, from buying and selling goods and services. They were variously the beneficiaries and the victims of "impersonal" forces that dominated the marketplace—of supply and demand, technological change, population growth and change, rises and falls in commodity and retail prices. In such a context even the larger and more aggressive buyers and sellers were essentially barterers and brokers—that is, "transactional leaders"—in an economic environment beyond their power of individual or, for a time at least, collective control.

But at times certain innovating leaders managed to transcend their environment and even transform it. The most conspicuous cases were doubtless men like Slater and Lowell, Livingston and Clinton, and their close associates. But the farmer who experimented with new seeds or crop rotation or tinkered out in the barn, the canal digger who discovered how to clear away trees and stumps, the southern planter who worked out more efficient methods of large-scale farming, the mechanic who tried out a new pulley arrangement on the banks of the Connecticut—all these in their different ways were altering the world in which they and their children would live. Some of these innovating leaders were acting for immediate self-interest, whatever the broader impact of their feats. Others were acting also for a broader purpose, even for a vision. The Erie Canal, the work of hundreds of New York State leaders supported by thousands of aroused followers, was a brilliant act of economic and technical planning—an act designed to achieve vast socioeconomic changes, an act that achieved them. Men like Francis Cabot Lowell and De Witt Clinton demonstrated that daring economic and political plans could be achieved in the 1820s just as they had been by leaders two generations earlier, in the 1780s.

If all this was something less than Jefferson's "moral superiority," it was something more than a "sounder calculating mind"—purposeful action aimed at explicit goals in response to human needs, somehow fashioned in the disheveled, conflict-ridden arena of American democracy. This remarkable physical and economic creativity almost matched the boldness of vision, genius of invention, and willingness to experiment of the founding fathers. The "economic miracles" of the 1820s and 1830s had their roots to some degree in the "political miracle" of the 1780s—the creation of a reasonably effective federal government operating in a liberated national economy. But the economic miracle had not been matched by constitutional creativity in the years of Monroe and the second Adams; rather the governmental system seemed static. The Framers had responded to the political and ideological imperatives of their time; the question fifty years later was how the leaders would respond to the imperatives rising out of Whitney's cotton gin, Clinton's ditch, Lowell's textile mills, Fulton's *Clermont,* and the innovations of thousands of other experimenters, inventors, and builders.

PART III
Liberty and
Equality

CHAPTER 9

The Wind from the West

AMERICANS were moving west. Restless, hopeful, yearning for another big chance somewhere out in the distant fields and plains where the rich soil ran six feet deep, so it was said, families sold off possessions from the "old place," loaded up horses and wagons, spoke farewells to a circle of envious, skeptical neighbors, and left to fulfill dreams of independence and abundance. People often moved in short jumps, from state to next-door state; sometimes they meandered up or down a fertile valley; but the great current flowed inexorably along parallel lines toward the nation's heartland, with the setting sun as its pole star.

Up-country yeomen of the Old South struck out for cheap and good land in Tennessee and Kentucky. Planters, their soil exhausted, moved through the Gulf states looking for new acreage to meet the demand for cotton stimulated by the gin, South Carolinians through the Saluda Gap into eastern Tennessee, Georgians into southern Alabama and Mississippi along two main routes linked at Fort Mitchell. They were helping to found a new cotton kingdom to the west of the Old South. Middle-staters used the Wilderness Road and the Cumberland Gap Road to debouch into the Ohio Valley and the farmlands of Indiana and Illinois. New Englanders spread westward in a steady stream into upper and central New York State, northern Pennsylvania, northeastern Ohio, and beyond into Michigan and even Wisconsin, planting churches and schools along the way.

For years the queen of the roads across the Alleghenies was the Conestoga wagon, with its four to six horses, its broad wheels to cope with muddy roads, and, between a high aft and stern, its ample low bed that kept families and goods from spilling out as the wagon pointed up and down steep hills. Many settlers had to do with less. Journeying along the National Road through Pennsylvania in 1817, Morris Birkbeck noted that with many families a "small waggon (so light that you might almost carry it, yet strong enough to bear a good load of bedding, utensils and provisions, and a swarm of young citizens,—and to sustain marvelous shocks in its passage over these rocky heights), with two small horses, sometimes a cow or two, comprises their all; excepting a little store of hard-earned cash for the land office of the district; where they may obtain a title for as many acres as they possess half-dollars, being one fourth of the purchase money. The waggon has a tilt, or cover, made of a sheet, or perhaps a blanket. The family are seen before, behind, or within the vehicle, according to the road or the weather, or perhaps the spirits of the party." Birkbeck noted also that some families traveled only with horse and packsaddle, and often "the back of the poor pilgrim bears all his effects, and his wife follows, naked-footed, bending under the hopes of the family."

In later years some families traveled in far grander style, as transportation improved on the waterways. Certainly the most extraordinary trip west was via the Allegheny Portage Railroad. Nothing really could compare with awakening in one's own canal barge on top of an Allegheny mountain. "The whole family was comfortably located in the cabin of their boat, which appeared to glide up the heights of the Alleghenies, unconscious of its being a fish out of water, whilst some of the family were preparing the coming meals and others were lying on their downy pillows," the *Hollidaysburg Aurora* wrote enthusiastically of the first trip. Next day "our boat and crew left the sunny summit and smoothly glided down her iron way to Johnstown, astonishing the natives." Another editor compared the mountaintop barge to Noah's Ark on Ararat. Even without hyperbole the portage railroad, with its huge hoists with stationary engines, carefully inclined planes, and elaborately balanced ascending and descending cars carrying barges, soon became world-famous.

But for most travelers the lasting memory was passage along the Erie Canal: gliding along mile after mile, watching the boy driver ahead manage the horses and keep the towline taut and untangled, talking with lockkeepers and farmers as the great basins were filled and emptied, stopping off in canal shops, showboats, and floating saloons, matching wits with thimblerig experts, gypsy fortune tellers, peddlers of tempting goods, . . . hearing the double blast of the cow horn as a packet captain signaled that he was "coming through," . . . chatting with the tobacco-chewing steersman as he kept his craft off-angle while avoiding rocks and abutments, . . . and enjoying a good meal prepared by a canalboat chef. And always the slowly passing scenery: the blue smoke in the morning rising from cottages and shanty boats, farmers pulling out stumps or sowing their cleared land with great sweeping movements of their arm, the "gentle slap of water against the boats, the riffle of towropes, the swish of wind in the water grass, the splash and murmur of widening circles when a muskrat slid into the canal, the warning horns of craft coming in from the feeders . . . the gentle tinkle of cowbells across open fields, the song of fiddle and jew's-harp, riding the wind, punctuated by the measured plop-plop of oxen hoofs as they plodded westward," in Madeline Sadler Waggoner's words.

And always the excited talk with other passengers about the adventures and opportunities lying ahead "out west."

Not all canal passengers traveled elegantly or comfortably. There was a kind of caste system among boats. The grandee of the Erie was the long and lean canal packet, carrying only passengers and hand luggage and offering good meals, "settles" on top of the cabin from which passengers could enjoy the canal scenery, and separate sleeping spaces for men and women. The emigrant's boat, or line boat, took on families and their furniture and stoves and chickens, and provided sleeping space on the floor at best. Next down in the hierarchy came the freighter, whose owner might live on board with the horses he carried along the canal; the cabin boat, built by the migrants to carry their families west; the shanty boat, a one-room hovel on a flatboat, which housed thousands of canallers along the Erie and moved occasionally by hitching a ride on another craft; and, lowest in caste of all, the timber raft, a collection of piles of logs lashed together and topped by a shanty for the crew.

But sometimes all passengers were tumbled into one existence, when the steersman's warning of "low bridge ahead," or bad weather, drove the nabobs out of their "settles" and into the cabin below. Because of the narrow beam of canalboats, the cabin was usually a jumble of clothes, bags, blankets, food, clotheslines, and people. Passengers had to sleep on foot-wide berths that appeared to Charles Dickens to be "hanging book-shelves, designed apparently for volumes of the small octavo size." Like most natives, the famous English visitor found he could get into his shelf, which was the bottom one, only by lying on the floor and rolling in. Dickens could cope with this, but not with the habits of his fellow passengers. "All night long, and every night, on this canal," he complained, "there was a perfect storm and tempest of spitting."

Spitting. This "filthy custom," as Dickens called it, repelled other visitors from abroad as well. "It was a perfect shower of saliva all the time," Fanny Kemble noted on *her* boat. Tobacco-chewing Americans seemed to spit everywhere—in carriages, boardinghouses, law courts, the Capitol, even on carpets in living rooms—but especially in the raw new towns of the West. Americans were slouchers too; they seemed to slouch sitting down. The "bearing and attitudes of the men" at the theater struck Mrs. Frances Trollope as "perfectly indescribable; the heels thrown higher than the head, the entire rear of the person presented to the audience, the whole length supported on the benches, are among the varieties that these exquisite posture-masters exhibit." Her remarks on slouching became so famous that American theatergoers spotting an egregious sloucher in the pit would set up the cry, "A trollope! a trollope!"

Americans, especially frontier Americans, were vulgar: this was the report brought back from the inscrutable continent to the west by many of the scores of visiting Europeans. Americans were also materialistic, avaricious, selfish, boastful, rude, gluttonous, cruel, violent. Yet other travelers —sometimes the same travelers—returned with different observations about the American character, especially on the frontier: "Jonathan" was friendly, generous, helpful, natural, unspoiled, hospitable, affectionate. Americans, in short, were complicated and contradictory.

Frontier people had a way of destroying generalizations and shibboleths. Not only European observers but also eastern Americans traveling into the West came to conclusions only to have them invalidated. American frontier people were long painted as rugged individualists, but these individualists were also resolute collectivists, or at least cooperators, in joining with their spouses and children in clearing land and building homesteads, with their townspeople in cabin raisings, logrollings, law enforcing, with the authorities in laying roads, fighting Indians, erecting forts, financing schools. Western settlers, supposed to be materialistic, set up schools and churches, libraries and literary societies, almost as fast as they established saloons and stables. Western frontier people were, on the whole, more daring, more restless, more mobile, more "middle-income" (the rich had the money to go West but little motive, the poor had the motive but no money) than the rest of the population. They were also generally outsiders who, it was said, had "sought the West to escape a society in which distinctions of birth and possession had put them at a disadvantage."

Their hallmark was diversity. They were diverse in their environments, for people were "settling in" behind a constantly moving frontier while hunters and trappers were advancing ahead of it. They were diverse in occupation: speculators, merchants, lawyers, farmers, riverboatmen, blacksmiths, flour millers, road builders, printers, distillers, teachers. They were self-contradictory, now friendly and now suspicious, generous and stingy, religious and blasphemous, nationalistic and parochial, hard-working and self-indulgent, rowdy and respectable. They were ambitious but lacking in lofty ambition, observers concluded. "They talked up liberty but restricted its practice. . . . They loved change but dreaded revolution. . . . They were avid readers but preferred newspaper gossip to literature. They were in a constant 'election fever' but cold to political principles. They had appetites but no passions." They knew how to make money but not how to spend it. They were, in short, bundles of complexities, contrarieties, and possibilities.

Out of the frontier rose a man—a migrant, an outsider, a hard worker, but also a man on the make—who embraced its contradictions. Born poor and fatherless in the Carolina uplands, Andrew Jackson rebelled from the start against schools, restrictions, and his mother's plans for him to become a Presbyterian minister. Foul-mouthed, mean-tempered, and combative even as a child, he grew into a wild youth who led his companions in wrestling, foot-racing, drinking, card playing—and in carting off neighbors' gates and outhouses. When provoked or thwarted, he choked with rage and could hardly speak. His mother, who had lost her husband four months before Andrew was born, suddenly left her last-born when he was fourteen in order to nurse American prisoners of war in far-off Charleston, and died there. This ultimate desertion left the boy more bellicose, restless, and mischievous than ever.

Yet there was always another side to Andrew Jackson. If he swore, he swore with style. If he bullied, he was the kind of bully who could win followers and even admirers. And if he was cruel and violent, it was the only way he knew how to cope with the wild frontier around him until it too could be mastered. He experienced that environment at a remarkably young age. A guerrilla at thirteen, he fought the British in bitter skirmishes; captured by the enemy, he was slashed across the head when he refused to clean a British officer's boots and demanded to be treated as a prisoner of war. Thrown into a prisoner-of-war camp, he was robbed of his clothes and, ravaged by smallpox, he was freed in an exchange, only to lose his remaining brother to the pox.

Somehow the youth was steeled by these ordeals rather than broken. At eighteen he read law; a year later he was practicing as a licensed attorney; and a year after that he was the public prosecutor for western North Carolina. Then he moved west, finally settling in Nashville, where he continued to prosper: attorney general for the Moro district at twenty-four, delegate to the Tennessee constitutional convention four years later, elected the first member of Congress from Tennessee at twenty-nine, United States senator at thirty, a judge in the Supreme Court of Tennessee a year later. During this meteoric rise, however, a wild outsider seemed to be struggling with the insider on the make. For years he and his after-work cronies acted the hooligans, stealing outhouses. He courted the vivacious Rachel Robards before she was divorced. He speculated recklessly in land, traded in slaves and cotton, brawled and quarreled incessantly, flirted with the Burr conspiracy, coolly and deliberately killed a man in a duel, fought others with cane, fists, and gun; maintained smoldering hatreds for Indians, Spanish, and Englishmen. He owned about eighty black men and women.

To old Republicans like Jefferson, Jackson was a dangerous man, a demagogue, utterly unfit to be President. Among those close to him, he could be elaborately courteous to men, gentle and courtly to women, and generous to a fault—he was often in debt for signing shaky notes for friends. To plain Americans, Jackson became—after the Indian campaigns and New Orleans—the nation's hero. If his views were hazy, his image was clear—a lean, ramrod figure topped by a seamed and wrinkled face, a hard-set lantern jaw, piercing eyes, under a corona of bristling white hair.

THE REVOLT OF THE OUTS

The simplest definition of politics is the conflict of outs versus ins. This is also the most simplistic definition, for the battle between those who hold office and those who seek it becomes enmeshed with ideological, policy, ethnic, geographical, religious, and other conflicts that may turn the contest into something more fundamental than a struggle to keep or seize power and pelf; some persons, indeed, reject office out of conviction. If ever a political contest was reduced to the simplest definition of politics, however, it was Jackson's campaign against John Quincy Adams in 1828, when a coalition of "insiders" united around a few great national issues was assailed by a coalition of outsiders agreed on hardly any issues at all.

Since the election sharpened not merely major policy issues but personal and psychological ones, it turned into the ugliest presidential contest in a generation. However divided, the outsiders were agreed on the man they wanted—Andrew Jackson—and they were united by the conviction that they had been excluded from the citadels of the political and financial system, from the centers of social status and deference. They were Westerners and Southerners incensed against the East; growers and consumers angered by abominable tariffs; mechanics and small businessmen indignant over "monopoly"; farmers hostile to middlemen and speculators.

Listen to young Congressman James K. Polk inveigh against what had come to be known as Adams' and Clay's American System: "Since 1815 the action of the Government has been . . . essentially vicious; I repeat, sir, essentially vicious." The American tripod was a "stool that stands upon three legs; first, high prices of the public lands . . . sell your lands high, prevent thereby the inducements to emigration, retain a population of paupers in the East, who may, of necessity, be driven into manufactories, to labor at low wages for their daily bread. The second branch of the system is high duties . . . first, to protect the manufacturer, by enabling him to sell his wares at higher prices, and next to produce an excess of revenue. The third branch of the system is internal improvements, which is the sponge which is to suck up the excess of revenue."

All of which sounded like the poor man against the rich, the People against the Elite, the rebels against the Establishment, until one looked at the Jacksonian leaders. They were—most of them—not mechanics or farmers or paupers but capitalists, planters, traders, landowners and speculators, slave owners, lawyers, journalists, and indeed men, like Jackson himself, who had already enjoyed the fruits of office as legislators and administrators. Still, they had acute feelings of political and psychological exclusion. And nothing had aroused both feelings as forcibly as Adams' and Clay's "deal" of January 1825—the deal that they were certain had kept Andrew Jackson out of the White House.

The campaign of 1828 began just after the "corrupt bargain" became known, when Jackson, fuming over the Judas of the West, resigned his Senate seat and started home. Neither time nor travel assuaged his feelings. He was weeping for his country's experiment in liberty, he wrote a friend, when "the rights of the people" could be bartered for promises of office. By the time he reached his Hermitage home he was talking darkly of "usurpation of power" and the "great constitutional corrective in the hands of the people" against it. Soon men in Nashville and Virginia and Washington and New York were laying plans for 1828.

A motley group was gathered behind the Old Hero—its acknowledged leader, Martin Van Buren. Small, amiable, plumpish, cautious, calculating, urbane, the New Yorker seemed almost the antithesis of the Hero, but both had made their way without much education, knew what it was to be on the outs with dominant factions in their states, and shared prejudices about bankers, entrenched federal officials, and Easterners unaware of the need to settle the western lands. Van Buren had shown himself a master political broker and coalition builder, as a leader of the "Albany Regency" and United States senator.

Jackson's old-time advisers had been mainly Westerners: Major John H. Eaton, a Florida land speculator and Tennessee politico; William B. Lewis, also of Tennessee, who had helped him as political lieutenant and fixer; Judge John Overton, an old confidant and loyalist. The most colorful by far was Thomas Hart Benton of Missouri. Expelled from the University of North Carolina for thieving from his roommates, he had moved to Tennessee, gained admission to the bar, won a seat in the state senate, served as Jackson's aide-de-camp, then moved to Missouri and within five years won election as United States senator. He and Jackson, who earlier had brawled ferociously in Tennessee, were now reconciled. A handsome, solidly built man, of considerable intellectual power, Benton had a vanity so grand and serene that friends came to accept it, like a national monument.

These men and their allies across the nation slowly worked out a simple but formidable double strategy to elect Old Hickory President. They would broaden out Jackson's personal coalition and entrench it solidly in the democratic and agrarian ranks of the old Republican party. Crucial to the first strategy was winning support from southern leaders disaffected by Adams, and the key man in this region was Vice-President Calhoun, who had broken with the President and plumped for Jackson. Although Calhoun had been elected Vice-President in 1824, he had been disturbed by the flouting of the popular will in Adams' selection by the House—and even more disturbed that two Adams terms, followed by two terms for the heir apparent, Henry Clay, would close off the presidency for sixteen years. Calhoun was already in his mid-forties. Within two years of Adams' (and his own) inauguration, having moved solidly into Jackson's camp, the dour South Carolinian was sending the Hermitage optimistic reports about 1828 prospects.

"Every indication is in our favor, or rather I should say in favor of the country's cause," he wrote Jackson in January 1827. "The whole South is safe, with a large majority of the middle states, and even in New England strong symptoms of discontent and division now appear, which must daily increase." He looked forward to the triumph of "the great principles of popular rights, which have been trampled down by the coalition." Within another year the general's lieutenants had extended their counter-coalition throughout the twenty-four states. The heart of this strategy was what Van Buren called an alliance between the "planters of the South and the plain Republicans of the North."

An even more crucial task was to build a firm foundation of popular support beneath the broadening cadre of Jackson's leaders. Van Buren & Co. decided on the bold strategy of the "substantial reorganization of the Old Republican party"—in plainer words, to build a *Jackson* party within the disheveled ranks of the cumbrous party of Monroe, Adams, and Clay. The key to this effort was unprecedented political organization. In Nashville, Jackson himself established and supervised a central committee composed of stalwarts like Lewis and Overton. In Washington, an informal caucus of members of Congress safeguarded Jackson's interests on Capitol Hill. Throughout the states, Hickory Clubs organized parades and barbecues and rallies, printed up handbills, pamphlets, and leaflets, and canvassed the voters in their homes. The Jackson men, ostentatiously taking their case "to the people," established an extraordinary number of new dailies and weeklies to combat the established newspapers that spoke for Adams and Clay. All this required money, but the Jacksonians seemed to have plenty of it. Edward Pessen estimated that the election of Jackson cost about one million dollars—a formidable sum in 1828.

The contest was largely devoid of issues, and it was meant to be. Jackson did not rally the masses by appeals to ideals of justice and equality; he stayed home and stayed quiet, except for occasional pieties and ambiguities. In vain did Adams supporters try to raise questions like the tariff and internal improvements. "The *Hurra Boys*" were all for Jackson, one Administration man sneered, but he had to admit that they constituted a "powerful host." The "National Republicans"—as the anti-Jacksonians came to be called—seemed unable to compete with a Hickory Leaf in every hat and hickory-pole raisings in every town square. Increasingly, the Jacksonians themselves were becoming known as "Democratic-Republicans," or simply "Democrats."

Slander and abuse pushed aside issues. Adams was called a monarchist, squanderer of the taxpayers' dollars on silken fripperies, Sabbath breaker, pimp. Partisans of the President in turn labeled Jackson as blasphemer, bastard, butcher, adulterer. As usual, the invective had a tiny morsel of truth. *John Quincy Adams* a *pimp?* Well, it seemed that in St. Petersburg, corrupted as he was by his long service in sinful foreign capitals, he had "prostituted a beautiful American girl to the carnal desires of Czar Alexander I." A fiction, of course, but a rumor to be handled only by attributing even baser acts to Jackson. The *Old Hero* an *adulterer?* Well, Jackson had indeed married Rachel Robards before she was divorced, and he may have done so knowingly, but the Jackson men had to put out sworn statements as to his innocence.

In a contest of invective and personality, no Adams could win out. Jackson beat him in the popular vote, 647,292 to 507,730. The general won the electoral college 178 to 83; Adams carried only New England and parts of the central Atlantic region. Jackson brought off a clean sweep of the rural hinterland west of New Jersey and south of the Potomac. Swept out of office by this gale of southern and "western" ballots, the National Republicans saw the results as presaging ominous changes, as their political fathers had twenty-eight years before. "Well," said an Adams backer, "a great revolution has taken place . . ." Another wrote: "It was the howl of raving Democracy."

It was, at least, the howl of the outsiders. With the approach of Inauguration Day 1829, plain people by the hundreds descended upon Washington, crowding the lodging places and thronging the streets. They massed in front of the Capitol to hear their hero pledge reform to all and the ending of the national debt. Then they followed the new President down Pennsylvania Avenue to the White House, pushed into the mansion, and fought their way toward the punch and the ice cream. As the visitors trampled on the chairs and carpets of the house just vacated by an Adams of Boston, as they smashed china and glasses, it seemed as though a new day had dawned in Washington. Truly the outsiders were now inside the citadel of power.

*   *   *

A political tempest had blown in from the west. Now the nation awaited Jackson with anticipation and apprehension. Nobody knew what he would do when he arrived in Washington, Webster wrote to friends in Boston. "My opinion is, that when he comes he will bring a breeze with him. Which way it will blow, I cannot tell. . . . My *fear* is stronger than my *hope.*" Old John Randolph of Roanoke, as passionate and apocalyptic as ever, cried that the country was ruined past redemption. "Where now could we find leaders of a revolution?"

Thousands of job seekers throughout the country had *their* idea of a good revolution: rotate the ins out of federal office, and rotate the outs in. Some stayed home in hopes of taking over as postmasters or customs collectors, but hundreds flocked to Washington, settled down in hotels and boardinghouses, and haunted the White House and the departments. "Spoilsmen" put heavy political pressure on the Administration. "I take it for granted that all who do not support the present administration you will not consider your friends, and of course will lose your confidence," a New York politico wrote to Van Buren. "The old maxim of 'those not for us are against us,' you have so often recognized that its authority cannot be denied." Arriving late in Washington to join the Administration, Van Buren was besieged by applicants who followed behind him into his room. Reclining ill on a sofa, he patiently heard them out.

A wave of fear passed through Washington officialdom. "The great body of officials," James Parton wrote, "awaited their fate in silent horror, glad when the office hours expired at having escaped another day. . . . No man deemed it safe and prudent to trust his neighbor, and the interior of the department presented a fearful scene of guarded silence, secret intrigue, espionage, and tale-bearing." From Braintree, Adams heard that a clerk in the War Office had "cut his throat from ear to ear, from the mere terror of being dismissed," and that another clerk had "gone raving distracted."

Two Kentucky job seekers ran into each other in Washington. "I am ashamed of myself," one said, "for I feel as if every man I meet knew what I came for." The other replied: "Don't distress yourself, for every man you meet is on the same business." Despite the furor, the number of actual removals was not large—less than 10 percent after the first eighteen months of the new administration. Probably a somewhat larger number of non-college men of lower socioeconomic station got hired. Some of the clerks and agents had been Jackson men; others had been neutral. Many other changes resulted simply from death or retirement. But a few removals were enough to put Washington in shock.

Jackson defended the removals on the ground of principle, not party. Men long in office, he said, were apt to become indifferent to the public interest: "Office is considered as a species of property, and government rather as a means of promoting individual interests than as an instrument created solely for the service of the people. . . . The duties of all public officers are, or at least admit of being made, so plain and simple that men of intelligence may readily qualify themselves for their performance. . . . In a country where offices are created solely for the benefit of the people no one man has any more intrinsic right to official station than another." Pitching his case on the level of good republicanism did not endear the President to Washington bureaucrats—or win support from old Jeffersonians like Madison, who privately criticized rotation.

The new President's inaugural address had given little concrete idea of his plans, aside from revamping of the civil service. He had straddled the issues of internal improvements, the tariff, the currency, all in a voice so low that it reminded veteran Washingtonians of Jefferson's inaudible remarks twenty-eight years before. Jackson did promise a proper regard for states' rights, economy in government, and a "just and liberal" policy toward Indians, but this was standard politicians' fare. Nor did his cabinet-building offer many clues. The two principal appointees, Van Buren as Secretary of State and Samuel D. Ingham at Treasury, came from the swing states of New York and Pennsylvania. John Eaton, Jackson's old Tennessee friend, was the new Secretary of War; other appointees came from North Carolina, Georgia, and Kentucky. Pro-South in substance, anti-Clay in sentiment, the Cabinet hardly looked like an instrument for governing. It met infrequently, usually on major occasions, but less to deliberate than to hear Jacksonian pronouncements worked up in the inner circle. Administrative policy questions were usually settled by the President and department heads in private conferences. The Cabinet rarely discussed major policy issues in the manner of a council of state.

It was the "kitchen cabinet" that both expressed and shaped the President's program. This was not a cabinet, nor of course did it meet in the kitchen; it was, rather, a shifting group of advisers on whom Jackson called as he needed them. The most influential was Amos Kendall. Born on a poor Massachusetts farm in 1789, Kendall had attended Dartmouth, taught at Groton, and studied law; unrequited by both the girl and the profession he loved, at the age of twenty-five he moved to Kentucky, where he was befriended by Mrs. Henry Clay and made tutor to the Clays' children. Later he turned to newspaper work and soon became editor of the

Argus of Western America in Frankfort. For years a supporter of Clay and Adams, Kendall finally was caught between the Clay and Jackson factions. For reasons of both opportunism and principle he broke with Clay, moved to Washington, and was taken on as fourth auditor of the Treasury.

Another key adviser—and another former Kentuckian—was Francis Preston Blair. He looked like Kendall's political clone, having broken with Clay, embraced Jacksonian oppositionism, and succeeded Kendall as editor of the *Argus.* He was brought to Washington to edit the new Democratic paper, the Washington *Globe,* whose columns he filled with "demonstrations of public opinion" drawn from remote country newspapers that allegedly he penned himself. Less close to Jackson was Isaac Hill, born of an impoverished New Hampshire family, a scourge of the New Hampshire squirearchy as editor of a small Concord weekly, until he moved to Washington.

It was an unlikely-looking lot: Kendall, nearsighted, asthmatic, prematurely white-haired, bundled up in a white greatcoat even on a blazing hot day; Hill, short, cadaverous, and lame; Blair, with an elfin body of hardly a hundred pounds. They had been outsiders to a society that prized good appearance in face, form, manners, and speech. But they were the perfect instruments to a President who needed men both committed and skeptical, both articulate and polemical, to help him with his speeches and papers, and often with his decisions. Many a morning the President would lie in bed, under a portrait of his lost Rachel, blurting out his ideas, chewing and spitting or puffing out great clouds of acrid smoke from his long pipe, while Kendall or others would take down the words, smooth them out, read them back over and over until their chief was satisfied. Several other aides helped too—Lewis and others from the old Tennessee days carried on for a time—and Van Buren had a most powerful triple role as the leading cabinet member, head of the foreign-policy-making establishment, and member of the inner group.

Personal and social squabbles in Jackson's first year were harbingers of the storm to come. A few weeks before the Inaugural, Secretary of War John Eaton had married Margaret (Peggy) O'Neale Timberlake, the vivacious daughter of a Washington tavernkeeper and the widow of a navy purser who had recently committed suicide. Rumors were put out—by Jackson's political enemies, it was said—that Timberlake had cut his throat on discovering Peggy's involvement with the wealthy young Eaton. Jackson had approved the marriage as a way of stilling the rumors, but the enamored pair waited only four months after the purser's death. Tongues waggled faster than ever as Washington watched to see if the wife of John Eaton would be received in society. Floride Calhoun, consort of the Vice-

President, proceeded to shun Peggy Eaton, and the cabinet wives followed suit. It was the kind of situation—as Jackson's enemies should have known —guaranteed to tap his unbounded concern for young women treated cavalierly, as he believed his wife Rachel had been. For Jackson's adored —and in his view maligned—wife had died only a few weeks before he was inaugurated.

"I did not come here," he asserted, "to make a Cabinet for the Ladies of this place, but for the Nation." Van Buren, himself a widower, moved into the breach by acting the gallant toward Peggy, while the President blamed first Clay, and then Calhoun, for the embarrassment.

The great battles of Jackson's presidency began with the congressional session that got under way in December 1829. From then on, the President took on the barons of the Senate—Clay, Hayne, and the others—his own Vice-President, his own Cabinet, the opposition party, the banking elite, the Supreme Court, secessionists. At the end, Clay himself would cry out that Jackson had "swept over the Government, during the last eight years, like a tropical tornado." But if Jackson's presidency was filled with conflict, it was in large part because he embodied it, and so did the men he confronted. It was a blast out of the west that precipitated the sectional storm that would dominate the rest of Jackson's first term.

THE DANCE OF THE FACTIONS

The chamber of the United States Senate, noon, Tuesday, January 26, 1830. An air of high expectancy hangs over the packed hall, as Washington personages push their way in from the blustery cold outside and crowd into the aisles and vestibules. A score or more fashionably dressed women, their round bonnets trimmed with drooping plumes, look down from the front row of the balcony. They are watching Senator Daniel Webster of Massachusetts, a full, almost portly figure in his old-fashioned long-tailed coat with bright gilt buttons, buff waistcoat, and large white cravat. Webster is looking toward the Vice-President of the United States, John Calhoun, in the presiding chair, erect and stern. All the Washington notables seem to be here, except for the distant man in the White House—famous senators like Hayne of South Carolina, Benton of Missouri, Woodbury of New Hampshire, celebrities of the past like John Quincy Adams and Harrison Gray Otis still haunting Washington, and so many visitors from the House that little business can be done there.

The occasion is Webster's reply to Hayne of South Carolina. A week earlier, Webster had dropped into the Senate, after finishing his legal business in the Supreme Court just a few steps away, in time to hear the

South Carolina senator call for an alliance of the West and the South against the "selfish and unprincipled" East. Over the next few days, while Benton, Hayne, Webster, and other senators argued over the usual questions of national politics—public lands, internal improvements, the tariff —Webster became aware that a far more ominous set of issues was dominating the debate: those of nullification, secession, the very nature of the American Constitution. Even so, the famous orator, affluent and successful, recently remarried after the death of his first wife, might have shunned the battle except that Hayne, unusually impassioned, sarcastic, and aggressive for a young man ordinarily so moderate and courteous, had dealt him some punishing blows.

Now Webster would answer Hayne's climactic speech. Hayne's supporters were so elated by their champion's performance that Webster's own backers became apprehensive. But not Webster. When his friend Supreme Court Justice Joseph Story called on him to offer help, he replied, "Give yourself no uneasiness, Judge Story! I will grind him as fine as a pinch of snuff." And the next morning, asked on entering the Senate whether he was "well charged"—a reference to the four fingers of powder needed to charge a muzzle-loading gun—the orator replied jauntily, *"Seven* fingers!"

The long-gathering conflict now culminating in this debate was explosive enough. It had its main source in dramatic social and economic changes in the South—especially in South Carolina—which had set that section in a radically different direction from the North. A decade or two before, South Carolinians had exhibited much the same constellation of interests and attitudes as most other states in the Union. Highly nationalistic, they gloried in the fame and achievements of John Calhoun and the other southern war hawks of 1812. As consumers of products from abroad, they hated tariffs, but many South Carolinians grew or made their own products that needed protection, and they also accepted tariffs as strengthening American manufactories in the event of war.

As for slavery, most members of the South Carolinian delegation in Congress favored the compromise of 1820. To be sure, old Charles Pinckney—the same Charles Pinckney who had brought his young bride to Philadelphia in 1787 and helped write the Constitution there—warned that if Congress was ever accorded the right even to consider the subject of slavery, "there is no knowing to what length it may be carried," but most of the state's political leaders shared the moderate attitudes of nationalists like Calhoun and William Lowndes.

Then—almost overnight, it seemed later—the mood of South Carolina had altered sharply. For rice and cotton growers, the 1820s were a time of rapid economic change, price and demand instability, credit squeezes, and depression, all tending toward a rising sense of social and economic insecurity, which in turn fostered a powerful parochialism and sectionalism. The Tariff of 1828 excited the worst southern fears; it was to them literally a tariff of abominations, to be despised and shunned. In a decade of peace they could no longer accept the tariff as a defense measure. Federal policy on internal improvements and other questions also continued to antagonize South Carolinians. But behind all the old issues always loomed the specter of northern interference with slavery. An alleged slave conspiracy, led by Denmark Vesey of Charleston, along with rumors of other planned slave revolts, aroused dread over threats from inside; the stepped-up efforts of the American Colonization Society in the North aroused fears over threats from outside.

By the late 1820s the balance of South Carolina politics had changed. If the cleaving issue in the state, and in much of the South, had been nationalism versus sectionalism, that issue now was: what kind of sectionalism? to be carried how far? and how accomplished? Steadily shifting away from his old nationalism, Calhoun still had to deal more with fire eaters who wanted secession than with moderates who wished to attain South Carolina's aims within the Union. News of the abominable tariff catalyzed powerful forces already building. Calhoun wrote a brilliant tract—the South Carolina Exposition—in which he flayed national tariff policy as unconstitutional and oppressive, "calculated to corrupt the public virtue and destroy the liberty of the country"; contended that no government based on the "naked principle" of majority rule could "preserve its liberty even for a single generation"; and claimed the right of "interposition" by state governments—that is, to declare null and void "unconstitutional" acts of the national government. If the federal government did not recognize the constitutional powers of the states, South Carolina would claim the right of nullification. South Carolinians had waited through Jackson's first year, hopeful that he—a slave owner himself, after all—would redress their grievances, but in vain. Hayne's hard line in the Senate, reflecting Calhoun's arguments, showed that southern patience was running out.

So now, Webster waited to take the floor. The chamber hushed as the Vice-President recognized him. Standing majestically as he faced the chair, resting his left hand on his desk while swinging his right hand up and down, he spoke in a low but compelling tone. The orator held the floor for three hours, pausing only once or twice to consult some notes. He ridiculed Hayne's fear of federal tyranny. "Consolidation!—that perpetual cry, both of terror and delusion—consolidation!" The federal government, he declared, was the instrument not of the will of the states but of "We the People"; the national interest was the controlling one; the effort of a state to nullify a law of Congress was a revolutionary and illegal act.

As Webster warmed to the attack, his granite face seemed to come alive; his eyes burned with fervor; his "mastiff-mouth" bit off his sentences with the finality of a spring trap. A connoisseur of all the arts of oratory, he moved from exposition to argumentation to irony to banter to scorn to eloquence to pathos. When he said, "I shall enter on no encomium upon Massachusetts; she needs none," but proceeded to do so, Bay State men clustered in the gallery were said to "shed tears like girls." Webster had never felt an audience respond more eagerly and sympathetically. His peroration would soon be on New England schoolboys' lips:

"When my eyes shall be turned to behold, for the last time, the sun in heaven, may I not see him shining on the broken and dishonored fragments of a once glorious Union; on States dissevered, discordant, belligerent; on a land rent with civil feuds, or drenched, it may be, in fraternal blood! Let their last feeble and lingering glance, rather, behold the gorgeous ensign of the republic, now known and honored throughout the earth, still full high advanced, its arms and trophies streaming in their original lustre, not a stripe erased or polluted, not a single star obscured, bearing for its motto no such miserable interrogatory as, What is all this worth? Nor those other words of delusion and folly, Liberty first and Union afterwards; but everywhere, spread all over in characters of living light, blazing on all its ample folds, as they float over the sea and over the land, and in every wind under the whole heavens, that other sentiment, dear to every true American heart—Liberty *and* Union, now and forever, one and inseparable!"

A few weeks later, Calhoun & Co. received another oratorical setback. The Webster-Hayne debate had been an interparty encounter, and politically the Massachusetts senator could be dismissed as a New Englander and an old Federalist. But what was the attitude of Andrew Jackson, a Southwesterner and a Democrat? Rather rashly, states' rights Democrats organized a celebration of Jefferson's birthday for April 13, 1830, in Washington to glorify their cause and symbolize the Democratic party alliance between East and West. Jackson and Van Buren attended, along with an array of other party leaders. The banquet in Brown's Indian Queen Hotel was hardly over and chairs pulled back from the board when the Southerners launched into speeches and toasts that evoked the Jefferson of the Alien and Sedition Acts. Defying Jackson to his face, George Troup, a Georgia planter-politician and states' rights extremist, toasted the government of the United States as more absolute than the rule of Tiberius, but as less wise than that of Augustus, and less just than that of Trajan.

All eyes turned to Jackson. Scowling at Calhoun as he signaled the crowd to rise, the old general toasted, "Our Federal Union—*it must be preserved.*" Van Buren, who had climbed up on a chair to witness the scene, saw the noisy company turn utterly silent, dumbfounded. Calhoun's hand shook, spilling a little wine down the side of his glass. But he was ready with his answering toast: "The Union—next to our liberty the most dear. . . ."

* * *

A great Virginia reel of politics was under way, as politicians chose partners and changed them, in a dance of sections and interests, issues and ideologies. Not for half a century had the nation possessed such compelling sectional leaders—the spare, consecrated Calhoun, champion of the South; the droll, sparkling, restless Clay, still "Harry of the West"; New England's hero, the imposing, magnetic Webster, "the great cannon loaded to the lips," as Emerson pictured him; the consummate politician Van Buren, keen, dexterous, opportunistic, the supple representative of New York and the other swing states. But these men were more than leaders of sections. They were statesmen with a vision of the national purpose, and they were politicians who hungered for the presidency. Hence they had to protect their standing in their state and section, while gaining national recognition and building national coalitions. They were trapped in the rising sectional feeling of Americans. And they had to deal with the unpredictable, prickly, opinionated man in the White House.

The speeches of Webster and Hayne in the Senate, the toasts of Calhoun and Jackson at Brown's Indian Queen Hotel, were the opening salvos of the 1832 presidential election campaign. Van Buren had attached his fortunes firmly to the President's, and the political foxiness of the "Little Magician," combined with the leonine presence and power of the President, made an invincible combination. Jackson struck first at Clay, his old western rival. The issue was the venerable one of internal improvements. In his December 1829 message to Congress, Jackson had questioned the constitutionality and the desirability of federal aid to roads and other projects. When Congress passed a bill authorizing government subscription of stock in a turnpike connecting Maysville and Lexington and lying wholly within Kentucky, the President vetoed it. Clay was outraged. Not only was he the author of the "American System" but only the year before he and his family had spent four days negotiating the steep curves and bottomless mud of the existing Maysville road. Still, the deliberate slap administered by Jackson helped confirm Clay as the National Republican candidate for President. Webster backed him too.

"On the whole, My Dear Sir," Webster wrote Clay two days after the veto, "I think a crisis is arriving, or rather *has arrived.* I think you cannot be kept back from the contest. The *people* will bring you out, *nolens volens. Let them do it. . . ."*

Jackson's most dangerous enemy was still Calhoun. Each man thought the other was plotting against him. If there was a "plotter," it was Van Buren, who had every reason to widen the break between the President and Vice-President. In fact, political issues, temperaments, and ambitions were the main dividers, but the Secretary of State was quick to take advantage of them. The Peggy Eaton business sputtered along for some time, as she was ostracized not only by Floride Calhoun and cabinet wives but even by Emily Donelson, the wife of Jackson's nephew, who served as White House hostess for the President. Van Buren went out of his way to accept the Eatons. He coyly made his chief privy to the proceedings. "Tell Mrs. Eaton," he wrote Jackson, "if she does not write me I will give her up as a bad girl."

Even more divisive was the resurrection of decade-old charges that Calhoun as Secretary of War had wanted General Jackson to be censured for improper conduct in pursuing Seminole Indians during the invasion of Florida. The President now asked Calhoun for an explanation. Incensed that this old issue would be revived by his enemies, Calhoun properly challenged the right to question his conduct as Secretary of War; but he wrote fifty more pages trying to defend his action. Having prejudged the affair, Jackson coldly ended any further discussion of it. If Calhoun seemed paranoid about attempts to isolate him, he really did have enemies. Blair was chosen to set up the Washington *Globe* as a Jackson organ, to counter the *United States Telegraph,* edited by Duff Green, a Calhounite. Federal officials were told to take the *Globe* or lose their jobs. They took the *Globe.*

With the Jackson-Calhoun feud heating up, and with the Peggy Eaton wounds still throbbing, Van Buren made an adroit move, offering to resign from the Cabinet so the President could refashion it. Realizing that he could thus eliminate the Calhoun influence in his inner circle, Jackson agreed, on condition that Van Buren become Minister to Great Britain so that the Calhounites would gain no satisfaction. The plan worked. Jackson was now able to create a Cabinet of past and future notables: Edward Livingston as Secretary of State; Louis McLane, Treasury; Lewis Cass, War; Levi Woodbury, Navy; Roger B. Taney, Attorney General. Calhoun got a brief revenge when Van Buren's nomination as minister came before the Senate; as presiding officer, he cast the deciding vote against the New Yorker.

"It will kill him, sir, kill him dead. He will never kick sir, never kick," Calhoun said to a friend. But he was quite wrong. On hearing of the rejection, Jackson erupted into a stream of denunciations of the South Carolinian. And he planned his own revenge: the substitution of Van Buren for Calhoun as Vice-President.

Calhoun had a more portentous situation to deal with in his home state. Anti-tariff and anti-abolitionist feeling had steadily been rising in South Carolina; polarization between unionists and nullifiers had sharpened to the point that the two factions called each other "submissionists" and "secessionists" and even held separate Fourth of July celebrations. No longer could the Vice-President bridge the gap. He was a leader; he must go with his state, or his followers would abandon him. Under intense pressure from the nullifiers, he wrote his "Fort Hill Letter"—an announcement to the nation that he was taking his stand for nullification. For Calhoun, in William Freehling's words, "the collapse of presidential prospects was a shattering experience. The bright young man who had always enjoyed success at last endured the agony of overwhelming setback. The signs of his despair were visible everywhere: in the slouch of his shoulders as he paced the Senate corridors; in his increasing tendency to make conversations into soliloquies, in his long dirges on the decline of the Republic." Still, he would be the southern candidate for President, if only to strengthen the hand of the nullifiers.

Henry Clay, John Quincy Adams' successor as head of the National Republican party, proposed to be the national candidate for President. On the eve of 1832 his party met in convention in the saloon of the Atheneum in Baltimore, with 155 delegates present from virtually all the states outside the Deep South. Former Democrat Peter Livingston of New York placed Clay's name in nomination in what was probably the first nominating speech in convention history. Clay was unanimously chosen. At another convention in Washington several months later, Clay accepted the nomination, in a speech warning that "the fate of liberty, throughout the world, mainly depends upon the maintenance of American liberty." Proudly the National Republicans presented their credo: against the spoils system, executive tyranny, and Jackson's treatment of the Indians; in favor of American capitalism in general, and in particular, of a protective tariff to foster American industry—which they defended as protecting workers as well as owners—internal improvements at federal expense, the use of public land revenues for such improvements, the maintenance of the national banking system and a stable and uniform currency.

The Democrats also met in convention in Baltimore, but the large number of delegates—334, from every state save Missouri—compelled a move to a Universalist church. The convention did not nominate Jackson; it simply "concurred," amid much enthusiasm, in a nomination already made in many states. The delegates adopted a two-thirds rule for the nomination of a Vice-President—the only real issue before the convention —and a unit rule, authorizing the majority of each delegation to cast the entire vote of the state. Van Buren easily scored far more than two-thirds of the votes on the first ballot. They did not need a positive platform; Jackson and Van Buren would run against the bank and the "aristocratic influences" favored by the National Republicans.

So the two parties confronted each other, but each was beset by factional problems. Calhoun threatened to draw votes from Jackson; and the leaders of the Webster faction, while publicly supporting Clay, were privately pessimistic about his chances and looking forward to a Webster candidacy in 1836, if not somehow in 1832. But the greatest threat to Clay lay in the strangest faction of all, a movement that called itself the Anti-Masons. For years Americans had been suspicious of secret societies, including the Masons, even though Washington and other heroes had been members. In the fall of 1826, an upstate New Yorker named William Morgan, an apostate Mason who had threatened to "expose" the secrets of Masonry, had been spirited away in a yellow carriage, driven to the Niagara frontier, and so disposed of that no trace of him was ever found.

The resulting uproar precipitated an explosive movement of moral protest, centered in New York but radiating powerfully throughout the Northeast. The movement received much of its force from antislavery and temperance New Englanders and New Yorkers, and much of its direction from a remarkable array of leaders including William H. Seward, Thurlow Weed, and Thaddeus Stevens. Even before the National Republicans and the Democrats had convened in Baltimore, the Anti-Masons had met there, in the first presidential nominating convention in history, and chosen as their candidate William Wirt, a dignified sixty-year-old Virginia Republican of the old school. Wirt had been on his way to the National Republican convention, ready to vote for Clay; he claimed to be shocked at his nomination by the Anti-Masons, but nonetheless accepted the honor.

Which of the presidential candidates could pull enough factions and sub-factions together to win a majority in the electoral college? As the campaign heated up during 1832, it became apparent that Jackson was in control. For one thing, the Democrats in the states seemed far more enthusiastic and organized than the followers of Calhoun, Clay, or Wirt. For another, the President proved himself a master in taking a moderate but clear-cut position on the issues that left other candidates appearing to be extremists. As the election campaign neared, the Administration took a more benevolent view toward reducing the tariff, lowering the cost of public lands, and even toward internal improvement.

Jackson even seemed conciliatory toward nullification, as a curious episode suggested. For years land-hungry Georgia settlers had been encroaching on Indian lands, and for years the Cherokees in particular had been resisting the tide, even to the point of setting up a kind of independent state under treaties with the federal government. Georgia refused to recognize Cherokee autonomy. Two New England missionaries were convicted and sentenced to four years at hard labor when they defied a Georgia law that compelled white residents in the Cherokee country to obtain a license and to take an oath of allegiance to the state. On the condemned men's appeal to the Supreme Court, old John Marshall, speaking for the majority, held that the national government had exclusive jurisdiction and that the Georgia law was unconstitutional. The prisoners were ordered released. When Georgia defied the decision, Jackson aided and abetted the nullifiers. "John Marshall has made his decision," he was reported to have said, *"now let him enforce it."*

Still, mollifying nullifiers and other factions was not much of a campaign strategy. What Jackson needed was a single, compelling issue that would transcend the ordinary play of interests and sections—an issue that would mobilize an electoral majority behind his cause. And he found it, by conviction and by contingency, in Nicholas Biddle's Second National Bank of the United States.

The first and second banks had always been a staple of Republican party controversy, and few were surprised when Jackson, determined as he said to "prevent our liberties" from being "crushed by the Bank," challenged the bank's constitutionality in his first message to Congress in 1829. With the bank's charter not due to expire until 1836, the President was content to ask Congress to curb the power of the bank and thus to delay a showdown with it until the second term. He knew that Biddle was a power in the politics of Pennsylvania and other key states. Webster and Clay knew this too, and for that reason they advised Biddle to call Jackson's hand before the 1832 election by forcing him either to support the bill for recharter or to face the power of the bank at the polls. The bank chief initiated hostilities by having a recharter bill introduced in Congress, which passed it by strong majorities after a long and angry debate.

Visiting Jackson in the White House, Van Buren found the old general lying on a couch looking pale and exhausted. "The bank, Mr. Van Buren, is trying to kill me," he said, *"but I will kill it."*

Kill it he did, with a veto and a bristling message that attacked monopoly and special privilege and boldly accepted the challenge of the "rich and powerful" to make the bank the central issue of the campaign. His own appeal would be to the "humble members of society—the farmers, mechanics, and laborers—who have neither the time nor the means of securing like favors for themselves." Thus the people would decide. This was the first time, according to Robert Remini, that a President "had taken a strong stand on an important issue, challenging the electorate to do something about it if they did not approve his position." Even Jackson was surprised by the popularity of his stand on the bank. "The veto works well," he said, "instead of crushing me as was expected and intended, it will crush the Bank."

Calhoun and his fellow nullifiers handed Jackson the other great national issue of the campaign. As feeling about the tariff and slavery issues boiled over in South Carolina during 1832, the nullifiers won a legislative majority in favor of a state convention that would adopt an ordinance canceling national tariff legislation. Hayne prepared to resign as United States senator, to be elected governor; Calhoun would resign as Vice-President, to succeed Hayne in the Senate. Jackson, after taking military precautions in South Carolina, prepared a "Proclamation to the People of South Carolina" that termed nullification an "impracticable absurdity" and ended flatly, "Disunion by armed forces is *treason.*"

The Jacksonians versus Philadelphia bankers and southern nullifiers—how could the Democrats lose? The response of the voters was decisive. Sweeping the electoral college over Clay, 219 to 49, Jackson won the electoral votes of sixteen of the twenty-four states and ran well ahead of Clay in the popular vote, 687,000 to 530,000. Jackson polled strongly in the South (except in South Carolina), well in the West, fairly well in the middle Atlantic states, and decisively in the swing states of Pennsylvania and New York. Aside from his own Kentucky, Clay's main strength lay in southern New England. Still, considering Jackson's position as national hero, and his brilliant positioning of his administration on the issues of the day, as well as the siphoning off of National Republican votes by the Anti-Masons, Clay had done well in the popular vote—a harbinger of the day when a revitalized Whig party would rise out of the ashes of the National Republicans.

* * *

Armed with his election mandate, Jackson now moved against nullification. The reaction of Carolina hotheads against his proclamation—the "mad ravings of a drivelling dotard," Congressman George McDuffie called it—only hardened his will. Although the nullifiers put up a show of resistance, enlisting 25,000 volunteers and even setting up a cannonball factory, it was clear that they were not eager for a military confrontation, especially after learning that the rest of the South opposed drastic action.

In mid-January 1833 the President asked the Congress for a "Force" bill that would allow him to enforce the revenue laws by military action if necessary, but the bill actually tried to avert the use of force by working out procedures, including "floating customs houses" off Charleston, to avert encounters in the city.

The Force bill produced in the Senate another brilliant debate, rivaling the Hayne-Webster forensics. This time Webster took on Calhoun, who had been liberated from the silence of the presiding chair, and the remorseless logic-chopping of the new senator from South Carolina was judged to have bested the fulsome rhetoric of the New Englander. John Randolph, sitting in the gallery, found his view obscured by a lady's bonnet. "Take away that hat," he bleated, "I want to see Webster die, muscle by muscle."

A combination of forces was working now against an explosion. Calhoun was pulling back from his earlier extremism, Van Buren was restraining Jackson from exercising his dearest wish of trying and hanging the secessionist leaders, and—most important of all—Henry Clay, the old compromiser himself, was coming in with a tariff bill designed to conciliate the Carolinians. The President signed both the Force bill and the compromise tariff bill on March 2, 1833, two days before he took the oath of office for a second term. Once again he had shown a masterly ability both to manipulate factions and to rise above them, to take a national and presidential posture, and to know when to stand firm and when to compromise.

But Andrew Jackson of Nashville was in no mood to compromise on the other great national issue. Nor was Nicholas Biddle of Philadelphia.

Only a historical novel, not history itself, could have plausibly pitted Jackson against so contrasting an antagonist. Born into an affluent old Quaker family of Philadelphia in 1786, Biddle entered the University of Pennsylvania at the age of ten; denied a degree three years later because of his youth, he gained admission to Princeton and won his degree there at fifteen. Successively a traveler in Europe, secretary to Minister James Monroe in London, and a Philadelphia lawyer, politician, and littérateur, he had married an heiress and moved into and upward through Philadelphia banking circles. He was everything Jackson was not: wellborn, superbly educated, urbane, genteel, and young. But both men were leaders, one in the world of politics, the other in that of economics.

Before confronting Biddle, the President decided on a trip north into the old Federalist hinterland. Like presidential heroes before him, he received the cheers of Baltimore, Philadelphia, and New York, but this presidential party traveled by steamboat, canal barge, and train—Jackson's first train ride. The party even invaded Boston, where they expected the coolest of receptions. Greeted at the Massachusetts border by young Josiah Quincy, who had reluctantly accepted the duty of escorting the dragon, Old Hickory so charmed Josiah and other Bostonians that the young man's father, President Quincy of Harvard College, called his overseers together and voted Jackson a degree of Doctor of Laws. Overseer John Quincy Adams boycotted the ceremony in Harvard Yard. He would not be present to watch Harvard's disgrace, he said, in conferring "her highest literary honors upon a barbarian who could not write a sentence of grammar and hardly could spell his own name." Despite serious hemorrhaging of the lungs, Jackson moved on up the North Shore to Lynn and Salem and finally Concord, New Hampshire, where he collapsed and had to be borne back to Washington by steamer.

He was not too sick, however, to resume the project he had got under way soon after his inauguration: removing the government deposits from Biddle's bank. Why did Jackson pursue the bank further, after his "veto victory" of '32? In part because he feared that Biddle might use the three years remaining before charter expiration to manipulate money and politicians to gain recharter, or even to precipitate a financial panic just before the 1836 election and thus help pro-bank candidates. Withdrawing the sizable government deposits in the bank would be a body blow to Biddle's "monster" financially—and a symbol around which Jackson men could rally.

But the President's decision had a deeper, more personal source. He was immovably, fanatically, emotionally committed to breaking Biddle's bank. Delegations of businessmen and bankers who came to ask him for relief could hardly get their first sentence out of their mouths before he would break in with his harangue. "Relief, sir!" he would burst out. "Come not to me, sir! Go to the monster. . . . You would have us, like the people of Ireland, paying tribute to London. . . ." Would to God all the "stock-jobbers, brokers, and gamblers [were] swept from the land!" He always came back to the monster. "I've got my foot upon it and I'll crush it." Over and over again he declaimed that he would never—never—never give in. Jackson's fanaticism, Michael Rogin has theorized, issued from a ferocious inner struggle that had its sources in childhood deprivation and adult trauma and conflict.

And he was officially almost alone. Treasury Secretary McLane had made clear from the start that he was against removal, so he was smoothly shifted to Secretary of State in the spring. Vice-President Van Buren, facing every day the full panoply of Democratic party factions arrayed in front of his Senate rostrum, dragged his heels, concerned as he was with the implications of the new struggle for party harmony and his own presidential ambitions. Jackson chose William J. Duane, a Philadelphia lawyer, to carry on the fight for repeal, only to discover that his new Treasury Secretary had no stomach to take on his fellow Philadelphian. The President sacked him, and substituted Attorney General Taney, who, along with Kendall and other members of the "kitchen cabinet," had been a close adviser on the program. Late in September, Taney instructed federal tax collectors in Philadelphia, New York, and Boston to stop using the bank as a depository within five days. That was the kind of action Jackson liked.

Somberly Nicholas Biddle watched these proceedings from deep within the bowels of his marble, Corinthian-columned temple on Chestnut Street. Fighting desperately on both the political and economic fronts, he saw to it that his banking friends and allies inundated Congress with clamoring delegations and a shower of petitions, memorials, and letters. He worked so closely with Webster politically that the senator, after much consultation back and forth, often served as his Washington agent, so closely financially that Webster borrowed from the bank and complained at the height of the removal battle that "my retainer has not been renewed, or *refreshed,* as usual." (Webster asked Biddle to burn all letters; Biddle replied primly that he did so "scrupulously," but only when asked.) Through the Massachusetts senator Biddle had access to free legal advice from a United States Supreme Court justice, Webster's friend Joseph Story.

Biddle's loftiest political hope was that the great Senate triumvirate of Webster, Clay, and Calhoun would amalgamate their forces against the "banditti" in the White House. "I only repeat what I have said again & again that the fate of this nation is in the hands of Mr. Clay Mr. Calhoun & yourself," he wrote Webster. "It is in your power to save us from the misrule of these people in place, but you can only do it while you are united." He added that the enemies of the bank were hanging on every whisper of hostility among them. Here Biddle miscalculated. The celebrated trio were too far apart on major issues like slavery and the tariff, too self-protective of their own presidential ambitions, too suspicious of one another, to organize a grand coalition behind the bank. At most they managed to organize some committees hostile to Jackson in the new Congress that met in December 1833.

On the economic front Biddle could move on his own, and more boldly. During late 1833 the bank initiated a credit reduction that was in part a response to the Treasury's deposit removals, but even more, enemies charged, an effort to put pressure on the government through the whole credit structure. The money pressure in the business world became so acute that leading Boston and New York merchants met with Biddle and charged to his face that the contraction gave no protection to the bank and represented a transparent effort to extort a new charter from the government. Soon the bank returned to expansion.

The last act of the drama took place in the Senate. No one there had been more dismayed by Jackson's exercise of presidential power than his great rival from the West, Henry Clay. The day after Christmas 1833 the Kentucky senator rose to offer resolutions of censure of the President. Jackson, Clay said, had seized powers not granted him under the Constitution, powers dangerous to popular liberty. He had abused the right of veto, made arbitrary appointments and removals, treated the judiciary with contempt, and had made the Treasury Secretary responsible to himself rather than to Congress. At this rate, he said, the great republic would become an elective monarchy, "the worst of all forms of government." He closed with stirring and portentous warnings—of approaching tyranny, of a land filled with spies and informers, where people no longer spoke "in the fearless tones of manly freedom, but in the cautious whispers of trembling slaves." Unless Congress acted quickly, "we shall die—ignobly die! base, mean and abject slaves—the scorn and contempt of mankind—unpitied, unwept, unmourned!"

After three months' debate, during which the Jacksonians tried to pose the key issue as rechartering the bank rather than the Constitution, the Senate passed censure by decisive majorities. The President was furious, but bided his time. Then the Democrats swept the congressional elections of 1834, increasing their majority in the House. The result was seen as a test of Jackson's bank policy; Biddle's bank was now doomed. But the President tasted the full sweets of victory only when his fellow Democrats pulled the obnoxious resolution out of the archives, directed that heavy black lines be drawn around the offending words, and ordered the censure E X P U N G E D.

JACKSONIAN LEADERSHIP

Like all strong leaders, Jackson became the target of ferocious criticism. His National Republican foes, showing a new skill at cartooning, pictured him as a maniacal king sitting on a crumbling throne beside a hovering bat and behind deserting rats; as a doctor, scalpel in hand, lancing Uncle Sam, with blood and specie flowing from the wound; as a tyrant receiving a crown from Van Buren and a scepter from the devil.

Inevitably, he divided the American people and polarized American politics. More than any other President, more even than Jefferson, he was loved and he was hated, and many of those who had loved Jefferson and

were still living—though by no means all—also loved Old Hickory. Like all
great leaders, he not only caused conflict, he cultivated it and embodied it.

Jackson's divisive impact was so powerful, indeed, as to serve as the
catalyzing force in a reordering of parties. Twice beaten at the polls, the
National Republicans were demoralized after his re-election, but the Jacksonian "tyranny" helped bring them back to life in the mid-1830s as the
Whig—and proudly Whiggish—party. Unable to agree on slavery or tariffs
or internal improvements or even the bank, the Whigs could unite against
"King Andrew." A hodgepodge of old-time Federalists, conservative
Democrats, staunch National Republicans, and opportunistic Anti-
Masons, eastern capitalists and labor, conservative midwestern farmers,
southern merchants and planters, the Whigs could unite against the city
rabble, the backwoodsmen, the spoilsmen, the non-gentlemen who, they
felt, dominated the Democratic party.

But what could the Whigs unite *for?* Could they get behind a candidate,
a platform, and a major effort to win control of the federal government?
One resource the Whigs possessed in abundance was leadership, or really
a cornucopia of leaders. Aside from the "Big Three," all of whom were still
politically in their prime, the Whigs could boast of a second cadre of men
of keen political insight: Senator Hugh Lawson White of Tennessee, onetime friend of Jackson's, a strict constructionist of the old school, a critic
and rival of Van Buren; Edward Everett, magnetic preacher and orator who
had been chosen pastor of Unitarianism's Brattle Street Church before he
was twenty, then had become an influential congressman, in sentiment
pro-bank and anti-"Levellers," as he termed them; William Henry Harrison of Ohio, famed Indian fighter, hero of the Battle of Tippecanoe, more
recently a United States senator and diplomat; Supreme Court Justice John
McLean, some kind of Republican-Democrat-Whig, now sheltered from
partisanship by the court, but available.

Jackson's expected choice of Van Buren as his heir apparent brought the
Whig leaders into a fleeting unity. Not yet a truly national party, even more
sectional than the Democrats, the Whigs decided on an ingenious strategy
for winning in 1836: running several candidates who were strong in their
states and who could capitalize on regional hostility to Jackson and Van
Buren. Collectively, they hoped, the Whig candidates would rack up
enough electoral votes to throw the issue into the House of Representatives, where they could combine against the Jacksonians. Henry Clay, still
ambitious for the White House but doubtful of beating Van Buren, stood
apart from these strange proceedings, as a nationalist and unifier. Heavily

pressured by Webster's friends, a caucus of 315 Whig members of the Massachusetts legislature unanimously nominated Webster for the presidency. A caucus of anti-Jackson congressmen in Tennessee nominated White, who accepted the call despite threats from Jackson that he would ruin this apostate Democrat if he did. A Whig state convention in Pennsylvania endorsed William Henry Harrison. By early 1836 all the Whig parties were off and running.

Under Jackson's stern eye, and with Van Buren's manipulative hand, the Democrats had little difficulty in uniting their forces. Unlike the Whigs, who declined to hold a national party convention because it would have dramatized their divisions, the Democrats were happy to convene in Baltimore in May 1835 to eulogize Old Hickory and anoint his successor. But the meeting was more than a celebration; it was an opportunity for 600 or more third-cadre Democrats—town and county notables, local professional men, farm and business leaders—to come together, exchange views and information, and then return to their home bailiwicks ready to do their part in the battle ahead.

It was not much of a battle, with several regional candidates providing scant direct confrontation to the "Little Magician." Since personalities abounded, the campaign became largely one of invective. The young Whig leader in New York, William H. Seward, called Van Buren "a crawling reptile, whose only claim was that he had inveigled the confidence of a credulous, blind, dotard, old man." Van Buren's running-mate, Senator Richard M. Johnson of Kentucky, though billed by the Democrats as the personal slayer of Tecumseh, was pilloried by southern Whigs as a man who had taken up with a mulatto woman and, when she ran off with an Indian (Tecumseh's revenge?) and was recaptured, had her sold down the river while he moved on to her sister. Still, some of the orators and editorial writers were able to rise above invective and to present the voters with a fairly coherent sense of choice between Whiggism and Jacksonianism.

The election outcome demonstrated anew that political leaders, like military ones, must unite their armies. Van Buren won 170 electoral votes, a clear majority over the combined total of Harrison with 73, White with 26, Webster with only 14. Political analysts noted the electoral strength of Harrison, the weakness of the celebrated senator from Massachusetts. Van Buren carried the popular vote by 763,000 to 736,000 over his combined opponents—a narrow margin, but well distributed. Democrats and Whigs each picked up some strength in the opposition's areas, helping produce a "converting election," as Gerald Pomper called it, that reflected a shifting voter coalition and heralded the shape of presidential contests to come.

For the moment, at least, sectional politics seemed to be declining, national party politics rising.

*   *   *

On Inaugural Day, Jackson and Van Buren rode together to the Capitol in a gleaming carriage behind four splendid grays. People were struck by the contrast between the two men as they alighted at the entrance to the Capitol, the one gaunt, careworn, ailing, the other half a foot shorter, plump, bouncy, but looking all his fifty-four years with his once reddish hair receding and his sideburns turning gray. The crowd seemed little stirred by the new President's inaugural words, which stressed the need for forbearance and harmony, but it still appeared mesmerized by Jackson; when he moved slowly down the steps to his carriage bystanders broke into thunderous applause and cheers. Watching from a side window, Thomas Hart Benton was transfixed. Most such pageants were unreal and fleeting, empty and soulless, but "this was reality," as Arthur Schlesinger wrote of Benton's feeling, "the living relations between a man and his people, distilled for a pause in the rhythm of events, rising for a moment of wild and soaring enthusiasm, then dying away into the chambers of memory."

Could Van Buren as leader *engage* his followers as Jackson had done? Buffed and burnished in his long years of state and national politicking, a believer in the political system in which he had risen steadily as Columbia County surrogate, state senator, New York state attorney general, United States senator, and, briefly, governor, a canny operator in the New York Regency, he had come to look on government as a vast network of pulls and pressures that needed only constant oiling for the clanking machinery and balm for the harried operatives. Thus he was above all a transactional leader—harmonizer, conciliator, consolidator, a man who, unlike Jackson, believed in dampening fires rather than kindling them. He saw the Democratic party as a means of unifying disparate groups and bringing them into accord behind a national program. Since Van Buren did not want or expect much action from the national government, he would not put much pressure on the political system. Clearly this kind of leadership would not engage the hearts and souls of Democrats. But could it cope with change and crisis?

The answer came with brutal impact within weeks of Van Buren's Inaugural. He had hardly had time to collect a Cabinet around him—he kept most of Jackson's men—when a financial disaster struck the nation. For some time danger signals had been warning that the boom conditions of the mid-1830s—the expansion of banks and bank loans, the mounting debts of planters and merchants alike, the dizzying rise of prices, especially for farmland—would tumble into financial chaos. Even as Van Buren took office, jobless New Yorkers were protesting against high rents and fuel and even sacking the city's flour warehouses. In May the jerry-built state banking system favored by Jackson collapsed under the pressure for specie. Banks closed their doors; bustling ports along the Atlantic and Gulf coasts fell idle; men lost their jobs and crops rotted in the fields. The country seemed stunned; the conquest of the land by a foreign power, the British minister wrote home, could hardly have produced a wider sense of "humiliation and grief."

Here was a dramatic test of leadership for the new President, but already there were signs that Van Buren would fail it. During his last year in office Jackson had issued a "Specie Circular" providing that payment to the government for public lands would be mainly limited to gold and silver. The circular was a clear expression of Jackson's and "Old Bullion" Benton's hard-money policy. As pressure on the state deposit banks rose during late 1836, Whigs helped push a rescinding of the circular through the Senate and House, but Jackson pocket-vetoed the measure. Now Van Buren was President, and pressure mounted on him to repeal the circular. Wavering between the pro and con arguments, Van Buren seemed haunted by Old Hickory, who from the Hermitage made known his opposition to repeal. The new President gave in to the old.

What then to do? With both his Cabinet and his party divided over possible measures, Van Buren decided to convene a special session of Congress. He cast about for a solution to the continuing panic, now flattening down into a depression. To ask for a rechartering of the national bank was unthinkable for a Jacksonian Democrat; to propose a tidying up of the state bank deposit system, which now lay almost in ruins, was equally unthinkable. But he hit upon a scheme advanced by William M. Gouge, a young Philadelphia editor and economist, who in his popular *History of Paper Money and Banking* had proposed that public funds should be kept in public custody and not deposited in private banks. This idea—the divorce of the government "from all connection with Banks"—Van Buren made the centerpiece of a spate of reforms that he presented to Congress.

For a time, prospects in Congress for the Independent Treasury, as it was called, seemed auspicious. Van Buren made the proposed divorce of Treasury and bank a party issue, and the Democrats seemed firmly in control of both chambers. In the Senate, Silas Wright, the plain-spoken Regency leader and longtime cohort of Van Buren, presided over the Finance Committee. In the House, another young New Yorker and ally of the President's, Churchill C. Cambreleng, chaired the Committee on Ways and Means, and loyalist James Polk was Speaker. On the face of it, moreover, the Independent Treasury bill seemed the answer to a Democrat's prayers. It carried on the hard-money tradition of the party; it blunted the charge that the Democrats were unduly influenced by state banks; it refreshed the Democrats' claim that they spoke for the great number of people. Thus Cambreleng argued that the bill would keep the government "in the hands of the planting, farming, and laboring classes and save it from becoming a mere gambling machine to fill the country as in England with 'palaces, poorhouses, and prisons.'"

Led by their forensic gladiators, Clay and Webster, the Whigs put up a furious resistance to Democratic dogma. Not only did they offer specific arguments that the Independent Treasury bill would draw specie out of circulation, unduly restrict loans and credits, and of course provide the Democrats with more patronage jobs. They maintained that government had positive obligations to help the people—to establish and maintain a sound currency, to secure and stabilize the nation's financial system, and certainly not, in Webster's words, to confine the constitutional obligation of government to the "mere regulation of the coins" and the care of its own revenues. He felt that "this could not be America when I see schemes of public policy proposed . . . leaving the people to shift for themselves. . . ."

In the end, though, it was Democrats rather than Whigs who doomed the divorce of state and bank. All along Van Buren had been forced to fight a rearguard action against a group of Democratic Conservatives who were clinging stubbornly to old Jacksonian hard-money positions. Led by Senator William Cabell Rives, a patrician Jeffersonian from Virginia, and Nathaniel P. Talmadge of New York, the conservatives denounced the Independent Treasury as really a new national bank in disguise, a Biddletype institution that would threaten the rights of the states. The divorce bill passed the Senate by a comfortable vote, but failed in the House as Democratic conservatives voted with the Whig opposition. In two years an Independent Treasury bill would pass both houses and receive Van Buren's signature, but by then it would be too late for the President and his party.

Somehow Van Buren had failed to find a transcending issue in the economic crisis, one that would raise Congress and the people above the lesser questions dividing them in order to grapple with the kind of central question—or visible enemy—that Jackson had so brilliantly dramatized. Van Buren had found himself harmonizing myriad factions that could not easily be brought together, mediating among ideologies that did not want conciliation. Democrats were split sectionally, doctrinally, ideologically; even the small band of conservatives were divided. Some of the financial issues, hideously complex, were easy prey to facile simplification and demagoguery. And looming ominously over all the debate was the old, unresolved, and bitter issue of states' rights, and behind that, the question of slavery.

A Calhoun Democrat from South Carolina, Francis Pickens, stoked the suppressed fire when he was allowed to give the first speech in the House on Van Buren's Treasury scheme. Expected to reiterate Calhoun's defense of the divorce bill in the Senate, the thirty-two-year-old congressman almost ignored the Treasury bill and, as "if drawn by some ineluctable force," in James Curtis' words, went on to a tirade against the North and a passionate defense of slavery. The whole banking system in the North, he declared, "is a political substitute for the standing armies of Europe. . . . We are not compelled to resort to those artificial institutions of society by which non-slave-holding regions seek to delude and deceive their victims. No, Sir, we avow to the world that we own our black population, and we will maintain that ownership, if needs be, to the last extremity!" Few in the House that day could have doubted the resolution of this young owner of several hundred slaves.

*   *   *

He could see in Jackson an approaching tyranny, Henry Clay had cried out during his Senate call for the censure of the President. "The land is filled with spies and informers; and detraction and denunciation are the orders of the day. . . . The premonitory symptoms of despotism are upon us; and if Congress do not apply an instantaneous and effective remedy, the fatal collapse will soon come on. . . ."

Every senator knew what Clay was talking about. Jackson had indeed swept into Washington like a tropical tornado. By the end of his two terms not only did Clay's censure resolution lie expunged but Jackson had forced on Congress the key policies he wanted and vetoed those he did not; his twelve vetoes, indeed, would serve as the presidential record until the regime of the beleaguered Andrew Johnson. Jackson was no less a tornado to his Cabinet, breaking and remaking it almost at will, or to the bureaucracy, forcing officials out of office and putting his own men in. He got rid of one Vice-President and chose a new one, and even in the most delicate area of all, "states' rights," he recognized the claims of Georgia and denied those of South Carolina.

Andrew Jackson was one of the nation's "strongest" Presidents, most historians agree, and probably one of the six or seven "greatest." Some observers at the time viewed him as a dictator, some as the tool of Kendall or Van Buren or others, and historians have supported both arguments.

But it took someone of Nathaniel Hawthorne's insight to write: "Surely he was a great man, and his native strength, as well as of intellect as of character, compelled every man to be his tool that came within his reach; and the more cunning the individual might be, it served only to make him the sharper tool." Most of the public at the time saw him either as Tyrant or as Hero; there was little middle ground. The Jacksonian model of the presidency would become for at least a century and a half the model for the "strong" President.

But for what purposes was the Jackson presidency used? With what results? In terms of what vision or values or fundamental goals? If historians agree about the Jacksonian model of the strong President, they sharply disagree over the central thrust of the Jacksonian leadership. Were the Jacksonians mainly a great coalition of poor farmers and eastern labor against entrenched capitalists? Or were they capitalists themselves, seeking only to share more of the booty of an expanding prosperity? Or were they mainly agrarians, dreaming the Jeffersonian dream of the small, independent, simple yeoman farmer who would constitute the base of a virtuous, limited, decentralized republic—a dream already being punctured by the cotton gin and the steam engine? Above all, was the climactic struggle between Jacksonians-Democrats and Federalists-National Republicans-Whigs a battle between equality and laissez-faire liberty, between People and Property?

The answers to these questions have been elusive because Jacksonian leaders operated at three levels of political discourse and action, and the middle level—the vital "linking" level—is still hazy and vacuous. At the upper level of rhetoric and declamation, the Jacksonian message came across with power and clarity. To denounce Biddle and the "monster bank," the southern nullifiers, the Whiggish "aristocrats," came easily to the "outsiders" and nationalists from the West. Through their rallies and conventions and newspapers, moreover, the Jacksonian leaders knew how to carry their message back to the voters in their communities and homes. Van Buren, indeed, believed in a deliberate strategy of bypassing old party leaders and directly mobilizing the "mass of the parties" in order to substitute out leaders for in.

At the bottom level, the level of day-to-day policy making and administration, the positions of the Jacksonian leaders were also clear. Absolute opposition to soft money, destruction of the national bank, guarded and opportunistic opposition to high tariffs, limited support of internal improvements, opposition to privileged corporate charters, fear of public debt, doubt about public enterprise, antagonism to monopoly—these positions were solidified in congressional debate, executive action, party platform, and press. While the Jacksonians often compromised policy in the play of pressure-group and party faction, both their positive and negative policies left an indelible imprint on governance.

But few Jacksonian leaders had a comprehensive, consistent philosophy that could support a coherent program. Like their Jeffersonian forebears, they believed in liberty and equality, but it was not clear how these supreme values would be achieved—by strengthening government or minimizing it, by curbing business or favoring it, by protecting property or regulating it or destroying it. These general questions became specific options in the everyday consideration of practical policies—questions, for example, of how to deal with what kind of business or property, owned by whom, serving whose interests, with what actual economic or social effects —but explicit, substantive principles to guide these options were deficient. Jacksonianism was full of ambiguities. Thus a powerful belief in laissez-faire gripped the Jacksonian leadership, as it had the Jeffersonian. But these agrarian individualists feared business power as much as they did governmental. "Instead of setting man free," Amos Kendall said, business power had "only increased the number of his masters."

Jacksonian confusion over philosophy and program was reflected in his veto message returning the recharter bill to Congress. "It is to be regretted that the rich and powerful too often bend the acts of government to their selfish purposes," the President said. "Distinctions in society will always exist under every just government. Equality of talents, of education, or of wealth cannot be produced by human institutions." He inveighed against governmental award of exclusive privileges that would "make the rich richer and the potent more powerful. . . ." He went on: "There are no necessary evils in government. Its evils exist only in its abuses. If it would confine itself to equal protection, and, as Heaven does its rains, shower its favors alike on the high and the low, the rich and the poor, it would be an unqualified blessing." But how turn government, which the Jacksonians controlled, into at least a qualified blessing? Should the government give special protection to the "humble members of society—the farmers, mechanics, and laborers," as Jackson called them, if Heaven and nature and the rich alike did not?

So in the end, the Jacksonian "wind from the west" blew noisily but left the structure of American capitalism largely intact. Nor did it move that other citadel of power, the slavocracy. Jackson and Van Buren carried the old North-South axis of the Republican party into the Democratic—the alliance built largely by Virginians and New Yorkers and devoted to Jeffersonian agrarianism, individual liberty, states' rights, and non-interference with liberty. Western leaders and voters did not upset this political balance; rather they fortified it. Thus the southern Democrats were left with a veto against any effort, gradual or radical, to curb slavery and possibly head off an explosion. Such was the price of Democratic party union, the price of national Union—a price that could not yet be calculated.

The Whigs were hardly more coherent in their own political philosophy, in part because as a party of opportunistic anti-Jacksonians they took on much of the ideological eclecticism of their Jacksonian opponents, a movement originally of opportunistic outsiders, as the two parties tangled—and became entangled—with each other. Like the Democrats, Whigs could deliver grand rhetoric through the mouths of their Websters and Clays, and like the Democrats, they advanced a spate of concrete policies. But the middle, linking level was absent here too. If the Jacksonian leaders lacked a foundation of philosophical radicalism, the Whigs lacked that of philosophical conservatism. The materials of a class system—the aristocracies, peasantries, and proletariats—that had empowered European ideologies were absent in the United States; much of the combat on the American terrain lined up entrepreneurs against entrepreneurs. No wonder Louis Hartz was reminded of "two boxers, swinging wildly, knocking each other down with accidental punches."

Still, Jacksonianism embodied an explosive force that Whiggism lacked. The Democratic leaders posed democracy itself as the ultimate issue and pitched their appeal to the masses. Jackson as an outsider "went to the people," and as a popular hero he easily mobilized support from the masses. Van Buren contended that those "who have wrought great changes in the world never succeeded by gaining over chiefs; but always by exciting the multitude. The first is the resource of intrigue and produces only secondary results, the second is the resort of genius and transforms the face of the universe." By the people the Jacksonian leaders still meant "adult white men only," of course, but within those limits they were willing to guide and to follow the popular will as they defined it.

Sustained rhetoric, if honestly meant, has its own impact; orators may come to believe in what they say. As the leaders continued to apotheosize Mankind, the People, Popular Rule, the Majority of the People, and all the other targets of their windy appeals, they bound themselves politically and morally to respond to new popular majorities mobilizing behind rising new leaders.

Thus the Jacksonians were forced to look ahead. The Whigs, more skeptical of popular rule, more cautious about extending the suffrage to poorer persons, were less captive to their own rhetoric about Mankind. Hostile to presidential power, they rejected the kind of majority rule that could be most directly implemented through a plebiscitary presidency.

They had a powerful rhetorical appeal of their own in "Liberty and Union," but their notions of liberty were as cloudy as their foes', and the two parties matched each other in their nationalistic appeals. During the 1830s the Whigs could find no national coalition builder to match Jackson or even Van Buren; indeed, they lost their own intellectual hero when John Marshall, still Chief Justice, died in July 1835.

It was said that the great bell in Philadelphia's old State House—the bell that proclaimed "Liberty throughout all the land unto all the Inhabitants thereof "—was overtaxed as it tolled Marshall's obsequies, leading to the fatal crack that appeared a decade later on Washington's birthday. Symbolists could make of this what they wished. With his belief in national power, an independent judiciary, limited suffrage, rights of property, gradual abolition of slavery (while recognizing its constitutional validity), the old Federalist had become the Perfect Whig. Like the Whigs, he believed in "Liberty *and* Union," in "ordered liberty," but on the relation between these two—in a clear definition of these values in all their dimensions and amplitude, on the way in which these values could be realized so that they would broaden and strengthen rather than vitiate each other—on these matters of principle and purpose the Whig leadership was as divided and nebulous as were the Jacksonian leaders on the relationship of Liberty and Equality.

Lacking the political and intellectual leadership in either party that could engage with these transcending questions, the "People" one day might have to decide them, but again the question was posed—with ballots or bullets?

CHAPTER 10

Parties: The People's Constitution

C HARLES DICKENS would never forget his astonishment when, early in
January 1842, he opened the door of his stateroom on the steam
packet *Britannia* and gazed inside at the tiny chamber hardly bigger than
a cab, at the two horsehair seats fixed to the wall, the narrow slabs for
sleeping, the pillows no thicker than crumpets. He could not believe that
"this utterly impractical, thoroughly hopeless, and profoundly preposterous box, had the remotest reference to, or connection with, those chaste
and pretty, not to say gorgeous little bowers, sketched by a masterly hand,
in the highly varnished lithographic plan hanging up in the agent's counting house in the city of London. . . ." The world-famous author of *Pickwick
Papers* and *Oliver Twist* suffered more disillusionments as the steam packet
encountered terrible January storms that tore the planking out of the
paddle wheels and left the usually exuberant Dickens prostrate with sea-
sickness.

Although the steam packet was a British ship carrying Her Majesty's
mails to Halifax and Boston, she was also the start of Charles Dickens' first
tour of America, and the start of a long series of disenchantments he would
undergo in the New World, of which he expected so much. Lionized on
arriving in Boston, he liked much of what he first saw with his imaginative
novelist's eyes—the bright and gay houses with their "very red" bricks and
"very white" stone and "very green" blinds and railings; the handsome
State House and other public buildings; the quiet and benevolent and
rational influence of the "University of Cambridge"; the healthy young
factory girls of Lowell, with their serviceable bonnets, good warm cloaks
and shawls, and clogs and pattens; Hartford, where the legislature, Dickens
reported gleefully, once had enacted "Blue Laws" that barred a citizen
from kissing his wife on Sunday; New Haven, the City of Elms; and finally
New York Harbor, "a forest of ships' masts, cheery with flapping sails and
waving flags."

Slowly the disenchantment took over. Dickens made a point of visiting prisons and insane asylums and, while often impressed by American
innovations, he was shaken by the plight of the inmates he interviewed.

Escorted by police officers, he prowled through the brothels and thieves' dens of the Five Points section near the Bowery. In Philadelphia he was appalled by a "pioneering" and dreadful system of solitary confinement. His repulsion mounted in Washington, the region of "slavery, spittoons, and senators—all three are evils in all countries," he wrote later. He was impressed by John Quincy Adams, Henry Clay, and some "noble specimens" from the West, but he hardly had time for the President of the United States, and he reserved his most impassioned criticism for members of Congress. Did he see an assembly of honest patriots trying to correct some of the vices of the Old World? Not at all.

"I saw in them, the wheels that move the meanest perversion of virtuous Political Machinery that the worst tools ever wrought. Despicable trickery at elections; under-handed tamperings with public officers; cowardly attacks upon opponents, with scurrilous newspapers for shields, and hired pens for daggers; shameful trucklings to mercenary knaves. . . . in a word, Dishonest Faction in its most depraved and most unblushing form stared out from every corner of the crowded hall. . . ." So fierce and brutal was the strife of politics that "sensitive and delicate-minded persons" had to stand aloof, leaving the battle to the selfish.

For Dickens, the supreme evil was slavery, and the supreme hypocrisy that of men who shamelessly displayed the Declaration of Independence, "which solemnly declares that All Men are Created Equal," and then would censure a member of Congress for having once risen up and called out to the lawmakers, "A gang of male and female slaves for sale, warranted to breed like cattle, linked to each other by iron fetters, are passing now along the open street beneath the windows of your Temple of Equality! Look!" Where now, asked Dickens, was the pursuit of Liberty and Equality?

Dickens traveled west, taking the canalboat across Pennsylvania and the famed portage railway over the Alleghenies. He was struck by Pittsburgh's great ironworks—"like Birmingham"—and the "great quantity of smoke hanging about it." He admired Cincinnati, the "prettiest place" he had seen save for Boston, and "honourably famous for its free-schools." He marveled at the size of the Mississippi, an "enormous ditch, sometimes two or three miles wide, running liquid mud, six miles an hour: its strong and frothy current choked and obstructed everywhere by huge logs and whole forest trees." He admired the old French portion of St. Louis and fulfilled his "great desire to see a Prairie." He was properly struck by Niagara Falls, and he took time to take a steamboat up the Hudson and then ride overland to Lebanon, where he inspected the Shakers and their austere community. But he had become increasingly fatigued and dispirited during the trip, and he seemed more repelled by the ugliness of the pious and "stiff-necked" Shaker matriarchs than impressed by their husbandry and fraternity.

Always his thoughts returned to the blight of slavery. He copied scores of advertisements from the newspapers: "Ran away, Negress Caroline. Had on a collar with one prong turned down" . . . "Ran away, a black woman, Betsy. Had an iron bar on her right leg" . . . "Ran away, the negro Manuel. Much marked with irons" . . . "Ran away, a negro boy about twelve years old. Had round his neck a chain dog-collar" . . . "Detained at the police jail, the negro wench, Myrna. Has several marks of LASHING, and has irons on her feet" . . . "Ran away, a negro woman and two children. A few days before she went off, I burnt her with a hot iron, on the left side of her face. I tried to make the letter M" . . . "Ran away, a negro named Arthur. Has a considerable scar across his breast and each arm, made by a knife; loves to talk much of the goodness of God." . . .

Reflecting on his travels in America, Dickens tried to sum up his estimate of the general character of the American people and their social system. He found Americans as a whole "frank, brave, cordial, hospitable, and affectionate." The more educated and refined, the more warm and ardent "to a most remarkable degree, which renders an educated American one of the most endearing and most generous of friends." But these qualities were "sadly sapped and blighted" among the great mass of men. Americans as a whole were too distrustful of one another; overly practical and impressed by "smart men," no matter how rascally; dull and gloomy in temperament; subject to a vicious and rapacious press; and always meanly suspicious of worthy public men.

"There's freedom of opinion here, you know," Dickens quoted Americans saying to him when he chided them on their suspicion of their governors. "Every man thinks for himself, and we are not to be easily overreached." Dickens respected this independence, but he was appalled by the sweaty, stinking, spitting, venal, leveling tendencies of the American people.

This burning question—equality in America—excited the curiosity of scores of European visitors in the 1830s and 1840s. And Americans were even more curious about what the visitors reported about them. Europeans, after all, had a detachment, a perspective, and a basis of social comparison no American observer could match; they were virtually anthropological in their merciless dissection of American manners and customs. Frances Trollope, with her sharp eyes for domestic manners, missed little, nor did Harriet Martineau, despite her ear trumpet through which people had to shout, nor did Fanny Kemble, with her special concern with the lives of women. Unhappily, the findings of these and a hundred other visitors were quite mixed.

Americans were variously found to be friendly, generous, rude, vulgar, solemn, dull, cold, violent, selfish, boastful, thin-skinned, practical, curious, vigorous, unrefined, materialistic, anti-intellectual. But the findings were often so self-contradictory that the visitors seemed to be describing the human condition, not merely the American. In sum it was a portrait, in Edward Pessen's words, "of a good-natured but essentially shallow man: clever but not profound, self-important but uncertain, fond of deluding himself, living almost fanatically for the flesh (although not knowing too well how), straining every fibre to accumulate the things he covets and amoral about the methods to be used, a hypocrite who strains at gnats and swallows camels, an energetic and efficient fellow albeit a small one, who takes comfort in—as well as his standards of behavior from—numbers."

The visitors noted the cosmetics of equality, but no one probed behind the superficial manners and customs to cut to the social bone of the real questions about equality in America: What kind of inequality existed, economic, social, political, or other? What was the awareness of inequality, as against the existence of it? To what extent did a rigid class or caste system exist, to what extent was economic and social mobility eroding these systems? No one even tried to come to grips with such major questions, save for an unrenowned twenty-six-year-old French aristocrat who journeyed to America with a friend in the spring of 1831.

Born of noble parents who barely escaped the guillotine during the Revolution, Alexis de Tocqueville grew up in an aristocratic family that clung to the traditions of the Bourbons even while providing their son with a solid Catholic education, a fine library, and the opportunity to study the classics at the *lycée* at Metz and law in the courts of Paris. With a friend, Gustave de Beaumont, Tocqueville attended the lectures of François Guizot and absorbed the historian's view that history was governed by inexorable laws and that the progress of bourgeois democracy was inevitable. Rejecting both the House of Bourbon and the Orléanist dynasty that came to power after the uprisings of 1830, the young lawyer, now a magistrate, decided with Beaumont on a long tour of the rising young republic to the west, ostensibly to study and report on the advanced penitentiary system that was believed to exist in the United States. They arrived in New York in mid-May 1831, during the growing conflict in Andrew Jackson's first term over the question: Should "People" or "Property" rule?

EQUALITY: THE JACKSONIAN DEMOS

Looking for democracy and equality, Tocqueville plunged into a nation that was sharply unequal in its distribution of wealth. An hour's carriage ride through any of the big cities of the East would show striking contrasts between the lives of the rich and the poor. Wealthy Americans lived in fine town houses; dined well on the best food served on imported china and silverware; spent lavishly for clothes, entertainment, travel. The very rich were attended by liveried servants. Not far away, in slums and stews, fifty or more poor families might live in a decaying tenement, with perhaps one privy. Scores of "destitute homeless wretches" had been seen "lying on bulks or under the sheds about the markets of New York and Philadelphia." Debtors were still being thrown into jail. Five thousand paupers lived in the stews of Boston, not far from the mansions on Beacon Hill. In 1830 the most affluent 10 percent of the nation's families probably owned at least two-thirds of the country's total wealth.

How was it possible, then, for Tocqueville to report, in the very opening sentence of his *Democracy in America,* "Among the novel objects that attracted my attention during my stay in the United States, nothing struck me more forcibly than the general equality of condition among the people"? How could he speak of equal *conditions?* In part because paupers and nabobs were relatively few; the great bulk of Americans lived somewhere between the two extremes. In part because the extremes of poverty and wealth that Tocqueville had witnessed in Europe made American inequality seem relatively benign. In part because Tocqueville, perhaps searching for a kind of Jeffersonian arcadia, perceived Americans as mainly rural, middle-class, homogeneous, agrarian, and he little noticed the beginnings of industrialization and urbanization, with their enormous implications for equality in America.

But the main reason Tocqueville and other observers underplayed the extent of inegalitarianism in America lay in the tendency of economic inequality to be tempered and cushioned, in both appearance and substance. The crucial fact was not the absence of class distinctions but the transcending of them, Henry S. Commager wrote; wherever men and women "met in typical gatherings—camp meetings, militia drills, Grange picnics, political conventions, church sociables, Chautauqua assemblies—they met on a basis of equality." It almost seemed that the American male—in his typically slouching posture, in his eternal smoking and chewing and spitting in even the most refined places, in his constant and indiscriminate handshaking, in his habit of saying "Yes, sir," to high and low—was trying to prove his membership in a great classless mass.

The most striking social buffer was the decline of deference. Free Americans would not bow or scrape or pull their forelocks, no matter whom they were addressing. On this score the relationship of master and servant particularly impressed Tocqueville. He had heard that in the North, especially in New England, in contrast with the slave domestic service of the South, servants performed their duties "without thinking themselves naturally inferior to the person who orders them." The servants had enough respect for themselves not to refuse their masters the promised obedience; on their part, masters "do not ask for marks of respect . . .; it is enough that, as servants, they are exact and honest." The free-and-easy egalitarian way of Westerners in dealing with visiting notables was widely known, and doubtless influenced behavior in the East.

It was not that Jacksonian America lacked classes. "There are upper classes and working classes," John Quincy Adams told Tocqueville bluntly. Class distinctions were visible in dress, speech, grooming, carriages, housing, residence area, as well as in income, education, social status. Social lines grew rapidly in western cities too, Richard Wade noted, though not drawn as tightly as in the East. Seating in theaters was partitioned on the basis of class; even applause was given by class. The United States had the makings of a caste system, with black men enslaved in the South and segregated in the North, illiterate immigrants sealed off in the worst jobs and the poorest housing, women set apart politically and psychologically in their own class pyramid. Visiting the Tombs in the Bowery, Dickens asked a warden if he put men in the bottommost, unhealthy cells of this infamous jail, and was reassured: "Why, we *do* only put colored people in 'em."

Save for the blacks and the very poor, what Jacksonian America as a whole lacked was a class system—a stratified social structure that set people off into separate and conflicting ideologies, economic statuses, rigid social structures. Most Americans *behaved* as though they existed in a culture of equality, even though they also existed in an economy, and to a considerable extent a society, of inequality. They responded, in their class roles, not directly to economic reality but to their perception of their class status, to their perception of others' class status, and to their perception of others' perception of their own class position.

Tempering tendencies toward class rigidity, to some degree, was the nation's social inheritance: a large, open, bourgeois middle class, without an upper class of aristocrats or a lower class of proletarians. "The great advantage of the Americans," Tocqueville observed, was that "they have arrived at a state of democracy without having to endure a democratic revolution; and that they are born equal, instead of becoming so." Born equal! The United States had no inherited nobility in the European sense; its farmers were not peasants in the French sense; its workers were not proletarians in the English sense. Tocqueville noted another reason for softened class lines—America's vast lands and abundance: "Their ancestors gave them the love of equality and of freedom; but God Himself gave them the means of remaining equal and free by placing them upon a boundless continent." Then too, poor Americans clung to the rags-to-riches myth. Stories were told of men who had struck it rich in land speculation, in banking, in manufacturing. A hard-working man could rise through the ranks, or if opportunity were closed to him, he could move west. "In America," Tocqueville reported, "most of the rich men were formerly poor."

The young Frenchman exaggerated. Neither social nor geographical mobility was as simple as he and many Americans thought. Wealth, jobs, and status were inherited by sons enjoying special access to colleges, family connections, social networks, their fathers' wills. Going west and buying a farm required more money than most poor men had. But Tocqueville, with his usual insight, understood the myths that moved Americans, if not always the hard facts that validated or eroded the myths. And the heady idea of the self-made man was at the heart of the mystique of Jacksonian Democracy.

*　　*　　*

Tocqueville had come to America to see democracy at work, for in the young republic, he believed, "the *demos* ruled in its unadulterated state." Democracy in America, he decided, was inexorably producing powerful egalitarian impulses and conditions, because democratic societies in general tended more and more toward equality and "dragged" everyone along with it. To some degree he welcomed this trend; ". . . after all," he said, "it may be God's will to spread a moderate amount of happiness over all men, instead of heaping a large sum upon a few." But even more he feared probable consequences of egalitarianism: a vast leveling down, conformity, mediocrity, one large, homogeneous middle class without "poetry or elevation." All this in turn would lead to something Tocqueville feared most of all—the "tyranny of the majority."

Leveling and mediocrity also discouraged great leadership, Tocqueville felt. He wrote of the brilliant leadership, a generation earlier, of Thomas Jefferson and his Federalist adversaries. These were men of principle, with lofty ambitions for themselves and their country. But if America had once had great parties and leadership, she had them no longer; men were occupied by their petty, material ambitions, and the country "swarms with lesser controversies." Doubtless Andrew Jackson in the White House seemed a narrow and quarrelsome figure to the young French aristocrat. He had to grant Jackson's skill and tenacity, however, in standing by his policies and arousing popular support.

In fact, the nation had strong leadership in the first cadre of Jackson and the other national Democratic figures like Van Buren and Benton, and in their great Whig antagonists like Clay and Webster. It had a robust second cadre of congressmen, state officials, partisan newspaper editors, party managers, federal and state officials, who carried on healthy, partisan combat. The vital test of Tocqueville's fears about leadership lay in the third cadre—the grass-roots activists who sustained and invigorated democracy at its foundation.

A remarkable mushrooming of grass-roots leadership occurred in a group that might have seemed least potent in a nation still mainly agricultural—the working people of the big eastern cities. Ever since the Revolution, craft unions had been organizing, agitating for better conditions, conducting strikes and boycotts, and then usually disappearing after a brief existence. Trade unionism revived in the more liberal and democratic climate of the 1820s. In 1824 weavers seeking higher wages left their looms in Pawtucket, Rhode Island, in the first known strike of women workers. By this time tailors, carpenters, cordwainers, hatters, riggers, and other craftsmen had formed somewhat durable unions. Working people were reaching out toward wider unities. After fifteen Philadelphia unions in 1827 banded together to form the first city central trade council, unionists in a dozen other cities moved to organize their own.

Local union leaders became more and more aware, as Jackson and other national leaders battled over issues of concern to working people, that they could not realize their goals through trade union action alone, but must enter the political arena as well. Here again, Philadelphia workers led the way, forming a workingmen's party out of the central trade council in 1828. Suddenly other movements, calling themselves workingmen's parties, People's Party, Farmer's and Mechanic's Society, or just Working Men, were springing into life in scores of cities in Pennsylvania, New York, New England, Ohio, and elsewhere. Typically these parties advanced a broad range of political demands: abolition of imprisonment for debt; equal, free, tax-supported, universal education; prohibition of licensed monopolies; equal taxation on property; revision or abolition of the militia system (which bore heavily on workers); and often a host of local needs, such as better working conditions and more "hydrant water" for the poor.

Leaders of these workers' parties knew what they wanted; the question was how to get it. And here the parties took a drastic step that set them off from a multitude of other interests pressing their demands. This was to nominate their own candidates for office, and then elect them. Such a strategy not only required a massive electoral effort from relatively small organizations, but presented the leaders with endless practical and philosophical dilemmas. Should they operate completely separately from political parties—that is, maintain their doctrinal purity at the expense of being isolated, or at least outvoted, politically? If they cooperated with existing political parties, on what terms? To what extent should the workers' parties broaden their own ranks beyond their own trade union members? To what extent should they press for policies that would benefit the general public, or at least the poor, and not unionists alone? Should the parties actually try to win elections, or act mainly as goads and gadflies to the existing major parties?

Bitter quarrels broke out over such issues. The question of including non-workers was especially vexing. Some workers wished to exclude lawyers, bankers, brokers, and employers. Others argued that the crucial factor was a man's views, not his job. The Philadelphia party decided that while employers might be present at meetings, they should be barred from holding office. But a member complained, "If an employer superintends his own business (still more if he works with his own hands) he is a working man."

Resolving such tough strategic questions—questions that have daunted all third parties before and since—required a rare degree of creative leadership, and this the workers' parties did not possess. Although the various city organizations produced vigorous and committed local leaders, they were heavily localized movements incapable of elevating and supporting leaders who could plan a national strategy and mobilize workingmen behind it. The workers' parties fell between stools—too inclusive in some places and too exclusive in others, too inexperienced in "practical" politics, too exposed to outside attack, too doctrinaire for some workers and yet too pragmatic for others. But their primary handicap was the readiness of the major parties—especially the Jacksonian Democrats—to appropriate their less controversial and less radical ideas as soon as it became politically expedient to do so. Within a few years the workers' parties were declining and disappearing almost as quickly as they had arisen.

If the workers' parties suffered from too few adequate leaders, radical movements of the day seemed to suffer from too many. Jacksonian leadership hastened popular ferment and protest, especially in New York City, a magnet to rebels looking for ways to spread their heretical ideas. These radicals were united by little but their hatred for the "haves" and their concern for the "have-nots." In a book, *Sources and Effects of Unequal Wealth,* Langdon Byllesby, contending that the laboring man shared almost none of the goods he produced, denounced both the credit system and labor-saving machinery. Thomas Skidmore attacked property that was not shared equally by the whole community; he urged that all existing land and goods be surrendered to the state and then reallocated equally as part of a "General Division." Robert Dale Owen, son of the organizer of the innovative but paternalistic factory at New Lanark in Scotland and later of the community of New Harmony in Indiana, edited *The Free Inquirer* and argued for liberalized divorce laws, education for workers, and a fairer distribution of wealth. Another British native, George H. Evans, founder of the *Working Man's Advocate* in New York, preached atheism, land reform, and the rights of wage earners.

The star of the New York radicals was a dedicated abolitionist, militant anti-cleric, popular lecturer, indefatigable social reformer—and a woman. Frances Wright had lived a remarkable life in Scotland even before she came to New York in 1830 to edit *The Free Inquirer* with Owen. Left without parents at the age of two, but with a large inheritance, she had traveled and written extensively while still in her teens, visited America in 1818 and again with General Lafayette in 1824, urged her plan of emancipation on Jefferson and Madison, and then carried out her own experiment in emancipation by purchasing slaves in the United States and colonizing them in Tennessee and, later, Haiti.

She was a tall, slender woman, whom Walt Whitman years later would call one of the sweetest of his memories, "graceful, deer-like . . . beautiful in bodily shape and gifts of soul." An eloquent foe of religion and of the influence of the Church in politics, she opposed the existing American educational system based on authority and the denial of equal rights for women. For insisting that the legal obligation of marriage should be replaced by a union based only on moral obligation she was called the "great Red Harlot of Infidelity."

Radical leaders in Massachusetts made up an even more variegated group. In the western hinterland of the state, where hard times and re-called mortgages reminded old men of the days of Shays's Rebellion, Theodore Sedgwick had been a boy of hardly six in Stockbridge when some of Shays's men ransacked the house of his father, Judge Sedgwick. Deserting his father's conservative doctrines, except for a common belief in emancipation, the young man became increasingly sympathetic to the needs of wage earners, including improved working conditions, public education, and temperance. He became as committed and outspoken a radical Democrat as the judge had been a conservative Federalist.

Fifty miles to the northeast, in Northfield, a disillusioned ex-pastor and ex-congressman, Samuel Clesson Allen, who had begun protesting the plight of the local farmers after he quit Congress in 1829, soon discovered —and asserted—that not only farmers but all producing workers were cheated by the diversion of wealth to the wealthy. Poverty, he contended, resulted from artificial limits on production. "The natural limit of production," he said, "is the wants of the consumers. Till these are supplied there is no reason why production should stop." Allen had hopes for Jackson's administration.

In Northampton, down the Connecticut River from Northfield, another kind of reformer was undergoing political transformation during the early thirties. The son-in-law of a wealthy Springfield capitalist, a Harvard man, a member of the intellectual elite of Cambridge, George Bancroft had returned to Northampton to found a progressive school and to write. For a time he played Whiggish politics while espousing radical and working-man doctrines, but then he took a position against Biddle's bank, deserted the Whig party for good, and declared himself against the moneyed aristocracy, to the consternation of Springfield high society. In Boston a trio of radical Democrats—Frederick Robinson, William Foster, Theophilus Fisk—directed their reformist arguments both at fellow Democrats and at organized workingmen. Another Boston reformer, Robert Rantoul, had started life among Federalist Essexmen, attended Phillips Andover and Harvard, and settled among wealthy Whigs, only to veer sharply toward humanitarianism, Jacksonianism, workers' rights, free markets, and a kind of genteel moralistic radicalism, including opposition to liquor and capital punishment.

These men—and this woman—had little in common except a burning sense of injustice. They divided over many social and moral questions; most of them were sympathetic to the wage earner's plight and took part in workingmen's parties, but were repelled by the revulsion of many a worker against their radical views on marriage, divorce, religion, women's rights. Many of them worked closely with the Jackson Democrats but were offended by the compromises and evasions of major-party coalition building and electioneering. Most were high-minded moralizers who had to recognize that they would lose their working-class audiences unless they were also willing to talk the hard language of wages, hours, working conditions, strikes, and boycotts. On one cardinal question the radicals and reformers were united—in economics they were egalitarians. They helped to make equality the burning issue of Jacksonian democracy.

By the mid-1830s the outcome of the popular thrust toward equality still lay in the balance. Although in everyday social contacts the farmers and workers, having long since given up habits of deference, could mingle with upper-class men on the basis of almost easy familiarity, rich and poor were still separated by class distinctions, income, residing place, and style of life. Genuine equality of *opportunity* had been dramatically posed by radicals and Jacksonian Democrats as perhaps the transcending national issue, but equality of *condition* was still sharply limited and perhaps declining under the impact of industrial and agricultural changes. Equality before the law was guaranteed in the constitutions and formally protected in the courts, yet not always realized in concrete situations where poor men were pitted legally against rich. If economic and social and legal equality were, on balance, still largely unrealized in the Jacksonian "Age of Equality," would the impetus of *political* equality be likely in the years ahead to broaden the other dimensions of equality?

*   *   *

Political equality meant that all men and women would have the right to vote. It meant that they would have the right to vote for all elective offices, at every level of government, local, county, state, and federal, on a regular, prescribed basis, at an appropriate time of year. It meant that the polls would be located reasonably near the voters; that voters would be subjected neither to corruption nor to intimidation; that they could vote in secret—which meant voting by paper ballots rather than orally, and with plain ballots that could be marked, folded, and deposited without anyone but the voter seeing them. It meant, more broadly, that voters could choose among candidates who took clear and forthright positions in competitive contests offering real alternatives, in elections the outcome of which would significantly affect the course of government, economic policy, social change.

Such political equality barely existed in America before the Revolution. A half century later, it was only partially achieved. It might never be wholly realized. Certain political equalities were hardly conceivable even in Jacksonian days. Women and slaves and Indians could not vote, nor could most freed Negroes in the North. Certain offices—especially the presidency and United States senatorship—were rendered by constitutions only indirectly subject to popular balloting. Certain elections would remain noncompetitive, no matter what the procedures. Even so, political equality was immensely expanded during the half century following the Declaration of Independence.

The central general issue was whether all adult white males should have the right to vote. The crucial specific issue was whether adult white males without property should have the right to vote. This issue aroused the most pressing philosophical, political, and practical questions. The powerful eighteenth-century doctrine of natural rights dictated that the franchise must be considered a fundamental right of all men. If all men were naturally endowed with reason, on what grounds could some be excluded from the process of self-government? In America, where "all men were created equal" and endowed with certain inalienable rights, this question took on a special urgency. Other philosophers argued, however, that only those men with a real and continuing economic stake in a society should vote, that the property-holding middle class must serve as the great stabilizing force, that men without property would, if given the ballot, ultimately turn democracy into dictatorship.

The practical question was how, if certain men were not allowed to vote, the criteria excluding them should be established. Should men be granted the right to vote on the basis of the money they had, the property they owned, or the taxes they paid? What if a man had property one year and lost it the next—did he lose the right to vote too? Critics of the property requirement liked to tell an old story of Tom Paine's: "You require that a man shall have sixty dollars' worth of property, or he shall not vote. Very well, take an illustration. Here is a man who today owns a jackass, and the jackass is worth sixty dollars. Today the man is a voter and he goes to the polls and deposits his vote. Tomorrow the jackass dies. The next day the man comes to vote without his jackass and he cannot vote at all. Now tell me, which was the voter, the man or the jackass?"

The political question was simpler: if the vote is given to these new voters, are they likely to vote for "our" side or the opposition? Related to this calculation, however, was an ingenious political argument used over and over again and with telling effect by opponents of full male suffrage. The argument was that if the right to vote was extended to the poor, the rich would buy the votes of the poor, and hence extending the vote to the poor was in reality extending it to the *rich*. Blackstone was solemnly cited as the great authority on the question—Blackstone who said that the "true reason of requiring any qualification with regard to property in voters, is to exclude such persons as are in so mean a situation as to be esteemed to have no will of their own." This argument was directed particularly against the enfranchising of industrial workers, who were seen as especially vulnerable to pressure from their employers.

Historians like to tell stories with exciting beginnings and endings, and any chronicler of Jacksonian democracy would wish to picture a mounting grand finale to the Fight for the Ballot, with the villain named Property being undone at the height of the era. In fact, the fight was not one central struggle but thousands of tiny skirmishes in a score or more states over a long stretch of time. Dismantling property restrictions in particular was a lengthy effort, often with three steps forward, one back, and one sidewise. Half a dozen states had adopted suffrage reforms by the end of the Revolutionary era, when poor soldiers had shown that they could fight as bravely as the rich, but three states passed more conservative suffrage requirements. The framers of the Constitution forced suffrage reform into at least thirteen channels by ingeniously providing that members of the new House of Representatives would be elected by those voters eligible to elect the lower houses of the various state legislatures, thus leaving the struggle for the vote largely in the hands of the states.

Some suffrage restrictions fell during the Jeffersonian era, with its emphasis on equal rights, and during the war with England, when soldiers argued that "if they were good enough to fight they were good enough to vote." Property requirements were replaced by taxpaying requirements, which in turn gradually faded away. Further extensions of male suffrage were pushed through the states during the Jacksonian era, but in Pessen's summary, "Well before Jackson's election most states had lifted most restrictions on the suffrage of white male citizens or taxpayers. Jackson was the beneficiary rather than the initiator of these reforms." Still Virginia, Louisiana, and Mississippi lagged; in the Old Dominion the 1831 suffrage extension still left a third of the white male population without the vote.

Conservatives fought a desperate rearguard action against the "tyranny of numbers." The state senate, declared the redoubtable conservative James Kent to the New York constitutional convention of 1821, "has hitherto been elected by the farmers of the state . . . by the free and independent lords of the soil. . . . We propose now to annihilate at one stroke all these property distinctions and to bow before the idol of universal suffrage." He drew a dismal picture of the day when the "owners of the soil" would be impotent, the poor would plunder the rich, the debtor would ignore the obligation of contract, the majority would tyrannize over the minority, the "motley and undefinable population of the crowded ports may predominate in the assembly." John Randolph, ravaged by drink, his eyes glowing with passion in a face of parchment white seamed by a mass of wrinkles, rose to heights of eloquence as he played perhaps his finest hour upon the stage. "I would not live under King Numbers," he proclaimed to the delegates to the Virginia convention of 1829, evoking the Burkean ideas he exalted. "I would not be his steward, nor make him my task-master. . . ."

Rhode Island lagged behind in suffrage reform, and it suddenly gave the nation a sharp warning as to the price of such delinquency in an industrializing state with large numbers of propertyless workers. It had held out against joining the new union after 1787; now it was resisting the currents of suffrage reform sweeping other states. In 1840, at the end of the "Jackson decade," Rhode Islanders were still operating under an archaic charter granted by King Charles more than 175 years before. Under a heavy freehold requirement, almost half the adult male white population could not vote. A rotten-borough system favoring the rural population left urban voters seriously underrepresented in the lower house. The charter lacked even a bill of rights. All this was accompanied by extensive corrupt influence at the polls.

The voteless men of Rhode Island needed their champion, and he came in the unlikely personage of Thomas Dorr, a wealthy young Exeter and Harvard graduate, of Whiggish disposition politically but philosophically a son of the Enlightenment. After trying vainly to work for reform within the charter system, Dorr led a move to draft a "People's Constitution" that extended the vote to all adult white male citizens if resident in the state for one year; it boosted the representation of Providence and other urban areas in the lower house; it required the use of the secret ballot—but withheld the ballot from blacks and women, and left a property requirement for voting in city and town elections.

Conservatives responded by drafting a less reformist charter. Both charters were submitted to the people, who voted Dorr's up and the conservatives' down.

Soon bewildered Rhode Islanders had two governments, one under the establishment, the other under Dorr as the "People's Governor." Constitutional comic opera turned deadly serious when the old government began arresting leaders of the new. Dorr escaped to New York to enlist aid from reform and radical leaders, and returned with promises of military assistance, including the dispatch of a thousand men from New York to Rhode Island by steamboat. Soon the Dorrites, hardly two hundred in number, attacked the Providence Arsenal, but the desperate, vainglorious effort, reminiscent of Shays's attack on the Springfield Arsenal, failed. Dorr's men left for home, and the leader escaped over the border. When the old government put through a liberalized constitution, he returned despite the price on his head, only to be arrested, indicted for high treason, found guilty, and sentenced to solitary confinement at hard labor for life. But the old government had overreached itself, and by the act of a Democratic legislature, Dorr was released after a year's confinement, and the oligarchy granted the people still another, and now heavily liberalized, charter. Decades late, Rhode Island had finally joined the parade toward full manhood suffrage.

*   *   *

It was because constitutions like Rhode Island's archaic one—and even more, the Constitution of the United States—embodied fundamental compromises with human liberty that abolitionist leaders like William Lloyd Garrison rejected constitutional processes, even voting. Garrison opposed any concerted political action; rather, he proposed that truth and right would prevail by waging the moral struggle through meetings and newspapers, especially his *Liberator.* His strategy was to be absolutely uncompromising. The first issue had proclaimed, "I am in earnest—I will not equivocate—I will not retreat a single inch—and *I will be heard.*" By 1843 the Massachusetts Anti-Slavery Society, under his influence, was resolving that the United States Constitution was a "covenant with death and an agreement with hell."

Another New England abolitionist leader, Theodore Dwight Weld, summarized the radical position. Slavery, he said, was pre-eminently a moral question, arresting the conscience of the nation. "As a question of politics and national economy, I have passed it with scarce a look or a word, believing that the business of the abolitionists is with the heart of the nation, rather than with its purse strings." Such a stance cut this brand of radical off from others who believed philosophically that moral and economic and political forces must be seen in their interaction, and who calculated practically that persons suffering various forms of deprivations had to be brought together into some kind of alliance.

Another "solution" to the slavery problem isolated not only the reformers but the problem. This was the colonization of freed slaves and free blacks. Founded in 1817, the American Colonization Society within a decade or so bought hundreds of slaves and transported them and hundreds of other freed blacks to Liberia, with money raised from churches, state legislatures, and individual donors. People of means tried private experiments in emancipation and colonization. Frances Wright, increasingly concerned about the plight of the blacks, took $10,000, a third of her inheritance, and bought 2,000 acres of dry, rolling land in the densely forested area of western Tennessee. She also purchased five male slaves and three female slaves who were to work cooperatively on the land. Her plan was to raise $41,000 from supporters and eventually settle a hundred slaves. With the hope of eventual freedom before them, the blacks would work off their purchase price and then emigrate to a colony of their own. The settlement would grow until all slaves in the South would be free.

With several white friends, Wright moved into one of two cabins she had built, the blacks into the other. "We have raised buildings for immediate use, cleared and fenced round them, planted and fenced an apple orchard of five acres, planted in potatoes a vegetable garden—opened fifteen acres for corn and planted two of old ground in cotton." The forest formed a thick, dark wall around the little settlement, and to one observer, it was "desolate." But Frances Wright's "mind was so exclusively occupied by the object she had then in view that all things else were worthless"; her enthusiasm for the project bordered on "religious fanaticism." She had isolated the settlement deliberately, as many planters were hostile to her experiment.

The experiment failed. The forbidding mosquito-infested environment took its toll; Wright became ill and had to leave the management to associates, who allowed it to end in disrepute and failure. She eventually colonized in Haiti the slaves she had purchased.

State Politics: Seedbed of Party

By the 1840s, Jefferson's "People," the Jacksonian Demos, Hamilton's "Beast," had been enthroned—the white male half of it, that is. Not only had the suffrage been immensely broadened, but the electoral college—now chosen directly by the voters—and other institutions had been made more directly and democratically responsive to the electorate. Nevertheless, the rising Demos still needed political organization strong enough to throw the People's collective power into the political scales, yet stable and firm enough to curb the Beast when occasion might demand. Americans required a political vehicle to organize and mass the people, to fight election contests, to unify their fragmented governments, to translate popular needs and aspirations into public policy and social change. For fifty years such a vehicle had been in the process of being invented and developed, a process as slow and halting as the extension of the suffrage. That vehicle was the political party.

In 1787 a few dozen men had met in Philadelphia and struck off a new constitution that soon was ratified in a dozen state conventions. During the half century after that year, many thousands of men (and lamentably few women), in tens of thousands of local, state, and national meetings, worked out a second charter that may be called a "party" or a "people's" constitution. The contrasts between the formal Constitution of 1787 and the party constitution of the 1780s to the 1830s are sharp and significant.

The Constitution was deeply rooted in centuries of intense moral, political, and legal thought in Europe and America; the party charter had impoverished intellectual roots. The former represented a central, strategic idea —an idea with the intellectual credentials of a Locke, a Montesquieu, a Harrington, and other philosophical giants, carefully applied to the needs and aspirations of the people of a young republic; the national party constitution was shaped without central plan or purpose, in opposition to the accepted wisdom of the day, in meetings held for more limited and parochial purposes. The Constitution was conceived and dedicated by the most illustrious and respectable leaders—men like Washington and Madison inside the Philadelphia convention hall, men like Adams and Jefferson outside. The party charter was spawned outside the establishment, often outside the law, and hence, born a bastard and growing up as a political orphan, it never became quite respectable.

The Constitution was accepted from the start, and indeed soon became a revered symbol of national unity and a mechanism of national unification. The party charter encountered sharp opposition from the established leadership of the new republic. Not only did leaders like Washington and Madison oppose parties as fractious, selfish, turbulent, divisive, but they also opposed or misconceived the essential theory of parties—the theory of majority rule, party rotation in office, party authority, party opposition, party distribution of power, the alternation of elites—that made the party charter in effect a *constitution*. The strategy of the Framers was to tame power by granting necessary authority to national officers responsible to conflicting constituencies, and to reserve authority to state and local officers who also had conflicting constituencies—all with an eye to curbing power by splitting it into pieces and balancing the pieces. The strategy of the party constitution was to control power by granting authority to electorally victorious parties that would have to compete against active opposition parties and be subjected to popular confirmation or repudiation in regular, open, and democratic elections. And that too was a difference— perhaps the fundamental difference—between the two constitutions.

To refer to the party charter as a general strategy and set of procedures would imply that a single central document existed somewhere, as the formal Constitution does under glass in the National Archives. In fact the party charter was more like the British constitution—a collection of laws, institutions, regulations, usages, understandings, traditions, to be found in diverse places. The party founders had no strategy shaped out of political theory; they found one later in practice.

The Constitution created a new national government and left the state governments in place, with their own constitutions and governments. But by fragmenting power, it made national parties necessary at the same time that it made them impossible—necessary because parties, with their coalition building and other unifying tendencies and machinery, could provide essential teamwork among the constitutionally separated branches of government, impossible because the existing parties (actually factions) were further fragmented and pulverized as they acted upon, and were acted upon by, those separated branches. By establishing two levels of constitutional and governmental authority—the national level and the state level —the Constitution also indirectly established two levels of party activity— in effect would create a *party* federalism as well as a constitutional and governmental federalism. Since state governments and political systems already existed (though somewhat altered after 1787), all this meant in effect that state political systems continued to exist for a time in roughly their pre-Constitution form while a new national political system slowly took shape.

Considering that both Federalist and anti-Federalist leaders opposed the idea of strong national parties, it was remarkable that a Federalist and a Republican party developed so quickly, even before Washington quit the presidency—remarkable that rudimentary state and national party organizations would be formed, rising leaders would exploit intensifying and widening conflict to sharpen two-party competition, Jefferson would assemble and lead a partisan administration, Congress would come to be organized roughly on party lines, the congressional caucus, established on a partisan basis, would become the central nominating mechanism for Presidents; and even the idea of a loyal party opposition would begin to be accepted, at least by some.

The party constitution was by no means fully shaped during the first twenty years of the new republic. Party leadership did not fully mobilize party followership, in part because the party leaders did not have a strategy of party, or even a commitment to it. Party organization was rudimentary; parties were not fleshed out with leaders, officials, whips, activists. Party feeling was often intense but also unstable, unevenly distributed, lacking in depth. There were parties, but not a party *system,* not an institutionalized party ramifying through leadership cadres, levels and branches of government, into mobilized mass followings. Hence it was possible for a partisan President like Jefferson to be succeeded by a lackluster partisan like Madison and in turn by a partyless man like Monroe. And it was perhaps inevitable that the party structure beginning to be erected by the end of John Adams' presidency would be in decay by the start of John Quincy Adams'.

It was at the state level that the party charter continued to be shaped, parties persisted, party systems and structures began to develop. It was at this level that a fundamental transformation of American politics was precipitated.

New York State served as the great testing ground for party. If downstate Virginians had been the main intellectual fathers of the formal Constitution, upstate New Yorkers were the leading experimenters and shapers of the second, "people's" constitution. Perhaps it was natural that this state, embracing social diversity and robust political life, should be the vanguard in the shift from the politics of the 1790s to the politics of the 1830s. New York was already a polyglot land, with its inflows of English and French and Rhinelanders, its Dutch Reformed, Huguenot, and other major religious groupings, its busy ports along the Hudson, capped by Albany and Troy; its spreading settlements on Long Island and in Westchester County; its estates of Dutch patroons and English squires; its enormous hinterland peopled by Indians, trappers, and traders; its vigorous, factious, independent, and dynamic politics reflecting the social and economic life of its people.

Even so, New York after the Revolution, continuing through the Federalist years and well into the Jeffersonian Republican epoch, epitomized not the politics of "modernity" but that of the mother country and its colonies. This was the politics of family and faction, patrician leaders and dutiful followers, hierarchy and deference. It was a politics of large patriarchal families controlling power and patronage in a narrow arena of governmental decision, and hence it was a politics of consensus within the upper socioeconomic stratum—in essence an upper-class politics, cloaked in a politics of compelling personality.

De Witt Clinton personified this kind of politics. Son of a Revolutionary War major general and nephew of George Clinton, the first governor of New York State, De Witt Clinton after graduating from Columbia rose quickly with his uncle's help. At the age of twenty, "he had arrived at a position of considerable political influence without having been obliged to serve an apprenticeship in the humble ranks of party workers, a circumstance," according to a biographer, "which may account for certain defects as a tactician which he showed in later life." In the personalistic wars of the New York Montagues and Capulets, he took on the Livingston, Jay, and other patrician families, and bolted the Republican ranks to become Federalist candidate for President in 1812. He ended up in low repute with both parties. Aristocratic in bearing, snobbish in attitude, resentful of criticism, he was, however, just the man to capitalize on his own vision, elite status, and network of personal supporters to drive through the planning and building of the Erie Canal. Having switched back to Republicanism, he was rewarded with the governorship in 1820 and in 1822.

The man who was to take the measure of Clinton as a politician, and lead the way in dissolving for good Clinton's kind of elitist, personalistic politics, hardly looked like a worthy challenger to the patrician six-foot "Magnus Apollo," as Clinton was called. Small, smooth, sandy-haired, Martin Van Buren had become an astute judge of human nature listening to great talkers in his father's tavern, but he had no advantage of social status or commanding presence. What Van Buren did possess was a new concept of democratic politics—the concept of party. And he had a group of followers who shaped with him a remarkable party organization that came to be known as the Albany Regency. These adherents—Silas Wright, William Marcy, Azariah Flagg, Franklin Butler, and perhaps a dozen others—were little known outside the Albany-Troy area where most of them lived and politicked. But they knew what they were against: Clinton and his whole system of politics.

And these "Bucktails" knew what they wanted: a united party organization, collective leadership and responsibility, strong party loyalty and discipline, competition between a majority party and a worthy opposition party, and an extensive party apparatus and network. Regency members subordinated their individual interests and even careers to the demands of party as determined by a majority in the legislative caucus. Editors of party newspapers, such as the famed Albany *Argus* or the New York *National Advocate,* were expected to follow the party line, and they generally did so; when editor Mordecai Noah of the *Advocate* quit over alleged interference with the business aspect of his work, he relented under pressure, returned to his post, and stated, "I yield, as I have ever done, with deference to the wishes of the party, when expressed through its accredited organs." Regency Republicans in the legislature were also expected to vote the party position (when the party had a position), even at risk to their careers. When seventeen legislators stood against a popular measure opposed by the Regency, in response to Van Buren's request that they "magnanimously sacrifice individual preferences for the general good," the lawmakers deliberately staked their posts. A few actually failed of re-election. The only reward for these potential martyrs was a banquet where, as Marcy wrote Flagg, "something approaching to divine honors were lavished on the Seventeen."

Party solidarity and loyalty came naturally to these men. They trusted one another, consulted with one another, respected one another's opinions and advice. They played as well as worked together. "Their families interchange civilities," it was noted, "their females kiss each other when they meet—their men shake each other heartily by the hand—they dine, or drink, or pray, or take snuff" with one another. As governor, Marcy read his proposed speeches to party colleagues in advance for their approval; Van Buren consulted closely with his associates. This kind of collective counsel was especially impressive in light of the quality of these men, no robots or pawns or party hacks but a group of unusually clear-headed, purposeful, thoughtful, honest men of considerable educational attainments and social standing.

Perhaps the most remarkable achievement of these leaders was to shape, as much in practice as in advance theorizing, a formidable concept of party government and majority rule. That concept embraced the propositions that competition between two strong, unified, disciplined parties was not dangerous to a democracy but vital to its health and maintenance; that harmony and consensus were undesirable and undemocratic when fundamental issues divided the people; that the absence of parties, or the amalgamation of them, would sap the foundations of liberty, especially freedom of speech and press; that party competition, spirit, and discord stimulated popular interest and dispelled apathy; that the parties—a governing party monitored and checked by an opposition party—served as a vital, extra-constitutional set of checks and balances.

Party advocates also emphasized the role of parties as watchdogs. The organized parties, Governor Enos Throop said, "watch and scan each other's doings, the public mind is instructed by ample discussion of ample measures, and acts of violence are restrained by the convictions of the people, that the prevailing measures are the results of enlightened reason." Above all, the theorists believed in majority rule, within and between parties.

The ultimate question, however, was what parties stood *for,* as platform makers and policy shapers. It has long been supposed that Van Buren and other Regency leaders during these early years took radical, egalitarian positions on public issues. More recent analysis, however, shows that behind their rhetoric about "Democracy versus Aristocracy," and "Republicans against Hartford Feds," was a strongly conservative cast. The Regency's loudest war cry, as late as 1830, was for states' rights; Van Buren and associates took conservative positions on the leading reform issues of imprisonment for debt, free public education, and presidential electoral reform. Under the doctrine of party government and majority rule, the crucial test was not what parties were for or against at any particular time, but whether they could serve as vehicles for political leadership, popular mobilization, and governmental action in the face of new needs and changing public attitudes.

That test came suddenly in July 1832, with Jackson's dramatic veto of the United States Bank recharter. For years the Regency had been accused of protecting its own "monsters"—its own state banks and Freemasonry. Now Jackson had handed it a new, far more spectacular, and easily hateable Monster, Biddle's national bank. After the veto message showed the way, Lee Benson wrote, the Regency's strategy was obvious: "Jump on board the antimonopoly bandwagon, guide it down the state rights road, and crush the Monster in its Greek temple on Chestnut Street, Philadelphia." In effect the Democrats had "dished the Whigs"—had dished even more the Anti-Masons and Workingmen, who had sought to monopolize the egalitarian, anti-"Monster" thunder.

Thus a spectacular national act had catalyzed party conflict in New York State, with powerful implications for national party realignment and competition. Whether Jackson's act, which immediately transformed 1832 presidential campaign strategy, would have a long-run effect on the American parties as a whole would depend on events also in other states.

*   *   *

Massachusetts, with its established patrician families and newly arrived Irish, its multitudes of farmers and factory hands and fishermen, its Beacon Hill and Brattle Street Brahmins who looked down on the social-climbing elites up and down the Atlantic seaboard, was almost as variegated as New York. The old commonwealth was developing industrially faster, probably, than any other state. Cotton mills were multiplying; railroads were radiating out from Boston; bankers and merchants were thriving and looking for places to put their money; Yankee captains and missionaries were searching for trade and heathen across the seven seas. If political families and factions were less contentious than in New York, religious groups were perhaps more so, as conservative and radical Unitarians debated each other, and orthodox Congregationalists held their ground against dissenting Baptists, Methodists, and Quakers; and all the Protestant sects closed ranks against the expanding Catholic population.

Massachusetts resembled New York and other states, however, in its passage from the old elitist politics of deference to the new politics of egalitarian rhetoric and wider political participation. The passage was illustrated by the contrast between Daniel Webster and the Jackson brand of politician. Webster, product of Exeter and Dartmouth, protégé of Boston notables, an admired insider in Beacon Hill society, Senate spokesman first of New England merchants and later of manufacturers, was the quintessential elitist transcending superficial popular favor. The widening of the suffrage and the rising winds of equality helped bring a new breed of politician to the fore.

David Henshaw was typical. Born not in Federalist Boston but in the hinterland near Worcester, apprenticed to a druggist at sixteen after a meager education in the village academy, he quickly rose in business and politics to become a powerful voice against the political establishment. Rewarded by Jackson with the patronage-rich collectorship of the port of Boston, Henshaw built a party machine not unlike the Albany Regency, especially in its appeal to rural voters outside the Yankee coastal region, and in its use of a party press, including Henshaw's own paper, the Boston *Statesman.* A stocky man of medium height and two hundred pounds, Henshaw believed in party leadership, regularity, and loyalty. He was also a conservative, as were many of the early Jackson men in the Common-wealth, but here too Jackson's bank veto catalyzed state Democrats and produced a swing toward radical rhetoric.

Massachusetts illustrated how, in a system that sustained party federalism as well as constitutional federalism, state politics refracted back upon national. The experience of Kentucky was quite different, but this frontier state also became part of an overall pattern of the decline of deference, the rise of grass-roots parties, and the complex interrelation of state and national politics.

Kentucky had seemed particularly vulnerable to boom and bust. All a Kentuckian needed to set up a bank during the post-1812 war years, some said, was a charter and a printing press. Land-hungry pioneers had borrowed from the state banks to buy more acreage; state banks expanded their circulation to meet demand; the newly re-established national bank in Philadelphia undertook its own liberal program of credit expansion, but then suddenly shifted toward contraction. The Panic of 1819 had left Kentucky with dozens of beleaguered state banks that in turn pressed their debtors harshly. Responding to desperate need, the legislature passed measure after measure to help debtors, most notably a "stay" law giving them an extra two years to pay off notes. Indignant creditors, turning to the courts for relief, won from circuit judge James Clark a ruling that a key debtor-relief law was unconstitutional.

Then followed a battle of Checks and Balances. A committee of the legislature denied the right of the judge to veto a deliberate measure of the government and recommended his removal. This move did not gain the needed two-thirds vote in the legislature. When the court of appeals sustained Clark, the legislature tried to remove the whole court, and failed again. A "relief party" then appealed to the people in the election of 1824. Showing a striking ability to organize a campaign and to engage with the needs and hopes of the voters, rejecting the old politics of deference in favor of mass campaign techniques, the relief party won the governorship and a majority in both houses of the legislature. Once again the reliefers tried to remove the erring judges from office, but could not secure the elusive two-thirds. Finally, arguing that if they could not remove the judges from their seats, they could remove the "seats from the judges," the relief party in the legislature removed the old court and authorized the governor to appoint a new one.

Out of the crisis and conflict in Kentucky had arisen a whole new leadership cadre, headed by Amos Kendall and Francis Blair. An editor, slaveholder, and conservative Republican, Kendall had been cool to debt-relief measures, but later he changed his mind, especially when he had to borrow $1,500 from his old friend Henry Clay and several thousands more from his new friend Martin Van Buren. Once enlisted in the debtors' cause, Kendall became its fiery leader. He pilloried the "court" party as a pack of conspirators and speculators, directed his appeals straight to the dirt farmers and the "common man"—and got chased in his editorial offices by an anti-relief lawyer brandishing a hickory stick. He and Blair also denounced high tariffs and federal improvements, thus widening the breach with their mentor Henry Clay.

The election year of 1828 brought Kendall his supreme opportunity to link up with Jackson. Bypassing the local elite, whose political power was based on a system of self-perpetuating county courts that controlled local appointments, he set up a central committee in Louisville to call for a state convention that would agree on a statewide ticket of Jackson electors. He organized mass meetings of Jackson voters who would meet in local conventions, as well as local committees headed by county and district leaders who reported to state committees.

Kendall, in short, built an integrated mass party in order to outflank the political dominance of the gentry. Where his own party following was inadequate he built alliances with Old Court men. It was only natural that, as the architect of Jackson's big victory in Clay's own state, Kendall would move to Washington and join his new mentor. And it was only natural that this fiery editorialist, who had won political influence by demagogic appeals to the common man, should make Jackson's bank recharter veto message a political arrow that flew straight to the emotional heart of the electorate.

Behind all the sound and fury in Kentucky politics, historians have found a rational grass-roots demand for economic relief and change, a popular urge for meaningful democratic participation in politics, strong "social and economic aspiration burning in the hearts of Kentuckians." Although Jackson would fail to carry Kentucky against native son Clay in 1832, the politics of the state had been changed for good, with an organized, competitive two-party system replacing the oligarchical politics of deference. Like Kentucky, each of the other states was unique but virtually all were forced to move toward Jacksonian democracy. And all the states, as they sent to Washington politicians like Henshaw and Kendall and a host of enterprising senators and congressmen, were helping to shape a new national political system, even while they were being shaped by it.

MAJORITIES: THE FLOWERING OF THE PARTIES

How and why Americans shaped a national party system—how they framed their second, or "people's," constitution—is one of the most complex and perplexing developments in American history. The storyteller would surely prefer to recount the wonderful tale of the great men who met in Philadelphia in 1787 and struck off their constitution in one glorious summer than to follow the labyrinthine process by which little-known men built parties in many places over a long period of time. Then, too, historians disagree about the nature of this party building, even though—or perhaps because—exceptionally talented scholars have pursued their historical studies in the Jeffersonian-Jacksonian period of party formation. They differ over basic questions of causation—whether the direction and shape that parties took during the first fifty years of the national existence was a product mainly of ideological forces, economic factors, intellectual effort, political calculation, institutional changes, chance, or interplay among some or all of these variables.

In exploring these causes it would be well to keep in mind that no economic development or institutional change or "great idea" in itself directly builds a political party. Transportation improvements, for example, helped make it easier for widely dispersed men to come together in party conventions, but no improved stagecoach or locomotive built parties. Party "as such is a product of human ingenuity and not simply a natural growth," in William Chambers' words. "It must be built by the efforts of skilled political craftsmen, including major leaders at the center and hundreds or thousands of lesser leaders in outlying localities, who must at least know that they are devising co-ordinated means to their immediate ends, although they may not be wholly aware of the fact that they are shaping a party in the process." Those who built parties were neither the celebrities of the age nor local nobodies; party did not emerge as a result of mass action at the grass roots. Parties were formed by leaders experimenting with new ways of gaining office and power.

The first parties were largely networks of leaders, mostly notables. Born and bred in the old politics of colonial days, the political leaders of the 1790s still operated in a system of deference to established notables, of family "connections" and influence, of limited participation by "average" farmers, workers, and clerks, even less involvement by women, and none at all by black slaves and white paupers. How was it that leaders who embodied and personified the politics of elitism and deference could themselves be instruments for change? The answer lay in sharply growing issue conflicts that raised the political consciousness of millions of Americans. As long as Americans were broadly agreed about national policy, as they were during most of Washington's presidential years, political competition was muted. Strong sentiments for or against Jefferson and Adams, and the burning issues over relations with the French and the British—issues that evoked powerful feelings and memories and loyalties—acted as catalysts cutting across regional and local attachments. The national Federalist and Republican parties were born out of this kind of conflict, which took on a new intensity with the War of 1812.

During this period Americans had national parties but not a national party system. Presidents, senators, and representatives typically acted and talked like good Federalists or good Republicans. The press was highly partisan. Congressional Republicans, at least, were well organized in their caucus. A few states had developed party organizations. But all this did not make a system: Parties were not generally seen as legitimate. Party leaders in office did not recognize the legitimacy of opposition parties. Party organization in most states was rudimentary. While many activists were highly partisan, settled party conviction and commitment among the electorate were limited to a few places in a few states. One could detect a "party in office," in short, but only a feeble party organization nationwide, and limited party affiliation among the electorate. And linkages that might make for strong and persisting structures—integrated national-state-local machinery, unified electoral and organizational effort, strong and stable party memberships—were rudimentary or absent.

As dramatic conflict over national issues declined following the War of 1812, so did the central role of national party leadership and organization. With the Federalist party almost dead outside New England, and with the Republican party reduced to state and factional in-fighting, Monroe's presidency was a time of heightened factional dispute but blurred party division. Party was left in the care, sometimes benign and sometimes casual, of the states. National party unity and organization fell into disarray.

The congressional caucus for nominating Presidents and Vice-Presidents—potentially the most powerful agency of national party power—both fostered and reflected this disarray. The caucus had started as early as 1792, when some Republican congressmen, after taking soundings in the states, met in Philadelphia to choose George Clinton to run against Vice-President John Adams. The Republicans held no caucus in 1796 because Jefferson was the unquestioned choice. Four years later, forty-three senators and representatives meeting at Marache's boardinghouse again agreed that Jefferson was pre-eminently their man, and formally endorsed Burr for Vice-President. The congressional caucus of 1804 routinely endorsed President Jefferson and substituted Clinton for Burr. In 1808, when the Republicans chose Madison overwhelmingly over Monroe, at least the caucus had a decision to make, but in 1812 its re-endorsement of Madison was unanimous. The 1816 caucus was actually a contest, with Monroe besting Crawford in a relatively close vote, but hardly a fifth of the members even showed up at the 1820 caucus. In 1824 the caucus was unable to perform its most essential function of uniting support behind one candidate. The Federalists had had even less success with a congressional caucus.

The reign of "King Caucus" had been brief, its rule weak. It died during the period of consensual, partyless government under Monroe. Only a pervasive conflict could create the conditions of raised political consciousness within which party competition could flourish, and that conflict came with the nomination and election of Adams in 1824, as a result of intense opposition to him, the apparent deal against Jackson, and the growing and divisive influence of Old Hickory first as candidate, then as the tribune of the common man, and finally as the opponent of Biddle.

In what institutional form this rising political conflict and election competition would be expressed became the crucial question in the 1830s. The nation's politics might have reverted to the "King of the Rock," "Winner Take All" politics of earlier years—the elitist politics of faction, personal following, closed caucus, the politics of family influence, social class, economic elitism. Profound changes in the foundations of American politics, however, made such a reversion impossible. The egalitarian issues posed by Jefferson and Jackson had permeated the electorate and immensely raised its political consciousness. The widening of the suffrage in the states, along with other measures of democratization, had expanded the number and broadened the class membership of voters that candidates had to attract. The very feel and aroma of politics had changed, with the new hucksterism and vote cadging, the decline of the gentry and of deference, the rise of the political professional who made politics his life and his living, the proliferation of patronage jobs, the profusion of small caucuses, conventions, election rallies, political parades and picnics and paraphernalia. All this amounted, in Richard McCormick's words, to a "hidden revolution" in the political environment.

This hidden revolution was intellectual, too—an upheaval in leaders' concepts of the role of faction, interest, party. The framers of the "Constitution" abhorred the ideas underlying the second, or people's, constitution—government by parties—as tending toward faction, turbulence, selfishness. Consciously or not, they wrote a constitution that would pulverize and crush parties. Even in founding the Republican party Jefferson would not recognize the legitimacy of party *opposition.* It took hundreds of men, working at the state and local grass roots of politics, to repudiate the anti-party doctrine of the Framers, whom they otherwise revered. They built their state and local parties against the prevailing elitist thought of the day.

One man stood out in his conceptualizing of the "party constitution"— Martin Van Buren. The "red fox of Kinderhook" may have been sly and slippery in some of his political machinations, but intellectually he was a hedgehog, in Archilochus' terms as interpreted by Isaiah Berlin. Van Buren had one big idea, the concept of what party was and could be. Although lacking clear philosophical guidelines, he developed his ideas on a kind of ad hoc, day-to-day basis. In later years he fleshed out his views, just as the Framers did about the Constitution in their retirements, but as early as 1827 Van Buren was arguing that a general convention would be better than the congressional caucus to concentrate the anti-Adams vote. He maintained that a convention would lead to the "substantial reorganization of the Old Republican Party," substitute "party principles" for "personal preference," and strengthen Republicanism in New England and the Republican political coalition between North and South.

Ultimately Van Buren developed virtually an ideology of party as the essence of a democracy of liberty and virtue. In a most hedgehog-like fashion, he broadened his party concept in arguing that free competitive parties were essential to the public interest, inseparable from free government, necessary to prevent abuse of private power, and conducive to the moral discipline of institutional loyalty and personal self-restraint. He believed parties must pursue high principle as well as low patronage, must compete vigorously with one another, must generate a clash of platforms as well as personalities. Above all—the highest test of a believer in the second constitution—he not only accepted but welcomed the idea of a continuing, responsible, and legitimated opposition. If earlier the "fundamental cause for the failure to create a national organization was intellectual," in James Chase's words, the critical factor in the later formation of a national party system was also conceptual and intellectual.

The creation of the presidential nominating convention provided the keystone for the party arch. Here again New York and other states had experimented with ways of moving party nominations out of the relatively small and unrepresentative legislative caucuses into conclaves of delegates chosen in state and local meetings. By the mid-1830s state conventions were well established in the central states and in Ohio and Kentucky; conventions for local nominations were widely employed in New England; they were, however, slow to be established in most of the South. After the Anti-Masons experimented with the first presidential nominating convention in 1831, in Baltimore, the Democrats staged their own the next year in the same city for the renomination of President Jackson, and for the nomination—appropriately—of Martin Van Buren for Vice-President. This convention pioneered in adopting the two-thirds rule for nominations, and in agreeing to a non-binding unit rule that allowed a majority of delegates from a state to cast the entire vote of the state. These rules, little considered at the time, would become critical to the Democrats in later years. The Whigs, emerging out of the National Republican party that had held its national convention in 1831, were forced to adopt the presidential convention as a permanent fixture.

So by the late 1830s Americans had a party *system*. National, state, and local parties were linked through a pyramid of local, county, and congressional-district conventions sending delegates to state and national conventions. Party consciousness was high among both party leaders and party followers. Strong cadres of leaders developed at every level. Party competition was intense and strengthened partisan feeling on both sides. The parties were well balanced against each other not only nationally but also in most of the states—a degree of national political unity that would not be seen again for four decades. The linkage within and between parties was almost complete.

On the surface, at least, the two parties looked splendid, with their national conventions topping the pyramids of state, county, and local committees and caucuses and conventions, their sonorous platforms rhetorically thwacking their foes hip and thigh, their national and state leaders skilled in the arts of intra-party negotiation and compromise, their robust local activity full of parades and picnics and speechifying and occasional fisticuffs and barroom brawls. Behind the façade lay certain weaknesses, existing and potential.

It was not wholly clear by the end of the 1830s what the parties were, what they were for and against. More than ever the Democrats claimed to be the "party of the common man," despite the fact that it did not engage with the average woman or the blacks or the really poor; nor did these people engage with the Democrats. The Jacksonians had made some effort to appeal to the expanding wage-earning class, especially in Van Buren's executive order establishing a shorter working day on federal public projects, but the Democracy was still largely an agrarian party. The Whigs, an unstable coalition of old Federalists, Anti-Masons, mercantile and industrial elements, and a congeries of other groupings, found it much easier to denounce Jackson's executive "usurpation" and Van Buren's partisanship than to develop a positive program of their own. Both parties had weaknesses at their foundations. Political change and realignment had occurred so quickly during the 1830s that large numbers of Americans were left in a void between or outside the two major parties. State and local parties lacked organization and vigor in a number of areas, especially in the South and parts of the West.

The main weakness of party as the second, or "people's," constitution lay in its awkward embrace with the first. The organized two-party system of the late 1830s was potentially strong enough to be a vehicle for popular majority rule. Theoretically a winning majority party takes over the government and rules until at least the next election. But the Constitution was craftily designed to thwart majority rule. Winners of a presidential election could take over the White House but not necessarily the Congress. Representatives were elected out of their own, often independent constituencies; only a third of the senators were even chosen in the same year as the President. The Supreme Court, as John Marshall had demonstrated, lay beyond the reach of transient popular majorities. Even if one party achieved the feat of winning control of the whole federal government, a profusion of states, counties, cities, and towns had their own counterbalancing and conflicting constituencies.

The party "constitution," in short, was designed to concentrate power, the formal Constitution to disperse it. Only a centrally organized and powerfully led and united party could overcome the separation of powers and checks and balances stitched into the American national and state constitutional systems, and neither the Whigs nor the Democrats were such a party. Thus the first constitution rent the second far more than the second constitution knit together the first. To a great extent, indeed, different parts of the two parties enhanced fragmentation by providing a local or state party foundation for the dispersed efforts of independent legislators or elected officials.

Still, the republic was only half a century old by the end of the 1830s;

it was still young, changing, experimental. The question was the future potential for majority rule through party government. Voting turnout rose so strongly and dramatically during the 1830s as to seem to make the "people's" constitution ultimately more viable. The participation of more and more low-income people in voting also made more possible a national party, whether Democratic or Whig or something else, that could provide the nation with a genuinely radical, democratic, popular national government that might, if given enough time and sense of commitment, unite the separated organs of government behind a comprehensive national effort to meet the needs and aspirations of the great number of lower-income people.

CHAPTER 11

The Majority That Never Was

S IXTY years after the Declaration of Independence, Americans still had a revolutionary credo without a revolutionary movement, a radical rhetoric without a radical party. At the Fourth of July celebrations of 1836, during President Jackson's last year in office, orators evoked the egalitarian phrases of the Declaration with little heed to the considerable inequality around them. The eras of Jefferson and Jackson would come to be described as "revolutions," but these at most were political rather than economic or social overturns. During these eras men had been revolved in and out of office, legislative and bureaucratic elites joined and sometimes displaced by more plebeian and populist types, banking and other establishments challenged, smaller enterprisers given a better chance to rise to the top. But the structure of society and government remained unchanged.

So did the essential condition of freed and enslaved blacks, middle-class and lower-class women, and the urban and rural poor. Together these people comprised the great majority of the population. These blacks and women and poor could hardly have been more different from one another. They could barely communicate with one another or even recognize each other, much less sympathize with one another. Some would hate one another. Yet the three groups had some things in common—they were in many ways impotent, economically, socially, politically, legally. They all were living in a great republic that preached and practiced its own peculiar form of majority rule. And they, together with Indians both subjugated and unvanquished, made up a popular majority in contrast to the cadres of middle-class and upper-class white men running the affairs of the republic. In the expanding democratic consciousness of the 1830s and 1840s, was there any chance for some kind of collective revolutionary or radical or even reformist impetus from people who shared only their powerlessness?

Historians have enough trouble dealing with events that did happen without trying to consider events that might have happened but did not, or should have happened and could not. But occasionally, like the dog that did not bark in the night, supremely important developments that might have occurred, and in the eyes of many should have happened but in the end did not, must be considered in the balance accounts of history. This must be done not only to grant a kind of retrospective historical justice to such groups, but even more because in the stream of history the causal agents that are blocked or diverted are entwined with those that are intensified and accelerated. Knowing the potential forces that never came into being helps us understand those that did.

"If ever America undergoes great revolutions," Tocqueville wrote, "they will be brought about by the presence of the black race on the soil of the United States; that is to say, they will owe their origin, not to the equality, but to the inequality of condition."

The potential reformist or radical or revolutionary forces that never came to realization—how can they be measured? First by assessing the "objective" conditions of people suffering major deprivations. Then, and more difficult, by analyzing how people responded subjectively to the unsatisfied wants and needs arising from those conditions. Finally, and most difficult of all, estimating the leadership, institutional, ideological, and other external forces that influenced the motivation and ability of people to reform, radicalize, or revolt.

The capacity to measure "objective" conditions has been enormously enhanced by the joint efforts of historians, archivists, demographers, geographers, and others. Through memoirs, diaries, account books, tax rolls, and the like, sophisticated analysis has provided better insight into the everyday lives of lower-class persons than do some of the lurid and partisan accounts of the past. These latter reports have often described exceptional situations, because they were more easily dramatizable and publishable. But they ignore the experiences of the great number of persons studied—experiences that ultimately affected the course of history.

Consider, for example, the "slaver." All too familiar are the horrifying tales of those floating slave pens whose smell of human squalor could be picked up miles downwind. On some slavers black persons sickened and died by the scores, were brutalized sexually and in other ways, thrown overboard on the approach of a naval vessel, left to die of thirst by deserting crews, were flogged, mutilated, hanged, and shot after any show of resistance. But for most slaves *La Fortuna* was a more typical introduction to life and death in America.

On *La Fortuna,* a ninety-ton schooner bound out of the Rio Pongo for Cuba, everything was efficiency, for maximum profit. Before embarkation the heads of all Africans, male and female, had been neatly shaven, and their bodies lightly branded with pieces of silver wire forming the recipient merchant's initials. Given a final big "feed" in the African slave pens, they had been taken out to the ship in canoes and stripped naked. The men were sent into the hold, the women to a cabin, and children left on deck. At mealtime, rice or farina or yams or beans, depending on tribal origin, were served in a large tub. The slaves dipped into it and swallowed on commands from a monitor, to prevent "inequality in the appropriation of nourishment." Every morning a dram was given to prevent scurvy, and thrice a week mouths were washed out with vinegar. At sundown the blacks were stowed below, in spoon position, each head in the next person's lap. Shackles were used as little as possible, and only for full-grown men, as it was believed that the more a slave was ironed, the more he deteriorated.

This trip was profitable for Captain Canot. After deducting expenses of $10,900 for his human cargo, $6,200 for the ship and her outfitting, and the pay of officers and crew, he fetched $77,469 for his cargo and $2,950 for the ship, netting $41,439.

Data from rich and diverse sources enable historians to think their way back into the existential conditions even of those who left few formal records. Any retrospective view is partial, distorted, and limited by the cultural blinders of the twentieth-century Western mind, but enough is known about the "objective" circumstances of existence and deprivation to permit speculation about how persons experienced those circumstances at the time, and why they behaved as they did, why they acted or failed to act.

BLACKS IN BONDAGE

Reverend Charles Colcock Jones, the owner of Montevideo, a 941-acre rice and Sea Island cotton plantation on the coast of Georgia, liked things run in an orderly and efficient manner. On a summer morning, as sea breezes drifted through the gray Spanish moss bearding the majestic live oaks, magnolias, and cedars that surrounded the plantation settlement, a single blast of a horn broke the stillness in the slave quarters. The summer sun would be burning as forty or so slaves, after a hurried breakfast, walked from their quarters to the plantation gates. In the fields, Cato, the black foreman, directed the field hands and assigned tasks for the day. Reverend Jones and his family would have fled the summer heat for higher ground at Maybank. Only the slaves, with their white overseer, remained to work the canals, ditches, and dams of rice culture in the malarial, mosquito-ridden swamps.

Cato directed the slaves at a variety of tasks, such as "working the roads, raising the river dams, cutting new ground, making fences, overseeing carpentry, planting cotton, breaking in corn, rice, and hops." Slaves had to be able to reach the most distant field in an hour's walk—one reason why Jones and other planters had split their holdings into two or three separate plantations under separate white overseers. Planters often rated a faithful, experienced driver such as Cato more valuable than white overseers, who tended to move from plantation to plantation.

At noon, Cato ordered the slaves to break for dinner, always eaten in the fields; at night, he would tell them to quit. Like other black drivers and foremen, he maintained the agricultural equipment by checking it and noting which implements needed repair. The driver estimated the size of the crop his labor force would produce, supervised the ginning of cotton and the harvest of corn, kept the keys to the barn, dairy, smokehouse, cotton house, gin house, corn house, rice house, winnowing house, and mill house at Montevideo. He kept track of the cattle, poultry, and other livestock holdings of the plantation.

At night, after the day's work was done, the driver policed the quarters, usually crudely built log cabins with dirt floors. Planters often crowded seven or eight slaves into the two-room cabins. Enlightened men like Jones supplied their slaves with sufficient though badly prepared and monotonous food—rice, fat pork, and clabber. After they had eaten their evening meal, the driver would blow a horn, signaling that every slave must be in for cabin check. Cato made a nightly report to the overseer.

The Montevideo slaves, like the majority of blacks in slavery, could support one another, maintain some community life, and build a certain group solidarity at work and at night in the slave quarters because they lived with other blacks in plantation units of twenty or more. By 1860 more than half of the 3,954,000 blacks listed as slaves lived with more than twenty other slaves; one-fourth of all the bondmen worked on plantations holding more than fifty slaves, while only one-fourth lived on small farms of ten slaves or less. The overwhelming white majority and superior white firepower would have made revolt suicidal, but blacks could maintain their own cultural and spiritual world within the group, and the group, in many cases, was led by one of their own—a black driver or foreman.

Slaves at Montevideo also gathered often in the small chapel built by Reverend Jones for religious meetings. "Your people all seem to be doing very well," wrote Cato. "They attend praise and go to church regularly whenever there is preaching in reach." Even in winter, Jones was often absent from Montevideo, preaching and teaching ecclesiastical history at a Columbia, South Carolina, theological seminary. In his absence, slaves received religious instruction from visiting white preachers who used Jones's "slave catechism" and his widely circulated work, *Suggestions on the*

Religious Instruction of the Negroes in the Southern States. Slaves often heard the favorite text of Reverend Jones: "Servants, obey in all things your masters according to the flesh; not with eyeservice, as men pleasers, but in single-ness of heart, fearing God. And whatsoever ye do, do it heartily, as to the Lord, and not unto men. . . ." Recalcitrant blacks were brought before the local minister, who "cited them in front of the next church service."

Religion was as important to many slaves as it was to their white masters, if for different reasons. Reverend Jones could not understand the "extrava-gant and nonsensical chants, and hallelujah songs of their own compos-ing" in the black praise meetings on his plantation. The cultural blend of African tribal customs with evangelical religion created a unique personal area for slaves that the white master could neither comprehend nor con-trol. The singing of spirituals in praise meetings expressed and heightened the slaves' sense of autonomy and hunger for liberty. Fearing religion as a potentially dangerous force, planters required white preachers such as Jones to lead the worship of slaves. To encourage slaves to listen to white ministers, owners often yielded to their demands for black assistant preachers in praise meetings and worship services. Black ministers formed a third cadre of black leadership, helping to hold their people together under duress.

Always in the consciousness of field hands loomed the "Big House," with its white masters and black servitors. About one-fourth of all the slaves in the South were house servants, including coachmen and garden-ers, Eugene Genovese has estimated. Reverend Jones's body servant, Tom, dressed his master every morning and attended the family. Some body servants slept at the foot of their master's bed so as to be ready for his call. Each member of the family had a personal servant. Jones's son owned a body servant, George, who at times traveled alone on the railroad to Savannah, protected by a written pass from his owner.

Built upon a concept of blacks as inferior and childlike, slavery encour-aged owners to promote feelings of dependence. "Will you please keep George, if convenient, with you on the island, about the house," young Jones wrote to his father, "as I do not wish that he should forget his training. I want him to acquire a house look, which you know is not the acquisition of a day." Young Jones asked his mother to have slaves make four shirts for George. Later he wrote, "The 'general's' garments fit him admirably and he emphatically looks a little Corporal Trim. . . . He expects to excite by his fine raiments quite the jealousy of his own sex, and the admiration of the fair sex of kindred extraction." In some slaves this kind of treatment produced virtual infantilization, but more often blacks only pretended to be dumb, childlike, and ignorant. Donning the grinning, head-bobbing, shambling role of Sambo was another way to resist oppression.

House servants enjoyed better food and clothing than field hands, because they received the leftovers from the master's table and the family's castoff clothing. Yet they had to pay a heavy psychological price for their greater material comforts. Living in such close proximity to whites, they were under constant surveillance. They had always to acknowledge their master's supremacy by deference and docility. Some house servants were obsequious; others put on a mask of submissiveness and spied on the master and his family for their fellow slaves in the quarters. Others openly resisted. In such cases, the responsibility of the driver to discipline his own people for the benefit of the white master made his life ambiguous and difficult. Jane, an eighteen-year-old house servant of Reverend Jones, gave "constant trouble." Jane's mother and father, Phoebe and Cassius, had also "occasioned trouble" before. Cato had earlier reported that "Cash has given up going to prayers" and was "cited before the next Meeting" for swearing.

Mary Jones, Reverend Jones's wife, wished to sell Jane because of her tendency to run away, but would not separate her from her family. Mary Jones especially valued Jane's mother, Phoebe, an accomplished house servant. "Much as I should miss the mother," Mary Jones wrote, "I will not separate them if I can help it." Jane eventually did run away, took the name of Sarah, and with the help of black friends found work as a house servant in Savannah. She pretended that her master had allowed her to find work in the city and pay him her wages. This was known as "hiring her time." The city constable learned of her runaway status and arrested her, receiving a thirty-dollar reward. On learning of her arrest, the Jones family had her sent to a slave broker and the auction block.

Slavery seriously compromised black family life. The power of owner over slave was absolute, and if a bondman ran away, the owner, not the law, administered punishment. Whether he administered it benevolently or harshly depended upon his nature. Rather than trifling with slaves who showed any inclination to flee, planters often sold them with or without their families, sometimes into the Deep South, where there was little or no chance for escape to freedom.

Since owners could sell slaves away from families at any time, there were no legal marriages among the bonded, and planters occasionally pressured a slave woman to cohabit with a black man not of her choice, to breed new slaves. Many years later, when she was in her nineties and blind, Rose

Williams still hated a Texas owner, Hall Hawkins, who kept her family together but wanted her to "marry" a man she despised:

Dere am one thing Massa Hawkins does to me what I can't shunt from my mind. I knows he don't do it for meanness, but I allus holds it 'gainst him. What he done am force me to live with dat nigger, Rufus, 'gainst my wants.

After I been at he place 'bout a year, de massa come to me and say, "You gwine live with Rufus in dat cabin over yonder. Go fix it for livin'." I's 'bout sixteen year old and has no larnin', and I's jus' igno'mus chile. I's thought dat him mean for me to tend de cabin for Rufus and some other niggers. Well, dat am start de pestigation for me.

I's took charge of de cabin after work am done and fixes supper. Now, I don't like dat Rufus, 'cause he a bully. He am big and 'cause he so, he think everybody do what him say. We'uns has supper, den I goes here and dere talkin', till I's ready for sleep and den I gits in de bunk. After I's in, dat nigger come and crawl in de bunk with me 'fore I knows it. I says, "What you means, you fool nigger?" He say for me to hush de mouth. "Dis my bunk, too," he say.

"You's teched in de head. Git out," I's told him, and I puts de feet 'gainst him and give him a shove and out he go on de floor 'fore he knew what I's doin'. Dat nigger jump up and he mad. He look like de wild bear. He starts for de bunk and I jumps quick for de poker. It am 'bout three feet long and when he comes at me I lets him have it over de head. Did dat nigger stop in he tracks? I's say he did. He looks at me steady for a minute and you's could tell he thinkin' hard. Den he go and set on de bench and say, "Jus' wait. You thinks it am smart, but you's am foolish in de head. Dey's gwine larn you somethin'."

"Hush you big mouth and stay 'way from dis nigger, dat all I wants," I say, and jus' sets and hold dat poker in de hand. He jus' sets, lookin' like de bull. Dere we'uns sets and sets for 'bout an hour, and den he go out and I bars de door.

De nex' day I goes to de missy and tells her what Rufus wants and missy say dat am de massa's wishes. She say, "yous am de portly gal and Rufus am de portly man. De massa wants yu-uns fer to bring forth portly chillen."

I's thinkin' 'bout what de missy say, but say to myse'f, "I's not gwine live with dat Rufus." Dat night when he come in de cabin, I grabs de poker and sits on de bench and says, "Git 'way from me, nigger, 'fore I busts you brains out and stomp on dem." He say nothin' and git out.

De nex' day de massa call me and tell me, "Woman, I's pay big money for you and I's done dat for de cause I wants yous to raise me chillens. I's put yous to live with Rufus for dat purpose. Now, if you doesn't want whippin' at de stake, yous do what I wants."

I thinks 'bout massa buyin' me offen de block and saving' me from bein' sep'rated from my folks and 'bout bein' whipped at de stake. Dere it am. What am I's to do? So I 'cides to do as de massa wish and so I yields.

Rose had two children by Rufus and then left him. "I never marries," she said later, "'cause one 'sperience am 'nough for this nigger."

The black infant mortality rate was almost double that of whites, yet the slave population between 1830 and 1860 grew by 23 percent every ten years. Slaves married earlier. Many slave women bore children when they were thirteen and fourteen years of age, so that by twenty some had produced five children. Planters gave bounties and prizes to women who boosted the slave population. Mothers had little opportunity to develop a real attachment to their children, since the usual practice was to press the mother back into service one month after childbirth and put the baby in the plantation nursery, where old slave women or slave children cared for the very young.

Because Reverend Jones considered marriage vows among blacks as sacred as among whites, he decided to sell the disobedient family of Phoebe and Cassius as a unit, for "we cannot consent to separate them." The slaves would have brought much more money if sold separately, but Jones resolved to take an economic loss. Jones then priced the family: "Cassius, Senior, age 45, good field hand, $800; Phoebe, Mother, age 47, accomplished house servant, $1,000; Cassius, Junior, good field hand, age 20, $1,000; Jane, daughter, age 18, house servant, $900; son, field hand, age 16, $800; daughter, Victoria, age 14, active field hand; Lafayette, age 12, smart active boy. . . ."

Wright, the slave broker, returned much lower estimates to the Joneses for the slaves (approximately $750 apiece), saying: "The estimates given must necessarily be subject to greater or less modification. The size, soundness of teeth, etc. are all to be considered." Jones wrote that he must have $800 for each, and they must be kept together. He had engaged a man to take them to Savannah by wagon: "Jackson says he will put them in a yard and feed them where he usually stops, and they will be safe, and at a trifling expense."

Slaves were a large investment, and slave-trading was a profitable business. The price for prime field hands was $1,250 in Virginia and $1,800 in New Orleans by the late 1850s, owing to the high demand for slaves in the new cotton fields of the Gulf states. Slave traders often earned commissions and profits of from 5 to 30 percent on the sale price of slaves.

Pressing for the speedy sale of his slaves, but wanting his price too, Jones wrote his son in Savannah to spruce up the appearance of the family for sale, as was the common practice. "You did right in procuring the shoes, and I wish you get of Mr. Lathrop striped Negro winter cloth the same as we bought for the people: six and a half yards apiece, and three yards of cotton homespun apiece and some buttons and thread, and have it given to them. Phoebe and Jane can make it up in a few days." The expense of keeping them at Wright's ran to $200 and Jones wrote his son to accept an offer of $4,000 supposedly from an up-country planter who would keep the entire family on his plantation. A professional slave trader, however, quietly bought the family through an agent and took them to New Orleans for separate sale.

Phoebe dictated a message from New Orleans to her adult daughters, Clarissa and Nancy, who, married with families of their own, were left behind on the Jones plantation. Her letter reveals the love that blacks held for their families. "Please tell them that their sister Jane died the first of Feby we did not know what was the matter with her. . . . Clarissa, your affectionate mother and Father sends a heap of Love to you and your Husband and my Grand Children Phebea. Mag. and Cloe. John. Judy. Sue.," wrote Phoebe from the slave trader's quarters in New Orleans. Many slaves, such as Jane, lost their lives in the slave trade. Others resisted. Some tried economic sabotage and covertly slowed down their work or maimed animals or broke tools or stole goods from the master. To run, to conspire, to revolt—these were the more dramatic ways of fighting back.

As a young slave, Nat Turner had fled a cruel and demanding overseer. He hid in the dark swamps of Southampton County, Virginia, to escape the slave patrols and bloodhounds. Thirty days later, Turner walked out of the swamps, not to freedom but back to slavery on the plantation of his master, Benjamin Turner. When asked why he returned, Nat Turner told his astonished fellow slaves, "The Spirit appeared to me and said I had my wishes directed to the things of this world, and not to the kingdom of heaven, and that I should return to the service of my earthly master." He had returned to lead his people, as an "exhorter" at their religious gatherings. Five feet seven inches tall, slender at 150 pounds, Turner seemed to mesmerize with his blazing, deep-set eyes and spellbinding oratory.

In 1822, Nat Turner was sold away from his wife and children to a new master, Joseph Travis, who demanded heavy, backbreaking labor in the fields. He did allow Turner to preach on Sundays to meetings in neighboring slave churches, which enabled him to learn the Virginia countryside and to tell many free blacks of a judgment day when he and all of his followers "should arise and prepare myself and slay my enemies with their own weapons."

Turner and his followers met, August 21, 1831, deep in the Southampton County woods to plan their revolt. It was a steamy, hot day, and they knew the whites would be tired that evening from a Sunday of visiting and drinking. The slaves waited. At midnight they struck, taking farm after farm by complete surprise. Beginning with Nat Turner's own master and his family, the band killed seventy white men, women, and children within twenty-four hours. State and federal militia finally overpowered them and jailed them in Jerusalem, the seat of Southampton County. Slave-hunting patrols killed more than two hundred blacks, many of whom had no knowledge of Turner. He himself escaped into the woods again, but this time he was captured. On November 11, after a short trial, Nat Turner was hanged as an immense crowd watched.

Now the planters closed ranks. The southern slave system became so repressive that no more rebellions broke out after Nat Turner's revolt in 1831. If he, a trusted slave, could mount such a terrifying rebellion, so might others. States enlarged their patrol and militia systems. Slaves caught without passes could expect twenty lashes from the patrols. The South passed laws abridging freedom of the press and speech for all. In Virginia, anyone printing or circulating literature for the purpose of persuading slaves to revolt was subject to prosecution. The slave codes tightened against not only bondmen but also free blacks throughout the South. In Mississippi, as in much of the lower South, no black person could own a grocery, inn, or tavern or any place where blacks could meet and plot rebellion. It was against the law for a free black to sell liquor or work in a printshop. If detected, the printer was liable to a fine, the black person to the death penalty.

*   *   *

In the North, free blacks managed a meager existence, often little better than in slavery. Northern whites segregated freedmen in the North even as they condemned slavery in the South. The number of free blacks North and South increased slowly from 434,000 in 1850 to 482,000 in 1860. Every new state admitted after 1819 restricted voting to whites. Only five New England states—Massachusetts, Rhode Island, Maine, New Hampshire, and Vermont—provided for equal voting rights for black and white males. Illinois, Ohio, Indiana, Iowa, and California prohibited black testimony in court if whites were a party to the proceeding. Massachusetts, though advanced in voting rights for blacks, banned intermarriage of whites with blacks and enforced segregation in hotels, restaurants, theaters, and transportation. A black man noted that "It is five times as hard to get a house in a good location in Boston as it is in Philadelphia, and it is ten times as difficult for a colored mechanic to get work here as in Charleston."

Whatever the discrimination in the North, to thousands of slaves it was still the place of liberty, or at least of hope. A few escaped, traveling at night, sleeping in barns, stealing corn from fields along the way, sometimes taking weeks and even months to reach safety. Some escapes were carefully plotted. Slaves stole horses, forged identity cards, wore disguises, sometimes boldly traveled by steamboat or stayed at the best hotels. Some had themselves shipped in large wooden boxes and a few of these almost suffocated. Some escaped simply by walking north, at night following the North Star. Relatively few fugitives were assisted by the mysterious Underground Railroad. Reputed to speed thousands of slaves north through hidden depots, midnight journeys, telegraphed messages, this "railroad" consisted rather of sporadic local efforts, significant more for raising abolitionist morale than for channeling armies of slaves to freedom. Most slaves made it on their own, or through black communities with the help of other blacks, slave or free. Despite southern fears and abolitionist claims, probably not more than a thousand slaves escaped to freedom in a typical year.

One of these was Fred Bailey; his escape indicated the possibilities and problems facing a black seeking to flee even from a border state with a large population of freedmen. Brought up by grandparents, he had never known his father and barely known his mother. He had luck enough to be sent to Baltimore, where his mistress, a kind and pious woman, began to teach him his letters, until her husband angrily told her to stop, for reading would "spoil the best nigger in the world." A chip of fate, Frederick was thrust back and forth from plantation and household, but in the process he learned to read, to teach other blacks, to become expert as a ship's caulker, and even to stand his master off physically to avoid a beating. The master hired him out to a Baltimore shipyard, where white workers tolerated him only because his wages went to his owner. Becoming increasingly independent, self-reliant, and proud, he borrowed papers given to free black seamen coming ashore in southern ports, donned sailor's clothes, and boarded a train for Philadelphia and freedom. Abolitionists in New York helped him move on to New Bedford and its shipyards.

Frederick Douglass, as he now called himself, could not ply his trade there because white workers threatened to strike, so he had to pick up odd jobs as a common laborer. Finding the Methodist Church segregated, he joined the Zion Methodists, where he became a class leader. Soon he was reading Garrison's *Liberator*, attending abolitionist meetings, and talking with his friends at church.

In the summer of 1841, abolitionists held an antislavery convention on the island of Nantucket. Douglass attended—mainly for the holiday, he said later—and was invited to speak. How the crowd was electrified by this dynamic young man with his rich, commanding voice—how they were mesmerized by the story of his years in bondage—how he was hired on the spot to speak for the Massachusetts Anti-Slavery Society—how he spent years on the abolitionist speaking circuit, with Garrison often sharing the platform—how he broke with Garrison and founded his own newspaper, *North Star*—how for years he gave other blacks a forum in his paper for their opinions—all this and much else became the stuff of one of the great personal histories of the nineteenth century.

Still, abolitionism was faltering even as Douglass, Garrison, and others were achieving their greatest renown. Nothing seemed to thwart Slave Power—not abolitionism or colonization or compromise or slave escapes or revolts. No single effort or strategy was enough to overcome the *system* of slavery. Could a united effort on the part of all major reformist and deprived elements overcome that system? Perhaps the most remarkable fact about Frederick Douglass, who might well have spent his life absorbed in the cause only of blacks, was that he reached out to other groups— especially to women and their rights.

WOMEN IN NEED

At about the same time that the horn was sounding outside the slave quarters of Montevideo, women on millions of farms throughout the nation were starting their day's chores in kitchens and outside. Despite the rise of the factory system, most American working women by mid-century were still farm women, and most farm women were still drudges. While their husbands bought steel plows, mowers, threshers, seed drills, and cultivators, farm wives shared little in labor-saving advances. The box stove that came into use in the late 1830s freed some city women of certain vexatious aspects of cooking, but stoves were not yet common in the country. While city women could import Frederic Tudor's ice from Boston, the country woman had no refrigeration except perhaps a nearby spring or family icehouse. Meat was preserved by curing and smoking it for thirty or forty hours. Milking, churning, pickling, preserving, and sun-drying of vegetables were also the lot of the country woman. On the frontier, women were scarce and hence highly valued but often had to shoulder men's tasks. On wagon trains going west, they could be seen with ankle-length skirts often hanging in tatters as they yoked cattle, pitched tents, loaded wagons, lifted heavy iron pots onto crossbars over the campfires.

Along with the house and farm chores many country women still made clothes for their families, at least until ready-made clothing began to penetrate the more remote rural towns by the 1840s. Girls started weaving thread into cloth as early as their fifth year. An older and steadier hand was required to gauge the amount of flax to spin: if too thick, the thread would bunch up; if too thin, it would break. To spin enough for a single square yard of cloth required one full day. Weaving was faster, five or six square yards a day. Women made sheets, blankets, towels, and rugs as well as the family clothing.

A farm woman typically was expected to rear six children on a two-and-one-half-year cycle of childbirth from her early twenties to her late thirties. The emotional and physical burden of repeated childbirth overwhelmed many women, resulting in ill health and premature aging if not in death. Although conscious family limitation was occasionally practiced, a historian noted, effective contraception was not available, and "custom, myth, religion, and men" acted to limit birth control. "I would it were not thus," Millicent Leib Hunt, wife of a prominent Detroit settler, complained on the birth of still another child. "I love my liberty, my ease, my comfort and do not willingly endure the inconveniences and sufferings of pregnancy and childbirth," but these were "God's ways" and she reproached herself for daring to complain. Before the birth of each of her five children she expected that either she or the baby—or both—would die.

Mothers had constantly to confront illness and death in the home. Children by the thousands died in epidemics of scarlet fever, cholera, ague, bilious fevers: the younger they were, the more vulnerable. Of the deaths recorded in South Carolina one year, nearly one-half were children under the age of five, nearly one-fourth children under one year.

Some women managed to escape all this—at least for a time. The growing factories of the Northeast continued to recruit women. Immigrants and farm girls flocked to Lowell and other mill towns. The work they turned to liberated other women as well, for they could now replace a large part of their labor time with manufactured clothing. Every time a woman left home to work in the mills she expanded both the labor reserve and the market for the specific goods of her industry. Every worker who swelled the ranks of the mill dimmed the prospects of better working conditions or even the success of the whole lot. By the 1840s, the bloom was off the social experiment that was to have been a shining example of the Yankee ideal of profit combined with virtue.

Alterations in the means and mode of production lay at the root of the change. As the owners faced sharpening competition, the pressure came to be unrelenting, forcing heavier workloads on women who were paid at piece rates. In the 1820s and 1830s, each operator was expected to handle two looms, allowing some relief and rest; later they were compelled to handle three or four. In 1834 the Lowell management, taking advantage of the labor pool, announced a 15 percent wage cut. Hours had always been long; but the speedup combined with wage cuts made conditions in the mills almost intolerable. The women worked amid an infernal racket, in rooms polluted by flying lint particles and fumes from whale-oil lamps and kept oppressively warm and humid because the threads had to be damp to prevent breakage. Although the mill girls had been vaccinated against smallpox, nevertheless typhoid, dysentery, and especially tuberculosis took their toll in the crowded factories.

As textile operations expanded, the repressive aspects of the old Yankee paternalism persisted while the more personal and benign elements faded. Mill owners could ignore women's problems of illness, exhaustion, restlessness, simple desire for change, because all knew that many workers would sooner or later be returning to homes elsewhere and would take these sorts of problems back with them. The fact that the owners' concept of factory labor ultimately turned on the basic premise that they were simply buying one more object—human labor—became increasingly blatant. Stepped-up mechanization and widening routinization within the factories were beginning to produce a class of proletarians far removed from the early image of the happy mill girl.

Would the mill workers become conscious of their altered status? The historian usually was left to speculate about the "short and simple annals of the poor." But in this case the factory women left a superb legacy of writings—not only letters and diaries but a "literature of the mill." The best side of Yankee paternalism— the concern for "enlightening" and "elevating" the mill girl—had a remarkable effect. The night-school classes, Improvement Societies, Lyceum lectures given by Emerson, Everett, Horace Mann, Robert Owen, and other notables, the subscriptions to circulating libraries, even the Sunday-school classes, all helped produce an outpouring of writing in the operatives' own magazine, the *Lowell Offering,* and elsewhere. They were exposed to all kinds of socialist, democratic, and utopian thought, the labor movement, abolition, poverty, budding class consciousness. The editor of the *Offering,* Harriet Farley, was expected by management to maintain strict neutrality, but the feelings of the mill hands, and especially their rising consciousness of the nature of factory life, burst through.

Thus a "fictional" account of a mill girl's first day at work:

"The next morning she went into the Mill, and at first the sight of so many bands, and wheels, and springs in constant motion, was very frightful. She felt afraid to touch the loom, and she was almost sure she could never learn to weave . . . the shuttle flew out, and made a new bump on her head; and the first time she tried to spring the lathe, she broke out a quarter of the treads."

Letters also revealed feelings.

"Dear Friend," wrote a mill worker to a confidante back home, "according to my promise I take my pen in hand to Write to you to let you no that i am A Factory girl and iwish you Was one idont no But thaire Will be aplace For you in a fortnigh or three Weeks and as Soon as thaire is iwill let you no and as soon as you Can board With me We will have first rate fun getting up mornings in the Snow Storms. . . . Elisebeth is a lot of hansome fellows here. . . . for pitty Sake dond Show this letter to any body for the girls are talking So that idont no What iWrite."

"Dear Harriet," wrote H. E. Back to a friend in New Hampshire. "With a feeling which you can better imagine than I can describe do I announce to you the horrible tidings that I am *once more a factory girl!* yes; once more a factory girl, seated in the short attic of a Lowell boarding house with a half dozen of girls seated around me talking and reading. . . . I almost envy you happy sundays at home. A feeling of loneliness comes over me when I think of *my home,* now far away; you remember perhaps how I used to tell you how I spent my hours in the mill—in imagining myself rich and that the rattle of machinery was the rumbling of my charriot wheels but now alas, that happy tact has fled from me and my mind no longer takes such airy and visionary flights for the wings of my imagination have folded themselves to rest. . . ."

The writings of the mill girls mirrored their mounting unrest. Their feelings were often too strong for the *Offering.* An outspoken mill worker, Sarah Bagley, attacked the magazine for accepting corporation subsidies and presenting a rosy picture of life at Lowell. "One would suppose," she wrote, "that the Lowell mills were filled with farmers' daughters who could live without labor and who go there merely as a resort for health and recreation, instead of a large portion of poverty's daughters whose fathers do not possess one foot of land, but work day by day for the bread that feeds their families."

Workers complained more and more of the denial of their liberty. "The

evils and abuses of the present system of factory labor," Mehitable Eastman told her fellow workers in 1846, "have accumulated too rapidly to be
passed by in silence. I have been employed by a manufacturing company,
for eight years,—have been subject to its increasing heartlessness and
cruelty, and from bitter experience can affirm that a change cannot be
effected too soon. . . . We have witnessed from time to time the cruelties
practiced by brutal Overseers and selfish agents upon defenceless operatives, while they dare not speak in self-defence lest they should be deprived
of the means of earning their daily bread. . . ."

A poem, "The Factory Bell," published in the *Factory Girl's Garland* in
Exeter, New Hampshire, remarks on the relentless ringing of the factory
bell calling the workers, as it sometimes seemed, up to death's door, which
was equated with the factory gate:

> . . . Sisters, haste, the bell is tolling,
> Soon will close the dreadful gate. . . .

The poem continues with a comment on the relentless ding-dong-ding all
day long: bells for meals; bells for return to work; and, finally, "our toil
is ended, Joyous bell, good night, good night."

Lucy Larcom had loved her factory life at first—"even the familiar,
unremitting clatter of the mill, because it indicated that something was
going on. I liked to feel the people around me . . . I felt that I belonged
to the world, that there was something for me to do in it, though I had not
yet found out what. . . ." But later she would put her feelings about the
routine and the crowdedness into verse.

The persons who uttered their grievances, in prose and poetry, were the
more articulate women, potential leaders of their sisters. Much depended
on whether the Sarah Bagleys, Lucy Larcoms, and the like could arouse
their fellow-operatives to full consciousness of their lack of liberty and
equality. And here the owners' system itself played into the militants'
hands. The homogeneity of the women—the great majority were native-
born New Englanders—their segregation from the rest of the population,
their closeness in age, their communal housing, and above all their mutual
dependence on one another for social and psychological support—all
strengthened the bonds of sisterhood. Although this closeness had its
drawbacks in lack of privacy and tranquillity, and conformity was often the
price of acceptance, "much of our happiness, nay, *everything,*" as Sarah
Bagley said, "depends on our social existence. . . . Our *whole* life is interwoven, with each other, in a greater or lesser degree. . . ."

The test was whether the rank and file could be organized for economic
action. Occasional sporadic strikes broke out. In the winter of 1834, eight

hundred of Lowell's female operatives turned out to protest the 15 percent wage cut. They marched on other mills and held an outdoor rally, to persuade fellow workers to join them. Their statement of principles, headed "UNION IS POWER," invoked the spirit of our "Patriotic Ancestors" who had preferred privation to bondage, and asserted that the "oppressing hand of avarice would enslave us." The mill owners were aghast. Describing the strikers' procession as an "amazonian display," the agent of the Lawrence Company complained that "a spirit of evil omen" had prevailed over the "friendly and disinterested advice" that had been given by the company to the "girls of the Lawrence mills." The owners coolly waited, adamant, and the strike spluttered out as women returned to work or left town. Other walkouts were hardly more successful.

Turning to political action, women mill hands sought to achieve the ten-hour day through state legislation. The leader in this effort, the indefatigable Sarah Bagley, was described as a "fiery and persuasive leader, as effective in a small committee meeting as she was addressing a crowd." Working closely with other militants such as Mehitable Eastman and Huldah Stone, Bagley founded the Lowell Female Labor Reform Association and soon attracted several hundred members. She edited *The Voice of Industry,* a labor newspaper originally published by the New England Workingmen's Association but later purchased by the LFLRA. Hoping to build a united New England labor movement, LFLRA leaders began organizing branches in a half dozen mill towns in Massachusetts and New Hampshire.

Their main target was the Massachusetts legislature in general and in particular William Schouler, chairman of the Committee on Manufactures. After the LFLRA had collected 2,000 signatures on a petition denouncing working conditions in Lowell and calling for the ten-hour day, Schouler headed an investigating committee that vaguely favored shorter workdays and better ventilation but concluded that "the remedy is not with us. We look for it in the progressive improvement in art and science, in a higher appreciation of man's destiny, in a less love for money, and a more ardent love for social happiness and intellectual superiority." When Schouler was beaten for re-election, the LFLRA claimed a victory and moved that the voters of Lowell be formally thanked for consigning Schouler to "the obscurity he so justly deserves." Schouler then pursued a personal vendetta against Sarah Bagley in his paper, the Lowell *Courier.*

The fact that the women had to thank the voters of Lowell betrayed their central political weakness, for it was men they were thanking, men who had the vote. If women had their own concept of liberty—liberty from harsh working conditions, liberty to strike and protest—the political establishment had its concept: liberty of contract. When workers gained a ten-hour law in New Hampshire, the legislature included a free contract exemption at the request of the mill owners, who soon signed up women willing to work twelve hours. In Massachusetts, the indomitable Bagley finally gave up and faded from the labor scene. The Middlesex mills of Lowell again cut wages in 1850, by one-quarter, and this time the employers used the blacklist to punish protesters.

*   *   *

Factory women turned first to direct economic action, such as strikes, and only then to the political. Middle-class women stressed political action to meet their needs. Above all, leaders among middle- and upper-class women felt keenly their need and right of the ballot. In the heady political days of the mid-1830s, they had begun to organize, starting with charity clubs called "female fragment societies." Their concerns tended to be more diffuse than those of the mill workers. Education was central, and they were proud of Emma Willard's achievements in founding in 1821 a model school, the Troy Female Seminary, with a curriculum of science, mathematics, geography, and history said to equal that of the best men's colleges, and a teacher-training program that was superior. Oberlin began to admit women to higher education in 1833, though this was admittedly to help meet the needs of male scholars for meals and laundry—and for high moral conduct that would shame the male students out of indulging in the depravities of "monastic society." Middle-class women were also taking the lead in temperance movements, charity issues, and marital rights. But many focused on the two great political issues, slavery and the suffrage.

When the National Anti-Slavery Convention of American Women met in Pennsylvania Hall in Philadelphia in the spring of 1838, crowds hostile to the emancipation of slaves and women broke down the doors and set fire to the building. As the flames rose, the mob began to make its way to the home of Lucretia Mott, the demure Quaker preacher who had organized the Philadelphia branch. "I felt at the moment," she wrote later, "that I was willing to suffer whatever the cause required."

Several American antislavery societies sent women as delegates to the World's Anti-Slavery Convention held in London in June 1840. The convention refused to seat the women delegates with the men and assigned them seats in the gallery. Lucretia Mott, in her dove-gray coat and white cap, walked down Great Queen Street deploring this segregation arm and arm with another delegate, Elizabeth Cady Stanton, a graduate of the Troy

Seminary and a young bride of twenty-five, who had come to the convention with her abolitionist husband as part of their honeymoon. The two women agreed to hold a women's rights convention on their return to America. It was almost eight years before Elizabeth Cady Stanton, by then living in Seneca Falls in upstate New York and feeling rather isolated, had a chance to take up the question with Lucretia Mott, who was attending a Quaker meeting in the area. They agreed to put an advertisement in the *Seneca County Courier* calling for a "Convention to discuss the social, civil, and religious rights of women," on July 19–20, 1848, in the Wesleyan Chapel at Seneca Falls.

It was a faltering start. The chapel was locked when the organizers arrived—only by accident?—and Mrs. Stanton's nephew had to be boosted through a window to unlock it. The meeting was to be for females only, but forty men turned up with the two hundred and fifty women and had to be admitted. This was just as well, because no woman present quite dared to preside over the meeting and Lucretia Mott's husband, James, took the chair. Mrs. Stanton gave a maiden speech of ample proportions and noble sentiment.

In a brilliant stroke, the delegates proclaimed their principles in the form of a new Declaration of Independence for women: "When, in the course of human events, it becomes necessary for one portion of the family of man to assume among the people of the earth a position . . . to which the laws of nature and of nature's God entitle them. . . . We hold these truths to be self-evident: that all men and women are created equal. . . . The history of mankind is a history of repeated injuries and usurpations on the part of man toward woman, having in direct object the establishment of an absolute tyranny over her. To prove this, let facts be submitted to a candid world."

Then the list of grievances: man had not permitted woman to vote; had compelled her to submit to laws in the forming of which she had had no voice; had "made her, if married, in the eyes of the law, civilly dead"; had taken from her all right in property; had passed grossly unfair divorce laws; had denied her a college education; had excluded her from the ministry. The convention passed resolutions calling for equal rights in trades, universities, and professions; equality in marriage; equal rights as to property, wages, and children; equal rights to make contracts and to testify in court. But the suffrage? That resolution carried by only a small majority. Lucretia Mott herself dared not support it.

Other women's rights conventions followed: Rochester, Akron, Worcester, Syracuse. The journey to the voting booth would take far longer than the most pessimistic leader might have dreamed. Only one woman present at Seneca Falls would vote for President by living long enough to vote in 1920.

Of the score or more grievances proclaimed in their Seneca Falls declaration, middle-class women often felt most keenly their status as legally inferior in marriage. The wife "is compelled to promise obedience to her husband, he becoming . . . her master—the law giving him power to deprive her of her liberty, and to administer chastisement." Feminists were outraged by the common law, under which a married woman was unable to contract with her husband or with third parties, could not convey real or personal property to or from her husband, and hence by extension could not lawfully engage in trade without her husband's consent. While some of the harsher applications of common law were being corrected through equity jurisprudence on a state-by-state basis, the wife's relationship to her husband was much like that of ward to guardian.

Despite the handicaps a woman assumed thereby, nearly all of them did marry: save as homemakers and housekeepers, how could they keep themselves? Perhaps by teaching school, but these positions were limited. Spinsters usually stayed at home to care for elderly parents, or paid for their keep by domestic labor in the kitchens of brothers and sisters. Marriages were permanent, if only because the alternative was hardly thinkable. Divorce was almost impossible; in many states it required a special legislative petition, as did Rachel Robards Jackson's divorce. In most cases a woman relinquished property, home, and children to her ex-husband. While feminists had made some progress by mid-century in improving the status of married women—Lucretia Mott and Elizabeth Cady Stanton helped persuade New York to recognize a wife's right to her separate property—divorce remained almost immune to major reform.

For many middle-class women, the main block to self-realization was less the law than social and psychological circumstance. For some, rising affluence, and the goods and comforts that came with it, elevated their feelings of need rather than satisfied them. Family duties in particular barred them from rewarding occupations and professions. Millicent Leib Hunt in Detroit rebelled against her domestic chores, assuaging her anger by writing in a diary about her duty. She tried to deny her "selfish" wishes for pretty clothes. Of her husband she vowed "never to oppose his opinions but by gentle and affectionate reasoning." She would always "offer him the choicest morsels at table" and manifest a "quick and ready compliance with his wishes."

For a time, Lydia Maria Child seemed immune to this kind of problem.

In her early twenties, she published two popular novels, earning a literary reputation. At thirty-one she wrote a tract, *An Appeal in Favor of That Class of Americans Called Africans,* electrifying the antislavery world, but it lost her sales on her popular writing. Boston exacted its sternest penalty when the Atheneum canceled her free membership. Moving from Boston to New York, she edited during the 1840s the *National Anti-Slavery Standard,* a militant weekly. In her newspaper writings and numerous letters she displayed a penetrating intelligence and unusual compassion. She commented on everything—on the machinations of compromising party politicians, on abolitionist backsliders, on Fourier ("I think Fourier means that society ought to be so constructed that every passion will be excited by healthy action on suitable objects"), on the failings of the "Swig" hard-cider party, and always on the flowers and birds and trees that she loved. She knew and influenced the movers and shakers of reform.

But Lydia Maria Child was married—to David Lee Child, who shared her concerns and passions but apparently was frustrated in his own career and dependent on his wife. By 1850 she was writing a friend that the "experience of the last eight years has terribly shaken my faith in human nature" and "my own strong and electric nature." She had all along hoped, she wrote two years later, after retiring to the country, that the time would come when household work and cares would leave her enough time to earn something again by writing. "But what with cooking, taking care of milk, making butter, picking and preparing vegetables, keeping the house tolerably clean, washing dishes, seeing that nothing moulds, ferments or freezes, ironing clothes, making and mending clothes, for myself and David, &c. &c. I find that the treadmill *never* stops. . . . Six weeks often passes without my even looking into a book or touching a pen."

This was the vibrant voice of a middle-class woman. A few years earlier, Mehitable Eastman had spoken with equal feeling for working-class women: "Never while we have hearts to feel and tongues to speak will we silently and passively witness so much that is opposed to justice and benevolence . . . never, while we are conscious of powers undeveloped, affections hemmed in, energies paralyzed, privileges denied, usefulness limited, honors forfeited, and destiny thwarted . . ." Powers undeveloped, destiny thwarted—here spoke the authentic voice for the unfulfilled needs of women. But how could awareness of these needs be raised to a higher level of consciousness—and to a broader economic and political effort? It is a curious irony of life that the same conditions that create a potential for us and create our awareness of that potential, are the same conditions that stand most powerfully in the path of realizing that potential.

MIGRANTS IN POVERTY

When Frances Wright made her first trip to the United States, the voyage could hardly have been more pleasant, considering the conditions of ocean travel at that time. The twenty-three-year-old orphan and heiress was neither nervous nor seasick during the month-long crossing. She liked the kindly, weather-beaten old captain, the cheerful and obliging crew. Her ship—the American-owned packet *Amity*— was well named, she felt, as she never heard a dispute on board save for one evening when a young Scotsman fell into an argument with an older Englishman over the question of grace and predestination. She listened for a while, but "in the middle of a nicely drawn distinction on the part of the Englishman, between foreknowing and fore decreeing, I fell asleep, and waked to no other noise than the creaking of timber and lashing of the waves."

Arrival in New York Harbor was even more pleasant. She stared in admiration at the "magnificent bay, whose broad and silver waters, sprinkled with islands, are so finely closed by the heights of the Narrows, which, jutting forward with a fine sweeping bend, give a circular form to the immense basin which receives the waters of the Hudson," the purity of the air, the "forest of masts crowded round the quays and wharfs at the entrance of the East River." She was much taken by the young men, as she saw them tall and slender and agile, their large white shirt collars unbuttoned and thrown back on their shoulders, their broad-brimmed hats shading their handsome, sunburned faces, who rowed out in the fast little boats to greet the *Amity*. She was even more pleased by the many active tars who sprang from the yards and rigging of nearby ships to help the passengers land, seemingly satisfied with a kind "thank ye." Soon she was having tea and fruit in a boardinghouse and hearing with astonishment the chorus of katydids, crickets, and tree frogs outside.

Steerage life on the *Oxford,* a British cargo ship loaded with immigrants, was less appealing. The captain had packed three hundred people into rough pine bunks. Having prudently brought their own bedding and food, the immigrants lived below-decks for the forty or so days of passage, amid the fetid squalor of cooking food, tobacco smoke, straw mattresses, offal. If the *Oxford* passengers were unlucky, their death rate from typhus, cholera, or smallpox would be more than 10 percent, and they would risk death or injury when fire broke out from a man's pipe or a cook's candle. They paid fifteen or twenty dollars for the journey, compared with Frances Wright's "thirty guineas, wines included."

Debarkation in New York Harbor was a jolting experience for the immigrants. The *Oxford* had no sooner tied up at the dock than scores of rough-looking men who called themselves "runners" swarmed onto the ship to "help" the passengers with their luggage but in fact tried to inveigle them to boardinghouses that had promised the runners so much a head. On arriving at the boardinghouse the immigrant might be turned away, or robbed, or given false promises of employment. On the side, the runners profited greatly by stealing trunks from passengers—a game called "Trunkeloo"—and selling them "first class" canalboat tickets that turned out to be the worst accommodations on the slowest craft. It was to this aspect of American private enterprise that newcomers were first introduced.

The poorest of the poor immigrants—except for Africans, worse off than poor—were the Irish peasants who fled disease and death in the famine-ridden southern counties of Cork, Kerry, Galway, and Clare after 1835. They and others from the British Isles constituted about three-fourths of the 220,000 immigrants from Europe to the United States between 1815 and 1830. Immigration then soared; 2,500,000 people arrived between 1830 and 1850. During the fifties another 2,750,000 immigrants came; almost half of these were Irish. The Germans, the largest nationality group after the Irish, were more often skilled mechanics or thriving farmers who soon moved on to the Ohio Valley or Great Lakes region. The Irish were likely to stay in New York or eventually to work their way toward other cities in the Northeast.

New York was the big port of entry, for immigration routes tended to follow the shipping lanes. Most newcomers moved at once to neighborhoods where their fellow countrypeople lived, often settling in tenements abandoned by the slightly less impoverished. Needing to be close to work and lacking public transportation, immigrants flooded into tenement areas and shanty towns in lower Manhattan. Houses built for single families became multi-family, surrounded by flimsy new dwellings in backyards and alleys. The density of the seven lower wards of Manhattan rose from about 95 to about 164 people per acre between 1820 and 1850. By the end of the 1840s, 29,000 persons were living in cellars.

Fleeing poverty in the old country, plunged into squalor in the new, the newcomers struggled for jobs. New Jersey contractors recruited construction gangs among the Irish of New York City, and for sixty cents a day tens of thousands labored from sunrise to sunset in the swampy, disease-ridden lowlands. Some laborers turned to liquor, which was often near at hand because New Jersey contractors liked to pay off in whiskey. A doctor visiting New Jersey canal workers found a man in delirium. Was he in the "habit of drinking ardent spirits?" the doctor asked. "Nothing more than the allowance," the man said. The allowance turned out to be five glasses per day.

Some of these new Americans, brought up in country towns and villages, could not cope with urban conditions and fled. Others fought, or drank. Some sought help and stayed.

A little aid came from local authorities concerned for immigrants mistreated, scorned, and swindled—to the amount of an estimated $2,500,000 in one year alone in New York City. After decades of abuse on the docks, the city commissioner of immigration leased an old fort at the foot of Manhattan known as Castle Garden and restricted immigrants to this one landing. Here, officials gave the newcomers travel advice, helped safeguard their belongings, aided them with lodging problems, and sold them valid tickets to their destinations. Immigrants also received a helping hand from families from the "old country" who had settled before them, and from their churches and church societies. Irish laborers turned to Irish contractors for jobs and loans. Mutual assistance and dependency bound the immigrant communities more and more tightly together.

In spite of the newcomers' initial response to the need to survive which had forced them together, forming what could be characterized as tribal affiliations along ethnic and extended-family lines, however, the undertow of expanding potential for industrial and commercial enterprise was strong enough to provide impetus for reconstructing the class structure within the immigrant community. It was no coincidence that the notion of the "reserve army of the unemployed" arose during this period of intense competition, which characterized the supply side of the labor market at a time of meteoric expansion.

When the New Jersey canal workers struck against pay cuts and inhuman working conditions, the state militia moved in, a riot followed, and the strike leaders were jailed. Contractors brought in strike breakers from Manhattan to replace the malcontents. When canal work was completed, many of these Irish, striker and strike breaker alike, settled in nearby New Jersey towns, swelling the labor force of rising industrial cities like Newark and Trenton.

Immigrants who stayed in the city scrounged for jobs at the bottom of the pile. Blacks and whites competed not only for jobs on the docks but for menial jobs, serving New York's wealthy. WANTED, read an advertisement in the New York *Herald:* "A cook, Washer, and Ironer, who perfectly understands her business; any color or country except Irish." Many Irish worked in the clothing trades either in large warehouse-type factories or in piecework at home. Almost thirty thousand women, Irish and otherwise, made clothes, often working twelve to fifteen hours a day for thirty or thirty-five cents. A seamstress might produce six pairs of pants during the week and bring her bundle to a merchant's door, to receive only $2.35.

In the eyes of many middle-class whites, the inner-city immigrants were mere paupers. Many, indeed, *were* paupers. Often society's response was to group the poor with the crippled, diseased, helpless, dying—and to isolate as many as possible. For this purpose, New York had put up the largest structure in the city, an imposing gray-stone fortress called Bellevue, developed from a "Publick Workhouse and House of Correction" commissioned in 1734. The site had been purchased by the city in 1811 and was enclosed on three sides by an eleven-foot wall, with a fourth side bounded by the East River. Bellevue was built by debtors and convicts to warehouse the afflicted.

In 1860 the Bellevue Hospital Medical College, the first of its kind in the United States, was added but during the 1830s and 1840s the complex consisted of a penitentiary where paupers lived, two hospitals, a bakery, icehouse, greenhouse, soap factory, stables, and the city fire station. Here from one to four thousand feeble, diseased, and dying vagrants were put or took refuge at various times. Despite efforts by city officials to maintain order and cleanliness, smells of sickness and death pervaded the buildings.

As so often happens in institutions, a kind of class system prevailed. The superintendent separated paupers according to sex, health, "character," and race. Blacks were incarcerated in the dark and noisome cellars of the penitentiary. No marriages or promiscuity was tolerated, in theory at least, nor was idleness allowed. Work, indeed, was considered the moral and practical cure for pauperism; hence the city installed a treadmill in Bellevue to force the poor to move heavy grindstones. All paupers had to work in the gardens, bakery, or factory buildings in order to provide their own food and clothing. Disobedient inmates lost meal privileges; they were assigned extra workloads or thrown into solitary confinement in the "Dark Room" on bread and water; or had to wear "an iron wing around their leg, with a chain and wooden block fixed thereto."

Bellevue housed many children. Schoolteachers, sent by the Free School Society of New York City, taught young inmates spelling, reading, writing, and "the principles of religion and morality." A Protestant minister was in attendance too, paid by the city to teach old and young alike and especially Irish Catholic immigrants the virtues of industry and sobriety.

Feeling isolated and beleaguered in a hard, punitive, work-oriented society, many immigrants turned back into their communal life—to their churches, schools, benevolent societies, social organizations. And they turned to politics. The Irish often took the lead on this score, not having to cope with a foreign language and having well-developed political instincts after a century of dealing with the English in their mother country. Banded together, soon they were electing city councilmen, who then might use the dole or outdoor relief to build support among the poor. They turned more and more to Tammany Hall, which during Jacksonian days was taking positions on such popular issues as abolition of imprisonment for debt and was distributing food and clothing to the immigrants and the poor of New York City while doling out patronage. By the 1840s, the stage was set for a showdown within Tammany between its remaining Protestant leaders, who still harked back to the old Jeffersonian days, and the rising Irish.

This conflict came to a head in 1841, when a young Irishman named Mike Walsh challenged Tammany. Born in Ireland twenty-six years earlier, Mike had emigrated with his parents, who had apprenticed him to a printer. Rowdy and hard-drinking, Walsh had a talent for organization and a flair for leadership. His virtues, however, were not appreciated by the older Protestant leaders of Tammany, who saw him and his Irish battalions as a threat to their control. When the nominating committee of the Democratic party refused to choose Mike for a seat in the state legislature, he decided to appeal to the people at the county meeting. And when the committee there asked him not to speak, he threw down his hat from the platform and demanded to be heard. He had his "Spartan Band" with him to lend support.

To mingled shouts of "Go it, Mike" and "Turn him out," he warned that he and his followers could disrupt other speeches if he was not allowed to give his own. In the end, the meeting rejected Walsh's candidacy, but he continued to organize the Irish workingmen. In 1843 he founded his own newspaper, the *Subterranean,* where he carried on his abrasive brand of politics, going to jail twice for libel. Later in the decade he won the Tammany nomination for state legislator, and a few years after that he gained a seat in Congress, where he remained a spokesman for the poor. "The only difference between the negro slave of the South and the white wage slave of the North," he told an icily hostile House, "is that the one has a master without asking for him, and the other has to beg for the privilege of becoming a slave."

Many an immigrant who gave up the fight in the inner city and found a job on the canals or with the railroads or fled west could not escape conflict and discrimination. In 1842, Irish coal miners fought blacks in Pennsylvania for mining jobs; a decade later, armed black strike breakers replaced Irishmen on the Erie Railroad.

Some cities seemed more kindly than others to immigrants and other "paupers." Philadelphia appeared more hospitable than Boston, in part because in that city, whose 300,000 inhabitants in 1840 more than doubled in the next twenty years, there were many jobs available. Mill towns on

water-power sites outside the city had robbed Boston of some of its industry. Boston was also the city still of the Puritan. Bostonians were the
loudest in talking about rights and abolition, but there as elsewhere orphan
girls at the age of ten were bound out to wealthy families for eight years
to do menial household labor. Mistresses expected such servant girls to be
up at five and ready to labor until eleven in the evening six days a week,
with one-half day on Sunday for rest.

Few immigrants had any contact with the one large group of white
Americans who rivaled them in their poverty. These were the poor rurals
of the hilly regions of Georgia, Virginia, and the Carolinas. Many of them,
or their forebears, had once lived in tidewater areas or on the piedmont
and tried to compete with the large slavery operations of the plantations.
Some had tried to earn land, or at least a living, by working for large
planters as slave overseers. But many gave up and moved west to the
mountains, where they could live by hunting and fishing and marginal
farming. Poor whites, they came to be called, or piney woods folks or
sandhillers or clayeaters or rednecks or crackers. They might sell their
game or fish or farm produce for cash, or "hire out" to labor on more
prosperous farms at fifty cents a day. Or they might be paid in tobacco or
whiskey. At the base of the class hierarchy lay the landless woodcutters,
farm laborers, and squatters on the land.

Undernourished, uneducated, often afflicted by the parasitic hookworm,
housed in crude log cabins or shanties, these rural whites were often too
listless to scratch more than a bare existence from the red soil. But, like
the immigrant, they needed someone to look down on, and this usually was
the black. Despite their need for jobs, the poor whites refused to do certain
tasks, such as waiting on table in the homes or working in the fields of
nearby planters. Fearing the competition of black people if the slaves were
freed, they opposed any talk of emancipation. One of their hopes, indeed,
was to acquire slaves of their own.

Their one great solace was religion. Sundays and other times they would
come down from their hollows, the women barefoot in the summer and
wearing long homespun dresses, handkerchiefs spread over their shoulders, with men's hats on their heads; the men in shirt sleeves and barefoot.
After services, they would return home for middle-of-the-day dinners of
fresh pork and sweet potatoes, cut up and served in one large tin pan.

Some poor whites turned to politics, as increasingly they gained the right
to vote and as leaders grew among them, or came to them. One of the latter
was Franklin Plummer, who emigrated from New England to the pineland
belt of Mississippi and proceeded to build a political machine by cultivating
poor whites. Illiterate themselves, they valued Plummer's Massachusetts

education, calling him a "walking encyclopedia." He visited their log cabins, talked with the kinfolk, and seated the children on his lap to search for
"redbugs and lice in their hair." His cry of "Plummer for the people and
the people for Plummer!" won him a seat in Congress, but the poor whites
voted him out of office when he abandoned demagoguery to support the
Natchez banking interests.

There were other poor in America: marginal New England farmers
holding on to their rocky soil, frontier people, impecunious scholars, laborers at the bottom of the pile, and, always, Indians and blacks—a mélange. They were bound together in a great commonality of deprivation
—denied good homes and food and clothes, good health and nutrition and
education, and hence damaged in motivation, aspiration, and self-fulfillment. City "micks" and southern "crackers," in particular, had in common
an existential condition: contempt. They retreated into insularity and clannishness, and resorted to church and drink. The poor suffered many different types of poverty, however, stemming from diverse sources. They
lacked the most essential quality that might have alleviated their plight: an
awareness of the commonality of their suffering, a feeling of shared grievances, a sense of potential unity.

Leaders Without Followers

"We find ourselves oppressed on every hand—we labor hard in producing all the comforts of life for the enjoyment of others," an "Unlettered
Mechanic" protested to the "Mechanical and Working Classes" of Philadelphia in 1827, "while we ourselves obtain but a scanty portion, and even
that in the present state of society depends on the will of employers." After
twenty-five members of the Union Society of Journeymen Tailors in New
York were found guilty of conspiracy to restrain trade, a handbill proclaimed: "THE RICH AGAINST THE POOR! Judge Edwards, the tool of the
aristocracy, against the people! Mechanics and working men! A deadly
blow has been struck at your liberty!"

"The man over there says that women need to be helped into carriages,
and lifted over ditches, and to have the best place everywhere. Nobody
ever helps me into carriages, or over mud-puddles, or gives me any best
place! And ain't I a woman?" Sojourner Truth so addressed a women's
rights convention in Akron in 1851. A former slave who believed that she
had been called by the Lord to travel the land testifying to the injustices
against her people, she had claimed the floor after hearing ministers dwelling on the manhood of Christ and the lesser intellect of woman.

"Look at me!" she went on. "Look at my arm! I have ploughed and planted, and gathered into barns, and no man could head me! And ain't I a woman? I could work as much and eat as much as a man—when I could get it—and bear the lash as well! And ain't I a woman? I have born thirteen children, and seen them most all sold off to slavery, and when I cried out with my mother's grief, none but Jesus heard me! And ain't I a woman? . . ." Sojourner Truth's voice was her weapon; she had never learned to read or write.

"David has signed my will and I have sealed it up and put it away," Lydia Maria Child wrote to a close friend. "It excited my towering indignation to think it was necessary for him to sign it, and if you had been by, you would have made the matter worse by repeating your old manly 'fling and twit' about married women being dead in the law. I was not indignant on my own account, for David respects the freedom of all women upon principle, and mine in particular by reason of affection superadded. But I was indignant for womankind made chattels personal from the beginning of time, perpetually insulted by literature, law, and custom. The very phrases used with regard to us are abominable. 'Dead in the law.' 'Femme couverte.' How I detest such language! I must come out with a broadside on that subject before I die."

* * *

The unfulfilled wants and needs of poor and enslaved Americans and of middle-class women in the early nineteenth century seem to have been psychological as well as material—problems of damaged self-esteem as well as of physical survival. Slaves and the very poor in city and country often had unbalanced, monotonous diets, leading to malnutrition, disease, and death; severe hunger and open starvation were uncommon. There is ample evidence that the manner in which people responded to their material situation—to poverty amidst plenty, to being excluded from the American cornucopia—was more crucial to how they ultimately behaved politically than was the "objective" situation itself.

The sense of deprivation and damaged self-esteem intensified in a nation whose ideologues preached liberty and equality. During the whole pre-Civil War period the preamble to the Declaration of Independence remained "the single most concentrated expression of the revolutionary intellectual tradition," in Staughton Lynd's estimate. Jefferson, Robert Owen, Garrison, and other spokesmen invoked it; Lincoln referred to the Declaration as the "standard maxim for a free society." The sense of deprivation arose even more fundamentally from what Barrington Moore has called "a recurring, possibly pan-human, sense of injustice, which arises from the combined requirements of innate human nature and the imperatives of social living."

Given such conditions of material and especially psychological deprivation, how could individual feelings be converted into some kind of collective action? This was initially seen as a task of consciousness raising. Reading over the speeches, tracts, protest novels, convention debates, street-meeting oratory, and knowing of the immense amount of grumbling that went on among activists within the ranks of the poor and the enslaved, one marvels at the power of the written and spoken word, the force of the appeals to scripture, the intellectual clarity and logic of many of the more formal writings, the ability of some radicals and reformers to appeal eloquently to common men and women. And the protesting leaders did penetrate to the hearts and minds of hundreds upon thousands of Americans.

But they penetrated far too little for the purpose of converting widespread feelings of injustice and deprivation into self-expressed feelings of need—into hopes and expectations, into feelings of entitlement that could then be converted into effective demands on the political system. Far too little to build a militant minority movement that might serve as both pressure on and alternative to the authorities in power. And certainly far too little to build an organized, lasting mass movement on the left, or radical political party, capable of gaining enough votes in elections to win majority control of the government.

Where, then, was the failure of leadership? Certainly not in the qualities —the commitment, imagination, compassion, acuteness, courage, and articulateness—of the leaders themselves. Women with the leadership capacity of a Stanton, Mott, Child, Wright, a Sojourner Truth; men with the skills of a Douglass, Garrison, Walsh, Weld, with all their diverse talents and aims, were nothing less than adornments to the nation, whether or not recognized at that time. And this top cadre was almost matched by a second cadre of regional and state leaders, operating within the various abolitionist, women's, and other radical and reform organizations.

Some of the nationally known leaders sprang from unlikely roots. Sarah Moore Grimké and Angelina Emily Grimké, for example, were the daughters not of Boston abolitionists but of wealthy and conservative South Carolina aristocrats. Encouraged by Quakers to break away from the social and political constraints of Charleston, the sisters in turn broke with the Quakers over the Friends' equivocal attitudes toward abolitionism. By the late 1830s, both had enlisted heart and soul with Garrison, Weld & Co., overcome their initial timidity on the lecture platform, and won national attention as speakers for women's as well as black rights.

Nor could the national leaders of the various causes be faulted for failing to work, or at least communicate, with one another. Many noted feminists were also abolitionists. Frederick Douglass, after attending the Seneca Falls convention, wrote a *North Star* editorial in which, standing upon "the watch-tower of human freedom," he claimed for women the same political rights as for men. The Grimké sisters not only corresponded at great length with Weld; Angelina Grimké married him. Communication—and sometimes confrontation—occasionally occurred in subtle and personal ways. Lydia Maria Child noted some gossip about the well-known actress Fanny Kemble, who had retired from the stage after marrying Pierce Butler, heir to a large Georgia plantation, and who had been deeply revolted by slavery. "It seems she keeps tugging at her husband's conscience all the time, about his slaves," Child wrote after the Butlers had spent a summer in Stockbridge.

"One day he begged her to spare him—saying, 'You know, Fanny, we don't feel alike on that subject. If I objected to it in my conscience, as you do, I would emancipate them all.'

" 'Pierce!' exclaimed she, 'look me full in the face, and say that in your conscience you think it right to hold slaves, and I will never again speak to you on the subject.'

"He met her penetrating glance for a moment, lowered his eyes,—and between a blush and a smile, said, 'Fanny, I cannot do it.' "

Within a few years, Fanny Butler had left her husband.

There was amazingly good communication among the top leaders of the elite. The abolitionists and even the North and South thoroughly communicated, thoroughly knew one another's views. They understood each other only too well. This close communication, and collaboration among top women's rights leaders and abolitionist leaders—and their mutual understanding even when in full disagreement—was not matched, however, among large sectors of their movements. Thus it was symptomatic that abolitionists often excluded women or women's representatives from their meetings. At the Akron meeting some women begged the chair not to let Sojourner Truth speak for fear "every newspaper in the land will have our cause mixed with abolition," and one reason the ex-slave wanted to speak was that ministers at this meeting had opposed political rights for women " 'cause," as Sojourner Truth said, "Christ wasn't a woman!" ("Where did your Christ come from?" she demanded in her speech. "From God and a woman!") Many adherents of these two causes, as well as others

such as temperance and Sabbatarianism, followed a "one issue" strategy
—they feared dividing their own ranks by taking stands on other reform
issues, even though, as others pointed out, they might have built at least
a loose coalition behind a program of reforms.

By far the most fundamental reason for the failure of leaders lay in their
inability to engage with the masses of people who did not see any connection between women's or black rights and their own welfare. Only at the
end of the long roll of middle-class women's grievances in the Seneca Falls
declaration was there a reference to a bread-and-butter question—"securing to women an equal participation with men in the various trades, professions, and commerce"—and this resolution was listed as merely having
been offered and spoken to by Lucretia Mott. The declaration utterly
ignored the plight of women in industry or the condition of the poor.
There was virtually no organizational connection between the reform
groups and the craft unions or even workers' movements. Yet the potential
for collaboration was there, if only because of the common feelings of
deprivation and oppression. Thus a "Factory Tract" of the Lowell Female
Labor Reform Association protested:

"Much has been written and spoken in women's behalf, especially in
America, and yet a large class of females are, and have been, destined to
a state of servitude as degrading as unceasing toil can make it. I refer to
the female operatives of New England—the *free* states of our union—the
boasted land of equal rights for all—the states where no colored slave can
breathe the balmy air, and exist as such;—but yet there are those, a host
of them, too, who are in fact nothing more nor less than slaves in every
sense of the word! . . ."

Perhaps the connections that failed to be made at the higher level could
have been achieved at the lower, in states and localities, where rank-and-
file members of various organizations might have worked out local coalitions or at least collaborations. But there were relatively few members, in
large part because the national organizations had not built, in contrast to
the political parties, the kinds of local structures of leaders and activists—
the "third cadres"—that ultimately were required for national leaders to
build and engage with grass-roots constituencies.

Were there in the United States persons of rare potential leadership who
might have transcended the differences among the reform and radical
groups and built a coalition of the have-nots? We will never know, because
such a leader did not arise. But that the potential existed was indicated by
the career, among others, of the incomparable Frances Wright. She was a
cosmopolitan who enjoyed the friendship of the most eminent men of her
time—Lafayette, Jefferson, Madison, John Stuart Mill, Robert Owen. She

was a rationalist who advocated universal education to perfect a democracy in which the inequalities of sex, color, and class would wither away. She was fearless, whether boating down rivers, traveling alone on horseback in the wilderness, or, dressed in a plain white muslin dress that adorned her like the drapery of a Greek statue, facing down howling mobs in lecture halls and in the streets.

For a time it seemed that Fanny Wright might attract a national following. In the great cities of America she lectured to as many as two thousand people at a time. In Cincinnati only a few people, and scarcely one woman, showed up at her first lecture; the house was full for her second, as word raced around town; and five hundred people had to be turned away from her third. She began publication of her own newspaper, *The Free Enquirer,* in New York, and built her own lecture building, the Hall of Science. She seemed equally concerned for the needs of the black, the poor, and the female, and she was active in the causes of all three.

But Fanny Wright and the people around her had audiences rather than followers. It was not only that her advocacy of greater rights for women, more liberal divorce laws, equal education, "free" marriage, and less church influence in politics made her so unpopular that several times she was nearly mobbed. Her undoing was that she could not win the support of activist women, blacks, and immigrants in sufficient numbers to make a difference, and that few cadres of rank-and-file leadership were available to link her national, inspirational appeal to local needs and thus raise the political consciousness of the deprived. Deeply concerned about all deprived groups, she was yet not a coalition-builder. Mainly she walked alone. And ultimately, so did women, blacks, and the poor.

*   *   *

Historians tend to doubt that a massive, nationwide, organized collaborative reform or radical movement was possible in the United States in the 1840s or 1850s. The ideological and social and political makings of such a movement simply were not there, in this view. They point to the powerful inhibitors to social action: the essential powerlessness of the deprived groups, as in the inability to vote; racist and sexist biases that kept radicals separated; the American "pragmatic" tradition, as it came to be called, emphasizing day-to-day efforts and step-by-step progress rather than collaborative long-range political action; the fragmenting and pulverizing effect of the American political system on nationwide mass movements; the inhospitability of an essentially agrarian society to urban radicalism; the ideology of individualism, self-help, self-promotion, individual advancement; the hospitality of the American economy to individual effort; the frontier as a social and political safety valve and escape hatch.

The issue, then, is not that the American reformers did not achieve power. The issue is that they fell so far short of achieving remedies for their objective situation, their sense of deprivation, and the gap between what they had and what they were entitled to, measured by the patriotic ideals of liberty and equality.

The second quarter of the nineteenth century, moreover, was a time of contagious intellectual and political ferment in much of the Western world. During the late 1840s, workers revolted in Paris; Louis Philippe abdicated; revolutions swept Berlin, Milan, Venice, Vienna; Emperor Ferdinand fled; Kossuth was proclaimed president of the Committee for National Defense of Hungary; Rome proclaimed a republic under Mazzini; the German national assembly framed a constitution; revolts broke out in Dresden and Baden; England enacted the Great Reform Bill after street riots and political tumult. Marx and Engels published the *Communist Manifesto*. The Western world boiled with utopian, revolutionary, millennial, communitarian, reformist, anarchist, radical ideas and activity.

The dog that did not bark in the night was an American dog; it was the absence of that bark that had to be explained—and that suggested the different path Americans were taking from their forebears across the Atlantic.

A NEW
MAP OF THE
UNITED STATES
of America
1857

GOLD REGION
OF
CALIFORNIA

A NEW
MAP OF THE
UNITED STATES
of America
BY J.H. YOUNG.
PHILADELPHIA
PUBLISHED BY CHARLES DESILVER 251 MARKET S.T 1857

DISTRICT
OF
COLUMBIA

PART IV
The Empire
of Liberty

Moline Advertisements.

JOHN DEERE'S

CELEBRATED CENTRE-DRAFT
PLOWS.

CHAPTER 12

Whigs: The Business of Politics

A *broad valley outside Dayton, Ohio, September 10, 1840.* Under sunny skies General William Henry Harrison, the Whig candidate for President, is addressing a vast throng packed together on the field around him. Excited newspapermen report that 100,000 persons have gathered to hear the general—the largest political rally in the half century of the republic.

For days people have been streaming into Dayton, by carriages, wagons, and horses, by packets and freight boats via the Cincinnati canal. Hundreds of flags and streamers float from trees and housetops, proclaiming: HAIL TO THE HERO. Banners stretch 150 feet wide across Main Street: HARRISON AND TYLER—THE TYRANT'S FOES—THE PEOPLE'S FRIENDS. Others proclaim the union between industry and high tariffs. Curtis' mill has strung its own banner across to the rifle factory: PROTECT US AND WE'LL CLOTHE YOU. The banner of Pease's mill on one side demands no standing army, on the other proclaims: ETERNAL VIGILANCE IS THE PRICE OF LIBERTY. On the morning of the tenth a mammoth crowd surrounds the Hero as he rides his white charger to the speaking platform.

Though Old Tip looks slight and elderly, his voice seems to penetrate to the farthest edge of the crowd.

"I will carry out the doctrines of my party, although I will make no more pledges than Washington, Adams, or Jefferson would. I was never, ever a Federalist."

The crowd breaks into cheering.

"I am a true, simple Republican, aghast that the *'Government* under "King Mat"' IS NOW A PRACTICAL MONARCHY!"

Louder and longer cheering.

"As President I will reduce the power and influence of the National Executive"—ecstatic cheering—"At the end of one term in office, I will lay down . . . that high trust at the feet of the people"—cheering beyond the power of the reporter to describe—"And I will not try to name my successor"—nine cheers.

Old Tippecanoe cites his sponsorship of the Public-Land Act of 1800. "Was I a Federalist then?"—cries of NO, NO, NO—But "methinks I hear a soft voice asking: Are you in favor of paper money? I AM!"—shouts of applause—"It is the only means by which a poor industrious man may become a rich man without bowing to colossal wealth"—cheers—"But with all this, I am not a Bank man, although I am in favor of a correct banking system, able to bring the poor to the level of the rich"—tremendous cheering.

It was the climax of Harrison's campaign. At first, he had refused to go on the stump. For a presidential candidate, campaigning was undignified, unthinkable; it had never been done. But his managers hoped to demonstrate that this gray-haired sixty-seven-year-old was fit to be President, that he would be a tribune of the people and not, as Van Burenites were charging, the tool of invisible party bosses. Soon Harrison was on his way to Columbus to show himself to the people. There, in a suddenly arranged speech from the steps of the National Hotel, he gave what was probably the first presidential campaign speech in American history. Once he started campaigning he would not stop; off went the presidential caravan to Cincinnati, Cleveland, Dayton, to more crowds and parades and speeches.

"This practice of itinerant speech-making," old John Quincy Adams said glumly, "has suddenly broken forth in this country to a fearful extent." No *Adams* had ever *campaigned*.

The Whig speechifying and ballyhoo camouflaged a most ingeniously run campaign. Whig leaders knew only too well the sorry fate of those Federalists and National Republicans who had allowed Jeffersonians and Jacksonians to pose as the "friends of the people." Whigs would now be more populist than those populists, more pleasing to the people. And where were the people? In the countryside. America in 1840 was still overwhelmingly rural; only about a tenth of the populace lived in places with more than 2,500 inhabitants. The Whigs would strike directly into the rural hinterlands that had sustained the old Republican party.

So Harrison was transformed from an aged general-politico, who had been born into a distinguished Virginia family in a fine plantation manor, into a simple farmer. Transparencies—an exciting media device of the day—showed him seated in front of his log-cabin "birthplace," a barrel of hard cider at his side. "Log-cabin boys" were organized to produce loud huzzas for the speechifying. Horny-handed farmers lumbered to the stage to present a pitchfork to Harrison.

The campaign brought marvelous theater into the villages and hamlets. Songs glorified the "Hero Ploughman" and his "Buckeye Cabin." Hawkers sold Tippecanoe buttons, tobacco, lithographs, canes surmounted by a miniature barrel, whiskey bottles in the shape of log cabins. Whigs would have no truck with issues; their convention adopted no party platform. In the absence of genuine issues, invective flourished. Whigs routinely pictured "Old Van" as living in regal splendor, in a palace fit for Croesus, playing billiards with ivory balls. "Mr. Chairman," demanded Congressman Charles Ogle, the Whigs' chief billingsgate purveyor, "how do you relish the notion of voting away the HARD CASH OF YOUR CONSTITUENTS" for "SILK TASSELS, GALLON, GIMP AND SATIN MEDALLIONS to beautify and adorn the 'BLUE ELLIPTICAL SALOON'?" Soon the crowds were chanting:

> Let Van from his coolers of silver drink wine,
> And lounge on his cushioned settee,
> Our man on a buckeye bench can recline,
> Content with hard cider is he.

The Democrats, not to be outdone in bombast, attacked the Whigs as an unholy coalition of old Federalists and new abolitionists, scourgers of the poor and starvers of laborers. They charged that the victor of Tippecanoe was really "Old Tip-ler," a "sham hero," a "granny," a blasphemer, the sirer of half-breed children by Winnebago squaws. Van Buren did not deign to take the stump, but the top cadre of the Democracy—veteran warriors like Thomas Hart Benton and Vice-President Richard Johnson, young stalwarts like James K. Polk and James Buchanan—counterattacked their Whig foes, and even feeble old Andrew Jackson was exhibited at balls and barbecues to remind the voters what a *real* hero looked like.

Still, it was a battle more of party than of personality. Behind the scenes parties compiled master mailing lists of voters, mobilized state and local campaign committees, mustered the patronage brigades, ground out posters, leaflets, and propaganda tracts. Fifteen hundred newspapers—most of them partisan weeklies—carried news of the party battle even to the frontier. Whig newspapers were especially ingenious in publishing campaign sheets. Horace Greeley's *Log Cabin,* full of chatty news about Harrison and his campaign, quickly went through a first printing of 30,000 and then sold at a weekly rate of 80,000 copies. Stealing the tune of "Jefferson and Liberty," the *Log Cabin* published sheet music with lyrics ending "For HAR-RI-SON and LIB-ER-TY!"

The result was the greatest outpouring of voters the nation had seen. Harrison beat Van Buren by about 53 percent to 47 percent, by 234 electoral votes to the Democrats' 60. The Whigs carried the House elections, 133 seats to 102, and exactly reversed the Democrat's previous margin in the Senate, 28 to 22. Harrison won the swing states of New York and Pennsylvania. The turnout was perhaps more remarkable than the election results. Almost two and one half million voted—about 80 percent of the eligibles, compared with less than 60 percent four years before. Every state reached new peaks of participation, according to William Chambers, with New York achieving a turnout of almost 92 percent. Not until the crisis year of 1860 would such a large proportion of the eligibles vote again. Campaign organization plus campaign hokum had mobilized the electorate.

The Whig Way of Government

In out-huckstering the Democracy, the Whigs had opportunistically out-flanked the Democrats "on the left," through the use of democratic symbols rather than democratic substance. Their rustic, populist strategy had worked, at least for the moment. But to win one battle, they had disregarded, perhaps even betrayed, the essential conservatism of developing Whig doctrine, the elitist attitudes of many of its leaders, the skepticism about populist majorities the Whigs had inherited from the old Federalist party. Whiggery had tried to turn the shank of history. But history—a moving, organic network of causally related events—is hard to outwit or outflank. History embodies a logic and momentum of its own with resistances, rewards, and penalties. History soon outwitted the Whigs and left them in its dustbin.

In picking the aged Harrison for President, the Whigs had sacrificed political conviction and clear policy positions for a largely media-created war hero. They had gambled on the health of an old soldier who would be seventy-two by the end of his term. History was cruel. The new President, after giving a vacuous Inaugural Address that promised presidential impotence and left policy up to Congress—a two-hour speech that found bored politicians roaming around the platform stamping their feet to get the blood running—moved into the White House and into the ceaseless importunings of Whigs hungry for office. Fatigued and dispirited, he caught cold one morning while shopping in Washington's meat and fish markets, and the cold turned into pneumonia. Bled, blistered, cupped, leeched, and massaged, he died just one month after taking office. Vice-President John Tyler, ignored by Harrison, had been staying in Williamsburg in benign isolation. Summoned now to Washington, he arrived two days later after covering the 230 miles by boat and horseback.

So John Tyler was President. In Tyler, a Virginian of the old school, history resisted the Whigs' effort to outflank it. Raised amid the aristocratic republicanism of the tidewater, graduated from the College of William and Mary at the age of seventeen, Tyler had climbed the political ladder from the Virginia House of Delegates to the national House of Representatives, and later to the governorship and the United States Senate. He had come to be known as a strict constructionist and a leading member of the southern states' rights bloc in Congress; and as such he gave only tepid support to Jackson. Tyler shifted toward the Whigs when the Virginia legislature instructed him to vote for expunging the censure resolution of Jackson and Tyler resigned his seat rather than comply. Independent in doctrine and party, Tyler was as critical of Whiggish economic nationalism as he had been of Jacksonian executive power. He had remained close enough to Clay, however, and to his old states' rights ideology, to be chosen by Whig leaders as a ticket balancer with Harrison—although only after those leaders had offered the vice-presidential nomination to several other, more noted politicians.

Tyler at fifty-one was still determined, on entering the White House, to stick to his conservative, old Republican principles. He immediately proved that he was indeed a strict constructionist. Soon labeled "His Accidency" by his Whig foes, he insisted on being considered the new, constitutional President, rather than a Vice-President acting as President, thus setting a precedent for all later Presidents elevated by chance. On the other hand, the new President decided to retain Harrison's Cabinet intact —a Cabinet headed by Daniel Webster as Secretary of State and dominated by Webster, Clay, and other Whig senators and congressmen. Surrounded, as he said, by "Clay-men, Webster-men, anti-Masons, original Harrisonians, Old Whigs and New Whigs—each jealous of the others, and all struggling for the offices," he resolved to move cautiously and to "work in good earnest" to reconcile "the angry state of the factions toward one another."

It was not to be. The Whigs had plastered over their factional splits with thick gobs of campaign hokum. Now they split over hard policy choices. The battle erupted not merely between two wings of the party, but two wings ensconced in two institutions separated by the Constitution and by Pennsylvania Avenue.

Commander of the congressional wing clearly was Henry Clay. Now sixty-four years old, "Harry of the West" was still the engaging, impetuous, eloquent legislative leader who had electrified Congress three decades earlier in the days of the war hawks, though now more irascible and volatile. Clay was still cock of the walk in the Senate, chairman of the Finance Committee, policy spokesman for congressional Whigs, and leader of men occupying key positions in both houses. The Kentuckian had gone into a half-drunken rage when news of Harrison's nomination had reached him at Brown's Hotel in Washington. Pacing the room, shouting obscenities, he had denounced his friends as "not worth the powder and shot it would take to kill them," and called himself the unluckiest man in party history—"always run by my friends when sure to be defeated, and now betrayed for the nomination" when sure of election.

Clay's relationship with President Harrison deteriorated so rapidly that the two were at the point of a break when the general died. For a time it seemed that the senator and his old friend John Tyler might be able to work together despite their doctrinal differences. But history was remorseless: the Whigs' campaign preference for rhetoric rather than policy positions that might serve as rough guides to party policy makers; the Whigs' desire to balance their ticket even if it meant choosing a states' rights doctrinaire; the Whigs' antipathy to executive leadership, and their doctrine of legislative supremacy—all these combined to rob Whiggism of the fruits of its 1840 victory.

The crisis came over banking, still the most divisive political issue facing the nation. In accordance with the President's states' rights views, Tyler's Secretary of the Treasury, Thomas Ewing, presented to Congress a bill for a "Bank and Fiscal Agent" to be chartered by Congress in its capacity not as the national legislature but as the local government for the District of Columbia, to be authorized to establish branches elsewhere but only with the consent of the states concerned. Thus elaborately were Tyler's constitutional scruples cosseted. Clay was unimpressed. Like Tyler, he would repeal Van Buren's Independent Treasury Act, but in its place he wanted an effective and truly national bank. Tyler's idea for an agency that would have to beg a state to allow a branch to be set up within it—"What a bank *would* that be!" Clay wrote to a friend.

The two men—the President of the United States, who stuck gamely to his states' rights dogmatism but felt that Congress should make policy, and the "Great Pacificator," who considered himself a kind of prime minister —met in the White House. Neither would yield. The President's amiability broke under Clay's pounding.

"Go you now, then, Mr. Clay, to your end of the avenue, where stands the Capitol, and there perform your duty to the country as you shall think proper. So help me God, I shall do mine at this end of it as I shall think proper."

Clay did modify his bill to provide that, while no branch of the proposed bank could be established without the consent of the state, such consent would be presumed automatically granted unless the state legislature specifically opposed it at the next session. It was a reasonable compromise, but Tyler would have none of it. Increasingly captive to a "Corporal's Guard" of extreme states'-righters such as the Virginians Thomas W. Gilmer, Henry A. Wise, and Abel P. Upshur, he called Clay's compromise

a "contemptible subterfuge." Tyler's Cabinet—still Harrison's Cabinet—
wanted their chief to sign the bill.

Washington waited while Tyler teetered back and forth between assent
and veto. His veto, on August 16, 1841, set off a tumultuous debate in the
Senate. That evening Benton, Calhoun, and other Democratic senators of
the old school, delighted by Tyler's defiance of the congressional Whigs,
came to the White House to celebrate with Tyler over cigars and brandy,
but they were followed by a mob of Whig protestors who aroused the Tyler
family with their clamor and disbanded only after burning the President
in effigy.

The presidential and congressional Whigs mobilized against each other.
Chastising Tyler on the Senate floor, Clay moved unsuccessfully to over-
ride the veto. In the deadlock that followed, presidential-congressional
relations unraveled. Tyler allowed Webster and other cabinet members to
involve themselves in a compromise bill that easily passed both House and
Senate. "Give your approval to the Bill," his Attorney General, John J.
Crittenden wrote him, "and the success of your Administration is sealed."
Veto it, and "read the doom of the Whig party and behold it and the
President it elected, sunk together, the victims of each other, in unnatural
strife." Again Tyler vetoed, and again a great hue and cry broke out, as
Whig leaders throughout the country castigated the President, letter writ-
ers threatened assassination, and burning effigies swung from tree limbs.

Then, on a September afternoon, five of Tyler's cabinet members strode
into his office, one by one, and laid their resignations on his desk. The
President knew well that the walkout was devised and coordinated by Clay
in an effort to punish him—and even more, to force his resignation and
bring into the White House the president of the Senate, a Clay lieutenant.
Tyler became more determined to stay. One man who had not resigned
that day was Daniel Webster. Busy with delicate foreign negotiations,
reluctant to serve Clay's interests, the "Godlike Daniel" saw his own opportunities in the Tyler-Clay hostilities.

"Where am I to go, Mr. President?" Webster asked his chief.

"You must decide that for yourself, Mr. Webster," said the President,
with his usual reserve.

"If you leave it to me, Mr. President," the Secretary of State said, "I will
stay where I am."

"Give me your hand on that," said Tyler, rising from his chair, "and now
I will say to you that Henry Clay is a doomed man from this hour."

Total war had erupted between the two wings of the Whig party. Rid of
the Harrison and Clay men in the Cabinet, Tyler created a new one composed of conservative Democrats and states' rights Whigs. The congres-

sional Whigs struck back by officially expelling Tyler from the party. There followed a presidential-congressional battle in which constitutional checks served as the live ammunition. In place of Clay's kind of national bank, Tyler proposed a nonpartisan "Board of Control" designed to limit White House authority over the "public Treasury" and to protect the rights of the states against its branches, a plan quickly tabled in Congress and later defeated. The Clay party brought out two tariff bills in the summer of 1842; Tyler vetoed both. Some extremist Whigs—not Clay—threatened the President with impeachment; Tyler toyed with the idea of a third-party movement. By the fall of 1842 the President and Congress were almost deadlocked, amid the most savage polemics and mutual buck passing. Clay had the votes, it was said, and Tyler had the vetoes; but, in fact, each side had a veto over the other.

Some bills did overcome the obstacle course. The Independent Treasury Act was repealed; a bankruptcy law was passed for the relief of hundreds of thousands of debtors spawned by the depression; and distribution and pre-emption acts gave settlers the right to "squat" on 160 acres of land and ultimately to buy it at low prices, with the proceeds from the sale of public lands to be distributed to the states. These enactments were due to "masterly logrolling," in Glyndon Van Deusen's words, among sectional blocs—logrolling that ultimately brought a new tariff compromise bill, the price of which was to decimate the distribution act.

Whig unity was fading so quickly now that Tyler welcomed a Democratic party sweep of the 1842 congressional election as "the greatest political victory ever won within my recollection." Clay, still master of the Senate Whigs, had already quit the upper house to prepare to seek the presidency in 1844. Webster left the Cabinet hardly a year and a half after Tyler had retained him. By this time Tyler's administration had been reduced to a caretaker government.

*   *   *

The Whigs never regained their verve and momentum after their failures in government. Clay won the party nomination in 1844 but once again he enjoyed a brief but empty victory when Democrat James K. Polk defeated him handily in the electoral college, though narrowly in the popular vote. Four years later, Clay lost the Whig nomination to General Zachary Taylor, who won the White House for the Whigs but died of cholera within two years. Having won the presidency twice by nominating military heroes who proceeded to die in office, the Whigs tried the same tactic again in 1852 with General Winfield Scott, who was beaten by Democrat Franklin

Pierce. This time the general survived, it was said, but the Whig party did not.

How could a political party develop so strongly, win two presidential elections and almost a third, and then decline so quickly? The Whigs had brilliant leadership in Clay and Webster and in broad cadres of secondary and grass-roots leaders. At a time when the Democrats were enfeebled by their states' rights and localistic leanings, the Whigs had a potentially powerful nationalistic doctrine of direct utility to the rising industrial and mercantile elites of the nation. Their rapid monopolization of the opposition to the Democrats, and equally rapid capture of the presidency and Congress, attested to an electoral appeal that seemed likely to give the Whigs political dominance for a generation or two.

But the heart of the Whig party often seemed to beat feebly behind the lively façade of senatorial gladiators and log-cabin appeals. Springing into existence after Jackson's veto of the bank bill, the party attained true unity only in opposition to "presidential dictatorship"; no other doctrine could unite men so diverse in view and competitive in ambition as Clay, Webster, and Calhoun. Conceiving of party itself as more an occasion for oratory and camp meetings than a vehicle for policy leadership, most Whigs had little vision of the possibilities of partisan organization. Opposed to strong Presidents, the party allowed patronage and other political resources to slip into the hands of congressional leaders, and hence, in contrast to the Jeffersonian Republicans and the Jacksonian Democrats, a national party was never firmly built around the chief executive.

The party placed its future largely in the hands of Clay and his lieutenants, skillful in the give-and-take of group and sectional logrolling but far less adept in mobilizing the grand nationwide coalitions necessary for effective presidential politics. Ironically, the party that opposed executive power unwittingly demonstrated that strong Presidents are necessary to the existence of strong parties, just as strong parties comprise the political foundation for strong Presidents.

Certainly the Whigs had bad luck, both in the demise of their generalissimo-Presidents and in their felt need to appeal at the same time to plantation elites in the South and business elites in the North. But transcending leaders can turn misfortune to their own uses and avoid, or at least cope with, sectional entrapment—they can, in short, turn the shank of history. The Whig failure of leadership lay far deeper than in the presidential-congressional imbalance; it lay in the inability of the Whigs to break away from a bourgeois, genteel, respectable, establishment politics appropriate in an earlier day of social elitism and popular deference. The genius of that system lay in the character—the honor, dignity, responsibility, honesty, courage—of wellborn leaders. The genius of Jacksonian leadership lay in its appeal to numbers through the techniques of organization, propaganda, conflict, party discipline, and voter mobilization. The Whigs commanded neither the quality of the earlier leadership nor the quantity of the Jacksonian followership. The day of the independent public gentleman was over.

Challenged by the Jacksonians, the Whigs sought to unite all those who believed in the old kind of leadership, whether they were Calhoun nullifiers or Clay nationalists. "In so doing," according to Lynn L. Marshall, "they looked back longingly to a heroic era when leadership in politics was integral to leadership in society. . . . Thus was the party born dead in July 1832 and continued in that condition until 1836. Thereafter, however, a total transfusion of Jacksonian blood would bring it miraculously to life." This miracle faded away as Democratic party leaders sought to build coalitions of voters even at the expense of older doctrines of liberty and equality, as new leaders of both parties calculated more in terms of a multiplicity of economic interests than of either republican or aristocratic leadership.

THE ECONOMICS OF WHIGGERY

Sometime during the 1830s and 1840s—we will never know more exactly—the American polity underwent an almost invisible but pervasive sea change. During the first three or four decades of the republic, political leaders in Washington and the state capitals had made the key decisions that closely molded the shape and direction of people's lives. The brilliant constitutional planners of 1787, the state convention delegates voting thumbs up or down on the new Constitution, Washington and Adams and Jefferson and Madison and their hundreds of associates, the state leaders who made key political and economic decisions about the first canals and turnpikes and other enterprises, the early party builders—these men acted far more on doctrinal, and on political and practical grounds, than on narrowly economic. Jackson's bank veto represented one of the last of the great political intrusions into economic life; later, politicians more reflective of specific economic interest increasingly dominated national and state politics. At least at the leadership level, Economic Man seemed to take over from Political Man.

The change was not dramatic. Economic interests had affected public decision-making from earliest colonial days. And large political considerations would continue to impinge on economic policy long after the 1840s. But the nation went through a significant shift from a condition where economics was a factor *in* politics to a condition where politics could be defined mainly *as* economic interest.

In short, the enterprisers—the go-getters, the boosters—were taking over. In earlier years a relatively few men had shown the way—men like John Jacob Astor in the fur trade and Eli Whitney in cotton ginning—and they had won their places in the history books. An entrepreneur like the "Ice King" of Boston would be lucky to occupy a footnote. Son of a wealthy Boston lawyer, brother of three Harvard men, Frederic Tudor in his teens had rejected academic life for business. When one of his brothers idly wondered at a Boston party why ice was not harvested from local ponds and sold in the Caribbean, the twenty-one-year-old Tudor took up the idea, invested in a huge shipment of ice to Martinique, and lost $4,000 when the cargo melted. For two decades Tudor set himself to buying up New England ponds and Caribbean icehouses; he promoted a demand for ice cream, iced drinks, and ice-preserved food; he tested a variety of insulating materials such as wood shavings, straw, blankets, and finally—and successfully—sawdust. Another young businessman, Nathan Jarvis Wyeth, invented a horse-drawn ice cutter, pulled on runners notched with saw teeth, that could gouge out parallel grooves, enabling men with iron bars to break the ice off in even chunks. The two men teamed up to de-ice Fresh Pond in Cambridge.

By the end of the 1840s, Tudor had achieved prodigious feats: trading in candles, cotton, claret, and a host of other commodities; digging for coal on Martha's Vineyard off Cape Cod; devising a siphon for pumping out ships; designing a new hull for a ship; running a graphite mine; turning white pine into paper; setting up one of the first amusement parks in America; and bringing to New England the first steam locomotive, a toy affair of one-half horsepower. But above all, he remained the "Ice King" whose ships carried thousands of tons of packed chunks to the East Indies, China, Australia, India. He was a restless, flamboyant, imperious, aggressive promoter, no modest, prudent Horatio Alger hero, in Daniel Boorstin's judgment, and he would pay for his recklessness by languishing in debtor's jail. But he brought ice not only to equatorial lands but to millions of Americans; rid their homes of decaying meat and rancid butter; and permitted them fresh instead of dried food and salted meat, heavily spiced to disguise its age.

Other Bostonians were as resourceful with granite as Tudor was with ice. In earlier years they had built their stone churches by digging up huge boulders, heating them with fires, and smashing them with iron balls. Later they split off chunks of granite with gunpowder, and still later by drilling holes along a straight line and then splitting the stone along the holes.

Granite built the sixteen locks of the Middlesex Canal from Boston to Chelmsford, where the hard stone was mined. By the 1830s, Charles Bulfinch and other fine New England architects were designing churches and public buildings built of granite from Massachusetts quarries.

Solomon Willard, a jack-of-all-trades, became the king of granite. Son of a country carpenter, he made his way to Boston, and soon to success as a builder of spiral stairs, wood carver, and self-taught architect. Summoned in 1825 to design the Bunker Hill monument in Charlestown, he scoured the countryside for suitable stone until he came upon the granite of Quincy. To cut huge, monumental blocks of stone from this quarry he devised lift jacks, hoists, and other machinery, and to move the massive blocks to Charlestown, he used a crude wooden track covered with iron plates and resting on stone crossties. When Daniel Webster delivered a splendid address at the dedication of the Bunker Hill monument in 1843, the event celebrated granite as well as the Revolutionary battle. For the flinty stone was now being used in the most famous public buildings and hotels in the country, as well as in drydocks; and when tough paving stone became necessary for heavy transport, Willard had the satisfaction of laying blocks of Quincy granite in front of Boston's famous Tremont House.

Some of the powder used in quarrying doubtless came from the Du Pont Company far to the south, near Wilmington, Delaware. The Du Pont mills, separated by buffer zones to keep one from blowing up another, were strung for miles along the swift-flowing Brandywine Creek. Stone dams formed shallow pools that diverted water from the creek into canals running to the power machinery. The Du Ponts made their black gunpowder and blasting powder out of charcoal from nearby willow trees, sulphur from Sicily, and saltpeter from India. Founded by the son of Pierre Samuel Du Pont de Nemours, the celebrated physiocrat who had fled revolutionary France to start a new life in America, the firm was already becoming a company town that owned the houses and dominated the lives of its employees.

Invention and innovation seemed to be accelerating during the thirties and forties. The electric dynamo in 1831, Cyrus McCormick's reaper in 1834, John Deere's steel plow in 1839, the magnetic telegraph in 1843, the sewing machine in 1846—all these and a host of other devices set off little agricultural and industrial revolutions of their own. One of the most remarkable inventors was Samuel Finley Morse, educated at Andover and Yale, a noted portraitist, as celebrated at home and abroad as he was underpaid for his paintings. He might have lived out his life as a professor of art in New York City had it not been for a chance conversation with a fellow passenger on a voyage back from Europe in 1832, about work on electricity abroad.

Morse had been curious about electrical phenomena ever since he had attended Benjamin Silliman's lectures and demonstrations at Yale; now, his interest reawakened, he went to work on a contrivance to combine a sending device that would transmit signals by closing and opening an electric circuit; a receiving device, operated by an electromagnet, to record the signals as dots and spaces on a strip of paper moved by clockwork; and a code translating the dots and spaces into letters and numbers. At first the magnet would not operate at over forty feet, but with the help of a university colleague, Morse worked out a system of electromagnet renewers or relays. The artist-inventor went through several years of poverty, frustration, and even actual hunger before Congress voted for an experimental line from Washington to Baltimore, and more months of waiting and preparation before he transmitted to Baltimore from the Supreme Court room in the Capitol his famous declaration, "What hath God wrought!"

The most striking and significant of all the enterprises of this period came to depend heavily on Morse's invention. This was railroading. Few ventures have been so much the product of trial-and-error gradualism and innovation, over so many years. Rails and roads were pioneered long before boilers and pistons. For hundreds of years beasts and men, women, and children had hauled coal cars on wooden rails in English and German mines. Flanges had to be devised to hold wheels on the tracks, and wooden rails plated with iron to keep them from splintering. The French and English developed fantastic steam engines for land transport—mechanical legs were even devised to push a car from behind—until it was discovered that the weighty iron locomotives needed smooth rails on a smooth track. By 1829 the English engineer George Stephenson had achieved success with his famous "Rocket."

Much earlier an American steamboat inventor, John Stevens, had been transfixed by the vision of American railway development. Squeezed out of Hudson River steamboating by Livingston's and Fulton's monopoly, Stevens appealed to state legislatures up and down the east coast to pave the way for railroading. He had the temerity to urge a railroad on the Erie Canal Commission as cheaper to build. Railroads, answered Chancellor Robert Livingston, would be too expensive, dangerous, and impractical. The canal went ahead. Finally, the New Jersey and Pennsylvania legislatures passed railroad bills, but things moved so slowly that Stevens in 1825, at the age of seventy-six, built an experimental locomotive on his own estate in Hoboken. This, the first American-built locomotive, was never put into service on a railroad.

But all the while the tinkerers were innovating. When, in 1829, the Delaware & Hudson Canal and Railroad Company imported the "Stourbridge Lion," a fine big English locomotive, to use at its western canal terminus, the machine ran forward and backward for a mile or two, amid the booming of cannon (one of which shattered a mechanic's arm), but the six-ton "Lion" proved too heavy for American track and was hardly used again. Clearly, locomotives in America would have to be built lighter and more flexible, for frail wooden trestles and sharper curves. There were even experiments with locomotives decked out with sails and with a horse aboard working a treadmill to turn the wheels. Neither ran.

Then, in the winter of 1830–31, Horatio Allen, who at the age of twenty-seven had single-handedly operated the "Lion," put the American-built "Best Friend of Charleston" into service between the South Carolina capital and Hamburg. The next year John B. Jervis brought in his locomotive, the "Experiment," with a swiveling, four-wheel "bogie" truck under the front end of the boiler, allowing the machine to follow more easily the curves of the railroad. The "Experiment" worked.

American railroading was under way, with distinctly American problems. Unlike English locomotives, which ran on coal, the American engines feasted on the virgin timber cut down along the line. The wood-burners required a huge balloon stack, picturesque in etchings but menacing to dry forests, wooden bridges, and ladies' parasols. The biggest challenge to American railroading was sheer distance. With a national mania for speed already evident, locomotives were invented that could cut through gardens, farms, and even towns—which meant in turn the devising of grade crossings, gates, bells, whistles, and cowcatchers. America's technology of speed meant steeper grades, sharper curves, narrow gauges, fragile trestleworks—and hideous accidents.

The nation's twenty-three miles of railroad track in 1830 multiplied over a hundredfold in the next ten years. As the inventors settled down to devising better wheels, pistons, cylinders, valves, steam boxes, boilers, couplings, roadbeds, a host of local boosters and big-city promoters plunged into the scramble for railroad extensions and rights-of-way. Rich Boston merchants, eager to head off the threat of New York and the Erie Canal to their western trade, pushed a railroad westward to Worcester and Springfield and through the sloping Berkshire Mountains to the Hudson. George Bliss, Jr., a Yale graduate and Massachusetts legislator, had to devise ways of securing rights-of-way, attracting customers, avoiding accidents, and maintaining discipline. Robert Schuyler, grandson of the great manor lord Philip Schuyler, became president of the New York and New Haven line, and of the New York and Harlem. Despite competition from Hudson River steamboats, the New York City railroad magnates extended their lines up to Peekskill, Poughkeepsie, and Hudson. Other roads radiated from Manhattan up through Connecticut to Massachusetts. Railroad fever spread up and down the coast.

Extending out from the main cities, the railroads were not yet amalgamated into a system, or even fully connected. Local nabobs were still more interested in competing, or at least expanding, than in combining. When President Schuyler of the New York and New Haven advised President Charles F. Pond of the Hartford and New Haven that the New York railroad wanted to connect with Pond's, in order "to form the most expeditious as well as the most comfortable lines which circumstances permit," Pond evidently agreed only on condition of access by his company to the entire passenger business of Schuyler's road between New Haven and New York. "We cannot accept such arrangement as you wish" was Schuyler's curt answer to Pond.

Railroad expansion in the 1840s symbolized a people on the make and on the move. As hundreds of thousands of immigrants entered during the forties, the total population rose from 17 million to over 23 million. People were continuing to move westward in huge numbers, for the West alone gained almost half that increase, the South only a fourth. Agriculture was still the dominant enterprise by far, but it was declining relatively to mining, manufacturing, and construction. By the 1840s the United States had a "domestic market truly national in its dimensions," and economic growth sharply accelerated. If the country had not yet reached the point of an explosive takeoff, it was nearing the edge. The rise of an "American common market," in Stuart Bruchey's words, resulted not merely from economic change but also from deliberate political action.

*   *   *

"Of all the parties that have existed in the United States," Henry Adams said, "the famous Whig party was the most feeble in ideas." Here again, the Whigs were cornered by history. Whiggery had respectable intellectual roots in men like Alexander Hamilton and John Marshall, with their belief in national power and private property, and their awareness of the links between the two. It had national spokesmen of the caliber of Horace Greeley and William Henry Seward, and state leaders creative in economic policy and development; Georgia Whigs, for example, promoted the building of railroads to link cotton planters to seaports.

During the 1840s, however, the Whigs had become as opportunistic in their national economic credo as in their log-cabin-and-cider campaign tactics. Their arguments varied, depending on circumstance. Some Whigs held that the interests of rich and poor had become identical. Said Robert Hare, the noted Philadelphia chemist: "Never was an error more pernicious than that of supposing that any separation could be practicable between the interests of the rich and the working classes." The wealthy must serve the poor—and if "the labouring classes are desirous of having the prosperity of the country restored, they must sanction all measures tending to reinstate our commercial credit, without which the wealthy will be impoverished."

Others proclaimed not the interdependence of classes but the absence of them. All Americans were workers, all were capitalists—or if not, could become so. The "wheel of fortune," said Edward Everett, "is in constant motion, and the poor in one generation furnish the rich of the next." Even so, the lot of the rich was not all that happy. The Unitarian minister William Ellery Channing wondered if the hardships of the *poor* were exaggerated. "That some of the indigent among us die of scanty food is undoubtedly true," he said, "but vastly more in this community die from eating too much than from eating too little." After all, he added, lawyers, doctors, and merchants had their struggles and disappointments, and as for women—"how many of our daughters are victims of *ennui*, a misery unknown to the poor, and more intolerable than the weariness of excessive toil!"

Whig writers even found a happy pastoralism in the lot of the sturdy working people. The Boston *Courier* ran an ode to the Factory Girl, who would leave her hearth and vineyard for a bucolic stint in the mills and then return home with her dowry:

> . . . She tends the loom, she watches the spindle,
>   And cheerfully talketh away;
> Mid the din of wheels, how her bright eyes kindle!
>   And her bosom is ever gay.
>
> * * * * *
>
> O sing me a song of the Factory Girl!
>   Link not her name with the SLAVES. —
> She is brave and free as the old elm tree,
>   That over her homestead waves.

As a final strategy Whigs advanced a doctrine of personal, internal reform. Workers' elevation, Channing said, "is not release from labour. It is not struggling for another rank. It is not political power. I understand something deeper. I know but one elevation of a human being, and that is Elevation of Soul." Collective, organized action by the poor was unnecessary and undesirable. For conservative Whiggery, if religion was not the opiate of the masses, individual moral uplift was the sedative for the fractious.

The Whig doctrine of classlessness, or of class consensus or identity, was in part a political stratagem to gain worker support and divide the opposition. It was also a valid expression of a crucial reality in American society: the absence of deep-seated class conflict. As Louis Hartz argued in his astute study of American liberalism, there was no fixed aristocracy to revolt against, no persisting peasant class, no genuine proletariat that might form a revolutionary movement, but rather farmers who were incipient capitalists and workers who were incipient entrepreneurs. An instinct of friendship, Hartz said, "was planted beneath the heroic surface of America's conflict, so that the contenders in it, just as they were about to deliver their most smashing blows, fell into each other's arms. American politics was a romance in which the quarrel preceded the kiss."

In the absence of large and genuine social conflict, American political combat dissolved into numberless skirmishes and scuffles, mainly over the elevating issue of who got what, when, and how in slicing up the expanding American pie. Tariff schedules, internal improvements, state subsidies, and even banking legislation provided ideal arenas for the politics of brokerage. Many Americans were in fact landless and jobless, or living in penury, but their voices were muted, or lost in the social euphoria and political complacency of a people that seemed to be realizing, most of them, the Lockean ideal of free individuals in a state of nature, the Jeffersonian dream of a nation of small property holders. Still, the spectacle of Americans scrambling for jobs, tariff protection, subsidies, and other financial goodies was not wholly edifying to moralists of the old school.

Inevitably, it seemed, the rich and the better-off gravitated toward the Whig party. New England industrialists, middle state commercialists, skilled native labor, farmers closer to markets, many big cotton, tobacco, and sugar planters tended to embrace Whiggery. In the Ohio Valley, Van Deusen found, "the pushing, ambitious, go-ahead bankers and businessmen, canal promoters, landowning interests, lawyers with an eye to the main chance, and farmers anxious for internal improvements" were more likely than not to be found in the Whig ranks. While individual enterprise was far too dynamic to be contained within party lines—plenty of Democrats were go-getters too—Whig elites were more closely linked with big money and property.

The wealth of Boston Whiggery was revealing. An 1846 study of 714 Bostonians reputed to be worth $100,000 or more—in some cases far, far more—indicated that the overwhelming majority of those identified by party were Whigs. They were not only partisans but active ones, contributing to the party's war chest, serving as delegates to party conventions, running for office, and altogether exerting a pervasive influence on state and national policy. Wealthy New Yorkers also were heavily Whig. Democrats too, in these and other cities, numbered rich men—a fact that helped mute the conflict between parties—but to a far less degree than did the Whigs.

The economics of Whiggery pervaded a profession that was becoming more and more allied to business—the profession of law. On the Supreme Court, Justice Story had seconded Marshall in carving out the scope of national power; in Jackson's day he returned to Massachusetts, mourning that "I am the last of the old race of judges." Yet he continued to teach at Harvard, developing and adapting American common law in the areas of partnership, bills of exchange, promissory notes, and other areas vital to a growing commercial and industrial society. The ablest of Massachusetts judges was doubtless Chief Justice Lemuel Shaw, who further adapted common law to business requirements, such as the need of railroads for land lying along direct routes, involving the right of eminent domain. Other lawyers, with the views if seldom the talents of a Story or Shaw, made the common law a powerful ally of business interests. Workers fared less well. Shaw developed a "fellow-servant rule" that relieved the employer of liability for damage to an employee harmed by another employee on the job—a rule that delayed the development of workmen's compensation.

Whiggery did not lack other illustrious leadership. Edward Everett's was an extraordinary success story: minister of the Brattle Street (Unitarian) Church—the largest and most prestigious in the Boston area—at twenty; occupant of the recently established chair of Greek literature at Harvard a year or so later; editor of the *North American Review* while still in his twenties; a commanding orator; member of Congress for five terms; governor of Massachusetts for four terms; minister to the Court of St. James's from 1841 to 1845; president of Harvard; briefly Secretary of State and United States senator. Yet there was often a negative cast to Everett's thinking, whether he was criticizing abolitionism, lecturing workers, or warning of a "war of Numbers against Property." The intellectual leader William Ellery Channing served as a moral and religious influence on Whiggery, but Channing too, though liberal in theology, did not fully grasp the evils of slavery and advocated the kind of inward personal reform that was often both ephemeral and hostile to collective efforts toward social reform.

Men like Abbott Lawrence and Nathan Appleton were more typical of Whig economic leadership. Already a leading Boston merchant by the time he reached his early forties, Lawrence had the vigor and imagination to move into the thriving cotton and wool industry—he founded the textile city that would bear his name—and then took the lead in extending the Boston–Worcester railroad to Albany. An ardent Whig, he served in Congress as a Boston representative and provided a nexus between the party and the men of money. At a crucial moment he lent Harrison $5,000. Appleton too had made a fortune out of textiles, beginning with his involvement in Lowell's power mill in Waltham, and he too went on to Congress, where he became a vigorous defender of protective tariffs and the American System. Of a very different cast was Thurlow Weed, the little-schooled son of a poor farmer, who began as a printer's apprentice and became a newspaperman, Anti-Mason, Whig party leader and patronage dispenser in New York. Like many other Whig leaders, Weed was antislavery—and anti-abolition.

The pre-eminently typical Whig was always Daniel Webster—and much of the success and failure of Whiggery reflected his own. Once upon a time, as a Federalist leader of the old school, he had stood foursquare for a lofty, nationalist conception of the young republic, but as the years passed he had chosen to serve the growing commercial and industrial interests of his region rather than respond to the needs and aspirations of the poor throughout the nation. His loans and retainers from banks and businesses hardly affected the public decisions of a man who was, in a more philosophical sense, already bought. In calling for a consensus that could only be flabby, in condemning those Jacksonians who exploited recession in order to array class against class, the "Godlike Daniel" became a kind of caricature of the Whig politico who traded with any and every interest that might give him a small victory on the morrow, regardless of political doctrine.

Whiggery never seemed to have a real chance. Born in negativism, led by men who often divided it, politically unlucky as well as inept, faced ultimately with the power of a resurgent Democracy, the Whig party faded away as quickly as it began. History finally vanquished it. This was a pity, because Whiggery developed a positive, creative impetus, in its nationalism, in its frank engagement with expanding commercial interests, and above all, in its fecund concept that individual liberty could be protected not only against government, but through government, especially at the state and local level. Yet in the late 1840s and early 1850s the Whigs would have one more opportunity to take leadership in confronting the supreme moral issue of the time.

EXPERIMENTS IN ESCAPE

"Our farm is a sweet spot," Sophia Willard Dana Ripley wrote a friend on an August day in 1840. Even "my lonely hours have been bright ones, and in this tranquil retreat I have found that entire separation from worldly care and rest to the spirit which I knew was in waiting for me somewhere. We are nearly two miles from any creature, but one or two quiet farmers' families, and do not see so many persons here in a month as we do in one morning at home. Birds and trees, sloping green hills and hay fields as far as the eye can reach—and a brook clear running, at the foot of a green bank covered with shrubbery opposite our window, sings us to our rest with its quiet tune, and chants its morning song to the rising sun. Many dreamy days have been my portion here—roaming about the meads, or lying half asleep under the nut trees on the green knoll near by—or jogging along on my white pony for miles and miles through the green lanes and small roads which abound in our neighborhood. . . ."

Sophia Ripley was giving voice to a powerful longing of thousands of Americans during the second quarter of the nineteenth century—to escape from the increasingly busy, noisy, bustling, competitive, industrial, urban world into some pastoral retreat. This escapism was in part a reaction against Whiggery in both parties, but the rebels against prosperity and profit were influenced by Whig views more than they liked to admit, for they usually had to fight on their opponents' intellectual battlefield.

The 1830s and 1840s were a time of ferment in much of the Western world, as workers and peasants, caught in the gears of the industrial revolution, attempted diverse experiments in social and political change. In France, working men and women fought alongside soldiers and students to force the abdication of the nation's last divine-right monarch; the new king of the French was *invited* to reign. In England, businessmen, workers, liberal and radical intellectuals joined in demonstrations and mass meetings to force through a reform bill designed to abolish rotten boroughs and extend the vote. Belgians fought in the streets of Brussels to break away from the Dutch kingdom, but Italian protest was stamped out by the Hapsburgs and the Vatican, and Polish revolt by the Russians.

Americans did not revolt—they had no crown or aristocracy to revolt against. There was still no proletariat or peasantry to furnish the materials of revolution, only a slave population too disorganized to act as a militant class or caste. The high tide of Jacksonian radicalism had ebbed by the forties; the reform impetus now took several directions. Some Americans still carried the torch for revolutionary change, but they were small in number if large of voice. Many reform-minded Americans made gradual changes through their state and local governments. Some went west to new opportunities; some climbed up through the class system, still largely an open one. But some yearned to go back to the Arcadia of their childhood, when they lived and worked in their own pastures and vineyards, when Jefferson could say that those "who labor in the earth are the chosen people of God." Most of all, they longed for a family, a home, a *community*.

Pastoral communitarianism was hardly new in America. Labadists, authoritarian in organization and fanatically anti-sexual in doctrine, had settled in Maryland in the late seventeenth century but dissolved in conflict within two or three decades. Early in the next century German Seventh-Day Baptists founded Ephrata, near Lancaster, Pennsylvania, where the monastic orders of Sisters and Brethren practiced their Pietist beliefs, and on the side ran grist and other mills, a tannery, a book bindery, and even a printing press. About the same time Moravians settled a permanent community at Bethlehem, Pennsylvania, and fanned out to the west and south.

Rappites, eager to submerge their individual interests in the social good in order to plant God's kingdom on earth as a prelude to Christ's return, moved across the Appalachians to establish their Harmony community at the head of the Ohio Valley; finding the soil there poor for vine and other cultivation, they founded a new "Harmonie" on the banks of the Wabash in Indiana. All of these communitarian sects, however, were dwarfed in size and duration by the Quakers and by the Shakers. Then, in the early nineteenth century, Americans witnessed a new phenomenon: the nonsectarian communitarian experiment. And they witnessed a phenomenal leader, Robert Owen of New Lanark, who arrived in America in 1824.

The son of an ironmonger and saddler, Owen soon had made his way to Manchester, the center of a burgeoning cotton-spinning industry in the 1780s, and with borrowed capital set up a factory for making cotton-spinning machinery. By the age of twenty he had become manager of one of the largest mills in Manchester, and within a few years the possessor of a sizable fortune. He was the boy wonder of English capitalism. But he was also an industrialist who cared deeply about the education and social welfare of his employees, especially the hundreds of pauper children who worked in his mills. As he steeped himself in the intellectual and reformist ferment of Manchester, he became more and more critical not only of the poverty and dismal working conditions of English mill hands, but of the whole system of government, religion, and family that sustained social misery. The target of biting attacks from Tory ecclesiastics and industrialists, he wanted a fresh start in America, where he could experiment with the reconstruction of society.

That reconstruction would be broad in vision but local in application. He had "come to this country," Owen said, "to introduce an entire new State of society; to change it from the ignorant, selfish system to an enlightened social system, which shall gradually unite all interests into one, and remove all cause for contest between individuals." The object would be to secure the "greatest amount of happiness" for Americans and their children "to the latest posterity." No principle, he said, had "produced so much evil as the principle of *individualism.*" The competitive scramble alienated men from their work, their families, their communities—ultimately themselves. Economic and social inequality pitted one against the other, skilled workers against unskilled, employers against employee, farmer against operative. Harmony, association, cooperation—Owen always returned to this ideal. Somewhere in America he would realize it.

Owen arrived in America as a celebrity. In New York, intellectuals, politicians, editors, and visionaries gathered around him to hear of his plan. He steamed up the Hudson to visit De Witt Clinton in Albany and to observe the Shaker establishment at Niskayuna. In Washington, he met President Monroe and Secretary of State Adams; lectured twice in the Hall of Representatives, with the nation's most illustrious men arrayed in front of him; and on a return trip met Madison at Montpelier and Jefferson at Monticello—just a few months before the latter died. Meanwhile Owen traveled by stagecoach to Pittsburgh and by steamboat down the Ohio to Harmonie, which the Rappites had decided to abandon and for which he was negotiating. After surveying the Indiana village, with its 20,000 acres of woods and meadows, 180 houses of brick, frame, and log, and an assortment of shops and factories, the Englishman bought the whole settlement for $125,000. He renamed it New Harmony.

By April 1825 enough people had crowded into the little village for Owen to draw up his constitution for the "preliminary society." No matter that the newcomers comprised what Owen's son Robert Dale would later call a heterogeneous collection of "radicals, enthusiastic devotees to principle, honest latitudinarians, and lazy theorists, with a sprinkling of unprincipled sharpers thrown in." Good workers and craftsmen had arrived too, hopes were high, and spring was in the air. Under Owen's constitution, he would direct the experiment for a year, after which the members would begin to take control. They would provide their own household goods and small tools, invest their capital in the venture at interest, and would be credited on the books with any livestock they might contribute.

Reluctantly, Owen granted that there would have to be, for a time, "a certain degree of pecuniary inequality." The society would advance each member a credit of fixed amount at the community store; at the same time, their daily labors would be computed and recorded, and they would be debited for goods consumed. All members were to render "their best services for the good of the society, according to their age, experience, and capacity," but those who did not wish to work could buy credit by paying by cash in advance. Everyone, rich or poor, was enjoined to be "temperate, regular, and orderly," and all were to have "complete liberty of conscience," especially in religion.

For a time, life was good in New Harmony. People worked—not always too hard—at plowing, planting, vine culture, storekeeping, carpentry, hat making, and other pursuits. In the long soft evenings on the Wabash, people discussed their experiment as they gathered on the benches in front of the village tavern. Concerts, dances, sermons, and lectures filled the evenings. Advanced ideas were discussed at meetings of the Female Social Society and the Philanthropic Lodge of Masons. Doubtless the intellectual highlight of the first year was the arrival of the keelboat *Philanthropist,* bringing Thomas Say, the zoologist; William Maclure, geologist and educator; and a miscellany of artists and educators.

Above all, a heady feeling of toleration and liberty filled New Harmony. Visiting preachers of all persuasions vented their theologies in the village church, sometimes three on one Sunday. Maclure conducted exciting educational experiments in the classrooms. Owen welcomed the clash of ideas, and so did his followers. "I have experienced no disappointment," William Pelham wrote. "I did not expect to find every thing regular, systematic, convenient—nor have I found them so. I did expect . . . to be able to mix with my fellow citizens without fear or imposition—without being subject to ill humor and unjust censures and suspicions—and this expectation has been realized—I am at length *free*—my body is at my own command, and I enjoy mental liberty, after having long been deprived of it." A powerful sense of community and fraternity also pervaded New Harmony—and yet this noble venture was to last hardly more than a year.

In part, it was the inevitable falling off of novelty and esprit as the relative ease of summer gave way to winter discomfort and illnesses; in part, disillusionment with the workings of the complex system of credits and debits. So many individual exceptions were allowed that the entire system became suspect. New Harmony failed, however, primarily in its pretensions toward equality. Owen himself, while always hazy on the matter, was no extreme egalitarian. His concept of equality did not extend to "persons of color," who might be received in the association "as helpers, if necessary," but in his view might better go off to Africa or elsewhere.

Nor were all whites perceived as equal either. "No one is to be favored over the rest, as all are to be in a state of perfect equality," wrote Mrs.

Thomas Pears, reflecting the general sentiment of the community, but she went on to say in her very next sentence, "Oh, if you should see some of the rough uncouth creatures here, I think you would find it rather hard to look upon them exactly in the light of brothers and sisters." This experiment in equality, Arthur Bestor concluded, had the paradoxical result of opening wide fissures in the community.

Young men began to grumble over favoritism to older members. Arguments broke out over land boundaries, extreme egalitarians contending that no one should have any property at all; one of them, Paul Brown, opposed the very existence of bookkeeping and decided that Owen was nothing but a "speculator in land, power, influence, riches, and the glories of this world." Owen remained steadfastly committed to the great ideal, but he was away during a critical seven months, and when he returned the community was already splitting up. In its genteel way, New Harmony ended as a single community not in a grand upheaval but in a series of secessions as evangelical Methodists, then better-off "English farmers," and later young intellectuals, split away. Owen benignly granted land to the secessionists, but soon he too slipped away from the experiment he had founded.

Thus New Harmony ended in disharmony. But it was not the end of Owen or his movement in America. Other Owenite communities were founded in Indiana, Ohio, New York, and Pennsylvania in the 1820s and 1840s. The establishment of communities of all sorts—Owenite, foreign-language sectarian, and religious—seemed to abate in the 1830s, as though Jacksonian leadership in the nation and states was absorbing reform energies. But in the 1840s came a spate of community founding, mostly by followers of an exotic philosophy spun out of the feverish imagination of a Frenchman named Fourier and imported by an American named Brisbane.

Rarely has an intellectual leader seemed so unlikely to find followers as Charles Fourier. Born in Besançon in 1772 to a cloth merchant of small means and bourgeois aspirations, he grew up hating the commercial world of "chicanery and fraud" in which he was employed, despising later the revolutionaries who had ruined his financial prospects, and detesting the whole classical and rationalist heritage of the *philosophes* of the Enlightenment. Living alone in poverty, a lifelong bachelor, he set himself, day after day and year after year, to expounding a philosophy of the passions. Into a series of enormous books lacking tables of contents, consecutive paging, or even any apparent order, he poured his views that men's natural passions, arising out of deepest wants and needs, were fragmented, perverted, and crushed by bourgeois civilization. The more social institutions were made to respond to the true passions, he said, the more fulfilled and benign men would be.

Fourier was controversial enough with his view that sex was a fundamental passion to be expressed in all its infinite variations, from partners of two to orgies of ten, from heterosexuality to homosexuality, in complex networks of liaisons. He founded his philosophy on a cosmology that linked the history of the passions to tens of thousands of years of human history, to a future epoch of immensely expanded degrees of passionate gratification, to such phenomena as the transformation of the salty seas into a tangy sort of lemonade—ideas that invested Fourier's writings with an air of happy madness.

Every day, precisely at noon, until his death, Fourier awaited the philanthropist who would agree to try out his system. No benefactor came. But one man who did come was Albert Brisbane, a young New Yorker who had studied Hegel in Berlin under the master himself, and dallied with the reformist ideas of Saint-Simon, until he discovered Fourier. After two years of indoctrination, Brisbane returned to America to propagate the faith. Fourierian wine lost some of its headiness in Brisbane's importation. Purging the doctrine of such delightful fantasies as the fornication of the planets, Brisbane seized on his master's detailed plan for Phalansteries, rural communes that would each allow their 1,600 members to live together in a harmonious, joyful, sensual life of love and passion.

Brisbane preached Fourierism from lecture rostrums, through the columns of Horace Greeley's New York *Tribune,* and in books on "association" and the reorganization of industry. Even so, it is not wholly clear how and why this young idealist cut so deeply into popular minds and aspirations. Evidently people were responding to Brisbane's emphasis on association as an escape from capitalistic competition, industrial disorder, and social disarray. We do know that at least a score of Fourierian associations, phalanxes, unions, and colonies were founded in townships and villages throughout the Northeast and Midwest—none in the South—between 1840 and 1847. One of these was Brook Farm, where Sophia Ripley had communed so happily on an earlier August day. Some communities like Oneida lasted for a few decades, but most succumbed within a year or two.

Why this record of failure? Critics pointed to mismanagement, poor planning, laziness, irresponsibility, thievery, fires and other catastrophes —and the inability of human nature to conform to the plans of utopians. Others contended that communities stressing harmony, cooperation, sharing of profits and property, pastoral pursuits, agricultural produce, attention more to human needs than to human productivity, could not survive in a society tending more and more toward industrial productivity, urban growth, and competitive individualism.

Like poor persons' names in village graveyards, the demise of these societies was often their only act recorded in history. Lost to history also were many of the happier days of communal people who at least for a summer or two, until the mortgage callers and rent or tax collectors swooped down, had a taste of true brotherhood, genuine sharing, social and religious tolerance, individual and collective fulfillment. We know only enough about these communities to generalize modestly: they were the final product of brilliantly creative intellectual leadership that knew how to envision but not how to plan. They were rural in nature, arcadian in heritage and nostalgia, mainly agricultural in sustenance. They were self-consciously experimental. And, despite all their concern with harmony, they usually broke up in conflict, secession, and mutual hostility.

It was a bitter denouement for the communitarians who had, in Horace Greeley's admiring words, sought to achieve their goals not "through hatred, collision, and depressing competition; not through War, whether of Nation against Nation, Class against Class, or Capital against Labor; but through Union, Harmony, and the reconciling of all Interests, the giving scope of all noble Sentiments and Aspirations. . . ." It was precisely this aspiration of harmony, however, that was the target of criticism by a young German who had watched the communal experiments with interest. Karl Marx and his friend Friedrich Engels lauded Owenites and Fourierians for their attacks on competitive capitalism, on the treatment of employees as mere commodities, on the alienation of the worker from his labor and its product. But, in a document that would become far more famous and influential than anything Fourier or Owen ever wrote, Marx and Engels excoriated the communitarians for their very belief in harmony and unity:

"They want to improve the condition of every member of society, even that of the most favored," Marx and Engels wrote in the *Communist Manifesto* in 1848. "Hence, they habitually appeal to society at large, without distinction of class; nay, by preference, to the ruling class. . . .

"Hence, they reject all political and especially all revolutionary action; they wish to attain their ends by peaceful means, and endeavor, by small experiments, necessarily doomed to failure, and by the force of example, to pave the way for the new social gospel. . . . These proposals, therefore, are of a purely utopian character."

Class conflict, not communal harmony, was to Marx the driving social force in history, but neither Marx nor the harmonious anticipated the fundamental conflict that soon would rend American society.

CHAPTER 13

The Empire of Liberty

T HE quarter century following the War of 1812–15 was an era of relative
quiet in American foreign relations. The big powers across the Atlantic
were relatively pacific, as though they were restoring energies lost in the
carnage and chaos of the Napoleonic wars. The nation's leaders rejoiced
in the benignity of international affairs. "There has, indeed, rarely been a
period in the history of civilized man in which the general condition of the
Christian nations has been marked so extensively by peace and prosperity," said President John Quincy Adams in 1825. Americans seemed preoccupied with domestic problems and opportunities—especially the vast
lands to the west. Still, American war hawks repeatedly brought the country to a fever pitch against both France and Britain—and doubtless the
jingoes would have challenged the third great European power, Spain, if
Mexico had not gained its independence.

The brush with France came close to comic opera. For years Washington
had been trying to collect on claims against the French for American
commercial losses during the French Revolution. Although in 1831 Paris
finally agreed to pay, the French Finance Minister reneged on the first
installment for the plausible reason that the legislature had not appropriated the necessary funds. A year later that body balked at paying at all.
President Jackson—who had been compelled to stand by fuming as Biddle's bank assessed his government $170,000 for having presented an
unredeemed instrument—now exploded, shouting, so it is said, "I know
them French"—he had never been abroad—"they won't pay unless they're
made to." He told Congress that if the money was not forthcoming the
United States government should be authorized to seize French property.
Chauvinistic excitement swept the nation. The French minister demanded
his passport. The French legislature made the appropriation but withheld
payment until the President explained his language.

"Apologize? I'd see the whole race roasting in hell first!" was Jackson's apocryphal reply. Jingoes had a field day. "No explanations! No
apologies!"

It was rumored that Jackson blew up when he saw a French note with the words *je demande,* not realizing that *demande* meant "request." He ordered naval preparations. Paris assigned a squadron to the West Indies. By now the tiff had become so absurd as to fall of its own slight weight, and the British skillfully mediated. Jackson withdrew any possible imputation of insult to the French government in a way that enabled him to feel he had avoided apologizing. The French, their honor satisfied, arranged to pay the money. And the French chargé in Washington, Alphonse Pageot, who had indignantly departed for Paris with his little son, Andrew Jackson Pageot, returned triumphantly to Washington with his boy, name unchanged.

The encounter with the British was more serious. In 1837 Canadians led by William Lyon Mackenzie rebelled against British rule. Nothing could be calculated to appeal more to the hearts and minds of Americans—to their memories of their own insurrection, their missionary hope of bringing republicanism to their northern neighbors, the need of some for employment after the Panic of '37. Incidents multiplied. Enlisting in the rebel cause, Americans raided United States arsenals and handed weapons over to their comrades. When they started to use a small steamship, the *Caroline,* to transport supplies to the insurrectionists, aroused Canadian loyalists rowed across the Niagara River, set the *Caroline* afire, and let it drift downstream. The ship had been sent over the falls with men trapped inside, American newspapers screamed. Actually the steamer had sunk above the falls, and only one man, Amos Durfee, had been killed, but this was enough. Durfee's draped body was displayed in Buffalo. The Rochester *Democrat* demanded that the "outrage" be avenged "not by simpering diplomacy—BUT BY BLOOD. . . ."

Within a year tens of thousands of Americans, it was estimated, were active across the border from Vermont to Michigan, with the avowed goal of emancipating "the British Colonies from British Thralldom." Organized in "Hunters' Lodges," equipped with cryptic signs, passwords, and badges, the Hunters planned to invade Canada. Meantime, diplomacy had been at work. President Van Buren, as firm in dampening the war fever as the jingoes had been in inflaming it, demanded that American volunteers in Canada return home, asked the governors of New York and Vermont to call their militias into service, and sent General Winfield Scott to pacify the sympathizers. At the end of 1838 several armed bands crossed the border; they were quickly broken up. Rensselaer Van Rensselaer, an American "general," was sentenced to a year's imprisonment for violating the neutrality laws. Van Buren pardoned him—but only after his defeat in the 1840 election.

Feeling along the border eased a bit, only to flare up again late in 1840 when Alexander McLeod, a Canadian deputy sheriff, was picked up in New York State and incarcerated on the charge of having murdered Durfee in the *Caroline* raid. Downing Street formally demanded McLeod's release, amid warnings of most serious consequences if the Canadian was not liberated. The State Department might have been conciliatory, but New Yorkers bridled—and they had the body. There was not gold enough in Britain to take McLeod out of Niagara County, a New York legislator proclaimed. London huffed and puffed in reply; McLeod must be surrendered alive, announced *The Times,* or avenged if dead. Although Webster, on taking office as Secretary of State, tried to calm the British, he could not overcome the stubborn fact that New York as a sovereign state was determined to try McLeod. Once again war cries echoed through the borderlands. The English tried vainly to understand a federal system that would allow a single state to determine a matter of such international concern while the national government was forced to watch helplessly. McLeod was tried before an American jury—and acquitted in twenty minutes—and the war threat dissipated.

People of good sense were more and more convinced that Anglo-American relations could not be left in the hands of mobs, adventurers, chauvinists, and the unexpected fair-mindedness of a New York jury. The coming to office of Robert Peel as Prime Minister, and the appointment of the more conciliatory Lord Aberdeen as Foreign Secretary in place of Lord Palmerston only a few months after Webster had taken office, set the stage for an attempt to resolve the knottiest issue between the two nations. This was the dispute over the northeastern boundary between Maine and New Brunswick.

For decades this poorly mapped area had been in dispute. In 1827, after Americans and Canadians competed for land grants along the Aroostook River, London and Washington agreed to submit the boundary differences to the King of the Netherlands for arbitration; but when the King submitted his compromise award, the British accepted and the Senate balked. A bloodless "war" broke out as Canadian lumberjacks invaded the disputed area; amid the usual alarms both Maine and New Brunswick called up their militias, and once again the hawks of Washington called for war rather than national dishonor. A truce was hastily patched together until the matter could be settled by negotiation, a task to test Daniel Webster's vaunted skill at diplomacy. He was ready for it, having visited England in 1839 and met with its leaders. To parley with Webster, Aberdeen had chosen the agreeable Lord Ashburton, who had married an American belle and heiress,

Anne Bingham of Philadelphia, during George Washington's presidency.

Webster and Ashburton had little trouble working out a compromise; the problem was gaining acceptance by border chauvinists and by the British government, which insisted on a boundary that would allow the Canadians an overland route between Quebec and St. John. Rarely has an issue turned so much on accurate mapping, and rarely has mapping been so faulty or inadequate. Some old maps, one of which seemed validated by Benjamin Franklin himself, supported British and Canadian claims. In order to gain Maine's support for his planned compromise with Ashburton, Webster sent the historian Jared Sparks to Maine to persuade the political leaders to accept the deal or risk something worse. Ashburton paid almost $15,000 for Sparks's expenses. As it turned out later, authentic maps supported the original American claims; unlucky Maine had lost the battle of the maps.

All the parties gained from the treaty itself, however. After the protracted negotiations with commissioners from Maine and Massachusetts (which still had property rights in Maine after the separation of 1820), the treaty settled a wide range of issues. The St. John, Detroit, and St. Clair rivers and Lake St. Clair were open to navigation by both parties. An extradition article dealt with the old problem of fugitives gone to Canada. On an entirely different but intensifying problem, the two nations agreed to maintain a joint cruising squadron on the coast of Africa to help curb the slave trade, though Washington would not accept a mutual right of visit to ascertain the real identity of a suspected slaver. The heart of the Webster-Ashburton Treaty, however, lay in its settlement of the old boundary question. The United States received about 7,000 of the 12,000 square miles in dispute, and gained most of its claim to about 200 square miles of land around the head of the Connecticut River.

The treaty was a major achievement at a time of ill feeling between Americans and British. Sixty years after the Revolution countless Americans still hated the British—hated them for their aristocratic condescension, their exactions as creditors, their endless criticism of Americans and American ways. To many Britishers, the United States was still the land of drunks, duelers, spitters, anarchists, lynchers, thieves, gamblers, slave drivers, cattle rustlers, bumptious boasters and yarn spinners. The English and American languages set them apart orally, and verbally too, as each side could read in the press the scurrilous attacks by the other.

Given such attitudes on both sides of the Atlantic, it seemed remarkable that the two nations avoided a major shooting war. Britain and the United States were economically interdependent, of course, but such a relationship among nations had not always prevented war in the past. The explanation in large part lay with the nation's foreign-policy and diplomatic leadership. Sixty years after the founding of the United States, it was still widely accepted that diplomats and negotiators must have a considerably free hand in parleys with other envoys, for a democratic foreign policy is not necessarily a pacific foreign policy; the popular mind was extremely touchy, suspicious, excitable, and belligerent. Time and again the leadership in Washington exercised restraint, but ultimately this leadership depended on the people for support. And the people were taking some leadership in foreign policy, not only with their votes, but with their feet, as they moved into Indian territories and into borderlands to the northwest or southwest, gazing across frontiers with envy, fear, greed, hostility, and often with a consuming missionary zeal.

Trails of Tears and Hope

Now these people were gazing toward the Far West. By the 1840s the trek west had lengthened considerably from the days of the first trans-Appalachian pioneers, with their Conestoga wagons and frontier stockades. The settlers of the plains bordering the Great Lakes and the Gulf of Mexico also were more diverse, quicker to organize some kind of government, and more inventive in exploiting land than the Scotch-Irish piedmonters whom Daniel Boone had led through the Cumberland Gap. Boone had never known distances such as his grandchildren faced in the two-thousand-mile trek over the Oregon Trail. Undertaken primarily for private motives, the migration would have enormous public impact, as the settlements provided the rationale for a national war and tinder for a civil one.

Pioneers and settlers still tended to move along the latitudes. People from the Northeast headed toward the Great Lakes areas and the northern plains. Southerners traveled toward the Gulf seaboard but many turned northwestward in the direction of the lower tiers of Ohio, Indiana, and Illinois. The migrants were caricatured back East as unscrupulous traders or frontier ruffians; many a Boston or New York salon was titillated by tales of bowie knife fights, eye-gouging brawls, and general drunken mayhem, engaged in by ruffians who styled themselves "ring-tailed roarers, half-horse and half-alligator." But Tocqueville discovered a more literate pioneer: "Everything about him is primitive and wild, but he is himself the result of the labor and experience of eighteen centuries . . . acquainted with the past, curious about the future, and ready for argument about the present . . . a highly civilized being, who consents for a time to inhabit the backwoods, and who penetrates the wilds of the New World with the Bible, an axe, and some newspapers."

Many were looking for a new start: New Englanders escaping from falling crop prices and the loss of farmland to sheep pasture; Carolinians and Tennesseeans displaced by plantations and "King Cotton"; Irish and Germans and others who had settled in port cities and now were on the move again. They might start their trip by one of a dozen or so railroads from the East. Or take the Erie Canal, switch to the Welland Canal around Niagara Falls to Lake Erie, and then catch a boat to Toledo, move along the Maumee River to Fort Wayne and Peru in Indiana, and branch off on canals running to Indianapolis and Terre Haute. Or take the Chesapeake and Ohio Canal from Georgetown to Cumberland, Maryland, and pick up the Cumberland Road to Columbus and Indianapolis and points west. Fares were falling; the New Orleans–Louisville steamboat trip cost fifty dollars in 1825, about half that a decade later, while Pittsburgh–Cincinnati dropped from about twelve dollars to about six.

In the great flat, fertile area extending down from the Great Lakes, Americans were no longer pioneers but settlers. Gone were the days when frontier communities had to experience long years of isolation and self-sufficiency. Settlers in the Michigan woods and Illinois prairie were now only a week or less, rather than months, from New York and Philadelphia. And the West was creating its own market centers. Cities like Detroit, Chicago, and Indianapolis were growing with dizzying speed along with the new transportation network. Miners, tanners, lumberjacks, plowmen, and craftsmen of a thousand different styles elbowed aside the old pioneer jack-of-all-trades in his rough homespun.

Farther south, in the "New Counties" organized from the Indian cessions in Alabama and neighboring states, life for the settler was more cramped. Land was quickly given over to growing cotton and rice. The yeoman farmer did not enjoy the variety of opportunities found farther north, but it was still a region of feverish change, "full of the ringing of axes and the acrid smoke of new-grounds," wrote W. J. Cash. "Whirl was its king."

A farmer with several acres of cotton and one or two slaves might strike it rich in a few seasons and then set himself up as an old tidewater planter. Imitating the Charleston elite, the planter would build a house of lumber sawn on the place—perhaps not a very grand house, sometimes "just a box, with four rooms, bisected by a hallway, set on four more rooms. . . . But it was huge, it had great columns in front, and it was eventually painted white, and so, in this land of wide fields and pine woods it seemed very imposing." In good years the planter would acquire more land and slaves, broadcloth suits, silk dresses, and even a coach-and-six. North or South, the Yankee peddler made shoes, clocks, pails, patent medicines available to nearly everyone.

"The nervous, rocky West is intruding a new and continental element in the national mind," Ralph Waldo Emerson observed, "and we shall yet have an American genius. . . . It is the country of the Future . . . a country of beginnings, of projects, of designs, of expectations."

It was also a country of conflict, as the speed of change heightened the clash of economic interests natural to society. Replacing the three distinct waves of emigrants—the transient pioneer who occupied the land, the settler who cultivated it, and the man of capital and connections who fit it into a broader economic network—the entire progression now overlapped and intertwined in a single generation. Federal land policy after 1819 also served to heighten tensions among squatter, landowner, and capitalist, for the government's refusal to sell land on credit left many farmers without the means of gaining title to the rich new lands, while other settlers who could afford to buy tracts often arrived to find squatters already on their spread.

Politics was a ready escape valve for simmering conflict. Everyone could talk about it, take part in it, denounce it. Almost everyone "expected at some time to be a candidate for something; or that his uncle would be; or his cousin, or his cousin's wife's cousin's friend would be"; so that with frequent elections for numerous offices, people seemed constantly to be electioneering. Conflict also erupted in outright violence. Squatters chased owners off land, and in turn were driven off. In Illinois and Iowa, gangs of horse thieves and other outlaws fought little wars with the citizenry for control of land and even of county governments. The "slick law" of the vigilante ruled some of the New Counties of the South. In the western melting pot, violence was an accepted way to settle differences.

*　　*　　*

Violence was still the final arbiter in the civil war between red people and white. Gone were the days when President Jefferson could drink a toast to "The Red People of America—Under an enlightened policy, gaining by steady steps the comforts of the civilized, without losing the virtues of the savage state." Some Americans did continue to idealize, and perhaps patronize, the Indian. A small group of artists and writers, led by the painter George Catlin among others, depicted and sometimes romanticized the noble savage. In their Washington finishing school, Mary Rapine and her classmates thrilled to the adventures of the Pawnee warrior Petalesharo.

For more political reasons, men like Edward Everett and Theodore Frelinghuysen rose in the Congress to demand that the government honor its commitments to the red nations.

But Henry Clay struck closer to the prevailing national attitude in his view, as interpreted by John Quincy Adams: "There never was a full-blooded Indian who took to civilization. It was not in their nature. He believed they were destined to extinction, and although he would never use or countenance inhumanity towards them, he did not think them, as a race, worth preserving." Most settlers did not share even this benignly perverse, self-fulfilling attitude. Caught in the cycle of occupation, Indian retaliation, and white counter-retaliation, settlers hated the Indians and the pusillanimous, chicken-livered federals who made treaties with them.

Indians under Black Hawk learned once again the price of resistance. Removal of most of the northwestern tribes had proved easy, since their strength had largely been broken in the War of 1812–15. But Black Hawk, a man of such righteous dignity that he reminded Easterners of James Madison and even Sir Walter Scott, persuaded a number of tribesmen to remain by the fields and graves of their ancestors on the Illinois frontier. Forced over into Wisconsin by white depredations during the fall of 1831, Black Hawk found so little food and game there that he recrossed the Mississippi next spring with about a thousand of his tribe. When both state militia and regulars were called out, he tried twice to surrender, but each time his envoys were cut down by white volunteers. Trapped against the river, his people were driven into the water at bayonet point and shot as they struggled for air. At slaughter's end, 150 of the original thousand remained alive.

All this time there thrived in the Southeast a wondrous collection of tribes that gave the lie to the stereotype, benign or malign, of the Savage. About 60,000 Indians—Choctaws, Chickasaws, Cherokees, Creeks, and Seminoles—had established their own civilizations on some of the best lands in Florida, Georgia, Alabama, and Mississippi. They had adopted both the best and the worst of white culture. The Cherokees of Georgia owned 22,000 cattle, 2,000 spinning wheels, 700 looms, 31 gristmills, 10 sawmills, 8 cotton gins, 18 schools—and 1,300 slaves. The wealth of the tribes proved their undoing, as land-hungry white Southerners eyed their fields and buildings and agitated for their removal to the West. But these native Americans were not nomads; pioneering in the wilds of Arkansas and Oklahoma did not interest them. Their prime spiritual value was oneness with the land they lived on: "The mountains and hills, that you see, are your backbone, and the gullies and creeks, which are between the hills and mountains, are your heart veins."

In trying to resist removal, the Indians adopted another white device—formal, representative government. The forms of white rule—assemblies, voting, elected officials—were added to the old tribal structures. The Cherokees adopted a constitution and even applied for statehood. This tribe had some notable leaders, including Sequoyah, who invented a system of writing to fit the ancient tribal language and published a newspaper in Cherokee; and John Ross, who headed two delegations of protest to Washington and made his appeals with the eloquence of a Demosthenes.

All in vain. Federal treaties with the red people were ignored, federal agents assailed with threats and violence. Georgia barred Indian testimony in court, ruled that the tribal government was illegal, and sent the militia onto the Cherokee lands to enforce its decrees, seize the tribal press, and terrorize the Indians into submission. Ross was jailed when he tried to organize a third delegation to Washington. Both President Jackson and the state governor ignored a Supreme Court ruling in favor of the Cherokees. Protection of life, liberty, and property—freedom to organize and petition —the right to a free press and a fair trial—protection against government —the whole American conception of liberty was in shreds.

Savagely punished by the authorities, set upon with whips and clubs by poor whites, defrauded by officials and speculators, the Indians bade farewell to their beloved hills and mountains and struck out for "Indian territory" a thousand miles away through swamps and wilderness. It was a trail of tears. "I saw the helpless Cherokees arrested and dragged from their homes," an army private wrote, "and driven by bayonet into the stockades. And in the chill of a drizzling rain on an October morning I saw them loaded like cattle or sheep into wagons and started toward the west." More than a quarter of the tribe died on the way to the banks of the Arkansas and Red rivers.

The epic might have ended there, west of the Mississippi. But the "Five Civilized Nations," as they came to be called, were not yet defeated. They rebuilt their societies in the wilderness. Creeks and Cherokees retained their old governmental structures, modeled on the southern territorial governments. The Choctaws adopted some of the elements of Jacksonian democracy: every male Choctaw over twenty-one could vote to choose a chief and ten councilors in each district; measures passed by the council could be vetoed by the chiefs, subject to a two-thirds override. At the Choctaw Academy, students pursued not only the three R's but geography, natural philosophy, history, algebra, and Latin.

The final end of the tragedy, however, had simply been delayed. The remorseless advance of the whites continued, and within a few years the Five Tribes were forced to cede land to settlers in Kansas and Arkansas.

Soon these proud and accomplished people were removed to a "reservation" in Oklahoma.

*   *   *

During these years Texas was arousing national attention. As the Indians
were forced west, whites were moving on toward the Southwest and Northwest, driven by high hopes and economic need. By the mid-1820s Stephen
F. Austin was achieving in Texas a dream that his father Moses had hoped
to realize when he secured a commission from the feeble government of
New Spain to settle three hundred American families there. Settling in
Bexar, Stephen Austin offered a guarantee of good conduct by the Americans in exchange for grants of land and promises of religious freedom from
the Spanish, who wanted the empty land filled up as a buffer against
Indians and marauding frontiersmen.

 This deal, which threw Texas open to colonization by thousands of
settlers seeking her rich bottomlands, worked well until it was threatened
by Mexico's revolution against the mother country. For more than a year
Austin, ignorant of the language, the laws, and the leaders of the revolutionary government, haunted the chambers of the constantly changing
officialdom in Mexico City. Receiving some concessions, Austin returned
to Texas and served as a benign despot on his immense holdings, as well
as a trusted adviser to the other *empresarios.* Almost 20,000 Americans
flooded into the province. Operating nearly independently of Mexican
authority hundreds of miles away, the Texans seemed to some to have
virtually realized the Jeffersonian paradise of a small republic.

This near-idyll was shattered when the Mexicans, alarmed by an abortive
effort to establish the "Republic of Fredonia," barred the admission of
additional Americans into Texas or the introduction of more slaves. After
much agitation by the aroused Texans, a convention resolved that Texas
must become an autonomous state within the Mexican federal union. Austin carried the resolves to Mexico City, only to be thrown into jail. By the
time he was released months later, in the fall of 1835, war had broken out
in Texas much as it had in Lexington and Concord sixty years before.
Mexican soldiers had ridden into the hamlet of Gonzales with orders to
confiscate a small brass cannon, which the Texans were determined to
keep. They not only kept it but used it to fire on the Mexicans. The Texas
struggle became one for independence, as Sam Houston, proclaiming that
the "work of liberty has begun," issued a call for volunteers.

 Six thousand Mexicans under General Santa Anna marched against the
rebels. Reaching San Antonio late in February 1836, they found a company
of Texans holed up in the Alamo, under self-styled Colonel Buck Travis,

a pugnacious soldier-politico only twenty-seven years of age. Travis appealed to the "People of Texas and All Americans in the World" for help "in the name of Liberty," but no help came. With matchless determination and heroism the 187 Texans held off the assaulting force of 3,000 Mexicans for ten days, until they were overwhelmed and massacred. The bodies of Davy Crockett and James Bowie, as well as Travis, lay in the carnage. Santa Anna's forces now swept on with sword and torch, overrunning American settlements and reaching Galveston Bay. After fleeing toward the United States border, the Texans rallied on the banks of the San Jacinto. With the cry of "Remember the Alamo!" on their lips, they overran a detachment of Mexicans they surprised in their beds, killed six hundred of the enemy, and captured Santa Anna.

With the surrender of Santa Anna, the war seemed over, and the way prepared for joining the United States. But Washington was cool to the Texas petition for annexation. President Jackson feared that merely recognizing Texas would hurt relationships with Mexico and disrupt the Democratic party. John Quincy Adams charged on the floor of the House that the Texas revolution was part of a proslavery conspiracy. Already entangled in the internal politics of the United States, the Texans would have to await further foreign and domestic developments before they could gain admission to the Union.

The white occupation of the Northwest was more peaceful but no less adventurous. Ever since the expedition of Lewis and Clark, the two thousand miles of plain and mountain between the Mississippi River and the Pacific had been the home of a peculiar breed of half-traders, half-explorers. These were the mountain men, whose lives were later glorified in the stories of Kit Carson, Jim Bridger, and Jedediah Smith. A few of these pioneers had settled in Oregon and turned to farming under the watchful eye of Britain's Hudson's Bay Company, which controlled the territory north of the Columbia River. Others stayed in California, nominally a Mexican possession but in fact governed loosely by the local military. In California the mountain men were joined by a second group of Americans, Yankee merchants who arrived by sea. Prominent among these was "el Bostono," Thomas O. Larkin, the American consul at Monterey. Skilled in both business and diplomacy, Larkin created from a five-hundred-dollar loan a sprawling coastal trade in California hides, Hawaiian sugar, and New England imports, while his quiet influence on the military commandant and other important citizens slowly moved the local Mexicans toward yearning for an independent California.

A new element loomed in the Pacific territories during the 1840s, thanks to the golden reports sent back by travelers and settlers. Imaginations throughout the American West were stirred by descriptions of a land where "perpetual summer is in the midst of unceasing winter . . . and towering snow clad mountains forever look down upon eternal verdure." After many months of correspondence, several groups interested in emigration agreed to meet at Independence, Missouri. Most of the families who gathered at Independence that spring of 1843 and in following years were fairly prosperous; they would start the year-long trek across the continent with all the wagons, stock, and household goods needed to homestead the new land. Other young couples and single men, drawn to the adventure but lacking means to make the trip on their own, hired themselves out to wealthier pioneers as teamsters and laborers.

As good frontier democrats, the travelers elected the officers of their wagon trains. Campaign techniques were impromptu; candidates mounted a barrel and spoke in their own praise, and then the voters literally lined up behind the man of their choice. "These men were running about the prairie, in long strings," a journalist reported. "The leaders . . . doubling and winding in the drollest fashion; so that, the all-important business of forming a government seemed very much like the merry schoolboy game of 'snapping the whip.' "

These boisterous elections seldom produced the sort of leaders who could stand up to the hardships of the trail. As the path grew steeper and rockier, the oxen fewer and leaner, the Indians more adept at robbing a camp or hamstringing a horse, the trains broke down into small groups or individual families—who found the going even harder alone. Winter typically saw the pioneers still high in the mountains above the Willamette and Sacramento valleys, and the older settlers left their cabins time and again to rescue the new emigrants. The travelers lost their stock, their wagons, sometimes all of their possessions along the trail. They arrived in the new land penniless but confident that they soon would make good.

Relations between Larkin and the newcomers were strained, for the untutored chauvinism of the Americans worried the native Californians and undermined Larkin's scheme for independence. But another knowing settler, John Augustus Sutter, greeted their arrival with pleasure. But he had left Switzerland in the 1830s, drawn by the New World's promise of wealth and freedom. His dream took shape on the banks of the Sacramento River, where his ranch and trading post made him the effective lord of northern California. But he was a lord without subjects; the only inhabitants of his "New Helvetia" were a handful of half-breeds and broken-down mountain men. Now the wagon trains would bring him tenants and customers. Perhaps when they arrived in force he would be able to complete his perennial project of building a mill on the Sacramento.

In the meantime, Sutter sent a few hired hands out to dig a ditch and test another location for the millrace.

ANNEXATION: POLITICS AND WAR

The 1840s brought an extraordinary conjuncture of popular attitudes, political leadership, and diplomatic and military opportunity, the outcome of which would add over 1,200,000 square miles to United States territory. Within one decade—indeed, within one presidential term—Americans fought a diplomatic war in the Northwest and a shooting war in the Southwest that expanded their lands by well over one-third. Nothing like this could or would ever happen again.

The popular idea lying behind this expansionism gathered force rapidly in the 1840s. Later called "Manifest Destiny," it was a concept cloudy enough to appeal to many needs and hopes, compelling enough to sustain determined leadership. It meant expansion, legitimated by Heaven or the fates, inspired by economic interest, territorial greed, and missionary idealism—expansion toward the western coast, or over the whole North American continent, or perhaps even the whole hemisphere. Congressman Stephen A. Douglas of Illinois told Congress that he would "blot out the lines on the map which now marked our national boundaries on this continent, and make the area of liberty as broad as the continent itself." That was the alleged purpose of Manifest Destiny—to bring the blessings of liberty and democracy, of Christianity and commercialism, to backward peoples. All this was mixed with boosterism. Said an Indiana congressman: "Go to the West and see a young man with his mate of eighteen," and thirty years later "visit him again, and instead of two, you will find twenty-two. That is what I call the American multiplication table."

The acolytes of Manifest Destiny were less creative or talented than they were dogged and determined. James K. Polk, their exemplar, was the oldest of ten children of a prosperous North Carolina farmer; he had been a frail youngster, a dutiful student at the University of North Carolina, and a hard-working Tennessee lawyer, before starting his climb up the political ladder, from state legislator to congressman to Speaker of the House to governor of Tennessee. A Jackson man from first to last, he had the old general's aid in winning the Democratic party nomination in 1844 as the nation's first dark horse.

"Who is James K. Polk?" the Whigs scoffed, but they found he was a President of plan and purpose. At the start of his administration he was determined to achieve four measures: tariff reduction; the independent treasury; settlement of the Oregon boundary question; and the acquisition of California. Backed up by an equally determined Cabinet and staff, supported in Congress, where he still had influence, Polk won these four measures—and then quit.

Oregon came as an early test of Polk's determination. Both Britain and the United States had long laid claim to the magnificent spread of half a million square miles lying roughly between the 42nd and 54th parallels. Both claims were based mainly on early explorations—the British, most notably on George Vancouver's of 1792; the American, on Lewis and Clark's of 1803–06. So impressive was each side's case, and so tangled the issues, that Webster and Ashburton avoided the dispute in their 1842 negotiations. But American settlers in Oregon, especially in the lush Willamette Valley, were pressing for a settlement, and the British wished to clarify the status of their Hudson's Bay Company, which dominated the fur trade in the vast expanse.

The Americans had their champions in Congress. "Let the emigrants go on; and carry their rifles," declaimed Thomas Hart Benton. "We want thirty thousand rifles in the valley of the Oregon . . . to annihilate the Hudson's Bay Company, drive them off our continent, quiet their Indians, and protect the American interests."

Elected on a Democratic party platform that had sharpened the issue by flatly claiming "our title to the whole of the Territory of Oregon is clear and unquestionable," Polk proceeded to take a strong line in his public pronunciamentos while still trying to deal privately with London. The result was a deluge of jingoism as even small boys picked up the cry "Fifty-four Forty or Fight," and the British attitude stiffened. Congress passed a resolution authorizing the President to terminate joint occupation of Oregon. Throughout 1845 there was talk of war—over territory three thousand miles from Washington and many weeks of sailing time from England.

Still, the foreign policy makers were able to transcend the war clamor they had helped create. Polk authorized his Secretary of State, James Buchanan, to offer the British a division at the 49th parallel. This was not the first time Washington had made this proposal, but now it failed to include a concession of free navigation of the Columbia River. Richard Pakenham, the British minister in Washington, rejected the proposal out of hand without referring it to London. He was disavowed by his government, which then proposed arbitration, but by now Polk had *his* back up. He would wait for Britain to make some substantial concession. The "only way to treat John Bull," he told a congressman, "was to look him straight in the eye."

A series of events, more than men's statecraft, made a settlement possible. Stronger leadership by "little Englanders" in Britain, a decision by the Hudson's Bay Company to move its main depot from Fort Vancouver on the Columbia to Vancouver Island (thus strengthening Aberdeen's argument that a presence on the river was not crucial), and the rising concern over the gathering potato famine in Ireland, brought a new proposal of the 49th parallel from the British. Although Polk remained unyielding, most of his cabinet members wanted a settlement, urging the President to try a most interesting tactic—to refer the proposed agreement to the Senate for *previous* advice, rather than for ratification or rejection. This way, the senators would take the political heat, whichever way they decided. None too eagerly, Polk agreed.

The Senate took its advice-before-consent role seriously. Amid general surprise, the upper chamber advised the President to accept the British proposal as it stood. Polk complied. While by now the Oregon question had become entangled with slavery and Mexico, the simple result in the Northwest was that Americans had got neither "fifty-four" nor "fight" but a fair and lasting "forty-nine."

*   *   *

Seventeen parallels south of the 49th lay Washington's old treaty-line border with Mexico, and to the southeast of that line lay the great curving Rio Grande, flanking Texas. Tyler had hoped to turn Texas into the political rallying ground of his presidency, with nationwide support for annexation as the main prop of his re-election bid. But Calhoun, Secretary of State after the resignation of Webster and the death of his successor, Abel Upshur, chose to focus on protection of slavery as the main justification for annexation. The Senate rejected Calhoun's narrow sectional case after a bitter debate, thus leaving the explosive issue of Texas for Polk. Even more than Oregon, it was a divisive question, cutting across parties, regions, and factions. Accusing Tyler of a slaveholders' conspiracy to enlarge the dominion of bondage, abolitionists used the issue of annexation to arouse Northerners over slavery. In the election of 1844 Van Buren's opposition to annexation alienated his mentor Jackson and thousands of other Democrats.

Henry Clay, the Whig nominee, typically tried to straddle the issue and typically came to be labeled "proslavery" by the abolitionists and "opportunistic" by the South. The Democrats had taken a forthright stand, calling for the "reannexation of Texas at the earliest practicable period." And, with Polk, the Democrats had won.

Deserted by his party, lame duck John Tyler still had four months to go in the White House following the election, and he wanted to make the most of them. Fearing that an annexation treaty would again be defeated in the Senate, Tyler used the device of a joint resolution, requiring only simple majorities in House and Senate, to push through approval of an annexation agreement with Texas. Ignoring any need to gain Mexico's consent, the resolution provided that, with the agreement of Texas, as many as four additional states might be formed from her territory; Texas could retain her own public lands but must also pay her own public debt; and the Missouri Compromise line of 36°30′ would be extended to Texas.

Four days later Polk took the oath of office, and then the implacable escalation began.

March 28, 1845: Mexico breaks off diplomatic relations with the United States.

May 28: General Zachary Taylor receives orders to hold his troops in a state of readiness to advance into Texas.

June 15: Taylor is ordered to occupy a position on or near the Rio Grande.

July 4: A convention called by President Anson Jones of Texas accepts the annexation terms.

July 26: Taylor advances into Texas and establishes his base on the south bank of the Nueces.

The gathering crisis eased a bit in the autumn when the exhausted Herrera regime, beset by extreme nationalists, signaled a wish to parley. Mexican leaders, long concerned over Washington's partiality to Texas, were naturally indignant at the annexation treaty and at threatening U.S. military moves. Polk sent John Slidell, a Spanish-speaking Louisiana politician, to Mexico City with instructions to offer Herrera $5 million for New Mexico, $25 million or more for California, and agreement on the Rio Grande as the northeastern boundary in exchange for American assumption of claims held by its own nationals against Mexico. Slidell arrived in Mexico only to learn that he would not be received as minister plenipotentiary, since the Mexicans wished to negotiate *before* officially resuming relations. Polk, however, refused to change Slidell's status to that of a commissioner, and the Mexicans ignored the envoy. But Slidell's presence had helped to turn public opinion against the Herrera government, and as 1845 ended the nationalist general Mariano Paredes launched a successful coup. Playing to popular fears that Slidell's mission was not a gesture of conciliation but a foray to gain territory, Paredes declared he would fight for Mexico's claim to all of Texas.

The leaders in Washington and Mexico City now made a fateful set of decisions. On January 13 the War Department ordered Taylor to occupy positions on the Rio Grande across from Matamoras, where Mexican forces were camped; a few days later, Paredes sent General Mariano Arista north with reinforcements and secret instructions to push Taylor back beyond the Nueces. As it took about two weeks for messages from the Rio Grande to reach either capital, the soldiers were on their own. Actions in Texas were following a separate course from events in Washington and Mexico City.

Then events seemed to take command:

March 28, 1846: The American regulars camp on the Rio Grande.

April 12: The Mexican command warns that Taylor's is a hostile action.

April 15: Taylor blockades the mouth of the Rio Grande.

April 24: Arista arrives and orders the Mexican forces across the river.

April 25: Arista's troops trap one of Taylor's cavalry patrols and kill or capture sixty Americans. Taylor reports the situation to Washington and urgently requests reinforcements. The Mexican and American armies begin to maneuver for battle, as both commanders act on the assumption that war has begun.

Now Washington: May 9: Polk convenes the Cabinet and gains their approval for an immediate declaration of war. Only later that evening does Taylor's message, describing the Mexican attack, arrive from the Rio Grande. The President spends the Sabbath drafting his speech, which is delivered two days later. "A cynic might have felt that Polk's war message sounded as if it had indeed been written on Sunday, for it combined the self-righteous wrath of the Old Testament with the long-suffering patience of the New," David Pletcher wrote. It "epitomized Polk's whole policy toward Mexico since his inauguration, by assuming what was not yet proved, by thrusting forward to throw his adversary off balance, and by maintaining a show of reluctance and sweet reason to placate moderates and pacifists at home. . . ."

A few Whig congressmen called for time to consider the mass of evidence that accompanied Polk's message, but heavy majorities in the House and Senate voted for war at once. Suddenly the War Department found itself without a war plan, despite the fact that hostilities had been predicted for months. A strategy was hastily improvised. General Taylor would conduct the main offensive across the Rio Grande into the lightly populated northern reaches of Mexico. The Navy's Pacific squadron, which had standing orders to capture the port of Monterey if war broke out, would seize as much of the California coast as possible. General Stephen W. Kearny would launch an expedition into New Mexico and then California. Later General Winfield Scott would strike at Mexico City itself by way of Veracruz. The plan and its execution turned out to be a curious repetition of the War of 1812–15: attacks along the northern border, battles in western waters and coastlands (in this case California), amphibious invasion from the eastern ocean, capture of the enemy's capital. But this time the United States struck at the enemy heartland—and there was no Battle of New Orleans.

While Taylor, without even waiting for the congressional declaration of war, pushed the Mexicans back across the river with artillery barrages and bayonet attacks, General Kearny moved out toward Santa Fe. Another long march brought his small force to San Diego and Los Angeles, where it linked up with shore parties from the U.S. Pacific squadron and a group of local Americans led by the flamboyant Captain John C. Frémont.

In late September, Taylor drove the Mexicans out of Monterrey after a four-day siege and stout opposition. Lieutenant Sam Grant was moved to pity by the plight of the conquered Mexicans: "Many of the prisoners were cavalry, armed with lances, and mounted on miserable little half-starved horses that did not look as if they could carry their riders out of town. The men looked in but little better condition." The bankrupt Mexican government could not even begin to match the millions of dollars appropriated in Washington. The Americans did suffer from inadequate supplies, primitive provisions for sanitation and health, and other failings of a makeshift, volunteer army, but few American soldiers missed a meal or lacked a working gun; few Mexicans ever received either.

After Monterrey fell, Taylor concluded a local armistice with Santa Anna, subject to being disclaimed by either government. Polk promptly did disclaim it and added a reprimand. Now that Taylor was being mentioned by Whigs as a presidential possibility, the general suspected Polk was intriguing against him. His suspicions hardened when he heard that Scott would lead the attack on Veracruz. Acting largely on his own, Taylor pushed south toward a showdown with Santa Anna. At Buena Vista a vastly superior Mexican force attacked the 5,000 men under Taylor. Once again the Mexican soldiers fought valiantly but were let down by their leaders, who hesitated in the face of repeated charges by Jefferson Davis' Mississippi volunteers. When Santa Anna tried to disengage, the battle was converted into a rout. Taylor's success, however, only earned him another reprimand from Washington, so the general gave up his command and returned to the United States—where he gained a hero's reception.

In February 1847 Scott struck at Mexico's east coast in what would become a great military saga of the war. The soldiers in the small American armada faced the powerful fortress of Veracruz and, towering behind it, the mountain of Orizaba, whose white summit appeared to them "like a great liberty cap suspended in the air." On March 9, as the setting sun dyed the snowy liberty cap blood-red, 10,000 soldiers streamed ashore in the first massive amphibious assault ever launched by Americans. As one lieutenant in the first wave wrote home with delight, all went smoothly. "As fast as they got in, the boats fell behind the frigate Raritan and held on her till the signal should be given to land. This, I think, was the most beautiful sight I ever saw, as the boats fell in their places, the colors flying, the bands playing, etc. When the signal was made to land, as the boats cast off and stood for shore the navy and the 2nd and 3rd lines sent up cheer after cheer that might have been heard for miles." After five days of skillful maneuver and bombardment, the Americans forced the surrender of the fortress.

Then began the long advance to the west. In the midsummer heat Scott's men moved through lowlands and trudged up through towering mountain passes to the central Mexican plateau. Though a heavy force of Mexicans stood at the canyons around Cerro Gordo, Scott's young engineering officers—Joe Johnston, George McClellan, and the brilliant Major Robert E. Lee—found or built paths around the Mexican positions, flanking and routing the defenders. Scott pressed on to Jalapa and Perote, where the invasion ended in May. Disease and the departure of hundreds of men whose short-term enlistments had expired left Scott with only a few thousand effectives, and he had to pause for several months while reinforcements arrived piecemeal from the United States.

After the fall of Veracruz, Polk dispatched Nicholas P. Trist, chief clerk of the State Department, on a secret peace mission to Mexico. At first Trist had more difficulty parleying with the suspicious Scott than with the enemy, but after achieving an armistice with the general he negotiated a temporary one with the Mexicans. This effort soon collapsed, and Scott resumed the offensive. He had already routed the enemy in Contreras and overpowered them at Churubusco, with heavy losses on both sides. Mexico City lay just over the next rise: "The mists disappeared and there, before them, lay what Cortez's lieutenants had seen . . . a great garden, dotted with bright lakes, fields of emerald and the white domes and glittering spires. . . . A valley fifty miles wide, dotted with six large extinct volcanoes far to the south, gleaming with snow—tiny Mexican lancers moving slowly among olive groves and straggling villages."

Scott faced a hard choice between storming the heavily fortified stone causeways that led into the city across swamps from the south or using a route from the west defended by a height called Chapultepec. Though Lee recommended the former, Scott chose to assault Chapultepec and the fortress-palace that topped it. After a day of cannonading, assault groups clambered and shot their way up almost vertical slopes, through heavy musket fire, to a point where they could climb the palace walls with scaling ladders. Inside, "Los Niños," the young cadets of the Military College, disregarded Santa Anna's order that they be relieved, and stood their ground with the other defenders. The Americans could not be stopped. General Scott watched the assault with pride and wonder: "I am an idiot to bring artillery so far . . . when I have such soldiers." A savage bayonet charge brought the fall of the fortress. Next day, Mexican troops in the rest of the city gave in after more heavy fighting, and the invading forces took control of the capital. Soon United States Marines were guarding the "halls of Montezuma."

Although Trist had been ordered back to Washington, with the fall of Mexico City he stayed on without authorization. By the terms of the Treaty of Guadalupe Hidalgo, Mexico surrendered all claims to Texas above the Rio Grande and ceded California and New Mexico to the United States. Washington agreed to pay $15 million for the almost 1,200,000 square miles comprising those two states and Texas, and parts of what would become Arizona, Nevada, Utah, and Colorado. Considering the length and daring of the military expedition, the price was not unduly high: 15,000 casualties out of about 120,000 men in the total force, of whom about 45,000 were regulars and Marines. Considering the Mexicans' advantage of numbers and position, and the constant interference by Polk and other political luminaries, it was an unusually well-conducted war. Perhaps the principal reason was the quality of American military leadership that emerged among the officers in the field. Men like Lee, Sherman, Bragg, Longstreet, Meade, McClellan, and a score of others won their spurs in the battles with the Mexicans. Indeed, some of these West Point graduates regretted seeing the war end; Brevet Captain Ulysses S. Grant, for one, lamented that "there goes the last chance I ever shall have of military distinction!"

The Geometry of Balance

The Mexican War had slashed through the body of the nation's politics like a bayonet through a man's belly, leaving severed connections and inflamed wounds. During the war Northerners and Southerners alike, it seemed, had been less concerned over the eventual land settlement with Mexico than over the status of slavery in the lands coming to the United States as territories and later as states. No sooner had Polk requested $2 million from Congress to negotiate peace with Mexico than a Pennsylvania Democrat, David Wilmot, had risen in the House to move that slavery be barred from any territory received from Mexico. Though the Wilmot Proviso never passed Congress, Wilmot kept pressing for it and in the process he united the South against its northern adversaries. Large planters sought more slave states in the Union to balance the North. Small southern farmers wanted this—they also wanted assurance that someday, if need be, they could take their slaves with them to serve as cheap labor if they migrated into the big open country of the Southwest.

But the war did more than sharpen North-South animosities. Its implications for the extension of slavery put heavy pressure on the delicate balance between Whigs who wanted to continue to be a national party, embracing a coalition of moderate supporters North and South, and those who shrank further and further from any involvement with "slave power." The Democratic party too was increasingly divided over the slavery issue, but less so than the Whigs, for the national Democracy was more securely based in its old coalition of northern and southern Jeffersonians, Jacksonians, and Van Burenites.

The deepening polarization reached into the states, into the grass roots. The complex internal politics of New York, ordinarily revolving around mundane questions of taxation and trade and manufacture, was drawn into the vortex of national discord. The cleavage was even deeper in Massachusetts, where John Quincy Adams remarked on two divisions, "one based upon public principle, and the other upon manufacturing and commercial interests." Adams himself would not be around to lend his national stature to moral leadership in the antislavery cause. While listening in the House to the reading of fulsome resolutions expressing the gratitude of Congress to various Mexican War generals—and preparing to oppose them—"Old Man Eloquent" suddenly collapsed at his desk. He died two days later.

In his own lifetime, having moved from the Federalist party into the Republican orbit and then into the Whig, having moved from high-minded disapproval of slavery to ardent hostility to it, but always short of abolitionism, having maintained ties with most party and factional leaders but always able to transcend them, Adams personified the shifting but sinewy bonds and balances that held the Union together. These came under enormous strain from the disruption of the war with Mexico and its settlement.

These elements of equipoise were constitutional, institutional, sectional, economic, philosophical, forming a complex geometry of balance. The provision in the Constitution for apportionment of southern representation based on the three-fifths rule may have seemed to John Quincy Adams "that fatal drop of Prussic acid in the Constitution, the human chattel representation," but the provision nevertheless helped balance southern and northern power in Congress. Northern states held a clear majority in the House but only half the Senate seats, and the South would gain representation in both chambers from the new states carved out of the farmlands and deserts and mountain lands of the Southwest. If a northern majority should take over the Senate, Southerners could filibuster there. There were still warm memories of the fourteen-day filibuster against the United States Bank bill in 1842. And the Southerners had other built-in safeguards—their strength in the Supreme Court, for example, and, in Democratic national conventions, the two-thirds requirement for presidential nominations.

If the Supreme Court was not a southern court, it had a strong tilt toward Virginia republicanism of the old Jeffersonian school. Chief Justice Roger Brooke Taney, appointed by Jackson partly in reward for Taney's heroic aid in the fight against Biddle's bank, presided over a court that had shifted markedly from the Federalist bias in favor of property rights and national power. In the Charles River Bridge case, he held that rights granted by charters must be construed narrowly. "While the rights of private property are sacredly guarded," the Chief Justice pronounced for the court, "we must not forget that the community also have rights, and that the happiness and well being of every citizen depends on their faithful preservation." In a series of rulings on federal power he led the court in narrow interpretations that recognized the claims of "sovereign" states. In *Luther* v. *Borden* he used the doctrine of political questions to deny his court's jurisdiction over a case that emerged from Dorr's Rebellion in Rhode Island and involved rival claims to the government of the state. Abolitionists feared the day when this "southern Marylander" and his "southern court" would rule on a central question over slavery.

Political balances strengthened governmental ones. Both major parties had their roots in the South and North; both appealed to a variety of economic, social, sectional, and other interests besides the slavery and antislavery groups; both saw the need for building North-South coalitions if they were to realize their great objective—winning presidential elections. Hence each party was a big noisy machine for devouring, morselizing, and blending sharp ideological and local attitudes that otherwise might become indigestible. Each big party machine was a cluster of countervailing state and local parties, interests, classes. Inevitably such equipoises had a static, conservative bias toward the status quo. "Balance was organic," for leaders like Webster, in Robert Dalzell's words. "Its roots lay in the past. It grew and developed over time; continuity was its vital force."

This nationwide equilibrium of rival and conflicting interests, delicately balanced in national institutions and state and local constituencies, was ordinarily flexible and durable, but it was vulnerable too, especially to the single overriding, highly controversial moral cause that, unlike the ordinary conflicts the system devoured, could not be morselized. That kind of moral conflict rather threatened to shred the machine. Other powerful forces could shock the system—wars, migration of population, severe economic depression. Two great forces, however, ordinarily provided elements of continuity and stability and predictability to the system of balances—the major parties; and the quadrennial presidential elections, which forced even the more extremist politicians to moderate their causes and their tongues, broaden their platforms, build coalitions with rival interests, and offer a candidacy of national appeal. Such an election seemed to be approaching in 1848.

1848! The equilibrium of Europe, at least, was sorely threatened as commotions and rebellions swept through Paris, Vienna, Prague, Venice, Milan. Suddenly established authority on the Continent was demonstrating its impotence. Louis Philippe abdicated; Emperor Ferdinand I escaped to Innsbruck, and then abdicated; Pius IX fled to Gaeta. New leaders were emerging, like Lajos Kossuth in Hungary and Louis Napoleon in France. And in London two men, little known except within international left-wing movements, put out a document called the *Communist Manifesto*. All this was a lesson to Americans that even the most venerable and seemingly stable institutions were open to change. But Americans were hardly listening, save for a fringe of humanitarians who focused their reform activism on the campaign against slavery.

Abolitionists had been agitating against slavery for decades; in the 1840s many resolved that the time had come for political action. It was not an obvious or easy decision. Purists in the movement had argued for years that the Constitution and the government themselves must be considered the enemy, that to take part in electoral and party battle was to be fatally compromised by the proslavery system it defended. And if antislavery militants did lead their movement into political action, further harsh strategic questions arose: Should antislavery men fight for abolition of all existing slavery, or simply for restrictions on the extension of slavery? Should they pursue the tactic of "one-ideaism"—concern themselves only with slavery—or work with reformers pursuing other and sometimes related causes, such as free education, temperance, women's rights, penal reform? Should they form their own party, or work within one or both of the major parties? This last was perhaps the hardest question, for antislavery leaders knew of some Democrats and even more Whigs who were as hostile to slavery as they were.

By 1840 at least some antislavery leaders were ready for political action, if only because their nonpolitical activity had proved so unrewarding. Meetings of abolitionists organized a loose-knit "Liberty party" and nominated James G. Birney for President. Birney epitomized the problems and progress of antislavery. A onetime slave owner himself, he had moved to Alabama, entered politics, and advocated the use of legislative power to emancipate slaves and prohibit their interstate sale. Later he sold his plantation and slaves and became an agent for the American Colonization Society. Increasingly convinced that colonization would expand the slave trade, he returned to Kentucky, freeing his last few slaves, helped form the Kentucky Anti-Slavery Society, and called for united action against the evil. As an activist who favored working within the political system, he was a logical candidate for President in 1840. The Liberty-ites, however, polled barely 7,000 votes, and had minimal effect on the outcome. Four years later the party won almost ten times as many votes, but ironically it may have given the election to Polk by cutting into Clay's Whig support in the crucial New York race.

By 1848 Texas, the war, Oregon, and calls for "Free Soil" had immensely enlarged the antislavery movement. In the Democratic party the movement now included the "Barnburners," so named because they had repudiated a New York Democratic convention in 1847 rather than accept its conservative platform, on the model of the Dutch farmer who had burned his barn to get rid of the rats. This action had left "Hunkers"—conservative party regulars—in control of a diminished Democracy. As the radical wing of the party, Barnburners turned increasingly toward antislavery in their national posture.

The Whigs, based more in the North, were even more divided over slavery than the Democrats. For some years there had been developing within that party an antislavery movement enjoying the agreeable designation "Conscience Whigs." Arrayed against them in increasing numbers were the "Cotton Whigs," so called for their support of cooperation with southern moderates and their close financial and political connections with the cotton growers of the South. Spiritually and intellectually based in Boston's Unitarianism and Concord's Transcendentalism, Conscience Whiggery took a moral stand on slavery that aroused compassionate Americans throughout the North and Northwest. Leaders of the two Whig factions seemed often to hate each other more than the common Democratic foe. It was not a Democrat but a Whig who labeled Cotton Whig moderation as a conspiracy between "the lords of the lash and the lords of the loom."

As 1848 approached, antislavery leaders within and outside the major parties stepped up their efforts to offer a presidential candidate clearly opposed to the extension of slavery. What should be the strategy? Purist abolitionists clung to their policy of scorning parties and elections in favor of moral appeals. Old Liberty party leaders and anti-extension Democrats and Whigs began to think the unthinkable—abandoning their parties and joining a new movement pledged to the Wilmot Proviso. The old "Liberty men" faced difficult choices. Should they exchange the moral impact of their intense single cause for the wider electoral support they could gain through coalition? Under the leadership of Salmon P. Chase, a forty-year-old Cincinnati lawyer who had fought the 1793 fugitive-slave law up to the Supreme Court (and lost), many Liberty men moved toward a broad Free-Soil movement. They would pay the price of compromise through collaboration, for despite all their vaunted militancy the Free-Soilers would be, as Eric Foner has pointed out, the first major antislavery group to avoid the question of Negro rights in their national platform. But it was this kind of concession that made it possible for the Free-Soil movement to embrace strong anti-extensionists, moderate Conscience Whigs, and those Barnburners who were far more concerned with the impact of slavery on whites than on blacks. The desertion of their parties by anti-extension Democrats and Whigs eased tensions within the two major parties, which continued their middle-of-the-road strategy of conciliating pro- and anti-extension delegates in their presidential conventions.

With basic strategic choices made, presidential election politics now unfolded as if following a master scenario.

November 1847: The Liberty party convenes in New York and nominates Senator John P. Hale, New Hampshire apostate Democrat, for President.

May 1848: The Democratic national convention, fiercely divided over slavery extension, meeting in Baltimore, promptly splits apart over the question of seating contested delegations of Barnburners and Hunkers from New York; when compromise efforts fail, neither delegation sits in the convention. When the convention nominates Lewis Cass, veteran Democrat, ex-general, opponent of Free Soil, advocate of "squatter sovereignty," the Hunkers pledge their support; the Barnburners pointedly do not.

Early June: The Whig national convention assembles in Philadelphia to decide among the often nominated but never elected Henry Clay and a choice of two generals of Mexican War fame, Zachary Taylor and Winfield Scott. The Whigs, like the Democrats the month before, oppose congressional power to control slavery in the territories. They choose war hero Taylor.

Now into this scenario intrudes a new anti-extensionist leader but a moderate of yore—the old fox of Kinderhook, ex-President Martin Van Buren himself. As the master organizer and unifier of the Jacksonian Democratic party, Van Buren had always taken a soft position on slavery; in particular, he had fought the abolition of slavery in the District of Columbia, amid the taunts of the abolitionists. Since his defeat in 1840 he had reluctantly moved toward a strong anti-extension position. Old Democratic party comrades broke with him, but he had the support of his handsome and personable son John, who doubled as a kind of Democratic party Prince Charming and as an eloquent adversary of slavery. Could the old man now be trusted? Free-Soilers asked, and the verdict was generally yes. Besides, he was immensely available, with his big national reputation and following.

Late June: The seceding Barnburners hold their own convention in Utica and nominate Van Buren for President.

August: Liberty-ites, Barnburners and other antislavery Democrats, and Conscience Whigs hold the national convention of the Free-Soil party in a huge, broiling tent in Buffalo and also nominate Van Buren for President, after sidetracking Hale. The Free-Soilers proclaim their slogan: "FREE SOIL, FREE SPEECH, FREE LABOR, FREE MEN!"

November: Taylor defeats Cass by 1,360,000 to 1,220,000 in the popular vote, 163 to 127 in the electoral college.

A striking aspect of the 1848 results was the mottled voting pattern; Taylor carried eight slave states and seven free; Cass, eight free and seven slave. Hence the Whigs, like the Democrats under Polk and Van Buren, would govern with their political support and obligation fixed in slaveholding as well as anti-extension constituencies. Another key outcome was Van Buren's failure to carry a single state with his 291,000 votes. His main role —ironic for the Democracy's supreme organization man—was to help pull his old party down. The Barnburners were gleeful—they had set fire to a big barn and they had punished some proslavery rats. But to what avail was this, if a huge new log cabin packed with southern and Cotton Whigs stood in its place?

Americans had come to expect a period of calm following presidential elections. The arguments had been made; the people had spoken; let the new man show what he could do. But the election of 1848 seemed to bring little surcease. Late in January 1849, even before Taylor took office, a caucus of southern senators and representatives, under the leadership of John Calhoun, after heated debate issued a "Southern Address" that charged the North with "acts of aggression" against southern rights. If the North did not moderate its position on fugitive slaves and territorial slavery, the address proclaimed to the South, "nothing would remain for you but to stand up immovably in defense of rights, involving your all—your property, prosperity, equality, liberty, and safety. . . ." At heart the address legitimated the need for southern separatism on the ground that the North was bent on demanding emancipation and racial equality. When Congress convened in December the House immediately became the theater of a struggle between southern Democrats and northern Whigs over the Speakership. Only after sixty-three ballotings and bitter threats on both sides was Democrat Howell Cobb of Georgia chosen over Whig Robert C. Winthrop of Massachusetts.

*   *   *

Three thousand miles to the west, something had happened that would affect all the calculations of the geometry of balance. Sutter's man James Marshall, boss of the mill, had looked into the stream and seen golden specks dancing amid the churning tailrace. Gold! Marshall rushed to Sutter, and soon the news was sweeping through the valley and out into the world.

Indians had often brought small quantities of gold dust to the Spanish missions in California, and white settlers in the early 1840s made two strikes that had aroused little excitement. But as the water coursed through the millrace near the Sacramento River, it led the way to a billion-dollar fortune. By midsummer of 1848, the U.S. military governor reported that "mills were lying idle, fields of wheat were open to cattle and horses, houses vacant, and farms going to waste" the entire length of the territory, as most of the population hurried to the gold fields. The prospectors pried nuggets from the ground with knives and picks, or built dams to uncover the grains of gold in the streambeds. They sifted heavy gold dust from the black river gravel with any tool from a pan to an elaborate wooden frame operated by several men. Word reached the East of yields of fifty or even a hundred dollars a day.

Easterners remained skeptical of the golden tales from California until December, when 230 ounces of almost pure metal arrived in Washington. Then newspapers, shipping lines, and thousands of citizens from every walk of life went wild. The gold seekers rushed to California by sea around Cape Horn, across Panama or Mexico by mule, over the Great Plains in wagons. More than 40,000 people arrived in 1849, with even more to follow in the succeeding years. In San Francisco Bay lay five hundred ships abandoned by their crews, while the sleepy village of San Francisco became a city of several thousand inhabitants in just a few months.

As adventurers from every state and a dozen nations scrambled to reap the golden harvest, law and order broke down. The white and Mexican Californians watched with anguish as the newcomers seized their lands, murdered and hanged one another, and trod over the local Indians in the race for gold. The territory needed government, and quickly. In August 1849 voters from each district met to choose delegates—lawyers, farmers, merchants, and a scattering of professional men—to a convention on state-hood. When they gathered in Monterey in September, the town had no hotels and some of the state-makers had to sleep under the open skies. The delegates' deliberations were brief and occasionally stormy. Everyone wanted the state capital to be located in his district; the Mexicans, remem-bering Frémont's Bear Flag revolt, objected to the inclusion of a bear on the state banner. Nonetheless, all agreed to a constitutional provision that "neither slavery nor involuntary servitude . . . shall ever be tolerated in this state."

The Californians' decision on slavery accelerated the conflict in Wash-ington. President Taylor urged Congress to admit California into the Union with its free-state constitution. Southerners bridled at the idea of admitting a free state without compensation to southern rights. Debates in the House and Senate raged over slavery extension. When Representa-tive Charles Allen, Massachusetts Free-Soiler, mocked the Southerners for their vain threats against the Union, asserting that "their united force could not remove one of the marble columns which support this Hall," H. W. Hilliard of Alabama rebuked him: "I say to him and to this whole House, that the *Union of these States is in great peril.*" He had never known such deep and settled feeling in the South, Hilliard added. If the North persisted in its threats to the South, "THIS UNION CANNOT STAND." The Northerners were accused of an act of aggression against the South. To many persons, North and South, the nation appeared on the verge of war.

By 1850 the great balances of the American system seemed to be collaps-ing. Constitution, parties, Congress, the presidency were no longer acting as resilient, stabilizing foundations for the flexible bonds of union. It was at this point of extreme crisis that two men who had embodied the spirit and calculus of compromise appeared on the scene for one last titanic effort.

Early on the evening of January 21, 1850, Henry Clay plodded through a Washington snowstorm to visit Daniel Webster in the latter's house. Clay had a bad cough; he was leaner now, an old man entering his mid-seven-ties, but he was as courtly and charming as ever, and although the visit was unexpected, the two rivals fell into an intense discussion. Clay had a plan —to gather all the issues dividing Congress into one omnibus package of conciliation that might unite it. Clay would admit California as a free state, compel Texas to relinquish its claim to New Mexico but reward it with federal assumption of Texas' unpaid debt, leave slavery untouched in the District of Columbia but abolish the slave trade in the District, enact a more effective fugitive-slave law, have Congress declare that it had no power to deal with the interstate slave trade, and, as for the rest of the territory acquired from Mexico, Clay would grant it territorial governments with no slavery provisions at all. For some time the two men talked—Clay lean and nervous, as a witness remembered, the play of emotion on his expressive face; Webster grave, intent, inscrutable. Encouraged by Webster's response, Clay began planning his speech to the Senate.

Eight days later, Clay presented his omnibus proposal to the Senate. The chamber was so jammed with people that the temperature rose to 100 degrees. He had witnessed many periods of anxiety and peril, he said, but he had "never before arisen to address any assembly so oppressed, so appalled, so anxious." Clay seemed almost like a death's-head, with his long, iron-gray hair, sunken cheeks, pinched nose, and black costume. Yet he was able to talk for three hours that day and the next, presenting his plan in detail and beseeching Congress to rise above its sectional animosities. He admitted that the omnibus proposal offered more to the South than the North; the richer and more powerful North could afford to be generous. His final words were to "conjure gentlemen . . . by all their love of liberty" and for posterity to draw back from the precipice, and he implored Heaven that if the Union should dissolve, "I may not survive to behold the sad and heart-rending spectacle."

Even the Great Pacificator's oratory seemed inadequate now. Senators still put their own sectional claims above union, and Congress soon again dissolved into a war of factions. Abolitionists in the North and proslavery extremists in the South were loudly calling for dissolution. Most moderate southern Whigs and northern Democrats favored Clay's plan, while northern Whigs stood by President Taylor in opposition. Jefferson Davis spoke for southern ultras: the South would yield nothing. On March 4 John Calhoun came to the Senate, though mortally ill. His speech had to be read for him, but the message came through strongly. If California should be admitted, it could only be "with the intention of destroying irretrievably the equilibrium between the two sections," and the South would be forced to leave the Union.

Three days later, Webster rose in a chamber even more oppressive and crowded than when Clay had spoken. Fashionable women sat in any available chair and gathered around the steps leading to the rostrum. The nation's notables were there: "Old Bullion" Benton, Clay, Lewis Cass, Davis, Stephen A. Douglas, and a flock of personages from the House. Webster thanked another senator who had yielded his place so that Webster could speak, and began:

"Mr. President, I wish to speak to-day, not as a Massachusetts man, nor

as a northern man, but as an American. . . . I speak to-day for the preservation of the Union. 'Hear me for my cause.' . . ." It was a long speech,
studded with historical allusions, references to increasing disunion such as
the rift within the Methodist Church, constitutional arguments. On occasion Calhoun feebly intervened, but for the most part, peering out of
cavernous eyes shrouded by a mass of snow-white hair, he sat in deathly
stillness. Webster's address was, in effect, a long historical essay, in which
he handed out praise and blame variously to South and North, like some
supreme arbiter. He ended on a personal note. What would happen if the
Constitution actually were overthrown? What states would secede? What
would remain American? Where would the flag remain? "What am I to be
—an American no longer?" He ended with poetry's tribute to his great
love, *Union:*

> Now, the broad shield complete, the artist crowned
> With his last hand, and poured the ocean round;
> In living silver seemed the waves to roll,
> And beat the buckler berge, and bound the whole.

If Congress were good theater, the marvelously conciliating speeches of
Clay and Webster and others would have come to an early climax in
dramatic confrontations as final votes were taken on the omnibus proposal.
But Congress was not good theater. Rather, through the complex, fractur-
ing effect of powerful committees, legislative procedures, and personages,
the omnibus was stripped apart and converted back into individual measures, which could be picked off in turn by shifting majorities. To make
matters worse for the Unionists, President Taylor, while supporting some
of the proposals individually, opposed Clay's omnibus compromise as
such. The proposals seemed headed for defeat when Taylor suddenly died
of cholera a few days after taking part in the festivities of a Fourth of July
celebration of the building of the Washington Monument. Eager to
strengthen his relationship with northern Whigs, Taylor had been willing
for Webster to be denounced by New Englanders as a traitor and moral
renegade for his compromising stand.

The new President was Millard Fillmore, a conciliatory fifty-year-old
New Yorker who had been pursuing a lackluster career as a state and
congressional politico when he was tapped to balance a presidential ticket
led by a southern soldier. Fillmore was more agreeable to the omnibus
proposals than Taylor. Unlike his predecessor, he was not expected to veto
a general compromise. By now Clay, tired and ailing, and Webster, newly
appointed as Fillmore's Secretary of State, were no longer the central
figures on the congressional stage. The measures had passed into the

hands of younger, more practical men who may have lacked the grand Union vision of a Clay or Webster but who knew how to bargain and maneuver, wheedle and pressure. The compromise that Clay and Webster, as supreme transactional leaders, had seen emerging from a carefully calculated geometry of balance, bringing sections and interests and ideologies into a stable and creative equilibrium, the new men saw as a matter of arithmetic, adding here, subtracting there, in a linear series of transactions. California admission, the fugitive-slave bill, and the other key measures went through in a rush in September 1850. The Great Compromise —tattered, battered, mutilated, but still a great compromise—was law.

Something of a lull followed. "There is rejoicing over the land; the bone of contention is removed; disunion, fanaticism, violence, insurrection are defeated," Philip Hone wrote in his diary. "The lovers of peace, the friends of the Union" had sacrificed sectional prejudices and prevailed. The presidential election of 1852 had little of the excitement and conflict of 1848. The Democrats nominated a party wheelhorse, Franklin Pierce of New Hampshire, the Whigs another general, sixty-six-year-old Winfield Scott. Both parties supported the Compromise of 1850 and opposed any further agitation of the fugitive-slave question. After a campaign in which neither candidate spoke out on controversial issues, Pierce won the election, carrying all but four states.

California cast four electoral votes for Pierce in 1852, a reminder that the United States now truly did span the continent. Californians celebrated their entry into the Union with cannonades. Those who hoped that order would follow statehood were cruelly disappointed. In California, liberty often came to mean license for the strong and unscrupulous to seize property or pleasure. The individual, reckless and self-confident, was supreme—until he was murdered, as were 4,200 whites and uncounted numbers of Indians during the 1850s.

John Sutter watched, helpless, as prospectors stripped his wheat fields for feed for their horses, thieves butchered and sold $60,000 worth of his cattle, and business agents swindled him out of vast sums. Finally, one summer evening, fire struck the Sacramento office that held his land grants and deeds. A fire bell in the night mocked Sutter's reliance on law.

Bitter debate in Washington; reckless individualism in California— would the flame burning in New England, kindled by a group of vigorous thinkers and writers, add to the heat of these other fires? Or would it light the way to a deeper understanding of the benefits—and the burdens—of liberty?

CHAPTER 14

The Culture of Liberty

"THERE was not a book, a speech, a conversation, or a thought" in Massachusetts from 1790 to 1830, Emerson noted with poetic license. During the second quarter of the nineteenth century, however, a potent alchemy of human forces transmuted the flinty soil of New England thought into a seedbed for intellectual and artistic growth. New England, after undergoing the struggles first of a military revolution and then of an industrial one, seemed to be heeding John Adams' admonition to himself: "I must study politics and war that my sons may have liberty to study mathematics and philosophy . . . geography, natural history and naval architecture, in order to give their children a right to study painting, poetry, music, architecture, statuary, tapestry and porcelain." At its height in the early 1850s the flowering of New England would bring forth Hawthorne's *The Scarlet Letter,* Melville's *Moby-Dick,* Thoreau's *Walden,* and other notable works.

Only a convergence of powerful forces could produce such a transformation. One was economic. The same mercantile and industrial development that had turned people's minds toward the shipyard and the counting-house had fostered a more diversified economy that in turn encouraged a more diversified culture, with room at its joints and in its interstices for dissent and experimentation. In particular, the ample fortunes of New England philanthropists, prodded by Puritan duty, made possible the founding of libraries, the patronage of artists, the endowment of academic chairs, the higher education of sons—and occasionally daughters—in painting, poetry, music, and other lively arts.

The maturing New England mind was seasoned and sharpened by conflict. Boston Federalists and their Whig descendants had thundered against the Jeffersons and Jacksons, the Van Burens and Polks, but the fiercest disputes arose over religious doctrine. Congregationalist Calvinism had long been wracked with disputes between conservative belief in literal scriptural and ecclesiastical authority, in the divinity of Jesus, in the depravity of man, and in revelation, as against an ethical-humanitarian Christianity that stressed the potential of individual reason as a guide to truth, the unity rather than the trinity of God, the individual as a source of reason and conscience, and the possibilities of the regeneration and even the perfectibility of man. For Bostonians this dispute had come to a head over a professorial appointment to the Hollis Chair of Divinity at Harvard in 1805. A pitched battle for support among the Harvard overseers had produced a narrow victory for the liberals and the appointment to the Harvard Divinity School of a string of Unitarian professors of theology. Outvoted, the conservative ministers seceded from Harvard and founded the Andover Theological Seminary, which proceeded to conduct genteel battle with the divinity school. Eloquent theologians reached far beyond their congregations to arouse students, businessmen, writers, and lawyers to higher doctrinal and political consciousness.

But affluence and conflict alone could not account for the flowering of the New England mind; rather they might have degraded or fractured it, save for one other decisive factor—the rise of an intellectual base, an institutional school that supported a system of collective intellectual and artistic leadership. This is what distinguished the collectivity of literary genius in the 1840s from the individual geniuses earlier in the century.

In that early period Washington Irving, growing up in New York City, found no literary companionship that might have lifted him above the level of his witty but superficial writing. Only in England and on the Continent, in Sir Walter Scott and lesser lights, did he find intellectual collegiality. After years abroad, he returned home a literary hero, but as Vernon Parrington wrote, he had "gently detached himself from contemporary America, and detached he remained to the end of a loitering life." Nor had James Fenimore Cooper found in New York a milieu that drew on his highest intellectual and artistic powers. Born of a rich, manorial family in rural New Jersey, Cooper moved from Mamaroneck to Cooperstown to Scarsdale and then to New York. In 1826, after four years in New York, he left with his family to travel and write in Europe. Later he returned, alienated from his compatriots, to conduct a long running war with his critics and detractors. Affronted by the frontier squalor of America, its bumptious manners, vulgar egalitarianism, debased press and politics, he lived out his days, intellectually and politically isolated, in Cooperstown. William Cullen Bryant was another intellectual semi-isolate. Reared in a small country town in the western Massachusetts mountain land, he had a year's education at Williams—then a college of four faculty members and a lean curriculum —before family penury forced him to give up higher education. In his early twenties he wrote a much-heralded poem—*Thanatopsis*—and, moving to New York, he soon emerged as the nation's leading poet of nature. Still, his poetic range was narrow and his poetic creativity limited, essentially of a "self-pollenizing nature," in Parrington's words.

Boston and Cambridge, on the other hand, provided a luxuriant bower for its creative men and women—a shelter against the hostile world, a place for mutual artistic communication, criticism, and stimulation, an array of support services. Boston was full of works by the architect Charles Bulfinch, who had built the first theater before the turn of the century, the elegant State House with its portico and dome, and the Athenaeum housing a superb private library. Boston had the Handel and Haydn Society, the Anthology Society, the Massachusetts Historical Society, a host of literary clubs, the magisterial *North American Review.*

Cambridge had Harvard and all that went with it. Many of the rising young literary figures had rubbed shoulders and crossed forensic swords in classes in the Yard. Cambridge was still a sedate country town where, it was said, on a quiet day one could hear the booming of guns from the Boston navy yard and the waves breaking on the ocean beaches a few miles away. Cambridge even had a small port on the Charles, where sloops deposited produce from the hinterland for Harvard tables and logs from the coast of Maine for Harvard fireplaces. Harvard had historians, moral philosophers, theologians, classicists. Above all it had great teachers who were intellectual leaders, acting as prods and mentors to a rising generation of literary geniuses.

The most colorful of these teachers was George Ticknor. The son of a wealthy Boston merchant who was himself a man of letters, the young Dartmouth graduate had toured the mideastern states and even visited Jefferson, and then in 1815—armed with letters of introduction from the sage of Monticello and accompanied by his friend Edward Everett—he left for Europe. There he met Byron, Chateaubriand, Goethe, Scott, Wordsworth, and a dozen other literary luminaries; he studied foreign languages assiduously. Appointed *in absentia* as the Smith Professor of Belles-Lettres at Harvard, he persuaded the college, on his return, to establish a program of modern languages and literature. At his stately Boston home overlooking the Common from Beacon Hill, Ticknor received students—including the daughters of his friends—in his huge library entered through a marble hall by a marble stairway. He displayed his literary opinions and his vast knowledge of the intellectual resources of Europe, and gave advice to aspiring students. Of equal stature to Ticknor was his traveling companion Edward Everett, who had been appointed to a Harvard chair of Greek literature even before he sailed, and in Europe received the first Ph.D. to be granted by Göttingen to an American. Back home, Everett came to edit the *North American Review,* even while he continued to hold his Harvard students spellbound. One of them was named Ralph Waldo Emerson.

But the greatest intellectual leader in Boston and Cambridge during this period was William Ellery Channing. A powerful intellect in behalf of Unitarianism, he had delivered an epochal sermon, "The Moral Argument against Calvinism," roundly attacking the notion that human nature was fundamentally depraved and incapable of progress and moral improvement. Channing was sensitive to the quiet but powerful revolutionary changes at work throughout the world. Experience must not be the only guide, he warned; men must also experiment. "There are seasons in human affairs of inward and outward revolution, when new depths seem to be broken up in the soul, when new wants are unfolded in multitudes and a new and undefined good is thirsted for. These are periods when the principles of experience need to be modified, when hope and trust and instinct claim a share with prudence in the guidance of affairs, when in truth to *dare* is the highest wisdom."

So all these forces—affluent and benevolent families, religious and philosophical collegiality and conflict—produced a culture in which literary fellowship and artistic creativity could thrive. There was one other powerful, though often invisible or unnoticed force—the existence of liberty both as a means and as an end. It was because liberty existed in Massachusetts, in the form of tolerance of dissent and of constitutional and judicial protection of political and religious liberty (save occasionally for abolitionists and other militants), that teachers could teach as they wished and students could argue. But liberty was more than a means, a process. In the form of a noble individualism, of the capacity of a person for self-fulfillment, liberty was the ultimate goal, the loftiest value.

It was because he saw in man "a great nature, the divine image, and vast capacities, that I demand for him means of self-development, spheres for free action—that I call society not to fetter, but to aid his growth," Channing said. But he saw eminently practical ways of teaching self-improvement along with preaching: learning to write good simple English, for example. One of his students, Oliver Wendell Holmes, would not forget

> Channing, with his bland, superior look,
> Cold as a moonbeam on a frozen brook,
> While the pale student, shivering in his shoes,
> Sees from his theme the turgid rhetoric ooze.

THE ENGINE IN THE VINEYARD

On a fall day in 1835, driving his chaise on dusty roads through groves of coloring maples and birches, Ralph Waldo Emerson brought his bride of one day from her house in Plymouth to their new home in Concord.

Together Waldo and Lydia Emerson—whom he renamed Lidian because it seemed more poetic—looked at the place where he would dwell for forty-seven years, she for another ten years after that. And their new neighbors looked at them—at Waldo, thin and tall, with his tomahawk nose, large, deep-seated eyes, thin curving lips—and at Lidian, not a beauty, all agreed, but refined and unaffected. He was in his thirty-third year, she in her thirty-fourth.

Their house stood half a mile east of Concord center, at the junction of the Cambridge Turnpike and Lexington Road, along which the stages ran to Boston. On these roads sixty years earlier British troops had marched, occupying Concord center before their repulse by Revolutionary guerrillas at the North Bridge a mile to the west. A few weeks before marrying Lidian, Emerson had bought their house from John Coolidge for $3,500. Soon the couple made it their own. Sitting by a curving window in their second-floor bedroom, Lidian could see their garden, with its grape arbor, pear trees, and flower beds. On the first floor Emerson established his study, lined with hundreds of books in freestanding shelves that could be readily carried out in case of fire. Emerson worked at a round table, in front of a fireplace of black Italian marble. Sitting in his rocking chair, he could revolve the table as he filled drawers with his journals. But his greatest joy was the garden, which led down to a brook and to low meadowlands that stretched toward Walden Pond, two miles away.

Emerson was at home in Concord. His grandfather, the Reverend William Emerson, descended from the first minister in Concord during the mid-1600s, had been a Revolutionary patriot and builder of the Old Manse near the center of town. Young Waldo, as he came to be called, had grown up in Boston, where his father—another William—had been minister of the First Church. Waldo's childhood had been scarred by frustration and tragedy. A mediocre, unsettled student, he lived in an aspiring family that set high demands on his scholarship and piety. He loved his rambles in Boston, picking up shells beside the wharves below Summer Street and exploring the North and South ends even at the expense of encountering bellicose Irish boys guarding their precincts, and he loved even more the trips to his ancestral home, where he explored the Concord River in the summer and followed the huge plodding ox teams clearing the snows of winter.

Life turned drear for the Emerson family when father William died and Waldo's mother was forced into a hard, peripatetic life of moving from place to place taking in boarders. Admitted to Harvard at the age of fourteen, Waldo had to scratch out a living tutoring even younger students, waiting on table at Commons, and serving as errand boy for President Kirkland of Harvard, beneath whose study he lived for a time. His work at Harvard was scattered and irregular until he came under the influence of Channing, Ticknor & Co., who were prime forces moving him, as he said later, "from the Unconscious to the Conscious; from the sleep of the Passions to their rage."

Graduated, Emerson still seemed unable to find himself. He taught at boys' and girls' schools, with little satisfaction, and attended divinity school in Cambridge, with less. He experienced rheumatic pains, serious loss of vision, lung troubles—psychosomatic perhaps, but no less painful for that. He traveled restlessly, preached evocatively, wrote feverishly—but could not find a center to his life. When the fetching girl he married at seventeen, Ellen Tucker, died of tuberculosis within seventeen months, he felt emptied of life. He quit the Unitarian ministry. By the time he remarried, a beloved brother was already dead of "consumption," another dying of it.

Somehow Emerson steadied himself. After traveling in Europe and meeting his heroes Coleridge, Carlyle, and Wordsworth, he resolved to break with his life in Boston and find the center of things in Concord. In the fall of 1834, a year before he brought his new wife to Concord, he and his mother had come there to board with grandfather Ezra Ripley in the Old Manse. In a corner room overlooking the river and the embattled bridge, under a great willow tree that tossed and "trumpeted" in the storms, he set himself to pulling together ideas gleaned from his musings, his travels, his readings—above all from his immersion in Kant, Swedenborg, Goethe, Coleridge, Carlyle. "Hail to the quiet fields of my fathers!" Emerson wrote in his diary. Moving across town to his new home, with Lidian and his mother, only brought him closer to the fields stretching toward Walden Pond. The result was *Nature,* a short book that became the clarion call for the small band of transcendentalists in Concord, Cambridge, and Boston.

Nature was, above all, a paean to Nature, the great organ through which the universal spirit speaks to the individual. If a man wishes not to be alone, stay not in his study but look at the stars; if a man would cast off his years, he must go to the woods, for in the woods, "we return to reason and faith." The moral influence of nature on every person is that amount of truth that it illustrates to him. The "Supreme Being does not build up nature around us, but puts it forth through us, as the life of the tree puts forth new branches and leaves through the pores of the old."

A powerful secondary theme forces its way through these beatitudes— the central role and thrust of *man.* The power to produce the delight of fields and woods does not reside in nature, but in man, "or in a harmony of both." The whole of nature is in fact a metaphor of the human mind.

Nature's dice are always loaded, but it also "offers all its kingdoms to man as the raw material which he may mould into what is useful" to man. "Who can set bounds to the possibilities of man?" Man, with access to the entire mind of the Creator, is himself the creator in the finite. Emerson's address "The Method of Nature" a few years later, panegyrized man, his talent, his genius. "O rich and various Man! thou palace of sight and sound, carrying in thy senses the morning and the night and the unfathomable galaxy; in thy brain, the geometry of the City of God; in thy heart, the bower of love and the realms of right and wrong. An individual man is a fruit which it cost all the foregoing ages to form and ripen. . . ."

As the years passed, Emerson forged his doctrine of man into a compelling doctrine of transcendental individualism. True divinity lay in the soul of a person. "Every man had his magnetic needle," as Van Wyck Brooks summed up his views, "which always pointed to his proper path, with more or less variation from other men's. He was never happy or strong until he found it, and he could only find it by trusting himself, by listening to the whisper of the voice within him." Emerson wrote on self-reliance: "Trust thyself: every heart vibrates to that iron string. . . . Society everywhere is in conspiracy against the manhood of every one of its members. . . . Whoso would be a man, must be a nonconformist. . . . Nothing is at last sacred but the integrity of your own mind. . . . Insist on yourself; never imitate." Within the divine whole of the universal, and in congruence with nature, each man was his own center, life-giving and life-receiving.

A circle of Transcendentalist thinkers formed around Emerson. The most unworldly of these was Amos Bronson Alcott. Born in a log cabin in Connecticut, meagerly educated, he went South to teach school but with little success. To Virginia planters, it was said, he owed a later courtliness of manner that never left him, and to North Carolina Quakers a faith in individual aspiration and transcendence that became the foundation of his life's work. Returning North, Bronson taught school in a number of towns; an inveterate reformer, he introduced children's libraries and the honor system, beautified the schoolrooms, and restricted the use of corporal punishment. In a Boston school he tried to draw rational ethical thoughts from his children instead of imposing doctrine on them. For these acts, and for his own extreme transcendental and mystical idealism, he attracted the wrath of Boston press and intelligentsia alike. His move to Concord in 1840, with his wife and growing family, brought him closer to Emerson, whom he both revered and criticized.

Equally controversial was the Transcendentalist Unitarian minister Theodore Parker. Grandson of the celebrated Captain John Parker who had fought the British at Lexington, young Theodore was largely self-taught in botany and astronomy until he walked to Harvard from Lexington, passed the entrance examination, and, too poor to enroll, was allowed to take the examinations. He had largely or wholly mastered twenty languages by the time he graduated from Harvard Divinity School in 1836, but he was denied their pulpits by certain Boston ministers because of his demand that "we worship, as Jesus did, with no mediator, with nothing between us and the father of all." Some of his sharpening social views, on slavery, war, divorce, education, and the like, made him as unpopular as did his call for a new creed of the perfection of God and the perfectibility of man.

The most remarkable member of the Transcendentalist circle was Margaret Fuller. Born in Cambridgeport near Boston, force-fed on Ovid at the age of eight, she came to be regarded by friends as a brilliant conversationalist, by a later Bostonian as "an unsexed version of Plato's Socrates"—and by all as a critic and rebel. For a course of "conversations" she brought together a large group of intellectual Boston women—"gorgeous pedants," Harriet Martineau called them—in Elizabeth Peabody's room in West Street. With Emerson and others she founded *The Dial,* the organ of the New England Transcendentalists, thus enlarging Emerson's circle even more. A passionate lover of women in general and in particular, Margaret Fuller brought out in 1844 *Woman in the Nineteenth Century,* in which she demanded sexual equality and spoke frankly about marriage, divorce, and physical passion, to the distress of Boston bluestockings. *The Dial* died in a few years, when she left Boston for New York.

All through the 1840s Emerson wrote, lectured, edited, corresponded —and as he developed in the fullness of his moral and intellectual powers, he gained fame throughout the United States—even in remote western towns—and Europe. His call for an enriching, fulfilling individualism lifted the hearts of his readers and listeners everywhere. Yet Emerson's popularity magnified the impact of the ambiguities and ambivalences in his moral philosophy. His faith in individual self-realization could easily be twisted, during a period of rising entrepreneurship, into a defense of ruthless, dog-eat-dog competitiveness. Like Jefferson earlier in the century, his doctrines could be expropriated by leftists, centrists, rightists, by believers in collective political action and by philosophical anarchists. He left open the question: Is man to be fulfilled only to liberate himself from government, the church, society, or is he to be fulfilled in order to help liberate others—women, slaves, immigrants, Indians—and not merely liberate but *help?*

Emerson would not be dismayed by his ambivalences. It was, after all, the seer of Concord who wrote, "A foolish consistency is the hobgoblin

of little minds, adored by little statesmen and philosophers and divines."
Still, it was disconcerting to some that the Panegyrist of Nature could
accept so exuberantly the impact of technology, especially the railroad.
Man "paves the road with iron bars," he rhapsodized, "and, mounting a
coach with a ship-load of men, animals, and merchandise behind him, he
darts through the country, from town to town, like an eagle or a swallow
through the air. . . ." He saw inventions as proof of man's power to impose
his will upon history. Yet, in the end, Emerson seemed ambivalent about
this too:

> 'Tis the day of the chattel,
> Web to weave, and corn to grind;
> Things are in the saddle,
> And ride mankind.
> There are two laws discrete,
> Not reconciled, —
> Law for man, and law for thing;
> The last builds town and fleet,
> But it runs wild,
> And doth the man unking.

*   *   *

As Henry Thoreau was sitting in his hut one summer afternoon, looking
out at Walden Pond, he could see hawks circling around his clearing,
pigeons darting about and perching restlessly on the boughs of the white
pines behind his hut, a fish hawk "dimpling" the glassy surface of the pond
and bringing up a fish, the sedge bending under the weight of the reed
birds as they flitted about. Here he could listen for sounds too, or remember them—the faint, sweet melody of the bells of Concord and Bedford,
the distant lowing of a cow, the whippoorwills "chanting their vespers,"
the *hoo hoo hoo, hoorer hoo* of owls, the trump of bullfrogs, the distant
rumbling of wagons over bridges.

Thoreau could hear something else too: the rattle of railroad cars about
a quarter mile away, and above the rattle the whistle of the locomotive,
"like the scream of a hawk."

In his rustic setting Thoreau pondered the sound of this railroad. He
used its causeway so often to go into town that the railroad workers would
"bow to me as to an old acquaintance," taking him for "an employee; and
so I am." The whistle informed him that restless city merchants were
coming into town, shouting their warning to get off the track.

"Here come your groceries, country; your rations, country-men! . . . And here's your pay for them! screams the country-man's whistle; timber like long battering rams going twenty miles an hour against the city's walls, and chairs enough to seat all the weary and heavy laden that dwell within them. With such huge and lumbering civility the country hands a chair to the city. All the Indian huckleberry hills are stripped, all the cranberry meadows are raked into the city. Up comes the cotton, down goes the woven cloth; up comes the silk, down goes the woolen; up come the books, but down goes the wit that writes them. . . ."

Thoreau cries out against the thundering "iron horse," the defiantly snorting "fire-steed," shaking the earth with his feet, breathing fire and smoke from his nostrils. Yet he is also enticed by it, as in the very use of the horse metaphor—by the engine's "steam cloud like a banner streaming behind in golden and silver wreaths," by the electrifying atmosphere of the depot, by the precision of the passing of the cars, so that farmers set their clocks by them. It almost seemed as if a new race was arising worthy of this technology. But in the end the man of Walden drew back. All these were arresting means—but to what ends? The steam clouds were rising higher and higher toward heaven—while the cars were going to Boston. If the pastoral life was being whirled away, he must "get off the track and let the cars go by"—

> What's the railroad to me?
> I never go to see
> Where it ends. . . .

Thoreau was not so much against tools as he was opposed to people becoming the "tools of their tools." Implicit in his essays and journals, in Max Lerner's summary, "is a devastating attack upon every dominant aspect of American life in its first flush of industrial advance—the factory system, the corporations, business enterprise, acquisitiveness, the vandalism of natural resources, the vested commercial and intellectual interests, the cry for expansion, the clannishness and theocratic smugness of New England society, the herd-mindedness of the people, the unthinking civic allegiance they paid to an opportunist and imperialist government." Thoreau did not pretend that technology could be stopped. "We have constructed a fate," he said of the railroad, "an *Atropos,* that never turns aside." Rather he would escape it.

The way in which he escaped it was audacious and, in the long run, enormously effective. He turned a retreat—his retreat to Walden—into a mighty intellectual advance. When Thoreau borrowed an ax late in March 1845, cut down some tall young white pines on Emerson's land at the edge of Walden Pond, bought the shanty of James Collins, an Irishman working on the railroad, for its boards, and put up his "tight shingled and plastered house, ten feet wide by fifteen long, and eight-feet posts, with a garret and a closet, a large window on each side, two trapdoors, one door at the end, and a brick fireplace opposite," as he described it, he wanted to embrace nature, to front only the essential facts of a simple existence, "to live deep and suck out all the marrow of life." But he wanted to do much more. He desired to conduct an "experiment in human ecology" that, if successful, he would publicize in every way he could—in his writings, in his travels, in his dramatic and unconventional behavior. And that is just what he did.

The Concord gentry muttered that the Walden Pond hermit was not that much of a hermit. He sometimes stayed with his mother in town, he often dined at the Emersons', he had a stream of visitors from the town and outside. He was eccentric; he could be seen gazing at clouds chasing clouds at two-thirty on a moonlit morning. Possibly he was dangerous; he had set off a woods fire by accident—or *was* it an accident? James Russell Lowell bluntly attacked Thoreau's claim to solitude and autonomy. The "experiment" presupposed, Lowell complained, "all that complicated civilization which it theoretically abjured. He squatted on another man's land; he borrows an axe; his boards, his nails, his bricks, his mortar, his books, his lamp, his fishhooks, his plough, his hoe, all turn state's evidence against him as an accomplice in the sin of that artificial civilization which rendered it possible that such a person as Henry D. Thoreau should exist at all." But this was to miss the point—that Thoreau was an artificer in dramatizing his rebellion against industrialism through his return to nature.

Thoreau had always been different, something of a rebel. He was Concord-born, to be sure, and of course went to Harvard, but on graduating in 1837 had returned to teach in the town school, only to shock parents by trying to instill discipline not through the ferule but through moral suasion. When a member of the school committee protested, Thoreau suddenly whipped several pupils—to dramatize the absurdity of whipping—and that evening quit the school. To Concord farmers, Thoreau, with his usually unkempt whiskers, large sloping nose, rough, weather-beaten face, rustic, ill-fitting dress coat, hardly looked like—well, like Emerson. Concord suspicions came to a pitch the day that Henry went to jail.

That act of civil disobedience was almost comical in nature but it became the stuff of legend, influencing even Tolstoi and Gandhi. He had "declared war on the State" by refusing to pay his poll tax. The "State" waited some years but finally, one day when Thoreau was on his way to the cobbler, the State in the person of neighbor Sam Staples, the jail keeper, led him to the lockup. A veiled woman—it turned out to be Thoreau's aunt, fearful that he might catch sight of her—rapped at the jail door and quietly paid the tax, but by that time Sam had got his boots off and was "sittin' by the fire, and I wasn't goin' to take the trouble to unlock after I got the boys all fixed for the night."

Thoreau had a pleasant and interesting night in jail, but the legends sprouted. The best of these was that Emerson came along and said, "Henry, what are you doing in *there?*" And Thoreau replied, "Waldo, what are *you* doing out *there?*"

By such symbolic acts—retreating to Walden, refusing to pay a tax— Thoreau would arouse men to consciousness of nature, of their place in nature, of the possibilities of a simple, natural existence and autonomy, of their capacity to take control of their lives, of their need for a spiritual awakening. And to arouse others to such consciousness, he had to arouse himself. Even the "economy" sustaining his life at Walden, like his withdrawal to nature, Sherman Paul observed, "was not an ultimate abdication from social life; it was only the means of the self-emancipation, which many, accepting social bondage as the inevitable condition of life, did not find necessary." *Walden,* rather than a renunciation of society, was an affirmation of social responsibility. After two years on the pond he returned to his parents' house, his experiment concluded.

He returned also—though he had never really left it—to the tight intellectual world of the Concord literati, and to the wider world of the town, almost as tight. Concord had its Lyceum, Social Library, its cracker-barrel philosophers, its temperance and antislavery societies. All the famous of Concord, including Emerson and Thoreau, lectured at the Lyceum, along with such visiting celebrities as Theodore Parker, Horace Greeley, and George Bancroft, the historian. But mostly the Concord greats talked to one another—and to themselves. They kept enormous diaries and journals, filled with profundities and trivia. They walked and dined with one another, criticized one another's work—Margaret Fuller actually rejected an essay of Thoreau's—and corresponded with one another during travels out of town. Thoreau's relationship with Emerson, half disciple, half critic, continued to be close. Under an oak on the riverbank, Thoreau read Emerson chapters from a new work, "Excursions on Concord & Merrimack Rivers." Emerson found the work invigorating, broad and deep, "pastoral as Isaak Walton, spicy as flagroot."

Thoreau stayed at the Emersons' after Walden, occupying a small room at the head of the stairs. A young writer named Nathaniel Hawthorne resided in the Manse with his bride. Bronson Alcott, with a houseful of lively and restless daughters, lived down the street. Margaret Fuller was in and out of town. Emerson liked having literary guests, provided they did not interrupt his inviolate mornings, when he wrote. He pleaded with a younger friend to visit him. "I cannot communicate with you across seventeen miles of woods and cornfields."

*   *   *

A year or so before Thoreau at Walden had heard the locomotive's whistle like a hawk's scream, Nathaniel Hawthorne had walked out to Concord woods not far away called "Sleepy Hollow." In his notebook he recorded meticulously what he could observe around him—a thriving field of Indian corn, a pathway "strewn over with little bits of dry twigs and decayed branches," the sunshine glimmering through shadow and the shadow effacing sunshine. His ear was alert to rustic sounds too—mowers whetting their scythes, the village clock striking, a cowbell tinkling. "But hark! there is the whistle of the locomotive—the long shriek, harsh. . . ."

An eerie presaging of Thoreau's experience—yet Hawthorne's reaction was different from his friend's. The whistle, he wrote, "tells a story of busy men, citizens from the hot street, who have come to spend a day in a country village; men of business. . . ." Hawthorne seemed to welcome the "startling shriek . . . in the midst of our slumbrous peace." His reaction to such events would usually be different from Thoreau's and Emerson's. His background was different.

Hawthorne was born not in Boston or Cambridge or Concord but in Salem, and he attended not Harvard but Bowdoin. Like Emerson, he grew up in a bereaved family—his father, a shipmaster, had died of yellow fever on a distant trip—but unlike Emerson, in a depressed city stricken by the embargo and by the War of 1812. With his mother immobilized for years in her bedroom, Hawthorne lived for a time amid a "cursed" solitude. He had ample leisure to explore the port, with its old wharves and custom house, its drays and longboats smelling of tarred ropes and briny bilge water, its decaying, often deserted mansions behind. Salem was already an old town, full of ghosts and legends from the days "of the magistrates who awoke each morning to the prospect of cropping an ear or slitting a nostril, stripping and whipping a woman at the tail of a cart, or giving her a stout hemp necklace or a brooch in the form of a scarlet letter," Van Wyck Brooks wrote. Young Hawthorne could ignore none of this: his great-great-grandfather had been a judge at the witchcraft trials. Out of the shadowy world of Salem, Hawthorne later formed his most powerful novel, *The Scarlet Letter.*

After years of solitary writing in Salem and restless travel, Hawthorne managed to land a job in the Boston Custom House and then, hoping to work close to nature but in an orderly, creative environment, he joined the Brook Farm community, the experiment in communal life in Roxbury.

Hawthorne had come to know the celebrated Peabody sisters, who had ancestral roots in Salem—Elizabeth, variously friend and aide to Channing and Alcott and the painter Washington Allston; Mary, engaged to Horace Mann; and the witty, artistic, charming linguist, Sophia, who became Nathaniel's love. He married her and took her to live in Concord. There followed doubtless the happiest years of his life but Hawthorne, still restless and searching, and badgered by landlord and creditors, moved his family back to Salem, where he took a job in the custom house there. Here he wrote about Hester Prynne and the Reverend Arthur Dimmesdale and Roger Chillingworth, about sin and guilt and justice, in the novel that made him famous. But Salem and success were not enough—or perhaps too much. Soon he moved to Lenox in the Berkshires, where he wrote *The House of the Seven Gables* and came to know Herman Melville, who was working nearby on a long, philosophical saga about a great white whale.

Hawthorne played up the pastoral theme of Emerson and Thoreau, but he went beyond it. He had been captivated, in a trip to the Berkshires in 1838, by the factory life of North Adams—by the mills, "supremely artificial establishments, in the midst of such wild scenery," by the mill girls looking out at Greylock, the northern crown of the Berkshires, while the machinery whizzed behind them, by the factory steam engine "supposed to possess a malignant spirit," that catches a man's arm and pulls it off, or catches a girl by the hair and scalps her. The story Hawthorne wrote years later, "Ethan Brand," pitted against the pastoral and mountain landscape an engine of a different sort—the fiery kilns on Greylock that converted white marble into lime.

But Hawthorne was pursuing here another, even more powerful dualism —the individual in society, individual self-realization amid collective aspiration, brotherhood versus ambition and alienation—ultimately, individual liberty in an increasingly industrialized, interdependent culture. The people in "Ethan Brand" were lonely, isolated people: the rude lime burner and his son, the alcoholic doctor, the ex-lawyer whose hand had been "torn away by the devilish grip of a steam-engine," a shabby old man desperately looking for his runaway daughter, a Wandering Jew—and Ethan Brand himself, a former lime burner who had once loved both man and nature. After communing with a satanic figure that lurked in the lurid blaze of his kiln, Brand went forth to discover the nature of the Unpardonable Sin, and in the quest he became an educated man, an intellectual, indeed a world-renowned scholar. But in that quest too he lost his sense of brotherhood, his sympathy for mankind, his "hold of the magnetic chain of humanity." Rather he became an ambitious, manipulative man, converting people into his puppets and coldly corrupting them, looking on them as merely "the subject of his experiment."

And that—cutting himself off from humanity—was the Unpardonable Sin.

*　　*　　*

In a week or so, Herman Melville wrote Hawthorne in June 1851, he would go to New York, "to bury myself in a third-story room and slave on my 'Whale' while it is driving through the press. . . .

"By the way," Melville continued, "in the last 'Dollar Magazine' I read 'The Unpardonable Sin.' He was a sad fellow, that Ethan Brand. . . ." As he wrote, Melville seemed to be connecting Hawthorne's themes to his own. There was a "frightful poetical creed that the cultivation of the brain eats out the heart. . . . I stand for the heart. To the dogs with the head. . . . The reason the mass of men fear God, and *at bottom dislike him,* is because they rather distrust His heart, and fancy Him all brain like a watch. . . ."

Melville scribbled on. In reading some of Goethe's sayings, "so worshipped by his votaries," he had come across this: *"Live in the all."* Get out of yourself, Goethe was saying, spread and expand yourself, reach out to the flowers and woods, etc. "What nonsense!" Melville exploded. "Here is a fellow with a raging toothache. 'My dear boy,' Goethe says to him, 'you are sorely afflicted with that tooth; but you must *live in the all,* and then you will be happy!' " Melville went on: "As with all great genius, there is an immense deal of flummery in Goethe, and in proportion to my own contact with him, a monstrous deal of it in me." Melville added teasingly: "P.S. 'Amen!' saith Hawthorne."

The man Hawthorne had come to know in Pittsfield and Tanglewood cut a different figure from the literary types of Salem and Concord. Born in New York in 1819, almost a generation behind Emerson and Hawthorne, into a distinguished but impecunious family, left without a father at twelve but with a mother who, he said, hated him, young Melville quit school at fifteen and knocked about in various jobs until he went to sea. His hard, daunting life on the *Acushnet* as a whaleman, followed by an idyll in the South Seas, left him with material for his feverish storytelling, and with an outlook both romantic and skeptic.

A number of specific and general themes run through Melville's work: alienation of man from his life and work; authority, on a warship, at least, as a system of "cruel cogs and wheels" systematically grinding people up in one common hopper; existence as an ordinary seaman in a disciplined, totalitarian unit; the tendency of the Age of Machinery to transform men into objects; the rise of expansionist capitalism in an underdeveloped country. But the most significant theme was the role and rights of the individual in an increasingly technological, industrial, urban, and collective society. For Melville was inquiring, Q. D. Leavis has said, "what alternatives are available which allow one to combine some kind of social life with self-respect once one has perceived—as is essential—how fraudulent all relations and institutions generally are." Or, in Leo Marx's words, in the end in *Moby-Dick* as in *Walden,* the American hero is either dead or wholly alienated from society.

Ultimately the fame of Emerson and Thoreau, of Hawthorne and Melville, would come to turn on the manner in which they wrestled with transcending philosophical dualisms and ambivalences—good and evil, freedom and fate, order and change, technology and nature, "civilization" and "savagery," guilt and innocence, appearance and reality, as well as the individual in society. They resolved none of these questions, but they posed them so dramatically, through such compelling essays and stories, as to bring their fellow Americans to a higher consciousness of the supreme moral and political choices facing them.

But those Americans—including the other writers who aped or criticized or ignored the celebrated authors—were not passive receptacles. Some of these moral and political issues reached straight to their physical and spiritual needs and others did not. Events too would be in the saddle, as domestic and foreign crises forced Americans to make choices. Those needs and those crises would make the general issue of individualism in society, of liberty under government, the central issue for the 1850s. The narrow issue would be the relationship of liberty and equality. Thousands of educators and editors and ministers, having read about Walden Pond and Brook Farm, about Hester and Ahab and (later) Billy Budd, would have to make their own moral judgments and political decisions in the days to come.

Still, on the central, perplexing issues of liberty, the celebrated writers of the day left a legacy of intellectual leadership that was as ambiguous in content as it was evocative in tone. Emerson's individualism could be defined as an enriching self-fulfillment or as the liberty to climb over the backs of others to embrace the bitch-goddess success. Thoreau's retreat to Walden could be seen as an effort to achieve a creative autonomy or as a device to deny his dependency on—and evade his responsibility to—the wider community. Hawthorne viewed the pursuit of self-interest as fundamental in human character but inadequate as the moral foundation of a stable community; on the other hand, reformers' attempts to replace competition and social distinction with harmony and communal equality could end up doing more harm than good. These literary men had ambivalent feelings toward the railroads and factories, the authority and the discipline, that came with the Age of Machinery and would have colossal influence in both narrowing and broadening people's liberties. Thus the literary culture of liberty gave out mixed signals to people trying to find the elusive border lines between individual freedom and communal needs.

RELIGION: FREE EXERCISE

A church somewhere in the "burned over" area of western New York, 1830. Charles G. Finney is preaching. His voice thunders; his great eyes seem to burn into the very souls of the hundreds watching him. He seems to be speaking to each and all directly, personally, assuring them that salvation is possible for all, not just for the limited elect; if they repent and embrace the Lord they could escape the terrible guilt and awful consequences of sin. Near Finney stands his famous "anxious seat," waiting for sinners ready to undergo conversion. As Finney rises to a passionate climax, his tall body straight and erect and his great arms outflung in the image of the cross—and had not Finney's life been threatened too?—people are crying out, bursting into tears, fainting, falling into trances.

While the pundits and philosophers of Concord and Boston were reaching thousands of persons through the printed word, the parsons and preachers of trans-Appalachia were attracting tens of thousands of persons through the spoken. New York's "burned over" district was so called because it had been so often kindled and rekindled by flaming revivalists. Easterners viewed western religion with hope and dismay. Many of their own sons—Finney for one—had migrated west. As wave after wave of settlers swept beyond the Appalachian frontier, eastern ministers had called for missionaries to take the gospel to them. Society there, Theodore Dwight Bozeman noted, was " 'in its forming state,' lacking moral ligaments, susceptible to rank growths of 'wild fanaticism,' and painfully needing lessons in the security and quiet of good community."

Reverend Timothy Dwight, president of Yale College, saw only three types of people on the frontier as he traveled through upstate New York in 1810: hunters and trappers "impatient of the restraints of law, religion, and morality; farmers who worked the land for a while and then moved on; and permanent settlers who stayed to prosper on the land." Only the last group, wrote Dwight, were God-fearing, and they lacked pastors to guide them. The churches must sponsor religious missions to "soften and humanize" the hearts of western settlers and win them back to religion.

Easterners were used to the flowing and ebbing of worship. There had been a "very wintry season" for religion everywhere in America after the Revolution. Ninety percent of the people lay outside the churches. Political events eclipsed religion, as people concentrated on establishing the new nation and winning the War of 1812. The outstanding men of the country such as Jefferson, Madison, and Monroe were statesmen, not ministers. Embracing the rationalism and deism of the Enlightenment, the Founding Fathers instituted religious freedom and welcomed conflict among the churches as a positive good—as the way to differentiate truth from error.

Democratic ideals of the Revolution shaped religion. Nowhere else in the world, Protestants felt, did they enjoy the freedoms they had in America after the Revolutionary War—freedoms guaranteed in the Constitution. The First Amendment put first among its list of liberties: "Congress shall make no law respecting an establishment of religion, or prohibiting the free exercise thereof." Article VI of the Constitution prohibited religious tests "as a Qualification to any Office." Revolutionary political beliefs had made state control of religion unacceptable, and the growing number of denominations made legal establishment of churches impossible. Earlier the churches had looked to the state for legal support in a wild and open land. When the Constitution separated church and state, choice of religion became an individual one. There seemed to be a price: With voluntary associations and denominations, and no exclusive national church, church attendance—even inherited membership—seemed to weaken as people moved to the frontier. Some feared that liberty had fatally impaired religion.

On the moving frontiers, each minister worked far from the power and status of his church; as civilization followed, ministers could join into Presbyteries, Ministeriums, Conventions, or Conferences. Ministers in America were persuasive and political. As Tocqueville learned, everywhere "you meet with a politician where you expected to find a priest." Ministers in the colonial period had looked to the state for financial as well as legal underpinning, but as state after state disestablished the churches and withdrew funds for support, it seemed to many ecclesiasts such as Timothy Dwight that religion had suffered another hard blow. The laity provided a minister with support and a salary, but, according to Dwight, "a voluntary contribution, except in a large town, is as uncertain as the wind; and a chameleon only can expect to derive a permanent support from this source."

As settlers cut themselves off from family roots and familiar surroundings to move to the frontier, they needed all the more a religious faith that could move with them and fortify them for their harsh battles with an unforgiving wilderness. Religion, by preparing people for another world, could make the troubles and hardships of the present one less burdensome. The churches were the key to neighborhood stability, ordered family life, and the education of children on the frontier, defenses against instability and indiscipline in an unsettled land.

Religion served as solace and security in the East too. Mill workers found it easier to work their twelve-hour shifts, the ministry believed, if they looked to religion for comfort. Factory owners erected churches in the mill towns, making Sunday attendance compulsory for their hands in the belief that churchgoing conveyed spiritual comfort—and greater stability in the work force. With the rise of the plantation system, many a slave owner brought religious worship to his slaves—religious worship that counseled obedience to the master, for a slave's obedience would mean entrance to heaven, that other world which promised to be so much better than the present one.

In 1800, Congregationalists, Presbyterians, Anglicans, Baptists, and Methodists were all established denominations, but the largest and most powerful were the first two. Between them, Congregationalists and Presbyterians controlled half the total number of congregations in America. They had founded, or helped to found, six of nine colonial colleges. Their assertive ministers—men such as Timothy Dwight—supported order against universal manhood suffrage, labor unions, poor relief, public education, western disorder, and other facets of liberty and equality. They retained the strict Calvinism of the Puritans, teaching that humanity, sinful by nature since Adam's fall, was inescapably predestined to eternal damnation. The death of Jesus Christ made atonement for sins and admission to heaven a free act of God's sovereign grace, but only for a limited few who underwent a transforming "election experience" and maintained a consistent life afterwards. To Congregationalists, Presbyterians, Methodists, and Baptists, this election experience, "being born again," was the greater part of religious life, more important than good deeds or sacraments. These churches, gathered around the elect, carried the name "evangelical."

Religious teachings and methods had to change before they could appeal to the frontier men and women who often disdained church hierarchies, formal worship services, and an intellectual clergy. Yet settlers on the frontier yearned for the stability, community, and comfort of religion. Presbyterians were the first Protestants to minister to western settlers, sending missionaries to the West during the French and Indian War of 1756. To bring people together from scattered settlements to listen to ministers, Presbyterians created the camp meeting. Two Presbyterian ministers, James McGready and Barton W. Stone, organized the famous Cane Ridge Revival in Kentucky.

It was the apogee of the Great Revival at the turn of the century—ten to twenty thousand people gathering in Bourbon County to hear dozens of preachers—Presbyterian, Baptist, and Methodist—all speaking together from platforms, wagons, stumps, and logs. Between one and three thousand people were "brought to the ground," or experienced conversion, at Cane Ridge. Kentucky ministers carried the revival message and camp meeting method to the Western Reserve, where Baptists and Methodists, but not Presbyterians, drew the most converts from the Awakening.

The Presbyterians fell behind in the struggle to save souls on the frontier, but came to scorn the extreme emotionalism of the western revivals. Although the first to use the camp meeting, they required a trained and educated ministry and a rigid presbyterial polity. The presbyterial governance took disciplinary measures against ministers who led emotional meetings, and in 1837–38 Presbyterians split into Old School, or consistent Calvinists who clung to the doctrine of limited election, and New School, or Arminians who challenged the Old School on election and free will. Between 1834 and 1836, the church lost 27,000 members. Its influence, however, remained greater than its membership, for it appealed to the rising industrial and commercial classes.

Methodists and Baptists preached salvation for all. God would grant salvation if persons repented and pledged their lives to service. This emphasis on voluntary individual choice appealed to the independent frontiersmen, and found its most concrete and dramatic form in the revival, designed to stir sinners to repentance. The Methodists and Baptists had begun in America as dissenting churches, never enjoying state support. With clergy and workers from the frontier folk—Methodists employed itinerant ministers—they grew with the country.

The most visible churchman was the circuit rider. Of all the religious men on the frontier, he was among the best known and the best loved. With his wide-brimmed light fur hat, high collar, long waistcoat, short breeches, and stockings, he could be spotted a mile away as he galloped on horseback to cabins on his hundred-mile circuit. Each rider carried the Bible and Wesley's *Sermons,* which he might read as he rode. Priding himself on being a graduate of "Brush College," the school of practical experience, a rider boasted of knowing all the forests and streams of his area so that he could reach his destination on time. For four years, the devoted preacher had to ride his circuit, spreading the gospel and ministering to the people as he preached every day in the week, twice on Saturday, and twice on Sunday. The presiding elder kept track of the rider's punctuality, for a crowd might be waiting, a crowd that would not return if a rider were late.

During the "harvest time of Methodism," 1820, circuit riders held one thousand camp meetings throughout the country. Multitudes, trying to escape the loneliness of the frontier, would gather to sit on planks laid across tree stumps at the meeting place. Bonfires illuminated the night as visiting clergy preached. "The uncertain light upon the tremulous foliage . . . the solemn chanting of hymns swelling and falling in the night wind; the impassioned exhortations" were not the reasoned, written sermons of the eastern ministers but electrifying appeals to people with deep spiritual needs.

Baptists recruited local persons as clergy to reach frontier people, in the form of farmer-preachers who had "received the call" and been "raised up" by their churches with a license to preach. The Council of Brethren would then examine a preacher and ordain him by prayer. The preachers were unpaid, self-supporting, and mobile, able to move with their congregations to new areas or back into the unchurched older areas without financial support or direction except from the Baptist regional associations. The principal difference from Methodism was the adherence to baptism by immersion, but frontier preachers debated election, grace, and free will, at times widening the difference between denominations.

Peter Cartwright, a famous Methodist circuit rider, ministered to Methodist and Baptist frontier people. Cartwright had grown up in the wilds of Logan County, Kentucky. Though his mother was a devout Methodist, he had loved horse racing, card-playing, and dancing until his conversion at a camp meeting. Soon after receiving an exhorter's license at age seventeen, he became a traveling preacher, riding the Red River Circuit in Kentucky, the Waynesville Circuit in Tennessee, the Salt River and Shelbyville Circuit in Indiana, and the Scioto Circuit in Ohio. He continued in Kentucky and Tennessee until 1824, when he requested the Sangamon Circuit in Illinois, owing to his hatred of slavery. During his fifty years of preaching Methodism against rival sects, he was forty-five years a presiding elder, twice a member of the Illinois legislature, and in 1846 ran for the United States Congress against Abraham Lincoln on the issue of Lincoln's "infidelism."

Cartwright wrote in his autobiography of the time he was to preach in an old Baptist church. "When I came," Cartwright remembered, "there was a very large congregation. While I was preaching, the power of God fell on the assembly, and there was an awful shaking among the dry bones. Several fell to the floor and cried for mercy. . . . I believe if I had opened the doors of the Church then, all of them would have joined the Methodist Church." But Cartwright had to ride on, and the Baptists sent three preachers to the place to retrieve Cartwright's twenty-three converts. "For fear these preachers would run my converts into the water before I could come round," the Methodists summoned Cartwright to return. He presented himself to the Baptist preacher for membership. "At the last moment, however, in the hearing of all, he declared that he still believed in infant sprinkling, forcing the Baptist minister to reject him. At the sight of his rejection, his twenty-three converts returned to the Methodist fold." Theological controversy ran deep on the frontier.

Evangelical Protestantism grew so strong on the frontier that by 1850 it was the national religion, claiming 4 million of a population of 27 million. The Methodists, with 1,324,000 members, were the largest denomination; the Baptists were second, with 815,000 members in primarily rural and southern areas—the ten most populous Baptist states were slave states in 1854. Presbyterians were third with 487,000 members; Congregationalists fourth with 197,000; Lutherans fifth with 163,000. In 1800, one of every fifteen Americans belonged to a church; by 1850, one of every six.

New England experienced a Second Great Awakening, in the form of revivals, renewed spiritual seriousness, and new efforts at moral reformation. Settled ministers, not itinerants as on the frontier, conducted sober revivals before middle- and upper-class congregations. The region continued to produce brilliant ministerial leadership. Timothy Dwight, grandson of Jonathan Edwards, the New England divine who had begun the first Great Awakening, served as president of Yale College from 1795 until 1817 and won Yale over from rationalism to Calvinism. As a student he had tutored at Yale and had devoted himself to the dignified asceticism of the earlier Puritan ministers, eating only two mouthfuls of food at dinner, sleeping on the floor, studying long hours each day. His harsh regimen may have contributed to his almost total loss of eyesight. For even this he was thankful, saying it helped him develop the powers of observation he used to describe the people and country in his *Travels in New England and New York,* and also caused him to shift emphasis in his lectures to Yale students from doctrine and scholarship to pastoral care. There is a certainty man will sin, Dwight preached, but he has the power not to. He asked for a simple yes-or-no conversion decision from his students, managing to convert over one-third of Yale students to a religious life.

Dwight's students carried the idea of revivals to their own churches. Nathaniel Taylor and Lyman Beecher, Dwight's most famous students, and others led a Calvinistic revivalism in the Congregational colleges of New England. Their teachings had political implications, as they sought to preserve religion and morality against the threat they perceived in Jeffersonian Republicanism and the popular-democratic, egalitarian tendencies it embodied. Any change in the social order, according to Dwight, had to begin with the moral reform of the individual. He had founded what came to be called the New Haven theology to make Calvinism more approachable to those well versed in Christianity. Salvation, as Calvinism had stressed, was for the few.

Such doctrines had little appeal to urban workers, many of whom were Roman Catholic immigrants from Ireland. Catholics had numbered only about 25,000 at the time of the Revolutionary War. By 1850, the Roman Catholic Church in America numbered 1,750,000 adherents—preponderantly Irish, collected mainly in the great eastern cities, as the Irish, ravaged by land enclosure and the potato famine at home, emigrated to the United States.

Even Catholicism fragmented in the pluralistic American environment. In the early national period, the hierarchy of the Church was largely French owing to the influx of priests fleeing the French Revolution. The cultured, aristocratic French clerics distrusted the poor Irish immigrants who began to swell their congregations, and the Irish communicants liked French priests no better. They wanted their own clergy. Roman Catholic churches had followed the earlier Protestant model of putting parochial affairs—title to church property—under the control of the laity; Catholics felt they should also select their spiritual leaders. Rome refused to allow this "trusteeism," but the Irish did not force the issue; their priests began to replace French clergy, in any case, as a consequence of their numbers. The hierarchy of the Church was a path of advancement to the ambitious Irish immigrant, with many an Irish man becoming a priest and many an Irish woman a nun.

Roman Catholics found religious freedom but not toleration in America. Native groups pressed them to assimilate, to abandon their alleged allegiance to a foreign potentate, even to renounce their Catholicism itself. In particular, the Irish immigrants—numerous, visible, filling the boardinghouses and tenements of the great eastern cities—were vulnerable to Protestant hoodlums. In 1831, a mob burned down St. Mary's Catholic Church in New York City, and two years later another group attacked the Ursuline Convent in Charlestown, Massachusetts. The convent included a popular school run by cultured Ursuline nuns that had attracted the daughters of a number of wealthy Protestant families, particularly Unitarians rebelling against the rigid Congregationalism of the public school system. The popularity of the Ursuline school had angered the orthodox ministers of Boston, especially Lyman Beecher, pastor of Hanover Street Church, who directed such fiery sermons against Catholics that his church became known as the Brimstone Corner.

After a rumor circulated in Boston newspapers that a nun had tried to escape from the convent and been detained against her will, Beecher delivered three violently anti-Catholic sermons in three churches in Boston. Other clergy followed his lead. Next day a mob stormed the imposing brick convent school on Ploughed Hill in Charlestown and set it on fire. The following night the mob returned to burn fences and trees around the school. Troops were called in to prevent an assault on the nearby Catholic church.

Rioting against Catholics broke out in Philadelphia in 1844, leaving thirteen persons killed, many injured, a Catholic seminary, two churches, and blocks of Catholic homes in ruins. Outbursts continued into the 1850s; mobs killed ten men in St. Louis, Missouri, and one hundred Catholics on "Bloody Monday" in Louisville, Kentucky. The Know-Nothing political party was forming to oppose what they saw as the rise of Catholic influence in the schools and in politics.

Bigotry found other targets besides Catholicism. From the day that Joseph Smith, a moody teenager, told the clergy in his western New York town that he had seen a vision in the nearby woods, and had been instructed to join no church but wait for the fullness of the gospel to be revealed to him, he was treated with harsh words. In 1830 he established his own church with six members and published *The Book of Mormon,* reportedly drawn from golden tablets revealed to him from on high. As the little band slowly expanded amid the fast-changing, booming economy of the Erie Canal area, it aroused hatred for its doctrines and for its alien practices—baptism of the dead, marriage for eternity, rule by an ecclesiastical oligarchy, and above all its rumored polygamy. Moving to Kirtland, Ohio, and then to Missouri, the Mormons could not escape from persecution. The governor of Missouri announced that they must be treated as enemies and either driven from the state or exterminated. Now numbering 12,000 souls, the Mormons moved to Nauvoo, Illinois, where they built a large Mormon temple, mills, foundries, power and navigation dams, community farms, even hotels. Here Smith ruled grandly, and apparently took unto himself (though secretly) a number of wives. But his virile leadership began to deteriorate into megalomania, and when his private army destroyed the offices of a newspaper critical of the sect, he and his brother were thrown into a Carthage jail, surrounded by a mob, and shot dead. A year later a mob of 1,500 armed ruffians besieged Nauvoo and killed Mormons and non-Mormons alike. The surviving Mormons, now under the leadership of Brigham Young, fled as Illinois frontiersmen occupied and looted the ruined town. Young, who had grown up in western New York among the fiery revivals of the Methodists and then converted to Mormonism, organized the survivors for the long trek west to Utah. Only in this final chosen land did the Mormons find some refuge from religious hatred.

Clearly there were sharp limits to American tolerance of religious diversity, and boundaries to the effective reach of the First Amendment. Protestants beset Catholics; Methodists persecuted Mormons; the head of the Mormons assaulted an opposing newspaper; Protestant sects "stole" members from one another. Yet the vast number of Americans who attended church and camp meeting did so without harassment. The various sects seemed indeed to thrive amid competition—a competition, Sidney Mead wrote, "that helped to generate the tremendous energies, heroic sacrifices, great devotion to the cause, and a kind of stubborn, plodding work under great handicaps, that transformed the religious complexion of the nation." Such competition could thrive only in an environment of liberty.

There was as well a latent but powerful strand of egalitarianism in American Protestantism. By the 1830s and the 1840s this moral tradition was confronting slavery more and more directly. Theodore Weld, a zealous convert of Charles Finney's, had traveled to Ohio in 1829 as an agent of the Society for Promoting Manual Labor in Literary Institutions, looking for a site to build a western manual labor theological seminary. The place chosen in southern Ohio was Cincinnati, where the society established Lane Seminary and called as its first president Lyman Beecher.

While Beecher was absent on a fund-raising tour in 1834, several Lane students, led by Weld, conducted an antislavery revival meeting to debate immediate abolition or colonization. The decision was for emancipation. When Beecher returned to find the trustees angered over the meetings, he dissolved the antislavery society, and Lane rebels withdrew in 1835 to found Oberlin College. Charles G. Finney was its first professor of theology and later president. Weld's band of followers also founded the Ohio State Abolition Society and determined to "burn down by backfires the city." So aroused was the populace by revival meetings against slavery that within one year the Ohio State Abolition Society swelled to 15,000.

If to many church members slavery was a sin and an evil, for others abolitionism was worse. The issue began to divide churches into northern and southern wings, although the Roman Catholic Church stood largely aloof from the controversy. The main plank in the abolitionists' platform asserted that slaveholding and even allowing slavery to persist were sins. "Faith Without Works Is Dead," preached Weld, as abolitionists began to call more and more for action, for immediate repentance and immediate freedom for the slave. The Quaker poet John Greenleaf Whittier spoke for many church members when he wrote: "We do not talk of gradual abolition, because, as Christians, we find no authority for advocating a gradual relinquishment of sin. We say to slaveholders—Repent Now—today—Immediately; just as we say to the intemperate—'Break off from your vice at once—touch not—taste not—handle not—from henceforth forever . . .' Such is our doctrine of immediate emancipation. A doctrine founded on God's eternal Truth—plain, simple and perfect."

Schools: The "Temples of Freedom"

The cultural change that touched and transformed most Americans in the first half of the nineteenth century was the emergence of a common, uniform, public school system. Two paradoxes marked this transforming change. It was an experiment in pure socialism, if socialism is defined as governmental ownership of certain facilities, and governmental hiring and firing of persons employed in those facilities, in order to carry out purposes of the state. The government was taking over not an impersonal service like a communications or transportation system, but the education of innocent and vulnerable children handed over by their parents to the tender mercies of Leviathan. In an era before socialism became an ideological issue within and among nations, this particular socialist experiment was conducted in other guises and for other purposes.

But what purposes? Herein lies a second paradox. The political, educational, religious, and intellectual leaders who brought about this transformation had diverse goals, so that a conflict of purpose centrally affected the formative period of education and has affected it ever since.

For some, common school education was intended to serve the political needs and purposes of the new republic. In his Farewell Address George Washington had urged the people to promote, "as an object of primary importance, Institutions for the general diffusion of knowledge. In proportion as the structure of a government gives force to public opinion, it is essential that public opinion should be enlightened." Jefferson made the point more pithily: "If a nation expects to be ignorant and free, in a state of civilization, it expects what never was and never will be." Some leaders stressed the practical need to educate the "jurors, magistrates, legislators, governors" who would run the new republic. It was argued too that as a matter of republican principle, *"the education of the whole becomes the first interest of all."* Or as Governor Edward Everett said, ". . . the utmost practicable extension should be given to a system of education, which will confer on every citizen the capacity of deriving knowledge, with readiness and accuracy, from books and documents."

For others, however, education as part of the republican experiment raised a more profound question—what were the purposes of the republic? Those who answered with the classic goals of "liberty and equality," as many did, believed that popular or universal education was vital to these purposes. Schoolhouses were seen as "Temples of Freedom," as both the source and the guardian of liberty. Even higher hopes were held for education as a product and protector of equality, especially in the light of the educational privileges of the elites. William Manning, the Billerica tavern-keeper, went to the heart of the matter: "Larning is of the greatest importance to the seport of a free government," he wrote, "& to prevent this the few are always crying up the advantages of costly collages, national aca-dimyes & grammer schooles, in ordir to make places for men to live without work, & so strengthen their party. But are always opposed to cheep schools & woman schooles, the ondly or prinsaple means by which larning is spred amongue the Many." This view, which was too strong for even the Jeffersonian press to print, anticipated the egalitarian thrust of the 1830s.

Still others looked on schooling as a means of achieving diverse goals or changes: as the way toward moral regeneration, or at least curbing vice; as an agency for inculcating patriotic values; as a training ground for republican leadership; as a practical preparation for earning a better livelihood. Education for leadership had a special appeal to early republicans, in the absence of the kind of aristocratic system that took care of the training of princes in monarchies. In providing for three years of elementary public education for all children, Jefferson's "Bill for the More General Diffusion of Knowledge" aimed at selecting potential leaders from the mass of the people.

Still other Americans, usually Federalist or Whig, sometimes Republican or Democratic, had a less elevated view of the purpose of schooling. Their aim was to control and discipline the children of an unruly, democratic people. Heirs to the Framers, who feared faction, disorder, and turbulence, these persons saw the public school less as a means of expressing and realizing the aspirations of the people, more as a means of carrying out the purposes of the state. Some radicals of the time understood this basic purpose. Defining the attitudes of certain of the workingmen's groups of the 1830s, Rush Welter wrote: "Whereas republican educational institutions had been intended to serve the *needs* of the people, democratic institutions were much more likely to respond to their *wants.*" Doubtless too, many parents were happy to let the schools take over the function of discipline, or at least of inculcation of proper values.

The "Common School Awakening" of the 1830s reflected a sharp diversity of purpose. The upper-class leaders of the movement wanted to provide a free elementary education for all white children, to create a trained educational profession adhering to a single standard, and to establish state control over local schools. States could then create uniform criteria for buildings, curricula, and teachers. States could also enforce the attendance of children. While leaders wanted social control, supporters of the movement believed advancement would come with common schooling. In educational opportunity the lot of the worker had declined since colonial times. Colonial authorities had bound out orphans, children of indentured servants, and even four- and five-year-olds as apprentices to learn a trade with a master, but apprenticeship faded with the onset of mechanization in the North and slavery in the South. Finding their wages, businesses, and status undermined by industrialization, skilled workers and small shopkeepers wanted their children to attend better schools, if possible with the scions of the wealthy.

Labor leaders made free, equal, and state-supported schools their cardinal goal. Robert Dale Owen, fresh from the failure of New Harmony, became an inspirational leader in the New York labor struggles of the 1830s and an advocate of common schools. In urging the Working Men's party to place tax-supported schools at the head of the platform, Owen proposed an audacious system of education in which the state would lodge all children in boarding schools, providing them with equal food, clothing, and instruction. Only through boarding schools could the environment of every child be equalized.

"I believe in a National System of Equal, Republican, Protective, Practical Education," Owen proclaimed, "the sole regenerator of a profligate age, and the only redeemer of our suffering country from the equal curses of chilling poverty and corrupting riches, of gnawing want and destroying debauchery, of blind ignorance and of unprincipled intrigue." Clearly the schools for Owen would be another utopia. His six essays on education received wide publicity, although his bold plan for boarding schools was far too visionary for the Working Men's party.

Responding to their leaders' calls for educational reform, craftsmen and small shopkeepers used their recently acquired suffrage to demand education for their children. In Pennsylvania, they argued the necessity of a free system of education, already established in Philadelphia. In 1834, a milestone bill providing for free education passed on a statewide level, only to meet violent opposition among the wealthy, who produced 32,000 signatures for repeal. When the Senate voted for another bill providing for free education of only the poor, Representative Thaddeus Stevens opposed it on the grounds that education should be free to all. After a denunciation of class hostility toward free public schools he carried the legislature, and the original act stood.

Although education had changed in colonial days from a dependence on family, church, and apprenticeship to more public, official arrangements, no part of the country before 1815 had a comprehensive school system. In New York and other middle Atlantic states, public funds had gone to benevolent organizations such as the Free School Society of New York City, which sponsored charity schools for the poor. To attend charity schools, children had to take pauper oaths, and the poor objected to charity schools so much that they boycotted them. As late as 1828, more than 24,000 children between the ages of five and fifteen received no education in New York City; in Delaware, New Jersey, and Maryland the number was even greater.

States had left responsibility for schools to local districts. The district schools received meager funds from local taxes, hardly enough to pay a teacher and maintain a schoolhouse. Parents were assessed rates according to the number of their children in school; those unable to pay could still send children as charity pupils. In Massachusetts, one-third of the districts, 1,000 in all, had no schoolhouses. By 1840, it is estimated, one-half of the schoolchildren of New England and the middle Atlantic states were receiving free education, as were one-sixth of those in the old Northwest.

Private schools for children whose parents could pay tuition flourished throughout the Northeast. Children of the wealthy attended private "dame schools," to avoid associating with the poor. In both district and private schools, instruction was all recitation by rote—students memorized a page from the text and recited to the teacher. In district schools, there was no age grading, since all ages learned in the one-room schoolhouse. Nor did uniform school books exist, at least at first; teachers taught from whatever books were at hand. In the 1830s, however, William McGuffey, a professor of languages, developed the renowned McGuffey's Readers, a series of six textbooks for the elementary grades. The Readers mingled entertainment with moral and patriotic lessons, and they became the chief introduction to learning for several generations of American schoolchildren.

Teachers usually had no direct training for their work. As one school board member wrote in 1847 of a teacher: "he thinks of turning peddler, or of working at shoemaking. But the one will expose him to storms, the other he fears will injure his chest. . . . He will nevertheless teach school for a meagre compensation." Such problems were less prevalent in the better-funded private schools where children of the well-to-do studied classical languages. In 1837, the Connecticut educational leader Henry Barnard estimated that 10,000 wealthy children attended private schools, at an expense greater than all the funds appropriated for the other 70,000 children of the state.

But members of elite groups often led reform. Leaders of the common school movement in the several states shared similar backgrounds and views on the purpose of education. They were members of the established professions—law, medicine, education, religion—and members of the Whig party. Horace Mann of Massachusetts, Henry Barnard of Connecticut, and Calvin Wiley of North Carolina were Whig legislators before they became state superintendents of education. As Whigs, they supported an active role by government in industrial growth, protective tariffs, internal improvements—and education.

Reformers hoped to bring every child into school through the establishment of the "free school," supported by taxes and state grants—free so that no child would be identified as pauper and the poor would attend, and free so that the rich would not object to mixed economic classes since they would be paying for the schools anyway through taxation. Raising taxes for schools was unpopular everywhere, and reformers had only limited success, as wealthy people who could educate their children privately often opposed common schools. It took a lawyer-educator-politician with the moral standing and political skill of a Horace Mann to enlist manufacturers in the common school movement in Massachusetts.

Mann contended that education would create better workers. "Education has a market value . . . it may be turned to a pecuniary account: it may be minted, and will yield a larger amount of statutable coin than common bullion." Mann's influence on educational thought and practice was immense through his use of publicity to popularize his beliefs. In 1837, at a financial sacrifice, he relinquished his seat in the Massachusetts legislature to become secretary of the Massachusetts Board of Education. Two years later he secured the first state-supported American normal school at Lexington, Massachusetts, and by 1845 he had formed a state association of teachers in Massachusetts, as well as founding and editing the *Common School Journal.*

Mann's accomplishments in Massachusetts were formidable. When he became secretary of the board of education, one-sixth of the children of the state were being taught in private academies, about one-third had no significant schooling at all, and in many districts the school term was only two or three months. Under Mann's leadership, a minimum school year of six months was established by statute; schoolhouses and equipment were improved; teachers' salaries raised by over a half; and the ratio of private school spending to public halved. The professional training of teachers was improved and educating by rote reduced.

Mann took on all comers. A Unitarian, he asserted that the Bible should be read in school, but without comment. A Puritan humanitarian with genuine sympathy for the poor and underprivileged, he believed that education would right the wrongs of society. The poor were miserable because of ignorance and lack of education, he felt, not because of injustice in the social system, and so the poor must work to better themselves. Democracy could succeed only if there was a free and universal school system teaching the work ethic; all should attend the public schools, and all would if the public schools surpassed the private schools in excellence. Inevitably Mann provoked fierce opposition not only from private schools but from many churchmen, who accused his board of education of creating a godless system of education.

Mann's leadership was matched in southern New England by Henry Barnard, who centralized and improved common schooling in two states. Barnard had received an excellent private school education, followed by study at Yale and a year abroad. Elected to the Connecticut legislature, he introduced a bill in 1838 to centralize the school system with a state board of commissioners to oversee it. As secretary of the board, he carried out the law and worked to change public sentiment in its favor. Through public schools, Barnard maintained, rich and poor might achieve mutual under-standing, and thereby reduce conflict. In 1842, he accepted the post of Commissioner of Public Schools in Rhode Island, where again he secured the passage of a school act. He wanted above all the "complete education of every human being without regard to the accidents of birth or fortune." With an inheritance that permitted him to spend $40,000 a year on educational publications, Barnard founded and edited the *Connecticut Common School Journal.* He went on to further leadership: chancellor of the University of Wisconsin, president of St. John's College, and the first United States Commissioner of Education.

Leaders of the Common School Awakening in the South were moderate businessmen, former yeomen farmers, who supported internal improvements and greater economic growth for the region. Reformers wanted the South to build home industries and businesses with cheaper money and free itself from New York factors and shippers who were "strangling the South" by controlling the cotton shipment to England and the shipment back of manufactured goods. A better business environment could not grow in the South, they feared, as long as the planter class controlled the state legislatures, for planters disdained commerce and internal improvements. Education of the masses would help all to see through the planters' values and allow the South to grow. Poor whites, if educated, would be less likely to follow demagogic leaders calling for war, and war was bad for business and economic growth.

"Let the sun of universal education shine upon it [North Carolina], and the matchless resources of the state, by works of improvement, be made to minister nutriment to its wants, and soon its bright blossoms will imparadise the soil from which its sturdy trunk has sprung, and its green, unfading foliage furnish umbrageous retreats for the weary of the earth," wrote Calvin Wiley, superintendent of North Carolina schools in the North Carolina *Reader*. Wiley believed education would develop resources and found a new prosperity in North Carolina. A lawyer and newspaper editor, he was a member of the North Carolina state legislature in the early 1850s when he was elected superintendent of schools. He established the *North Carolina Journal of Education* and the first teacher-training institution in North Carolina.

Only state or local schools for paupers existed in most districts in the South. Children of planters received elementary education from private tutors; others had no education at all. The southern rate of illiteracy for whites was double that of the North in the period before the Civil War. In the 1840s the South made an effort to apply greater resources to education, but it fell behind other regions because it was the poorest section of the country. In 1860 a white child received approximately eleven days of schooling per year in the South, as compared to fifty in the North.

In the West, evangelical ministers advanced common schooling as part of a crusade against ignorance. Young Congregationalist ministers of the American Home Missionary Society who traveled to the Northwest frontier to convert the settlers were amazed at the illiteracy they found, and dispatched letters home to urge the society to send schoolteachers to the West. New England, priding itself on its educational heritage, sent forth numerous apostles of intellectual training.

For the first time, women began to serve as missionary teachers. Catharine Beecher, daughter of the eminent Congregationalist minister Lyman Beecher, began to send circulars in 1835 to county newspapers and clergymen throughout the East asking for names of women who would serve as teachers. In the West she asked for the names of towns and villages where a teacher would be welcome. She organized local groups of church women to raise a one-hundred-dollar donation to train and place one teacher in the West. Carrying the endorsements of Horace Mann and Henry Barnard, Catharine Beecher would present her case to a town's most eminent official, and after gaining his endorsement she would build a local committee.

In Boston, the Ladies' Society for Promoting Education at the West donated several thousand dollars to the cause. The Organization for Promoting National Education, Catharine Beecher's committee, received funds from local committees, arranged a brief training period for the teachers, and eventually sent 450 teachers to the West.

Missionaries, schoolmasters, college presidents, and lecturers "swarmed out generally flying over the mountains and alighting beyond wherever there was a job, often trusting to the future to develop a salary." Horace Mann spent the last four years of his life administering Antioch College in Ohio. The "Father of the Indiana School System," Caleb Mills, was a minister who answered a call to save the West; he knelt in the snow one winter day in 1833 with the founders of Wabash College in Crawfordsville, Indiana, to dedicate their lives to the cause of education and "the service of the Master whose followers they were."

Born in Dunbarton, New Hampshire, in 1806, the son of a wealthy farmer, Caleb Mills, after studying at Dartmouth and Andover Theological Seminary, answered an advertisement in the *Home Missionary Journal* for a minister who could preach on Sundays and teach in a new college being organized in Crawfordsville, Indiana. In 1833 he went there with his wife and three young women whose purpose was to "go west to teach." His preparatory class of twelve young men was the first class at Wabash, where Mills was professor of Greek and Latin until 1876.

Indiana had the highest rate of illiteracy of any northern state, and although numerous laws for common schooling existed, the school system was still only on paper. "One of the People" was the signature on the first educational message that Mills sent to the Indiana state legislature. In his six annual messages, 1846–51, he called upon the legislature to establish public schools. Mills popularized the argument of Horace Mann and other educational leaders that education of the common people would ensure the survival of the nation: "We can better meet the expense of the proper education of the rising generation, than endure the consequences resulting from the neglect of it."

The messages and the resulting support brought forth a new bill before the legislature providing for compulsory taxation for schools, a central elementary system, uniform textbooks, and a superintendent of public instruction. The lawmaker who helped guide the bill through the legislature and spoke persuasively in its behalf was the ubiquitous Robert Dale Owen, the early leader of workingmen's demands for education.

The founder of the Michigan system of public schools was also a Congregationalist minister, John Pierce. Born in Chesterfield, New Hampshire, Pierce lost his father when very young and was sent to live with a grandfather on his New England farm, where he received only eight weeks of schooling. Resolving at age twenty to earn an education, Pierce graduated from Brown University, and from Princeton Theological Seminary three years later; then, as an ordained minister, he accepted a call to serve as a missionary in the Michigan Territory.

At the constitutional convention that met to apply for Michigan's statehood, Pierce helped persuade the chairman of the committee on education to support common schooling in the state. Appointed the first state superintendent of public instruction in 1836, he submitted a report for the organization and support of primary schools, for a University of Michigan with branches, and for disposing of the common school lands. Pierce's report became the basis of the Michigan school system, although twenty years elapsed after the plan was adopted before free schools existed in the townships, and then only for three months a year. In 1838, Pierce began publication of the *Journal of Education.*

Religion was a powerful force in the Common School Awakening in urban areas. In New York City, pious men of the Public School Society, worried about the masses of poor people separated from the moral influences of the church, resolved to create an alternative influence to educate the people in morality and virtue. The society received state funds to staff eleven free schools for 20,000 children. The society claimed that the religious teaching offered in its schools was nonsectarian, and it opposed state money going to any schools maintained by religious denominations. Its schools were New York City's only real public schools, but the increasing numbers of Roman Catholic immigrants boycotted them.

In 1834, Bishop John Hughes found across from the Roman Catholic cathedral in New York City a half-empty school run by the society. If he could supervise the teaching and the books used in the school so that anti-Catholic sentiment would be erased, Hughes promised to bring in Catholic children. Governor William Seward, valuing the discipline, socialization, and routine of education for poor children, supported Bishop Hughes. On this issue, Seward stood alone against his Whig party. The New York school law of 1842 provided for a New York City Board of Education to receive state funds, to tax, to build schools, and to distribute money to schools meeting certain requirements. No school with sectarian religious teaching would receive funds, but the Protestant Bible, viewed by the board as nonsectarian, could be used for instruction in the schools. The Catholics objected, and decided to create their own system of parochial schools.

Conflicting purposes continued to mark the movement for common schooling. Whig businessmen and reformers stressed the redemptive social purpose of education. Not only would common schooling create better workers to operate the new industrial system; it would fuse society together with shared morals and values. Some educational reformers, however, saw uneducated lower-class people as a threat to American democracy—and immigrants and the increasing numbers of factory laborers as a threat to the status quo. The powerful influence of schooling, they believed, was necessary to educate the poor in the values of hard work, individualism, thrift, and morality. Common schooling would relieve social problems without altering the social structure. The reformers focused on changing the person, not the society, as the root of the problem; the individual child was to conform to society's values. The common school could, therefore, include everyone without large cost or threat to the privileged.

The "middling" classes who were in favor of the common school movement supported the reformers, voted for the extension of public educational services, and sent their children to the public schools, but they wanted an educational system that would set their children apart from the lower classes. With only elementary schools opened to all, they turned to the high school with its entrance and graduation requirements, its teaching of the classics and American values, as the institution to maintain the advantage of their children over the poor. The latter usually could not attend high schools, for by that age a child of poor parents had gone to work. The 80,000 elementary schools had 90,000 teachers and 3,300,000 pupils in 1850; in contrast there were only 6,000 secondary schools with 12,000 teachers and 250,000 pupils.

By the 1850s, another purpose was intruding into the consciences of reformers: improving the lot of the poor. How could the mass of people be informed or reformed, trained or restrained, when more than three million persons remained in bondage and ignorance? "Our motto used to be 'the cause of education, the first of all causes,'" Horace Mann said in his farewell to Massachusetts teachers in 1844. "Recent events, however, have forced upon the public attention the great truth, that before a man can be educated, he must be a free man." The movement for common education did not reach out to the children of slaves. Horace Mann could not wait for education to effect that change; in 1848 he resigned his educational office to win election to Congress and join the political battle for the liberty and equality of black people.

Could the schools expand liberty, increase prosperity, create better workers, safeguard property, prevent revolution, and at the same time blur class lines, lift the poor, foster equality? The contradictory purposes of the common school movement, with its lack of even a rough sense of priorities, were to plague education in the United States for years to come. Yet the movement, divergent and contradictory as it was, brought important gains in several states; a public school system, if only in skeleton form, was established; common schooling was a step away from a class system in the nation; the door of education partially opened to the middle classes and to the poor.

LEADERS OF THE PENNY PRESS

"What is the liberty of the press?" Alexander Hamilton had asked in the *Federalist*. It depended first of all on public opinion, answered this foe of revolution. Conditions in the 1830s, however, seemed ripe for a newspaper revolution. The egalitarian, individualistic, participatory temper of Jacksonian politics had quickened the interest of larger numbers of people in party combat, public issues, and political personalities—and quickened also their appetite for news of scandal, crime, disasters, sports, explorations, scientific discoveries. Liberty of speech and press was still largely honored in fact as well as in the national and state constitutions. Editors could freely assail the government, opposing parties and politicians, and one another. Newspaper editors who denounced politicos as crooks and liars, and one another as prostitutes and panderers, ran far greater danger of being knocked down or horsewhipped in the streets by their victims than of being taken off to jail by the local constable. Abolitionist editors, of course, were never safe from mob violence.

Other conditions were creating the potential for change. Newspapers, so needful of rapid transportation and communication, expanded along with the railroad and telegraph. The new journalism would be as dependent on a big-city environment as the Concord literati were on a village one, and this was a time of rapid urbanization. By the late 1840s Manhattan was approaching a population of 515,000, with another 97,000 people in Brooklyn. Newspapers needed a concentrated volume not only of readers but also of advertisers, pressmen, and craftsmen. New York alone employed 2,000 workers in printing and publishing by 1840.

The great mercantile dailies, serving primarily the business world through their ample coverage of ship arrivals and departures, stock and commodity prices, and business dealings, had hardly changed in decades. Subscribers purchased these papers by the year, at six cents a copy delivered to their homes; it was difficult to buy single numbers. The established newspapers were overdue for change. The presses themselves were about to be outmoded. In Britain the old-time hand press had been superseded by steam-powered cylinder presses that rolled back and forth over a flat type bed, and were capable of two to four thousand impressions an hour.

Innovating leaders and daring experimenters were needed as the catalysts for real change in journalism. The crucial act was an idea—the idea that tens of thousands of middle- and low-income people would buy newspapers if the papers were cheapened in content and price. This notion of a "penny press" came to a number of persons around the same time. Two of these were a brother and sister in Boston, Lynde and Cornelia Walter, who founded and established the *Transcript* at the low price of four dollars a year. But Boston, with a population in 1830 of only 61,000, was not the place for a mass-circulation paper. It took a metropolis like New York, and a man like Benjamin H. Day.

A onetime apprentice on Samuel Bowles's Springfield *Republican,* Day had come to New York at the age of twenty and worked at the case in the offices of several papers until he could set up shop as a job printer. Cholera and a bank crisis cut into his business so badly that in desperation he decided to try out an idea he had flirted with since his days as a compositor —putting out a one-penny newspaper, to be sold on the streets. Almost single-handedly, working in a small room on William Street, Day got out his first issue of the *Sun* on September 3, 1833. Only eight by ten inches in size and four pages long, it was hardly a sensation. The left-hand of its three columns on the first page listed steamboat advertisements—to Albany for one dollar, to Hartford by the "splendid low-pressure steamboat WATER WITCH," to New Orleans and Liverpool and Le Havre. Most of the rest of the front page offered the story of an "Irish captain." But up on the right side of the masthead was the magic phrase "PRICE ONE PENNY."

Day had sensed the great popular appetite for "human interest" stories, and soon the *Sun* was dishing them up. Most popular were young George Wisner's police-court reports:

". . . Bridget McMunn got drunk and threw a pitcher at Mr. Ellis, of 53 Ludlow St. Bridget said she was the mother of 3 little orphans—God bless their dear souls—and if she went to prison they would choke to death for the want of something to eat. Committed."

"Catharine McBride was brought in for stealing a frock. Catharine said she had just served out 6 months on Blackwell's Island, and she wouldn't be sent back again for the best glass of punch that ever was made. Her husband, when she last left the penitentiary, took her to a boarding house in Essex st., but the rascal got mad at her, pulled her hair, pinched her arm, and kicked her out of bed. She . . . got drunk and stole the frock out of pure spite. Committed."

". . . Bill Doty got drunk because he had the horrors so bad he couldn't keep sober. Committed."

Soon the *Sun* had its imitators, the most notable and successful being James Gordon Bennett's New York *Herald.* Scottish-born, Bennett had knocked about as a teacher in Nova Scotia, bookstore clerk in Boston, reporter in New York, translator of Spanish-American newspapers in Charleston, and a Washington correspondent for the New York press, before resolving to publish his own newspaper. Two ventures failed before he began publication of the *Herald* in May 1835. Acting as editor, reporter, proofreader, and folder, he put out the first issue in a Wall Street cellar, with a plank across two flour barrels serving as business and editorial desk. His paper, he proclaimed, was "equally intended for the great mass of the community, the merchant, the mechanic, working people. . . ."

The *Herald* seemed at first as sensationalist as the *Sun,* but Bennett outdid Day as a newspaperman. He developed a first-class financial section, a lively letters column, a reasoned and informed editorial column, wide political, society, and sports coverage. He attacked Nicholas Biddle, and he took on a local financier so fiercely that twice the money man assaulted him in the street. He was not above devoting entire issues of his paper to sensational murder cases, as in the trial of a notorious man-about-town for the killing of a prostitute in a brothel. And he took on church, political, and financial establishments. Within a year the *Herald* boasted a daily circulation of 30,000.

As the penny press expanded, printing technology advanced with it, in turn making possible even larger and faster outpourings of newspapers. The Hoe "lightning press" of 1847 had a revolving printing surface, with type ingeniously locked into the curved cylinders by means of V-shaped column rules. Men stood on four tiers on both sides of the huge cylinder, feeding in pages from tilted tables. In 1849 Bennett installed a Hoe press with six cylinders capable of 12,000 impressions an hour. The cost of such presses—at least $20,000—threatened to end the days when young editors could start a newspaper for a few hundred dollars, and the cost also made advertising more important.

Innovating publishers competed feverishly to speed up their news gathering and distribution. They sent sloops out to meet ships bringing news from abroad. When one New York combine of publishers set up a semaphore system from the Sandy Hook sloop base to the Battery, a rival publisher ran a pony express between the two points. *Sun* reporters dispatched carrier pigeons out of a dovecote on top of their plant. The telegraph changed much of this. The first telegraphic dispatch published in a newspaper appeared in the Baltimore *Patriot* in May 1844, from Wash-

ington: "ONE O'CLOCK.—THERE HAS JUST BEEN MADE A MOTION IN THE HOUSE
TO GO INTO COMMITTEE OF THE WHOLE ON THE OREGON QUESTION, REJECTED,
—AYES, 79; NAYS, 86."

Selling the penny papers was even more competitive. Ragamuffin news-
boys paid the publishers sixty-seven cents for a hundred copies and
hawked them on the streets; their shrill cries became a vivid part of the
urban clamor. Papers could be found in "every hotel, tavern, counting-
shop," in the hands even of porters and draymen and boys old enough to
read. The post office distributed newspapers free, or at heavily subsidized
rates, in rural areas—a beneficence that did not stop publishers from
complaining of poor postal service. Reliance on the postal service had its
risks too, as abolitionist editors discovered when southern postmasters
refused to deliver their papers.

New York kept its leadership in the newspaper world, but the Baltimore
Sun, founded in 1837, quickly won a reputation for excellent reporting
from Washington—and a circulation of 12,000. The Philadelphia *Public
Ledger,* established the next year, fearlessly attacked local corruption and
abuses, at the cost of libel suits and even a mob attack. The *Ledger* carried
on the Philadelphia image of tolerance by defending the rights of Catholics
against rioters and those of abolitionists against lynchers. Boston's new
Daily Times gained a circulation of 12,000 in four months, in part by ped-
dling its copies throughout eastern Massachusetts towns. The Boston *Post*
continued as the great Democratic organ. Southern cities, especially
Charleston, developed fine newspaper traditions.

The press had long followed flag and flatboat. "Wherever a town sprang
up," Frank Luther Mott wrote, "there a printer with a rude press and 'a
shirt-tail-full of type' was sure to appear as by magic." By the 1850s rapidly
growing cities like Cincinnati and St. Louis had half a dozen or more
papers each. In Chicago, in 1840, John Wentworth, an Exeter and Dartmouth graduate, had walked the lake beach into town with thirty dollars
in his pocket; within three years he owned the weekly Chicago *Democrat* and
a year later converted it into a daily. In 1847 three businessmen founded
the Chicago *Daily Tribune,* which they sold a few years later to Joseph
Medill, Alfred Cowles, and several partners. Newspapers were already
sprouting in the territories to the west—in Green Bay and Milwaukee and
"Du Buque," in St. Paul and Sioux Falls and down in Leavenworth and
Lawrence, Kansas.

Publishers adapted themselves to local conditions and crises. The first
newspaper in Oklahoma was a Baptist missionary organ printed in an
Indian dialect. The staff of the San Felipe *Telegraph and Texas Register* had
fled for their lives on the approach of the Mexican army, which seized their

printing press and threw it into a nearby bayou, but the *Telegraph* carried on with another press. The Santa Fe *Republican* published two pages in Spanish and two in English. The *Weekly Arizonian* had to suspend publication for two years when one of its publishers was shot for resisting arrest for a stage robbery. The *Deseret News* in Salt Lake City had great trouble obtaining a steady supply of paper over the mountains. California newspapers, stimulated by the gold rush, exploited the pony express—a total of seventy-five mustangs and their riders relaying mail and newspapers between stations fifteen miles apart, all the way from Missouri, in half the time that stagecoaches required.

The famous old newspapers of the East did not fold in the face of the rise of the penny press and the westward movement. Great mercantile dailies, often still charging six cents for home delivery, carried on. The even more noted partisan papers—the historic Democratic triumvirate of the Washington *Globe,* the Richmond *Enquirer,* and the Albany *Argus,* and such Whig organs as the *National Intelligencer* in Washington, the Springfield *Republican,* and the Louisville *Journal*—conducted a party debate that broadly set the shape of national political conflict. Americans were discovering once again that new ideas, institutions, and inventions did not have to replace the old; the country was vast enough for the old and new to live side by side.

The new, popular press did run into heavy criticism for its sensationalism, vulgarity, even blasphemy. Bennett's *Herald* was a particular target. Ministers who hated him for his irreverent coverage of religious news, politicians who feared his editorial pen, and rival editors who envied his circulation triumphs—these and others opened up a "moral war" against this "venomous reptile," this "obscene vagabond," this "polluted wretch," as one editor gently labeled him. After losing both advertising and readership—he saw a third of his circulation go, it was said—Bennett toned down some of his more strident coverage. His circulation climbed back toward 33,000 by 1849, in part because of the Mexican War, which enabled the *Herald* and other papers to demonstrate their news-gathering enterprise.

Critics of the penny press feared that its truckling to the baser instincts of the masses would enable it to drive out the quality ones, as cheap money drives out dear. Yet the penny papers, even while exploiting the popular appetite for news of crime and vice, also drew tens of thousands into the newspaper-reading habit. They awakened the aspirations and expectations of large numbers of lower-income and less-educated people, bringing them to political self-consciousness during and after the Jackson years. Indeed, fears of the degrading of the whole press by the penny press were soon quieted by the journalistic feats of one man: Horace Greeley.

He was an unlikely-looking editor in a profession that professed to be composed of gentlemen—"my clothes were scanty and seedy," he remembered, "my appearance grim and unprepossessing." But ever since his earliest years on a stony New England farm Horace Greeley had been in love with the printed word—he could "read fluently" at the age of four, he said later, "and quite passably with the book upside down—an absurd practice." Arriving in New York with his personal possessions wrapped in a bandanna slung over his shoulder, he spent years in short-term jobs, one of which consisted of editing the *Jeffersonian* while steamboating up and down the Hudson, and another of typesetting, from which he was sacked because, it was said, the boss caught sight of him in the composing room and cried, "For God's sake, fire him; let's have decent-*looking* men around here, at least!" But through sheer doggedness, intense ambition, a fecund editorial imagination, and a good deal of experimentation, Greeley fought his way to the top of the tough, competitive world of Manhattan journalism. In April 1841, with his own savings and borrowed money, he launched the New York *Tribune.*

The *Tribune* would be a penny paper, but with a difference. Although Greeley had worked closely with Whig leaders for years, he wanted a paper free of "servile partisanship" as well as of "gagged, mincing neutrality." He would shun sex and celebrity stories, scandals, quack medical advertisements, and police reports in favor of serious, responsible, high-minded journalism. Greeley's list of causes was lengthy: liberty, egalitarianism, a vague form of socialism, the rights of labor, the agrarian movement, free distribution of government lands to settlers, certain women's rights, internal improvements, cooperativism. He believed that leaders among the privileged should engage literally in Social Uplift: the "great, the all-embracing reform of our age," he preached, "is the Social Reform—that which seeks to lift the Laboring Class, as such—not out of labor, by any means—but out of ignorance, inefficiency, dependence, and want."

His list of dislikes was even longer: landlordism, capital punishment, human exploitation, monopoly, both wage and bond slavery, liquor, tobacco, and—alas—the theater, as a place of intoxication and assignation, full of "libertines" and "courtezans." But he was much more than a moralist; a literary leader too, he assembled a brilliant staff, including Margaret Fuller, published major book reviews, book extracts, and lectures, and hired Karl Marx as a London correspondent. He was a trainer of younger writers, advising them never to publish a book until asked by a bookseller and offered "current cash of the realm," and to remember that even though they might "write with an angel's pen," their writings would not sell unless they were known and talked about as authors. Hence they must write for the magazines; Mr. Emerson, he said, would have been twice as much read if he had done so, "just to let common people know of his existence."

Certainly Greeley let them know of his; the *Tribune* picked up a circulation of 11,000 within seven weeks. He also published the weekly *Tribune*, whose national readership soared to over 100,000 by the mid-1850s.

As he became editorially and politically more powerful, Greeley did not bother to change his style to suit the fashionable. He remained "a strange, child-like figure," in Vernon Parrington's words, "with his round moon-face, eyes blinking through spectacles and a fringe of whiskers that invited the pencil of the cartoonist—yet carrying the sorrows of the world in his heart. . . ." Nor did Greeley forget the poverty of his earlier days. A believer in Fourierism, he encouraged his staff to share in the profits of the paper. Writing was remunerative for only a very few at the time; young reporters were lucky to earn eight dollars a week. Most of the famous authors of the period, for that matter, lived on other income—Emerson on his lecturing, Hawthorne on patronage, Melville on a small bequest from his wife's father.

The penny press was still an urban phenomenon. As people moved away from closed parochial communities—where everyone knew everyone else and what each was doing—into the impersonal city, the demand for penny papers grew. The anonymity of the environment whetted urban dwellers' appetites for more newspaper coverage of events, more human-interest stories at a cheaper price. As the factory had made cheaper, mass-produced goods available to a growing market, so did the penny press make mass-circulation papers available to every urban dweller. Railroads and the Erie Canal opened the midwestern market as publishing became a big business centralized in the eastern cities.

Literary magazines proliferated, catering mainly to women; *Godey's Lady's Book* had 150,000 subscribers in 1860, the prestigious *North American Review* only a few thousand. Domestic novels written by women authors sold thousands of copies. *The Wide, Wide World* by Susan B. Warner launched the wave of best-selling novels by and for women, followed by *The Curse of Clifton* by Mrs. E. D. E. N. Southworth, *The Lamplighter* by Maria S. Cummins, and *Tempest and Sunshine* by Mary J. Holmes. The total sales of all the works of Hawthorne, Melville, Thoreau, and Whitman in the 1850s did not equal the sales of one of the more popular domestic novels.

The special journal flourished as reform sentiment grew—Benjamin Lundy's *Genius of Universal Emancipation*, William Lloyd Garrison's *Liberator*, labor organs such as Frances Wright's *Free Enquirer* and George Henry Evans' *Workingman's Advocate*. But the penny press, with its low price, high circulation, emphasis on human-interest stories, and advertisements, appealed most to the growing urban middle class in the Jacksonian age.

No matter how intent on mass circulation and moneymaking, or on exploiting freedom of the press in fierce local disputes, the press could not wholly escape the moral issue of slavery. And some editors did not want to. Elijah P. Lovejoy, son of a Congregational minister and student at Princeton Theological Seminary, published a religious paper, the St. Louis *Observer*. In 1836, he had to move his press from St. Louis to Alton, Illinois, twenty-five miles up the Mississippi River, after mobs attacked his newspaper for assailing injustices to blacks. Supported by prominent businessmen, Lovejoy continued his crusades in the Alton *Observer*, against intemperance, "popery," mob violence, and slavery, as opposed to God's law. By 1837, after mobs had destroyed two additional presses, Alton citizens called a public meeting, condemned the mob action, and pledged money for a new press. A third press was shipped for Lovejoy to a warehouse protected by sixty armed guards. But a mob broke through, smashed the new press, set the building afire, and killed the editor.

ABOLITIONISTS: BY TONGUE AND PEN

Lovejoy's murder electrified the antislavery leadership. It was a "shock as of any earthquake throughout this continent," said John Quincy Adams. To some, the mob had struck a blow not merely against the antislavery movement but against liberty for all. Never mind that Lovejoy himself was an anti-Catholic extremist who viewed slavery as a papist plot—bigots too had their rights. "To say that he who holds unpopular opinions must hold them at the peril of his life," asserted the New York *Evening Post*, was "to strike at all rights, all liberties, all protection of law." In Boston, William Ellery Channing, backed up by a committee of 100 notables, asked the city authorities for the use of Faneuil Hall, the "cradle of liberty," to mourn Lovejoy's death as a threat to liberty of tongue and pen. The mayor and aldermen turned him down.

"Has Boston fallen so low?" Channing implored in an open letter. "May not its citizens be trusted to come together to express the great principles of liberty for which their fathers died?" When Channing mobilized his influentials, the city gave way. After five thousand or more people crowded into Faneuil Hall to hear Channing's declarations, the attorney general of the commonwealth of Massachusetts gained the floor to castigate Boston's blacks as lions, tigers, hyenas, jackasses and monkeys, to praise the South for subjugating their own "wild beasts of the menagerie," and to call the Alton mob as glorious as the Revolutionary patriots who had dumped John

Bull's tea into Boston Harbor. Authority would exercise its right to free speech too.

It was a challenge thrown into the teeth of the abolitionists in Faneuil Hall—Channing, Maria Chapman, Benjamin Hallet, and others lesser known. One of these was a handsome, sandy-haired young man named Wendell Phillips. Under the influence of Garrison—whom he had seen dragged through the streets of Boston by a rope—and of his abolitionist wife, Anne Greene, Phillips had embraced the antislavery cause, to the consternation of his aristocratic friends of Harvard, Beacon Hill, State Street, and the law. During the cacophony of applause and hoots that followed the attorney general's speech, Phillips pushed his way forward through the crowd and leaped up on the platform. Speaking quietly, slowly gaining the attention of the crowd, Phillips seemed to intoxicate himself and the crowds.

"Sir, when I heard the gentleman lay down principles which place the murderers of Alton side by side with Otis and Hancock, with Quincy and Adams, I thought those pictured lips"—here Phillips pointed to portraits of the apostles of liberty—"would have broken into voice to rebuke the recreant American—the slanderer of the dead. . . ." The audience burst into applause and catcalls. Channing's resolutions carried and Phillips left the hall a celebrity. "Sublime, irresistible, annihilating," Garrison called the speech.

Abolitionism thrived on news of tragedy and martyrdom: the burning of abolitionist churches, the return of terrified fugitive slaves, the congressional ignoring of petitions, the murder of Lovejoy and others. By the 1840s the American Anti-Slavery Society numbered more than 1,200 societies in the national organization, with a membership of about a quarter million persons. As abolitionism expanded, the central questions of ends and means that once could be debated in isolation now took on enormous theoretical and practical importance. Literary and forensic abolitionists could find larger audiences for their speeches, books, and articles. Wendell Phillips quickly reached the first rank of the brilliant leadership of antislavery, and was one of the boldest and most articulate on questions of strategy.

These questions were as complex as they were compelling. They were questions of ultimate goals, of strategy, and of tactics in realizing strategy. Should abolitionists and other radicals concentrate on seeking equality and liberty for all deprived persons—women and Indians and newspaper editors as well as blacks—or focus on arousing public opinion only against the most dramatic and egregious sin, slavery? In either case, should abolitionism seek to accomplish its aims by gradually reforming society—that is, cleansing it of its impurities—or by reconstructing it? And in either of those cases, should radicals work within the existing system of political parties, elections, fragmented constitutional government, at the risk of being corrupted or compromised by it, or bypass the system and emphasize direct political action and propaganda?

Garrison and others had long denounced the constitutional compromise over slavery. Phillips saw the whole political system as biased toward certain outcomes. "Every government is always growing corrupt," he said. Every Secretary of State was "an enemy to the people of necessity, because the moment he joins the government, he gravitates against that popular agitation which is the life of a republic." Phillips held liberty to be as essential to a republic as a republic was to liberty; hence antislavery agitation was part of the machinery of the state. "The Republic which sinks to sleep, trusting to constitutions and machinery, to politicians and statesmen, for the safety of its liberties, never will have any."

Phillips understood the clashing roles of reformer and politician. "The reformer is careless of numbers, disregards popularity, and deals only with ideas, conscience, and common sense," he said. ". . . He neither expects nor is overanxious for immediate success. The politician dwells in an everlasting NOW. His motto is 'Success'—his aim, votes. His object is not absolute right, but, like Solon's laws, as much right as the people will sanction. His office is not to instruct public opinion, but to represent it."

The abolitionists would instruct, preach, inspire, elevate public opinion; they were wary of electoral activity because even ad hoc alliances with other parties or movements for achieving practical, short-run ends through government, would help the enemy by legitimizing *its* institutions. *"Moral* influence," said Lydia Maria Child, "dies under *party* action." Because the militant abolitionists were above all moralizers and preachers, they impressed some of their contemporaries—and some historians—as dogmatic, humorless, rigid, aggressive, and even neurotic, responding more to their internal psychological needs than to the social and economic needs of the masses. They can better be understood as persons who, because of their social, educational, and religious backgrounds, took the values of liberty and equality with the utmost seriousness; saw slavery as the monumental repudiation of these values that it was; and cast about unceasingly for moral or political solutions to an evil that seemed to be spreading.

Inevitably, abolitionists tended to be earnest, committed, single-minded. Some, like the New York capitalist Lewis Tappan, often were morally arrogant, obstinate, cliquish, and abrasive. But many seemed notably reasonable, gentle, good-humored, personable. Maria Chapman was a beautiful person in almost every meaning of the phrase; Wendell Phillips showed all the graces of his birth and breeding; Lydia Maria Child's devotion to justice was matched by her love of nature; the Grimké sisters were sensitive and compassionate, if determined; even Garrison revealed himself in his letters as a frequent conciliator and occasional wit. Aileen Kraditor saw them as "a group of people intensely earnest in their struggle against slavery but also capable of poking fun at their own seriousness and laughing at their own vagaries."

The abolitionists lived amid conflict—conflict not only with proslavery opponents but among themselves. Their disagreements over gradualism versus immediatism, over moral agitation versus political coalition-building, over reconstructing society versus purifying it—these and other disputes erupted in meeting after meeting. But they were also distinguished by their ability to listen to one another. They corresponded among themselves indefatigably, editorialized in their own newspapers and wrote letters to their opponents', talked and talked endlessly at their conferences. Debates went on within families too; James Russell Lowell and Wendell Phillips were but two who admitted the influence on them of their wives. "My wife," said Phillips, "made me an out and out abolitionist."

Dedicated to transcending leadership, educated and invigorated by conflict, united in a great intellectual collective, firmly grounded in a "third cadre" of rank-and-file activists throughout the Northeast and Midwest, the abolitionists of the 1830s and 1840s constituted a leadership group surpassed only by the men who earlier had built the nation's political system. Rather than operating through institutions, however—especially after the failure of the Liberty party in the 1840s—these men and women appealed directly to the public, through their speaking and writing, in order to raise people's consciousness of the evil of slavery. The object, said Lydia Maria Child, was "to change public opinion on the subject of slavery, by the persevering utterance of truth." This change would then show itself "in a thousand different forms:—such as conflict and separation in churches; new arrangements in colleges and schools; new customs in stages and cars; and new modifications of policy in the political parties of the day." Instead of staking their hopes on any of these developments, she said, abolitionism must control the public opinion that dominated them all. "The business of anti-slavery was, and is, to purify the *fountain,* whence all these streams flow; if it turns aside to take charge of any *one* of the streams, however important, it is obvious enough that the whole work must retrograde."

Ultimately, the abolitionist leaders were strategists of propaganda. Since even their incessant editorializing and lecturing could not reach masses of people, much depended on men and women who could. To some degree the antislavery writings and sentiments of Emerson and Thoreau had penetrated the popular consciousness. James Russell Lowell's poetry and prose—especially *The Biglow Papers*—and John Greenleaf Whittier's poems against slavery expansion influenced public opinion, as did Richard Hildreth's 1834 novel *The Slave, or, Memoirs of Archy Moore.* But their combined impact could hardly compare with that of a tiny woman, lately of Cincinnati, of a deeply religious family, who had been antislavery though not abolitionist, but who reacted passionately to the fugitive-slave provisions of the Compromise of 1850. The author earlier principally of books on housekeeping and "domestic science," she now penned a sentimental novel about two well-meaning but negligent southern masters, a cruel, New England–born villain named Simon Legree, a faithful black couple called Tom and Eliza, and a little white child named Eva. Harriet Beecher Stowe's *Uncle Tom's Cabin* sold three thousand copies on the day of publication, one hundred times that within a year, perhaps a million copies in Britain alone. Inspired by moral conviction and religious fervor, filled with gripping banalities, the book (and the play based on the book) became probably the most effective piece of propaganda in American history.

Whatever their differences and conflicts, antislavery people were united in their belief in moral persuasion and their opposition to the use of force. Some indeed made a fetish of nonviolence and "nonresistance." By the advent of the 1850s, however, powerful antislavery propaganda, intensifying abolitionist feeling, deepening southern intransigence, and a constitutional and political system that seemed to satisfy neither side, combined to raise storm clouds on the horizon. Not only nonresisters had responded to Lovejoy's murder. At a memorial meeting in Ohio a man of thirty-seven had risen at the end of the ceremonies to raise his hand and vow to consecrate his life to the destruction of slavery. His name was John Brown.

PART V
Neither Liberty
Nor Union

"Am I not a Woman and a Sister?"

CHAPTER 15

The Ripening Vineyard

I N October 1852, in his big house overlooking salt marshes stretching toward the Atlantic, hardly a dozen miles north of the Pilgrim landing, Daniel Webster lay dying of cirrhosis of the liver. His stomach and legs were swollen; he could barely sit up; he vomited blood even as five or six leeches sucked away. But the old warrior would die as he had lived, acting the parts of squire, orator, and statesman. Even prostrate on a sofa the Secretary of State seemed as imposing as ever in his blue coat, buff vest, black pantaloons, white cravat and turned-down collar. He spent hours watching as his ox and sheep were paraded past his window, and he supervised the daily activities of house and farm, gazing raptly at the stars and stripes of a miniature Union flag fastened to the masthead of a tiny boat in his pond. Toward the end, after completing his will and assembling family and servants around his bed, he delivered an oration on immortality. Drowsily closing his eyes for a moment and then opening them, he cried out, "Have I—wife, son, doctor, friends, are you all here?—have I, on this occasion, said any thing unworthy of Daniel Webster?"

The old gladiator died in bitter political disappointment. Vexed and humiliated by the Whig convention's nomination of General Winfield Scott earlier in the year, he had written his son that he was determined to quit as Secretary of State "and either go abroad, or go into obscurity . . ." President Fillmore kept him on until the end. Webster predicted that the Democrats under Pierce would sweep the country. As a *national* party," he said, "the Whigs are ended."

But not only the Whig party was dying in the early 1850s; a way of government was dying with it. The three resplendent leaders who had, in their different ways, acted for union were gone. Calhoun had died within a few weeks of Webster's great speech of March 7, 1850, still doubting that "two peoples so different and hostile" could "exist together in one common Union," while hoping that the North might make the necessary concessions for the nation to continue. Henry Clay, the very symbol of union, had died only four months before Webster. During most of their public lives these three leaders had fought to save the Union, even at the sacrifice of high principles like liberty and equality, as they defined them.

But now, in the early 1850s, the air was filled with the voices of those who proclaimed that the Union was but a means to higher ends—and what lofty ends was *this* union serving? Ralph Waldo Emerson happened to be on the beach at Plymouth the Sunday morning when Webster died, looking out across the rough water whose spray was blowing onto the hills and orchards. Not since Napoleon, Emerson reflected, had Nature "cut out such a masterpiece" as Webster, a strong leader, the teacher of the nation's legislators in style and eloquence, the model for young adventurers. "But alas!" as he wrote in his journal, "he was the victim of his ambition; to please the South betrayed the North, and was thrown out by both."

At dawn that Sunday morning the great bell of the Marshfield parish church loudly rang out. People stood transfixed; someone had died. The bell tolled three times three strokes, the signal for the death of a male. Then, indicating his age, it pealed seventy times. Webster! Born a few years before Shays' Rebellion and the drafting of the Constitution, he had, along with Clay and Calhoun, dominated the last forty years of Congress. A friend, walking around Webster's farm with him, once noted that the Marshfield land was not rich by nature, but rich with the money and manure the senator had lavished upon it. Webster had made a *fainéant* national government work too, after a fashion. Emerson mused: "He brought the strength of a savage into the height of culture."

THE CORNUCOPIA

By the 1850s in the upper Mississippi Valley, the endless work to clear and plow the land, the desperate struggles with bugs and blizzards, the risky financial gambles with machines and middlemen—all this effort was paying off. A twelve-year-old boy in Wisconsin, John Muir, would never forget the joys and woes of pioneer Wisconsin farm life: planting corn and potatoes and spring wheat while the nesting birds sang in the mild soothing breeze, the oaks behind "forming beautiful purple masses as if every leaf were a petal"; then the heavy summer work, sweaty days of sixteen or seventeen hours grinding scythes, chopping stove wood, fetching water from the spring, harvesting and haying under a burning sun; in the winter, rising in a bitterly cold house, squeezing throbbing, chilblained feet into soggy boots, hauling and chopping and fencing in the frozen wastes and yet still relishing the wonderful radiance of the "snow starry with crystals."

Farming remained the main occupation of Americans—about three-quarters of the nation's 24 million population were still "rural"—but the agricultural heartland was moving west. In what Allan Nevins called the Northwestern Surge, land-hungry settlers had broken through the Appalachians to seize the flat and later the rolling prairies to the west. Illinois began the 1850s with fewer people than Massachusetts and ended the decade with almost half a million more. Wisconsin jumped ahead of New Jersey. The population of Iowa soared from 200,000 to almost 700,000. With 2,340,000 inhabitants, Ohio became the third biggest state of the Union. The irresistible magnet was the soil, dark and black, fertile from age-old grassland vegetation and deep root systems, six and even ten or twelve feet deep. The climate, while occasionally cruel, was just about right for rich yields.

Improved farm machinery boosted production during the 1840s and 1850s. The steel plow was the decisive weapon in breaking up the prairie land, replacing eastern-type cast-iron plows that would not scour effectively. John Deere had fashioned his first steel plow from a saw blade in 1837; a decade later this plow, manufactured by the thousands in the East, was rapidly coming into use in the prairie region. In the late 1850s farmers even tried to substitute a steam plow for the ox-driven plow, but the ungainly contraption was not a success. The most dramatic change on the prairie came with the improvement of the reaper. Hussey's reaper, the most widely known in 1840, was mounted on two large drive wheels from which extended a platform with its cutting knife on the forward edge. The grain fell on this platform and had to be quickly raked away by half a dozen men. With Cyrus McCormick's improved reaper, the grain was raked from the side of the platform, thus forestalling the need to bind before the machine came around again. Reapers often were deployed together by the scores, with hundreds of men, women, and children harvesting the golden grain behind them.

Everything ultimately turned on the intelligence, daring, and persistence of the farm people. James Baldwin left a striking record of his farm days, as portrayed by Allan Nevins: "Here is a sober, hardworking Quaker farmer of Indiana, living in a log cabin with stick-and-clay chimney—but with the skeleton of a new frame house near by." About it stretched the "big woods," especially thick down by the watercourses, two large cornfields speckled by charred stumps, other fields marked for "tree deadenin'," and a full-grown orchard. "The farmer's speech is Hoosier dialect. Yet like the Yankee squire he is proud of his shelf of books: the *Journals* of George Fox and John Woolman, Walker's *Dictionary,* standard texts like Noah Webster's blue-backed spelling book, Pike's *Arithmetic,* and Lindley Murray's *English Reader;* some volumes of McGuffey; old classics like *Robinson Crusoe;* and in due time Dickens. Though his daily dress is blue jeans, he has a 'go to meetin' suit of drab homespun and a gray beaver hat in which he takes on a mien of dignity."

Out of this magical mix of men and machines and moisture with sun and soil was arising the granary of the world—a cornucopia of corn and wheat, of oxen and horses, of pork and beef, and later of poultry, and the products of grain, especially whiskey. At first corn was king, then wheat. The corn crop of 1839 came to 377 million bushels, while that of 1849 was almost 600 million. Wheat production in the next decade rose by 75 percent to about 175 million bushels, while the rate of increase of corn production fell somewhat. Illinois led the nation in corn and later in wheat. By the 1850s that state and Indiana and Wisconsin were far outstripping New York and Pennsylvania in wheat output. One stockman alone, B. F. Harris of Urbana, raised annually about 500 cattle and 600 hogs on his four-thousand-acre farm.

The prairie land seemed to pulsate with energy. The air was filled with the clatter of revolving wooden horse rakes, threshing machines, seed drills, corn planters, harrows, sulky plows, self-scouring disks, and—in the farmhouse—hand-washing machines and chain-bucket pumps. Farm people flocked to agricultural fairs to see new machines, inspect livestock and produce, hear political orators. Energy radiated outward. The railroads and canalboats that brought people and machines west returned east loaded with hogs and foodstuffs. Cattlemen trying to save money drove huge herds of steers overland, pasturing their beeves on roadside grass and in hired meadows, trying frantically to keep them out of farmers' fields. With a sixty-day drive from Illinois to eastern cities, however, stockmen increasingly chose to sell their hogs and cattle in western cities instead. Alton and Peoria and especially Chicago were rapidly becoming the slaughtering centers of the nation.

This Northwestern Surge in agriculture produced a powerful social and economic undertow in the East. Farmers in the Northeast were accustomed to change; many had shifted from a self-sufficient home economy to a market economy as the seaboard cities expanded. Now they were faced with a more severe challenge as grain from the West cut heavily into the market for their cereals, and their holdings of swine and sheep fell off. The drovers of Long Island, Connecticut, New Jersey, and Westchester, who had once hustled their herds into the cattle market at Bull's Head Village in lower Manhattan, had to stand by helplessly as wholesale slaughterers brought in cattle and hogs by the hundreds of thousands via canals—especially the Erie—and railroads from the West. Some farmers could not make the transition, and they—or at least their sons and daughters—escaped to the city or to the West.

But others proved that Yankee resourcefulness was still alive. They stepped up their production of milk and apples and berries and market vegetables. They bred some of the best sheep and blooded horses and poultry and cattle—Guernsey, Durham, Devon, and other breeds. Upstate New Yorkers produced cheddar good enough for the export trade, and built more than a score of cheese factories during the 1850s. New England farmers made money out of the rich tobacco lands along the Connecticut River, out of maple sugar, cranberries, butter, vegetables. Canneries, using tin canisters—later "tin cans"—preserved lobsters, oysters, fruit jellies, peas, tomatoes, sweet corn, some of which was bought by whalers for their long voyages. The Yankees were quick to take advantage of farm fads. One of these was "hen fever"—unbridled speculation in blooded fowls. Shanghai chicks, Cochin Chinas, and other fancy Oriental poultry brought from $75 to $100 a pair at the Boston Fowl Show in 1852.

Many of these efforts were experimental, and not all ended well. Ephraim Bull of Concord spent years perfecting an early-ripening variety of the wild northern fox grape. After eleven years of planting, selecting, and testing his stock, he exhibited his "Concord grape" amid much acclaim in the Massachusetts Horticultural Hall. But Bull was better at inventing than profit-making, for commercial nurseries moved in on his trade in seedlings and bested him in competition. The embittered Bull at least had the last word. On his gravestone in Concord cemetery is carved the epitaph: "HE SOWED, OTHERS REAPED."

While northwestern farming surged, and northeastern agriculture adapted, much of southeastern farming lagged behind. A South Carolinian in 1857 summed up the situation in an address to his state's agricultural society, in much the same words of warning used by other farm leaders: "Our present system is to cut down our forest and run it into cotton as long as it will pay for the labor expended. Then cut down more forest, plant in cotton, plough it uphill and downhill, and when it fails to give a support leave it. . . . Then sell the carcass for what you can realize and migrate to the Southwest in quest of another victim. This ruinous system has entailed upon us an exhausted soil, and a dependence upon Kentucky and Tennessee for our mules, horses, and hogs, and upon the Northern States for all our necessaries from the clothing and shoeing of our negroes down to our *wheelbarrows, corn-brooms and axe-handles.*" The South was still self-sufficient in food, but already in 1859 the wheat and corn crops of Illinois and Ohio exceeded those of all seven states of the Deep South combined.

Slavery was keeping the South excessively rural, with an unbalanced economy dominated by dangerous speculation in cotton, tobacco, and sugar. Southerners could not break out of their economic prison, walled in by poor communication and transportation, depleted soils, limited capital, lack of diversification, a slower population growth, and, first and last, a great sluggish under-class of poor whites and under-caste of blacks. Moreover, the large plantation owners lacked an incentive to break out of the pattern, for the prices of cotton and tobacco rose steadily between 1850 and 1860, even while production doubled. King Cotton brought prosperity—at least to a few—and made it possible to ignore the underlying problems.

The southern "rim states" were somewhat more successful in agriculture. Northwestern Virginia and the Shenandoah Valley produced heavy crops of wheat; small farms were thriving in Tennessee and Kentucky; Arkansas and Florida were boosting their cattle and hog production; the piedmont country of Virginia and North Carolina displayed agricultural diversity in its market gardening and livestock raising; Texas was rapidly becoming a livestock empire by itself. By 1856 Texans were driving their longhorns overland to the slaughterhouses of Chicago. By the end of the decade the "outer" South was, in agricultural diversification and innovation, leaving the "inner" far behind.

Agriculture North and South showed the defect of its own virtue of abundance—colossal waste. Land was depleted by inefficient plowing, waste or improper use of manure and other fertilizers, single-cropping of the same land year after year, heavy leaching. It was easy to squander a commodity that seemed in endless supply. Throughout the nation, however, were men aware of this waste and inefficiency. Long active in their own states, in 1852 they formed the United States Agricultural Society to represent and assist the nation's agriculture and promote experimentation and education. As farm journals burgeoned—*Prairie Farmer, American Agriculturalist, American Farmer, Farmer's Register,* and *Cultivator*—editors preached better fencing, fertilizing, plowing, draining, rotating. Greeley's *Tribune* appointed an agricultural editor. The message was further spread at fairs and exhibitions. Scientific farming, however, remained in its infancy.

States began establishing agricultural courses, departments, and—in Michigan—a college of agriculture. The federal government largely stood aloof. Despite a tiny budget, the Patent Office promoted use of new seeds and new crops, such as sorghum cane, but bills to establish grants of public lands for higher education met a presidential veto. Agriculture—still the foundation of the American economy—was left primarily to private leadership and enterprise.

*   *   *

The British and Pennsylvania pig iron that helped mechanize much of the northwestern farmer's work supplied also the thousands of miles of rails that bound him closer to the markets of the East. The railroad fever and expansion of the 1850s was producing a virtual revolution in transportation. Hardly a town or large city did not harbor ambitions that the rails would come its way, bringing investors, buyers, jobs, and access to the whole railroad gridiron developing in the Northwest. The eleven thousand miles of railroad in existence in 1852 almost tripled in length by the end of the decade. The north-central states led the way in this expansion, followed by the Northeast, the south Atlantic states, and the old Southwest.

America's hundred-year romance with the railroad was well under way, although some people did not love the iron horse. "The railroad will leave the land despoiled, ruined, a desert where only sable buzzards shall wing their loathesome way," cried an orator. A state legislator waxed more evangelical than environmental: "Canals, sir, are God's own highway, operating on the soft bosom of the fluid that comes straight from Heaven. The railroad stems direct from Hell. It is the Devil's own invention, compounded of fire, smoke, soot, and dirt, spreading its infernal poison throughout the fair countryside. It will set fire to houses along its slimy tracks. It will throw burning brands into the ripe fields of the honest husbandman and destroy his crops. . . ."

But, as Bismarck once remarked, it is not by speeches and parliamentary resolutions that the great questions of the day are decided but by blood and iron, and the iron rails continued to chop through the countryside, at a national average of almost forty miles a week. Each mile cost from $20,000 to $40,000, but capitalists and civic leaders in the big eastern cities and the growing inland towns raised the money, with aid from European financiers. The local citizen helped out too; during the 1850s Wisconsin farmers mortgaged their property for almost $5 million to invest in railroad building. Politicians and capitalists and townspeople alike felt well rewarded when the first iron horse arrived in town. Church bells rang, bands played, and politicos gave speeches as the hissing monster rumbled into the new depot. And when the Erie Railroad completed its 450-mile main line stretching from the Hudson to the Lakes in 1850, President Fillmore and Daniel Webster themselves rode the train—Webster seated on a rocking chair fastened onto an open flat car—to the end of the line at Dunkirk, where they were greeted by a parade, a barbecue, and a twenty-one-gun salute from the U.S.S. *Michigan.*

Cities wanted railroads—and railroads built cities. Chicago, perfectly situated at the center of the northwestern heartland, and at the southern tip of Lake Michigan around which east-west traffic to the north had to detour, had not a single railroad tie in 1850. Within five years it became the terminus for 2,200 miles and had 100 big trains arriving and departing each day. Its grain elevators, trackside warehouses, lake and canal facilities meshed with its railroads radiating out like spokes in a wheel. Soon trains out of Chicago were jumping the Mississippi into Iowa, steaming down to Cairo and points south, invading Missouri, and linking with the great northern arms of the Father of the Waters.

Lake Michigan served as a broad seaway south to Chicago, tapping the wilderness to the north; two other nautical boulevards, Lakes Ontario and Erie, pointed directly at Chicago from the east. But these inland seaways were not connected and hence could not serve heavy transportation until man intervened. As the constantly improved Erie Canal disgorged people and freight from the east, more and more Lake Erie steamers navigated its shallow and frisky waters. The opening of the Canadian-built Welland Canal enabled steamboats to pass around Niagara Falls between Ontario and Erie. But the most momentous development for Chicago and all the other Great Lakes cities was the extraordinary feat, conceived and engineered by a young Vermonter named Charles T. Harvey, of building the Sault Ste. Marie Canal to bypass the rapids between huge Lake Superior and Lake Huron. Soon lake steamers were toting vast quantities of copper and iron ore from the mines on Superior's shores to points east. By the late 1850s Chicago, Detroit, Cleveland, Buffalo, and scores of smaller cities were battening off this new lake commerce, and ships were carrying western products from Chicago to Liverpool over the thousand-mile seaway stretching toward the northeast.

Not only grimy ore boats plied the lake waters. Fine lake steamers were built to carry first-class passengers in style, as well as immigrants below-decks. "The handsomest of the lake vessels by the middle fifties," Nevins wrote, "the *Western World,* was 348 feet long, with powerful engines and beautiful interior fittings. She and her peers, the *Plymouth Rock,* the *Western Metropolis,* and others, with several hundred staterooms each, competed in luxury and entertainment for those who could pay. Down the green lakes they slipped with dancing, gambling, flirtation, and feasting, the musicians in the ballrooms thrumming their guitars," to the chant:

> Old Huron's long, old Huron's wide,
> De engines keep de time.

Still, nothing could compete for romance with the river-boating a thousand miles south, on the Mississippi. Nevins pictured the river port scenes: "The mile-long expanse of boats smoking and throbbing at the St. Louis and New Orleans levees; the motley crowds of passengers—fur-traders, immigrants, soldiers, cotton-planters, land-speculators, gamblers, politicians, British tourists, Indians, and plain farmers; the avalanche of pork, grain, tobacco, cotton, and hides that the Illinois, the Cumberland, the Washita, the Arkansas, and the Red poured into the central Mississippi stream, cramming every deck; the lordly pilots, the hardbitten captains, the profane mates, the chanting roustabouts; the fierce races as the firemen tied down safety valves, the hands crammed fat-pine into the roaring furnaces, and the passengers cheered. . . ."

No lady, northern or southern, could ever forget those New Orleans riverboats—stepping down the long promenade deck with its view of hundreds of lights reflecting off the river water, or parading into the palatial dining saloon, with its glittering mirrors, shining candelabra, table settings of damask and silver, and bowers of fruits and flowers.

Romantic—but not altogether economic. The lower Mississippi was often a fickle and even faithless waterway as the water rose and fell unpredictably, channels silted up, and vessels grounded or waited for days in order to pass through. In St. Louis, crates, barrels, hogsheads of tobacco, bags of corn, and a great confusion of goods of all descriptions piled up for two miles along the winding riverbank, often delayed there by a water level that could rise or fall almost forty feet. St. Louis was far enough north to suffer from ice, far enough south to suffer from floods. Despite these difficulties the Missouri city, as well located among rivers as Chicago was among lakes, became by the 1850s one of the world's biggest centers for breaking and transferring freight.

As northern canals grew wider and longer, northern steamers bigger and deeper, northern ports more mechanized, northern capitalists bolder and richer, northern free workers more productive, the South fell behind in the competition to exploit the riches of the heartland.

* * *

Businessmen preferred economics to romance. They were making and selling and buying and importing their own cornucopia of goods. George W. Cable described a New Orleans wharf: "drays with all imaginable kinds of burden; cotton in bales, piled as high as the omnibuses; leaf tobacco in huge hogsheads; cases of linens and silks; stacks of rawhides; crates of cabbages; bales of prints and of hay; interlocked heaps of blue and red ploughs; bags of coffee, spices, and corn; bales of bagging; barrels, casks, and tierces; whiskey, pork, onions, oats, bacon, garlic, molasses, and other delicacies; rice, sugar—what was there not? . . ." Agriculture still dominated invention and production, but transportation and industry were becoming increasingly important. In 1854 the Patent Office issued fifty-six patents for harvesting implements, thirty-nine for seed planters, and sixteen for plows; in 1856 it issued forty for sewing machines, thirty-one for looms, and nineteen for locks.

Products that would become household names were being manufactured now in quantity: not only the McCormick reaper but the Colt revolver, the Remington rifle, Otis elevators, Goodyear's India-rubber fabrics, Baldwin locomotives. Cities were already specializing in their output. Cincinnati produced more than 125,000 chairs a year by the mid-1850s; Chicago about $2.5 million in ready-made clothes; Lynn, Massachusetts, about 4.5 million boots and shoes. Americans were ingenious in making machines that helped make machines—drills, saws, pumps, belts, milling machines, turret lathes. The American system specialized in interchangeable parts. By the end of the decade, manufactories were turning out 300,000 iron stoves a year, with interchangeable panels, tops, lids, fireboxes.

It was the age of iron—iron locomotives, ships, railroad rails, bridges, farm machinery, pianos—and buildings. Substituting iron beams for wood, Americans made the first multi-story iron building frames. Cast-iron beams were enormously heavy, however, and soon Trenton was using specially designed machines to roll wrought-iron ones. These beams were used in building Cooper Union and Harper Brothers' new building after the old one burned. James Bogardus' Manhattan foundry for making iron was made of iron.

Merchant princes were catering to family buyers, especially women. H. B. Claflin earned a fortune out of the dry-goods business. Charles L. Tiffany sold fine jewelry and silverware. Visitors in New York gaped at the huge department stores, with their plate-glass windows and marble pillars. There were a hundred piano manufacturers in New York City alone. But women produced for themselves—books, selling in the hundreds of thousands. "America is now wholly given over to a damned mob of scribbling women," Nathaniel Hawthorne wrote to his friend the publisher William D. Ticknor, "and I should have no chance of success while the public taste is occupied with their trash."

Fueled by enormous farm output, abundant natural resources, rising productivity, a thickening transportation grid, heavy inflows of cheap labor from abroad, and constant experimentation and innovation, the great economic boom roared on. Critical to expansion was the capital that flowed from foreign and eastern and—increasingly—western investors, from home savings, and from the nearly 27 million ounces of gold that were produced in the decade after James Marshall had looked into Sutter's mill stream with a wild surmise. Commodity output in agriculture, mining, manufacturing, and construction more than doubled during the two

decades after 1840. Economic historians differ as to which decade brought
the most significant economic "takeoff" or acceleration—the 1820s, 1830s,
1840s, or 1850s—but without doubt all the earlier forces making for
greater productivity came together most powerfully in the later years.

Such was the view from the top, but from the bottom Americans were
still making little progress toward equalizing the average family's share of
this cornucopia of farm, freight, and factory. By the end of the 1850s
masons, blacksmiths, stonecutters, and foremen or overseers were making
about two dollars a day; teamsters, quarrymen, blacksmiths' and boiler-
makers' helpers, and unskilled laborers about one dollar. The old patterns
of discrimination persisted: male weavers received 93 cents a day, female
weavers 65 cents. Women spinners got half a dollar a day. Some Americans
romanticized that the early years of the republic had been golden years of
equality, others that the labor and populist movements of the 1830s had
had an egalitarian impact. Sober statistics indicated that inequality in the
American republic in its first seventy years had simply been constant.

THE CORNUCOPIA OVERFLOWS

At the glittering Crystal Palace exhibition in London in 1851, the *National Intelligencer* reported proudly "our handled axes, hay rakes, grain
cradles, scythes and snathes, three-tined hayforks, solid steel hoes, road-
scrapers, posthole augers, fan-mills, smut-mills, sausage cutters, sausage
stuffers, tin-man's tools, permutation locks, wheel cultivators, carpenters'
tools, currycombs, corn-blooms, portmanteaus and trunks, ice-cream
freezers, axletrees, paint-mills," had established for American industry a
"character independent of and unlike that of any other nation." Most of
these products betrayed the hold that agriculture still had on American
industrial enterprise, but the Yankees also invaded the English market with
sewing machines, clocks, and even the Hoe printing press.

Farm commodities—cotton, wheat, pork, and the like—made up by far
the greater part of American exports across the Atlantic. Those exports
were soaring; during the 1850s America's foreign commerce more than
doubled. In exchange for their commodities Americans were importing
textiles, machinery, iron in the form of rods, bars, rails, and castings. Using
the great export routes of the Mississippi and the St. Lawrence, as well as
the Atlantic ports, Chicago and Cleveland and St. Louis and New Orleans
were shipping out their flour and pork and bacon at the rate of tens of
millions of dollars a year.

Eastern port cities boomed along with this commerce; so did the American merchant marine. The coastal trade flourished; richly decorated "floating palaces" were steaming along Long Island Sound to Connecticut ports, where passengers could link with the expanding railroad grid. New York City gained and held the lion's share of foreign commerce, followed by Boston, and then by Philadelphia and Baltimore in close competition. The glory of all these ports was the American merchantman—especially the packet, the brig, and the clipper ship. The packet was the most versatile vessel, so dependable that it could run on regular schedules, able to carry cabin passengers, best-paying freight such as textiles and fine goods, and sometimes bulkier freight. The brigs, great square-rigged vessels with two or three masts, were the workhorses of the marine fleet, majestic in size and speed, thrilling to see amidst the spume of the Atlantic. But the pride and the boast of American sailors was the clipper ship, narrow of beam, daintily concave in sides and bow, low and clean of deck, slicing through the water at fifteen knots or more, under a panoply of sails reaching two hundred feet above water.

London liked the grain and the goods that arrived on the packets; it was less enthusiastic about some of the people. The 1850s were a bumptious period in American diplomacy. The new American minister in London, James Buchanan, received instructions from the new Secretary of State, William L. Marcy, to appear at court not in gold braid and ostrich feathers but "in the simple costume of an American citizen." When Buchanan dutifully showed up in sober republican attire, aside from a dress sword he added so he would not be mistaken for a servant, a London newspaper upbraided the "puppyism" of "the gentleman in the black coat." American visitors in Europe were invincibly boastful. They felt they had much to brag about—especially after 1851 when the New York yacht *America* won her cup off the Isle of Wight in a duel with British yachtsmen.

Behind Yankee vainglory lay a surge of organized popular feeling. Since the mid-1840s a movement known as Young America had risen, primarily in the western wing of the Democratic party. Inspirited by the defeat of Mexico and the acquisition of territory, exuberantly nationalistic but also keenly sympathetic to the republican and revolutionary movements of Europe, Young America enjoyed thwacking the "Old Fogeys" in the party hip and thigh. There had been a Young England, a Young Italy, a Young Germany, they pointed out—why not a Young America? Led by a man of dubious reputation named George Sanders, a wealthy Kentucky Democrat, Young America mixed nineteenth-century liberal idealism and crassly materialistic expansionism into a heady brew that for a short time helped raise popular consciousness of America's "manifest destiny." By supporting the Hungarian patriot Kossuth and others "who had suffered in the cause of liberty," Young America both abetted and exploited a wave of popular feeling for Hungarian and other rebels against "oppression"—a feeling that amounted to a fad and even a Kossuth craze.

For these Americans too, the watchword was liberty. When Kossuth arrived in New York Harbor in December 1851, the health officer who boarded the ship saw fit to welcome "Noble Magyar! Illustrious Kossuth!" to the land of free speech and action, and as the hope and trust "of the friends of liberty in every nation and clime." Said the New York *Herald:* "National glory—national greatness—the spread of political liberty on this continent, must be the thought and action by day, and the throbbing dream by night, of the whole American people, or they will sink into oblivion." But liberty, as Americans defined it, seemed to have a variety of meanings and applications—liberty of speech and religion, liberty to take and exploit land, liberty of enterprise, liberty of foreigners to revolt against oppression, liberty of Americans to intervene in such revolts, liberty of Americans to spread liberty. And self-interest often seemed to lurk behind the lofty ideals. Thus William Seward could talk about the nation's "divine purpose" of spreading democracy, and almost in the same breath, of farmers' need of gaining markets for "our surplus meat and bread." And, aside from the abolitionists, all the talk of liberty seemed to have no relevance to slaves.

It was this seeming hypocrisy that especially galled foreigners. *Punch* portrayed a diabolical, cigar-smoking American, pistol in hand, whip tucked under his arm, blowing smoke rings that displayed lynch law, repudiation, dueling, and slavery. The caption: "THE LAND OF LIBERTY."

*　　*　　*

The mixed concepts of liberty as liberation, and liberty as exploitation, dominated the goals of American foreign policy in the early fifties. Everything seemed to conspire to make Cuba a tinderbox. This was a time, in the wake of the revolutions of '48 and the counter-insurgencies, when American liberals, North and South, could grieve over the sufferings of subjugated Cubans as well as the oppression of Hungarians, Italians, French, or Irish. To southern planters, however, Cuba was a slave dependency where Madrid, under pressure from London and Paris, occasionally threatened to emancipate the slaves, thus creating a "free soil" area to the south. And to other Americans, Cuba was a large and profitable-looking piece of real estate.

This was also a time when the President of the United States, instead of being predisposed against going to war, was wholly prepared to do so if necessary to protect "American national interests." Franklin Pierce, moreover, was a nationalist who had warned in his Inaugural Address that his administration would not be restrained "by any timid forebodings of evil from expansion." He was close to southern and western expansionists who were gaining increasing influence in the Democracy, and to leaders of Young America who set the tone of much of the debate.

Yet Pierce had to proceed warily. He had to husband the support of northern and southern moderates on slavery and expansion, both in dealing with Congress and in seeking to retain the presidency. And he had to work with two men in his own administration who dreamed of entering the White House. Secretary of State Marcy was a venerable Democratic party wheelhorse, three-term governor of New York, and an anti-abolitionist, who had won some notoriety for saying that he could see "nothing wrong in the rule that to the victor belongs the spoils." James Buchanan, Secretary of State under Polk, was modest and shrewd enough to accept the London ministry. Buchanan's compliance with Marcy's dress instruction was an early indication that neither man would allow the other—or the President—to outbid the jingo vote at home.

But the Cuban tinderbox lay waiting, and the spark that threatened to ignite it was struck early in 1854 when the Spanish authorities in Havana rather arbitrarily seized an American coastal steamer, the *Black Warrior*. The Spaniards had reason to feel edgy: For some years various filibusters, bearing the torches of liberty and realty, had been launching expeditions into Cuba expecting that the oppressed masses would rise against their overlords. Americans had been variously implicated in these efforts. Not for the first or last time, the Cubans failed to rise and welcome their deliverers. After the Havana authorities had executed a number of Americans among the invaders, a bellicose American mob assaulted Spaniards in New Orleans and sacked the Spanish consulate.

The Whig administration of the day had resisted demands for war and even offered Madrid an apology. But the patriotic Democrats were now in power, and they would not let the Spaniards off so easily. In Madrid itself there appeared one of the most remarkable products of American parochial politics ever to grace the diplomatic corridors of power: Pierre Soulé, a United States senator from Louisiana and a longtime leader of southern expansionists. Soulé was no swamp rat, but a well-mannered gentleman and fine conversationalist, a democrat who had fled monarchist France as a youth and developed ties with European radicals. Appointed Minister to Spain by Pierce, he arrived in Madrid amid much controversy, and promptly created a furor when the Duke of Alba and the French ambassador at a diplomatic grand ball made cutting remarks about Mrs. Soulé's plump figure and low-cut costume, leading the aggrieved husband to cross swords with the duke and then to shoot the ambassador in the leg. Talk about these duels had hardly died down when Soulé was presented with the *Black Warrior* provocation.

For a time the stage seemed set for American annexation of Cuba and war with Spain. Pierce sent Congress a truculent message alleging long-time Spanish insults to American rights and honor, and demanding indemnity, failing which he was prepared to use any means for redress that Congress would grant him. Marcy more calmly instructed Soulé to demand satisfaction. The Louisianian was beside himself with hope and excitement. This seemed to him—and to his fellow annexationists at home—the ideal moment to strike, for the outbreak of the Crimean War would divert British and French attention to their eastern crisis, and Madrid itself was preoccupied by a domestic military revolt. Soulé did his part by exceeding Marcy's instructions and bidding Madrid to agree to pay an indemnity and to dismiss the Havana officials—and to do so within forty-eight hours—or he would regard his demands as rejected.

But this was to be another day that a President did not go to war. Sensing that Soulé had overreached himself, the Spanish minister in Washington dealt directly with Marcy, while French and British diplomats closed ranks with the Spanish. Madrid, long expert at procrastination, used delay as a means of cooling tempers. The calls by southern press and politicians for seizure were matched by demands for a hands-off policy by Northerners aware of the proslavery implications of accession, and by some influential southern journals.

Frustrated, Pierce decided to convene a conference of his ministers in Madrid, London, and Paris. This trio—Soulé, Buchanan, and the Virginia expansionist John Mason—issued the Ostend Manifesto (actually neither a manifesto nor written in Ostend) calling for the American purchase of Cuba or, failing that, use of force to seize it. The manifesto turned out to be far too blatant, arousing a furor at home; "Manifesto of the Brigands," the *Tribune* called it. Defeated in the fall congressional elections, Pierce drew back. Marcy repudiated the document and rebuked Soulé. The Louisianian resigned. The affair was over. It remained for the London *Times* to write its epitaph: "The diplomacy of the United States," it observed, "is certainly a very singular profession."

The expansionist energies of Young America and other nationalists did not flag on the shores of Cuba. Eight hundred miles farther south lay the Isthmus. For centuries Americans, North, Central, and South, had dreamed of a waterway that would link the Atlantic and the Pacific. The dream became even more compelling when gold-rushers to California, to avoid the long trip around Cape Horn, took the tortuous and disease-ridden overland mule trail from ocean to ocean. Britain, however, also had interests and possessions—notably British Honduras—in Central America. After some angry incidents and confrontations Zachary Taylor's Secretary of State, John M. Clayton, and Britain's minister in Washington, Henry Lytton Bulwer, had signed a treaty by which the two nations renounced territorial ambitions in Central America, agreed to cooperate in constructing an isthmian canal, and promised never to gain or exercise exclusive control over the canal.

Democrats were still denouncing the treaty as an ignominious surrender and repudiation of the Monroe Doctrine when the American minister in Greytown, in the British protectorate of the Mosquito Coast, had his face cut open by a broken bottle during mob disorders. When an American naval commander demanded reparation and it was not forthcoming, he bombarded the town. Tempers cooled, but British-American relations were further embittered when the American filibuster William Walker made himself dictator of Nicaragua and talked of forming a Central American federation, and when New England fishermen jousted with Canadian authorities over fishing rights along the Newfoundland and Labrador coasts. Other incidents followed; the absorption of the British in the Crimean War, and of Americans in the widening split between North and South, may have helped avert serious confrontations.

*　　*　　*

If the Atlantic had been for Americans an ocean of commerce and an arena of conflict—an arena of invasions, sea battles, blockades, privateers, filibusters—the Pacific had been pacific. What was known of the largest of oceans, aside from the reports of explorers, had been learned in pursuing the prodigious source of a few rather specialized products: sperm oil for the brightest, purest kind of light, as in lighthouse beacons; spermaceti, for the better grade of candles; whalebone, for corsets, stays, whips, and umbrellas; ambergris, for perfumes and aphrodisiacs. The source for all these was the whale—the humpback, the bowhead, the right, and above all the sperm whale.

In their two- and three-year journeys to the southern and northern and western Pacific, whalemen explored new routes and charted distant islands, reefs, and shoals. They also left way stations and repair ports, the most important of which was Honolulu. By the 1850s, several hundred whalers were visiting the Hawaiian port every year. Its ship-repair facilities made it a vital naval station; inevitably Pierce and Marcy included Hawaii as part of the nation's manifest destiny. Whalemen from Massachusetts found on Hawaii a large and energetic band of missionaries from Boston, who had built out of coral blocks a large stone church, in the image of a New England meeting house, that served also as a landmark for sailors.

During this height of the era of whaling 600 whalers were bringing home over a quarter million barrels of sperm and whale oil a year, and 2.5 million pounds of whalebone. "Home" was a remarkably small number of ports —notably New Bedford and other New England seacoast towns and river ports like Poughkeepsie on the Hudson. Whaling flourished for a time in the island towns of Nantucket and Edgartown, but eventually they yielded ground to New Bedford. Collectively the whaling towns provided more than 15,000 men for crews and employed thousands more in building, outfitting, and repairing the slow, stubby, broad-beamed vessels strong enough to survive forty or more months of warring with wind, wave, and whale.

Herman Melville had shipped out of Fairhaven, across from New Bedford, on a whaler bound for the South Seas, and no one pictured the romance of whaling as evocatively as he did. The long-awaited, transcending moment of excitement came with the chase by the speedy little whaleboats:

> . . . The vast swells of the omnipotent sea; the surging, hollow roar they made, as they rolled along the eight gunwales, like gigantic bowls in a boundless bowling-green; the brief suspended agony of the boat, as it would tip for an instant on the knife-like edge of the sharper waves, that almost seemed threatening to cut it in two; the sudden profound dip into the watery glens and hollows; the keen spurrings and goadings to gain the top of the opposite hill; the headlong, sled-like slide down its other side;—all these, with the cries of the headsmen and harpooners, and the shuddering gasps of the oarsmen, with the wondrous sight of the ivory Pequod bearing down upon her boats with outstretched sails. . . .
>
> A short, rushing sound leaped out of the boat; it was the darted iron of Queequeg. Then all in one welded commotion came an invisible push from astern, while forward the boat seemed striking on a ledge; the sail collapsed and exploded; a gush of scalding vapor shot up near by; something rolled and tumbled like an earthquake beneath us. The whole crew was half suffocated as they were tossed helter-skelter into the white curdling cream of the squall. Squall, whale, and harpoon had all blended together. . . .

This was a romantic view of the whaler's life; the view from the forecastle was markedly different. The forecastleman shared the hardships of the ordinary seaman—sleeping and living in a tiny, stinking compartment, with swill and vomit washing about under the wooden bunks, with almost no ventilation or light during cold or stormy weather, with men of a dozen lands and tongues smoking, spitting, cursing, quarreling amid greasy pans, sea chests, soap kegs, in sweat-saturated underclothes. For the whalers, whose voyages were long, conditions were even worse than for ordinary seamen. Their water turned foul, butter rancid, meat rotten, with bread so full of worms that it became common practice to scald them out or—more agreeably—to pour half a pint of rum into the bread casket ahead of time. On the "Nantucket sleigh-ride" a man could drown or lose a limb. Pay was poor. Whalemen lived wretched, oppressed lives, second in misery only to the lot of Africans on the slaver.

The indomitable whalers sailed far beyond the Sandwich Islands to the Bonins, the South China Sea, and Japan. Ever since independence, and freedom from the British Navigation Acts, Americans had been conducting an active trade with the Chinese in tea and silks, working closely with the British, in the treaty ports of Canton, Shanghai, and other Chinese trading centers. A major obstacle in dealing with the Chinese was their conviction that the visitors were "foreign devils" and "barbarians," while the Americans looked on the Chinese as quaintly mysterious. The inscrutable Orient and Occident had similar problems in Japan. Several American whaling men who had survived a shipwreck off the Kuriles were incarcerated by the Japanese for a year, and required to trample on a tablet picturing the Crucifixion.

Yet trade was growing, and the Fillmore administration decided on a bold step: dispatching Commodore Matthew C. Perry to Japan to work out commercial understandings. The expedition cleared Norfolk in November 1852. Six months later the Japanese were awed by the spectacle of Perry's small fleet steaming up the Bay of Yedo (later Tokyo) against the wind. They were apprehensive too:

> Thro' a black night of cloud and rain,
> The Black Ship plies her way—
> An alien thing of evil mien—
> Across the waters gray.

Through a skillful mixture of diplomacy and firmness, Perry worked out a convention for shipwrecked sailors. It was a small start, and disappointing to some traders at home, but within a few years the consul general, Townsend Harris, tactfully negotiated a commercial treaty that set the direction of Japanese-American diplomacy for another half century.

"It Will Raise a Hell of a Storm"

The railroads that forked out of Chicago and rolled across Illinois pointed toward Missouri and Iowa—and toward the vast Kansas-Nebraska Territory that lay beyond. Settlers particularly fastened their gaze on the sandy clay of the fertile river bottoms in eastern Kansas. Slave owners in northwestern Missouri, flanking the winding Missouri River north and south, dreamed of growing hemp and tobacco in the reaches southwest of the river. Land-hungry homesteaders throughout the north eyed the bottomlands and the rich clay loam of the upland prairies beyond.

The territory in itself posed a hot issue, for the question of slavery there was still open. The area was also bound to lie in the vortex of other pressures rising throughout the land: the old issue of federal disposal of lands; the question of local and national treatment of long-beleaguered Indian tribes; and, in the frenzied transportation boom of the 1850s, federal choice of the routes for the transcontinental railroads that would link Atlantic and Pacific. In 1820 American politicians and their political system had handled such factors through a compromise that barred slavery north of 36°30′, and hence, by implication, Nebraska. In 1850 another compromise had endorsed the expedient of popular (territorial) control of slavery while seeming to leave the 1820 compromise intact. But the pressures now were more explosive and centrifugal than ever.

Standing most exposed in this controversy was no Clay or Webster but the forty-year-old chairman of the Senate Committee on Territories, Stephen A. Douglas of Illinois. Douglas looked like a giant who, beneath his great mane and high forehead, had been squashed flat into a broad swath of eyebrows, a wide mouth and neck, and dwarfed legs. Life indeed had tried to squash him flat. Fatherless shortly after his birth in Vermont, put out to farm work as a child by a taskmaster of an uncle, denied a full education, he wandered west, taking job after job, until he settled in Illinois to read law and enter politics. He lost a congressional election by thirty-five votes, and a Senate contest by five legislative votes, before winning a House seat in 1843 and a Senate seat four years later. In his one term in the upper chamber he had achieved a Senate and national reputation as a quick-witted, resourceful, and pugnacious debater and yet also as a conciliator between northern and southern Democrats. Trained as a boy in woodworking, in his short life Douglas had become a master craftsman in the more unruly fields of railroad promotion, tariff making, public land disposal, river and harbor subsidies.

Douglas had a most ingenious plan: to admit Nebraska as a territory, neither legislating slavery there nor legislating it out, leaving the decision on slavery to the people in the territory, and to do all this without openly repudiating the Missouri Compromise. This last requirement was crucial, because Douglas knew that millions venerated that compromise as virtually the holy writ of the Union, sanctified by Clay, Webster & Co. Yet Douglas could not act alone. He could only exert leverage among the great balances of the domestic mobile, and those balances were swinging against him as of January 1854. Two of these swung together: the growing southern influence over the machinery of Congress, and Pierce's weak presidential leadership. Moreover, time did not lie on Douglas' side; he was desperately eager to go about his principal business of organizing the Nebraska Territory before his enemies on both flanks could thwart him.

For a time, after Douglas introduced his Nebraska bill in the Senate early in January 1854, it seemed that he might pick his way through the thickets. Providing that Nebraska, when admitted as a state, should be received into the Union "with or without slavery," as its "constitution may prescribe" at the time of admission, the measure neither affirmed nor repealed the Missouri Compromise—it simply ignored it. Antislavery leaders were not unduly upset; it was hard to argue against local "popular sovereignty," and they doubted that the territory would be hospitable to slavery anyway. But now the leading proslavery senators swung into action, a formidable phalanx: Andrew P. Butler of South Carolina, longtime disciple of Calhoun, champion of nullification, chairman of the Judiciary Committee; two states' rights, proslavery Virginians, Robert M. T. Hunter and James M. Mason; and David R. Atchison of Missouri, a leader of the proslavery faction, chairman of the Committee on Indian Affairs, and bitter foe of Thomas Hart Benton, whom he had helped defeat for re-election in 1850. These senators lived and concerted together in Washington, in their famous "F Street Mess."

The phalanx saw its chance to strike the Missouri Compromise its death-blow. With their chairmanships, big Democratic majorities, and complaisant President, they could hardly expect such an opportunity again. Douglas, startled when proslavery Senator Archibald Dixon of Kentucky brought up an amendment that directly repudiated the compromise of 1820, pleaded with Dixon in the Senate chamber to avoid such a drastic step. Later, when Douglas asked Dixon to join him in a carriage ride so they could talk undisturbed, Dixon was so persuasive—he had the votes—that Douglas not only agreed to support Dixon's amendment but proposed to sponsor it.

"By God, Sir," Douglas said, "you are right. I will incorporate it in my bill, though I know it will raise a hell of a storm."

Why this flip-flop by the "Little Giant"? politicians wondered at the time, and historians ever since. To Douglas, it was not a change of heart but a recognition of where power lay in the Senate and House, of the need to placate that power in order to move ahead on railroad-building and western development. Critics charged that he yielded to the Southerners because of his presidential ambitions, but he was playing better short-term congressional politics than long-term presidential. Long before the term "pragmatist" became popular, Douglas was an expert in calculating short-run advantage and step-by-step movement. He had no strong feeling about slavery, and even less understanding of how others could feel so strongly on the matter. He preferred to leave the future of slavery up to "the laws of climate, and of production, and of physical geography. . . ." Material forces, not moral, would decide.

It remained only for Douglas and the Southerners to line up the Administration. Increasingly pressed for time, Douglas had only one day—a Sunday—to persuade the President, who would transact no business on the Sabbath. With the aid of Secretary of War Jefferson Davis, Pierce's reluctant assent was gained for a meeting with Douglas and a small group. Sensing that the measure would divide his party and the nation, but crippled by divisions within his Cabinet and within himself, the President could not resist the Senate junto; he even agreed in writing that the Missouri Compromise was inoperative. On January 23, 1854, Stephen Douglas brought in his Nebraska bill, embracing the fateful amendment.

Waiting for Douglas' move was a trio of antislavery senators: Chase, Wade, and Sumner. Salmon P. Chase of Ohio had been born in New Hampshire and had, like Douglas, lost his father in his early years; the uncle who took him in was the Protestant Episcopal bishop of Ohio. Settling in Cincinnati, Chase gained fame as the "attorney-general for runaway negroes" in his ardent defenses of fugitive slaves. A one-man antislavery party, he deserted the Whigs to work for the Liberty party in 1840 and the Free-Soilers in '48. The deaths of three wives, and of four of six daughters, seemed to deepen his compassion. His junior colleague from Ohio, Benjamin F. Wade, born in Massachusetts and in poverty, rough of mien and coarse of speech, was a Senate neophyte experienced nonetheless in Ohio politics. The most arresting of the trio was Charles Sumner, Boston-born, Harvard-educated, friend of his fellow Unitarians Channing, Longfellow, and Emerson. His longtime denunciations of the cotton Whigs as "the lords of the loom" still alienated him from Robert Winthrop and the rest of the Whig establishment in Boston. Well over six feet tall, large of frame, pedagogical and humorless of bearing, he spoke, said Longfellow, "like a cannoneer . . . ramming down cartridges," pressing a single idea with such doctrinal fervor that Francis Lieber complained of his "jacobinical abstraction" and Winthrop labeled him a "jesuit of the first water."

Chase and his Senate and congressional friends had ample time to prepare their counterattack. On January 24 Washington's *National Era* blazoned forth with their "APPEAL OF THE INDEPENDENT DEMOCRATS IN CONGRESS TO THE PEOPLE OF THE UNITED STATES."

"We arraign this bill," the appeal proclaimed, "as a gross violation of a sacred pledge; as a criminal betrayal of precious rights; as part and parcel of an atrocious plot to exclude from a vast unoccupied region, immigrants from the Old World and free laborers from our own States, and convert it into a dreary region of despotism, inhabited by masters and slaves. . . ."

This hyperbole set the tone for the whole manifesto. It offered little reasoned historical or legal analysis, or even a convincing attack on slavery, but rather paraded a series of horribles that would result from the bill: all unorganized territory would be open to slavery, territorial settlement would be slowed up, the transcontinental railroad would be sidetracked, the homestead law vitiated, the whole country placed under the "yoke of a slaveholding despotism." Again and again the address returned to its main charge: the bill was a diabolical conspiracy against freedom, a plot contrived by a servile demagogue truckling to the South for the sake of his presidential ambitions. "Shall a plot against humanity and Democracy, so monstrous, and so dangerous to the interests of Liberty throughout the world, be permitted to succeed?"

Editors and preachers and merchants had already been thundering against the assault on the Missouri Compromise; now the sheer force of this address, printed also in the New York *Times* and other newspapers, set off detonations across the North. Never mind the rhetorical absolutes in the address, the exaggerations and distortions, the conspiracy theory—its transcending moral conviction, its timeliness, and above all its reverberating call for the defense of liberty struck home to men and women determined, whatever their specific position on slavery, that this barbaric insult to freedom not be extended to "free soil." Horace Greeley in New York, Samuel Bowles in Massachusetts, Henry Ward Beecher in Brooklyn, Theodore Parker in Boston, Horace White in Chicago, were only the most noted of those who used the occasion to hurl their own thunderbolts from press and pulpit.

Still underestimating the power of this moral tempest, Douglas predicted that the "storm will soon spend its fury." It did not, because of its own intensity, because the bill lacerated the public as it wended its way through Senate and House, and because Douglas and his supporters, as well as the antislavery men and their allies, fought the congressional battle so furiously that the issue could not die. Douglas spent most of his time superbly managing the bill, but his angry speeches, laced with epithets, bristled in the press accounts. Greeley, fearing that the bill would "suffocate the moral force of liberty and equality within the young republic," in Jeter Isely's words, blasted the measure in a series of brilliant editorials—and watched his *Weekly* pick up another 35,000 readers nationwide during the first six months of 1854. The *Tribune*'s opposition could be expected; more significant was the spectacle of leading Democratic papers of Free-Soil tendencies—William Cullen Bryant's New York *Evening Post*, the Rochester *Union*, Buffalo *Republic*, Cleveland *Leader*, and others—almost overnight turning against the Democratic party leadership.

* * *

Would this wave of indignation pass over the North and then subside, like so many moral protests in the past? Or would it take form in some new and lasting political constellation? Looking back later, some historians saw an entire new movement and party spring to life as people mobilized against the Nebraska bill. Few did mobilize at the time, however. The editorial thunderbolts did not descend on people neatly arrayed in the Democratic and Whig parties. In the absence of strong party ideology or organization, Americans were perceiving and acting as members of a variety of subcultures.

They were divided not only over slavery but also over temperance, women's rights, keeping the Sabbath, prison reform, free land, tariffs, immigration, schools, banks, foreign policy, foreign relations. People's origins caused other divisions: natives and newcomers often hated one another, immigrants from the British Isles and continental Europe were wary of one another; German Catholics looked down on Irish Catholics; Irish resented Germans; and some Irish disdained other Irish.

The single most powerful antagonism in the early 1850s was native American hostility toward the newcomers who had been arriving each year by the hundreds of thousands—hostility toward their religion, their speech, their drinking, their very foreignness. And the fastest-growing party in the north was the Know-Nothing (or American) party, whose stated program was "Anti-Romanism, Anti-Bedinism, Anti-Pope's Toeism, Anti-Nunneryism, Anti-Winking Virginism, Anti-Jesuitism, and Anti-the-Whole-Sacerdotal-Hierarchism with all its humbugging mummeries. . . ."

Cutting through this welter of distrusts and conflicting concerns were

three dynamic forces that dominated the politics of slavery. One was abolitionism, rooted in New England preaching and writing and the Yankee
diaspora into western New York and Ohio and the northwestern states, an
abolitionism often expressed in a strident anti-southernism. The second
was the defense and protection of slavery, often reflected in a militant
anti-northernism. The third was an "anti-niggerism," shared extensively
by some Whigs and many Democrats and probably by most Know-Nothings—and even by some abolitionists, though it was hard for militant
abolitionists to accept this fact. Not everyone who wanted to free the slaves
was pro-black; millions of Americans were against slavery and also against
"niggers," because they saw the former as a moral wrong and the latter
as a threat. This attitude was most clearly reflected in Free-Soilism. Many
Free-Soilers strenuously resisted the Nebraska bill and its threat of allowing slavery onto free soil because they did not want blacks to invade
"white" territory, put their children into white schools, and compete for
white jobs. They did not want blacks next to them, slave or free.

These dominant groups defended their views in the name of liberty or
freedom. Nativists wanted to pursue their lives and their work free of
brawling, pushing, competitive Irishmen and Germans. Slave owners proclaimed their liberty to take their bondsmen into the new territories.
Homesteaders wished to move into a Nebraska free of "niggerism." Abolitionists continued to view slavery as the supreme affront to the whole ideal
of liberty. Thus liberty as a value still served as a source of intellectual and
political confusion rather than as a guide to coherent political action.

This disarray posed a severe problem for serious politicians. They could
not operate within the bounds of neatly polarized conflict. They had to win
state and local elections against rivals who could easily outdemagogue
them in the emotional politics of the early fifties. They had to calculate in
terms of possible coalitions, political balance sheets, electoral margins.
They had to deal with Americans as they were—with millions of persons
not logically arrayed in rational ideological combat but intent on immediate daily needs of survival and betterment and self-esteem, some alienated
from politics or apathetic toward it, parochial in outlook, variously cursing
Catholics, blacks, Southerners, Northerners, abolitionists, slave owners.

It would take, not a single event like the Nebraska bill, but a series of
powerful hammerblows over a number of years before this jumble of
attitudes could be heated and pounded into a viable political movement
or party. For a time, as Americans turned against the Democratic party
because of Nebraska, and the Whig because of its weakness and timidity,
people were in a state of political confusion. Many nevertheless stayed with
Whiggism or the Democracy. Others joined the Know-Nothings, either as

a way station to some other political destination or as a place to settle down. Some met in "anti-Nebraska" meetings and simply formed anti-Nebraska groups. Some met and talked about organizing new Independent or People's parties. Some pressed for a new Fusion party to embrace abolitionists, Know-Nothings, Conscience Whigs, Free-Soilers, Barnburners, and anyone else available for a coalition.

In Ripon, Wisconsin, fusionists proposed that merging anti-Nebraska groups adopt the name "Republican"; a plea was sent to the *Tribune* that it adorn its masthead with a Republican banner, but Greeley hedged. Thirty congressmen, meeting at Mrs. Cratchett's boardinghouse in Washington, discussed a new party to stop slavery expansion. "Republican," they thought, would make a good name for such a party. Meetings in Jackson, Michigan, and Worcester, Massachusetts, and elsewhere, held almost simultaneously, debated the need for a new party and agreed that "Republican," evoking memories of Jefferson and popular rights, would be a fine name for a party designed to attract a large variety of people.

But all these efforts would atomize rather than mobilize protest unless events brought more hammerblows—and events did. In Washington the Senate battle raged on, as Douglas pleaded, demanded, goaded, orated, his sharp sentences going "straight to the mark like bullets, and sometimes like cannon-balls, crashing and tearing," Carl Schurz wrote. As Douglas, the Southerners, and the White House mobilized all their influence, including party patronage, the anti-Nebraska forces lost battle after battle, including the final Senate roll call, when the bill passed 37 to 14. In the House, where the Administration applied whip and spur, and Douglas made his presence known, the tall, gaunt, shrill-voiced Alexander H. Stephens of Georgia applied his rapier-like logic and command of facts to win a closer victory for the measure, 113 aye to 100 nay. Each major event on the Hill, and especially the final roll calls, produced outbursts of delight, rage, threats, recriminations, and dire predictions among hundreds of editors, preachers, and politicians in the country.

The bill had hardly passed the House, in late May 1854, when the moral dimension of the issue was illuminated in Boston. Anthony Burns, a twenty-year-old slave and leader of his people on a Virginia plantation, had escaped by boarding a ship bound for Boston, been tracked down by his master, put in chains in a Boston jail, and subjected to the provisions of the Fugitive Act. This provided for not a jury trial but a summary hearing before a commissioner who could dispatch the fugitive back into slavery. While Burns awaited his hearing, Wendell Phillips and Theodore Parker whipped up a Faneuil Hall crowd to a pitch of indignation. A mob tried to free Burns, only to be beaten off. By the time the commissioner ordered

Burns returned to his master Boston was an armed camp, filled with cavalry, artillery, Marines, and police, and with outraged Bostonians and
hundreds of protesters from Worcester and other towns. Church bells
pealed and thousands watched in helpless fury as the trembling slave, his
face scarred and a piece of bone projecting from a broken hand, was taken
by cavalry and foot soldiers through flag-draped streets to his Virginia-
bound ship. This was only the latest in a series of horrifying fugitive-slave
recaptures, which in some cases had ended in the rescue of the runaway.

But it was in the far-off territory itself that shocking events now would
galvanize the nation and precipitate a transformation of party politics and
ultimately of the American political system.

*   *   *

"Come on, then, Gentlemen of the slave States," William H. Seward of
New York had cried out on the Senate floor shortly after the Nebraska bill
passed the House. "Since there is no escaping your challenge, I accept it
in behalf of the cause of freedom. We will engage in competition for the
virgin soil of Kansas, and God give the victory to the side which is stronger
in numbers as it is in right."

It was certain from the start of the Nebraska debate that the Kansas part
of the territory would be a combat zone. To publicize Kansas as an arcadia
for homesteaders and planters alike, and then to legislate that the people
in the territory would decide the burning issue of slavery on the basis of
squatter sovereignty, was to thrust two gamecocks into a rain barrel. Escalation began as soon as slavery men heard that the Massachusetts Emigrant
Aid Society was sending Yankees into Kansas in order to convert it into
a free state, and when antislavery men heard that Missouri planters were
dispatching "border ruffians" into Kansas with the opposite purpose. Each
side exaggerated the satanic purpose and effectiveness of the other.

Each side exploited its own advantages. When a territorial delegate was
to be elected, hundreds of Missourians crossed the boundary in buckboards and wagons, on horseback and on foot, to pick an anti-free-stater
as delegate. Proslavery men proceeded to organize a proslavery legislature, which promptly passed anti-antislavery legislation, including penalties for antislavery agitation. Antislavery colonists held their own
convention, declared the proslavery legislature illegal, asked admission to
the Union as a free state, and later met in convention to frame the free-
state Topeka constitution. By the end of 1855 Kansas had two governments—and two sides each arming itself rapidly, the antislavery men with
"Beecher's Bibles," considered more practical in combat than the Good

Book. As the last snows melted on the prairies in the spring, Kansas was headed for a showdown.

Then came the sack of Lawrence. Proslavery men had long considered the town a hotbed of abolitionism; armed with indictments against free-state leaders and two Lawrence newspapers—the *Herald of Freedom* and the *Kansas Free State*—sheriff's men and "border ruffians" occupied the town. Spoiling for a fight, furious at finding the leaders gone and the populace unresisting, the invaders threw printing presses into the river and bombarded the Free State Hotel into rubble. One man angered by the nonresistance to this invasion was John Brown, on his way to Lawrence with his small troop of Liberty Guards when he heard about the sacking. He resolved to take the drastic action that the cowardly antislavery people refused to take. Selecting a small band from his Liberty Guards, including several of his sons, exhorting them to "fight fire with fire," he led them to the houses of proslavery men and, while wives and children watched, dragged the victims out and hacked them to death with cutlasses. With the fifth murder Brown stopped; he had avenged the killing of six free-state men during Kansas' months of violence, including the one man who had died at Lawrence.

It is probable that, on the way to Lawrence, Brown was told of another assault by the "slave power," far away in Washington. This news could hardly have tempered his passion, nor explained his action. Brown was an enigma to his neighbors in Pottawatomie Creek, and would remain so long after: was he a fanatical moralist who as a boy had seen a young slave beaten with a shovel by his master, a stern Calvinist who had dedicated his life to a merciless effort to extirpate the evil of slavery; or was he simply a homicidal lunatic from a family of lunatics?

Each incident in Kansas provoked storms of oratory in Congress as both chambers became caldrons of sectional hatred and hyperbole. "Truly—truly—this is a godless place," Sumner lamented early in 1856. No one writhed under the oratorical lashes of Douglas and southern senators with a greater desire for vengeance than the Massachusetts lawmaker. Carefully he planned his climactic attack on the moral wickedness, the supreme sinfulness, of slavery. From his first words when he gained the floor in mid-May—"Mr. President, you are now called to redress a great transgression"—to his final reference to Virginia, "where human beings are bred as cattle for the shambles," his speech, "The Crime Against Kansas," was studded with provocative and offensive personal attacks on his foes. He attacked the phalanx, especially Butler, charging that the South Carolinian had chosen a mistress who, "though ugly to others, is always lovely to him

... the harlot, Slavery. . . ." When Douglas answered him in kind, Sumner ranted: ". . . no person with the upright form of man can be allowed—" He paused.

"Say it," Douglas shot back.

"I will say it—no person with the upright form of man can be allowed, without violation of all decency, to switch out from his tongue the perpetual stench of offensive personality. . . . The noisome, squat, and nameless animal, to which I now refer, is not a proper model for an American Senator. Will the Senator from Illinois take notice?"

"I will," Douglas replied, "and therefore will not imitate you, sir."

This was not the kind of grand Senate debate in which senatorial gladiators harangued each other on the floor and then walked through the cloakroom arm in arm. These adversaries loathed one another. As the bonds of civility snapped, as allies and constituents egged the antagonists on, Congress trembled on the edge of violence. Preston S. Brooks, a thirty-six-year-old congressman from South Carolina, a Mexican War veteran considered to be a moderate and agreeable man, had listened to some of Sumner's remarks. Incensed by Sumner's "insults" to South Carolina and to Brooks's admired uncle, Senator Butler, Brooks carefully planned vengeance. He would not challenge Sumner to a duel, because that would imply acceptance of the Massachusetts man as his social equal. He would simply thrash him, as he would any other inferior guilty of wrongdoing.

After gallantly waiting for some women visitors to leave the Senate lobby, Brooks strode up to Sumner's desk, where the senator was busy with correspondence, and rained twenty or thirty blows on Sumner's head with a gold-knobbed gutta-percha cane. Sumner rose convulsively, wrenching his bolted desk from the floor, and reeled about as Brooks broke his cane on his head and kept on striking him, until bystanders dragged the assailant away. Almost insensible, his head covered with blood, Sumner, with the help of friends, stumbled out of the Capitol into a carriage, a painful convalescence—and martyrdom.

THE ILLINOIS REPUBLICANS

Sacking a defenseless town, dragging helpless men out of their homes and hacking them to death, bloodying a United States senator pinioned under his desk—this explosion of baleful events sent new and irresistible shocks into the American conscience. Thirty months of rising conflict, culminating in these violent days of May, were arousing Americans to a consciousness of slavery as the supreme issue transcending all the others. The hurricane was whipping through the mainstream of American politics, washing out old waterways and carving new channels, wrenching people from ancient political moorings and leaving them adrift or clutching new ones.

Fundamental economic and social forces, as well as bitter conflict, seemed to be transforming America during the 1850s. The economic boom roared on through the middle of the decade, both satisfying needs and raising expectations. Population soared under the impact of foreign immigration and domestic fecundity. Rising prices altered long-established relationships among groups and classes. Massive immigration caused new anxieties and tensions. Intense railroad building not only was altering the face of the land but causing social dislocation, as the jobs of draymen and teamsters and rivermen evaporated in one place and employment for railroad builders and trainmen and telegraphers suddenly materialized hundreds of miles away.

The few Americans who were reading Karl Marx in the 1850s might have expected sweeping political change to follow economic and social, especially in the wake of the storm over slavery. A major political change indeed was in the making, as a few Americans tried a major political experiment —to create a new political party that would challenge the existing two-party system in elections. This had never been done. Earlier the Democratic party had gradually grown out of the old Republican party; the Whigs had never had to challenge a full-bodied Federalist party. Many politicians doubted that this new party—anti-Nebraska, or Fusion, or Republican, or People's—would have any more success than Liberty-ites or Free-Soilers. Only a Republican zealot would have dreamed in 1854 that the isolated protest meetings of that year would start the formation of what would become the dominant party for three-quarters of a century.

The question for Republicans by the end of 1854, indeed, was whether their movement would even survive. They faced not only the familiar Whigs and Democrats, Free-Soilers and Know-Nothings, but "Temperance men, Rum Democrats, Silver Gray Whigs, Hindoos, Hard Shell Democrats, Soft Shells, Half Shells," and assorted others, in David Potter's listing. Of the third parties, the Know-Nothings seemed most ascendant. In November 1854 they swept Massachusetts, scored well in New York and Pennsylvania, and elected a large number of representatives to the national House; after they won more victories the next year, some predicted that the nativists would take the presidency in 1856. Know-Nothings and anti-slavery representatives had enough in common in the new Congress to elect as Speaker Nathaniel P. Banks, a Massachusetts nativist and antislavery man who was once a Democrat, more recently a Know-Nothing, and now on his way to Republicanism.

All the parties indeed seemed immobilized by 1856. The Democrats, claiming to be the only truly national party, were bleeding at both ends as proslavery extremists deserted them in the South and "Free Democrats" seceded in the North. Whigs, still torn between conscience and cotton, were walking a tightrope on nativism, as they watched Democrats making inroads among immigrants and Catholics, and Know-Nothings exploiting bigotry. Some Whig leaders followed the high road; invited to address an anti-alien organization, Edward Everett not only declined but lectured his would-be host on the need to greet newcomers "in a spirit not of exclusiveness but of fraternal welcome." Other Whig leaders were less high-minded. The Know-Nothings, even in the flush of their victories, comprised the weakest party of all, for they were deeply divided over slavery. When the party adopted a proslavery platform in its convention in June 1855, northern delegates withdrew, and the party was on the road to extinction.

The parties were immobilized because their top leadership was immobilized, and the leaders were immobilized because they were enmeshed in state and local politics. If the leaders could have fought in one great arena, some bold and committed spirit might have taken an advanced position against slavery—even in favor of emancipation—knowing that someday the people would catch up with him. But the national politicians of the day had to fight their battles within the states, and within key cities and counties in those states. Men like Sumner or Chase or Seward did take the lead, but only when local conditions permitted. No great national leader arose to rally Whigs or Democrats behind a daring commitment to halt and eventually abolish slavery; rather, month after month and year after year, state and sectional leaders calculated, advanced here, retreated there, compromised, adjusted, as they competed with rivals within and outside their parties, and tried to survive in the three-dimensional maze of American electoral and party politics.

The task of party invigoration, of creative political response to the hurricane of events and the social dynamics of the 1850s, would fall on a cadre of activists who, amidst all the murk, had a clear vision of what they believed in, where they wanted to go, and how they proposed to get there. No state demonstrated their problems and their progress more vividly than Illinois.

*   *   *

Illinois seemed the distillation of America. Though it opened on the Great Lakes to the north and flanked hundreds of miles of the Mississippi on its west, already it was the quintessential heartland. Both its industry and its agriculture were booming in the 1850s, the two meeting in Chicago's grain elevators and McCormick's reaper factory. Illinois embraced sections and cultures: Chicago teemed with Irish and Germans; northern Illinois was dotted with towns more Yankee than Dedham; southern Illinois, touching Kentucky and reaching farther south than Richmond, was a land of people who still talked and thought as Virginians and Kentuckians. No one—no European traveler, no nationally ambitious politician, no immigrant heading west along the northern routes, no businessman looking for profit—could ignore Illinois.

If Chicago was the economic capital of Illinois in the 1850s, Springfield was the legal and political. Like Bloomington and Peoria and a dozen other places in central Illinois, it was a boom town, with its brand-new railroad connection to Chicago and New York, its population that was doubling while land valuation tripled. This town smack in the middle of the state was also the capital, with a proud new statehouse built of buff-colored stone that had been dragged by teams of twelve oxen from a nearby quarry. Springfield was still in part an unfinished frontier town: on a wet day people could sink to their knees in the prairie mud of the unpaved sidewalks; hogs ran wild in the streets, and in the business district imposing three-story shops stood next to ramshackle houses. The public square was crowded with buggies and sometimes by "movers" headed west in their covered wagons. Yet Springfield also had its aristocracy, dominated by wealthy old Whig families like the Stuarts, Edwardses, and Todds.

One of the Todds, Mary, a small and refined woman of quick temper, had married below her station in accepting a local lawyer, Abraham Lincoln, a man of tall frame, easygoing manner, hollowed cheeks, huge arms and hands, coarse black hair, and dowdy garb. Even after Lincoln was making good money as a lawyer, he could be seen currying his horse and milking his cow.

If you wanted to find Abe Lincoln in Springfield, you would look for a battered sign, LINCOLN & HERNDON, swinging on rusty hinges outside an office building downtown. You would climb a narrow flight of stairs, cross a dark hallway, and enter an office filled with a long, creaking sofa, a few old cane-bottomed chairs, and desks piled high with papers that overflowed the pigeonholes. If Lincoln wasn't there, his partner, William Herndon, might be. Billy seemed almost the opposite of Abe: youthful, nervous, verbose, something of a dandy, but admiring of "Mr. Lincoln." Lincoln might be down at the courthouse or the capitol, or visiting another law office, or some place where you might find him telling jokes that had a crowd in stitches—"he could make a cat laugh," someone said—or he might be sitting by himself in a state of such utter melancholy that no one would dare approach him.

If Lincoln was not in town, he was probably out riding circuit. Gone were the days when he might ride horseback through rain and snow for thirty miles or so. Now he could take trains, with his free pass, or drive a horse and buggy. In earlier times he had been lucky to find a farmhouse where he could put up overnight in the extra room; now he could often stay at a newly built hotel. He often traveled with other lawyers, and with David Davis, circuit judge of the judicial district, a huge man of three hundred pounds, cherubic face, and sharp, penetrating mind. At night Lincoln might have to share a bed with another attorney, but the judge had his own bed, as tribute to the principle of separating bench and bar.

Life on the circuit was hard but educational. Lincoln, arguing every kind of case under every kind of law, constitutional, patent, admiralty, and common, came to know virtually every economic interest and human problem in the heart of Illinois.

He became a respected lawyer, trusted with important responsibilities, arguing many cases involving human problems, including divorce, rape, murder, and both sides in fugitive-slave cases. But most of his cases dealt with property: disputed wills, railroad rights-of-way, foreclosures, debt collection, patent infringements, trespass violations, mortgages, property damages. While early in his career he represented rivermen against bridge and railroad enterprises, later he took so many cases for railroads—he represented the Illinois Central in eleven appeals to the Illinois Supreme Court—that by the mid-1850s he was known as a railroad lawyer. Yet he also sued the Illinois Central when they offered him a fraction of the fee he billed them, and won. A Whig, a man of property, he prospered in the economic boom of capitalist Illinois. He believed in individual liberty, initiative, and enterprise. It was best, he said, "to leave each man free to acquire property as fast as he can." Some would get rich, but a law to prevent that would do more harm than good.

But Lincoln was much more than an attorney for capitalism. A onetime state legislator, a Whig congressman in 1845-47, an unsuccessful candidate for the United States Senate, he had repeatedly subordinated his law practice to his desire to run for office. Herndon marveled at this man who could be so relaxed and casual at times but who seemed "totally swallowed up" in his greed for office. His ambition, Herndon said, "was a little engine that knew no rest."

Politically ambitious—and yet the soul of political caution. When news of the Nebraska bill reached Springfield, and Herndon and other militant young Whigs wanted to use aggressive, even desperate means to defend the cause of freedom, Lincoln urged them to do nothing rebellious or illegal. People all around him were breaking away from Whiggism to the Know-Nothing or Republican or some other party, but Lincoln would have none of it. Above all he feared being linked with abolitionists or other extremists, but he dared not offend the radicals, for they voted too. When Republicans and other antislavery leaders invited him to a Springfield meeting to form a state organization, he contrived to be out of town; and when they elected him to their state central committee, he declined the poisoned chalice.

He was not sure where he stood. "I think I am a whig," he wrote his friend Joshua Speed, "but others say there are no whigs, and that I am an abolitionist." As a congressman he had voted for the Wilmot Proviso forty times, he went on, and he had never heard of anyone trying to "unwhig" him for that. He simply opposed the *extension* of slavery, he insisted to Speed.

"I am not a Know-nothing. That is certain. How could I be? How can anyone who abhors the oppression of negroes, be in favor of degrading classes of white people?" Americans seemed to be degenerating. "As a nation, we began by declaring that *'all men are created equal.'* We now practically read it 'all men are created equal, *except negroes.'* When the Know-Nothings get control, it will read 'all men are created equal, except negroes, *and foreigners and Catholics.'*" At that point, Lincoln added, he would prefer to emigrate to some country like Russia, "where they make no pretense of loving liberty."

If he was politically immobilized, at least he could speak for himself, and when Stephen Douglas returned to Illinois late in 1854, Lincoln's competitive spirit was aroused by the man who had succeeded so brilliantly in politics as he had not. The Little Giant, after journeying to Chicago "by the light of my own effigy," Douglas related almost pridefully, tried to defend his Nebraska role to a mass meeting, only to be howled down. Farther south he found his audiences more friendly. When he defined his position to a wildly cheering audience at the state fair in Springfield early in October, Lincoln was there, sitting directly in front of him and listening intently to every word; at the end he rose and announced that he would respond to Douglas the next day, at the same time and place. He did, before a crowd as enthusiastic as Douglas', and the two men squared off again in Peoria—exchanges that would lead to a much more extended confrontation four years later.

Still, Lincoln continued to take a moderate position on slavery, far short of abolition, and to act as a conciliator among anti-Nebraska Whigs, fusion-

ists, and others, not to take leadership and certainly not to join the controversial Republicans. Few other moderate antislavery leaders of statewide
standing were willing to embrace Republicanism or radicalism. Yet within
a year a strong Republican party was growing in Illinois. What had happened?

The persons who built the Republican party in Illinois were not national
leaders—the Republicans still had none—nor were they noted state antislavery men—most of them were still standing by their old parties—but a
"third cadre" of militant grass-roots activists. These were the people who
organized meetings, put up posters, carried on antislavery correspondence, carried around petitions, got people to vote. One antislavery orator
alone, a man named Ichabod Crane, subsidized by an anti-Nebraska fusion
group in Chicago, spoke to more than a hundred rallies and probably many
more than 100,000 persons during 1854, and to almost another hundred
meetings during the next two years. The militants had a superb political
vehicle—the city or county convention. No one could stop them from
"issuing the call," organizing and holding the convention, adopting rules
of order, electing a chairman, conducting vigorous debate, passing resolutions, all before press and public.

Perhaps the most remarkable of the activists' meetings was held in the
winter of 1856 in Decatur by a group of anti-Nebraska newspaper editors,
mainly old-line Whigs. Only one politician was present—Abraham Lincoln, who had just declined to serve as an Illinois delegate to a Republican
national organizing convention in Pittsburgh. To Lincoln's satisfaction,
the Illinois editors took a moderate position, calling for restoration of the
Missouri Compromise but acceding to slavery in the South and the fugitive-slave law. Acting boldly as men who were political leaders as well as
editors, they called for a statewide convention, to take place in Bloomington in late May. While Lincoln was out of town, Herndon added his partner's name to the call. Told by old-line Whigs that he had ruined Lincoln,
Herndon anxiously wrote his partner: Did he approve?

"All right, go ahead," Lincoln replied. "Will meet you, radicals and all."

The Bloomington convention met in the wake of lurid accounts of the
sack of Lawrence and the caning of Sumner. The grass-roots activists were
still taking the lead; Lincoln came to Bloomington but was immensely
relieved when old-line Whigs and bolting Democrats showed up along with
radicals and abolitionists. At least he could play the role of conciliator. He
and Judge Davis and old-line Whig Orville Browning worked strenuously
behind the scenes to prevent splits among the polyglot delegations of
Whigs, anti-Nebraska Democrats, Know-Nothings, German immigrants,
and temperance reformers. The convention censured both the Nebraska

bill and nativism. Soon the call rang out for "Lincoln, Lincoln" to give the concluding address. The normally analytical attorney seemed to catch fire as he spoke. Men sat enthralled, reporters listened with their pencils transfixed while Lincoln gave perhaps his most galvanizing speech—a speech lost to history because of those frozen pencils.

By this time the national parties were wheeling into line, in preparation for the presidential election battle of 1856. After the Know-Nothings split into their northern and southern wings earlier in the year, the "South Americans" prepared to do battle behind Fillmore, and the "North Americans" looked toward other parties, especially the Republicans. As nativists, they could hardly look to the Democratic party, with its hospitality to immigrants and Catholics. The Democratic national convention met in Cincinnati early in June.

Pierce hoped to be renominated, but his weakness as President and flabbiness as a leader had disappointed even his southern friends in the party. The Southerners would rather reward the Northerner who had taken leadership on the Nebraska bill, fought for it, and put it through— the Little Giant. Southern support now was Douglas' undoing, however, for at this point the Democracy wanted to win a national election, not merely a congressional enactment, and a moderate safe-and-sane candidate was available in James Buchanan. The Pennsylvanian had worked closely with southern leaders, but less flamboyantly than Douglas. He had served in both House and Senate; he was experienced in foreign affairs as a former Secretary of State—and he had the great advantage of having been in London during the battle over Kansas. Keeping in close touch with the contest from Washington, Douglas learned over the telegraph of the successive ballots as Pierce fell behind and Buchanan forged ahead; then the Illinoisan, always a believer in party unity and discipline, asked that his name be withdrawn.

Two weeks later, in a fervency of moral indignation and high enthusiasm, two thousand Republican delegates and friends gathered in Philadelphia's Musical Fund Hall. This crusading new party was already proclaiming itself as a national movement but one look at the state standards revealed that it was embarrassingly sectional—not a single southern delegation was present. Unswayed by Democratic charges that they were a single-issue party, the Republicans adopted a platform of nine planks, most of which took a strong stand against slavery extension, but they did not neglect to call for government-aided construction of a Pacific railroad "by the most central and practical route." The convention quickly chose for President a man who seemed an ideal candidate—John C. Frémont, soldier, western explorer, famous as the "Pathfinder," and a moderate on slavery. True, he was politically inexperienced but he was young and bold and determined, just the right candidate, in Nevins' words, for a party that would be young, bold, and determined. The fact that he was married to the spirited Jessie Benton, daughter of the maverick Democratic senator from Missouri, seemed a fine little extra—until the senator announced that he was sticking by his party's choice of Buchanan and, to boot, that he loved his son-in-law "like a son" but flatly opposed him for President.

The presidency had now become such a glittering prize in American politics that parties were compelled to broaden their ranks and win over third parties. Already there were three parties in the 1856 field, but where were the Whigs and the North Americans? The latter threatened to hold their own convention and nominate their own candidate—a move that would divide the antislavery forces even further—until Thurlow Weed and other Republican managers contrived an adroit piece of political chess play. In a move that once again indicated the close affinity between Republicans and northern Know-Nothings, the leaders of the latter party had chosen Speaker Banks for President as a holding operation until the Republicans selected their own candidate. The maneuver worked; once Frémont was nominated by the Republicans, the North Americans soon dropped Banks and endorsed the Pathfinder.

The Whigs, broken as a major party, had their last hurrah in a September gathering of their leaders in Baltimore. There they fell back on their political and intellectual taproot—preservation of the Union. Denouncing both the Democratic and Republican parties as merely sectional and divisive, they endorsed Fillmore as a friend of the Union and of the Constitution, "without adopting or referring to the peculiar principles of the party which has already selected" him. So disappeared the northern leadership of the great Whig party in the bowels of the Know-Nothing party, for whose nativist prejudices it had little but contempt. It was the politics of nostalgia; these Whig "gentlemen," a Republican journalist observed, "are evidently incapable of the idea that the process now going on in the politics of the United States is a *Revolution.*"

By now the parties' orators and foot soldiers—Frémont's Republican–North Americans, Buchanan's Democrats, and Fillmore's Know-Nothing–Whigs—were locked in furious combat throughout the North. The Democrats were so strong in the South, the Fillmore forces so weak, and the Republicans so absent, that Buchanan won there by default, and the Democracy was able to deploy its finest southern orators in the battle of the North. That battle on the part of all three parties consisted, rhetorically, of systematic exaggeration and distortion of the positions of both foes. Although the Republicans in particular tried to moderate their position on slavery in order to capture the centrist vote, southern Democrats frightened the electorate with warnings of disunion and secession should Frémont win.

It was also a battle of cadres. Here the Democrats had the advantage, with their thousands of well-disciplined jobholders and their tens of thousands of stalwarts who could not forget the glory days of Jackson and Van Buren. But the Republicans had the advantage of enthusiasm, as their militants used press, pulpit, parades, and personal proselytizing to transmit their new gospel. They could call on some of the most eminent literati. In Concord, a group of Republican neighbors had gone to Emerson's house to ask him to join the Massachusetts delegation to the Republican national convention. They had done so in fear and trembling, for Emerson was known to be averse to "meddling with politics" in any partisan way. Though Emerson was not at home, Mrs. Emerson electrified her visitors by stating that of course Mr. Emerson would put aside his private affairs in this "momentous crisis."

But this election would not be decided in Massachusetts—all New England, and New York too, were expected to go Republican—rather in the great swing states in the center. Foremost of these was Pennsylvania, with its twenty-seven electoral votes, and its bellwether state elections three weeks before the presidential. The Democrats poured in vast sums of money, some of it scourged out of New York merchants in the southern trade; the Republicans brought in less money but battalions of orators. The Democrats' victory in the state election presaged Buchanan's win in November. Still the Republicans fought on. Women and clergymen were so militant in the cause that Democrats sneeringly dismissed them as "Pulpit and Petticoats." The militants took on a radical posture, appropriating the air of the "Marseillaise" and bringing audiences to their feet with the battle song:

> Arise, arise, ye brave,
> And let your war-cry be
> Free speech, free press, free soil, free men,
> Frémont and victory.

Illinois was the critical battleground of the West. Lincoln, Herndon, and other anti-Nebraska leaders canvassed the state, trying especially to bring old Whigs over to Frémont and the Republican state ticket. While Lincoln was disappointed in the outcome of the Republican national convention —Frémont was not conservative enough and Lincoln himself had lost as a favorite-son candidate for Vice-President—he was now enlisted in the Republican cause. Still, he was cautious and conciliatory. Even in 1856, he

did not speak of the Republican party, for fear of alienating Free Democrats and old-line Whigs; he solicited votes for the anti-Nebraska or Frémont cause.

History and geography, more than campaigning, dictated the presidential election results. The South went for Buchanan, the upper tier of northern states for Frémont, and Maryland for Fillmore. But the Democrats
carried Pennsylvania, Indiana—and Illinois. Republican disappointment
was tempered by elation over their 1.3 million popular votes, second to the
Democrats' 1.8 million, but far ahead of Fillmore's 870,000. Their "glorious defeat" had put them in the strategically crucial position of being the
major opposition party.

Lincoln pondered the election results. Illinois, a microcosm, had gone
Republican in the north and Democratic in the south, but had elected a
Republican state ticket. Lincoln's ability to moderate clashes among Free
Democrats, old-line Whigs, disaffected Germans, unreconstructed Know-
Nothings, and radical abolitionists left him as undisputed leader of the
Illinois Republican party. But what about the national party? Could it both
restrict slavery and preserve the Union?

"We don't want to dissolve" the Union, he had warned his foes in a
speech in Galena, "and if you attempt it, *we won't let you.*" The purse and
the sword would not be in the Southerners' hands. "We won't dissolve the
Union, and you shan't."

CHAPTER 16

The Grapes of Wrath

V IOLENCE in Kansas, mobs in Boston—but the eye of the storm was in Washington. The city was calm as President-elect Buchanan, escorted by army regulars, Marines, and state militias, rode with Pierce to the Capitol. Buchanan's Inaugural Address reflected the placidity and quietism of the capital. Clad in a well-publicized suit of rural homespun, he deplored the incessant agitation over the slavery issue, and offered the pious injunction that things would quiet down if the nation would allow the people in the territories to decide on slavery there, and leave the institution alone where it already existed.

For a capital already confronted by overwhelming questions of peace and war, it was a curiously unfinished city through which Buchanan and his escort paraded on their way to the White House. The Capitol was imposing, even noble, some felt, with its great classic dome and pillars and porticos, though two big wings, built to accommodate an ever-expanding House and Senate, were still uncompleted—great marble blocks lay scattered around the Hill, among pendant cranes. From the Capitol the Inaugural Day visitors could see a scattering of houses and shanties still surrounded by fields. The base of the new Washington Monument looked impressive but the shaft ended abruptly 150 feet up because funds had run out. Grand plans were under discussion to beautify the Mall, which still resembled a cow pasture. Pennsylvania Avenue, down which Buchanan rode, had gas lights; outlying streets did not. Washington was a city of magnificent avenues, patriotic monuments, and high pretensions; it was also a city where people threw swill and slops into the alleys, hogs scavenged in the roads and wallowed in the muck, and people gasped for breath, through handkerchiefs pressed to their faces, when winds whipped through the dirt roads during dry periods.

It was the unfinished capital of an unfinished government. Aside from the Capitol the most imposing building was the Patent Office, a center of attention for a people constantly tinkering, inventing, experimenting. If many of the other government buildings did not look like much, they did not do much. If the capital lacked focus and coherence, so did the federal government, which remained a collection of fragmented powers, traditional military and diplomatic functions and offices, a presidency and Congress often at odds with each other, a Supreme Court not yet confirmed in the fullness of its authority. The doctrine of states' rights, the unceasing opposition of southern Democrats to a major federal role in internal improvements, and the vigor of some northern states in improving transportation and subsidizing industry, had left a federal government hardly able to cope with its ordinary duties, much less its extraordinary ones.

No city in America seemed more pinioned between North and South. Though the new Smithsonian building had just been built on the site of the old slave pens, Washington was still a city where one encountered slaves—where a visitor like Frederick Law Olmsted could find that the aged, bent, infirm, and overworked black man bringing in firewood for Olmsted's hotel room was a slave hired by the hotel from the man who owned him. It was a city where "free" blacks applying for residence had to report within five days of arrival or risk a fine, the workhouse, and expulsion from the city; where secret meetings were forbidden; where after twenty-four "genteel colored men," in the words of the police record, held a charitable, nonpolitical meeting, several were sent to the workhouse, others were fined, and one was ordered to be flogged.

If the nation's capital appeared, all at the same time, to be monumental and unfinished, politically pretentious and socially diminished, the nation's leadership, gathered in Washington for Buchanan's inaugural, presented an equally mixed picture. The void left by Clay, Webster, and the other political monuments of the recent past had yet to be filled.

A still rising star, if no Calhoun, among the southern leaders in Congress was Jefferson Davis. Born in the closing year of Jefferson's presidency, later heir to a small Mississippi plantation, Davis had led an unexceptional early life as an army officer on the northwest frontier, a tour of duty distinguished mainly by his elopement with the daughter of his commandant, Colonel Zachary Taylor. His young wife soon died of malarial fever, but Davis, after ten years as a planter and an abbreviated term in Congress, brilliantly led the Mississippi Rifles in Mexico, under the command of his former father-in-law. A states'-righter who wanted to fashion an autonomous South in an overarching Union, he won election to the Senate, backed Polk and expansion, served as Pierce's resourceful Secretary of War, and in 1857 was about to return to the upper chamber. With his "slender, tall, and erect figure," Carl Schurz remembered, "his spare face, keen eyes, and fine forehead," he struck the editor with "the grace of his diction, and the rare charm of his voice—things which greatly distinguish him from many of his colleagues." Though on Capitol Hill he was admired and feared for his lucidity, his temper, his aloofness, and his touchiness over criticism of the South, he possessed neither a philosophical vision that might have balanced his prickly sectionalism nor a Jeffersonian confidence in the ultimate good sense of the people.

Davis' great rival from the North was William Henry Seward of New York. Short, rustic, seedy compared to the fastidious Mississippian, Seward was talkative, good-natured, and gay-hearted in dealing with fellow senators. Long a close associate of Thurlow Weed in New York's turbulent politics, he had risen rapidly: state senator at twenty-nine, governor at thirty-seven, senator ten years later. As governor he had brooked nativist wrath by pressing for public schools in which immigrant children could be instructed by teachers speaking the same language and professing the same faith. Now fifty-six, he was famous as a strong antislavery man, an excellent constitutional lawyer, and a moralist who had fluttered Washington dovecotes when he called for abolition of the slave system by gradual, compensated emancipation and appealed to a "higher law than the Constitution." He was also viewed as rash and unsteady in judgment, prone to shift erratically between moralistic pronunciamentos and devious party politics.

Charles Sumner and Stephen Douglas were doubtless the best-known senators, but Sumner was still convalescing from Brooks's attack in March 1857, and Douglas had been left isolated by the victory of Buchanan & Co. There were others: the aged John J. Crittenden of Kentucky, whose passion was the Union; the high-minded Alexander H. Stephens of Georgia, broad-minded in outlook but rather too stubborn in detail; the majestic-looking Salmon P. Chase of Ohio, as statesmanlike in Washington as deficient in popular appeal back home; the ancient warrior Lewis Cass of Michigan; the South Carolinian radical and secessionist Robert Barnwell Rhett; and a score of others of almost equal rank among the second cadre.

It was difficult, though, to find in Washington leaders who were equal to the deepening crisis—men with the power to appeal to the hearts and minds, to the fundamental wants and needs and aspirations of the people, able to apply steady moral and intellectual standards to the issues confronting them, able to combine moral earnestness and moderation of temper, able to live up to the leadership heritage of the founding fathers they constantly apotheosized. Washington as a capital city seemed unable to inspire and sustain that kind of leadership. Rather, it rewarded the political brokers and technicians on the Hill, the opportunistic bureaucrats in the agencies, the middlemen operating out of the endless enclaves and interstices in a fragmented system of government.

Washington simply preferred peace and quiet to extremism of any kind. After years of Jeffersonian and Democratic rule, the capital was a southern-oriented city, under a congressionally controlled city government under, in turn, a Democratic-controlled Congress. "The fiercer the storm blew roundabout," Constance McLaughlin Green wrote, "the greater the quiet at the center. It was like the stillness at the eye of a hurricane." But the storm was steadily rising, among proslavery and antislavery firebrands South and North, among ambitious, anti-extension Republican politicans in the West, and among a little republic of Southerners who had long expected and hoped that that storm would burst.

SOUTH CAROLINIANS: THE POWER ELITE

Southern fire-eaters had exulted over Preston Brooks's assault on the "blackguard" Sumner. While the South Carolina congressman was showered with tributes and gifts, northern editors and orators raged over this "ruthless attack" on "liberty of speech" and all decency. The House of Representatives passed a resolution of censure but failed to muster the two-thirds vote needed for expulsion. Brooks resigned anyway, ran in the special election in his district, won a smashing victory, and within two months was back in his old seat.

Brooks's vindication surprised few Southerners. South Carolina had long been the most militant state in the South, the quickest to defend its honor, the proudest of its civilization, the spearhead for southern nationalism and romanticism. Brooks represented the district that had sent John Calhoun to Congress forty-six years before. Some Carolinians frowned on Brooks's resort to violence; some of them wondered whether the congressman represented the Carolina they knew and loved.

That state defied the northern stereotype of it as merely a land of cotton plantations and slave drivers. Smaller than New York or Pennsylvania in area, South Carolina was at least as diverse physically. The most distinct section was the low country along the Atlantic, with its flatlands, placid rivers, endless tidal swamps, and sea islands strung along the coast. Thick growths of palmetto and cypress and gum, live oaks reaching out for sun and air, tangles of dangling vines and creepers, cascades of gray moss, all combined with stagnant pools and deep muck and bulbous cypress stumps to give the lowlands an air of haunting, mysterious, and ominous beauty. Fifty miles or so inland began the "middle country" of pine trees and freshwater swamps, a belt that slowly changed into a region of longleaf pine, sand hills, and a light sandy loam that made excellent cotton land. About the center of the state stretched the fall line, northwest of which lay the upland country of rolling prairies, steep hills, and rugged mountains. South Carolinians and their economy were as variegated as their scenery. Up-country people, an independent lot who felt well removed from the coastal nabobs, raised fruit, small grains, horses and cattle, and whatever else was manageable and profitable in their valleys and hollows. In broad reaches of the piedmont region, onetime yeomen had turned to cotton, following the bonanza resulting from Eli Whitney's gin. Typically owning few if any slaves, the piedmonters specialized in short-staple cotton. Some of these farmers, however, were entrepreneurs who had invested heavily in slaves in order to capitalize on the cotton boom. Their dreams and aspirations turned toward the coast, where the great rice and cotton plantations lay. The lowland planters specialized in fine luxury cotton, grown and harvested by gangs of slaves. Despite northern images of South Carolina as simply a cotton kingdom, many planters made their fortunes out of rice, which grew abundantly in those tidal swamps.

South Carolina's social pyramid consisted largely of a planter elite; a fringe of merchants, doctors, lawyers, and other upper-middle-class professionals; piedmont farmers and upland yeomanry; white mechanics, clerks, overseers, and others; free blacks; and a slave caste divided between household servants and field hands. Its social dynamics lay at the top and the bottom of this pyramid. The cotton planters along the coast and the rice planters along the rivers made up a genuine social, economic, and political elite that almost lived up to the Yankee caricature of it. Aping the airs and refinement of the English squirearchy, the rich planters, in William Freehling's portrait of them, smoked the best Spanish cigars and drank the choicest brandies and Madeira, hunted with hound and horn, frequented horse races and cockfights, and mixed with one another in ballrooms and drawing rooms, while their wives sang or performed on the piano, played chess, and lounged in living room or library. Comprising perhaps the most cosmopolitan group in America during the early decades of the century, the planters were well educated, having attended South Carolina College or a northern institution such as Yale or Princeton; they were well traveled, spending part of the winter in Philadelphia or New York, and summering in the mountains or in the North or in Europe; they were well read, especially in novels of chivalry and courage; and they conducted extensive correspondence among themselves and with friends in the northern states, Europe, and especially England. Many planters spent little time in their country seats, preferring to live in Charleston or points north, and most deserted their plantations entirely during the summer because of the heat and the swamp diseases.

The lives of the slaves on South Carolina plantations were much like elsewhere in the slave kingdom: organized, disciplined, hard, monotonous, occasionally benign, more often nasty, brutish, and short. But

Africans in the Carolinian black belt were a special breed. After South Carolina, alone among the southern states, had allowed the reopening of the slave trade before the constitutional interdiction took effect, Yankee and southern slavers had brought in tens of thousands of blacks—so many that the slaves formed a huge work force in the rice swamps and, speaking to one another in their Gullah dialect, which was almost incomprehensible to whites, salvaged parts of their African heritage. Then too, after the Vesey conspiracy of 1822, South Carolina had been left with heightened fears and suspicions of its black population, both slave and free. But black people's worst enemy in the swamplands was not their white masters but the malaria-carrying mosquito. One planter admitted that on his Savannah River plantation, slaves died faster than they were born.

Master and slave were locked in a forced embrace that brought out the worst qualities of each. Dependent on his bondmen for yields, many a planter left them to sicken and die in the swamps while he drank and gambled in northern and European cities. Too conscience-stricken to apply the lash himself, he left that task to his overseer. Unable either to endure their lot or to escape it, slaves resorted to devious means of coping. Frederick Law Olmsted, traveling through Marion County to the Great Pee Dee River, came across a line of slaves, mainly women, dressed in dirty gowns and pieces of blanket. As the overseer, carrying a rawhide whip, rode to one end of the line, the blacks at the other end stopped their heavy labor until the overseer returned.

"Clumsy, awkward, gross, elephantine in all their movements; pouting, grinning, and leering at us; sly, sensual, and shameless, in all their expressions and demeanor," Olmsted wrote, adding that he had never seen anything so revolting as the whole scene.

The patriarchal planter held his family too in subjection, if a more privileged kind. Wealthy wives were ornaments placed on an artificial pedestal. Daughters were educated for a decorative and domestic role. Fathers wanted their sons to learn to be leaders and rulers, yet kept them dependent and subordinate.

Patriarchs made their house servants and even their field hands part of their "family," to the point of conceiving mulatto children, but cotton pickers could still be literally sold down the river into the swamplands. Southern wives looked on, helpless but knowing. "Like patriarchs of old, our men live all in one house with their wives and their concubines . . ." Mary Boykin Chesnut noted in her diary. "Any lady is ready to tell you who is the father of all the mulatto children in everybody's household but her own." Mary Chesnut had come into money from her father's estate shortly after she was married, but it had gone to settle debts. She questioned why she should "feel like a beggar, utterly humiliated and degraded, when I am forced to say I need money." She railed at the patriarch who posed as the "model of all human virtues" to his wife and daughters but ran a "hideous black harem."

"You see," she added, "Mrs. Stowe did not hit the sorest spot. She makes Legree a bachelor."

Yet out of this patriarchal, caste-ridden, self-indulgent, elitist community had emerged one of the most cultivated and elegant societies in America. Its capital, Columbia, sitting astride the fall line over a hundred miles from the coast, was a city of handsome houses and gardens, wide, tree-lined streets, and sparkling social life. Thomas Cooper, aging but still vigorous, presided for years over the lively South Carolina College, which spread its maternal wings over the state and strengthened the ideological and political ties binding the Carolinian elite. The eminent political scientist Francis Lieber came to teach here. Small but brilliant groups of artists, scientists, architects, intellectuals, physicians thrived in the state, and many of these masters taught as well. By the mid-1850s educators had founded several women's colleges that taught classics and not merely comportment.

Probably the most cosmopolitan people in Charleston were the East Bay merchants in the great export and import houses in the Cooper River docks area. Their traditional family and financial ties to Londoners and Parisians, New Yorkers and Philadelphians, their close links to planters needing goods and loans, their involvement in the system of elite power, enabled the merchants to serve as moderating and mediating influences among the powerful forces long building up in the Carolinian lowlands.

Charleston, Carolinians liked to say, was the Athens of America, and the boast was not wholly idle. Here at the confluence of the Ashley and Cooper rivers flourished an active press, the stimulating *Southern Review,* the respectable Literary and Philosophical Society, the Apprentices' Association with its 10,000-volume library and lectures in science, about twenty-five churches, a bank, a theater, and a noted medical college. Here also were a slave auction house, jail with flogging block and treadmill, almshouse, orphan asylum, two arsenals, and noisome slums.

By the 1850s, however, some wondered whether the glory of Charleston and of the state lay in the past, in the eighteenth century rather than the nineteenth. Historians would differ as to just when the state seemed to mutate from the moderate and cosmopolitan community of old to the most bellicose, separatist, and politically homogeneous in the South, but the nullification crisis of the early 1830s seemed to lie at the center of this sea change. Perhaps it was only accidental that such cultural adornments as the

Southern Review and the Academy of Fine Arts died during this crisis. The fact that many Carolinians were willing separately to take on General Jackson's armies over the issue of the *tariff*—seemingly a mere matter of dollars and cents—reflected the depth and intensity of the feeling. The tariff was not the real issue, of course; the South feared that national majorities could be turned against slavery, that northern firebrands might incite slave revolts. Ten years earlier, South Carolinians had exorcised from their midst Denmark Vesey and thirty-four other blacks by hanging them for planning a revolt that never took place; years later they could not exorcise the great fear that still perturbed them.

The bonds that would snap between North and South a quarter century later were already fraying between Carolinians and other Americans. Calhoun's resignation as Jackson's Vice-President, Hayne's resignation as United States senator and selection as governor, and Calhoun's election to replace him in the Senate marked the turning away of these men from national to sectional leadership. In South Carolina the nullifiers now were top dogs. Seeking always to strengthen Carolinian solidarity in the face of external threats, nullifier leaders almost put through a test oath that would require all state officers to swear primary allegiance to a sovereign South Carolina. Any possible ties between Carolina slaves and the North were attacked by laws that forbade slaves to learn to read and write and that taxed out of existence peddlers who might traffic in tempting ideas as well as goods. Thus the planter elites tried to suppress criticism and choke off opposition.

The leadership now governing South Carolina was as powerful and unified as any the nation had seen for half a century. Its power and unity flowed from a political system that reflected an ideological solidarity so strong as to render most questions merely tactical disputes over how best to carry out an agreed-on strategy. The Carolinian structure of government was remarkable in a nation that worshipped the checks and balances. An almost omnipotent legislature selected the governor for a two-year term, at the end of which the incumbent was ineligible for re-election. The legislature chose other key state officers and court clerks, as well as local officials. The governor lacked the power of veto. This centralization of power in legislative elites might not have been unusual if the legislators operated in a competitive two-party system, or at least could expect to face opposition, but such was not the case. The absence of a statewide gubernatorial election that might stimulate grass-roots participation and unity, a doctrine of "virtual representation" that gave legislators wide leeway, the absence of a strong and continuing opposition party, the fear of any opposition at a time when Carolinians were mobilized against external and internal threats, the weakness of local government and voluntary associations, the partial diking off of state from national politics—all these intended and accidental factors drew South Carolina away from the mainstream of national competitive politics, immensely fortified the power of the slaveholding elites, and emasculated the old Unionist opposition.

* * *

Mightily sustaining the Carolinian power elites, and mightily sustained by them, was an ideology—a set of lenses through which the elites perceived the world, a system of doctrines by which they understood it, a hierarchy of values by which they measured it. South Carolinians needed such an ideology, a guide to political action and policy decision, and a way of rationalizing and justifying action taken. Under the intellectual leadership of John Calhoun, the Carolinians and Southerners allied with them shaped perhaps the single most potent ideology to appear in the nation since its founding—but an ideology so flawed at its very heart as to betray those who embraced it.

When Calhoun responded to President Jackson's famous toast, "Our Federal Union—*it must be preserved,*" with his own counter-toast, "The Union—next to our liberty the most dear," the South Carolinian was expressing the central value of his ideology. From Jeffersonian roots Calhoun had drawn a relatively generous and expansive concept of this supreme value. To him liberty was the goal because, in Charles Wiltse's words, "it was the liberty of the individual to seek his own betterment, to develop his own talents and skills, to realize his own fullest potentialities, that led to every advance in civilization and thereby improved the condition of the whole society." While this was a highly individualistic theory of liberty, it flowed powerfully from the historic defense of the rights of man against authority as expressed in the English, American, and French revolutions.

Carolinians warmly embraced Calhoun's idea of an elaborate mechanism to keep government off the back of the citizen—not only states' rights in general but state nullification of abhorrent federal law, not only the traditional checks and balances but the requirement of a "concurrent majority"—that is, agreement of all major sections and interests—in order for the federal government to act. Calhoun wanted two Presidents, representing two major sections of the country and each having an absolute veto over the other. Calhoun's was almost a caricature of the old notion of checks on government officials to stop them from interfering with individual liberty; once again the questions of checks against private abuse of individual liberty, and of the ready availability of "government by the people" to curb arbitrary use of private power, were left by the wayside, enveloped in a fog of theory.

The more, however, that Carolinians apotheosized liberty as individual opportunity, as defense against oppression, as the "unalienable right" written into the Declaration of Independence and signed by eminent Carolinians, the more they faced a flagrant political and intellectual contradiction —the subordination of women and especially of blacks in a caste society. Immensely sharpening this dilemma was the emphasis that Calhoun and others placed on the constant threat to liberty of excessive power, the tendency of those holding power to abuse it, the need to balance power with power. Where was the balancing power of slaves? For a century Carolinians had had to confront the taunting cry from the North: how could slaveholders talk about liberty?

It would take men of great intellectual power and resourcefulness to resolve this dilemma, and such men South Carolina had in abundance in the antebellum period. Calhoun had deposited his intellectual legacy with a group of thinkers who were at least as uncompromising as he and who criticized him, indeed, mainly for his expedient concessions to the North when he was seeking the presidency. There was William Gilmore Simms, a big, proud man with a bluff manner and slyly sarcastic tongue, shunned by the Charleston elite even after he "married into a good name." There was Edmund Ruffin, an archetypal Yankee-hater, a Virginia-born and -raised agriculturalist who served for a time as agricultural surveyor for South Carolina. There was James Henry Hammond, well wed to a woman who brought him a plantation of 7,500 acres and 148 slaves, a onetime fire-eater who called slavery "the cornerstone of our Republican edifice." An able politician and longtime champion of nullification and secession, Hammond started as the editor of a paper in Columbia, where he challenged one critic to a duel and horsewhipped another, and once advocated the death penalty for abolitionists. These men and other Carolinians, like Thomas Cooper, in intellectual communion with writers in other states, such as George Fitzhugh and Nathaniel Beverly Tucker of Virginia and William Lowndes Yancey of Alabama, wrenched the concept of liberty out of its old moral foundations to make it serve new political purposes.

Thus, where Calhoun contended that people were not all "equally entitled to liberty" but had to earn it, Simms added that liberty was "not intended to disturb the natural degrees of humanity," but was served only when a man was "suffered to occupy his proper place." Where Calhoun warned that liberty should not be overextended to those not yet ready for it, Simms would grant only "such liberty as becomes one's moral condition." Slavery was a benign institutionalization of natural inequality. Liberty was often defined simply as states' rights, in the Calhoun tradition, but this old doctrine too was flawed. If South Carolina demanded her freedom from national governmental control on the ground that she knew best how to govern her affairs, should not South Carolinians in their localities be guaranteed their liberty against *state* control—and how could that proposition be defended when the South Carolina legislature had almost total power over local officials?

There was a much simpler way to overcome the intellectual dilemma over liberty than reinterpreting and narrowing and trivializing it—to repudiate the concept entirely and with it the essence of Jeffersonian moral philosophy. "Liberty and equality are not only destructive to the morals," said George Fitzhugh, "but to the happiness of society." So much for the Declaration of Independence. Slavery, contended Albert Taylor Bledsoe, another non-Carolinian, was in effect liberty: "By the institution of slavery for the blacks, license is shut out, and liberty is introduced. . . ." It was even simpler to dispose of that dangerous concept of Mr. Jefferson's that "all men are created equal." Hammond simply denied it.

Whatever their attitude toward liberty in theory, Carolinians and other Southerners were unquestionably ready to abrogate it in fact. By the 1850s every southern state save Kentucky had passed laws limiting freedom of speech, press, and discussion. Hammond recommended "one way" to silence talk of abolition: *"Terror—Death . . ."* Even in Kentucky, Cassius Clay's antislavery *True American* was suppressed by other means, as a mob dismantled his presses and sent them to Cincinnati. Most southern editors applauded this clamp-down on their fellow journalists. The failure of the press to challenge the proslavery litany reflected—aside from the everpresent threat of the duel—a failure of the southern imagination to see alternative possibilities for its society.

The dragnet covered even the universities. When in Chapel Hill a chemistry professor remarked that he would vote for the 1856 Republican ticket if it should be run in North Carolina, there was a public uproar. The Raleigh *Standard* called for his ilk to be "silenced or . . . be driven out," students burned him in effigy, and he was hounded out of the university. The silencing of any independent critical voice, the absence of any of the "isms" sweeping the North, and the tendency of southern schools to become institutions of propaganda constituted crucial ways, in Clement Eaton's words, in which the "Southern people set up an intellectual blockade, a *cordon sanitaire.*"

By the time that slavery boiled up again as a national issue in the mid-1850s, the intellectual effort to reconcile slavery and liberty had become so extremist and even gymnastic that a simple and straightforward defense of slavery seemed more useful to southern elites. This defense took many forms. Some arguments for slavery were essentially debating points: that slavery was sanctioned in the Bible; that the founding fathers had owned slaves; that most of the abuse of blacks took place in southern cities, at the hands of owners who had never before had slaves. Other proslavery arguments were essentially biological: black men were innately inferior and even helpless, and needed white masters to look out for them. In a famous address to the United States Senate in 1858, Hammond argued that all societies required a "mud-sill" class of laborers and that Negroes were born inferior, while another Carolinian, William Henry Trescot, held that they were unfit to be educated. Still other arguments were philosophical: that the slaves were part of a "bygone pastoral Arcadia," in David Donald's words, that "had formerly flourished in the South before it was undermined by the commercialization of urban life on the one hand and by the increasing democratization and decentralization of the frontier on the other." Could not agrarian community and hierarchy and order be saved?

By far the most telling southern argument, however, was not the defense of slavery, but the attack on northern capitalism as a system of "wage slavery" far less just and humane than black slavery. Better to be a slave at the mercy of a master who must take responsibility for him, wrote "a Carolinian," than a wage worker subject to "no tyrant but the hard laws of demand and supply, stern and unchangeable." Southern writers triumphantly contrasted the slave cared for by his master in illness and old age, in hard times and good, with the wage slave abandoned by his employer on a minute's notice. As usual, Fitzhugh put the point the most tellingly, in his aptly titled tract *Cannibals All! Or, Slaves Without Masters.* Everywhere, he said, the strong took advantage of the weak—hence cannibals all—but the South had long recognized this and made provision for protecting the slave, while the North extracted full value from the worker and then tossed him into the ashcan. Capitalism, in short, was white slavery.

Candid Carolinians knew, however, that masters did not always provide for their bondspeople, as when planters for months left slaves to the mercy of overseers and malaria, or provided poor food or shelter, or sold off rebellious or inefficient field hands. Candid capitalists of the North knew that the "white slavers" were often as unjust as southern polemicists claimed. Behind the lofty pretensions of each lay an ignoble defense of the elite monopolization of property and profits. The tragedy of South Carolina was that, despite its possession of the finest intellects of the South, the defense of slavery was shallow and self-interested. The tragedy of the North was that it was too vulnerable to southern charges of "wage slavery" to be able to mount a respectable defense. The tragedy of both North and

South was that neither fully engaged with the other, neither treated the value of liberty analytically and multidimensionally, and neither linked it to equality and other principles in a well-considered hierarchy of values. Where a war of words was so inadequate, a war of weapons would seem likely to follow.

THE GRAND DEBATES

"Oyez! Oyez!" intoned the court crier as the Supreme Court justices, gathering their black robes around them, seated themselves behind their long bench. It was the same cry that had opened the court session for *Marbury* v. *Madison* a half century before, and all the sessions since; the high court still met in a drab, ground-level basement room beneath the Senate chamber; and the Chief Justice was about to render a decision as portentous and controversial as *Marbury*. Otherwise things were different. It was March 6, 1857, two days after Buchanan's inaugural. The court had grown from five members to nine. The case involved not a white clerk named Marbury, but a black slave called Dred Scott. And the court was about to invalidate not a minor procedural act of Congress, as in *Marbury*, but one of its towering achievements—the Missouri Compromise restriction on slavery.

The faces of the men behind the bench would have delighted Dickens: Taney's deeply seamed countenance of parchment yellow, set among shaggy eyebrows and graying locks, highlighted by large, world-weary eyes; the stern and swarthy visage of Virginia's apoplectic Peter V. Daniel; the genial and philosophical expression of John A. Campbell of Alabama; the dour, ruddy face of Robert C. Grier of Pennsylvania; the aristocratic features of the youthful Benjamin R. Curtis. Emerging out of the rough-and-tumble of American law and politics, the justices were mainly a collection of able, experienced mediocrities, notable more for their party and sectional background than their intellects. Flanking Taney were party men —six other Democrats, one Republican, and one Whig. Flanking him were sectional men—four other judges from slaveholding states, two men from the middle states, and one from Massachusetts. The last was the Whig Curtis, the ablest intellect among the associate justices. Dominating the scene—and the court—was Taney, born of the Maryland planting gentry, appointed Chief Justice by Jackson after the fight against the national bank, a devout Catholic who had long since freed his own slaves. Taney had proved to be the perfect heir to the Jeffersonian states' rights tradition, guiding the court away from the nationalist direction it had taken under Marshall's leadership.

Holding papers in his thin, tremulous fingers, Taney briefly reported the facts of the case. Behind his flat recitation lay a small human drama. No one, not Dred Scott himself, knew when and where he was born—probably in Virginia, probably around the turn of the century. Short, dark, uneducated and illiterate, he had been picked up, used, and moved around by white people according to their convenience: raised by a family in St. Louis, purchased by an army surgeon, John Emerson, taken to Rock Island, Illinois, when Emerson reported for duty there, removed to Wisconsin Territory, married to a slave woman named Harriet, then taken back to Missouri by the surgeon. When Emerson died, he bequeathed his slave to his wife and daughter. Then something stirred in Dred Scott; evidently he tried to buy his freedom and failed. His original owners sued Mrs. Emerson for Scott's freedom, on the ground that his earlier residence in Illinois and Wisconsin Territory—free soil—had made him free. That was the crucial issue that had brought the case to the high court, an issue that transcended slave and owner; as the case gained in importance, prestigious legal talent was enlisted on both sides.

Though his voice weakened and almost faded away, Taney went on for over two hours, but long before he ended proslavery people in the courtroom were exultant, and free-soil men indignant. Even while other justices were concurring and dissenting the next day, northern newspapers were headlining the essential results: SLAVERY ALONE NATIONAL—THE MISSOURI COMPROMISE UNCONSTITUTIONAL—NEGROES CANNOT BE CITIZENS—THE TRIUMPH OF SLAVERY COMPLETE. The decision was infinitely complicated, but three results stood out: Dred Scott was still a slave (he was soon manumitted, lived a year, and died of consumption); no black person could be a United States citizen under the Constitution of 1787; and Congress had no power to bar slavery in federal territories and hence the Missouri Compromise restriction was unconstitutional.

A storm of protest swept through the northern press and pulpits. The decision, said the New York Tribune, carried as much moral weight as "the judgment of a majority of those congregated in any Washington barroom." Pointing to the Democratic court, the Democratic Administration, and the Democratic House and Senate, the protesters smelled a plot. Had not Buchanan and Taney held a whispered conversation during a pause in the inaugural ceremonies? Were not the President and at least two of the associate justices as thick as thieves? And had not Buchanan said in his Inaugural Address that he understood the Supreme Court would soon rule on the issue of slavery in the territories, adding piously, "To their decision, in common with all good citizens, I shall cheerfully submit, whatever this may be"? The hypocrite! He knew right then how the court would rule.

So the protesters charged—and this time their conspiracy theory was justified. Two members of the court—and possibly Taney himself—had indeed given the President ample information in advance about the nature and timing of the decision.

Buchanan had done more: he had helped Taney "mass the court." The southern members of the court wanted to strike a mortal blow at the Missouri Compromise—but they feared that the blow would not be mortal if only the five southern members inflicted it. There must be six. The President urged his fellow Pennsylvanian Grier to join in a strong decision, and Grier did so. He wrote the President that he would try to persuade the three other justices also to back a strong position.

A broad position it turned out to be—so broad and strong and sweeping as to alter central currents of American history. As a legislative decision it recast the law of the land affecting both enslaved blacks and free. As a political decision it upset the delicate balance between North and South, exacerbated antagonism between proslavery and antislavery Democrats, and destroyed that superb device of compromise, squatter sovereignty, that had allowed politicians to evade the moral dilemma of slavery by condemning it while prating about states' rights or local popular authority. As a judicial decision, it was prospectively even more important, for the court now had struck down a major law enacted by the coequal legislative branch and endorsed by the coequal executive branch. The court's power to invalidate state legislation that it deemed unconstitutional, as in *Gibbons* v. *Ogden,* and to protect its own internal arrangements and integrity, had long been accepted. Now it was invading the federal lawmaking domain reserved, under democratic theory, to the elected politicians of House, Senate, and White House.

Why, observers wondered, had the court inserted itself into the political storm whirling around slavery? In part because the cautious legislative and executive politicians had left a vacuum that some force was bound to fill. But mainly because the Southerners wanted to surround and control that whirlwind. The thrust of the Dred Scott decision did not result from chance or gradualism. Behind Taney's penetrating, closely reasoned decision lay a deep rage against the antislavery men, a rage welling out of Taney's roots in the tobacco lands of Maryland, out of his Jacksonian heritage, out of his distaste for northern capitalism and the hypocritical reformers it seemed to breed. The pressures in him, if not on him, were southern pressures. He wanted this sweeping decision—and so did the four other Southerners and the one "dough face" on the court.

What the Northerners were now witnessing was southern power massed in the federal government. Numerically Democrats controlled the Supreme Court, the House, the Senate, as well as the presidency and the Cabinet. Concentrated within those Democratic majorities was a southern plurality, organized, purposeful, disciplined. If there was no southern "conspiracy" in the polemical meaning, there was a group of men living and working and conferring together who cut across the formal lines separating executive and judiciary and legislature. Just as a power elite now controlled South Carolina politics, so a wider power elite dominated the federal system.

This was no simple conflict between North and South; many Southerners opposed the extension of slavery and some even slavery itself, and many Northerners hated the black man, cared little about slavery, or at least were willing to leave it in its place. It was a conflict of philosophies, parties, and policies. Dred Scott was ultimately far more than a legal decision; it was an intellectual statement, a party manifesto, a policy paper, with all the tendentious reasoning, legal error, and opinionated argument found in such documents. It was one of a series of grand debates, in Congress, in the courts, in the press, and on the stump. And ultimately it must be answered less by legal than by intellectual and political power— it must be answered by opposition leadership.

*   *   *

It is not given to more than a few voyagers in the stream of history to influence its basic direction. The flow of events, moving within the embankments set by geology, biology, and climate, now hurries along, now placidly twists and winds its way, through numerous channels, ultimately debouching into some broad and distant water. Destroying old landmarks, shaping new ones, the stream of history engulfs most people who stand in its way but raises some to its surface. Of these a few will breast the current and perhaps divert or even transform it, but a far greater number will seek only to survive, through agility, ingenuity, and luck.

James Buchanan stood on the crest of events when he entered the White House; the question for him was whether he would become a maker of history or a victim of it. He possessed the ingredients of power: the executive and foreign-policy authority of the presidency, a large pool of patronage jobs, power to appoint Supreme Court and other federal judges as well as cabinet members and other high officials, influence over legislation mainly through his party leadership, the visibility and prestige of the White House. What he lacked was the capacity to be both principled and propitiatory, both consistent and conciliatory, at the appropriate time for each. He strongly hoped, Edward Everett wrote the President-elect, that he could "give the country a vigorous and conciliatory administration to check the present centrifugal tendencies." But Buchanan was not strong enough to contain the whirlwind. He dealt with slavery by evading it, in London, in his campaign, in his Inaugural Address.

But the issue of slavery could no longer be evaded. In Kansas the crisis would not simmer down. Ensconced in their rival "capitals," proslavery and antislavery Kansans eyed one another belligerently and boycotted each other's elections while the nation watched with excitement. Knowing that they were in the minority, the proslavery forces planned to hold a constitutional convention, rigged to overrepresent their side, that would protect slavery under the fundamental law. Held in Lecompton in the fall of 1857, this convention, recognizing that such a constitution would be defeated in a properly conducted popular vote, proposed to withhold the charter from the people and submit to them a special article that guaranteed the right of property in slaves. Even if the special article should be rejected, the right to hold property in slaves already in the territory would be protected. The proposition, a Kansan said, was "Vote to take this arsenic with bread and butter, or without bread and butter."

Once again the Free Soilers erupted in indignation. "The Great Swindle," thundered the Emporia *Kansas News*.

What would Buchanan do? He had sent to Kansas a governor, Robert J. Walker, who promised that any constitution adopted by a constitutional convention would have to be submitted to Kansans for a fair vote. Now he was in a box. He knew that by supporting Lecompton he would probably break his party into pieces. Yet southern ultras were demanding that the entire constitution be sent direct to Washington, where the Democratic Congress would legislate it and the Democratic President sign it. Most of the southern leadership, including Southerners in Buchanan's own Cabinet, supported the Lecompton forces. Buchanan was dependent on southern support politically; of his 174 electoral votes in 1856, 112 had come from the South. He would need southern support if he ran again in 1860; he would need southern support in the Democratic convention, with its two-thirds rule; he would continue to need southern support to get his bills through Congress. And beyond all these practical concerns was his fear that the South would secede if it lost the game in Kansas—already proslavery firebrands were making threats. Yielding to this massed southern power, the President publicly endorsed the Lecompton plan.

Stephen Douglas was in a terrible dilemma. His political ambitions too depended on southern favor. Still aspiring to the presidency, he might—with backing from his southern friends—head off Buchanan for the Democratic nomination in 1860. But he was also the celebrated spokesman for "squatter sovereignty," and now he waited only to know whether his doctrine had been violated. "The only question," he wrote a friend, "is whether the constitution formed at Lecompton is the act & will . . . of a small minority, who have attempted to cheat & defraud the majority by trickery & juggling." As chairman of the Committee on Territories, Douglas received constant intelligence from Kansas, and he did not have long to wait to learn the truth. The Lecompton plan, he decided, was a fraud, a mockery. He could not sanction it without "repudiating all the acts of my life." But to attack Lecompton now, he knew, would break his ties with the President and with the South, lead to his being cast out of the Democratic party leadership, and jeopardize his committee chairmanship in the Senate. Returning to Washington, he hurried to the White House. A stiff confrontation followed.

"Mr. Douglas," said Buchanan as the talk came to an end, "I desire you to remember that no Democrat ever yet differed from the Administration of his own choice without being crushed. . . ."

"Mr. President," replied Douglas, "I wish you to remember that General Jackson is dead, sir."

The clerk had barely completed reading the President's annual message to Congress, on December 8, 1857, when Douglas was on his feet to express his total dissent on the Lecompton issue. In his major address a day later the Illinois senator spoke once again for popular sovereignty. "I have spent too much strength and breath, and health, too, to establish this great principle in the popular heart, now to see it frittered away." The packed gallery and lobby broke into a tumult as he concluded, "If this constitution is to be forced down our throats, in violation of the fundamental principle of free government, under a mode of submission that is a mockery and an insult, I will resist it to the last."

Suddenly the Little Giant did not look so small to his old Republican and Unionist foes. A courtship followed, as Republican members of Congress called on Douglas and discussed common efforts against Lecompton. Horace Greeley visited him too, and speculation arose that more must have been discussed than parliamentary tactics. Would Douglas join the Republicans? Or could he persuade Republicans and old-time Whigs to swing over to his cause? In severing his ties with southern ultras, Douglas had bolstered his position as leader of the northern Democrats. While the southern junta laid plans to help defeat him in his Senate re-election race and to strip him of his chairmanship of the Committee on Territories, eastern Republicans talked openly of backing Douglas in his Senate race in 1858 and for the presidency in 1860.

These reports galvanized the Illinois Republicans into action. From Herndon in Springfield, Greeley in New York received an indignant letter.

Was Greeley backing Douglas? Was he going to "sell us out" in Illinois "without our consent to accomplish some *national* political purpose"? Greeley should not raise Douglas over the heads of long-term and well-tried Republicans, who had never flinched. "We want the man *that we want;* and it is not for N. York—Seward—Mass—Banks or any other state or man" to tell Illinois Republicans whom they should have. "We want to be our own masters."

It was a critical moment for Lincoln. Greeley's *Tribune* was influential in Illinois, with a circulation rapidly heading toward 20,000 in that state alone. Stealing Douglas from the Democracy, Lincoln knew, was a tempting thought for Illinois Republicans. It was a critical moment for Illinois Republicans too, and it was they—the "third cadre" of grass-roots activists —who now took leadership. By mid-1858 the rank-and-file leaders had come to like and esteem the tall, humorous, sad, tolerant, thoughtful man from Springfield. They liked him also because by now he had firmly embraced the Republican party, not merely the antislavery movement. With Lincoln's encouragement, but without his active leadership, Republicans meeting in scores of county conventions spontaneously called for him to be chosen to run against Douglas at the party's state convention to be held in Springfield. There was no precedent for using a state party convention to nominate a candidate for United States senator, but the Illinois Republicans, in a burst of political creativity, did that on June 16, 1858, by designating Lincoln the party's "first, last, and only choice" for senator.

"I want to see 'old gentleman Greely's' notice of our Republican Convention," Herndon wrote. "—I itch—I burn, to see what he says. . . ." The Illinois Republicans had happily defied the patronizing and meddlesome eastern press that was trying to sacrifice them to its national coalition building. The men of Illinois had done much more. They had launched Lincoln on his national career; they had turned a shank of history; and they had set the stage for the most significant debate—and the most remarkable public intellectual encounter—in American history.

*   *   *

Lincoln moved to the attack within a few hours of his nomination by acclamation at the state convention. The 1,500 delegates adjourned for supper, then reconvened in the stifling Representatives Hall. Some in the perspiring crowd urged him to move the meeting out to the front steps, but Lincoln persuaded them to stay inside because his voice was not in the best condition to reach a crowd outside. This night he wanted to be heard. He had long been shaping this speech in his mind, working over its phrases, and he had even rehearsed it the previous night before Herndon and other friends, only to be told that it was too radical, too incendiary.

Now he stood before the delegates, a gangling figure in frock coat, bow tie, rumpled vest and trousers. He wasted no time on pleasantries:

"If we could first know *where* we are, and *whither* we are tending, we could then better judge *what* to do, and *how* to do it."

Lincoln was reading from a manuscript with underlined key words.

"We are now far into the *fifth* year, since a policy was initiated, with the *avowed* object, and *confident* promise, of putting an end to slavery agitation." All recognized the reference to the Kansas-Nebraska act.

"Under the operation of that policy, that agitation has not only, *not ceased,* but has *constantly augmented.*

"In *my* opinion, it *will* not cease, until a *crisis* shall have been reached, and passed.

" 'A house divided against itself cannot stand.'

"I believe this government cannot endure, permanently half *slave* and half *free.*

"I do not expect the Union to be *dissolved*—I do not expect the house to *fall*—but I *do* expect it will cease to be divided.

"It will become *all* one thing, or *all* the other. . . ."

Free or slave. All one thing or all another. Suddenly this moderate, prudent man had started talking like an abolitionist. But Lincoln knew precisely what he was about. Intensely worried by the Republican flirtation with Douglas, he would destroy the middle ground on which Douglas was standing and indict the senator as part of a grand conspiracy to spread slavery throughout the nation. Lincoln's purpose emerged in his very next sentence:

"Either the *opponents* of slavery, will arrest the further spread of it, and place it where the public mind shall rest in the belief that it is in course of ultimate extinction; or its *advocates* will push it forward, till it shall become alike lawful in *all* the States, *old* as well as *new—North* as well as *South.*"

Lincoln spelled out the conspiracy he was alleging. With the repeal of the Missouri Compromise via the Kansas-Nebraska bill, the endorsement of that repeal by the Supreme Court, and the endorsement of the endorsement by President Buchanan, the plots, said Lincoln, lacked only "another Supreme Court decision, declaring that the Constitution of the United States does not permit a *state* to exclude slavery from its limits." Was it absolutely certain that Douglas and Pierce, Taney and Buchanan, had acted by "preconcert"? Well, said Lincoln, "when we see a lot of framed timbers" perfectly put together "by different workmen—Stephen, Franklin, Roger and James, for instance," it was hard to believe that the four had not worked on a common plan "before the first lick was struck."

Having centered his convention attack on Douglas and played down his own position, Lincoln kept on the offensive. To Douglas' vast irritation, he continued to dog the senator's footsteps, attend his speeches, and announce to Douglas' throngs that a rebuttal would follow later in the day. Late in July, hoping to share a platform with Douglas rather than following him, Lincoln challenged Douglas to more than fifty debates in all the places —at least fifty—Douglas was scheduled to appear. Ready for combat but unwilling to share so many audiences with Lincoln, Douglas proposed they debate at a central point in each congressional district in the state, save for Springfield and Chicago, where each had already spoken. That would mean seven debates—in Ottawa, Freeport, Galesburg, Quincy, Jonesboro, Charleston, and Alton. Lincoln accepted.

The debates that followed were grand theater. They were also a striking display of political craftsmanship on both sides; and they represented the intellectual climax of the grand debates over slavery that had been echoing throughout the land for decades.

Douglas supplied most of the theater. Merely traveling from town to town, the senator was a sight to see. When he arrived back in Chicago from Washington, artillery roared a 150-gun salute; banners hung from windows and over the streets; flags fluttered on ships and buildings. When he journeyed down to Springfield, a flatcar on his special train carried a twelve-pound cannon that continually boomed out across the prairie. Rockets and fireworks climaxed his evening speeches. The intensive railroad building in Illinois was already affecting campaigning; Douglas could rest or receive delegations in his ornate private car between speeches, and regular and special trains brought listeners by the thousands.

Still, the pastoral folk memory of the debates was valid too—the memory of farmers arriving in buckboards, buggies, carriages, and carts, of roads so enveloped in dust as to resemble great smokehouses, of farmers in overalls and their wives in hoop skirts and young mothers with babies at their breasts standing in the burning sun for two or three hours. With his homespun face, hollowed cheeks, and tangled hair, Lincoln looked more like the hired hand in Sunday garb than the wealthy attorney that he was; Douglas, with his shiny black hair, shiny top hat, shiny black vest, and shiny black footwear, appeared every inch the city man, traveled and worldly. Each respected the oratorical prowess of his adversary. Douglas was all force, pacing up and down the platform, tossing his huge head and locks, blasting out cannonades of questions and accusations. Lincoln was supple, sinewy, tenacious. Douglas himself took the best measure of his opponent, when informed of Lincoln's nomination:

"I shall have my hands full. He is the strong man of his party—full of wit, facts, dates—and the best stump speaker, with his droll ways and dry jokes, in the West. He is as honest as he is shrewd, and if I beat him my victory will be hardly won."

Like master chess players, each man tried to put the other on the defensive. In the first debate, in Ottawa, Douglas posed seven questions for Lincoln, centering mainly on the question of race. Here Douglas felt on safe ground, given the anti-Negro attitudes so widespread in the state. "I do not question Mr. Lincoln's conscientious belief that the negro was made his equal, and hence is his brother, but for my own part, I do not regard the negro as my equal, and positively deny that he is my brother or any kin to me whatever." Douglas' belief in the innate inferiority of blacks was the key to his entire approach to slavery. It enabled him to consider the issue a matter of local preference, of popular sovereignty. To soothe the troubled consciences of Illinois free-soil sympathizers, who were expanding in numbers, the senator argued that popular sovereignty would keep slavery out of the territories, since slavery had already reached its natural limits and would not thrive where the soil and climate were inhospitable.

"Diversity, dissimilarity, variety in all our local and domestic institutions," Douglas said, "is the great safeguard of our liberties." Lincoln's statement that the nation could not endure half slave and half free, said Douglas, would lead to a war of sections. "Why should the slavery agitation be kept up?" It only gave Republican politicians a hobbyhorse on which to ride into office.

Douglas' exploitation of the race issue put Lincoln on the defensive. He made clear he was not talking about full Negro equality, but of the rights guaranteed all people by the Declaration of Independence. Blacks were equal in the "right to life, liberty and the pursuit of happiness," in rights that extended beyond mere liberation from slavery, but they did not extend to full social and political equality. Lincoln made clear his opposition to intermarriage of blacks and whites, to blacks serving on juries, to blacks holding office or becoming citizens or voting in elections. Lincoln sought to keep Douglas on the defensive by pressing his accusation of a conspiracy to legalize slavery in every state in the Union. He charged Douglas with holding a "care not" position on slavery and of seeking to lull Northerners into moral indifference. Douglas indignantly denied the conspiracy charge.

And so the debates continued, lengthy, repetitious, with the audience chiming in with cheers, laughter, sharp comments, advice, cries of "good, good," "we stand by that," "you have him," "that's right," all duly noted down by the reporters. "Put on your specs," someone called out to Lincoln, who promptly obliged. The audience, indeed, was a vital part of the debates, responding, falling silent, audibly disapproving or doubting. A legend would grow that Lincoln vanquished his opponent, but each man really held his own. At one point Republican backers urged Lincoln to be more aggressive, and other orators were mobilized to assault Douglas. But as the debates proceeded, as charges were made and rebutted and specific questions raised and answered, the debates took on a broader moral and intellectual dimension, and here Lincoln emerged the superior leader, though a perplexed and flawed one.

Lincoln moved to a philosophical level in the debates in part because he was frustrated on the political. Douglas' doctrine of popular sovereignty was simply too tough to handle. That doctrine made it all too easy for the senator to label blacks inferior and at the same time express his dislike of slavery, but in the next breath to say, what did it matter?—the question should be left to the people in the states and territories, and it was none of his business how they decided. On this issue Douglas had been absolutely, indeed heroically, consistent, especially after Dred Scott, as his break with the Administration proved. His was a virtually unassailable position. Who could object to popular sovereignty? Even Republicans like Greeley—to Lincoln's acute political discomfiture—had to admit the force of this old Jeffersonian, Republican, states' rights doctrine.

"Has Douglas the *exclusive right,* in this country, of being *on all sides of all questions?"* Lincoln demanded amid great laughter. Was he "to have an entire *monopoly* on that subject?"

Frustrated, Lincoln found it politically necessary to "rise above politics" to the philosophical level of good and evil, to the moral level of right and wrong. "The real issue in this controversy—the one pressing upon every mind—is the sentiment on the part of one class that looks upon the institution of slavery *as a wrong,* and of another class that *does not* look upon it as a wrong." The Republican party, he said, took the first position. "It is the sentiment around which all their actions—all their arguments circle—from which all their propositions radiate. They look upon it as being a moral, social and political wrong. . . ."

Strong words. But the more Lincoln took this high ethical plane, the more he became trapped in a political and moral dilemma. Political, because he was seeking to hold a centrist position in the Republican party, because he was a constitutionalist who did not want to move outside the document bequeathed by the founding fathers, because he was a "process" Republican as well as a "principle" Republican. That is why in the very next words after the moral bugle call he had just sounded about "political wrong"—indeed, separated in the official transcript only by a semicolon—he went on: ". . . and while they contemplate it as such, they nevertheless have due regard for its actual existence among us, and the difficulties of getting rid of it in any satisfactory way and to all the constitutional obligations thrown about it. . . ." So what was the Republican party solution? "To *make provision that it shall grow no larger.*"

And here lay Lincoln's moral dilemma. If slavery was so evil, what about the millions of enslaved who would be left alone in their degradation? If, as Lincoln implied, slavery might not be extirpated under his policy of gradualism for another hundred years, what about the tens of millions of bondmen who would be trapped on southern plantations while the rest of the civilized world emancipated serfs and slaves? Lincoln believed in individual effort and growth, in room for talent—what about the potential for growth and creativity crushed in the minds and bodies of millions of persons who would otherwise have made the musicians and actors, the lawyers and doctors, the businessmen and politicians of the future? And what about the blacks already free, or who might be free? In the debates he saw a "physical difference between the black and white races" that would "for ever forbid the two races living together on terms of social and political equality." They could not intermarry or, presumably, otherwise integrate. But since Lincoln would also deny them the right of citizenship, the right to hold office, the right to vote, and the right to serve on juries, he was also denying them the political means of achieving greater liberty and equality, short of a century or so.

In effect, Lincoln would give black people economic rights, job rights, a property right in their own labor. Despite his reverence for the rights extended in the Declaration of Independence to *all* men—rights to life, liberty, and the pursuit of happiness—he would narrow them in the case of blacks. "I agree with Judge Douglas," he said in the Ottawa debate, that the Negro "is not my equal in many respects—certainly not in color, perhaps not in moral or intellectual endowment. But in the right to eat the bread, without leave of anybody else, which his own hand earns, *he is my equal and the equal of Judge Douglas, and the equal of every living man.*" Great applause burst forth from this audience of farmers, just as they cheered and laughed, in a later debate, when Lincoln said, "I do not understand that because I do not want a negro woman for a slave I must necessarily want her for a wife"—and proposed that, since only Illinois law could outlaw miscegenation, Judge Douglas' fear of intermarriage could be allayed by placing him in the *state* legislature.

It was all very demeaning to blacks and to Lincoln himself, who must have sensed it. His defenses were that he was admittedly an ambitious man who wanted to win an election, and politics was the art of the possible; that he must work within the Constitution and the political system, which allowed only for gradualism; and that his greatest love was for the Union, in the spirit of the Framers and Webster and Clay, and that forcing the issue would disrupt the Union. Lincoln, despite his supple and leathery argumentation, did not grapple with the question that had eluded so many other leaders: what was the Union *for,* if not for the ideals of the Declaration of Independence? And if in the spirit of national Union liberty and equality were national values, and if slavery was a national evil that flatly contradicted these values, then there should be national action to confront the evil. But Lincoln did not propose compensated emancipation or any other national program, however difficult to accomplish, that might serve as a response worthy of the Union.

"The planting and the culture are over," Lincoln said in a final speech, to friends back in Springfield; "and there remains but the preparation, and the harvest." For Lincoln, the harvest was plentiful but inadequate. The Democrats won a majority of the contests for the state legislature, which could hence be expected to re-elect Douglas to the United States Senate. The Republicans, under Lincoln's leadership, won elections for state treasurer and another statewide office, by popular vote. This did Lincoln no immediate good; once again he was a loser. But he had attracted wide attention; he had won praise as a fine debater of issues; and he had maintained his position in the dead center of the Republican party.

And if Douglas had ended as the political victor in the debates, Lincoln, with his finespun logic and his grasp of the complex relationships of ideas, institutions, and individuals, had emerged as intellectually the superior of the two. Neither emerged as a moral leader, capable of reaching into the minds and hearts of human beings, appealing to their more generous instincts, recognizing their fundamental wants and needs, and mobilizing their hopes and aspirations. Still, the American people were the real victors in this contest, for the Lincoln-Douglas debates became a model for vigorous but rational political discussion, and a treasure of the nation's intellectual heritage.

THE POLITICS OF SLAVERY

The economic boom roared through mid-decade, fueled by foreign capital, especially British, and by $300 million worth of gold from California. The nation's commerce, industry, and foreign trade expanded as they stimulated one another. There were booms in land, railroads, securities and commodities speculation—and in prices. When prosperity faltered a bit in 1854, the Crimean War boosted overseas orders for grains, metals, and livestock. Also fueling the boom were more than 1,300 banks, with an authorized capital of over $300 million. Trading on the New York Stock Exchange rose to a new intensity, as brokers, their arms swinging over their heads, bought and sold in their staccato lingo—"Sell 'em"—"Take 'em"—"Fifty More"—"I'll take your lot, buyer four months"—"Done!"

The boom brought the usual worries over the excesses of materialism. Moralists chided the ladies who crowded into Tiffany's to buy diamonds, Stewart's to buy laces, Ferrerro's to buy bonnets, or even worse, bought imported silks and laces and wines, or, worst of all, journeyed themselves to Paris and purchased

> Dresses for breakfasts, and dinners, and balls,
> Dresses to sit in, and stand in, and walk in;
> Dresses to dance in, and flirt in, and talk in;
> Dresses in which to do nothing at all;
> Dresses for Winter, Spring, Summer and Fall—
> All of them different in color and shape,
> Silk, muslin, and lace, velvet, satin, and crepe.

The surge in big fortunes, Emerson feared, might "upset the balance of man, and establish a new, universal Monarchy more tyrannical than Babylon or Rome."

But not all was Babylon. While Kansas bled and business prospered, Thoreau published *Walden,* Walt Whitman *Leaves of Grass,* Longfellow *Hiawatha,* William H. Prescott the first volumes of his *Philip II.* At decade's end, Hawthorne would bring out *The Marble Faun* and Emerson *The Conduct of Life. The Atlantic Monthly,* appearing in 1857 under the editorship of James Russell Lowell, promised to publish Emerson, Bryant, Prescott, Hawthorne, Melville, Oliver Wendell Holmes, Wilkie Collins, Harriet Beecher Stowe, Lydia Maria Child, and a score of other eminent authors. New York City was the book center of the country, with the big firm of Harper and Brothers issuing three million books a year; in New York State alone, books were distributed through four hundred or more booksellers or book outlets. Bibliophiles and litterateurs met at the Saturday Club in Boston, the Century Club in New York, Russell's Bookshop in Charleston. The South no longer could boast an Edgar Allan Poe, though it was rich in storytelling. But there was little communication between southern and northern men and women of letters.

Late in 1857 a panic suddenly swept through the whole edifice of American banking and commerce. First an old flour and grain house failed; then a prestigious life insurance company tottered; soon railroads—including the huge Illinois Central—went down; securities prices collapsed; depositors flocked to their banks to find closed doors; financial houses toppled; and within weeks fear was running throughout the American money system and to bankers, merchants, and investors abroad. Much human shock and misery followed. Businessmen could not borrow money to keep going; farmers found their commodity prices dropping almost overnight; workers were laid off; established Boston families were suddenly impoverished; western merchants waited in vain for their remittances from New York and Pennsylvania. Although southern banks held up more sturdily than northern or western, much to the satisfaction of "southron" leaders, hardly a segment of the nation's economy was left untouched.

So powerful were the forces sustaining the American economy, however —the resources, technology, enterprising workers and industrial leaders, the dependably high revenues from cotton, heavy demand from abroad, a continuing flow of gold from California—that the country had largely recovered by the summer of 1858. Still, the panic had left a residue of tension and ill feeling: farmers were angry at middlemen and eastern buyers, workers at coldhearted employers, depositors at faithless bankers. Farmers talked about laws restricting middlemen; workers in New York marched in militant processions demanding jobs; New England mill hands struck. There was little violence; the panic was too short-lived for that. Perhaps the deepest scar was left between North and South, as tobacco and cotton growers blamed the avaricious Yankee bankers, factors, and jobbers for robbing them of their profits.

Still, as prosperity returned late in 1858 and the election oratory quieted, sectional hostility seemed to soften a bit. The Kansas crisis faded away into anticlimax as Kansans finally and categorically rejected the Lecompton constitution, thus leaving themselves in territorial status. A "Southern Commercial Convention" in May 1859 urged the repeal of all laws illegalizing the foreign slave trade, but even the Buchanan administration opposed such a retrograde and extremist measure.

Then, in late October 1859, another act of violence disrupted the seeming calm. Unsatiated by his bloodletting in Kansas, John Brown had become more than ever possessed of a single fanatical vision—the liberation of the slaves. Somehow evading the "federal hounds" sent to track him down, he had moved from place to place throughout the North, raising a little money, collecting a few arms, and gathering another following. Monomaniacal, contemptuous of the cowards who fell by the way, he possessed a strange power of mesmerizing skeptics. After Boston abolitionists lionized him and Concord literati received him, he left New England scornful of all the extremist talk and, with a band that included two of his sons, ready for action.

His was a daring plan: to capture the federal arsenal at Harpers Ferry, arm the slaves that would flock in from the whole area, and prepare for revolution, or at least for liberation. The seizure of the arsenal, early in the morning in the sleepy Virginia town, came easily. Then Brown and his band settled down to await the blacks. But the people who arrived in the morning were not black but white—first a half-drunken mob from the town, then some militia units, and finally federal troops under the command of Robert E. Lee. After Lee demanded unconditional surrender, and while Brown finally parleyed for safe escape, the federal troops suddenly stormed the arsenal. Brown, struck down by a Marine lieutenant, was saved only because the officer had absentmindedly brought his dress sword rather than his battle weapon. Brown's two sons were killed in the action.

What were Brown's true intentions? He did indeed intend to liberate the slaves; he had tried to persuade his friend, the great black leader Frederick Douglass, to come with him, but Douglass had refused, warning him that he would be "going into a perfect steel-trap" and would never emerge alive. But Brown was intent even more on martyrdom—martyrdom to prove to himself that he truly possessed the heroic qualities he esteemed in a man, and to send a bugle call across the land. In both he succeeded magnificently. So courageous was his bearing after his capture, so candid his statements, that he won the admiration of his southern captors and hero worship in the North. Lydia Maria Child, while disapproving of violence, asked the permission of Governor Wise of Virginia to visit Brown and bind his wounds, on the ground that he was not a criminal but "a martyr to righteous principles." Wise politely turned down her request.

When Brown was hanged, church bells tolled across the North, black bunting was displayed from windows, gun salutes fired, offices closed, memorial meetings held. Emerson proclaimed that Brown would "make the gallows glorious like the cross"; Thoreau called him an "angel of light"; Wendell Phillips avowed that the "lesson of the hour is insurrection." Moldering in his grave in North Elba, New York, the "crazy, deluded, monomaniacal, fanatical" old man would have been pleased to know of all this. Let them hang him, he had said: "I am worth inconceivably more to *hang* than for any other purpose." And on the way to the gallows, sitting bound on the coffin that would soon contain him, he handed out a message for his countrymen: the crimes of this guilty land would never be purged away, "but with Blood . . ."

Already Southerners were seeing blood. The more northern abolitionists canonized Brown, the more the defenders of slavery responded with wrath. Correspondence that Brown carelessly—or deliberately—left behind revealed that New England eminences had encouraged and aided the "murderer," that leading abolitionists valued Brown as an abettor of disunion, that the bells tolling for Brown were proclaiming northern approbation of slave insurrection. The fact that Seward and Lincoln both repudiated Brown's violence, that moderates like Edward Everett and other northern notables were calling for conciliation at Union meetings, that some of Brown's backers thought he had planned liberation, not insurrection, had little effect on the rising feeling. The "Black Republicans" seemed to control northern politics. A spasm of fervent solidarity passed through the South. "Never before, since the Declaration of Independence," exulted a South Carolina paper, the *Watchman*, "has the South been more united in sentiment and feeling."

* * *

It had long seemed likely that 1860 would be a year of conflict, perhaps even of showdowns between slavery and antislavery forces, between Democrats and Republicans, between moderate and militant factions within those parties. The passion sweeping the country contained an explosive combination of anger and fear. Anger, because conflict over slavery was becoming increasingly polarized as the old compromises crumbled, because thoughts of Kansas still burned in people's minds, and now because of John Brown. Fear, because many Northerners suspected that the "slave power" was spreading its "tentacles"—and its peculiar institution —throughout the nation, and because, even more, many Southerners suspected that "Black Republicans" were threatening not only their way of life but their solidarity, by driving a wedge between slaveholders and poor whites and even, God forbid, between masters and slaves.

Anger was the keynote of the Thirty-sixth Congress, which convened on December 5, 1859, three days after Brown was hanged. The House was so divided that it took two months to elect a Speaker. Members of Congress talked freely of secession and disunion. They shouted one another down, obstructed legislative action, carried ill-concealed weapons onto the House floor. The Senate displayed hardly more civility. Republicans, bolstered in number in the 1858 elections, took the lead in pressing a homestead bill, a protective tariff bill, and a Pacific railroad bill; the first passed both chambers and was vetoed by Buchanan; the second passed the House and failed in the Senate; the third died in the legislative labyrinth. The lawmakers were now seeking sectional acclaim at the expense of practical policy-making.

Fears of Southerners for their own sectional unity were further aroused at this point by a bombshell in the form of a book—written by one of their own. Hinton Rowan Helper, son of a North Carolinian blacksmith, after travels throughout the North and West, had concluded that slavery was blighting the South, crippling its economic progress, and above all impoverishing and degrading the whites—especially the small farmers and skilled workers. He cared nothing for the plight of the slaves; they should be deported. He cared passionately about whites—all whites. He was long on convincing facts and figures, but also on moral concern. "Nonslaveholders of the South!" he wrote, "farmers, mechanics, and workingmen . . . the arrant demagogues whom you have elected to offices of honor and profit, have hoodwinked you, trifled with you, and used you as mere tools for the consummation of their wicked designs. . . ." Southern elites dreaded nothing more than a challenge to solidarity between rich and poor whites.

The solidarity was all the more important in the early months of this election year, for the unity of the organization that threw a great protective arm over the South, the Democratic party, was approaching a harsh test —the convention of 1860. Everything seemed to go wrong for the Democrats when they met in Charleston late in April. The city, crowded and intensely hot, had been made for finer things than this horde of Democracy's raucous, quarrelsome grass-roots activists. Nor was the political arithmetic encouraging. Now clearly the choice of northern Democrats, Douglas had the votes to control the convention but not enough for the two-thirds needed to nominate. Despite the desperate efforts of Douglas men to conciliate delegates who would not be conciliated, and despite a Douglas-backed platform that even left the issue of squatter sovereignty open, delegation after delegation of Southerners walked out of the convention.

Even with much of their southern opposition gone, Democrats were unable to nominate their man in fifty-seven ballots. The Charleston conclave adjourned, to meet again for a new try in Baltimore six weeks later. There the tragicomedy was re-enacted, as Douglas reasserted control of the convention and the Southerners and other anti-Douglas delegates walked out a second time. Now at last the Little Giant had enough votes for nomination, but it was a Pyrrhic victory. The secessionists promptly met in a nearby Baltimore hall, passed the proslavery platform that had been rejected in Charleston, and nominated John C. Breckinridge, Buchanan's Vice-President and an old-time Whig from Kentucky, for President.

Amid the heat and anger of their conventions the northern and southern

Democrats had tragically miscalculated each other's conviction; the Douglas men, for example, had thought only a few southern ultras would walk out. Between the two Democratic conventions another party met, also in Baltimore, but with a harmony and purposefulness that the Democracy no longer could command. This was the Constitutional Union party, inheritor of the great Whig tradition, organized by Senator John J. Crittenden, Henry Clay's successor both as a Kentuckian and as a Unionist. Delegates from twenty-three states agreed not to write a platform but simply to run —or stand—on the Constitution and on the Union. With Crittenden too old to campaign, the convention chose a ticket of John Bell of Tennessee and Edward Everett of Boston, both old-time Whigs.

And the Republicans? They were still a party of much promise and little performance, of compelling ideology but cloudy strategy. They were clearly now the antislavery party that wished to doom the evil to ultimate extinction nationally and let it wither in the South. They were increasingly the party of economic growth, expanding industrial capitalism, protection for business, western development through railroads and free homesteads; and most Republicans believed that liberty and equality could be achieved best through expanding the economic opportunity of the little man.

The Republicans, though, faced strategic dilemmas in the spring of 1860. To win the fall election they had to carry the swing states that had eluded them four years earlier, and to do that they must broaden their appeal not only geographically and economically but politically; they had to attract old Whigs, moderate nativists, antislavery Democrats, Fillmore men, all-out Unionists. But the more Republicans broadened their appeal, the more they would compete with opposition parties expert at compromise—Douglas' northern Democrats and Bell's Unionists. The alternatives were to move in a radical direction, in the hope that a militant program and candidate would bring out a huge, mobilized Free-Soil vote, but this course seemed risky judging from recent election returns; or to follow a strategy of political expediency, but 1860 was no time to divert this vigorous young party toward a fickle and shapeless opportunism.

Only moral, intellectual, and political leadership of the highest order could have readily solved such strategic problems, and the Republican party could claim no such leadership. The party did possess an array of presidential hopefuls, each of whom symbolized a plausible posture for the party. Seward was the front-runner. Although the New York senator was seeking to appear more conciliatory—he now spoke not of slave and free states but of "labor states" and "capital states"—he still symbolized the militant antislavery party that had its roots in the "upper" North. Toward the other end of the party spectrum, Edward Bates of Missouri stood for the Whiggish republicanism of old, with leanings toward nativism. Senator Salmon P. Chase of Ohio held a combination of low-tariff and antislavery views that made him less available than his rivals. Senator Simon Cameron of Pennsylvania came from the most pivotal state of all, but his reputation was mainly that of an opportunistic machine politician.

And then there was Abraham Lincoln, seemingly the most unavailable contender of them all, a much defeated, regional politician who had never managed anything larger than a company of militia. On second look, he appeared more promising: he was popular in Illinois, which would be a pivotal state; he stood at the center of the Republican mainstream; he had a rural mien and background, an advantage in campaigning; he had won something of a national reputation in his debates with Douglas; and if he still was less known than Seward or Chase, his relative obscurity at least meant that he had fewer enemies in the party. Lincoln was aware of his need for wider recognition, especially in the East, and he readily accepted an invitation to speak in New York City. His address at the Cooper Union was largely a legal and historical argument that the Framers opposed slavery, but it was delivered with such logic and moral earnestness that he drew an ovation from a sophisticated audience that included Greeley and Bryant. By the time he had finished a speaking tour of New England he had won considerable national attention, at least as an orator.

To plan strategy as a party, rather than as a collection of rival tongs each looking for its own main chance, the Republicans needed a means of making a collective and democratic decision. As Lincoln had said, to defeat the enemy "we must hold conventions; we must adopt platforms . . . ; we must nominate candidates, and we must carry elections."

The convention was not only the key means of national party decision; by mid-century it had become virtually an American art form. The arrival of flag-bedecked trains carrying state delegations, the delegates' march to the convention hall with bands playing and banners waving, the stentorian call to order in the bunting-draped hall, the points of order, the fiery debates over the platform, the deafening floor demonstrations for favorites, and then the suspense-ridden presidential balloting—suspenseful because the presidential choice was usually made in the balloting itself—were all firmly fixed in political folkore and practice. Conventions had a grimy side too—the flushed, sweating delegates who enjoyed their liquor as much as their politics, the pickpockets and prostitutes who infested the hotels and public places, the sordid deals—with both money and patronage jobs as currency—made with delegates.

Such, in all its tawdriness and grandeur, was the Republican conclave that opened in mid-May in the famous Wigwam convention hall in Chicago. Lincoln had been lucky in the choice of this city rather than an eastern one, and Illinois Republicans made the most of it. After Seward's delegates pulled into the station in thirteen train cars filled with merrymakers, Lincoln's men arranged for thousands of Illinoisans to flock in from Springfield, Peoria, and dozens of other towns. Seward had brought along someone else: Thurlow Weed, one of the most dexterous politicos of the day, widely experienced and connected, an old hand at conventions and convention deals. Lincoln's men—his old friend Judge David Davis, Republican state chieftain and railroad entrepreneur Norman Judd, Jesse Fell, Leonard Swett, and others—were mainly novices at big-time politics.

The Republicans established themselves as a truly national party during the convention's second day, when they voted through a platform with much wider appeal than the antislavery manifesto of four years earlier. Drafted by a group including Greeley and Schurz, the platform called for free homesteads, a tariff that would encourage industrial development, internal improvements, a Pacific railroad, Kansas' immediate entry into the Union, and other antislavery planks. It was a moderate, even conservative platform—so much so that the white-haired veteran Free-Soiler Joshua Giddings felt compelled to add a reaffirmation of the truths of the Declaration of Independence. When he was voted down and began to leave the hall in chagrin, a New York delegate rose to urge "gentlemen to think well before, upon the free prairies of the West, in the summer of 1860, they dare to wince and quail before the assertions of the men of Philadelphia in 1776." Shamed, the delegates now carried the motion unanimously, amid an explosion of cheers, and old Giddings resumed his seat.

Next day Seward led on the first ballot, as expected, but Lincoln was a strong second, as not expected. There followed a scramble for delegate votes, as Weed, Davis, and the other managers expended their political resources—patronage jobs, policy promises, future recognitions, even cabinet posts—in a wide-open distribution of loaves and fishes, using the hard currency of specific promises and the soft currency of hopes and expectations. "Make no contracts that will bind me," Lincoln had said to his managers, but Judge Davis allegedly told his colleagues, "Lincoln ain't here and don't know what we have to meet!" All managers played this game, but Lincoln's had the added advantage of handing out hundreds of counterfeit tickets in order to pack the Wigwam's gallery and out-hurrah the Seward rooters.

In the end, though, it was a set of more serious political factors—above all, Lincoln's "availability"—that brought him a surge of strength in the second ballot, and victory, as Cameron's Pennsylvania shifted to him, early in the third. More delegates jumped onto the bandwagon, and the nomination was made unanimous. A quiet fell upon the Wigwam as the delegates contemplated what they had done, then the cannon boomed from the roof and Illinoisans in the streets outside were swept up in a happy pandemonium.

Lincoln was waiting nervously in his Springfield law office when a telegram arrived: "TO LINCOLN YOU ARE NOMINATED." He studied it for long moments. "Well," he said, "we've got it."

What did Lincoln have? A worthless nomination, some said; he would probably lose, but if he won he would lose too, for the slave states would secede. Lincoln scoffed at this latter prospect. He and most of the other Republican leaders could not believe that the Southerners really meant secession and war. "He considered the movement South as a sort of political game of bluff, gotten up by politicians, and meant solely to frighten the North," a friend wrote after talking with him. " 'They won't give up the offices,' I remember he said, and added, 'Were it believed that vacant places could be had at the North Pole, the road there would be lined with dead Virginians.' " Seward and Schurz and others also were optimistic.

The Republican leaders were less dogmatic about winning. A four-party race was unprecedented and unpredictable. Some calculated that Lincoln would monopolize the antislavery vote and hence overcome the divided opposition. Others believed that Douglas and Bell would monopolize the moderate, pro-Union vote, especially if they could agree on fusion or coalition arrangements in some of the key states. In any event, Republican leaders agreed that their course was clear. Lincoln must "make no speeches," as William Cullen Bryant said, "write no letters as a candidate." Nothing must sully the image of Lincoln and his party as following a moderate, centrist path between the ultras of secessionism and the ultras of abolitionism.

Lincoln complied, publicly. Privately, he was busy meeting with party chieftains, bantering with reporters, sending out campaign suggestions, querying local politicos as to how the situation looked in their end of the "vineyard." And he allowed his image to be sharpened as "honest Abe," a son of the frontier, log cabin born, farm boy, rail splitter. The Republicans lived up to their Whig forefathers in organizing campaign processions carrying replicas of rails he had split, and presenting the "Wide Awakes," who provided song and spectacle. But Lincoln stayed in Springfield.

Douglas would not be so constricted. Leading half a party, facing probable defeat, he decided on intensive tours North and South. In city after city he called for Union, denounced the ultras, pictured the Democratic party as the only remaining vehicle of North-South harmony. His audiences seemed as spellbound as ever by the Little Giant, but he won few conversions from the Republican party in the North or Breckinridge's splinter party in the South. Douglas, who had spent so many years keeping his fences mended with the Southerners, was amazed by the hostility shown him in the slave states. He gave as good as he got, denouncing secessionist talk as traitorous. Early in October he was shocked to hear that Pennsylvania and Indiana had gone Republican in elections for state officials.

"Mr. Lincoln is the next President," Douglas told his secretary. "We must try to save the Union. I will go South." He was headed South anyway, but he intensified his efforts. Now he spoke for the Union rather than himself. The South must not secede. Aroused, desperate, as he saw his life's political work being swept away, he followed a killing pace—literally killing, for in eight months he would be dead of accumulated fatigue, untended illnesses, campaign overwork, and the heavy drinking and smoking that went with it.

On November 6, 1860, Abraham Lincoln won 1,866,000 votes; Douglas, 1,375,000; Breckinridge, 843,000; Bell, 590,000. Lincoln carried eighteen free states for 180 electoral votes, Breckinridge, eleven slave states for 72, Bell three border states for 39, and Douglas only Missouri, and three New Jersey votes, for 12. Studying the vote, newspaper editors could find some predictable patterns. Lincoln had won no electoral votes in the South, Breckinridge none in the North, though both had drawn huge popular votes in rural areas. The Democratic party now lay in fragments. Despite strong economic, ethnic, and religious views among the voters, the outcome was almost completely sectional. Geography was destiny.

But there was little time for analysis. On receiving news of Lincoln's election, South Carolina's legislature unanimously called for a state convention to be held in Columbia in late December. This convention declared without dissent that "the union now subsisting between South Carolina and the other States, under the name of the 'United States of America,' is hereby dissolved."

On January 9 Mississippi seceded, the next day Florida, the next day Alabama, followed by Georgia, Louisiana, and Texas. The Union was dissolved.

* * *

The Union was dissolved. The grand experiment seemed finished. Americans had created a union to achieve order, security, liberty, and equality. Now union was gone, and with it order and security. Liberty had been largely achieved, but not for blacks, Indians, or controversial ministers and editors. Equality had been partially achieved, but not for slaves, women, illiterates, masses of laborers in fields and factories. "The last hope of freedom in the old world is now centered in the success of the American Republic," Douglas had said during the campaign. Now the Old World looked on in mingled pity and glee.

What had happened? What could have happened, in a nation that had been put together like a Swiss clock, with power and energy so nicely distributed and positioned and balanced, precisely so that the nation could absorb pressures from without and within? The first answers, in the heat of the conflict, offered conspiratorial or even diabolical explanations: the catastrophe was due to southern planters, northern abolitionists, agitators in general. In later years, the explanation would often reflect the political ideology or intellectual environment of the time. Secession and civil war were due to class rule North and South, cultural conflict, lack of communication and understanding, modernization surges and lags, ideological differences over slavery and the "unfreedoms" and inequalities that it caused.

Much of this inquiry was inconclusive, however, because it searched for single causes in what was a web of influences or a channel of causation. It failed to differentiate between the givens of history—the geographical, racial, and economic forces that were inextricable and inseparable from the past—and the somewhat more tractable decision-making situations, where leaders might have decided differently, for example, in permitting the slave trade or agreeing to a three-fifths rule, and the more "open" crossroads situations where men had considerable choice in arranging their political institutions and in making decisions within them.

The immediate cause of the Civil War lay in the derangement of the nation's two political systems—the constitutional system of the 1780s and the party system of the 1830s—and in their interaction with each other. Both these systems rested on an intricate set of balances: the constitutional, on a balance between federal and state power and among the three branches of the federal government; the party, on a competitive balance between party organizations at the national and state levels. The genius of this double system lay in its ability to morselize sectional and economic and other conflicts before they became flammable, and then through incremental adjustment and accommodations to keep the great mobiles of ideological, regional, and other political energies in balance until the next adjustment had to be made. This system worked well for decades, as the great compromises of 1820 and 1850 attested. The system was flexible too; when a measure of executive leadership was needed—to make great decisions about the West, as with Jefferson, or to adjust and overcome a tariff rebellion, as with Jackson—enough presidential authority could be exerted within the system to meet the need. But the essence of the system lay in balances, adjustment, compromise.

Then, in the 1850s, this system crumbled. The centrifugal forces beset-ting it were so powerful that perhaps no polity could have overcome them; yet European and other political systems had encountered enormously divisive forces and survived. What happened in the United States was a fateful combination: a powerful ideology of states' rights, defense of slav-ery, and "southern way of life" arose in the South, with South Carolina as the cutting edge; this was met by a counter-ideology in the urbanizing, industrializing, modernizing states, with Illinois as the cutting edge in the West. While many issues were involved in this ideological confrontation —the tariff, federal support for internal improvements, nativism, religious differences, western development, temperance—less and less these issues modified the growing issue of slavery, and more and more they helped deepen that division.

As these ideological differences grew, the double system began to falter, and the more it faltered, the more the ideological conflict intensified. The two-party system assumed that within each party moderate and "extrem-ist" forces would grapple for control, but that the two parties would tend toward the center—and hence toward gradual adjustment and morseliza-tion—because of the need to win the support of centrist voters. The system in short depended on electoral competition in a diverse and balanced electorate. The 1850 election, however, began to throw the system askew. Because of weaknesses in the Whig party, which had never established itself at the grass roots to the degree the Democracy had, especially in the South, the Democrats won overwhelming control of Congress and South-erners won predominance within the party as a result of their unified control of caucuses, appointments of committee chairmen and member-ships, parliamentary rules and processes. This was the background of the Kansas-Nebraska bill, the passage of which showed the power of southern ultras and unsettled the system further.

If the "party constitution"—the competitive, two-party mechanism— had worked, the Democrats would have paid the political price in 1856: defeat at the hands of a moderate party that would have appealed to the voters for a mandate against southern extremism. But in 1856 the Whigs, plagued by their own sectional problems, and with their organizational heart beating feebly, were near the point of collapse, and the Republicans and Know-Nothings were minority parties. The Democrats won an un-deserved victory over splintered opposition, and this again played into the hands of the ultras. At the same time, the ultras virtually controlled the presidency, through the two-thirds rule in the convention and the choice of men, in Pierce and Buchanan, who were not expected to be strong Presidents. Even the presidential veto could be negated when congressional leaders, invoking party discipline (their own), could override the White House. There was never a strong Administration party that could build a solid link with moderate elements in the North and the border states.

Under the rising ideological-sectional pressures, this system exploded and revealed in naked outline what had been for some years the actual power configuration—a four-party or multi-party system, with its inherent weaknesses. In the four-party showdown of 1860, the Republicans won with a minority of the popular vote. In that election Stephen Douglas was the real hero, as he decided to fight for the Union even at the expense of his own candidacy, bypassed the southern ultras, and made a final effort to reach the great grass-roots Democracy, North and South, that had kept the nation together.

Much would be said later about a "blundering generation" of leaders, but these men were operating within the system they knew, as best they could, only to find that the constitutional and party system could not cope with the power of ideology. Nor could they fully understand an ideological battle in which extremists did not act rationally and prudently, in which every politician was vulnerable to the man on his "far right or left." Much would also be made later of economic and ethnic and religious forces that these leaders could not overcome, but these were precisely the forces that, as experienced transactional leaders, they had in the past overcome through gradual adjustment and accommodation.

At least the system did allow for a certain vital flexibility and potential —the coming to power of a strong President who could build his own presidential party and govern. As the southern states broke away from the Union, as the inauguration of a new President neared, eyes North and South turned toward the tall man in Illinois, and to another man in Mississippi, Jefferson Davis.

CHAPTER 17

The Blood-Red Wine

Two Westerners left their homes on February 11, 1861: Jefferson Davis and Abraham Lincoln. They had much in common. Both had been born in Kentucky. Both had prospered in the trans-Appalachian region as that region had prospered. Both had become famous throughout the nation; indeed, both had recently been elected Presidents, and they were now setting forth toward their posts. Davis and Lincoln had something else in common: Neither would live to come home again.

The day before, Jefferson Davis, as spare and erect as ever but with his light hair now turning gray, was helping his wife prune rose bushes on Brierfield, their plantation near Vicksburg, when a messenger rode in with a telegram. Her husband's face turned so desolate as he read the message that Varina Davis feared news of a death in the family. Davis was silent for long moments, then told her that he had just been chosen provisional President of the newly formed Confederate States of America. As an old soldier he had expected at most a military command, but as a good soldier he immediately packed to leave. Early next morning the plantation bell summoned the slaves of Brierfield to hear their master bid them farewell. Then Davis and his black manservant walked to a nearby Mississippi landing, rowed out into the river, and flagged a steamer for the ride north to Vicksburg.

Davis was beginning his long trip to Montgomery at a critical moment for the seven seceding states. Spurred as always by South Carolina's leaders, they had organized a new government with remarkable speed and efficiency. Their new charter, the Confederate Constitution, provided for the "sovereign and independent" nature of the individual states and protected slavery, though slave importation was barred to appease French and British opinion. Davis had been chosen provisional President over such fire eaters as William Yancey and Robert Rhett, with Alexander Stephens, an old Whig turned Democrat, as Vice-President. All this was in response to wild enthusiasm in the lower South, as orators called for secession, old soldiers formed military companies, women sewed flags, preachers fulminated from the pulpit about the mortal peril to the South, and news-papers mirrored the intense feelings at the grass roots. But states of the upper South, so critical to secessionists' hopes, were holding back.

Heading east, Davis could hardly ignore the geography of secession as he was forced to make a detour north into Tennessee—which still remained in the Union—southeast to Atlanta, and then doubled back southwest to Montgomery. Nor could he ignore the lower South's shortage of east-west railroad links, ominous for a region heading toward war. Even this run had no sleeping cars, so the President-elect rested, fully dressed, on a camp bed set up in a regular coach. He was immensely buoyed, though, by the "approbation" of the people crowding into stations where he paused, by the booming guns and bonfires that marked his way. At each of his twenty-five stops Davis repeated that "no reconstruction" of the Union was now possible and urged his listeners to prepare for war.

Yet he could not forget the "cooperationists" who opposed separate secessions by the states, favored collective action by all the South, and in many cases were willing to negotiate with the Republicans in search of some kind of last-minute compromise, even while they insisted on southern rights and their determination to repel any Union assault. Rolling through Tennessee, he could not forget that two days before he left Brierfield the people of that state had voted decisively against calling a convention to consider secession; and that a few days before, Virginians had dashed secessionist hopes with their own foot-dragging. Without the prestigious Old Dominion little could be done; certainly a Gulf Coast Confederacy would not be enough.

In Montgomery a delegation from the Confederate constitutional convention waited to greet Davis. Yancey grandly introduced him to the station crowd: "The man and the hour have met." Davis had only one day to prepare his inaugural address; then, as the strains of "Dixie"—played by a southern band for the first time—died away, he called the new nation the true embodiment of "the American idea that governments rest on the consent of the governed" and asserted that the southern people would preserve their political liberty at all costs. He hoped for good will between the Confederacy and the "Northeastern States of the American Union," but warned that if "lust of domination should cloud the judgment or inflame the ambition of those States," then the South would "maintain, by the final arbitrament of the sword, the position which we have assumed among the nations of the earth."

"Upon my weary heart," the new President recorded, "was showered smiles, plaudits, and flowers." But ahead he saw "troubles and thorns innumerable."

* * *

Lincoln had left Springfield amid a cold drizzle and an atmosphere of gloom. Umbrellas raised against the rain, a small crowd gathered around the rear platform of the single coach that, with engine and baggage car, comprised the President-elect's special train. The day before, Lincoln had grasped Herndon's hand and said, "If I live I'm coming back some time, and then we'll go right on practicing law as if nothing had ever happened." But he added, "I am sick of office-holding already." Now, standing on the rear platform, he looked down, his face wreathed in sadness, then looked up and spoke a few words of farewell. The wheels of the stubby little locomotive began to turn.

Lincoln's train meandered back and forth along the whole route to Washington, so that people and politicians could see him, and he them. As though strengthening himself for the ordeal ahead, he drew sustenance from encounters with Indiana farmers, Cincinnati immigrants, even traveling slaveholders; from Pittsburgh miners and ironworkers; from Albany Know-Nothings, New York merchants and pro-secessionists. Using a dozen different railroads, he rolled slowly across the country, zigzagging through the prairies and the Mohawk Valley, and down the flank of the Hudson. Sometimes he escaped the deluge of advice, admonitions, and job soliciting by withdrawing to his private quarters. His occasional melancholy was not shared by Mary Todd Lincoln, already aglow at the prospect of being the First Lady, or by their two young sons, whose pranks bedeviled train crew and passengers alike.

News from Washington told of drift, indecision, and paralysis, of a confusion of voices, proposals, manifestos, diatribes. With his Cabinet rid of Southerners, Buchanan could act more freely, but he hoped that Congress could solve the crisis, or that a new constitutional convention could be called, in the spirit of '87. Congress was too divided to do more than discuss attractive but utopian compromises.

The eyes of Washington were on the man who was still tacking back and forth as he headed east. But Lincoln had no solution either, and at first he seemed to play down the seriousness of the crisis. Conscious that the Inaugural Address would be his first major statement, he kept a draft of it in his pocket. To the crowds along the way he spoke from the train platform, groping for words, experimenting with various phrases. He told an Indianapolis gathering, "It is your business to rise up and preserve the Union and liberty, for yourselves, and not for me." In Cincinnati he promised to treat neighboring Kentucky's slaveholders just as "Washington, Jefferson, and Madison" had treated them. He argued to a Pittsburgh crowd that no crisis existed except an artificial one created by designing politicians. In Freedom, Pennsylvania, he invited a towering coal heaver up to the platform, and they stood back to back for the audience to judge who was taller.

In Philadelphia the President-elect raised a flag at Independence Hall and said: "I have often inquired of myself, which great principle or idea it was that kept this nation together. It was . . . something in that Declaration giving liberty, not alone to the people of this country, but hope to the world for all future time. . . . It was that which gave promise that in due time the weights should be lifted from the shoulders of all men, and that all should have an equal chance."

The militant and vocal crowds seemed to stiffen Lincoln's determination as he neared the capital. But Washington had little sense of this. It was boiling with contemptuous stories of Lincoln's western gaucheries and with rumors that Seward or some other cabinet eminence would control the new administration. Nor did Lincoln boost his prestige when, to evade a rumored assassination plot in Baltimore, he abandoned his train and slipped into Washington unannounced. Ensconced in a fine suite in the popular Willard's Hotel, he received border state delegations, giving them the pledges they wanted: that he would leave slavery intact and delay using force to bring the seceded states back into the Union. Acting in an atmosphere of heightened tension and polarization, Lincoln wanted to regain balance among the warring sides. But some Republicans in Congress were supporting a "Force Bill" to give the President full control over all federal and state troops—a measure almost certain to drive Virginia and other wavering states into secession with the lower South. Other Republicans, including Horace Greeley in his *Tribune,* were urging that the cotton states be allowed to "go in peace."

In this supreme crisis Lincoln, however much he might talk about liberty and equality, was determined above all else to save the Union, as something precious in itself. The Union to him was more than an ideal—it was bone of his bone, the great protecting shield for his family, the legacy of his revered forefathers, the house for his home. To preserve the balances of union he had chosen a unity Cabinet, with the now moderate antislavery Seward of New York as Secretary of State; the forthright Chase of Ohio for the Treasury; a border state loyalist, Edward Bates of Missouri, as Attorney General; a New Englander, Gideon Welles, as Secretary of the Navy; an-

other border state man, Montgomery Blair—a son of the old Jacksonian
—as Postmaster General; Pennsylvania's Simon Cameron as Secretary of
War; and an Indianan, Caleb B. Smith, as Secretary of the Interior.

But on March 4 he had a speech to give, an oath to take from Chief
Justice Taney. A statue of "Liberty," waiting to be placed on the unfinished
Capitol dome, lay on the grass before him as Lincoln delivered his Inaugural Address. He sought to reassure the South that neither he nor the
Republican party threatened it. He quoted the Republican platform plank
pledging not to interfere with slavery, and to enforce the fugitive-slave law
rigorously. But secession he flatly rejected, for it was the essence of
anarchy. "A majority, held in restraint by constitutional checks, and limitations," Lincoln said, was "the only true sovereign of a free people."

Much of the address read like a lecture in constitutional law, but toward
the end: "I am loth to close. We are not enemies, but friends. We must not
be enemies. Though passion may have strained, it must not break our
bonds of affection. The mystic chords of memory, stretching from every
battle-field, and patriot grave, to every living heart and hearthstone, all
over this broad land, will yet swell the chorus of the Union, when again
touched, as surely they will be, by the better angels of our nature."

But the Richmond *Enquirer* echoed almost every other southern paper
in labeling the address as "the cool, unimpassioned, deliberate language
of the fanatic." It continued: "Sectional war awaits only the signal gun."

The Flag That Bore a Single Star

At half-past four on the morning of April 12, 1861, a shell rose from a
mortar battery at Fort Johnson, arched in a fiery red parabola through the
dark air as its fuse spat out flame, and burst over tiny Fort Sumter in the
neck of Charleston Harbor. For the next thirty-four hours Confederate
batteries poured shot and shell into the fort occupied by federal troops.
From their rooftops Charlestonians watched the explosions. Well-dressed
ladies—if the *Harper's Weekly* artist was to be believed—lay prostrate in
tears, holding one another in their arms. And well they might. That mortar
shell was the signal for war.

It was a signal desperately feared by some, ardently sought by others,
long expected by almost all. For months now Sumter had loomed as a
symbol of southern determination and northern defensiveness, of the
clash between state and national sovereignty, of the collision between two
cultures. It seemed only fitting that a fort off Charleston should be the
fulcrum of conflict. Federal arsenals and garrisons throughout the South
had yielded to the secessionists, but Charleston was too important as a

port, and South Carolina too conspicuous in the leadership ranks of secession, for Washington to surrender Sumter. The pride of Unionists had
been stirred when Major Robert Anderson of the regular army led his little
force a mile across the water from vulnerable Fort Moultrie to Sumter, a
half-completed square of masonry. Even Buchanan had summoned
enough nerve to send an unarmed steamer in December with provisions
for the garrison, but fire from the shore batteries drove it away. After that,
the lame-duck President had been happy to leave the spiky problem to his
successor.

By the time of Lincoln's inauguration a South Carolinian "circle of fire"
surrounded Sumter. Forty-three guns, manned by several hundred amateur cannoneers, supported by several thousand volunteer infantrymen,
who in turn were backed by tens of thousands of militant Charlestonians,
ringed the fort. But Sumter's sixty cannons controlled the entrance to the
harbor. Now time was running out for Anderson, as his provisions were
low. Lincoln was torn between advisers counseling that the fort was inde-
fensible and should be evacuated, or at least allowed to be honorably
starved out, and others who urged that a relief expedition was both militarily feasible and politically necessary to back up the new President's pledge
to protect federal property and uphold the law.

As the Administration vacillated, rumors flew around Washington,
hopes and fears rose and fell, militants North and South pressed for decision. Some Southerners preferred not to leave the issue of peace and war
to Lincoln; Roger Pryor, a Virginia congressman, urged a Charleston
crowd to "Strike a blow!"—promising that the "moment blood is shed, old
Virginia will make common cause with her sisters of the South."

By this time Lincoln had decided. On April 8 Governor Francis Pickens
of South Carolina received presidential notice that a fleet was on its way
to Sumter with food, and that it would fight its way into the harbor if fired
upon. General Pierre G. T. Beauregard, commanding the forces besieging
Sumter, wired Montgomery for instructions. Now it was Davis who had to
face the issue of peace and war. Each side, North and South, preferred to
have its way without war; each side would go to war if denied its way; each
side wished the other to bear the onus of starting a war. But Jefferson Davis
overrode the uncertainty in Montgomery. His orders sped back to Beauregard: the fort must surrender or be reduced before the relief fleet arrived.

The Confederate general sent a delegation of notables, including Pryor,
to demand the fort's capitulation; after Anderson refused, the four emissaries rowed directly to the nearest shore battery. When the battery commander offered to let Pryor open the bombardment, the congressman
turned pale, saying, "I could not fire the first gun of the war." But Edmund

Ruffin, a Virginian who had become one of South Carolina's most fiery extremists, had no such qualms. It was his shell that burst on Sumter and awoke Charleston to the coming of war.

As the Confederate fire intensified, the fort became an inferno of exploding shells, crashing masonry, and acrid smoke. The garrison's stubborn defense won cheers from the Confederates, even from the Yankee-hater Ruffin. So skillfully did Anderson deploy his men that not one of them was killed. But the barracks caught fire several times, and even though the blazes were extinguished, Anderson feared that his powder magazine would be touched off and the whole place blown up. The surrender terms allowed the garrison to march out with drums beating and colors flying, to the ship that would take them to a hero's welcome in New York. Anderson had also requested and been granted a hundred-gun salute to the American flag. On the fiftieth round a gun exploded prematurely and killed Private Daniel Hough. He was the only casualty of Sumter, the first of 600,000 deaths to come.

*   *   *

"Well, boys," a New York farmer said, "it's Massachusetts and South Carolina. I'm a-going to take the train to Boston and enlist." Southern farm boys also rallied around the flag—a new Confederate flag that they christened with a song:

> We are a band of brothers, And native to the soil,
> Fighting for our liberty, With treasure, blood and toil;
> And when our rights were threatened, The cry rose near and far,
> Hurrah for the Bonnie Blue Flag, that bears a Single Star.

The attack on Sumter did what words had failed to do: it united and galvanized the North. Lincoln's call on April 15 brought 75,000 volunteers within a few days. People welcomed the end to the long weeks of indecision; "strange to say," Congressman John Sherman wrote to his brother, the war "brings a feeling of relief: the suspense is over." It seemed, said Allan Nevins, "a purifying hurricane which swept away all sordid aims. Idealists had been disheartened by the trickeries, bargains, and compromises of the past ten years; by the Ostend Manifesto, the Nebraska Act, the Lecompton swindle, the filibustering, the corruption, and the absorption in moneymaking. Now, they said, the flame of devotion to the principles of Washington, Hamilton, and Marshall was burning brightly again."

But Washington and the Fathers stood for Union. Now the house was divided, the Union broken in half. Or rather it was broken into two-thirds and one-third, for the population of the twenty-three northern and border states was now 22 million, and that of the South 9 million, of whom 3.5 million were slaves. The North predominated in economic power too, with its modernizing agriculture, growing industry, substantial railroad grid and merchant marine. The South's economy still depended on agricultural staples—especially cotton—and on banking capital that amounted to only one-third that of the North. But Montgomery had two vital military resources: an aroused citizenry with a great military heritage, and a brilliant officer corps, vastly augmented when Robert E. Lee declined Lincoln's offer of the federal field command and accepted leadership of Virginia's military forces.

Still, the two armies would be composed mainly of volunteers, officered by men who had seen little action, save for Indian expeditions, since the Mexican War. The Confederate volunteers ranged from the wealthy and wellborn members of the Washington Artillery Battalion, Louisiana's most prestigious militia unit, to Carolina backwoodsmen in homespun and drab butternut. Wade Hampton of South Carolina raised, trained, and equipped his own private army of infantry, cavalry, and artillery. Another set of volunteers who joined freely but reluctantly were the regular army officers from the border states of Virginia, North Carolina, Tennessee, and Arkansas. Albert Sidney Johnston left with his state—Texas—in secession. Others, however—Winfield Scott of Virginia, David Farragut of Tennessee —remained loyal to the Union, as did almost all the rank-and-file soldiers. Men from Missouri, Kentucky, and Maryland faced harsh dilemmas, since both North and South organized units in their states. Here indeed were literal cases of brother against brother, even in the family of President Lincoln's in-laws, the Todds.

While sergeants shouted orders on a thousand drilling fields, while quartermasters bought muskets and tents and britches and cannons, Lincoln and Davis and their commanders planned strategy. The northern plan as it developed was multi-pronged: to advance on Richmond in force; blockade southern harbors; and capture the Mississippi and Tennessee river reaches, in order to divide the Confederacy and isolate its main regions. Southern strategists planned to capture Washington and then strike north into Maryland and central Pennsylvania, whence they would seek to cut the Northeast off from the Northwest. . . . Twelve thousand miles away a superior student of the tricks of history, a Russian nobleman, bustled around his study, jotting down notes for the first draft of what would become a monumental work of literature. In *War and Peace* Count Leo Tolstoi would describe the chaos of battle—the accidents, missed orders, mistaken identities, loss of control, impotence of leadership—just as the amateur American soldiers would experience it in the first major clash of the war. That encounter occurred at Bull Run, in late July 1861.

By summer, as the ranks of the armies swelled, the war was taking on a momentum of its own. Soldiers and civilians were demanding immediate and decisive action from their governments. One quick march to battle and victory would follow. Northern troops were rushed into Washington to defend the capital, while Virginia volunteers occupied Alexandria and Harpers Ferry on the Potomac. There the two forces were poised in June, while the clamor for action continued to grow.

Bull Run was a small, muddy stream running southeast through pasture and weeds. The Warrenton Turnpike, a main road leading southwest from Washington, crossed the Run at a stone bridge, but the stream also could be forded in several places. South of Bull Run lay Manassas Junction, where rail lines from Richmond and the Shenandoah met. These railroads would shape the coming battle.

General Winfield Scott, the aged and corpulent commander in chief of the United States Army—a Tolstoian figure himself—ordered General Irvin McDowell to collect Union regiments around Washington and advance them on July 8 to seize Manassas Junction, in the face of General Beauregard of Sumter fame. If Beauregard's men retreated, McDowell could hold a grip on the railroads of northern Virginia; if not, then the public at least would have its fight. McDowell was reluctant to advance—his troops were green, his supply wagons too few, and his reinforcements not yet arrived. By July 16, however, he felt strengthened enough to start south with 30,000 men. As the Union columns marched through rolling hills and thick woods, Private Edwin Wyler of the 5th Massachusetts found blackberries to pick, milk to buy, and fresh lamb to purchase or "capture." Aside from the obstacles left by the retreating "rebs" and the blacks encountered in small, run-down hamlets, it seemed to him more like a picnic near his native Woburn than an invasion of the mysterious, hostile South. The masthead of Greeley's *Tribune* had exhorted: "Forward to Richmond!"—perhaps it would be this easy.

Outnumbered by McDowell three to two, Beauregard fell back to prepared defenses behind Bull Run. The old fire-eater Edmund Ruffin, now an infantry private in the 2nd South Carolina, recorded his comrades' anger on being ordered to retreat before the Yankees, but their spirits rose when they drove back the first incautious Union probes into the Bull Run lines, and when reinforcements arrived. General Joseph Johnston had been guarding the Shenandoah Valley with 11,000 men against a force nearly twice that size led by General Robert Patterson. While Patterson fretted, hesitated, and exchanged bombastic telegrams with Scott in Washington, Johnston with astute timing slipped brigade after brigade along a single-gauge railroad to the east. Jackson's Virginians, Bartow's Georgians, Bee's Mississippians and Alabamans were already joining Beauregard, as was Johnston himself.

McDowell's plan was to send his strongest columns around Beauregard's left flank, crossing the Run at and above the Stone Bridge. With an early start and a quick march, his men could seize Manassas Junction before Johnston could arrive by rail—or so the Union man thought. But things soon began to go wrong. Units became delayed and lost as they worked their way through jammed roads on the Confederate flank, so that the troops reached the battlefield exhausted. Once across the stream they encountered Colonel Nathan Evans' lone brigade guarding the enemy flank. Reporter E. P. Doherty, covering the 71st New York for the *Times*, noted that the Union men attacked bravely, but without much discipline, fighting in little knots and moving confusedly in and out of the smoke and underbrush. Soon a bloody stalemate developed.

Expecting McDowell to attack his right, and dismissing the noise of the mounting battle on his left as a diversion, Beauregard kept most of his troops guarding the crossings below the Stone Bridge. He did allow Johnston to shift several of his brigades to the left, much to the disgust of Johnston's men, who were lusting for battle and expecting it on the right. Instead they found themselves in the thick of the fray on the left, arriving just in time to shore up Evans' wavering line. Across the Run, Colonel William Sherman's troops had been equally frustrated, as they marched back and forth as decoys around the bridge, while only a few hundred yards away Georgians and New Yorkers shot and impaled one another. Watching a farmer and his dog hunting in the fields and Confederate horsemen splashing back and forth across the stream, Sherman felt for a moment that he was back in peacetime. Finally, early in the afternoon, he was allowed to take his brigade across the Run, onto the flank of Bee's and Bartow's Valley brigades. Pushing Bee's forces back, the Union troops advanced toward Henry Hill, the last position between them and the enemy's rear. Holding Henry Hill, however, were Thomas Jackson's 2,600 Virginians, and they were determined to stay. They did.

"See Jackson standing like a stone wall!" Bee shouted to his now fleeing men. "Rally behind the Virginians!" As the Mississippians closed ranks with their comrades, regiment after regiment of Union men were storming up the hill, only to break under the withering fire of the enlarged "Stonewall Brigade." When McDowell ordered two batteries of regular artillery forward to blast Jackson's men out of their positions, rebel cavalry charged down on the cannons but were driven away by Union infantry. Arthur Cummings' 33rd Virginia, which was closest to the northern guns on the hilltop, wavered. Fearful that his men could stand up under the fire no longer, Cummings, without orders, shouted, "Charge!"

The Union artillerymen, shrouded in their own gun smoke and confused by the cavalry charge, saw gray-clad troops appear through the haze on their right. Friend or foe?—some regiments in both armies wore gray. Cummings' men answered the question with a single volley that mowed down the gun crews and horses. The Confederates smashed through the battery, were thrown back, swarmed down again with the rest of Jackson's brigade, yelling at the top of their lungs. The battle surged back and forth, in bloody hand-to-hand combat. Soldiers drifted in, attracted by the sound of fighting; others pulled out, unarmed and bloodied, spreading word that all was lost. It was the critical moment of the battle, but they could not know this either.

From a tower above the center of the Confederate position, Captain Edward Alexander could see men streaming to the rear, and others hurrying forward, as the two sides fought amidst the wrecked Union batteries. Then, off to the southwest edge of the fight, he could see a great cloud of dust raised by a fresh unit marching toward the sound and the fury. Was it Union or friendly? As he watched a shell burst over the northern lines. The blue-clad troops recoiled before the fresh onslaught. It was Kirby Smith's brigade, just arrived from the Shenandoah. They had marched right from their trains into battle.

The Union soldiers, exhausted from fourteen hours of marching and fighting, now outnumbered and outflanked, had had enough. With little panic—but with little stopping—the Northerners retreated back across Bull Run. Some officers tried to hold them back with drawn sabers, to no avail. In a few places the retreat began to turn into a mad rout. Fearful that the rebels were right on their heels—actually, Beauregard's men were themselves too exhausted and bloodied to follow—the Union soldiers streamed toward Washington, meeting political celebrities and sightseers who had come to watch the rout of the rebels. The powder-begrimed soldiers became locked in a hellish traffic jam with the civilians, whose spotless carriages were laden with fashionable ladies and sumptuous picnic lunches. The army's retreat ended after a few miles, but the sightseers dashed back to the capital with wild tales of disaster.

Beauregard was left in possession of the battlefield. It was a scene of carnage. The dead, a Confederate noted, were scattered for three miles along the battlefield. "The countenances & postures generally indicated the suffering of agonizing pain. . . . Clotted blood, in what had been pools, were under or by almost every corpse. From bullet holes in the heads of some, the brains had partly oozed out." Men's faces had turned black, save for white froth on their mouths; horses lay about, tangled in their own intestines; as survivors approached, fly-covered corpses seemed to come alive as the flies sprang off together in a grotesque caricature of the dead. A terrible stench hung over the field.

*   *   *

Far from the battlefield, a wave of exultation swept through the South, while the sting of defeat produced shock, anger, and recriminations in the North. Horace Greeley, now castigated by his critics for his "Forward to Richmond" war cries in the *Tribune,* seemed to falter under the strain; he wrote Lincoln that after his "seventh sleepless night" he wondered if the Union could win, and that if the President felt it could not, he should ask for an armistice. Otherwise, "every drop of blood henceforth shed in this quarrel will be wantonly, wickedly shed, and the guilt will rest heavily on the soul of every promoter of the crime. . . ." Lincoln had lain awake too, on a sofa in the Executive Office, but he was already making plans for a broadening of the war effort.

Southerners indulged in some braggadocio. A "few more Bull Run thrashings" would bring the Yankees "under the yoke," said the Louisville *Courier-Journal,* "as docile as the most loyal of our Ethiopian chattels." The Confederates paid a price for their victory, however. Having won what was greeted as the decisive battle of the war, many recruits refused to re-enlist. But this was only a temporary loss. Their main problems were far more serious—problems of organization and ideology.

The difficulty was not simply that the Confederacy lacked adequate war factories, transport, medical supplies; this was partly made up by heroic effort and sacrifice, such as the donation of church bells to be recast into cannons. The trouble lay in a decentralized structure of government charged with prosecuting a war that increasingly demanded central direction and control. The Confederate constitution prohibited protective tariffs, spending for internal improvements, and export taxes, except by a two-thirds legislative majority, and it lacked a general welfare clause. Born and bred on the doctrine of states' rights, the Southerners still took it very seriously. Thus, the governor of Florida charged that central control of the army would "sap the very foundation of the rights of states." Davis' astute War Secretary, Judah Benjamin, warned that the only way to defend the states was "by a concentration of common strength under one head." But he was fiercely attacked for subverting the power of the states and for assuming dictatorial power.

Nor was the central government itself organized for war. The Congress was weak, and prone to argue over trivialities. The Cabinet was not strong as a unit, and the few effective members were occasionally at odds with the military, as in the case of Benjamin's altercations with both Johnston and Stonewall Jackson. Inevitably, Davis had to exercise strong presidential direction—even to the point of treating cabinet heads like clerks—only to be accused of "executive usurpation." In fact, Davis had to share his executive powers with the state governors, who also interfered in military operations. It was not surprising that the Confederacy was slow in furnishing arms to its men and in raising revenue. The Treasury fueled inflation by issuing much printed money—money printed on paper smuggled through the Union lines.

Behind a government in disarray lay an ideology in disarray. When the Southerners talked about defending their rights, they were referring to liberty in its various forms, constitutional, individual, local, sectional. All these liberties were defined negatively—as "leave us alone" against oppressive government, northern interference, and now the central Confederate government itself. Not only did the Southerners hold a limited and negative view of liberty, in common with most Americans of the day, and not only did their leaders offer little conception of the broad possibilities and creative dimensions of liberty, in common with virtually all intellectual leaders North and South; many Southerners confounded the problem even further by not comprehending the concessions they might have to make in wartime in order to protect even their own negative brand of liberty. Thus, libertarians railed against even Davis' highly selective and limited suspensions of habeas corpus. "Away with the idea of getting independence first, and looking after liberty afterwards," proclaimed Vice-President Stephens. "Our liberties once lost, may be lost forever."

The issue came to a head in the spring of 1862, when, after a string of military reversals and a lag in volunteering and re-enlisting, Davis called for conscription. The call touched the rawest nerves of the South. It would make "free-born citizens" the "vassals of the central power," alleged Governor Joseph Brown of Georgia. The Conscription Act, though passed by the Confederate Congress by more than two to one in mid-April, "brought into the open the deadliest conflict within the Confederacy," in Charles Roland's words, "that of state rights as opposed to Southern nationalism." Critics virtually equated individual, local, and states' rights, all defined as liberty or freedom *from*.

No one epitomized this confusion of thought better than Robert Barnwell Rhett of South Carolina. Jealous of Davis, angry that he had been left out of the Cabinet after years of fighting for southern independence, Rhett from the start was critical of the President's moderate policies. As time passed, he became increasingly strident in his attacks on what he characterized as the President's trend toward executive usurpation and even military despotism. But Rhett wanted a stronger prosecution of the war and hence approved the presidential call for conscription. Essentially Rhett reflected the militance of South Carolinians, their pride at having led the way for the whole South, their fierce devotion both to liberty as they defined it and to Confederate victory as they envisaged it.

And for a time it seemed that they and the rest of the Southerners would have both. In the summer of 1862 the Confederate Army under Lee's leadership went on to a series of brilliant victories. It was not clear at the time how a small, hastily established confederation, with all its economic and social weaknesses and organizational and ideological divisions, could mobilize and sustain one of the most versatile and telling military forces known to that time. It was still something of a mystery a century later. Perhaps a clue lay in the rural heartland of the South, upper and lower. Out of that heartland had come the votes for Breckinridge, just as Lincoln's votes sprang from the rural areas of the North. Out of that southern heartland came the farm boys hardened to the rough-and-ready life of the outdoors, accustomed to handling guns and horses and wagons, used to the ways of rutted roads and treacherous swamps, protecting a southern culture and way of life as compelling as it was unsettled, defending the land they loved and knowing the land they defended.

MEN IN BLUE AND GRAY

War is a great engine of change; the more nearly total the war, the faster and broader the flow of change tends to be. But the shape and texture of that change, economic, social, political, ideological, depends on human beings and how they respond to the "impersonal" forces streaming around them—whether they succumb or adjust to them, or try to guide or transcend or even transform them. Responding to change is a supreme test of leadership.

A shift in the fortunes of war was all too evident to Abraham Lincoln as he looked out of the White House windows at the beaten and exhausted Union soldiers, swaying in their saddles or slumping down on the steps of houses, who trickled into Washington in the days after Bull Run. The crisis brought out the iron in Lincoln's soul. "But the hour, the day, the night pass'd," Walt Whitman wrote later. "The President, recovering himself, begins that very night—sternly, rapidly sets about the task of reorganizing his forces, and placing himself in the position for future and surer work."

The war had already forced Lincoln to adapt his operational ideas to new conditions. As a Whig congressman he had opposed Polk's vigorous use

of presidential power. "Were I President," he had said, "I should desire
the legislation of the country to rest with Congress, uninfluenced by the
executive in its origin or progress. . . ." Now, as President, he turned the
Whig conception of the presidency upside down. In the first few months
he did not dominate Congress—he governed without it, by the simple
expedient of failing to call the lawmakers back to Washington for a special
session until many weeks after Sumter. During those intervening weeks he
expanded the Army and Navy, called for more volunteers, raised and spent
money, declared a blockade, and suspended habeas corpus. This "great
democrat, the exponent of liberty and of government by the people," said
James Randall seventy-five years later, "was driven by circumstances to the
use of more arbitrary power than perhaps any other President has seized."

But Lincoln knew what he was doing, and why. "Was it possible to lose
the nation and yet preserve the Constitution?" he asked. "By general law,
life and limb must be protected, yet often a limb must be amputated to save
a life; but a life is never wisely given to save a limb." The President also
knew that he would be charged with executive usurpation. He was so
pleased when Anna Ella Carroll, daughter of a former Maryland governor,
wrote a pamphlet upholding his executive authority and charging Congress with despotic tendencies, that he helped her publish it and put copies
into the hands of senators and congressmen.

By the time Congress met in late July, the impact of Bull Run united
executive and legislature at least for a time. In seventy-six public acts in
twenty-nine working days, Congress passed legislation of unprecedented
scope, authorizing an army of one-half million troops and a budget of over
$300 million. Lincoln had the support of some powerful senators pressing
for a stronger prosecution of the war. With every military setback their
voices became louder. Douglas had already helped rally Democrats behind
the war in this, his last and finest hour, and had gone home to die; his
support of the Union and the war effort had left a standard for others in
his party to follow. In the House the blunt, salty Thaddeus Stevens, chairman of the Ways and Means Committee, exhibited forceful legislative
leadership in driving through the big financial bills.

To the Commander in Chief fell the responsibility for strategic planning,
and Bull Run forced Lincoln to lay out explicitly what the North must do.
Over several days and nights, sitting on the sofa in his office or on the
lounge in the cabinet room, he penciled a program for immediate action:

*"Let the plan for making the Blockade effective be pushed forward with all possible
despatch.*

*"Let the volunteer forces . . . be constantly drilled, disciplined, and instructed
without more for the present.*

"Let Baltimore be held as now, with a gentle but firm and certain hand. . . .

"Let the forces in Western Virginia act till further orders according to instructions or orders from General McClellan.

"[Let] General Frémont push forward his organization and operations in the West as rapidly as possible. . . .

"Let the forces late before Manassas . . . be reorganized as rapidly as possible in their camps here and about Arlington. . . .

"Let new volunteer forces be brought forward as fast as possible. . . ."

Four days later, the President developed his plans further:

"When the foregoing shall have been substantially attended to: 1. Let Manassas Junction (or some point on one or other of the railroads near it) and Strasburg be seized and permanently held. . . . 2. This done, a joint movement from Cairo on Memphis, and from Cincinnati on East Tennessee."

Lincoln projected that, by year's end, the forces of the Union would be massed and the Confederacy cut off by sea. Northern columns were to reach eastern Tennessee and western Virginia, where Union sympathizers had organized to resist secession; another force would be poised in Memphis, ready to drive down the Mississippi River and cut the southern nation in two.

*   *   *

The President's plan called for a collective effort far beyond anything the American people had known. General George McClellan was given the most exacting job: command of the Union forces massed around Washington. In West Virginia the thirty-four-year-old former railroad executive had defeated two small rebel detachments, the first northern victories to offset Sumter and Bull Run; now he was called to build and lead the largest army ever assembled on the American continent. McClellan's first acts were to confine the troops to their camps, tighten discipline, and order a rigorous schedule of drills and parades. A few soldiers quit, and many volunteer officers unequal to the regular army routine found ways to get home, but the great majority of the men responded energetically to McClellan's combination of harsh demands and winning personal charm. Within a few weeks of Bull Run, the fruits of the general's labors were plain for all to see on the fields before Washington.

"Oh, but this is grand!" wrote one infantry captain. "Troops, troops, tents, tents, the frequent thunder of guns practising, lines of heavy baggage wagons, at reveille and tattoo the air filled with the near and distant roll of drums and the notes of innumerable bugles—all the indications of an immense army. . . ."

To provide all those drums and bugles—and rifles, rations, belt buckles, and the thousand other material requirements of McClellan's Army of the Potomac as it grew to number almost 200,000 men—was another unprecedented undertaking. The job fell to the War Department, which was soon inundated with requests, complaints, and contracts. Simon Cameron, though a wily politician, proved hopelessly inadequate as an administrator; his main contributions to the war effort, Washingtonians complained, were to lose memoranda and to find special deals for his cronies from Pennsylvania. As northern farmers and industrialists churned out war goods, the tiny bureaucracy in Washington was able to feed and equip the main Union forces, but only amidst massive confusion and waste. The Army received a mishmash of supplies, many of them shoddy and few of them uniform. The cost of the purchases—inflated by unnecessary orders, overlapping contracts, and fraud—cut dangerously into the $300 million appropriated by Congress.

McClellan was given green troops and substandard equipment, but western generals complained of receiving nothing at all. The federal government focused its supervision on the army around Washington while draining the West of troops, guns, and skilled officers. Lincoln appointed John Charles Frémont to command the main Union force in Missouri because of his prominence within the Republican party; similarly, he would relieve Frémont later in the year after the general quarreled bitterly with the Blairs.

Left largely to their own devices, the Westerners muddled through. Frémont put up $75,000 of his own money and bought what rifles he could find. In St. Louis two wealthy businessmen, James Buchanan Eads and Charles Ellet, began building a gunboat fleet that would give the Union control of the western waterways. And further south at Cairo, Illinois, where the Ohio and Mississippi rivers joined, a small man, of uncommanding presence, was drilling a small body of troops. Ulysses S. Grant had left the Army in disgrace several years earlier, his Mexican War heroism overshadowed by tales of drunkenness. He returned to his wife and children in Missouri, took up the backbreaking work of farming, but went bankrupt; he tried a few business ventures, but they failed; when Sumter fell, he was working as a clerk in his father's leather store. A local politician helped Grant to appointment as a colonel and then a brigadier in the new volunteer forces, but the job that he really wanted, on McClellan's staff in Washington, was closed to him because of his reputation. So in the autumn of 1861 Sam Grant supervised the training of his Illinois troops and waited for a chance to redeem himself.

While the armies prepared and waited, the Navy acted. Lincoln's head of the Navy Department, Gideon Welles, proved himself a superb organizer, his assistant, Gustavus Fox, a keen strategist. Having begun the war with 43 seaworthy ships, Welles bought or built 400 more of every size and description, from shallow-draft tugs to experimental ironclad gunboats. This motley array of vessels clamped a lid over the coast of the Confederacy, squeezing southern commerce until only a fraction of the prewar shipping was able to get through. Fox organized the Navy's best ships into an amphibious task force that struck sharp blows against the South. On August 29, 1861, an expedition seized Hatteras Island off North Carolina, and on November 7 a naval landing party hoisted the Stars and Stripes over Port Royal farther down the coast. These victories not only shook southern confidence and closed two ports; they gave the Navy advance bases from which it could tighten the blockade and strike again.

Lincoln, indeed, might be excused for thinking the Navy to be too aggressive, for one ship commander almost triggered a war with Britain. Captain Charles Wilkes had been patrolling the eastern Caribbean in the sloop *San Jacinto,* searching for Confederate commerce raiders, when he learned that two southern diplomats, James M. Mason and John Slidell, had slipped through the blockade and were on their way to Europe aboard the British mail steamer *Trent.* On his own initiative, and against the advice of his second-in-command, Wilkes intercepted the *Trent* in the Bahama Channel on November 8, stopped her with a shot across the bow, and sent a boarding party to bring Mason and Slidell back to the *San Jacinto.* The northern press applauded when Wilkes arrived in Boston with his prisoners, but the British government professed to be outraged. Lord Palmerston and his Cabinet tacitly sympathized with the Confederacy; the combination of southern cotton and northern insolence seemed an almost irresistible inducement to war. While the London *Times* breathed fire, and British troop transports prepared to sail for Canada, the Prime Minister demanded that the American government apologize and release the captive envoys.

The northern public, happy to turn against America's old enemy, showered Wilkes with gifts and testimonials. Lawyers, congressmen, and editors called upon Lincoln to defy the British ultimatum. Secretary of State Seward seemed taken with the idea of bringing the South back into the Union by starting a war with Europe. "We will wrap the whole world in flames!" he told *Times* correspondent William Russell. But neither popular pressure nor diplomatic cleverness swayed Lincoln. The President, wanting just "one war at a time," dictated a conciliatory reply to Palmerston. The note, although filled by Seward with references to Britain's violations of American neutral rights during the Napoleonic wars, disavowed Wilkes's action and "cheerfully" promised to release Mason and Slidell. In

London, Charles Francis Adams adroitly presented the American case, and Queen Victoria worked for peace; the crisis subsided.

While meeting one challenge with soft words, Lincoln brazenly ignored another. As an emergency measure in the days after Sumter, Lincoln had authorized the Army to seize and hold suspected traitors without regard to the right of habeas corpus. This action embroiled the President and the military in a clash with the courts, as represented by the nation's highest judicial official, still Chief Justice Taney. When soldiers from Fort McHenry arrested John Merryman, lieutenant in a secessionist militia company in Baltimore, Taney himself wrote out the writ of habeas corpus. He ordered the arresting officer to appear before him with Merryman, "certify and make known the day and cause of the capture and detention of said John Merryman," and then "submit to and receive whatever the said Court shall determine upon" concerning the arrest.

General George Cadwalader, commandant of McHenry, declined to appear before Taney; a messenger who tried to serve the court's writ upon the general was denied admission to the fort. The Chief Justice, having no troops of his own, could only dictate a scathing opinion. Congress, not the President, had the power to suspend habeas corpus under the Constitution; if Lincoln's action went unchallenged, then "the people of the United States are no longer living under a government of laws." Rather every citizen would hold "life, liberty and property at the will and pleasure of the army officer in whose military district he may happen to be found." Taney sent his opinion to the President, calling upon that "high official," whose oath of office the Justice himself had administered only months before, "to perform his constitutional duty to enforce the laws; in other words to enforce the process of this Court." Lincoln, knowing that the North held the Supreme Court in contempt because of Taney's ruling in the Dred Scott case, serenely ignored the command; the Chief Justice was as powerless as John Marshall had been thirty years earlier, when Taney's mentor Andrew Jackson had defied the court's ruling in the Cherokee lands case.

"Ambition must be made to counteract ambition," James Madison had written—and his strategy was working even amid civil war, as the crisis brought the Congress as well as the judiciary into conflict with the President. The foundations for a permanently large and powerful chief executive were building under the stupendous wartime pressures. In the long run, the increased scope of presidential power and the magnitude of the issues at stake in the war guaranteed that President and Congress would clash.

The first foretaste of the conflict was evident in July, when the lawmakers approved Lincoln's emergency measures only grudgingly and in part, in a last-minute rider tacked onto a military pay bill. Now in December, as they convened for the regular session, congressional leaders looked for ways to increase their influence on the war effort. In the House, the Committee on Government Contracts launched a series of investigations into the purchasing practices of the War Department, amassing eleven hundred pages of evidence of fraud and mismanagement. With these probes, and with its support of the civilian Sanitary Commission, which worked to improve conditions in the military hospitals and camps, Congress succeeded in saving money and lives.

Not all of the legislative initiatives were constructive. A group of radical Republicans led by Benjamin Wade and Zachariah Chandler organized a Joint Committee on the Conduct of the War, their goal being to push for a quick end to both the war and slavery. As the winter dragged on and the Union armies continued to drill, the Joint Committee began to question the loyalty of Union officers. General Charles Stone was imprisoned for six months at the committee's behest; his "crime" had been to send a patrol across the Potomac that ended in disaster and death for several hundred northern men—including Edward Dickinson Baker, a former senator and a close friend of Lincoln. Another old soldier, bedeviled by congressional witch hunters, wrote bitterly about serving a government "where to be suspected, merely, is the same as to be convicted."

Lincoln had to deal cautiously with the members of the Joint Committee; they had powerful support in Congress and in the country. The war had intensified the hopes of abolitionists across the North, and Wade's group championed their cause. Lincoln had to fend off antislavery agitation even in the Army itself, canceling emancipation orders issued by Generals Frémont and Hunter. To attack slavery before the Union Army was able to take the offensive against the South, the President feared, would be to lose the border states of Missouri, Kentucky, and Maryland—in his view, to lose both Union and abolition.

The radicals played into Lincoln's hands. Cameron, already on shaky ground as the inefficiency of the War Department became exposed, made a play for the abolitionists' support. Without White House consent he issued a call for the arming of freed slaves to help put down the rebellion. Racial war—the very thought terrified Unionist slaveholders and stiffened Confederate resolve. Cameron had overreached himself; Lincoln "reluctantly accepted his resignation," sent him to Russia as American ambassador to the Tsar, and appointed Edwin Stanton as Secretary of War. Cameron's interference with the war effort was ended, the radicals were temporarily discredited, and Lincoln gained some relief from congressional pressure.

The only way fully to satisfy Congress and the people, however, was to push the war to a victorious conclusion. In February of 1862 the northern forces finally began their offensive, advancing all across the broad front. The Navy led off, landing an amphibious force at Roanoke Island. In the West, a flotilla of gunboats and transports commanded by a saltwater sailor, Commodore Andrew Foote, carried Grant's division down the Cumberland River into Tennessee. Fort Henry on the Cumberland surrendered to the gunboats, and Grant's men trapped a small enemy army in Fort Donelson on the Tennessee River. The forty-year-old general became a national hero in mid-February when he accepted the "unconditional surrender" of 14,000 rebel soldiers at Donelson. A second northern force under Don Carlos Buell captured Nashville, and by the end of March most of Tennessee was in Union hands.

Confederate forces under Albert Sidney Johnston regrouped and counterattacked Grant's column, which had grown to an army of 50,000 men by the beginning of April. Both sides were mauled in the two-day battle at Shiloh Church—Johnston and 40,000 men in blue and gray were gunned down—but the Confederates were forced to retreat. The northern onslaught resumed. New Orleans fell on April 25 to units of David Farragut's fleet, which had run the batteries of the forts defending the city. Charles Ellet was killed when Confederate gunboats sortied to defend Memphis, but the ships that he had built for the Union cleared the way into that city. Farther west, a small Union army marched into Arkansas, destroying a mixed force of Confederates and Indians at Pea Ridge. On July 1 Farragut was able to sail upriver and join forces with the gunboat fleet at Vicksburg, the last Confederate stronghold on the Mississippi.

In the East, General Ambrose Burnside's amphibious force crossed from Roanoke Island to the North Carolina mainland, seized the port of New Bern, and threatened the interior of the state. But the focus of attention was the Potomac, where McClellan began to move his army. The main Union force descended the river in transports and landed at the tip of the York peninsula, where Cornwallis' surrender had ended the American Revolution years before. As McClellan pushed cautiously up the peninsula with 100,000 men, a second army occupied Manassas, while a third advanced into the Shenandoah Valley. By mid-May, the Union controlled most of northern Virginia, and the Army of the Potomac stood on the outskirts of Richmond.

Southerners responded to the Union invasion with éclat. They proved that the North had no monopoly on "Yankee ingenuity"; a single Confederate gunboat, its sides protected by several inches of iron plating, challenged the combined Union fleet at Vicksburg, crippled several ships, and escaped unscathed. A second ironclad, the rebuilt old frigate *Merrimac,* threatened to cut off McClellan's army on the peninsula, until the Union ironclad *Monitor* checked it in a duel off Hampton Roads. Nathan Bedford Forrest and other Confederate cavalry commanders were able to tie down and halt the Union forces in the West by raiding behind their lines, burning supplies, and sending false messages on the occupying army's telegraphs.

The leadership of two men, Robert E. Lee and Stonewall Jackson, saved the Confederate capital and finally reversed the spring tide of Union victory. Lee had fewer than 80,000 men to withstand the three advancing northern armies, yet he sent Jackson into the Shenandoah Valley with 18,000 men to divert what Union forces he could. Jackson and his soldiers performed brilliantly. Dancing around a cumbrous army twice their strength, they fought five battles in as many weeks, forced Lincoln to stop the Union force at Manassas from marching to join McClellan, and then rushed back to Richmond. At Jackson's return, Lee launched another desperate gamble. Again dividing his forces, he attacked the isolated northern wing of the Army of the Potomac, drove it back, and bluffed McClellan into withdrawing his entire force. After seven days of continuous fighting, McClellan's men found themselves back on the James River, camped on the plantation where President Harrison had been born; the bells of Richmond were no longer in earshot.

*   *   *

Presidents can plan, and generals can command, but the outcome of wars turns largely on the individual decisions of thousands of individual soldiers to advance or wait or retreat, to lead or follow or run. The men in blue and gray were, more often than not, still boys; the majority of them had not been old enough to vote in the election that precipitated the war. Charles Fair saw in the Civil War soldiers "a curious kind of naïveté," as though each was "too unguardedly himself, the villains obviously and totally villainous, the virtuous cleareyed and straight as strings, the country boys so rustic and simple one cannot believe them." That innocence would not survive four grinding years of war. In shaping the destiny of the Union, the soldiers—and through them the American people—would themselves be reshaped.

Most of the three-quarters of a million volunteers were farm boys. They brought with them their farm talk, their farm look, their farm knack of dealing with mules and horses. Since friends often enlisted together, they brought with them too their neighborhood associations and attitudes. The Army was a vast mosaic of neighborhoods and common interests. From Illinois alone came units of German immigrants, Galena miners, Bloomington teachers and students, and the "Preacher's Regiment," so called because it included many men of the cloth.

The men brought their own leaders too, for they often elected as captains and colonels popular local politicians from back home. Some proved utterly incompetent and were court-martialed; the soldiers themselves weeded out others. "We have *forced ten resignations* from officers," a Wisconsin private wrote home, "and put better men in their places." Some officers made speeches and courted votes, but civilian leaders often made poor military ones. Among the best leaders were the handful of West Point graduates. Thomas Jackson, wearing a shabby coat and a battered forage cap, drilled his men with spartan discipline and evangelical fervor; he considered "a gum cloth, a blanket, a tooth brush and forty rounds of cartridges as the full equipment of a gentleman soldier," a southern volunteer complained. The soldiers called Jackson "Old Blue Light" until he led them to victory; then they called him "Stonewall." Sam Grant's men referred to him as the "quiet man." When he took command of the 21st Illinois, the volunteers lined up to hear a speech. Grant gave them one: "Men, go to your quarters!"

Camp life as always was an organized bore: drilling, policing the camp, chopping wood for fires, eating salt pork and other staples. Most of the men lived in big tent cities; close quarters and poor sanitation left thousands ill and hundreds dead before the first battles were fought. Soldiers gambled, read, sang, listened to preachers, devised elaborate practical jokes. They came to know other men from very different backgrounds. Northerners who had hardly met a black man began to encounter the bondmen who crowded around the Union camps in Maryland and Missouri. The whites were not friendly, at least in the beginning. "I don't think enough of the Niggar to go and fight for them," wrote an Ohio volunteer.

The men spent most of their time talking; and mostly they talked about the impending warfare. Veterans of Bull Run pictured the fear and confusion, the awful carnage around the batteries on Henry Hill. When war came to many of these soldiers in the spring of 1862 it was initially like all wars: hurry up and wait. After exhausting marches through mud or across still-frozen fields, the regiment would halt, the men would scatter, pitch their tents, start fires for cooking—and wait. Suddenly the drums would beat the long roll, the soldiers would grab their rifles, deploy nervously—and then wait. Much of the fighting was at long range: marching through woods, firing across fields, glancing off an enemy unit, and then settling down for another long wait. Then, suddenly, infantry would find themselves in a bloody holocaust, shooting and stabbing at close quarters. Shiloh, a private remembered, was "one never-ending, terrible roar."

In the summer of '62 the war seemed to assume its old shape. Lee sent Jackson north again in August, this time toward Manassas. The Union troops had a second chance to fight at Bull Run—and once more they lost. Pushing his advantage, Lee united his forces and marched onward into Maryland. The stakes were piled high. Lincoln needed a victory in order to take a stronger posture against slavery and perhaps to save his administration; McClellan needed a victory to save his job; Lee had to find some way to finish off the North before its overwhelming weight of numbers and firepower could be brought to bear. As the two armies raced north, dodging and chasing and parrying each other, soldiers on both sides felt the mounting tension.

McClellan caught Lee's army near the town of Sharpsburg, astride a little stream called Antietam Creek. He hammered the Confederate lines with artillery fire, then sent 75,000 men forward, in three disjointed frontal assaults. On the right the two sides fought over a tiny cornfield, leaving it so strewn with corpses that hardly a patch of ground was left bare. In the center, the Union men pushed forward to a worn-down road, the Sunken Lane; after three hours of fighting, some of it hand to hand, they held the road but were too exhausted to press on. To the left, a handful of Confederates slaughtered Union troops as they tried to cross the single narrow bridge over the Antietam. The Northerners finally carried the bridge, only to stop when they smashed into a rebel unit dressed in captured blue uniforms. The last hours before nightfall brought more attacks, more resistance, more slaughter—and no decision.

McClellan claimed victory at Antietam, for Lee's forces were so battered they had to pull back to Virginia. Lee could claim a victory because he had saved his army despite being outnumbered two to one. But few soldiers were claiming victory the morning after the battle. They sprawled on the ground, averting their eyes from the dead and wounded lying amid the trampled cornstalks, bodies draped over the rubble of blasted stone walls, corpses floating in the watery muck of Antietam Creek. From 20,000 men flowed the vintage of blood.

THE BATTLE CRIES OF FREEDOM

This blood soaking into the mud of Antietam—why was it being shed? For food and clothing and shelter? The great majority of men on both sides had shared in the American cornucopia. For Union or Confederacy? Few of the soldiers wished to shed blood for a particular way of organizing the general government. For some supreme goal that transcended government—that was served by government? Yes, for liberty, freedom, justice

—this is what the soldiers were told. But confusion still prevailed. Not only were Northerners and Southerners wholly at odds with each other as to what constituted liberty, who should enjoy it, how it could be safeguarded and broadened. The northern leaders seemed divided and unsure among themselves.

Lincoln was no exception. "This is essentially a People's contest," he had told Congress. "On the side of the Union, it is a struggle for maintaining in the world, that form, and substance of government, whose leading object is, to elevate the condition of men—to lift artificial weights from all shoulders—to clear the paths of laudable pursuit for all—to afford all, an unfettered start, and a fair chance, in the race of life. . . ." But in answer to Horace Greeley's "Prayer of Twenty Million," in which the *Tribune* editor castigated the "preposterous and futile" idea of trying to put down a rebellion without extirpating the evil of slavery that caused it, the President wrote, "My paramount object in this struggle *is* to save the Union, and is *not* either to save or destroy slavery. If I could save the Union without freeing *any* slave I would do it, and if I could save it by freeing *all* the slaves I would do it; and if I could save it by freeing some and leaving others alone I would also do that. What I do about slavery, and the colored race, I do because I believe it helps to save the Union; and what I forbear, I forbear because I do *not* believe it would help to save the Union. . . ." Lincoln could hardly have stated his priorities more clearly, but what had happened to the priority of liberation—of elevating the condition of all men?

The imperatives of war did not allow the extended debate, philosophizing, legislating, compromising, adjusting inevitable in a pluralistic system of checks and balances. Decisions had to be made. Abolitionist pressure was mounting as the war lagged. European opinion—especially English liberal opinion—was waiting for Lincoln to take leadership against slavery. Senate and House might act if he did not; as early as August 1861 Congress had legislated for the emancipation of slaves who were used in arms or labor against the North, and within a year after that had acted to liberate slaves belonging to rebels or traitors. By midsummer 1862 the President had decided on some form of general emancipation. On July 22 Lincoln informed his Cabinet of his decision, adding that he had made up his mind on the main point but would hear suggestions as to details. As usual, the Cabinet was divided, but the President had to agree with the view that the emancipation proclamation must be issued only after a victory; otherwise it would seem an act of weakness and desperation—in Seward's words, "the last *shriek* on our retreat. . . ."

But where was the victory? Although a bitter disappointment to Lincoln,

Antietam was enough of a victory to permit public announcement of his emancipation intention; thus the blood shed in that battle acquired some meaning. Late in September the President summoned his Cabinet. After reading a few pages from the humorist Artemus Ward, to the non-amusement of Seward and Chase, Lincoln said he would now announce the proclamation. The Cabinet divided again. Bates, dreading any move toward black equality, held that forced colonization should accompany emancipation. Seward privately feared that the proclamation might incite a slave rebellion in the South and alienate moderate opinion in the North, but he supported the President. Blair was still concerned about its possible impact on Union supporters in the border states. Chase approved the idea as a moral necessity, Welles as a military one. Next day the President published his decree, warning that in one hundred days—on January 1, 1863—all slaves in any states or area still in rebellion would be declared free.

"We shout with joy," Frederick Douglass said, "that we live to record this righteous decree." Other abolitionists were pleased, though wary; they would maintain pressure on the President. Moderate and conservative Republicans were apprehensive, most Democrats hostile, and Confederate spokesmen enraged and yet pleased to be vindicated in their warnings about the Republicans' satanic intentions.

The "hundred days" proved the most harrowing in Lincoln's life, and perhaps in the Union's. Even as McClellan boasted of his "victory" at Antietam, the President was searching for a general who could *fight,* amid rumors of disaffection within the Union armies toward the Commander in Chief in the White House. There were more delays, stalemates, and reversals in western operations. The fall congressional elections went against the President. Republican senators were holding long and heated caucuses in which they criticized the President, denounced the moderates and incompetents around him, and discussed ways of gaining greater control of the war. Even worse, the Cabinet was split several ways, and, worst of all, factions within the Administration were tying in with congressional blocs. These centrifugal forces threatened to break the government apart. Then, in mid-December, came the frightful news of the slaughter at Fredericksburg, where Lee shattered Burnside's army—almost 1,300 Union soldiers killed, another 10,000 wounded.

Fredericksburg precipitated a government crisis. Caucusing senators asked that the Cabinet be reorganized; they criticized Seward so sharply for his moderate attitude toward slavery and his alleged influence on Lincoln that the Secretary of State felt obliged to tender his resignation. At a meeting with Lincoln the senators demanded a more active role for a reorganized Cabinet, and especially for their friend Chase. Lincoln quietly heard them out, asked them to return the following evening, and called a cabinet meeting for the next day. In an open discussion Lincoln gained the agreement of all—including Chase—to his claim that the Cabinet had seldom disagreed on basic issues. When the senators arrived that evening, they found Lincoln there with his Cabinet save for Seward. After reasserting that his cabinet members were fundamentally in harmony, the President called on the members to vouch again for this position. Cornered, Chase now contradicted the statements he had made to the senators on the Hill. The Senate delegation was left in disarray, Seward in vindication, Chase in humiliation.

Shortly, Chase returned to the White House. He had prepared his resignation, he told the President.

"Where is it?" asked Lincoln. Chase produced a letter but seemed reluctant to part with it.

"Let me have it," said the President, reaching out and snatching it. He was exultant. Now he had both Seward's and Chase's tenders. He would accept neither resignation. He had the balance he wanted. "I can ride now," he said to a friend. "I've got a pumpkin in each end of my bag."

It was a small triumph amid the gloom of December. Lincoln suddenly seemed drawn and aged. He spent hours waiting for news of battles, other hours in reflection, reassessing the course of the war. "The dogmas of the quiet past," he told Congress in his annual message, "are inadequate to the stormy present. . . . As our case is new, so we must think anew, and act anew. We must disenthrall ourselves, and then we shall save our country."

On New Year's Eve, the night before the Emancipation Proclamation was to be signed, Lincoln "tossed in fitful sleep, dreaming of corpses on a distant battlefield in Tennessee, of guns flashing in the night, of silent troops lying exhausted in the rain, of crowds reading casualty returns at Willard's Hotel." Next day, after the President had greeted a long procession of guests, his arm seemed almost paralyzed, and his fingers trembled so that he had to take a firm grip on the gold pen. "If my name ever goes into history," he said to the cabinet members and officials gathered around him, "it will be for this act." It was not an impressive-looking document, with its detailed exemptions and its admonition to slaves to refrain from unnecessary violence. But five words stood out in the order: after January 1, 1863, slaves in rebelling states and areas shall be "THEN, THENCEFORTH, AND FOREVER FREE."

A black preacher raced down Pennsylvania Avenue to read the proclamation to a crowd of blacks. They shouted, clapped, sang. Later, blacks and whites gathered in front of the White House and called for the President to appear. When he came to the window and bowed to them, ecstatic cheering broke out, and one black exclaimed that if he would only "come out of that palace, they would hug him to death."

* * *

1863. Somewhere around a campfire a Union troop was singing:

> Oh, we'll rally 'round the flag, boys, we'll rally once again,
>   Shouting the battle cry of freedom;
> We will rally from the hill-side, we'll gather from the plain,
>   Shouting the battle cry of freedom . . .
> We will welcome to our numbers the loyal, true, and brave,
>   Shouting the battle cry of freedom,
> And although they may be poor not a man shall be a slave,
>   Shouting the battle cry of freedom.

Somewhere in the South soldiers were singing, to the same tune:

> We'll meet the Yankee hosts, boys,
> With fearless hearts and true,
>   Shouting the battle cry of freedom,
> And we'll show the dastard minions
> What Southern pluck can do,
>   Shouting the battle cry of freedom.

Somewhere the 1st Arkansas (Negro) Regiment heard the President's proclamation.

> See, there above the center, where the flag is waving bright,
> We are going out of slavery; we're bound for freedom's light;
> We mean to show Jeff Davis how the Africcans can fight,
> As we go marching on!

Notes

PROLOGUE

p. 3 [*Pownall's map*]: T. Pownall, *A Topographical Description of the Dominions of the United States of America* (1776), Lois Mulkearn, ed. (University of Pittsburgh Press, 1949), pp. 25–26; see also (as referred to in Pownall) Edward Anthill, "An Essay on the Cultivation of the Vine, suited to the different climates in North America," *Transactions* of the American Philosophical Society (Wm. and Thomas Bradford, 1771), (O.S.) I, Section II, pp. 117–97.

4 [*Origin of first Americans*]: Harold E. Driver, *Indians of North America* (University of Chicago Press, 1961), Ch. 1.

[*Dispersion of Indian Americans across the continent*]: Geoffrey Barraclough, ed., *The Times Atlas of World History* (Hammond, 1979), pp. 36–37.

[*Nootkas on the tide*]: quoted in Richard B. Morris, ed., *Encyclopedia of American History* (Harper & Row, 1976), p. 10.

5 [*Types of Indians*]: Driver, Ch. 24.

[*Decimation of Indians on Martha's Vineyard and Block Island*]: Howard Zinn, *A People's History of the United States* (Harper & Row, 1980), p. 16.

[*Tideland and piedmont Indians*]: Bureau of the Census, *A Century of Population Growth* (Government Printing Office, 1909), pp. 39–40.

6 [*Joseph Brant and the Iroquois*]: Katharine C. Turner, *Red Men Calling on the Great White Father* (University of Oklahoma Press, 1951), p. 19; Angie Debo, *A History of the Indians of the United States* (University of Oklahoma Press, 1970), p. 71.

[*Great Lakes tribes*]: Debo, p. 13.

[*Treaty with Cherokees*]: U.S. Congress, House Committee on Indian Affairs, "Indian Territory, West of the Mississippi," *Reports of Committees, 30th Congress, 1st session*, no. 736 ([Albany?]: Wendell and Van Benthuysen, [1848?]), p. 1.

[*Creek-Seminole army*]: Angie Debo, *The Road to Disappearance* (University of Oklahoma Press, 1941), p. 44.

7 [*Population in the 1780s*]: Bureau of the Census, *A Century of Population Growth* (Government Printing Office, 1909, 1976).

[*Religious affiliation, 1775*]: Morris, p. 824.

8 [*Transportation and currency in the 1780s*]: *A Century of Population Growth*, pp. 20–23.

[*Taverns and drinking*]: Frank J. Klingberg, *The Morning of America* (Appleton-Century, 1941), pp. 295–301.

[*Patrick Henry as an "American"*]: quoted in Oscar Handlin, *The Americans* (Little, Brown, 1963), p. 150.

9 [*Catholic mass in Boston*]: John Thayer, *An Account of the Conversion of the Reverend Mr. John Thayer* (J. P. Cochlan, 1787), as cited in J. P. Brissot de Warville, *New Travels in the United States of America, 1788*, Durand Echeverria, ed. (Harvard University Press, 1964), p. 88.

[*Songs in America*]: James Truslow Adams, *The Epic of America* (Little, Brown, 1931), pp. 70–71.

[*Omaha leader's song*]: Alice C. Fletcher, *Indian Story and Song from North America* (Small, Maynard, 1906), pp. 24–25.

[*Americans in the 1780s*]: see also St. John de Crèvecoeur, *Sketches of Eighteenth Century America* (Yale University Press, 1925); Percy G. Adams, ed., *Crèvecoeur's Eighteenth Century Travels in Pennsylvania & New York* (University Press of Kentucky, 1961); James Schouler, *Americans of 1776* (Dodd, Mead, 1906); Marshall Davidson, *Life in America* (Houghton Mifflin, 1974), Vol. 1, passim; Marquis de Chastellux, *Travels in North-America in the Years 1780-81-82* (White, Gallagher, & White, 1827).

1. THE STRATEGY OF LIBERTY

13 [*Fiscal background of Shays's Rebellion*]: Jonathan Smith, "The Depression of 1785 and Daniel Shays' Rebellion," address before the Clinton, Mass., Historical Society, printed in pamphlet form by that Society (1905), and reprinted in *William and Mary Quarterly*, Third Series, Vol. 5 (January 1948), pp. 77–94; for a contemporary analysis, see Richard Cranch to John Adams, Oct. 7, 1786, John Adams Papers, Microfilm Reel 369, Massachusetts Historical Society, Boston.

14 [*Leadership of the rebellion*]: On Shays's role, reflected in a dialogue between him and General Rufus Putnam, as reported by Putnam to Governor Bowdoin, see Charles Oscar Parmenter, *History of Pelham, Massachusetts* (Carpenter and Morehouse, 1898), pp. 395–98. [*Collective nature of the rebel leadership*]: Richard B. Morris, "Insurrection in Massachusetts," in Daniel Aaron, ed., *America in Crisis* (Alfred A. Knopf, 1952), pp. 31–33.

[*Reaction of Massachusetts authorities to the rebellion*]: see especially extensive references in correspondence in the Henry Knox Papers and the Bowdoin-Temple Papers, Massachusetts Historical Society; see also Van Beck Hall, *Politics Without Parties: Massachusetts, 1780–1791* (University of Pittsburgh Press, 1972), pp. 210–12, and references therein. [*Statement of "respectable Bostonian"*]: Joseph Warren to John Adams, Oct. 22, 1786, Adams Papers.

[*Letter of anonymous Regulator to Gov. Bowdoin*]: Bowdoin-Temple Papers, anonymous to Bowdoin, n.d. The records of the Regulators are virtually nonexistent as compared to those of the authorities. See, however, George Richards Minot, *The History of the Insurrections in Massachusetts* (originally written 1788), 2nd ed. (Books for Libraries Press, 1970), letter, Eli Parsons to "Friends and Fellow Sufferers," Feb. 15, 1787, pp. 146–47; see also files of the many newspapers of the day. William Manning, *The Key of Libberty* (written in 1798), Samuel Eliot Morison, ed. (The Manning Association, 1922), offers the views of a "typical" farmer who was partial to neither authorities nor rebels.

[*Other sources on Shays's Rebellion*]: Neville Meaney, "The Trial of Popular Sovereignty in Post-Revolutionary America: The Case of Shays' Rebellion," in Neville Meaney, ed., *Studies on the American Revolution* (Melbourne: The Macmillan Co. of Australia, 1976), pp. 151–216; Robert J. Taylor, *Western Massachusetts in the Revolution* (Brown University Press, 1954); Josiah Gilbert Holland, *History of Western Massachusetts* (Springfield: Samuel Bowles & Co., 1855), Vol. 1.

The Great Fear

15 [*Washington's daily life at Mount Vernon, fall 1786*]: John C. Fitzpatrick, ed., *The Diaries of George Washington* (Houghton Mifflin, 1925), Vol. 3, passim; see also *Washington's*

Map of Mount Vernon (reproduced in facsimile from the original), Introduction by Lawrence Martin (University of Chicago Press, 1932).

15–16 [*Washington on the cause of the commotions*]: Washington to David Humphreys, Oct. 22, 1786, in John C. Fitzpatrick, ed., *The Writings of George Washington* (Government Printing Office, 1939), Vol. 29, p. 27; Knox to Washington, esp. quotation of Knox by Washington in Washington to James Madison, Nov. 5, 1786, *ibid.*, p. 51. [*Washington on inconsistency of man*]: Washington to David Humphreys, Dec. 26, 1786, *ibid.*, pp. 125–26. [*Washington to Madison on "thirteen sovereignties"*]: *ibid.*, p. 52.

16–17 [*Letters of John and Abigail Adams' correspondents, and the Adamses' responses*]: Adams Papers, Microfilm Reel 369, Massachusetts Historical Society; see esp. exchanges with Rufus King, Cotton Tufts, James Warren, John Jay, Thomas Jefferson, John Quincy Adams. [*Abigail Adams on Hyde Park*]: quoted in Page Smith, *John Adams* (Doubleday, 1962), Vol. 2, p. 642. [*John Quincy Adams on the governor as "Old Lady"*]: JQA to Abigail Adams, Dec. 30, 1786, Microfilm Reel 369. [*AA to JQA on "Poppa's" new work*]: AA to JQA, Jan. 17, 1787, *ibid.* John Adams' new work was published in his *Defence of the Constitutions of Government of the United States of America*, published in two volumes, 1787.

18–19 [*Reports to Jefferson about Shays's rebellion, and his response*]: see Julian P. Boyd, ed., *The Papers of Thomas Jefferson* (Princeton University Press, 1954–55), Vols. 9–11, passim; see also Dumas Malone, *Jefferson and the Rights of Man* (Little, Brown, 1951), pp. 156–66. [*Jefferson's and Adams' English tour*]: Boyd, Vol. 9, pp. 369–75; see also L. H. Butterfield, ed., *Diary and Autobiography of John Adams* (Belknap Press, 1961), Vol. 3, pp. 184–86. [*Abigail Adams to Jefferson on Shays's rebellion*]: AA to Jefferson, Jan. 29, 1787; and Jefferson's reply, Feb. 22, 1787, Adams Papers, Microfilm Reel, 369, Massachusetts Historical Society. [*Jefferson on revolution and the tree of liberty*]: Jefferson to William Stephens Smith, Nov. 13, 1787, Boyd, Vol. 12, p. 356.

19 [*The rebel attack on the Springfield arsenal*]: see detailed reports in the Henry Knox Papers, Massachusetts Historical Society; and a separate folder, "Lincoln-Bowdoin, Shays' Rebellion Campaign, 1786–1787," Massachusetts Historical Society, containing day-to-day reports from Gen. Lincoln to Bowdoin. See also General Shepard to Governor Bowdoin, Jan. 26, 1787, Massachusetts Archives, Vol. 190, pp. 317–18, reprinted in *American Historical Review*, Vol. 2, No. 4 (July 1897), pp. 694–95.

20 [*Events in western Massachusetts after the Springfield arsenal encounter*]: Robert J. Taylor, *Western Massachusetts in the Revolution*, pp. 162–63. [*Stockbridge episode*]: Electa F. Jones, *Stockbridge, Past and Present* (Samuel Bowles, 1854), pp. 193–98; newspaper clippings, Shays's Rebellion, city and town libraries, Berkshire County; Robert A. Burns assisted in this research. See also Thomas Egleston, *The Life of John Paterson* (G. P. Putnam's Sons, 1894), pp. 198–99. Edward Bellamy, *The Duke of Stockbridge* (Silver, Burdett, 1900), offers a fictionalized version of some of these events. See also Marion L. Starkey, *A Little Rebellion* (Alfred A. Knopf, 1955).

21 [*Alexander Hamilton on the question Americans must decide*]: *Federalist* No. 1, Edward Mead Earle, ed., *The Federalist* (Modern Library, 1937), p. 5.

[*Early Americans on their country as mission or venture*]: Arthur Schlesinger, Jr., Address to the American Historical Association, Washington, D.C., Dec. 29, 1976, reprinted under the title "America: Experiment or Destiny?" *American Historical Review*, Vol. 82, No. 3 (June 1977), pp. 505–22.

A Rage for Liberty

21 [*Franklin's home and addition in Philadelphia*]: Franklin to M. le Veillard, April 15, 1787, in Albert Henry Smyth, ed., *The Writings of Benjamin Franklin* (Macmillan, 1907), Vol. 9, pp. 558–62; on aspects and artifacts of his home, see Robert D. Crompton, "Frank-

lin's House off High Street in Philadelphia," *Antiques,* Vol. 102, No. 4 (October 1972), pp. 680–83; George B. Tatum, *Penn's Great Town* (University of Pennsylvania Press, 1961), p. 158 and illustration No. 15.

22 [*Description of Franklin*]: quoted in Carl Van Doren, *Benjamin Franklin* (Viking Press, 1938), p. 750.

[*The Philadelphia of Franklin's time*]: Edwin Wolf 2nd, *Philadelphia: Portrait of an American City* (Stackpole, 1975); George B. Tatum, *Philadelphia Georgian* (Wesleyan University Press, 1976).

22–23 [*Independence Hall*]: David W. Belisle, *History of Independence Hall* (James Challen & Son, 1859). [*Franklin on "hanging together"*]: John H. Hazelton, *The Declaration of Independence: Its History* (Dodd, Mead, 1906), p. 209.

23 [*Liberty as a precious jewel*]: cited in Bernard Bailyn, *The Ideological Origins of the American Revolution* (Belknap Press: 1967), pp. 62, 114.

[*Hamilton on the "rage for liberty"*]: quoted in John C. Miller, *Alexander Hamilton: Portrait in Paradox* (Harper & Brothers, 1959), p. 113.

24 [*Saxon origin of liberty*]: Gordon S. Wood, *The Creation of the American Republic, 1776–1787* (University of North Carolina Press, 1969), pp. 31, 228.

[*Congregationalists vs. Baptists*]: Bailyn, pp. 264–66. [*Baptists and Quakers vs. John Adams*]: ibid., 268–69. [*Virginia Declaration of Rights*]: ibid., p. 260.

[*Benjamin Franklin on "publick liberty"*]: quoted in Clinton Rossiter, *Seedtime of the Republic* (Harcourt, Brace, 1953), p. 299.

25 [*John Adams on liberty and property*]: from Adams, *A Defence of the Constitutions of Government of the United States of America,"* quoted in Francis W. Coker, *Democracy, Liberty, and Property* (Macmillan, 1942), p. 125. [*Continental Congressman on dilemma of liberty and luxury*]: quoted in Wood, p. 65.

[*Slavery in America, 1770s and 1780s*]: Donald L. Robinson, *Slavery in the Structure of American Politics, 1765–1820* (Harcourt Brace Jovanovich, 1971), Chs. 3 and 4; [*Samuel Johnson on "yelps for liberty"*]: quoted in Robinson, p. 80. See also Edmund S. Morgan, "Slavery and Freedom: The American Paradox," *Journal of American History,* Vol. 59, No. 1 (June 1972), pp. 5–29.

[*American self-image in the eighteenth century*]: quotations from Wood, p. 99; Bailyn, pp. 138–39.

26 [*"Evils and calamities" making for crisis*]: John Jay to George Washington, June 27, 1786, John Jay Papers, Columbia University; also in Henry P. Johnston, ed., *Correspondences and Public Papers of John Jay* (G. P. Putnam's Sons, 1891), Vol. 3, pp. 203–5.

[*The "mortal diseases"*]: James Madison to Thomas Jefferson, March 19, 1787, in Robert A. Rutland, ed., *Papers of James Madison* (University of Chicago Press, 1975), Vol. 9, p. 318.

[*Wood on shift to institutional concern*]: Wood, p. 463.

27 [*John Quincy Adams on the crisis as one of credit and contracts*]: quoted in Robert A. East, *John Quincy Adams: The Critical Years: 1785–1794* (Bookman Associates, 1962), pp. 85–86.

[*Contingency in history*]: Sidney Hook, *The Hero in History* (John Day, 1943); Edward Hallett Carr, *What Is History?* (Alfred A. Knopf, 1962); Isaiah Berlin, *The Hedgehog and the Fox* (Simon and Schuster, 1970). The Americans' "experiments" in different forms and powers of government have been described in detail by Wood, esp. Parts II–IV.

28 ["*Almost every pen*" *at work*]: quoted in Wood, p. 6. [*Madison's correspondence with fellow Virginians*]: see esp. George Washington to Madison, March 31, 1787, Rutland, Vol. 9, pp. 342–44; Madison to Edmund Randolph, April 15, 1787, *ibid.*, pp. 378–80; Madison to Washington, April 16, 1787, *ibid.*, pp. 382–87. See also relevant letters, *ibid.*, Vol. 10. [*Madison's suspicions of Patrick Henry and George Mason*]: *ibid.*, Vol. 9, p. 331, pp. 50, 55.

Madison's *Vices of the Political System of the United States* is reprinted in Rutland, *Papers*, pp. 348–57. I have drawn information and whole sentences on Madison's final weeks in New York and journey to Philadelphia from my *The Deadlock of Democracy* (Prentice-Hall, 1963), Ch. 1, and sources referred to therein.

Philadelphia: The Continental Caucus

30–1 [*Pinckney's trip to Philadelphia*]: Marvin R. Zahniser, *Charles Cotesworth Pinckney* (University of North Carolina Press, 1967), p. 87. [*Gerry's trip*]: George Athan Billias, *Elbridge Gerry: Founding Father and Republican Statesman* (McGraw-Hill, 1976), p. 156. [*Johnson's trip*]: George C. Groce, Jr., *William Samuel Johnson* (Columbia University Press, 1937), pp. 139, 172–73; see also Committee on Historical Publications, *Roads and Road-Making in Colonial Connecticut* (Yale University Press, 1933), Tercentenary Commission of the State of Connecticut, Pamphlet Series 1-15.

31 [*Washington's arrival in Philadelphia*]: Clinton Rossiter, *1787: The Grand Convention* (Macmillan, 1966), pp. 159–60.

[*Mason on Madison's early activities*]: Burns, p. 14. [*Blending of politician and scholar*]: *ibid.*, p. 15.

32 [*Some major works on the character and background of delegates to the 1787 convention*]: Charles A. Beard, *An Economic Interpretation of the Constitution of the United States* (Macmillan, 1929); Robert E. Brown, *Charles Beard and the Constitution* (Princeton University Press, 1956); Merrill Jensen, *The New Nation* (Alfred A. Knopf, 1950); Forrest McDonald, *We the People* (University of Chicago Press, 1958); Edmund S. Morgan, *The Birth of the Republic, 1763–89* (University of Chicago Press, 1956); Cecilia M. Kenyon, "Men of Little Faith: The Anti-Federalists on the Nature of Representative Government," *William and Mary Quarterly*, Third Series, Vol. 12, No. 1 (January 1955), pp. 3–43; Stanley Elkins and Eric McKitrick, *The Founding Fathers: Young Men of the Revolution* (American Historical Association, 1962); Arthur Taylor Prescott, *Drafting the Federal Constitution* (Louisiana State University Press, 1941), a topical analysis.

[*Gladstone on Constitution*]: John Bartlett, *Familiar Quotations* (Little, Brown, 1943), p. 450.

[*Biographical data on the delegates*]: Rossiter, Ch. 8.

33 [*Regulators in the Massachusetts elections*]: Hall, Ch. 8.

[*Madison on "wicked measures"*]: Madison to Edmund Pendleton, April 22, 1787, in Gaillard Hunt, ed., *The Writings of James Madison*, Vol. II (G. P. Putnam's Sons, 1901), p. 354.

34 [*Malcontents as "scum"*]: Wood, pp. 476, 498.

[*Main sources on proceedings of the federal convention*]: Max Farrand, ed., *The Records of the Federal Convention of 1787*, Vols. I–IV (Yale University Press, 1966); Gaillard Hunt, ed., *The Journal of the Debates in the Convention Which Framed the Constitution of the United States* (as recorded by James Madison), Vols. I–II (G. P. Putnam's Sons, 1908); Jonathan Elliot, comp., *The Debates in the Several State Conventions on the Adoption of the Federal Constitution . . .* , Vols. I–V (Lippincott, 1836), known as *Elliot's Debates*.

34 [*Randolph's proposals.*]: Farrand, Vol. I, pp. 20, 21.

35 [*Pinckney on question of abolition of state governments*]: *ibid.,* pp. 33-34.

[*Pierce on James Wilson*]: Farrand, Vol. 3, pp. 91-92.

36 [*Pierce on Paterson*]: *ibid.,* p. 90.

[*Paterson's speech*]: Farrand, Vol. 1, pp. 242 ff.

38 [*Rutledge on gentlemen's shyness in regard to the national executive*]: *ibid.,* p. 65. Pinckney, Sherman, Gerry, and Wilson discussion: *ibid., pp.* 65-66.

[*Gerry on choosing the executive*]: *ibid.,* p. 80.

[*National judiciary discussion*]: *ibid.,* pp. 119 ff.

39 [*Appointment of judges*]: *ibid.,* pp. 118 ff.; Vol. 2, pp. 41 ff.

[*Paterson on slaves as lacking personal liberty*]: quoted in Robinson, p. 192 (note Robinson's interpretation of Paterson's statement).

40 [*Robinson on white workers' attitude toward slaves*]: *ibid.,* p. 28.

[*Rossiter on the delegates and slavery*]: Rossiter, p. 267.

[*Franklin on sawing boards to make them fit*]: Farrand, Vol. 1, pp. 489, 499.

[*Lafayette to John Jay, August 4, 1787*]: John Jay Papers.

41 [*Hamilton on the need for a powerful national government*]: Farrand, Vol. 1, pp. 282-311.

2. THE THIRD CADRE

42 [*Franklin's remark at convention's end*]: Max Farrand, ed., *The Records of the Federal Convention of 1787* (Yale University Press, 1966), Vol. II, p. 648 (Sept. 17, 1787).

[*Washington taking leave*]: John C. Fitzpatrick, ed., *The Diaries of George Washington* (Houghton Mifflin, 1925), Vol. 3, p. 237.

[*Roger Sherman on the power of Congress not extending to the press*]: Charles Warren, *The Making of the Constitution* (Little, Brown, 1937), p. 508.

42-3 [*Transmission of Constitution by Congress to states*]: Clinton Rossiter, *1787: The Grand Convention* (Macmillan, 1966), p. 275. [*Lee's comment on the "unanimous" transmission*]: Richard Henry Lee to George Mason, Oct. 1, 1787, in James Curtis Ballagh, ed., *The Letters of Richard Henry Lee* (Macmillan, 1914), Vol. 2, p. 439.

43 [*Anti-Federalist (Melancton Smith) on twenty assemblies being equally respectable*]: Paul Leicester Ford, ed., *Pamphlets on the Constitution of the United States* (Brooklyn, N.Y., 1888), p. 115.

44 [*Alexander Hamilton, Madison, and the* Federalist]: John C. Miller, *Alexander Hamilton: Portrait in Paradox* (Harper & Brothers, 1959), Ch. 12; see also James Madison to George Washington, Nov. 18, 1787, in Robert A. Rutland, ed., *Papers of James Madison* (University of Chicago Press, 1975), Vol. 10, p. 254; Irving Brant, *James Madison: Father of the Constitution* (Bobbs-Merrill, 1950), pp. 170-71; Jacob E. Cooke, ed., *The Federalist* (Wesleyan University Press, 1961), Introduction, pp. xi-xviii; Marvin Meyers, "Founding and Revolution: A Commentary on Publius-Madison," in Stanley Elkins and Eric McKitrick, eds., *The Hofstadter Aegis* (Alfred A. Knopf, 1974), pp. 3-35.

[*Dropping of the* Federalist *by one newspaper*]: Cooke, p. 600.

[*Publishers on demand for* Federalist]: Cooke, p. xiv.

45 [Federalist *as America's greatest contribution to political philosophy*]: *ibid.,* jacket cover.

The Anti-Federalists

46 [*The anti-Federalist network*]: Robert Allen Rutland, *The Ordeal of the Constitution* (University of Oklahoma Press, 1966), Ch. 3. See also Jackson Turner Main, *The Antifederalists* (University of North Carolina Press, 1961), passim.

[*Madison on "respectable names" among his adversaries*]: Madison to Archibald Stuart, Oct. 30, 1787, Rutland, *Madison Papers*, Vol. 10, p. 232.

47 [*Ratification of the Constitution in Pennsylvania*]: the definitive source is Merrill Jensen, ed., *Ratification of the Constitution by the States—Pennsylvania*, Vol. 2 of *The Documentary History of the Ratification of the Constitution* (State Historical Society of Wisconsin, 1976).

48 [*Remarks of Robert Whitehill*]: *ibid.*, pp. 393–98.

49 [*Shuffling and stamping of feet in the Connecticut convention*]: Rutland, *Ordeal*, p. 85.

[*Ratification in Massachusetts*]: Van Beck Hall, *Politics Without Parties: Massachusetts, 1780–1791* (University of Pittsburgh Press, 1972), Chs. 9 and 10; Rutland, *Ordeal*, Chs. 5 and 6; George A. Billias, *Elbridge Gerry* (McGraw-Hill, 1976), Ch. 14; Robert Ernst, *Rufus King* (University of North Carolina Press, 1968); John C. Miller, *Sam Adams* (Stanford University Press, 1936); Samuel Bannister Harding, *Contest over the Ratification of the Federal Constitution in the State of Massachusetts* (Longmans, Green, 1896).

50 [*Gerry's style as too sublime*]: Ford, p. 1.

[*Federalist and anti-Federalist invective*]: quoted in Rutland, *Ordeal*, p. 73.

[*Richard Henry Lee to Samuel Adams on toiling in the "Vineyard of liberty"*]: Richard Henry Lee to Sam Adams, Oct. 5, 1787, and Sept. 2 (?), 1787, Samuel Adams Papers, New York Public Library.

[*Incident in Sheffield*]: Rutland, *Ordeal*, p. 79.

51 [*Gerry incident*]: Rutland, *Madison Papers*, Vol. 10, pp. 345, 376, 400–1; Billias, pp. 213–14; Rutland, *Ordeal*, p. 96.

[*Nasson on liberty*]: *Debates and Proceedings in the Convention of the Commonwealth of Massachusetts, 1788* (William White, 1856), pp. 235–36. On the third-cadre leaders in Massachusetts, see also Harding, pp. 63–65.

52 [*Maine observer*]: quoted in Rutland, *Ordeal*, p. 118.

[*Ratification in Maryland*]: Philip A. Crowl, "Anti-Federalism in Maryland, 1787–1788," *William and Mary Quarterly*, Third Series, Vol. 4, No. 4 (October 1947), pp. 446–69.

The Course Is Set

53 [*Ratification in Virginia*]: Rutland, *Madison Papers*, passim; Fitzpatrick, *Washington Diaries*, passim; John C. Fitzpatrick, ed., *The Writings of George Washington* (Government Printing Office, 1939), passim; Robert D. Meade, *Patrick Henry: Practical Revolutionary* (Lippincott, 1969).

[*Patrick Henry's speech to Virginia convention*]: quoted in Meade, p. 356.

54 [*A friend's warning to Madison to come home to run for election*]: Joseph Spencer to Madison, Feb. 28, 1788, Rutland, *Madison Papers*, Vol. 10, pp. 540–41.

[*Madison's answer to Henry*]: Gaillard Hunt, ed., *The Writings of James Madison* (G. P. Putnam's Sons, 1904), Vol. 5, pp. 125–26.

55 [*Anti-Federalist on "energy" and "liberty"*]: Rutland, *Ordeal*, p. 231.

[*Henry's final speech*]: *ibid.*, pp. 248–49.

55 [*Vote of the Allegheny men in favor of the Constitution*]: Dorothy Davis, *John George Jackson* (McClain Printing, 1976), pp. 13–18, 346 n. 44.

[*Monroe to Jefferson on Washington's influence*]: Rutland, *Ordeal*, p. 253.

[*Ratification in New York*]: Miller, *Hamilton*, Ch. 14; E. Wilder Spaulding, *His Excellency George Clinton* (Macmillan, 1938), Ch. 13; anon. (taken in shorthand), *The Debates and Proceedings of the Convention of the State of New York* (Francis Childs, 1788); Frank Monaghan, *John Jay* (Bobbs-Merrill, 1935); Linda Grant DePauw, *The Eleventh Pillar: New York and the Federal Constitution* (Cornell University Press, 1966).

56 [*Invective against anti-Federalists "daily going about to poison the tenants"*]: quoted in Rutland, *Ordeal*, p. 204.

[*Hamilton's appeal to Scotsmen*]: Harold C. Syrett, ed., *The Papers of Alexander Hamilton* (Columbia University Press, 1962), Vol. 4, pp. 645–46.

[*A Clintonian on opponents' invective*]: quoted in Rutland, *Ordeal*, p. 203.

[*Hamilton on elections going wrong*]: Hamilton to Gouverneur Morris, May 19, 1788, Syrett, p. 651.

[*A Clintonian on the "wellborn" lacking influence*]: James M. Hughes to John Lamb, June 18, 1787, John Jay Papers, Columbia University.

57 [*John Jay to Washington on Virginia victory*]: July 4, 1788, John Jay Papers.

[*Madison insists on "one adoption"*]: Miller, *Hamilton*, p. 214.

[*Anti-Federalists' amendments*]: John Jay to Washington, July 18, 1787, and July 23, 1787, John Jay Papers.

[*The parade in New York City*]: Miller, *Hamilton*, p. 213.

Vice and Virtue

58 [*"Women of the republic"*]: term from Linda K. Kerber, *Women of the Republic* (University of North Carolina Press, 1980).

[*Women's roles during this period*]: see Kerber, esp. Chs. 4 and 9; Mary Sumner Benson, *Women in Eighteenth-Century America: A Study of Opinion and Social Usage* (Columbia University Press, 1935); Pauline Maier, *The Old Revolutionaries* (Alfred A. Knopf, 1980).

58–60 [*Mercy Otis Warren*]: Vera O. Laska, *"Remember the Ladies"—Outstanding Women of the American Revolution* (Commonwealth of Massachusetts Bicentennial Commission, May 1976), pp. 36–60; *Notable American Women;* Kerber, Chs. 3 and 8.

[*Warren as a playwright who probably never saw a play*]: Laska, p. 45.

[*Warren's rationale for wider participation by women*]: quoted in Kerber, pp. 83–84.

59 [*Warren's authorship of attack on the Constitution*]: Mercy Warren to Catharine Macaulay, Sept. 28, 1787, and Dec. 18, 1787, Mercy Warren Letterbook, Massachusetts Historical Society; Charles Warren, "Elbridge Gerry, James Warren, Mercy Warren and the Ratification of the Federal Constitution in Massachusetts," *Massachusetts Historical Society Proceedings*, Vol. 64 (June 1932), pp. 143–64.

[*Warren's attack*]: "Observations on the new constitution, and on the Federal and State Conventions. By a Columbian Patriot," Richard Henry Lee, ed. (Quadrangle Books, 1962), pp. 1–19.

[*Quotations from "Observations . . ."*]: pp. 1, 8, 19, 3, resp.

[*Warren on "liberty delights the ear"*]: Mercy Warren to Catharine Macaulay, July 29, 1779, Mercy Warren Letterbook, Massachusetts Historical Society.

60 [*Framers defend social pluralism*]: Madison to Jefferson, Oct. 24, 1787, Hunt, Vol. 5, pp. 17–41.

[*Governmental tyranny*]: George W. Carey, "Separation of Powers and the Madisonian Model: A Reply to the Critics," *American Political Science Review*, Vol. 72, No. 1 (March 1978), pp. 151–64.

61 [*Pinckney on the one order of Commons*]: Charles C. Tansill, ed., *Documents Illustrative of the Formation of the Union of the American States* (Government Printing Office, 1927), p. 273.

[*Problem of representation in the Constitution*]: Jean Yarbrough, "Thoughts on the *Federalist*'s View of Representation," *Polity*, Vol. 12, No. 1 (Fall 1979), pp. 65–82; see also Robert A. Goldwin, ed., *Representation and Misrepresentation* (Rand McNally, 1968); Gordon S. Wood, *The Creation of the American Republic, 1776–1787* (University of North Carolina Press, 1969), passim; *The Federalist*, passim; Richard W. Krouse, "Two Concepts of Democratic Republicanism: Madison and Tocqueville on Pluralism and Party in American Politics," paper prepared for delivery at the 1977 Annual Meeting of the American Political Science Association, Washington, D.C., Sept. 1977.

62 [*Values of Federalists and anti-Federalists*]: Irving Kristol, ed., *The American Commonwealth* (Basic Books, 1976), esp. Martin Diamond, "The Declaration and the Constitution: Liberty, Democracy and the Founders," pp. 39–55; Jean Yarbrough, "Republicanism Reconsidered: Some Thoughts on the Foundation and Preservation of the American Republic," *Review of Politics*, Vol. 41, No. 1 (January 1979), pp. 61–95; George W. Carey and James McClellan, "Towards the Restoration of the American Political Tradition," *Journal of Politics*, Vol. 38, No. 3 (August 1976), pp. 110–27.

[*Jefferson on ward republics*]: Jefferson to Joseph C. Cabell, Feb. 2, 1816, quoted in Yarbrough, "Republicanism Reconsidered," p. 89.

63 [*Yarbrough on Jefferson's proposed local public forums*]: ibid., p. 90.

[*Virtue*]: John Agresto, "Liberty, Virtue and Republicanism," *Review of Politics*, Vol. 39, No. 4 (October 1977), pp. 473–504; Yarbrough, "Republicanism Reconsidered"; Douglass Adair, "Fame and the Founding Fathers," in Harold Trevor Colbourn, ed., *Fame and the Founding Fathers: Essays by Douglass Adair* (W. W. Norton, 1974), pp. 2–26.
    See, in general, Austin Ranney, " 'The Divine Science': Political Engineering in American Culture," *American Political Science Review*, Vol. 70, No. 1 (March 1976), pp. 140–48.

3. THE EXPERIMENT BEGINS

64 [*Washington informed of his election*]: Douglas Southall Freeman, *George Washington* (Charles Scribner's Sons, 1954), Vol. 6, p. 164.

[*Washington "oppressed with . . . anxious sensations"*]: Jared Sparks, ed., *The Writings of George Washington* (Little, Brown, 1858), p. 461. Quote is from missing diary entry for April 16, 1789.

[*Washington on Alexandria*]: Washington to Charles Cotesworth Pinckney, June 28, 1788, in John C. Fitzpatrick, ed., *The Writings of George Washington* (Government Printing Office, 1939), Vol. 30, p. 9. [*Washington forced to borrow money*]: John C. Fitzpatrick, ed. *The Diaries of George Washington, 1748–1799* (Houghton Mifflin, 1925), Vol. 4, p. 7.

[*Alexandria celebration*]: *Pennsylvania Packet*, April 23, 1789.

65 [*Washington's haste and preoccupation with the tasks ahead*]: Freeman, Vol. 6, pp. 167–68.

[*Crowd at Susquehanna crossing*]: ibid., p. 172. [*Ode at Trenton*]: ibid., pp. 175–76.

[*Washington on entry into New York*]: Washington Irving, *Life of George Washington* (Putnam, 1857), Vol. 4, p. 511.

66 [*Washington's inaugural suit*]: Frank Monaghan, "Notes on the Inaugural Journey and the Inaugural Ceremonies of George Washington as First President of the United States" (New York Public Library, 1939), passim.

[*Debate over protocol*]: James T. Flexner, *George Washington and the New Nation (1783–1793)* (Little, Brown, 1970), pp. 182–83.

[*Livingston announces "it is done"*]: Freeman, Vol. 6, p. 192.

67 [*Washington's Inaugural Address*]: Fitzpatrick, *Writings of Washington*, Vol. 30, pp. 281–96.

The Federalists Take Command

67 [*Washington's ambivalence about serving as President*]: Fitzpatrick, *Writings of Washington*, Vol. 30, passim.

[*Presidential election of 1788–89*]: Congressional Quarterly, *Presidential Elections Since 1789* (Congressional Quarterly, Inc., 1975); Merrill Jensen and Robert A. Becker, eds., *The Documentary History of the First Federal Elections* (University of Wisconsin Press, 1976), Vol. 1, p. xi.

68 [*Hamilton's interference in the vice-presidential election*]: Hamilton to James Wilson, Jan. 25, 1789, in Harold C. Syrett, ed., *The Papers of Alexander Hamilton* (Columbia University Press, 1962), Vol. 5, pp. 247–49; see also Hamilton to Theodore Sedgwick, Jan. 29, 1789, *ibid.*, pp. 250–51. [*Reaction of John Adams*]: Page Smith, *John Adams* (Doubleday, 1962), Vol. 2, pp. 759–60.

[*Electing the 1st Congress*]: Jensen and Becker, Vol. 1, esp. Chs. 1 and 2. [*Madison's election*]: James Madison to George Washington, Jan. 14, 1789, in Gaillard Hunt, ed., *The Writings of James Madison* (G. P. Putnam's Sons, 1904), Vol. 5, pp. 318–21; see also Madison to Thomas Jefferson, March 29, 1789, *ibid.*, pp. 333–38.

69 [*Pennsylvania elections*]: Jensen and Becker, pp. 227–429.

[*Washington on obtaining lodgings*]: Washington to Madison, March 30, 1789, Fitzpatrick, *Writings of Washington*, Vol. 30, pp. 254–56. [*Abigail Adams at Richmond Hill*]: Smith, p. 770.

[*Washington on Congress as "the first wheel of government"*]: draft of proposed address to Congress [April? 1789], in Fitzpatrick, *Writings of Washington*, Vol. 30, pp. 299–300.

[*Maclay vs. Adams on reference to President's address*]: Edgar S. Maclay, *Journal of William Maclay* (D. Appleton, 1890), pp. 10–11; Smith, pp. 750–51.

70 [*Washington on the judicial branch as keystone of the national polity*]: Washington to John Jay, Oct. 5, 1789, Fitzpatrick, *Writings of Washington*, Vol. 30, pp. 428–29. [*John Jay's early activities as Chief Justice*]: correspondence with Justice Cushing, Nov. and Dec. 1789, and Jay to Richard Law, March 10, 1790, John Jay Papers, Columbia University.

[*Organizing and manning the new government*]: see, in general, Leonard D. White, *The Federalists* (Macmillan, 1948).

71 [*Adams' denial of patronage to friends*]: Smith, p. 762. [*Washington on nepotism*]: Washington to Bushrod Washington, July 27, 1789, in Fitzpatrick, *Writings of Washington*, Vol. 30, p. 366.

[*Washington on national government being organized*]: Washington to Gouverneur Morris, Oct. 13, 1789, *ibid.*, p. 442.

[*Washington on reasons for his trip*]: *ibid.*, pp. 446–47. [*Basic sources for information on the trip*]: *ibid.*, pp. 450–56; Fitzpatrick, *Washington Diaries*, Vol. 4, pp. 20–52; William Spohn Baker, *Washington after the Revolution, 1784–1799* (Lippincott, 1898), pp. 150–61; Freeman, Vol. 6, pp. 240–45; Flexner, pp. 227–31.

72 [*Roads and taverns in New England, 1789*]: see esp. George F. Marlowe, *Coaching Roads of Old New England* (Macmillan, 1945), and Forbes and Eastman, *Taverns and*

Stagecoaches of Old New England (State Street Trust Co., 1954), 2 vols. See also the relevant portions of Fitzpatrick, *Washington Diaries.*

72 [*Ports and farmers*]: Rollin G. Osterweis, *Three Centuries of New Haven, 1638–1938* (Yale University Press, 1953), p. 171; Richard J. Purcell, *Connecticut in Transition* (American Historical Association and Oxford University Press, 1918), pp. 98–99, 120.

[*New Haven c. 1789*]: Purcell, pp. 120–21; Albert P. Van Dusen, *Connecticut* (Random House, 1961), p. 175. On the changing character of town politics in this period, see Edward M. Cook, Jr., *The Fathers of the Towns: Leadership and Community Structure in Eighteenth-Century New England* (Johns Hopkins University Press, 1976), esp. p. 191.

[*Slavery in Connecticut*]: Robert A. Warner, *New Haven Negroes: A Social History* (Yale University Press, 1940), p. 5.

[*Washington's remark at Wallingford, Connecticut*]: Fitzpatrick, *Washington Diaries,* Vol. 4, p. 26.

73 [*Colonel Wadsworth's "Woolen Manufactory"*]: William B. Weeden, *Economic and Social History of New England, 1620–1789* (Riverside Press, 1891), Vol. 2, p. 853.

[*Manufacturing in Hartford*]: Purcell, pp. 120–21, which comments as well on the state of manufacturing throughout Connecticut at this time.

[*Springfield and its arsenal*]: Weeden, Vol. 2, p. 792; Marlowe, p. 49.

[*Isaac Jenks's tavern*]: Marlowe, pp. 42–43. [*Washington quote on houses in the Connecticut Valley*]: Fitzpatrick, *Washington Diaries,* Vol. 4, p. 30.

[*Massachusetts agriculture during this period*]: Flexner, p. 229; James T. Adams, *New England in the Republic, 1776–1850* (Little, Brown, 1926), pp. 184, 186–88, 190. [*The small farm*]: Adams, p. 191.

[*The incident at the Boston town line*]: Justin Winsor, ed., *The Memorial History of Boston, 1630–1880* (Ticknor, 1886), Vol. 3, pp. 197, 573; for Washington's own remarks, see Fitzpatrick, *Washington Diaries,* Vol. 4, pp. 33–34, along with the appended footnotes.

74 [*Washington vs. Hancock*]: Fitzpatrick, *Writings of Washington,* Vol. 30, pp. 451–53; Baker, pp. 154–55. For a description of Hancock, see Winsor, Vol. 3, p. 201; for skepticism concerning his "gout," see Smith, Vol. 2, p. 782, and Harold and James Kirker, *Bulfinch's Boston, 1787–1817* (Oxford University Press, 1964), p. 104.

[*Life in Boston at the time of Washington's visit*]: Jean Pierre Brissot, "Boston in 1788," *Old South Leaflets* (The Directors of the Old South Work, n.d.), Vol. 6, pp. 2–10; Weeden, Vol. 2, pp. 848, 851–52, 863; Marjorie Drake Ross, *The Book of Boston: The Federal Period* (Hastings House, 1961), pp. 46, 49, 68; Samuel Eliot Morison, *The Maritime History of Massachusetts, 1783–1860* (Houghton Mifflin, Sentry Edition, 1961), pp. 30, 43.

[*Harvard in 1789*]: Brissot, pp. 7–8. [*Higher education in New England*]: "Education," *Dictionary of American History,* rev. ed. (Charles Scribner's Sons, 1976), Vol. 2, pp. 394–95, 397.

75 [*Washington on playing-card factory*]: Fitzpatrick, *Washington Diaries,* Vol. 4, p. 38. [*Shoe manufacturing in Massachusetts*]: B. E. Hazard, *Organization of the Boot and Shoe Industry* (1921), *passim.* [*Fishing and whaling*]: Morison, pp. 32, 134–35, 141, 396 (table). [*Commerce and trading in New England as a whole*]: Walter B. Smith and Arthur H. Cole, *Fluctuations in American Business, 1790–1860* (Harvard University Press, 1935), p. 4.

[*Cotton in Beverly*]: Robert W. Lovett, "The Beverly Cotton Manufactory: Or, Some New Light on an Early Cotton Mill," *Bulletin of the Business Historical Society,* Vol. 26, No. 4 (December 1952), pp. 220–37.

75 [*Washington on the "factory girls"*]: Fitzpatrick, *Washington Diaries*, Vol. 4, pp. 37–38.

[*Newburyport and Portsmouth in 1789*]: Joshua Coffin, *A Sketch of the History of Newbury, Newburyport, and West Newbury* (1845) (Peter E. Randall, 1977), pp. 260–61; Benjamin W. Labaree, *Patriots and Partisans: The Merchants of Newburyport, 1764–1815* (Harvard University Press, 1962), pp. 66–67, 70–71, 84, 89; Nathaniel Adams, *Annals of Portsmouth* (C. Norris, 1825), pp. 288–89.

[*Sources on New England shipbuilding*]: reports on the industry submitted to Secretary of the Treasury Hamilton; see esp. Joseph Whipple to Hamilton, Dec. 19, 1789, Syrett, Vol. 6, pp. 19–24; Benjamin Lincoln to Hamilton, Dec. 22, 1789, *ibid.*, pp. 27–31; and an unknown citizen of Massachusetts to Hamilton, Oct., 1789, *ibid.*, Vol. 5, pp. 479–81. See also J. T. Adams, p. 201.

[*New Hampshire industry*]: George D. Nash, *Issues in American Economic History* (D. C. Heath, 1964), p. 117; Rolla M. Tryon, *Household Manufactures in the United States, 1640–1860* (University of Chicago Press, 1917), p. 135.

[*Washington's visit to Andover*]: Fitzpatrick, *Washington Diaries*, Vol. 4, p. 47; see also the entries under "Phillips, Samuel" in *Dictionary of American Biography*, Dumas Malone, ed. (Charles Scribner's Sons, 1934), Vol. 14, p. 543, and *The National Cyclopedia of American Biography* (James T. White, 1900), Vol. 10, p. 94.

[*Phillips Academy in 1789*]: Mary E. Brown and Helen G. Brown, *The Story of John Adams, a New England Schoolmaster* (Charles Scribner's Sons, 1900), pp. 36, 45, 53–54.

76 [*The Lexington school*]: D. Hamilton Hurd, comp., *History of Middlesex County, Massachusetts* (J. W. Lewis, 1890), Vol. 2, p. 621. [*State of American schools in 1789*]: "Education," pp. 394–97.

[*Lexington c. 1789*]: Hurd, pp. 614, 630–31, 634, and Charles Hudson, *Abstract of the History of Lexington, Massachusetts* (T. R. Marvin & Son, 1876), p. 22.

The New Yorkers

76 [*Major sources on New York City, 1789–90*]: Sidney I. Pomerantz, *New York: An American City, 1783–1803* (Columbia University Press, 1938); Frank Monaghan and Marvin Lowenthal, *This Was New York* (Doubleday, Doran, 1943).

[*Federal Hall*]: Bruce Bliven, Jr., "Federal Hall" (National Park Service, 1975); Pomerantz, passim; Monaghan and Lowenthal, passim.

[*Washington's assurances against a military dictatorship*]: Address to the New York Legislature, June 26, 1775, Fitzpatrick, *Writings of Washington*, Vol. 3, p. 305.

[*Daily life in lower Manhattan*]: Monaghan and Lowenthal, passim, and sources cited below. Mrs. Ellen Yager assisted me in identifying sources and conducting research in New York City libraries and archives.

77 [*Washington on the trappings of office*]: quoted in Freeman, Vol. 6, p. 252.

[*Where leaders lived in New York City*]: Rufus Rockwell Wilson, *New York: Old and New* (Lippincott, 1909), Vol. 1, pp. 270–73.

78 [*Federal officials and employees*]: White, Ch. 24.

[*Samuel Provoost*]: James Grant Wilson, ed., *Memorial History of the City of New York* (New York History Co., 1893), Vol. 3, p. 100; Rev. Morgan Dix, *Trinity Church Bicentennial Celebration* (J. Pott, 1897), p. 31. On religious life generally in New York City, see Pomerantz, pp. 372–95.

78 [*New York City tavern life*]: W. Harrison Bayles, *Old Taverns of New York* (Frank Allaben Genealogical Co., 1915), pp. 346–47, 356–57, 376–77.

[*Social life and organization*]: Bayard Still, *Mirror for Gotham* (New York University Press, 1956), esp. pp. 58–69; the observer of "three distinct classes" is cited on p. 60 of this work.

[*Entertainment*]: Pomerantz, Chs. 8 and 10.

79 [*Competitive, factious background of New York politics*]: Patricia U. Bonomi, *A Factious People: Politics and Society in Colonial New York* (Columbia University Press, 1971), and sources cited therein.

80 [*New York merchants observing ships starting through the Narrows*]: Maxwell F. Marcuse, *This Was New York* (LIM Press, 1970), pp. 145–46. [*Visiting English actor on daily life of merchants*]: Hugh E. Macatamney, *Cradle Days of New York* (Drew & Lewis, 1909), p. 124; Still, p. 69.

[*Manufacturing in New York*]: Pomerantz, pp. 194–99.

[*Alleged Dutch exclusiveness*]: Macatamney, p. 124.

81 [*Jewish leadership*]: Pomerantz, pp. 386–87; *Encyclopaedia Judaica*, Vol. 12 (Macmillan, 1971), p. 1070.

[*Black leaders*]: *Dictionary of American Biography*, passim.

[*Tammany in 1789–90*]: Gustavus Myers, *The History of Tammany Hall* (published by the author, 1901); M. R. Werner, *Tammany Hall* (Doubleday, Doran, 1928); the initiation song is quoted from Werner, p. 12.

82 [*Tammany goals*]: Werner, p. 10.

The Federalist Thrust

83 [*John Adams on the need for ceremonial*]: Smith, p. 754.

[*Washington's display in New York City*]: Freeman, Vol. 6, pp. 226–27.

[*Mercantile interests among the Federalists*]: William Appleman Williams, *The Contours of American History* (World, 1961), pp. 149–62; see also Fred Moramarco, "Hamilton and the Historians: The Economic Program in Retrospect," *Midcontinent American Studies Journal*, Vol. 8, No. 1 (Spring 1967), pp. 34–43.

84 [*Madison's tariff proposals*]: "Speeches in the First Congress—First Session, Duties on Imports," Hunt, Vol. 5, pp. 339–55.

85 [*Machiavellian aspect of Hamilton*]: John C. Miller, *Alexander Hamilton: Portrait in Paradox* (Harper & Brothers, 1959), p. 227.

[*Sources of Hamilton's economic proposals, and earlier correspondence*]: Syrett, Vol. 5, pp. 439, 464–65, 538–57; *ibid.* (1962), Vol. 6, pp. 51–65; see also Miller, Ch. 16.

85–6 [*Jackson's attack*]: Broadus Mitchell, *Alexander Hamilton: The National Adventure* (Macmillan, 1962), p. 78. [*Madison's "desertion"*]: John C. Miller, *The Federalist Era* (Harper & Row, 1960), p. 41. On assumption of state debts, see Whitney K. Bates, "Northern Speculators and Southern State Debts: 1790," *William and Mary Quarterly*, Third Series, Vol. 19, No. 1 (January 1962), pp. 30–48.

86 [*Hamilton's banking policy*]: see in general Bray Hammond, *Banks and Politics in America* (Princeton University Press, 1957); Thomas Francis Gordon, *War on the Bank of the United States* (Burt Franklin, 1967); Herman E. Krooss, ed., *Documentary History of Banking and Currency in the United States* (McGraw-Hill, 1969), Vol. 1.

86 [*Text of Hamilton's report on a National Bank*]: Syrett, Vol. 7, pp. 236–342

87 [*John Fenno's poem*]: *Gazette of the United States*, Feb. 23, 1793, quoted in L. Michael Golden, "Precedent, Conflict, and Change: A Case Study of the National Banking System" (Williams College, 1978).

    [*Madison on Hamilton's national bank proposal, February 2, 1791*]: Hunt, Vol. 6, p. 36.

88 [*Jackson on the harmful effect of the bill*]: quoted in M. St. Clair Clarke and D. A. Hall, *Legislative and Documentary History of the Bank of the United States* (Gales and Seaton, 1832), p. 37.

    [*Hamilton's defense of the constitutionality of the bank bill*]: Syrett, Vol. 8, pp. 97–134.
    [*Washington's deliberateness*]: Miller, *The Federalist Era*, p. 58.

    [*House request for Treasury Plan*]: *The Debates and Proceedings in the Congress of the United States* (Gales and Seaton, 1834), Vol. 1, p. 1058.

89 [*Hamilton's inventory*]: Mitchell, Ch. 8; see in general Williams, pp. 162–70.

    [*Proposed anti-civil-libertarian constitutional amendments*]: Miller, *The Federalist Era*, p. 21.

90 [*Adoption of the Bill of Rights*]: See in general Irving Brant, *The Bill of Rights* (Bobbs-Merrill, 1965); Rutland.

    [*Newspapers in 1790*]: Donald H. Stewart, *The Opposition Press of the Federalist Period* (State University of New York Press, 1969), Ch. 1.

91 [*Washington's mediation between Hamilton and Jefferson*]: Miller, *The Federalist Era*, p. 95; Fitzpatrick, *Writings of Washington*, Vol. 32, pp. 130–31, 185–86.

    [*Lack of theoretical understanding of potential role of parties in a republic*]: Richard Hofstadter, *The Idea of a Party System* (University of California Press, 1969), passim; Daniel Sisson, *The American Revolution of 1800* (Alfred A. Knopf, 1974), esp. Ch. 2.

    [*Jefferson and Madison's "botanical" expedition of 1791*]: James MacGregor Burns, *The Deadlock of Democracy* (Prentice-Hall, 1963), pp. 26–27, and sources cited therein.

92 [*Jefferson urges Washington to stay on*]: Jefferson to President, May 23, 1792, in Paul Leicester Ford, ed., *The Writings of Thomas Jefferson* (G. P. Putnam's Sons, 1895), Vol. 6, p. 5.

    [*Coinage with figure of liberty instead of Washington*]: Miller, *The Federalist Era*, p. 8.

The Deadly Pattern

92–3 [*Washington's birthday ball*]: James T. Flexner, *George Washington: Anguish and Farewell (1793–1799)* (Little, Brown, 1969), pp. 13–14. ["*Tranquility reigns*"]: Freeman, Vol. 6, p. 321. [National Gazette *attack*]: Flexner, *Anguish and Farewell*, p. 15.

93 ["*Invitation*" *to settle in the Southwest*]: Madison to Washington, March 26, 1789 (enclosure), in Hunt, Vol. 5, pp. 331–33.

95–6 [*John Quincy Adams on policies toward Indians*]: quoted in George Dewey Harmon, *Sixty Years of Indian Affairs* (University of North Carolina Press, 1941), p. 362. [*President Washington's policy*]: Francis Paul Prucha, *American Indian Policy in the Formative Years* (Harvard University Press, 1962), esp. pp. 43–50. [*Wars with Indians*]: Keith Irvine, general ed., *Encyclopedia of Indians in the Americas* (Scholarly Press, 1974).

96 [*Red Jacket's remarks*]: Katharine C. Turner, *Red Men Calling on the Great White Father* (University of Oklahoma Press, 1951), p. 12. [*Aupaumut's plea*]: *ibid.*, p. 25. [*Image on medal*]: *ibid.*, p. 15.

See also Angie Debo, *A History of the Indians of the United States* (University of Oklahoma Press, 1970); Dale Van Every, *Disinherited: The Lost Birthright of the American Indian* (William Morrow, 1966).

97–8 [*Congressmen oppose excise*]: Leland D. Baldwin, *Whiskey Rebels* (University of Pittsburgh Press, 1939), pp. 64–65. [*Washington on minority threat*]: quoted in John A. Carroll and Mary W. Ashworth, *George Washington*. Vol. 7: *First in Peace* (Charles Scribner's Sons, 1957), pp. 186–87. [*Bradford described*]: *ibid.*, p. 185. [*Role of Democratic societies in Whiskey Rebellion*]: Eugene Perry Link, *Democratic-Republican Societies, 1790–1800* (Octagon Books, 1973), pp. 145–48 and passim.

98–9 [*Washington on Republicanism*]: Fitzpatrick, *Writings of Washington*, Vol. 34, pp. 98–99. [*Washington to Ball*]: *ibid.*, Vol. 33, p. 506. ["*Self-created societies*"]: *ibid.*, Vol. 34, p. 29. [*Jefferson on whiskey campaign*]: Dumas Malone, *Jefferson and His Time* (Little, Brown, 1962), Vol. III, p. 188. [*Jefferson to Washington*]: Entry for Aug. 2, 1793, in Thomas Jefferson, "The Anas," in Ford, Vol. I, p. 253. [*Madison on speech*]: Hunt, Vol. 6, p. 223.

Divisions Abroad and at Home

99 [*Another feather in liberty's cap*]: Boston *Gazette*, Sept. 7, 1789, quoted in Charles Downer Hazen, *Contemporary American Opinion of the French Revolution* (Johns Hopkins University Press, 1897), p. 142 (Johns Hopkins University Studies in Historical and Political Science, Extra Vol. 16).

[*Jefferson on the French Revolution*]: Jefferson to Diodati, Aug. 3, 1789, Julian P. Boyd, ed., *The Papers of Thomas Jefferson* (Princeton University Press, 1958), Vol. 15, p. 326.

100 [*Adams on French Revolution*]: quoted in Smith, Vol. 2, pp. 785–86.

[*Hamilton on thinking in English*]: Hamilton conversation with George Beckwith, Oct. 1789, Syrett, Vol. 5, p. 483. [*Cause of France as cause of man*]: Republican leader quoted in Miller, *The Federalist Era*, p. 130.

[*John Adams on later revolutionary developments*]: quoted in Hazen, p. 254. [*Jefferson on the higher stakes*]: quoted in Miller, *The Federalist Era*, p. 127. [*Celebration of the executions of king and queen*]: Hazen, pp. 183, 258.

[*Washington on transcending party animosities (in Inaugural Address)*]: Fitzpatrick, *Writings of Washington*, Vol. 30, p. 294. [*Washington on "Internal dissensions" and pleas for harmony*]: Washington to Jefferson, Aug. 23, 1792, and Washington to Hamilton, Aug. 26, 1792, *ibid.*, Vol. 32, pp. 128–34.

101 [*Hamilton as "deeply injured party"*]: Hamilton to Washington, Sept. 9, 1792, in John C. Hamilton, ed., *The Works of Alexander Hamilton* (John F. Trow, 1851), Vol. 4, p. 303.

[*Hamilton on Madison as little acquainted with the world*]: Hamilton to George Beckwith, Oct. 1789, in Syrett, Vol. 5, p. 488. [*Jefferson's appeal to Madison*]: Letter of July 7, 1793, Ford, Vol. 6, p. 338.

[*Citizen Genêt's activities*]: Harry Ammon, *The Genêt Mission* (W. W. Norton, 1973); see also, especially for domestic political implications: Harry Ammon, "The Genêt Mission and the Development of American Political Parties," *Journal of American History*, Vol. 52, No. 4 (March 1966), pp. 725–41.

103 [*The Jay Treaty*]: Jerald A. Combs, *The Jay Treaty* (University of California Press, 1970). [*Washington on reception of the Jay Treaty*]: Private letter to Hamilton, July 29, 1795, Fitzpatrick, *Writings of Washington*, Vol. 34, p. 262.

104 [*Washington on his knowledge of the Constitution*]: address to the House of Representatives, March 30, 1796, in Worthington C. Ford, ed., *The Writings of George Washington* (G. P. Putnam's Sons, 1892), Vol. 13, pp. 177–80. [*Madison's response*]: speech in Congress, April 6, 1796, Hunt, Vol. 6, p. 272.

[*Other sources*]: Paul A. Varg, *Foreign Policies of the Founding Fathers* (Michigan State University Press, 1963); Alexander DeConde, *Entangling Alliance* (Duke University Press, 1958); Gilbert L. Lycan, *Alexander Hamilton and American Foreign Policy* (University of Oklahoma Press, 1970); Albert H. Bowman, "Jefferson, Hamilton and American Foreign Policy," *Political Science Quarterly*, Vol. 71, No. 1 (March 1956), pp. 18–41.

4. THE TRIALS OF LIBERTY

106 [*John Adams in Quincy*]: Page Smith, *John Adams* (Doubleday, 1962), Vol. 2, pp. 894–97. [*Thomas Jefferson at Monticello*]: Nathan Schachner, *Thomas Jefferson* (Appleton-Century-Crofts, 1951), p. 576.

107 [*Jefferson's alleged lack of ambition to govern men and his hope to come in second to Adams*]: Jefferson to Rutledge, December 27, 1796, in Paul Leicester Ford, ed., *The Writings of Thomas Jefferson* (G. P. Putnam's Sons, 1896), Vol. 7, p. 94.

108 [*Hamilton's effort to "waste" Adams' support*]: Leonard Baker, *John Marshall: A Life in Law* (Macmillan, 1974), p. 212; George A. Billias, *Elbridge Gerry* (McGraw-Hill, 1976), pp. 249–53.

[*Bache on Washington*]: quoted in Smith, p. 909.

109 [*Washington on criticism of himself*]: Letter to Thomas Jefferson, July 6, 1796, in John C. Fitzpatrick, ed., *The Writings of George Washington* (Government Printing Office, 1939), Vol. 35, pp. 118–22.

[*President John Adams*]: Zoltán Haraszti, *John Adams and the Prophets of Progress* (Harvard University Press, 1952); John Adams, *Defence of the Constitutions of Government of the United States of America* (1787), 2 vols.; John Adams Papers, Massachusetts Historical Society, Boston; Smith, passim.

[*Adams' view of liberty*]: Russell Kirk, *The Conservative Mind* (Henry Regnery, 1953), pp. 86–87.

Philadelphians: The Experimenters

110 [*Philadelphia background*]: Louis B. Wright, *The Atlantic Frontier* (Alfred A. Knopf, 1947); Frederick B. Tolles, *Meeting House and Counting House* (University of North Carolina Press, 1948); Carl Bridenbaugh, *Cities in Revolt* (Alfred A. Knopf, 1955); Carl and Jessica Bridenbaugh, *Rebels and Gentlemen* (Reynal & Hitchcock, 1942); James Lemon, "Urbanization and Development of Eighteenth Century Southeastern Pennsylvania and Adjacent Delaware," *William and Mary Quarterly*, Third Series, Vol. 24, No. 4 (October 1967), pp. 501–42.

[*Adams on City Tavern*]: Smith, p. 168.

[*Philadelphia's "firm adherence" to liberty*]: Richard B. Morris, "Independence," Government Printing Office (for National Park Service), 1976.

[*The historic city*]: Richard B. Morris, "Independence" (Government Printing Office, 1976). [*Franklin Court*]: Robert H. Wilson, *Franklin Court* (Swarthmore Press, 1976).

111 [*Minister quoted on outspoken laborers*]: Jacob Duché, quoted in Bridenbaugh, p. 99.

[*William Penn on education*]: quoted in Wright, p. 245.

112 [*The Philadelphia press*]: Margaret Woodbury, *Public Opinion in Philadelphia, 1789–1801* (Seaman Printery, 1919).

113 [*Aurora editor on no news in Philadelphia*]: quoted in *ibid.*, pp. 7–8.

113 [*William Penn on need of civil liberties*]: quoted in Jack P. Greene, ed., *Settlements to Society, 1584–1763* (McGraw-Hill, 1966), p. 170, reprinted from *Minutes* of the Provincial Council of Pennsylvania, Vol. 2, pp. 56–59.

114 [*Du Bois on the condition of blacks in Philadelphia*]: W. E. Burghardt Du Bois, *The Philadelphia Negro* (first published 1899) (Benjamin Blom, 1967), pp. 11, 15.

115 [*Income distribution in Philadelphia*]: Richard G. Miller, *Philadelphia—The Federalist City* (Kennikat Press, 1976), Ch. 1.

[*Division of the classes into "the cream, the new milk . . ."*]: quoted in Thomas Scharf and Thompson Westcott, *History of Philadelphia, 1609–1884* (L. H. Everts, 1884), Vol. 2, p. 910; see also Bruce Laurie, *Working People of Philadelphia, 1800–1850* (Temple University Press, 1980).

[*Warner on the private search for wealth*]: Sam Bass Warner, Jr., *The Private City* (University of Pennsylvania Press, 1968), p. x.

116 [*Franklin on the pains of the moment*]: quoted in Bernard Fay, *Franklin: The Apostle of Modern Times* (Little, Brown, 1929), p. 511.

[*Franklin on making experiments*]: quoted in Verner W. Crane, *Benjamin Franklin and a Rising People* (Little, Brown, 1954), p. 201.

117 [*Tom Paine and his fellow radicals*]: Eric Foner, *Tom Paine and Revolutionary America* (Oxford University Press, 1976), passim; Philip S. Foner, ed., *The Complete Writings of Thomas Paine* (Citadel, 1945), 2 vols.; see also Joseph Dorfman, "The Economic Philosophy of Thomas Paine," *Political Science Quarterly*, Vol. 53, No. 3 (September 1938), pp. 372–86; Howard Penniman, "Thomas Paine—Democrat," *American Political Science Review*, Vol. 37, No. 2 (April 1943), pp. 244–62.

[*Bailyn on Paine's* Common Sense]: Bernard Bailyn, "Common Sense," *American Heritage*, Vol. 25, No. 1 (December 1973), p. 36.

[*English constitutional thought and the social and political balances*]: aside from the standard editions of Hobbes, Locke, Filmer, etc., and of secondary and tertiary thinkers such as Charles Herle and Marchamont Nedham, see W. B. Gwyn, *The Meaning of the Separation of Powers* (Tulane University Press, 1965) and M. J. C. Vile, *Constitutionalism and the Separation of Powers* (Clarendon Press, 1967).

118 [*Nedham on freedom*]: quoted in Gwyn, p. 22.

[*Farmers and "leathern aprons" being more reasonable*]: quoted in Gordon S. Wood, *The Creation of the American Republic* (University of North Carolina Press, 1969), p. 86.

[*Foner on Paine's rejection of governmental checks and balances*]: Eric Foner, p. 91.

[*The colonial gentry's loss of power*]: Miller, p. 20.

119 [*Radical and anti-radical debate over the Pennsylvania constitution of 1776*]: quoted in Wood, pp. 442, 431, 441, 430; the last two citations refer to quotations of Benjamin Rush.

[*Pennsylvania's struggle over the Constitution of 1776*]: Miller, Ch. 2.

Quasi-War Abroad

120 [*Foreign affairs at the time John Adams entered the presidency*]: Alexander DeConde, *The Quasi-War* (Charles Scribner's Sons, 1966), Ch. 1. See also Alfred L. Burt, *The United States, Great Britain and British North America, 1783–1812* (Yale University Press, 1940).

[*Adams' inaugural warning*]: Walter Lowrie and Matthew St. Clair Clarke, eds., *American State Papers, Foreign Relations* (Gales and Seaton, 1832), Vol. 1, p. 39.

121 [*Adams' Cabinet*]: Manning J. Dauer, *The Adams Federalists* (Johns Hopkins University Press, 1953), esp. pp. 121–24; Gerard H. Clarfield, *Timothy Pickering and American*

Diplomacy, 1795–1800 (University of Missouri Press, 1969); Bernard C. Steiner, *The Life and Correspondence of James McHenry* (Burrows Brothers, 1907).

121 [*Hamilton's advising of Adams' Cabinet*]: Harold C. Syrett, ed., *The Papers of Alexander Hamilton* (Columbia University Press, 1962), Vol. 20 (fall 1796 and early winter 1797).

[*Mission of Pinckney, Marshall, and Gerry*]: Dauer, pp. 124 ff.; DeConde, Ch. 1. [*On Elbridge Gerry*]: Billias; Samuel Eliot Morison, "Elbridge Gerry, Gentleman-Democrat," *By Land and By Sea* (Alfred A. Knopf, 1953). [*John Marshall*]: Baker; [*C. C. Pinckney*]: Marvin R. Zahniser, *Charles Cotesworth Pinckney* (University of North Carolina Press, 1967).

121-2 [*Talleyrand as a "cloven footed Devil"*]: quoted in DeConde, p. 179. [*Pinckney's response to Talleyrand*]: Alexander DeConde, *A History of American Foreign Policy* (Charles Scribner's Sons, 1963), p. 68; Lowrie and Clarke, Vol. 2, pp. 161–62.

122 [*John and Abigail Adams at home*]: Smith, Ch. 72.

124 [*Pickering on Gerry*]: John C. Miller, *The Federalist Era* (Harper & Row, 1960), p. 214.

[*Adams' message to Congress*]: Lowrie and Clarke, Vol. 2, p. 199.

[*Hamilton as Washington's second-in-command*]: see Washington to the Secretary of War, July 4, 1798, Fitzpatrick, Vol. 36, pp. 304–11, plus other references in the Washington and Hamilton papers.

125 [*John Adams' gloomiest summer*]: Smith, p. 985.

Semi-Repression at Home

125 [*Political invective and extremism of 1790s*]: James Morton Smith, *Freedom's Fetters* (Cornell University Press, 1956), pp. 101–4, 116.

126 [*Naturalization Act*]: ibid., p. 435. Appendix includes entire act. [*Federalist fear of immigrants*]: John C. Miller, *Crisis in Freedom* (Little, Brown, 1951), p. 44. [*Jefferson denounces Alien Bill*]: Smith, *Fetters*, p. 53.

[*Sedition Act*]: ibid., pp. 441–42. Complete act in appendix.

127 [*Ardent ambition of Harrison Gray Otis*]: Samuel E. Morison, *Harrison Gray Otis, 1765–1848: The Urbane Federalist* (Houghton Mifflin, 1969), p. 101.

[*Washington supports acts in general*]: Marshall Smelser, "George Washington and the Alien and Sedition Acts," *American Historical Review*, Vol. 59, No. 2 (January 1954), pp. 322–34, esp. p. 333; see also Washington to Alexander Spotswood, Nov. 22, 1798, Fitzpatrick, Vol. 37, pp. 23–24.

[*Hamilton's attitude toward Sedition Act*]: John C. Miller, *Alexander Hamilton: Portrait in Paradox* (Harper & Brothers, 1959), p. 484. [*Adams and Jefferson on act*]: ibid.

128 [*Bill induces some foreigners to leave*]: Frank M. Anderson, "The Enforcement of the Alien and Sedition Laws," *Annual Report of the American Historical Association, 1912*, pp. 115–26.

[*Abigail Adams resents Bache*]: Smith, *Fetters*, p. 9.

[*Act enforced in New England*]: ibid., p. 187. [*High percentage of convictions*]: Leonard W. Levy, *Legacy of Suppression* (Belknap Press, 1960), p. 131.

[*Bache case*]: Smith, *Fetters*, pp. 188–204, quoted at pp. 192, 198, 203.

129 [*Baldwin case*]: ibid., p. 271, italics added. [*Newark newspaper on liberty*]: ibid., p. 272.

[*Cooper case*]: Miller, *Crisis*, pp. 202–10. [*Adams on Cooper's "libel"*]: Smith, *Fetters*, p. 311.

130 [*Federalists on Sedition Act*]: Miller, *The Federalist Era*, p. 231.

130 [*Debate over constitutionality of Alien and Sedition Acts*]: see Mark D. Howe, review of Smith's *Freedom's Fetters*, in *William and Mary Quarterly*, Third Series, Vol. 13, No. 4 (October 1956), pp. 573–76.

131 [Kentucky Gazette *calls for mass meeting*]: James M. Smith, "The Grass Roots Origins of the Kentucky Resolution," *William and Mary Quarterly*, Third Series, Vol. 27, No. 2 (April 1970), p. 222.

132 [*Jefferson on nullification of assumed, undelegated powers*]: Schachner, Vol. 2, p. 611. [*Smith on "practical politics"*]: Smith, "Grass Roots," p. 239.

[*Virginia resolution*]: Irving Brant, *James Madison: Father of the Constitution, 1787–1800* (Bobbs-Merrill, 1950), p. 461.

[*Central argument of the resolutions*]: Frank M. Anderson, "Contemporary Opinion of the Virginia and Kentucky Resolutions," *American Historical Review*, Vol. 5, No. 2 (December 1899), pp. 225–52.

133 [*Washington on Virginia and Kentucky Resolutions*]: Fitzpatrick, Vol. 37, p. 87 (confidential letter to Patrick Henry, Jan. 15, 1799). [*Abigail Adams on "mad" resolutions*]: Smith, *John Adams*, Vol. 2, p. 998. [*Hamilton suggests sending troops*]: Hamilton to Theodore Sedgwick, Feb. 2, 1799, Syrett, Vol. 22, pp. 452–53.
    See also Richard Hofstadter, *The Idea of a Party System* (University of California Press, 1969), Chs. 2 and 3; Richard Buel, Jr., "Freedom of the Press in Revolutionary America: The Evolution of Libertarianism, 1760–1820," in Bernard Bailyn and John B. Hench, eds., *The Press and the American Revolution* (American Antiquarian Society, 1980), pp. 59–97.

The Ventures of the First Decade

133 [*George Washington's death*]: John C. Fitzpatrick, ed., *The Diaries of George Washington* (Houghton Mifflin, 1925), Vol. 4, p. 320; James Thomas Flexner, *Washington: The Indispensable Man* (Little, Brown, 1969), pp. 392, 396–402.

134 [*Origins and early shaping of the American party system*]: Major sources consulted include: Hofstadter; Roy F. Nichols, *The Invention of the American Political Parties* (Macmillan, 1967); Noble E. Cunningham, Jr., *The Jeffersonian Republicans* (University of North Carolina Press, 1957); Joseph Charles, *The Origins of the American Party System* (Institute of Early American History and Culture, 1956); Morton Borden, *Parties and Politics in the Early Republic, 1789–1815* (Thomas Y. Crowell, 1967); William Nisbet Chambers, *Political Parties in a New Nation* (Oxford University Press, 1963); a collection of essays, Norman K. Risjord, *The Early American Party System* (Harper & Row, 1969).

135 [*Jefferson on not going to heaven but with a party*]: Jefferson to Francis Hopkinson, March 13, 1789, Ford, Vol. 5, pp. 75–78.

136 [*Rise of national parties in Congress*]: John F. Hoadley, "The Emergence of Political Parties in Congress, 1789–1803," *American Political Science Review*, Vol. 74, No. 3 (September 1980), pp. 757–79; Rudolph M. Bell, *Party and Faction in American Politics: The House of Representatives, 1789–1801* (Greenwood Press, 1973); Mary P. Ryan, "Party Formation in the United States Congress, 1789 to 1796: A Quantitative Analysis," *William and Mary Quarterly*, Third Series, Vol. 28, No. 4 (October 1971), pp. 523–42. Cf. Ronald P. Formisano, "Federalists and Republicans: Parties, Yes—System, No," typescript, 1980, 62 pp.

[*Politics of deference*]: Ronald P. Formisano, "Deferential-Participant Politics: The Early Republic's Political Culture, 1789–1840," *American Political Science Review*, Vol. 68, No. 2 (June 1974), pp. 473–87; and in one state, Richard R. Beeman, *The Old Dominion and the New Nation, 1788–1801* (University Press of Kentucky, 1972).

137 [*Democratic and Republican societies*]: Eugene P. Link, *Democratic-Republican Societies, 1790–1800* (Columbia University Press, 1942).

137 [*Washington on the Democratic societies*]: quoted in Miller, *The Federalist Era*, p. 161.

138 [*Case of Matthew Lyon, the "Spitting Lyon"*]: Henry Adams, *The Life of Albert Gallatin* (Lippincott, 1879), pp. 191–92; Miller, *The Federalist Era*, pp. 208–9.

139 [*The Virginia and Kentucky resolutions as contradiction of two-party strategy*]: James MacGregor Burns, *The Deadlock of Democracy* (Prentice-Hall, 1963), pp. 31–32.

[*Manning's tract*]: William Manning, *The Key of Libberty* (The Manning Association, 1922). On Manning himself, see Foreword to this volume by Samuel Eliot Morison.

140 [*Idea of America as an experiment*]: Arthur Schlesinger, Jr., Address to the American Historical Association, Washington, D.C., Dec. 29, 1976, reprinted under the title "America: Experiment or Destiny?" *American Historical Review*, Vol. 82, No. 3 (June 1977), pp. 505–22, quoted at p. 514.

[*Patrick Henry on "work too great for human wisdom"*]: quoted in Benjamin R. Barber, "The Compromised Republic: Public Purposelessness in America" (Kenyon Public Affairs Forum, Kenyon College, 1976), p. 6.

[*Impossibility of one code of laws*]: ibid.

[*Barber on experiment*]: ibid., p. 9.

[*Madison on lessons of experience*]: ibid.

142 [*French traveler on slaves*]: J. P. Brissot de Warville, *New Travels in the United States of America* (J. S. Jordan), p. 284.

[*Polish poet at Mount Vernon*]: Julian Niemcewicz, quoted in Herbert Aptheker, *American Negro Slave Revolts* (Columbia University Press, 1943), p. 125.

143 [*Abigail Adams on women as "Lordess"*]: quoted in Smith, *John Adams*, Vol. 2, p. 1006.

[*John Adams on the subordination of women and children*]: ibid., pp. 1016–17.

[*John Randolph's credo*]: quoted in Robert Dawidoff, *The Education of John Randolph* (W. W. Norton, 1979), p. 32.

144 [*Washington on religion and morality*]: Fitzpatrick, *Writings of Washington*, Vol. 35, p. 229.

[*William Manning on education*]: Manning, pp. 61, 20–21.

Showdown: The Election of 1800

144 [*Jefferson to Aaron Burr on the "Eastern" states*]: Jefferson to Burr, June 17, 1797, Ford, Vol. 7, pp. 147–48.

145 [*Jefferson on laying purpose and pen to the cause*]: Jefferson to James Madison, Feb. 5, 1799, ibid., p. 344.

[*Intra-party factionalism*]: Daniel Sisson, *The American Revolution of 1800* (Alfred A. Knopf, 1974), pp. 363 ff.

146 [*Hamilton on Adams' pardon of Fries*]: Miller, *Alexander Hamilton*, p. 507.

[*Adams to McHenry on Hamilton*]: quoted in Smith, *John Adams*, pp. 1027–28.

147 [*Burr's election activities*]: Burns, p. 34.

[*Jefferson on role of the central states*]: Jefferson to Madison, March 4, 1800, Ford, Vol. 7, p. 434.

[*Jefferson's refusal to answer "lies"*]: Jefferson to James Monroe, May 26, 1800, ibid., p. 448.

148 [*Marching women and children to the polls*]: Miller, *The Federalist Era*, p. 264.

148 [*Hamilton on not being overscrupulous*]: Hamilton to John Jay, May 7, 1800, in Henry Cabot Lodge, *The Works of Alexander Hamilton,* Constitutional Edition (G. P. Putnam's Sons, [1917]), Vol. 10, pp. 371–74; Frank Monaghan, *John Jay: Defender of Liberty* (Bobbs-Merrill, 1935), pp. 419–21.

[*Electioneering in 1800*]: Burns, p. 34.

The section on Gabriel's revolt of 1800 was drafted jointly by the author and Stewart Burns.

[*Gabriel's revolt*]: See in general Aptheker, pp. 219–26; Nicholas Halasz, *The Rattling Chains* (David McKay, 1966), pp. 87–100; Thomas W. Higginson, *Black Rebellion* (Arno Press, 1969), pp. 185–214; Gerald W. Mullin, *Flight and Rebellion: Slave Resistance in Eighteenth-Century Virginia* (Oxford University Press, 1972), passim; Willie Lee Rose, *A Documentary History of Slavery in North America* (Oxford University Press, 1976), pp. 107–14.

[*"Othello" on liberty*]: Carter G. Woodson, ed., *Negro Orators and Their Orations* (Associated Publishers, 1925), pp. 14–15.

149 [*Du Bois on "the Preacher"*]: quoted in Eugene D. Genovese, *Roll, Jordan, Roll: The World the Slaves Made* (Pantheon Books, 1974), p. 258.

[*Black resistance and white controls*]: Aptheker, pp. 140–49; Raymond A. Bauer and Alice H. Bauer, "Day to Day Resistance to Slavery," in Robert V. Haynes, ed., *Blacks in White America before 1865* (David McKay, 1972), pp. 235–57.

[*Gabriel Prosser described*]: Aptheker, p. 219. [*Election of leaders by slaves*]: Mullin, p. 148.

150 [*Rebel leader on right to fight for liberty*]: Aptheker, p. 220. [*Brother Martin quotes Scripture*]: Rose, p. 114.

[*Rebels to spare those "friendly to liberty"*]: ibid.

151 [*Insurrection organized on "true French plan"*]: Higginson, p. 199. [*Monroe seeks advice*]: Monroe to Thomas Jefferson, Sept. 15, 1800, in Stanislaus M. Hamilton, ed., *The Writings of James Monroe* (G. P. Putnam's Sons, 1900), Vol. 3, p. 209.

[*Jefferson on execution of rebels*]: Jefferson to James Monroe, Sept. 20, 1800, Ford, Vol. 7, pp. 457–58.

[*Monroe on Gabriel's stoicism*]: Monroe to Colonel Thomas Newton, Oct. 5, 1800, Hamilton, Vol. 3, p. 213. [*Rebel on endeavor for liberty*]: Aptheker, p. 224.

[*Story about Adams' mistresses*]: Smith, *John Adams,* p. 1034.

[*Invective against Jefferson in 1800 campaign*]: Charles O. Lerche, Jr., "Jefferson and the Election of 1800: A Case Study in the Political Smear," *William and Mary Quarterly,* Third Series, Vol. 5, No. 4 (January 1948), pp. 467–91; see also Cunningham, p. 239.

152 [*Jefferson's political stands during election of 1800*]: Jefferson to Elbridge Gerry, Jan. 26, 1799, Ford, Vol. 7, pp. 327–29.

153 [*George Cabot to Hamilton, on Burr and Jefferson*]: letter of Aug. 10, 1800, Syrett, Vol. 25, pp. 63–64.

[*Miller on the feeling for Burr*]: Miller, *The Federalist Era,* p. 269.

[*Jefferson's letters after receiving election results*]: Jefferson to Robert R. Livingston, Dec. 14, 1800, Ford, Vol. 7, pp. 462–66; Jefferson to Aaron Burr, Dec. 15, 1800, and Feb. 1, 1801, *ibid.,* pp. 466–68 and 485–86, resp.

[*Jefferson as a moderate*]: Sisson, p. 407.

[*Hamilton on Burr*]: quoted in Miller, *The Federalist Era,* p. 270.

154 [*Jefferson on the Federalist effort to "debauch" Burr*]: Jefferson to Mary Jefferson Eppes, Jan. 4, 1801, Ford, Vol. 7, p. 478.

[*Burr and the election of 1800*]: works cited above; Sisson; John S. Pancake, "Aaron Burr: Would-be Usurper," *William and Mary Quarterly*, Third Series, Vol. 8, No. 2 (April 1951), pp. 204–13.

[*Marshall's angling toward presidency in 1800 elections*]: Albert J. Beveridge, *The Life of John Marshall* (Houghton Mifflin, 1916), Vol. 2, pp. 540–43.

[*Jefferson's indirect assurances to Federalists about his presidency*]: Jefferson to Benjamin Smith Barton, Feb. 14, 1801, Ford, Vol. 7, pp. 489–90; Jefferson Papers, Library of Congress, Vol. 109, p. 18739; Matthew L. Davis, *Memoirs of Aaron Burr* (Harper & Brothers, 1858), Vol. 2, pp. 129–33; Schachner, p. 658.

155 [*Jefferson on the "revolution" of 1800*]: quoted in Sisson, p. 21.

5. JEFFERSONIAN LEADERSHIP

159 [*Conrad & McMunn's boardinghouse*]: Dumas Malone, *Jefferson the President* (Little, Brown, 1970), pp. 3, 29; James Sterling Young, *The Washington Community, 1800–1828* (Columbia University Press, 1966), Ch. 5, esp. pp. 100–1.

[*Jefferson as "all ends and angles"*]: Marshall Smelser, *The Democratic Republic* (Harper & Row, 1968), p. 1.

[*Jefferson's Inaugural Address*]: Paul Leicester Ford, ed., *The Writings of Thomas Jefferson* (G. P. Putnam's Sons, 1897), Vol. 8, pp. 1–6.

160 [*John Marshall's Inaugural Day letter to Charles Pinckney*]: quoted in Leonard Baker, *John Marshall: A Life in Law* (Macmillan, 1974), pp. 359–60.

161 [*Reactions by opposition leaders and publicists to Jefferson's assumption of office and Inaugural Address*]: Malone, pp. 4–5; Smelser, pp. 18–19.

[*Jefferson on the "sprig of grass"*]: quoted in James MacGregor Burns, *The Deadlock of Democracy* (Prentice-Hall, 1963), p. 25; see general sources quoted therein, in Sources, on Jefferson. I have used occasional sentences or phrases from this work in describing Jefferson.

162 [*Smelser on liberty as Jefferson's guiding star*]: Smelser, p. 13.

163 [*Celebrations of Jefferson's inaugural*]: Malone, pp. 29–32.

"The Eyes of Humanity Are Fixed on Us"

164 [*Jefferson on the newness of things*]: Jefferson to Joseph Priestley, March 21, 1801, Ford, Vol. 8, p. 22.

[*Jefferson on the storm through which the "Argosie" had passed*]: Jefferson to John Dickinson, March 6, 1801, *ibid.*, p. 7.

[*Jefferson on the "event of our experiment"*]: Jefferson to Governor Hall, July 6, 1802, *ibid.*, p. 156.

[*Jefferson's attempt to heal party schisms while expecting new opposition to arise from within Republican ranks*]: Jefferson to John Dickinson, July 23, 1801, *ibid.*, pp. 75–77; Jefferson to Wilson C. Nicholas, March 26, 1805, *ibid.*, pp. 348–49; Jefferson to Thomas Cooper, July 9, 1807, *ibid.*, Vol. 9, pp. 102–3.

[*Jefferson's desire to unite Federalists and Republicans he felt he could win to his purpose*]: see Jefferson to Horatio Gates, March 8, 1801, *ibid.*, Vol. 8, pp. 11–12.

165 [*Jefferson's characterizations of his high Federalist adversaries*]: *ibid.*, pp. 41, 147, 169.

165 [*Jefferson on separating "patriotic" Federalists from their congressional leaders*]: Jefferson to Thomas Lomax, Feb. 25, 1801, *ibid.*, Vol. 7, p. 500. [*Jefferson on avoiding shocking Federalist feelings*]: Jefferson to William B. Giles, March 23, 1801, *ibid.*, Vol. 8, p. 26. [*Jefferson on the "Essex Junto"*]: Jefferson to Levi Lincoln, July 11, 1801, *ibid.*, p. 67. [*Jefferson to Du Pont de Nemours on consolidating great body of people*]: *ibid.*, Jan. 18, 1802, p. 126 n.

[*Jefferson on likely extinction of Federalist party*]: Jefferson to Du Pont de Nemours, Jan. 18, 1802, *ibid.*

[*Relationship of Jefferson and Madison*]: Adrienne Koch, *Jefferson and Madison: The Great Collaboration* (Alfred A. Knopf, 1950), passim.

166 [*Jefferson on "appointments and disappointments"*]: Jefferson to Benjamin Rush, March 24, 1801, *ibid.*, p. 31. [*Jefferson on making ingrates and enemies*]: Jefferson, Jan. 13, 1807, quoted in Leonard D. White, *The Jeffersonians* (Macmillan, 1951), p. 349. [*Jefferson on simple questions*]: Jefferson, July 12, 1801, quoted in White, p. 352. See White for extensive discussion of Jefferson's personnel and patronage policies.

166-7 [*Smelser on New Haven as the Vatican City of Federalism*]: Smelser, p. 49. [*Jefferson on his "painful office"*]: quoted from his answer to the remonstrance of a committee of the merchants of New Haven, Jefferson to Elias Shipman and others, July 12, 1801, whole text in Ford, Vol. 8, pp. 67–70; see also White, pp. 351–52.

167 [*Collective leadership of Jefferson with his Cabinet*]: Noble E. Cunningham, Jr., *The Process of Government Under Jefferson* (Princeton University Press, 1978), Chs. 2–3.

[*Jefferson on public administration as simple*]: White, p. 4; Jefferson to James Monroe, May 29, 1801, Ford, Vol. 8, p. 59.

[*Newspaper description of President's house*]: Alexandria *Advertiser*, quoted in Malone, p. 38.

168 [*Federalist charge that Jefferson collected rent from his guests in the President's house*]: Irving Brant, *James Madison: Secretary of State* (Bobbs-Merrill, 1953), p. 42.

[*Jefferson on Washington, D.C., as pleasant country residence*]: Jefferson to Joel Barlow, May 3, 1803, Ford, Vol. 8, p. 150. [*Jefferson to son-in-law on same*]: Jefferson to T. M. Randolph, June 4, 1801, quoted in Brant, p. 42.

[*Pennsylvania Avenue as "streak of mud"*]: Brant, p. 41. See also Young.

169 [*Jefferson on paying off "Hamilton's" debt*]: Jefferson to Du Pont de Nemours, Jan. 18, 1802, Ford, Vol. 8, p. 127 n.

[*Johnstone on causes of Republican disunity in Congress*]: Robert M. Johnstone, Jr., *Jefferson and the Presidency* (Cornell University Press, 1978), p. 119. [*Significance of congressmen living in separate boardinghouses*]: Young, esp. Ch. 6. See also Cunningham, pp. 282–86. [*John Quincy Adams on typical Republican legislator*]: quoted in Johnstone, p. 118.

170 [*Jefferson's views on the role of the legislature in a tripartite balance*]: Thomas Jefferson, *Notes on Virginia* (Harper Torchbooks, 1964), pp. 110–24; Jefferson to James Madison, June 20, 1787, Ford, Vol. 4, pp. 390–96; Jefferson to Spencer Roane, Sept. 6, 1819, *ibid.*, Vol. 10, pp. 140–43; Jefferson to Abigail Adams, Sept. 11, 1804, in H. A. Washington, ed., *The Works of Thomas Jefferson* (Townsend Mac Coun, 1884), Vol. 4, pp. 560–62.

[*Jefferson's pledge to carry out the legislative will*]: reply to notification of election, Feb. 20, 1801, in Saul K. Padover, ed., *The Complete Jefferson* (Duell, Sloan & Pearce, 1943), p. 383.

[*Jefferson's dinner invitations to Republicans and Federalists*]: Young, p. 169.

[*John Quincy Adams on his 1804 dinner with Jefferson*]: Charles Francis Adams, ed., *Memoirs of John Quincy Adams* (Lippincott, 1874), Nov. 23, 1804, Vol. 1, p. 316. [*Adams on his later dinner*]: *Memoirs*, Nov. 3, 1807, quoted in Francis Coleman Rosenberger, ed., *Jefferson Reader* (E. P. Dutton, 1953), pp. 60–61.

172 [*Johnstone on flow chart*]: Johnstone, p. 121.

[*Jefferson's party leadership*]: See in general Noble E. Cunningham, Jr., *The Jeffersonian Republicans in Power* (University of North Carolina Press, 1963), esp. Ch. 4. For a sharply dissenting view, see Young.

To Louisiana and Beyond

172 [*Madison on the Mississippi*]: quoted in Malone, p. 266.

173 [*Jefferson's "peculiar confidence" in western men*]: Jefferson to J. P. G. Muhlenberg, Jan. 31, 1781, in Julian P. Boyd, ed., *The Papers of Thomas Jefferson* (Princeton University Press, 1951), Vol. 4, p. 487.

[*Jefferson on America's favored international position, in Inaugural Address*]: Ford, Vol. 8, p. 3 (text here spelled out from abbreviated form in Ford).

[*Jefferson on having nothing to do with European interests*]: Jefferson to George Logan, March 21, 1801, Ford, Vol. 8, p. 23.

[*Jefferson on "unwise" French policy of regaining Louisiana*]: Jefferson to James Monroe, May 26, 1801, *ibid.*, p. 58.

[*The Jefferson administration's reaction to French policy in Saint Domingue*]: Carl Ludwig Lokke, "Jefferson and the Leclerc Expedition," *American Historical Review*, Vol. 33, No. 2 (January 1928), pp. 322–28. [*Jefferson's fear of implications of independent black republic*]: Arthur Burr Darling, *Our Rising Empire* (Yale University Press, 1940), pp. 415–16; Lokke, p. 324.

174 [*Jefferson's warning to France against taking possession of Louisiana*]: Jefferson to Robert R. Livingston, April 18, 1802, Ford, Vol. 8, p. 145.

[*Jefferson's military preparations in response to recession of Louisiana*]: Mary P. Adams, "Jefferson's Reaction to the Treaty of San Ildefonso," *Journal of Southern History*, Vol. 21, No. 2 (May 1955), pp. 173–88.

[*Handlin on New Orleans as a fulcrum*]: Oscar Handlin, "The Louisiana Purchase," *Atlantic Monthly*, January 1955, p. 47.

[*Louisiana policy of the Spanish court*]: *ibid.*, pp. 48–49.

175 [*Jefferson's notification to Monroe of his appointment*]: Jefferson to Monroe, Jan. 10, 1803, Ford, Vol. 8, p. 188. For the formal communications and instructions from the Administration to Livingston and Madison, see Gaillard Hunt, ed., *The Writings of James Madison* (G. P. Putnam's Sons, 1908), Vol. 7, passim. [*Monroe's inability to resist the call to duty*]: Harry Ammon, *James Monroe: The Quest for National Identity* (McGraw-Hill, 1971), pp. 204–5.

176 [National Intelligencer *on Louisiana treaty, July 8, 1803*]: quoted in Malone, p. 297.

[*Jefferson on peace*]: Jefferson to John Sinclair, June 30, 1803, quoted in *ibid.*, p. 295.

[*"Fabricus" in the* Columbian Centinel, *July 13, 1803*]: quoted in *ibid.*, p. 297.

177 [*Paine on constitutionality of power to acquire territory*]: Paine to Jefferson, Sept. 23, 1803, in Philip S. Foner, ed., *The Complete Writings of Thomas Paine* (Citadel, 1945), Vol. 2, pp. 1447–48.

[*Jefferson on "written laws"*]: Jefferson to John Calvin, Sept. 20, 1810, Ford, Vol. 9, p. 279.

[*Jefferson's draft of a proposed constitutional amendment*]: quoted in Malone, p. 316.

[*Jefferson's willingness to acquiesce in not following constitutional amendment route*]: Jefferson to W. C. Nicholas, Sept. 7, 1803, quoted in Johnstone, p. 73.

177 [*Jefferson's curiosity about soil, fauna, etc., of Louisiana Territory*]: Jefferson to Meriwether Lewis, April 27, 1803, Ford, Vol. 8, pp. 193–99; see also references to remainder of this section.

178 [*The Lewis and Clark expedition*]: the key documentary sources are the notes and diaries of the two leaders. Of the several editions, I have used James K. Hosmer, ed., *History of the Expedition of Captains Lewis and Clark 1804–5–6*, reprinted from the edition of 1814 (A. C. McClurg, 1902), Vols. 1 and 2; and Ernest Staples Osgood, *The Field Notes of Captain William Clark, 1803–1805* (Yale University Press, 1964). John Bakeless, *Lewis & Clark: Partners in Discovery* (William Morrow, 1947), usefully summarizes these and other sources.

179 [*Jefferson's concern about the fur trade*]: Ralph B. Guinness, "The Purpose of the Lewis and Clark Expedition," *Mississippi Valley Historical Review*, Vol. 20, No. 1 (June 1933), pp. 90–100.

   [*Jefferson on Meriwether Lewis*]: from "Life of Captain Lewis by Thomas Jefferson" (written in 1813 and included in Hosmer, Vol. 1, pp. xli–lvi, at xlvi).

   [*Jefferson's instructions to Lewis*]: Jefferson to "Merryweather" Lewis, June 20, 1803, Ford, Vol. 8, pp. 194–99.

181 [*Indian chief on not whipping Indian children*]: quoted in Bakeless, p. 124.

182 [*Jefferson-Lewis exchange at end of expedition*]: Lewis to Jefferson, Sept. 23, 1806, quoted in Bakeless, p. 376; Jefferson to Lewis, Oct. 20, 1806, Ford, Vol. 8, p. 476.

Checkmate: The Federalist Bastion Stands

183 [*Major sources on judicial review and the Marshall Court*]: Robert K. Carr, *The Supreme Court and Judicial Review* (Farrar and Rinehart, 1942); Gottfried Dietze, ed., *Essays on the American Constitution* (Prentice-Hall, 1964), esp. Ch. 1; Edward S. Corwin, *John Marshall and the Constitution* (Yale University Press, 1921); Richard E. Ellis, *The Jeffersonian Crisis: Courts and Politics in the Young Republic* (Oxford University Press, 1971); Robert Kenneth Faulkner, *The Jurisprudence of John Marshall* (Princeton University Press, 1968); Charles Warren, *The Supreme Court in United States History* (Little, Brown, 1924), Vol. 1; Benjamin F. Wright, *The Growth of American Constitutional Law* (Houghton Mifflin, 1942).

   [*Jefferson's reaction to Federalist "court packing"*]: Jefferson to William B. Giles, March 23, 1801, Ford, Vol. 8, pp. 25–26; Jefferson to William Findley, March 24, 1801, *ibid.*, pp. 27–28; Jefferson to Benjamin Rush, March 24, 1801, *ibid.*, pp. 31–33; Jefferson to Elbridge Gerry, March 29, 1801, *ibid.*, pp. 40–43. [*The "one act of Mr. Adams's" that displeased Jefferson*]: Jefferson to Abigail Adams, June 13, 1804, *ibid.*, Vol. 8, pp. 306–8.

184 [*Gouverneur Morris on Federalists' need to cast anchors*]: quoted in Johnstone, p. 172.

185 [*Justice Chase on judicial power*]: quoted in Baker, p. 379.

   [*Jefferson's designation "sweeping Republicans"*]: cited in Schachner, p. 683.

   [*Giles on the Federalist "fortress"*]: William B. Giles to Jefferson, June 1, 1801, Jefferson Papers, Library of Congress.

186 [*Jefferson's involvement in repeal of Judiciary Bill*]: Johnstone, p. 175.

   [*Reaction of Supreme Court justices to Republican judicial measures*]: Baker, pp. 378–79.

186–8 [*Marshall opinion in Marbury v. Madison*]: William Cranch, *Reports of Cases Argued and Adjudged in the Supreme Court of the United States*, known also as *Cranch Reports* (Banks Law Publishing Co., 1911), Vol. 1, pp. 152–80. [*Withholding of Marbury commission*]: *ibid.*, p. 161. [*People's "original right"*]: *ibid.*, pp. 175–76.

188 [*Peltason on Marshall stating the question so that the answer was obvious*]: Jack W. Peltason and James MacGregor Burns, *Government by the People* (Prentice-Hall, 1952), p. 107.

188 [*Boston* Independent Chronicle *on Marbury*]: quoted in Baker, pp. 409–10.

189 [*Jefferson's executive leadership and his quotations thereon*]: Johnstone, pp. 86, 56.

190 [*Jefferson on harmony in his Cabinet*]: Jefferson to Destutt de Tracy, Jan. 26, 1811, Ford, Vol. 9, p. 307.

[*Jefferson on President's power of decision*]: ibid., p. 308.

[*Cunningham on Jefferson as Republican party unifier*]: Cunningham, *Jeffersonian Republicans in Power*, p. 304.

[*Jefferson's moderate appointment policy*]: Ellis, p. 234.

191 [*Jefferson on likelihood that Republican party would split*]: Jefferson to Joel Barlow, May 3, 1802, Ford, Vol. 8, p. 150. [*His tendency to equate the Republican party with the nation*]: Jefferson to William Duane, March 28, 1811, ibid., Vol. 9, pp. 310–14.

192 [*Hamilton-Burr duel*]: Milton Lomask, *Aaron Burr* (Farrar, Straus & Giroux, 1979), pp. 346–55.

[*Jefferson on majority rule in his Inaugural Address*]: Ford, Vol. 8, p. 2 (reprinted in abbreviated note form in Ford).

6. THE AMERICAN WAY OF WAR

194 [*Coronation of Napoleon*]: Frederic Masson, *Napoleon and His Coronation* (Lippincott, [1907]), pp. 171–240; Vincent Cronin, *Napoleon Bonaparte: An Intimate Biography* (William Morrow, 1972), pp. 246–54.

[*French attack to the east*]: Theodore A. Dodge, *Napoleon*, Vol. 2 in Great Captains series (Houghton Mifflin, 1904).

[*British court and politics*]: John Brooke, *King George III* (Constable, 1972).

195 [*Nelson's victory at Trafalgar*]: David Walder, *Nelson* (Dial Press, 1978), Ch. 33.

[*Jefferson on "chance"*]: Jefferson to Barnabus Bidwell, July 5, 1806, quoted in Robert M. Johnstone, Jr., *Jefferson and the Presidency* (Cornell University Press, 1978), p. 132.

[*Jefferson on inexperience of American diplomats*]: cited by Dumas Malone, *Jefferson the President* (Little, Brown, 1970), Vol. 4, p. 299, as Jefferson to Madison, March 19, 1803; cited in ibid., Vol. 5, *Jefferson the President: Second Term, 1805–1809*, p. xviii, as of date of Nov. 19, 1803.

[*Barbary pirates*]: Louis B. Wright and Julia H. MacLeod, *The First Americans in North Africa* (Princeton University Press, 1945); Ray W. Irwin, *The Diplomatic Relations of the United States with the Barbary Powers* (University of North Carolina Press, 1931).

196 [*Burr, Wilkinson, and western adventurism*]: Thomas P. Abernethy, *The Burr Conspiracy* (Oxford University Press, 1954); James Ripley Jacobs, *Tarnished Warrior* (Macmillan, 1938); Nathan Schachner, *Aaron Burr* (Frederick A. Stokes, 1937); Isaac J. Cox, "Hispanic American Phases of the 'Burr Conspiracy,'" *Hispanic American Historical Review*, Vol. 12, No. 2 (May 1932), pp. 142–75.

197 [*Frederick Jackson Turner on Wilkinson*]: quoted in John A. Garraty, ed., *Encyclopedia of American Biography* (Harper & Row, 1974), p. 1204.

[*Jefferson's proclamation against the conspiracy*]: Paul Leicester Ford, ed., *The Writings of Thomas Jefferson* (G. P. Putnam's Sons, 1897), Vol. 8, pp. 481–82 (Nov. 27, 1806).

"The Hurricane . . . Now Blasting the World"

198 [*The "broken voyage"*]: A. L. Burt, *The United States, Great Britain, and British North America from the Revolution to the Establishment of Peace After the War of 1812* (Yale University Press,

1940), pp. 218–24; see generally Eli F. Heckscher, *The Continental System* (Humphrey Milford, 1922).

198 [*Identifying English deserters on American ships*]: Thomas A. Bailey, *A Diplomatic History of the American People* (F. S. Crofts, 1941), p. 112; James F. Zimmerman, *Impressment of American Seamen* (Longmans, Green, 1925), passim.

199 [*Jefferson on public opinion following the* Chesapeake *incident*]: Jefferson to Du Pont de Nemours, July 14, 1807, cited in Bailey, pp. 116–17; Jefferson to William Duane, July 20, 1807, Ford, Vol. 9, p. 120.

[*Jefferson and the embargo*]: Dumas Malone, *Jefferson the President: Second Term, 1805–1809* (Little, Brown, 1974), Ch. 26; Louis Martin Sears, *Jefferson and the Embargo* (Duke University Press, 1927).

200 [*Impact of the embargo and New Hampshire song*]: Bailey, pp. 119–120, quoted from p. 119.

[*Jefferson's failure to elicit full support for the embargo from his colleagues*]: Johnstone, p. 266.

201 [*Jefferson's "un-Jeffersonian" behavior in enforcing embargo*]: ibid., p. 284.

[*Poetic attack on Jefferson by William Cullen Bryant*]: William Cullen Bryant, *The Embargo*, "By a Youth of Thirteen" (Printed for the Purchasers, 1808); quoted in part in Malone, *Jefferson: Second Term*, p. 606.

[*Jefferson on the sudden unaccountable revolution*]: Jefferson to Thomas Mann Randolph, Feb. 7, 1809, Ford, Vol. 9, p. 244.

[*Jefferson on "hurricane . . . now blasting the world"*]: Jefferson to Caesar Rodney, Feb. 10, 1810, ibid., p. 271.

202 [*Impeachment of Justice Chase*]: Johnstone, pp. 182–87. [*Chase on "mobocracy"*]: quoted in Nathan Schachner, *Thomas Jefferson* (Appleton-Century-Crofts, 1951), Vol. 2, p. 778.

[*Jefferson as political leader*]: Johnstone, passim; Dumas Malone, *Thomas Jefferson as Political Leader* (University of California Press, 1963).

[*The Marshall court*]: Albert J. Beveridge, *The Life of John Marshall* (Houghton Mifflin, 1919), Vol. 3; Charles Warren, *The Supreme Court in United States History* (Little, Brown, 1924), Vol. 1.

[*Trial of Aaron Burr*]: Richard B. Morris, *Fair Trial* (Alfred A. Knopf, 1952); Francis F. Beirne, *Shout Treason: The Trial of Aaron Burr* (Hastings House, 1959); cf. Julius W. Pratt, "Aaron Burr and the Historians," *New York History*, Vol. 26, No. 4 (October 1945), pp. 447–70.

203 [*Jefferson on the Madison-Monroe friction*]: Jefferson to Monroe, February 18, 1808, Ford, Vol. 9, p. 177–78.

[*Election of 1808*]: Irving Brant, "Election of 1808," in Arthur M. Schlesinger, Jr., ed., *History of American Presidential Elections* (Chelsea House, 1971), Vol. 1, pp. 185–246.

The Irresistible War

204 [*Dolley Madison's interposition between the French and English ministers*]: Irving Brant, *The Fourth President* (Bobbs-Merrill, 1970), p. 404.

[*Origins of War of 1812*]: Bradford Perkins, *Prologue to War, 1805–1812* (University of California Press, 1961); George R. Taylor, "Agrarian Discontent in the Mississippi Valley Preceding the War of 1812," *Journal of Political Economy*, Vol. 39, No. 4 (August 1931), pp. 471–505; William Appleman Williams, *The Contours of American History* (World, 1961), pp. 192–96. Roger H. Brown offers a somewhat different analysis in *The Republic in Peril: 1812* (Columbia University Press, 1964).

204 [*War of 1812*]: Patrick C. T. White, *Nation on Trial: America and War of 1812* (John Wiley & Sons, 1965); Reginald Horsman, *The War of 1812* (Alfred A. Knopf, 1969); Harry L. Coles, *The War of 1812* (University of Chicago Press, 1965).

205 [*John Randolph as legislative leader*]: William Cabell Bruce, *John Randolph of Roanoke* (G. P. Putnam's Sons, 1922), Vol. 1, Ch. 7.

206 [*Tension earlier between Madison and Monroe*]: Harry Ammon, *James Monroe: The Quest for National Identity* (McGraw-Hill, 1971), Ch. 15; Brant, *The Fourth President*, Ch. 40. [*Monroe's appointment as Secretary of State*]: Ammon, pp. 454–56; Irving Brant, *James Madison the President* (Bobbs-Merrill, 1956), Ch. 18.

[*Boston* Columbian Centinel *on western "hypocrisy"*]: quoted in Bailey, p. 135.

208 [*Benton on question of war*]: Thomas Hart Benton to Henry Clay, Feb. 7, 1810, in James F. Hopkins, ed., *The Papers of Henry Clay* (University Press of Kentucky, 1959), Vol. 1, p. 447.

[*Clay on conquest of Canada*]: *ibid.*, p. 450.

[*Macon on the governments of England and France*]: quoted in Bailey, p. 137.

[*Madison on going to war against England and/or France*]: James Madison to Thomas Jefferson, May 25, 1812, Gaillard Hunt, ed., *The Writings of James Madison* (G. P. Putnam's Sons, 1908), Vol. 8, p. 191.

[*Monroe's anonymous letter*]: Washington *National Intelligencer* editorial, April 14, 1812, Hopkins, Vol. 1, p. 645; originally thought to have been written by Clay, it has been proved to be the work of Monroe.

[*Madison's war message*]: Hunt, Vol. 8, p. 198.

209 [*John Quincy Adams on impressment*]: Perkins, p. 428. [*Calhoun on same*]: *ibid.*, p. 434. [*Fourth of July toast*]: *ibid.*, p. 435.

[*Election of 1812*]: Norman K. Risjord, "The Election of 1812," in Schlesinger, pp. 249–72.

212 [*Madison on "Experimentum crucis"*]: Madison to Thomas Jefferson, Oct. 14, 1812, Hunt, Vol. 8, p. 220.

213 [*English commander on regulars*]: Coles, p. 157.

215 [*The American way of war*]: Merle Curti, *Peace or War: The American Struggle, 1636–1936* (W. W. Norton, 1936); Russell F. Weigley, *The American Way of War: A History of United States Military Strategy and Policy* (Macmillan, 1973); Walter Millis, *Arms and Men* (G. P. Putnam's Sons, 1956).

[*Jay on the supreme need for safety*]: *Federalist* No. 3, in Edward Mead Earle, ed., *The Federalist* (Modern Library, n.d.), p. 13.

216 [*Relative size of American and European military efforts*]: John K. Mahan, *The War of 1812* (University of Florida Press, 1972), p. 325.

Waterside Yankees: The Federalists at Ebb Tide

217 [*The Hartford Convention*]: Henry Adams, *History of the United States, 1813–1817* (Charles Scribner's Sons, 1891), Vol. 2; James M. Banner, Jr., *To the Hartford Convention: The Federalists and the Origins of Party Politics in Massachusetts, 1789–1815* (Alfred A. Knopf, 1970); David H. Fischer, *The Revolution of American Conservatism* (Harper & Row, 1965), pp. 177–78 and passim; Samuel Eliot Morison, *Harrison Gray Otis* (Houghton Mifflin, 1969), esp. Ch. 17.

[*Monroe's effort to monitor the convention*]: Ammon, pp. 341–42.

218 [*Waterside Yankee leaders*]: my portraits are drawn mainly from Fischer's brief biographies of old Federalists in Fischer, pp. 245–59. [*Ames as "lethargic," etc.*]: *ibid.*, p. 21.

219 [*Salem in 1790*]: Samuel Eliot Morison, *The Maritime History of Massachusetts* (Houghton Mifflin, 1921), p. 79. [*Marblehead*]: Samuel Eliot Morison, *By Land and By Sea* (Alfred A. Knopf, 1953), p. 183.

220 [*Other ports*]: Robert G. Albion, William A. Baker, and Benjamin W. Labaree, *New England and the Sea* (Wesleyan University Press, 1972), passim; see also David T. Gilchrist, ed., *The Growth of the Seaport Cities, 1790–1825* (University Press of Virginia, 1967).

[*Plymouth rope making*]: Samuel Eliot Morison, *The Ropemakers of Plymouth* (Houghton Mifflin, 1950).

[*The sight of Boston*]: quoted by Morison from unnamed source, in Morison, *Maritime History of Massachusetts*, p. 42.

[*Connecticut Valley trade*]: Margaret Elizabeth Martin, *Merchants and Trade of the Connecticut River Valley, 1750–1820* (Smith College Studies in History, Vol. 24, October 1938–July 1939).

221 [*Yankee merchants*]: Arthur Meier Schlesinger, *The Colonial Merchants and the American Revolution, 1763–1776* (Longmans, Green, 1918); see also George E. Brooks, Jr., *Yankee Traders, Old Coasters and African Middlemen* (Boston University Press, 1970).

[*Yankee merchants' preoccupation with commerce*]: Brissot de Warville, 1788, quoted in Morison, *Maritime History of Massachusetts*, p. 43.

[*Mariner's life*]: Albion, Baker, and Labaree, p. 86.

[*Social deference in the port towns*]: Fischer, p. xiv; for a broad view of a specific social order, that of the merchants of Newburyport, see Benjamin W. Labaree, *Patriots and Partisans* (Harvard University Press, 1962); see also Albion, Baker, and Labaree, pp. 50–53.

222 [*Boston and Cambridge cultural scenes around 1815*]: Van Wyck Brooks, *The Flowering of New England, 1815–1865* (E. P. Dutton, 1936), Chs. 1–2, quoted at p. 8. See also Vernon L. Parrington, *Main Currents in American Thought* (Harcourt, Brace, 1930), Vol. 2, Book 3, Part I.

223 [*The Essex Junto*]: David H. Fischer, "The Myth of the Essex Junto," *William and Mary Quarterly,* Third Series, Vol. 21, No. 2 (April 1964), pp. 191–235.

[*Essexmen as conservatives*]: Fischer, "Myth of the Essex Junto," p. 199.

224 [*John Quincy Adams on Essexmen's selfishness*]: J. Q. Adams to Josiah Quincy, Dec. 4, 1804, cited in Edmund Quincy, *Josiah Quincy* (Fields, Osgood, 1869), p. 64.

[*John Adams' instructions to himself on the proper pursuit of knowledge*]: L. H. Butterfield, ed., *Diary and Autobiography of John Adams* (Belknap Press, 1961), Vol. 1, p. 73 (diary notation of a Tuesday in Jan. 1759).

225 [*Adams' moral instructions to himself*]: ibid., p. 72 (same date).

[*Adams on individual self-interest versus public virtue*]: quoted in Page Smith, *John Adams* (Doubleday, 1962), p. 234.

[*Wood's summary of reasons for balanced government*]: Gordon S. Wood, *The Creation of the American Republic, 1776–1787* (University of North Carolina Press, 1969), p. 198.

226 [*John Adams on executive power*]: see Manning J. Dauer, *The Adams Federalists* (Johns Hopkins University Press, 1953), esp. Ch. 3.

[*Adams' fear of the few*]: Adams to Jefferson, March 1, 1778, Adams Papers, Massachusetts Historical Society, Boston.

[*Adams quoted on liberty*]: Smith, pp. 78–79.

226 [*Adams on equality*]: quoted in Smith, Vol. 1, p. 259, from Charles Francis Adams, ed., *Works* (Little, Brown, 1854), Vol. 9, pp. 375-78 (Adams to James Sullivan, May 26, 1776).

[*Adams on property as a liberty*]: quoted in Dauer, p. 42.

[*Adams' views in general*]: see also Zoltán Haraszti, *John Adams and the Prophets of Progress* (Grosset & Dunlap, 1964); Clinton Rossiter, *Conservatism in America* (Alfred A. Knopf, 1955).

Federalists: The Tide Runs Out

227 [*Federalist party*]: Fischer, *The Revolution of American Conservatism*, passim; see also Linda K. Kerber, *Federalists in Dissent* (Cornell University Press, 1970); Shaw Livermore, Jr., *The Twilight of Federalism* (Princeton University Press, 1962).

228 [*Fischer on Adams' "curious relationship"*]: *The Revolution of American Conservatism*, p. 17.

[*Adams' puzzling motives*]: Ebenezer Mattoon to Thomas Dwight, March 2, 1801, quoted in Fischer, *The Revolution of American Conservatism*, p. 18.

[*Adams on his Federalist foes' "stiff-rumped stupidity"*]: John Adams to John Quincy Adams, Dec. 14, 1804, Adams Family Papers, Reel 403, Massachusetts Historical Society.

[*John Quincy Adams' alienation from the Federalist party in Massachusetts*]: Samuel Flagg Bemis, *John Quincy Adams and the Foundations of American Foreign Policy* (Alfred A. Knopf, 1949), pp. 138-50.

[*Samuel Chase on liberty*]: Fischer, *The Revolution of American Conservatism*, p. 358.

229 [*Samuel Lyman on "nothing so unequal as equality"*]: *ibid.*, p. 251.

[*Sewall on security*]: *ibid.*, p. 256.

[*Ames on "Madam Liberty"*]: *ibid.*, p. 26.

[*Ames on disorganization of Federalists*]: *ibid.*, p. 53.

[*Federalist satire of the "Grand Caucus"*]: *ibid.*, p. 57.

[*Federalist attempts to organize a party mechanism*]: See in general Linda K. Kerber, "The Federalist Party," in Arthur M. Schlesinger, Jr., ed., *History of U.S. Political Parties* (Chelsea House, 1973), Vol. 1, pp. 3-29. See also Fischer, *The Revolution of American Conservatism*, Ch. 3.

[*Jeremiah Smith on "red hot feds"*]: *ibid.*, p. 64.

230 [*Pickering's secession "plot" of 1804*]: Fischer, "The Myth of the Essex Junto," pp. 229-32.

231 [*Hartford Convention finale*]: Banner, Ch. 8; Morison, *Harrison Gray Otis;* review of Banner by Fischer in *American Historical Review*, Vol. 75, No. 6 (October 1970), pp. 1778-79.

[*Hartford Convention report*]: quoted in Richard B. Morris, ed., *Encyclopedia of American History*, rev. ed. (Harper & Brothers, 1961), p. 153.

[*Madison on hearing of the proposed Hartford Convention*]: Brant, *The Fourth President*, p. 582.

[*Jefferson on Hartford Convention*]: Ford, Vol. 8, p. 67.

7. THE AMERICAN WAY OF PEACE

232 [*Gallatin at Ghent*]: Henry Adams, *The Life of Albert Gallatin* (Lippincott, 1879), pp. 508–48.

[*Negotiations at Ghent*]: A. L. Burt, *The United States, Great Britain, and British North America* (Yale University Press, 1940), Ch. 15; Samuel Flagg Bemis, *John Quincy Adams and the Foundations of American Foreign Policy* (Alfred A. Knopf, 1949), Chs. 9 and 10.

[*J. Q. Adams on his colleagues' drinking and smoking habits*]: Charles Francis Adams, ed., *Memoirs of John Quincy Adams* (Lippincott, 1874), Vol. 2, p. 656 (diary entry of July 8, 1814).

[*Albert Gallatin as peacemaker*]: Viscount Bryce, ed., *A Great Peace Maker: The Diary of James Gallatin* (Charles Scribner's Sons, 1914), p. 28.

[*France as a political volcano*]: William H. Crawford to Henry Clay, May 15, 1814, in James F. Hopkins, ed., *The Papers of Henry Clay* (University Press of Kentucky, 1959), Vol. 1, p. 911.

233 [*Clay on being surrounded by a British garrison*]: Clay to William H. Crawford, July 2, 1814, *ibid.*, p. 939.

[*Gallatin on the lot of 100,000 American citizens in the proposed buffer area*]: Bryce, p. 28 (diary entry of Aug. 8, 1814).

[*Wellington on American naval power on the Great Lakes*]: Thomas A. Bailey, *A Diplomatic History of the American People* (F. S. Crofts, 1941), p. 150 (Wellington to Castlereagh, Nov. 9, 1814).

234 [*"Dreadful day" and Wellington's alleged note to Gallatin*]: Bryce, p. 34 (diary entry of Nov. 28, 1814); see also pp. 34–35 (diary entry of Dec. 12, 1814).

[*Bailey on the treaty as a truce of exhaustion*]: Bailey, pp. 151–52.

[*Concluding festivities*]: Bryce, pp. 35–36 (diary entries of Dec. 24, 1814, Christmas Day, 1814); see also Adams, *Memoirs*, Vol. 3, pp. 127, 131, 137–39.

Good Feelings and Ill

234 [Niles' Weekly Register *and New York* Evening Post *on the news from Ghent*]: quoted in Bailey, pp. 154–55. [*The treaty of Ghent as one of the most popular of treaties*]: *ibid.*, p. 155.

235 [*London* Times *laments treaty*]: quoted in Glenn Tucker, *Poltroons and Patriots* (Bobbs-Merrill, 1954), Vol. 2, p. 671.

[*Disarmament of the Great Lakes*]: Burt, quoted at p. 388.

[*Madison's message to Congress*]: December 5, 1815, Gaillard Hunt, ed., *The Writings of James Madison* (G. P. Putnam's Sons, 1908), Vol. 8, pp. 337–38.

236 [*John Randolph versus a national bank*]: quoted in William Cabell Bruce, *John Randolph of Roanoke* (G. P. Putnam's Sons, 1922), Vol. 1, p. 431.

[*Williams on Gallatin's reports*]: William Appleman Williams, *The Contours of American History* (World, 1961).

[*Madison's shifting economic views*]: Madison to D. Lynch, June 27, 1817, Hunt, Vol. 8, p. 392.

237 [*The Second United States Bank*]: Bray Hammond, *Banks and Politics in America* (Princeton University Press, 1957), esp. Ch. 9.

[*Madison on America's fortieth year as an independent nation*]: Eighth Annual Message, Dec. 3, 1816, Hunt, Vol. 8, pp. 375–85, 383–84.

237 [*Clay on the establishment of the national character*]: Clay to Officials of the City of Washington, Sept. 18, 1815, Hopkins, Vol. 2 (1961), p. 63.

238 [*Monroe on the experiment of war*]: quoted in Harry Ammon, *The Quest for National Identity* (McGraw-Hill, 1971), p. 344.

[*New York State politics*]: Shaw Livermore, Jr., *The Twilight of Federalism* (Princeton University Press, 1962).

239 [*Monroe's Inaugural Address, March 4, 1817*]: Stanislaus Murray Hamilton, ed., *The Writings of James Monroe* (G. P. Putnam's Sons, 1902), Vol. 6, pp. 6–16.

[*Monroe on parties as unnecessary*]: Monroe to Andrew Jackson, Dec. 14, 1816, Hamilton, Vol. 5, p. 346.

[*Monroe on inviting Federalists to rejoin the "family of the union"*]: Rives Papers, July 27, 1817, Library of Congress, quoted in Ammon, p. 377.

[*Biddle on the follies of faction*]: quoted in Ammon, p. 367.

241 [*Clay on "entrance of the sovereign"*]: Henry Clay, "Speech on Internal Improvements," March 7, 1818, Hopkins, Vol. 2, p. 452.

[*Clay on Monroe's constitutional arguments*]: *ibid.*, March 13, 1818, p. 483.

[*Clay on Monroe's anti-party beliefs*]: *ibid.*, March 7, 1818, p. 452.

[*Bank politics and comments*]: Hammond, Chs. 9 and 10, quoted at p. 259.

242 [*Politics of slavery*]: Glover Moore, *The Missouri Controversy* (University Press of Kentucky, 1966); Donald L. Robinson, *Slavery in the Structure of American Politics, 1765–1820* (Harcourt Brace Jovanovich, 1971).

[*Role of Rep. James Tallmadge*]: James Tallmadge Papers, New-York Historical Society; see also John W. Taylor Papers, New-York Historical Society.

243 [*Moore on the nature of the North-South agreement*]: Moore, p. 111.

[*Jefferson on the fire bell in the night and having the wolf by the ears*]: Jefferson to John Holmes, April 22, 1820, in Paul Leicester Ford, *The Writings of Thomas Jefferson* (G. P. Putnam's Sons, 1897), Vol. 10, p. 157.

Adams' Diplomacy and Monroe's Dictum

244 [*Madison on Spanish hostility toward his administration*]: Madison to John Graham, circa June 1, 1816, Hunt, Vol. 8, p. 345.

245 [*East and West Florida as a pistol aimed at the Mississippi*]: Bemis, p. 302.

[*Conversation between Adams and Castlereagh*]: Bemis, p. 304. I have used Bemis' rendition of Adams' indirect quotation of these (and other) conversations into direct quotations, drawn from Adams' *Memoirs.* I have also retained Bemis' italics.

[*Turmoil in Florida*]: Bailey, pp. 167–68.

[*The Seminoles*]: see Robert Spencer Cotterill, *The Southern Indians* (University of Oklahoma Press, 1954); Edwin C. McReynolds, *The Seminoles* (University of Oklahoma Press, 1957); John R. Swanton, *Early History of the Creek Indians and Their Neighbors*, Bureau of American Ethnology, Bulletin 73 (Government Printing Office, 1922).

246 [*Jackson to Monroe on seizing Florida*]: quoted in George Dangerfield, *The Awakening of American Nationalism* (Harper & Row, 1965), p. 46; see also Bemis, pp. 313–14.

[*Rush reports English resentment toward Jackson*]: Bailey, pp. 169–70.

[*Niles' Weekly Register on Jackson's popularity*]: *ibid.*, p. 170.

247 [*Clay's views*]: see esp. Clay's speech in the House of Representatives on the Seminole War, Jan. 20, 1819, Hopkins, Vol. 2, pp. 636–60.

[*Monroe on his three main goals after the Florida incursion*]: Monroe to James Madison, Feb. 7, 1819, Hamilton, Vol. 6, pp. 87–88.

[*Adams-Onís negotiations*]: see Philip Coolidge Brooks, *Diplomacy and the Borderlands: The Adams-Onís Treaty of 1819* (University of California Press, 1939).

248 [*Adams on the most important day of his life*]: Adams, *Memoirs*, Feb. 22, 1819, Vol. 4, p. 274.

249 [*Internal British politics and foreign policy prior to the Monroe Doctrine*]: Dangerfield, Ch. 5, passim. See also Bemis, Ch. 18. [*Canning's proffer of Anglo-American cooperation*]: see esp. Richard Rush to John Quincy Adams, Sept. 19, 1823, Hamilton, Vol. 6, pp. 377–86.

[*Madison on liberty and despotism*]: Madison to Jefferson, Nov. 1, 1823, *ibid.*, pp. 395–96.

[*Cabinet discussion of proposed Anglo-American cooperation*]: Adams, *Memoirs*, Vol. 6, pp. 177–81, as rendered by Bemis, pp. 384–85. Italics are Bemis'.

[*Expectation that European powers will not interfere in America*]: Adams, quoted in Bemis, p. 387.

250 [*Key provisions of the Monroe Doctrine*]: Hamilton, Vol. 6, pp. 328, 340, italics added.

251 [*European response to enunciation of the Monroe Doctrine*]: quoted in Dangerfield, p. 190; in Bailey, p. 189 (Metternich); in Bemis, p. 403 n. (Lafayette to John Quincy Adams).

[*Economic aspects of the Monroe Doctrine*]: Williams, esp. pp. 215–18.

[*The Monroe Doctrine*]: Dexter Perkins, *A History of the Monroe Doctrine* (Little, Brown, 1955); Donald Marquand Dozer, *The Monroe Doctrine: Its Modern Significance* (Alfred A. Knopf, 1965); Worthington C. Ford, "John Quincy Adams and the Monroe Doctrine," *American Historical Review*, Vol. 7, No. 4 (July 1902), pp. 676–96; William S. Robertson, "The Monroe Doctrine Abroad in 1823–24," *American Political Science Review*, Vol. 6, No. 4 (November 1912), pp. 546–63; Marie B. Hecht, *John Quincy Adams* (Macmillan, 1972), Ch. 15.

252 [*Salvador de Madariaga on the Monroe Doctrine*]: quoted in Dozer, p. vii.

[*Sources and dilemmas in American foreign policy and strategy*]: Hans J. Morgenthau, *In Defense of the National Interest* (Alfred A. Knopf, 1952); Felix Gilbert, *To the Farewell Address* (Princeton University Press, 1961); Paul A. Varg, *Foreign Policies of the Founding Fathers* (Michigan State University Press, 1963); Robert E. Osgood, *Ideals and Self-Interest in America's Foreign Relations* (University of Chicago Press, 1953).

253 [*Hamilton on morality of nations*]: quoted in Morgenthau, pp. 14–18, italics in original.

254 [*Morgenthau on John Quincy Adams*]: Morgenthau, p. 22.

Virginians: The Last of the Gentlemen Politicians

254 [*The Crawford incident*]: diary entry of John Quincy Adams, Dec. 14, 1825, Adams, *Memoirs*, Vol. 7, pp. 80–81; Samuel L. Southard to Samuel L. Gouverneur, Sept. 3, 1831, quoted in Ammon, pp. 543–44.

255 [*Description of Jefferson in his last years*]: quoted in Nathan Schachner, *Thomas Jefferson* (Thomas Yoseloff, 1951), p. 997.

[*The Virginia environment and history*]: Matthew Page Andrews, *Virginia: The Old Dominion* (Doubleday, Doran, 1937); Edmund S. Morgan, *Virginians at Home* (Colonial Williamsburg, 1952); Louis D. Rubin, Jr., *Virginia* (W. W. Norton, 1977); Richard L. Morton, *Colonial Virginia* (University of North Carolina Press, 1960), Vol. 2.

255 [*Virginia, social and political aspects*]: Robert E. Brown and Katherine Brown, *Virginia 1705-1786: Democracy or Aristocracy?* (Michigan State University Press, 1964); Abbot Emerson Smith, *Colonists in Bondage* (University of North Carolina Press, 1947).

256 [*Collective intellectual leadership in Virginia*]: Richard Beale Davis, *Intellectual Life in Jefferson's Virginia* (University of North Carolina Press, 1964), p. 4.

[*Robert Carter's library*]: Louis Morton, *Robert Carter of Nomini Hall* (University Press of Virginia, 1945), pp. 214-16. [*Bernard visit*]: *ibid.*, p. 216.

[*Never be born than ill bred*]: quoted in Davis, p. 8; see also Andrews, p. 255, on private schools.

[*Morton on "curious contradiction"*]: Morton, p. 214.

257 [*Henry Adams on the excellence of upper-class education in Virginia*]: quoted in Davis, p. 1.

[*Individual education*]: Morgan, pp. 16-18. [*William and Mary*]: Andrews, p. 323.

258 [*Schools of Virginia Federalists*]: David H. Fischer, *The Revolution of American Conservatism* (Harper & Row, 1965), pp. 370-87.

[*Life of John Randolph*]: Robert Dawidoff, *The Education of John Randolph* (W. W. Norton, 1979).

[*Malone's description of Randolph*]: Dumas Malone, ed., *Dictionary of American Biography* (Charles Scribner's Sons, 1932), Vol. 8, p. 366.

[*Randolph's philosophy*]: Dawidoff, pp. 32-33.

259 [*Marshall in* McCulloch v. Maryland]: quoted in Richard B. Morris, ed., *Encyclopedia of American History*, rev. ed. (Harper & Row, 1961), p. 158. [*Ruling in* Gibbons v. Ogden]: *ibid.*, p. 489.

[*The Yazoo claims and* Fletcher v. Peck]: C. Peter Magrath, *Yazoo: Law and Politics in the New Republic* (Brown University Press, 1966).

[*Randolph denounces Yazooists*]: *ibid.*, p. 46.

260 [*Marshall on Georgia's obligations*]: *ibid.*, p. 78.

262 [*Madison's definition of tyranny*]: James Madison *et al.*, *The Federalist* (E. P. Dutton, 1937), No. 47, p. 245.

263 [*First- and second-generation intellectual leadership in Virginia, in relation to constitutional experimentation and development*]: Davis, passim; Brown and Brown, passim; John T. Agresto, "Liberty, Virtue, and Republicanism: 1776-1787," *Review of Politics*, Vol. 39, No. 4 (October 1977), pp. 473-504; George W. Carey, "Separation of Powers and the Madisonian Model: A Reply to the Critics," *American Political Science Review*, Vol. 72, No. 1 (March 1978), pp. 151-64; Richard W. Krouse, "Two Concepts of Democratic Republicanism: Madison and Tocqueville on Pluralism and Party in American Politics," paper prepared for delivery at the Annual Meeting of the American Political Science Association, Washington, D.C., Sept. 1977; Clinton Rossiter, *The American Quest, 1790-1860* (Harcourt Brace Jovanovich, 1971).

This section was written with the assistance of Jeffrey P. Trout.

The Checking and Balancing of John Quincy Adams

I have used this same title as a section title to describe James Madison's presidency, in *The Deadlock of Democracy* (Prentice-Hall, 1963). I now consider this title more appropriate for John Quincy Adams' presidency.

264 [*William Plumer's electoral vote for John Quincy Adams in 1820*]: Samuel Flagg Bemis, *John Quincy Adams and the Union* (Alfred A. Knopf, 1956), p. 12.

264 [*J. Q. Adams on William Crawford as a "worm," etc.*]: *ibid.*, p. 16, or Adams, *Memoirs*, Vol. 5, p. 315.

[*Preliminary developments, election of 1824*]: James F. Hopkins, "Election of 1824," in Arthur M. Schlesinger, Jr., ed., *History of American Presidential Elections* (McGraw-Hill, 1971), Vol. 1, pp. 349–409; Hecht, Ch. 16; Bemis, *John Quincy Adams and the Union*, Ch. 2; Hopkins, Vol. 3, passim.

266 [*Schoolteacher's comment on the election*]: Henry D. Ward to Ephraim Cutler, April 14, 1824, quoted in Dangerfield, p. 220.

[*Results of 1824 presidential election*]: Svend Petersen, *A Statistical History of the American Presidential Elections* (Frederick Ungar, 1963), pp. 17–18.

[*Dangerfield on Clay's boardinghouse electioneering*]: Dangerfield, p. 224.

267 [*J. Q. Adams' campaigning for support*]: Bemis, *John Quincy Adams and the Union*, pp. 36–37.

[*Clay to correspondents on the electoral situation*]: Adams to James Erwin, Dec. 13, 1824, Hopkins, Vol. 3, p. 895; Clay to George McClure, Dec. 28, 1824, *ibid.*, p. 906.

[*Webster's mediation*]: Schlesinger, p. 380; see Smith (cited below), p. 185.

[*Randolph on election*]: Dangerfield, p. 228.

[*Jackson on the "Judas of the West"*]: Jackson to William B. Lewis, Feb. 14, 1825, John S. Bassett, ed., *Correspondence of Andrew Jackson* (Carnegie Institute, 1928), Vol. 3, p. 276.

[*John Adams' reaction to election*]: Bemis, *John Quincy Adams and the Union*, p. 48.

268 [*Notification of J. Q. Adams of his election*]: *ibid.*, p. 51; see Margaret Bayard Smith, *The First Forty Years of Washington Society*, Gaillard Hunt, ed. (Charles Scribner's Sons, 1906), p. 186.

[*Adams' use of the term "National" government*]: Bemis, *John Quincy Adams and the Union*, p. 61.

[*Adams on the "perilous experiment"*]: Adams, *Memoirs*, Vol. 7, p. 63 (diary entry of Nov. 26, 1825).

[*Congressional politics*]: Tallmadge Family Papers, New-York Historical Society; John W. Taylor Papers, New-York Historical Society.

269 [*President Adams' lack of political support*]: Bemis, *John Quincy Adams and the Union*, Ch. 5; Hecht, Ch. 18; Dangerfield, Ch. 9; Adams, *Memoirs*, passim.

[*J. Q. Adams to his son on bewaring of "Trap doors"*]: Adams to George Washington Adams, Dec. 31, 1826, quoted in Bemis, *John Quincy Adams and the Union*, p. 88.

[*Politics behind the "tariff of abominations"*]: Robert V. Remini, *Martin Van Buren and the Making of the Democratic Party* (Columbia University Press, 1959), pp. 170–85. See also Dangerfield, pp. 275–87; see generally Joseph Dorfman, *The Economic Mind in American Civilization* (Viking Press, 1946), Vol. 2, Ch. 22; Frank W. Taussig, *Tariff History of the United States* (G. P. Putnam's Sons, 1931), pp. 82, 92.

[*Congressional tariff role*]: Robert V. Remini, "Martin Van Buren and the Tariff of Abominations," *American Historical Review*, Vol. 63, No. 4 (July 1958), pp. 903–17; Williams, pp. 230–35.

270 [*John Randolph on manufacturing a President*]: quoted in Bemis, *John Quincy Adams and the Union*, p. 90.

[*Dangerfield on Adams' signing of the "tariff of abominations"*]: Dangerfield, p. 283.

Jubilee 1826: The Passing of the Heroes

270 [*Biblical admonition to celebrate the half-century*]: Leviticus 25:10.

271 [*John Adams on his life drawing to an end*]: Adams to Jefferson, Jan. 14, 1826, in Lester J. Cappon, ed., *The Adams-Jefferson Letters* (University of North Carolina Press, 1959), Vol. 2, p. 613.

[*Adams-Jefferson exchange on the "homespun"*]: *ibid.*, pp. 290-93.

[*John Adams' exchanges with Mercy Warren*]: Page Smith, *John Adams* (Doubleday, 1962), Vol. 2, pp. 1087-88; "Mercy Otis Warren," *Dictionary of American Biography* (including Adams' comment on history as not the province of ladies).

[*Adams and Jefferson on children and on Abigail Adams' death*]: Cappon, pp. 508, 529.

272 [*Adams-Jefferson exchanges on checks and balances, parties, liberty*]: *ibid.*, pp. 334, 337, 340, 351, 534, 550.

[*Jefferson on the Declaration of Independence*]: quoted in Fawn M. Brodie, *Thomas Jefferson: An Intimate History* (W. W. Norton, 1974), p. 468.

[*Celebrations of the Fourth of July in 1826*]: John Murray Allison, *Adams and Jefferson* (University of Oklahoma Press, 1966), Ch. 7.

273 [*Death of Jefferson*]: Brodie, p. 468. [*Death of Adams*]: Smith, pp. 1136-37; Allan Nevins, ed., *The Diary of John Quincy Adams* (Frederick Ungar, 1951), pp. 360-61.

8. THE BIRTH OF THE MACHINES

274 [*Whitney's trip to Georgia*]: Jeannette Mirsky and Allan Nevins, *The World of Eli Whitney* (Macmillan, 1952), pp. 50-55.

[*Eli Whitney on "moral world"*]: Whitney to Josiah Stebbins, quoted in *ibid.*, p. 130.

[*Southern agriculture in 1790*]: John Allen Krout and Dixon Ryan Fox, *The Completion of Independence* (Macmillan, 1944), pp. 7-8.

[*Whitney on cotton boll*]: letter of Eli Whitney to Eli Whitney, Sr., quoted in Mirsky and Nevins, p. 66.

[*Whitney's "little model"*]: *ibid.*

275 [*Whitney's fight to protect rights to his cotton gin*]: *ibid.*, pp. 93-97.

[*Impact of the cotton gin on the American economy*]: Douglass C. North, *The Economic Growth of the United States, 1790-1860* (Prentice-Hall, 1961), p. 8.

[*Rise of the price of cotton and expanding cotton production in the South*]: Paul W. Gates, *The Farmer's Age: Agriculture, 1815-1860* (Holt, Rinehart and Winston, 1960), p. 8.

[*Southern journal on "indissoluble cord"*]: *De Bow's Review*, quoted in Paul S. Taylor, "Plantation Laborer before the Civil War," *Agricultural History*, Vol. 28, No. 1 (January 1954), p. 3.

[*Trade of New York City, Philadelphia, and Boston*]: Krout and Fox, pp. 11-22.

276 [*Early career of Francis Cabot Lowell*]: Hannah Josephson, *The Golden Threads* (Duell, Sloan & Pearce, 1949), pp. 15-17.

[*Lowell's leadership in cotton manufacture*]: Robert K. Lamb, "The Entrepreneur and the Community," in William Miller, ed., *Men in Business: Essays on the Historical Role of the Entrepreneur* (Harper & Brothers, 1951), pp. 106-7.

[*Early difficulties of transportation*]: Edward C. Kirkland, *A History of American Economic Life* (Meredith, 1969), p. 133.

277 [*Early experiments in steam navigation*]: described in Krout and Fox, pp. 229-30.

277 ["*Mania*" *for steam engines*]: *ibid.*, p. 230.

[*Traveler in Northwest Territory*]: Samuel Williams of Chillicothe to Samuel W. Young, Esq., of Hillsboro, Virginia, in *Niles' Weekly Register*, Vol. 11, No. 324 (January 11, 1817), quoted in Roscoe Carlyle Buley, *The Old Northwest: Pioneer Period, 1815–1840* (Indiana Historical Society, 1950), Vol. 1, p. 57.

Farms: The Jacks-of-All-Trades

278 [*Description of sheep shearing at Clermont*]: Elkanah Watson, *Men and Times of the Revolution, or Memoirs of Elkanah Watson* (Dana, 1857), p. 394, quoted in George Dangerfield, *Chancellor Robert R. Livingston of New York, 1746–1813* (Harcourt, Brace, 1960), p. 434. *Description of Clermont estate*: Alf Evers, *The Catskills: From Wilderness to Woodstock* (Doubleday, 1972), p. 239.

279 [*Average tenant farm and rent on Clermont estate*]: Dangerfield, p. 190.

[*Excerpts from the diary of Thomas Coffin*]: Robert H. George, "Life on a New Hampshire Farm, 1825–1835," *Historical New Hampshire*, Vol. 22, No. 4 (Winter 1967), pp. 3–5.

[*Amount of wood needed by farmers each winter*]: Paul W. Gates, "Problems of Agricultural History, 1790–1840," *Agricultural History*, Vol. 46, No. 1 (January 1972), p. 37.

[*Spring tasks on New England farm*]: listed in George, p. 9.

[*Description of average northern farm and farming methods*]: Krout and Fox, pp. 92–93.

280 [*Jefferson on production of laborers*]: James A. Henretta, "Families and Farms: Mentalité in Pre-Industrial America," *William and Mary Quarterly*, Vol. 35, No. 1 (January 1978), p. 18.

[*Limits placed on farm production by rudimentary implements*]: Gates, *The Farmer's Age*, p. 287.

[*Coffin's comment on haying day in July*]: George, p. 6.

[*Report of English agriculturist on American hogs*]: Paul Leland Haworth, *George Washington, Farmer* (Bobbs-Merrill, 1915), p. 57.

281 [*Traveler's comment on Yankee farmers*]: Joseph Holt Ingraham, *The South-West. By a Yankee* (Harper & Brothers, 1835), Vol. 2, p. 89.

[*Economic pressures on New England farm families*]: Henretta, p. 7.

[*New England farm land values*]: Gates, *The Farmer's Age*, p. 29.

282 [*Cotton prices, 1815–27*]: Stuart Bruchey, ed., *Cotton and the Growth of the American Economy: 1790–1860* (Harcourt, Brace & World, 1967), Table 3-A.

[*Population growth in the Gulf states*]: Stuart Bruchey, *The Roots of American Economic Growth, 1607–1861* (Harper & Row, 1965), p. 156.

[*Crowding of small farmers by planters migrating to the Southwest*]: Gates, *The Farmer's Age*, p. 9.

[*Description of cotton planting by slaves*]: Dr. J. W. Monett, "The Cotton Crop," in Ingraham, p. 281.

283 [*Tendency of overseers and planters to use the whip as discipline*]: Monett, p. 287, and Eugene D. Genovese, *Roll, Jordan, Roll: The World the Slaves Made* (Pantheon, 1974), pp. 64–65.

[*Cotton-picking on the Dabney plantation*]: Susan Dabney Smedes, *Memorials of a Southern Planter*, Fletcher M. Green, ed. (Alfred A. Knopf, 1965), pp. 53–55.

[*Estimate of average amount of cotton picked by a field hand*]: Monett, p. 287.

284 [*Dabney's efforts to make his plantation self-sufficient*]: Smedes, pp. 55–60.

284 [*Evading of overseer by slaves*]: Monett, p. 286.

[*Small farmers in Mississippi*]: Ingraham, p. 26.

[*Statistics on cotton shipments to New Orleans*]: Bruchey, *Roots*, p. 156.

[*New England journalist on commission merchants*]: Ingraham, p. 93.

286 [*Shortage of investment capital in South*]: Bruchey, *Roots*, p. 40.

[*Georgia writer quoted on sterility of land*]: Gates, *The Farmer's Age*, p. 142.

[*Historian on the iron plow*]: Clarence H. Danhof, quoted in Bruchey, *Roots*, p. 178.

[*Southern visitor to New York State fair on importance of iron plow*]: Gates, *The Farmer's Age*, p. 283.

287 [*Growth of national market for farm products*]: Bruchey, *Roots*, pp. 153–60.

Factories: The Looms of Lowell

287 [*Whitney on his debts and business setbacks*]: Mirsky and Nevins, pp. 145–46.

[*Whitney's heartbreak over Catherine Greene*]: *ibid.*, p. 284.

288 [*Description of Whitney's first factory, Mill River*]: *ibid.*, p. 313.

[*Whitney's attitudes toward his laborers*]: *ibid.*, p. 190. [*Need to supervise every detail*]: *ibid.*, p. 225.

[*Wages for armorers*]: Felicia Johnson Deyrup, *Arms Making in the Connecticut Valley* (George Shurnway, 1970), p. 242.

[*Summary of average wages for unskilled workers in Pennsylvania*]: William A. Sullivan, *The Industrial Worker in Pennsylvania, 1800–1840* (Pennsylvania Historical and Museum Commission, 1955), p. 75.

289 [*Diversions at Harpers Ferry armory described*]: Merritt Roe Smith, *Harper's Ferry Armory and the New Technology* (Cornell University Press, 1977), p. 65.

[*Contributions of John Hall and Simeon North to interchangeable parts manufacture*]: Smith, p. 325.

[*Community of Salem, North Carolina, in 1799*]: Frank P. Albright, *Johann Ludwig Eberhardt and His Salem Clocks* (University of North Carolina Press, 1978), pp. 3–6.

290 [*Control which the Elders Conference exercised over morals in Salem*]: *ibid.*, pp. 12–13.

[*Dependence of Salem on Philadelphia wholesale houses for manufactured articles*]: *ibid.*, p. 64.

[*Eli Terry's methods of producing clocks by machine*]: Dirk J. Struik, *Yankee Science in the Making* (Little, Brown, 1948), p. 147.

291 [*Value of Whitney's estate*]: Mirsky and Nevins, pp. 312–13.

[*Slater's introduction of cotton-spinning machinery into the United States*]: Daniel J. Boorstin, *The Americans: The National Experience* (Vintage Books, 1965), p. 27.

292 [*Power loom adopted by Lowell for cotton mills*]: Robert Brooke Zevin, "The Growth of Cotton Textile Production after 1815," in Robert William Fogel and Stanley L. Engerman, eds., *The Reinterpretation of American Economic History* (Harper & Row, 1971), pp. 139–41.

[*Site of the Waltham mills described*]: Steve Dunwell, *The Run of the Mill* (David R. Godine, 1978), pp. 30–33.

294 [*Building of Lowell*]: Lamb, p. 107.

[*Lucy Larcom and conditions in Lowell factories*]: Lucy Larcom, *An Idyll of Work* (James R. Osgood, 1875), passim. See also Dunwell, pp. 42–49.

294 [*Lowell as a social experiment*]: Benita Eisler, ed., *The Lowell Offering* (Lippincott, 1977), p. 15, quoted in Anna D. Socrates, "The Women of Lowell: A Study in Leadership and Consciousness-Raising" (Williams College, Nov. 1979).

295 [*Merchants' pursuit of stable investment returns from the Waltham-Lowell system*]: Robert F. Dalzell, Jr., "The Rise of the Waltham-Lowell System and Some Thoughts on the Political Economy of Modernization in Ante-bellum Massachusetts," *Perspectives in American History*, Vol. 9 (1975), pp. 229–68.

296 [*Skepticism of Cabots and Lowells toward Francis Cabot Lowell's plans for a textile mill*]: Ferris Greenslet, *The Lowells and Their Seven Worlds* (Houghton Mifflin, 1946), p. 156.

Freight: The Big Ditches

296 [*Maiden voyage of the* Clermont]: Dangerfield, pp. 407–9, and John S. Morgan, *Robert Fulton* (Mason/Charter, 1977), pp. 140–43; see also Robert R. Livingston, "The Invention of the Steamboat," *Old South Leaflets*, Vol. 5, No. 108 (Old South Meeting House, 1902), pp. 161–76 (which includes letters by Robert Fulton).

[*Skepticism about the steamboat*]: quoted in Morgan, p. 140. [*Speed of the* Clermont *and the reactions of amazed bystanders*]: ibid., p. 142.

[*Fulton on his plans to use steamboat on the Mississippi River*]: ibid., p. 143.

297 [*Fulton's early interest and training in navigation*]: ibid., pp. 41–42.

[*Livingston's New York State monopoly on steam navigation*]: Dorothy Gregg, "John Stevens, General Entrepreneur," in Miller, p. 135.

[*Description of building the* Clermont]: Louis C. Hunter, *Steamboats on the Western Waters* (Harvard University Press, 1949), p. 66.

298 [*Comparatively low cost of steamboat construction*]: Gregg, p. 133.

[*Livingston's interest in steam navigation*]: Dangerfield, p. 287.

[*Fulton's careful study of records of other inventors in steam navigation*]: Morgan, pp. 156–58.

[*Prohibitive cost of freight transport by wagon*]: Kirkland, p. 136.

299 [*Settler digging clay from the middle of the road*]: Buley, p. 459.

[*Livingston's influence in securing a monopoly of steam navigation on the lower Mississippi*]: Dangerfield, p. 417.

[*Roosevelt's difficulties in building the Mississippi steamboat*]: Morgan, pp. 168–69.

300 [*Sinking of the* New Orleans]: Morgan, p. 170.

[*Speed of the* Washington *as compared to keelboats*]: Buley, p. 413.

301 [*Steamboats' failures in transporting heavy freight*]: Buley, p. 427.

[*Lincoln's flatboat trip to New Orleans*]: Stephen B. Oates, *With Malice Toward None* (Harper & Row, 1977), pp. 14–15.

302 [*Rise of cities on the Ohio and Mississippi rivers*]: Louis Bernard Schmidt, "Internal Commerce and the Development of National Economy before 1860," *Journal of Political Economy*, Vol. 47, No. 6 (December 1939), pp. 798–801.

304 ["*Wedding of the waters*" *at Erie Canal celebration*]: Ronald E. Shaw, *Erie Water West: A History of the Erie Canal, 1792–1854* (University Press of Kentucky, 1966), pp. 186–91.

[*Song* " '*Tis done* . . . "]: Madeline Sadler Waggoner, *The Long Haul West* (G. P. Putnam's Sons, 1958), p. 128.

[*The Pennsylvania Canal*]: Kirkland, pp. 146–47; Waggoner, Ch. 11.

The Innovating Leaders

305 [*Forman's interview with Jefferson*]: David Hosack, *Memoir of De Witt Clinton* (J. Seymour, 1829), p. 347; Jefferson to Clinton, Dec. 12, 1822, *ibid.*, pp. 347–48.

307 [*Robert Lamb on role of extended family in decision-making process*]: Lamb, p. 93.

[*Broadus and Louise Mitchell on root-cutting technique*]: Broadus Mitchell and Louise Pearson Mitchell, *American Economic History* (Houghton Mifflin, 1947), p. 353.

[*Role of state governments in economic development and promotion*]: Carter Goodrich *et al.*, *Canals and American Economic Development* (Columbia University Press, 1961), passim; Roger L. Ransom, "Interregional Canals and Economic Specialization in the Antebellum United States," *Explorations in Entrepreneurial History*, Second Series, Vol. 5, No. 1 (Fall 1967), pp. 12–35.

308 [*Elkanah Watson*]: Hugh M. Flick, "Elkanah Watson's Activities on Behalf of Agriculture," *Agricultural History*, Vol. 21, No. 4 (October 1947), pp. 193–98; Watson is quoted at p. 194.

[*Appeal of Erie Canal proposal to group interests*]: Julius Rubin, "An Innovating Public Improvement: The Erie Canal," in Goodrich, quoted at pp. 53–54.

309 [*The new triangle of trade*]: Schmidt, p. 821; see also Douglass C. North, "The United States in the International Economy, 1790–1850," in Seymour E. Harris, ed., *American Economic History* (McGraw-Hill, 1961), pp. 181–205.

310 [*"Impersonal" economic forces dominating the marketplace*]: Zevin, passim.

9. THE WIND FROM THE WEST

315 [*Migration west*]: Oscar Handlin, *The Americans* (Atlantic Monthly Press, 1963), Ch. 14; Harry J. Carman, Harold C. Syrett, and Bernard W. Wishy, *A History of the American People* (Alfred A. Knopf, 1964), Vol. 1, Ch. 12; Ray Allen Billington, *Westward Expansion* (Macmillan, 1960).

[*Morris Birkbeck on the small family wagons*]: quoted in Carman, Syrett, and Wishy, p. 361.

316 [*Hollidaysburg* Aurora *on the Allegheny Portage Railroad trip*]: quoted in Madeline Sadler Waggoner, *The Long Haul West* (G. P. Putnam's Sons, 1958), pp. 196–97.

[*Sights and sounds of the Erie Canal*]: Waggoner, p. 155; my description of passing through the canal is mainly drawn from this work; and from Ronald E. Shaw, *Erie Water West* (University Press of Kentucky, 1966).

317 [*Dickens on canal-barge life*]: Waggoner, pp. 152, 153.

[*Spitting*]: Edward Pessen, *Jacksonian America: Society, Personality, and Politics* (Dorsey Press, 1969), p. 23. [*Mrs. Trollope on slouching*]: *ibid.*, p. 23.

318 [*Individualism on the frontier*]: Ray Allen Billington, *The American Frontier Thesis: Attack and Defense* (American Historical Association, 1958), p. 36.

[*Westerners as outsiders*]: Frederic Austin Ogg, *The Old Northwest: A Chronicle of the Ohio Valley and Beyond* (Yale University Press, 1919), pp. 101–2; see also Robert E. Riegel and Robert G. Athearn, *America Moves West*, 4th ed. (Holt, Rinehart and Winston, 1964), pp. 78–80.

[*Contradictions of frontier people*]: Pessen, pp. 34–35.

[*Character of frontier people*]: see also Louis B. Wright, *Culture on the Moving Frontier* (Indiana University Press, 1955); Marvin Meyers, *The Jacksonian Persuasion* (Stanford University Press, 1957); Richard Hofstadter and Seymour Martin Lipset, eds., *Turner and the Sociology of the Frontier* (Basic Books, 1968); Robert E. Riegel, *Young America,*

1830–1840 (University of Oklahoma Press, 1949); Dale Van Every, *The Final Challenge* (William Morrow, 1964).

319 [*Andrew Jackson's life and character*]: Marquis James, *Andrew Jackson: Portrait of a President* (Bobbs-Merrill, 1937); Michael Paul Rogin, *Fathers and Children: Andrew Jackson and the Subjugation of the American Indian* (Alfred A. Knopf, 1975); Robert V. Remini, *Andrew Jackson and the Course of American Empire, 1767–1821* (Harper & Row, 1977).

The Revolt of the Outs

320 [*Polk on the "American tripod"*]: James K. Polk, in the House of Representatives, March 29, 1830, 21st Congress, 1st session, *Register of Debates*, pp. 698–99, quoted in Arthur M. Schlesinger, Jr., *The Age of Jackson* (Little, Brown, 1945), p. 62.

321 [*The Jackson men as insiders and outsiders*]: Pessen, Ch. 8, passim. See also Sydney H. Aronson, *Status and Kinship in the Higher Civil Service* (Harvard University Press, 1964).

[*Jackson's comments on the "corrupt bargain"*]: Jackson to John Coffee, Feb. 19, 1825, in John Spencer Bassett, ed., *Correspondence of Andrew Jackson* (Carnegie Institute of Washington, 1928), Vol. 3, pp. 277–78; Jackson to James Buchanan, June 25, 1825, *ibid.*, p. 287.

[*Election of 1828*]: Robert V. Remini, *The Election of Andrew Jackson* (Lippincott, 1963); Edward Pessen, *New Perspectives on Jacksonian Parties and Politics* (Boston: Allyn and Bacon, 1969); Robert V. Remini, "Election of 1828," in Arthur M. Schlesinger, Jr., ed., *History of American Presidential Elections* (Chelsea House, 1971), Vol. 1, pp. 413–92. On New York State and national aspects of the campaign, I have used the John W. Taylor Papers, New-York Historical Society; the Amariah Flagg Collection, Columbia University Library; and the A. C. Flagg Papers, New York Public Library. For a Massachusetts Whig view, see the Edward Everett Papers, Massachusetts Historical Society, Box 3, Folders 1 and 2.

322 [*Calhoun on prospects for 1828*]: Calhoun to Jackson, Jan. 24, 1827, Bassett, Vol. 3, p. 332.

[*Van Buren on a North-South coalition and reorganization of the old Republican party*]: Remini in Schlesinger, *Elections*, Vol. 1, p. 417.

323 [*"Hurra Boys" for Jackson*]: Remini, *Election*, p. 111.

[*Campaign slander and abuse*]: Remini in Schlesinger, passim; Glyndon G. Van Deusen, *The Jacksonian Era* (Harper & Brothers, 1959), pp. 26–27.

[*Jackson's marriage to Rachel Robards*]: Remini, *Jackson and the Course of American Empire*, Ch. 5.

[*Reactions to the 1828 election outcome*]: Remini, in Schlesinger, *Elections*, p. 434.

324 [*Webster on Jackson's "breeze"*]: Daniel Webster to Ezekiel Webster, inclosure, Feb. 1829, in C. H. Van Tyne, ed., *Letters of Daniel Webster* (McClure, Phillips, 1902), p. 142.

[*Randolph on finding leaders of a revolution*]: John Randolph to J. Brockenbrough, Jan. 12, 1829, Feb. 9, 1829, in Hugh A. Garland, *Life of John Randolph of Roanoke* (D. Appleton, 1855), Vol. 2, p. 317.

[*New York politico on patronage*]: William L. Mackenzie, *The Lives and Opinions of Benj'n Franklin Butler . . . and Jesse Hoyt* (Cook, 1845), pp. 51–52.

[*Van Buren besieged by job seekers*]: Martin Van Buren, *The Autobiography of Martin Van Buren* (Government Printing Office, 1920), *Annual Report* of the American Historical Association for the Year 1918, Vol. 2, pp. 231–32.

[*Parton on wave of fear*]: James Parton, *Life of Andrew Jackson* (Mason Brothers, 1860), Vol. 3, p. 212.

324 [*Adams on the officialdom in terror*]: Charles Francis Adams, ed., *Memoirs of John Quincy Adams* (Lippincott, 1876), Vol. 8, p. 144 (April 25, 1829).

[*Conversation of two job seekers*]: Amos Kendall, *Autobiography*, William Stickney, ed. (Lee and Shepard, 1872), p. 308.

[*Jackson's appointment policy*]: Aronson, passim.

325 [*Jackson's defense of removals*]: James D. Richardson, *Compilation of the Messages and Papers of the Presidents* (Bureau of National Literature, 1897), Vol. 2, pp. 1011-12 (Dec. 8, 1829).

[*Madison on rotation*]: Gaillard Hunt, ed., *The Writings of James Madison* (G. P. Putnam's Sons, 1910), Vol. 9, pp. 539-40 (Aug. 29, 1834).

[*Jackson's Cabinet*]: Leonard D. White, *The Jacksonians* (Macmillan, 1956), Ch. 5.

[*Jackson's "kitchen cabinet"*]: Richard P. Longaker, "Was Jackson's Kitchen Cabinet a Cabinet?" *The Mississippi Valley Historical Review*, Vol. 44, No. 1 (June 1957), pp. 94-108.

326 [*Blair filling columns with "public opinion"*]: Harriet Martineau, *Retrospect of Western Travel* (Harper & Brothers, 1838), Vol. 1, p. 155.

327 [*Jackson on not making a cabinet for the ladies*]: Jackson to J. C. McLemore, April 1, 1829, Andrew Jackson Papers, Library of Congress, 2nd Series.

[*Clay on Jackson sweeping over the government like a tornado*]: *Register of Debates* (Gales and Seaton, 1837), Vol. 13, 24th Congress, 2nd session, Jan. 16, 1837, p. 438.

The Dance of the Factions

327 [*The Webster-Hayne debate*]: Claude M. Fuess, *Daniel Webster* (Da Capo Press, 1968), Vol. 1, Ch. 15; Theodore D. Jervey, *Robert Y. Hayne and His Times* (Macmillan, 1909), Chs. 9-14; Charles M. Wiltse, *John C. Calhoun, Nullifier, 1829-1839* (Bobbs-Merrill, 1949), Ch. 4.

328 [*Hayne on "selfish and unprincipled" East*]: ibid., p. 365.

[*Webster's statements before the climactic debate*]: quoted in Fuess, pp. 372, 374.

[*Economic, social, and political change in South Carolina*]: Charles S. Sydnor, *The Development of Southern Sectionalism, 1819-1848* (Louisiana State University Press, 1948), passim; William W. Freehling, *Prelude to Civil War* (Harper & Row, 1965), Part I.

[*Pinckney on slavery*]: Freehling, p. 109.

329 [*Calhoun's "South Carolina Exposition"*]: Richard K. Crallé, ed., *Reports and Public Letters of John C. Calhoun* (D. Appleton, 1855), Vol. 6, pp. 1-59 (consisting of original draft of the Exposition, adopted with alterations by the South Carolina Legislature, Dec. 1828), passim.

[*Webster on the cry of "Consolidation!"*]: *The Writings and Speeches of Daniel Webster*, National Edition (Little, Brown, 1903), Vol. 5, p. 257.

[*Webster's sense of audience response in the Senate*]: Webster to Jeremiah Mason, Feb. 27, 1830, in Charles M. Wiltse, ed., *The Papers of Daniel Webster, Correspondence 1830-1834* (University Press of New England, 1977), Vol. 3, pp. 18-19; Fuess, Vol. 1, p. 374.
[*Bay State men cry over "encomium upon Massachusetts"*]: Fuess, p. 378.

330 [*Webster's climactic words*]: *Register of Debates* (Gales and Seaton, 1830), Vol. 6, 21st Congress, 1st session, Jan. 27, 1830, pp. 58-80.

[*The toasts at the Indian Queen Hotel*]: Van Buren, *Autobiography*, pp. 413-17; Freehling, p. 192.

331 [*Emerson on Webster*]: *The Journals of Ralph Waldo Emerson,* eds. E. W. Emerson and W. E. Forbes (Houghton Mifflin, 1912), Vol. 7, p. 87

[*Henry Clay and the Maysville Turnpike*]: Clement Eaton, *Henry Clay and the Art of American Politics* (Little, Brown, 1957), pp. 10, 96–97.

[*Webster on the coming crisis*]: Webster to Clay, May 29, 1830, in Wiltse, *Papers of Daniel Webster,* Vol. 3, p. 80.

332 [*Van Buren on Mrs. Eaton*]: Van Buren to Jackson, July 25, 1830, quoted in John A. Munroe, *Louis McLane: Federalist and Jacksonian* (Rutgers University Press, 1973), p. 293.

[*The break between Jackson and Calhoun*]: Wiltse, *John C. Calhoun,* Ch. 6; Van Deusen, p. 45.

[*Calhoun: "It will . . . kill him dead"*]: quoted in Thomas H. Benton, *Thirty Years' View* (D. Appleton, 1856), Vol. 1, p. 219.

333 [*Freehling on the collapse of Calhoun's presidential hopes*]: Freehling, pp. 226–27.

[*Clay on the fate of liberty throughout the world*]: quoted in Schlesinger, *Elections,* Vol. 1, p. 507.

334 [*Nomination of Wirt by Anti-Masons*]: John P. Kennedy, *Memoirs of the Life of William Wirt* (Lea and Blanchard, 1850), Vol. 2, pp. 299–315.

335 [*The authority of Georgia in Cherokee territory*]: *Worcester* v. *Georgia* (6 Peters 515), in Richard Peters, *Reports of Cases Argued and Adjudged in the Supreme Court of the United States* (Banks Law Publishing, 1917), Vol. 6, pp. 515–47.

[*Jackson on Worcester v. Georgia*]: quoted in Horace Greeley, *The American Conflict* (Case, 1866), p. 106; Greeley claims that the remark was related to him by Congressman George N. Briggs of Massachusetts.

[*Jackson on preventing liberties from being "crushed by the Bank"*]: quoted in Schlesinger, *Elections,* Vol. 1, p. 499. On the origins of the bank war, see Donald B. Cole, *Jacksonian Democracy in New Hampshire, 1800–1851* (Harvard University Press, 1970), Ch. 5.

[*Clay and Webster urging Biddle to call for bank recharter*]: Daniel Webster to Nicholas Biddle, Dec. 18, 1831, in Wiltse, *Papers of Daniel Webster,* Vol. 3, p. 139; Eaton, p. 99.

[*Jackson on killing the bank*]: Van Buren, *Autobiography,* p. 625.

[*Jackson's appeal to the "humble members of society"*]: quoted in Schlesinger, *Elections,* Vol. 1, p. 500. [*Remini on Jackson's stand on issues*]: *ibid.,* p. 500. [*Jackson on the veto working well*]: *ibid.,* p. 510.

[*Nullification proclamation*]: Richardson, *Messages and Papers,* Vol. 2, pp. 1203–19.

336 [*Election of 1832*]: Schlesinger, *Elections,* Vol. 1, p. 574.

[*Reaction of South Carolina extremists to nullification proclamation*]: Freehling, pp. 267–78; McDuffie quoted, p. 267.

337 [*John Randolph on seeing Webster die, "muscle by muscle"*]: quoted in Wiltse, *John C. Calhoun,* p. 194.

[*Contrast between Biddle and Jackson*]: James, pp. 250–52.

[*Jackson's trip through the Northeast to New England*]: James, pp. 340–49. [*John Quincy Adams on Jackson as a Harvard degree recipient*]: quoted in John T. Morse, *John Quincy Adams* (Houghton Mifflin, 1899), p. 241.

338 [*Jackson's reasons for renewing the bank war after his re-election*]: Schlesinger, *Age of Jackson,* p. 98.

338 [*Jackson's response to visiting delegations*]: *ibid.*, p. 109; Bray Hammond, *Banks and Politics in America* (Princeton University Press, 1957), p. 430. [*Rogin on Jackson's fanaticism*]: *Fathers and Children*, Ch. 9.

[*McLane shifted to State Department*]: Munroe, Ch. 12.

339 [*Relationship of Biddle and Webster*]: Wiltse, *Papers of Daniel Webster*, Vol. 3, passim; on the retainer, Webster to Biddle, Dec. 21, 1833, p. 288; [*on burning letters*]: *ibid.* and Biddle to Webster, Dec. 25, 1834 (actually 1833), p. 292; [*on the need for unity among Webster, Clay and Calhoun*]: Biddle to Webster, Dec. 15, 1833, p. 285.

340 [*Henry Clay's censure speech against Jackson in the Senate*]: *Register of Debates*, 23rd Congress, 1st session, Dec. 26 and 30, 1833, pp. 58-94; Calvin Colton, ed., *The Works of Henry Clay* (Henry Clay, 1896), Vol. 5, pp. 576-620.

Jacksonian Leadership

341 [*The Whig party*]: Eber M. Carroll, *Origins of the Whig Party* (Duke University Press, 1925); see also studies of state and sectional origins.

[*Edward Everett*]: Edward Everett Papers, Box 2, 1819-27, Massachusetts Historical Society.

342 [*Drafting of Webster*]: Sydney Nathans, *Daniel Webster and Jacksonian Democracy* (Johns Hopkins University Press, 1973), pp. 91-92.

[*Jackson's threats to Hugh Lawson White*]: Dumas Malone, ed., *Dictionary of American Biography* (Charles Scribner's Sons, 1936), Vol. 10, p. 106.

[*Seward on Van Buren*]: New York *Evening Post*, Nov. 2, 1836, quoted in Schlesinger, *Age of Jackson*, p. 214.

[*Election of 1836*]: Schlesinger, *Elections*, Vol. 1, p. 640.

[*Pomper on 1836 as a "converting election"*]: Gerald M. Pomper, *Elections in America* (Dodd, Mead, 1968), pp. 112-13.

343 [*Schlesinger on "the living relations" between leader and followers*]: *Age of Jackson*, p. 215.

[*Van Buren and his administration*]: James C. Curtis, *The Fox at Bay* (University Press of Kentucky, 1970); Charles Francis Adams, ed., *Memoirs of John Quincy Adams Comprising Portions of His Diary from 1795-1848* (Philadelphia: Lippincott, 1876), Vols. 9-10; and other works cited previously in this chapter.

344 [*British minister's report on public reaction to the panic*]: quoted in Curtis, p. 73.

[*Jacksonian finance*]: John M. McFaul, *The Politics of Jacksonian Finance* (Cornell University Press, 1972); Curtis; Hammond; Walter B. Smith, *Economic Aspects of the Second Bank of the United States* (Harvard University Press, 1953).

345 [*Cambreleng on the Independent Treasury bill*]: Cambreleng to Van Buren, Nov. 18, 1837, quoted in Van Deusen, p. 126.

[*Webster statements*]: *Congressional Globe*, 25th Congress, 1st session, Sept. 28, 1837, Appendix, p. 169; *ibid.*, 25th Congress, 2nd session, Jan. 31, 1838, Appendix, p. 606.

346 [*Pickens on northern banking and southern slavery*]: *ibid.*, 25th Congress, 1st session, Oct. 10, 1837, Vol. 5: Appendix, p. 178, quoted in Curtis, p. 106.

[*Clay on "symptoms of despotism"*]: Senate speech of Dec. 26 and 30, 1833, in Colton, Vol. 5, p. 620.

[*Jackson's veto record*]: Richard M. Pious, *The American Presidency* (Basic Books, 1979), p. 207; William M. Goldsmith, *The Growth of Presidential Power* (Chelsea House, 1974), Vol. 1, pp. 329-31.

346 [*Historians' evaluation of Jackson*]: Arthur M. Schlesinger, Jr., *Paths to the Present* (Macmillan, 1949), Ch. 5; Arthur M. Schlesinger, Jr., "Our Presidents: A Rating by 75 Historians," *The New York Times Magazine* (July 29, 1962), p. 12.

347 [*Hawthorne on Jackson*]: quoted in Clinton Rossiter, *The American Presidency* (Harcourt, Brace, 1956), p. 150.

[*Controversy among historians over Jacksonianism*]: Pessen, *Jacksonian America*, pp. 384–93; see also Marvin Meyers, *The Jacksonian Persuasion* (Stanford University Press, 1957), pp. 2–3; McFaul, Ch. 1; Charles G. Sellers, Jr., "Andrew Jackson versus the Historians," *Mississippi Valley Historical Review*, Vol. 44, No. 4 (March 1958), pp. 615–34.

[*Van Buren's strategy of directly mobilizing followers*]: Notebook, Martin Van Buren Papers, Library of Congress, cited in Schlesinger, *Age of Jackson*, p. 51.

348 [*Kendall on business power limiting man's freedom*]: quoted in Schlesinger, *Age of Jackson*, p. 319, from the Washington *Globe*, Sept. 24, 1840.

[*Jackson's philosophy as reflected in his veto of the recharter bill*]: quoted in Richard Hofstadter, *The American Political Tradition* (Alfred A. Knopf, 1948), p. 62.

[*Jacksonians and the North-South axis*]: Richard H. Brown, "The Missouri Crisis, Slavery, and the Politics of Jacksonianism," *South Atlantic Quarterly*, Vol. 65 (1966), pp. 55–72.

349 [*Hartz on the parties as wildly swinging boxers*]: Louis Hartz, *The Liberal Tradition in America* (Harcourt, Brace, 1955), p. 90.

[*Van Buren on those who had wrought great changes in the world*]: Van Buren Papers, quoted in Schlesinger, *Age of Jackson*, p. 51.

10. Parties: The People's Constitution

351 [*Dickens on his* Britannia *stateroom*]: Charles Dickens, *American Notes* (Chapman and Hall, 1891), p. 5.

[*Dickens on Boston and on New York City harbor*]: ibid., pp. 23, 64–65.

352 [*Dickens on "slavery, spittoons, and senators"*]: Dickens to Charles Sumner, March 13, 1842, quoted in Norman and Jeanne MacKenzie, *Dickens: A Life* (Oxford University Press, 1979), p. 120.

[*Dickens on Congress*]: *American Notes*, p. 98.

[*Dickens on slavery and the Declaration of Independence*]: ibid., p. 97.

[*Dickens on Cincinnati*]: quoted in Norman and Jeanne MacKenzie, p. 123.

[*Dickens on western cities*]: *American Notes*, pp. 131, 137, 140.

353 [*Dickens' quotations from advertisements for runaway slaves*]: ibid., pp. 184–85.

[*Dickens on the general character of the American people*]: ibid., pp. 193–94.

354 [*Pessen's summary of Europeans' collective portrait of Americans*]: Edward Pessen, *Jacksonian America: Society, Personality, and Politics* (Dorsey Press, 1969), p. 34.

[*Tocqueville*]: Jacob Peter Mayer, *Alexis de Tocqueville: A Biographical Essay in Political Science* (Viking Press, 1940); George Wilson Pierson, *Tocqueville and Beaumont in America* (Oxford University Press, 1938).

Equality: The Jacksonian Demos

355 [*The plight of the destitute and the debtors*]: Pessen, p. 48. [*Distribution of wealth*]: Daniel E. Diamond and John D. Guilfoil, *United States Economic History* (General Learning Press, 1973), p. 82; Herman E. Krooss, *American Economic Development* (Prentice-Hall, 1955), p. 24.

355 [*Tocqueville on equality of conditions*]: Alexis de Tocqueville, *Democracy in America* (Alfred A. Knopf, 1960), Henry Reeve Text, Phillips Bradley, ed., Vol. 1, p. 3.

[*Tocqueville's underestimation of the beginnings of industrialization and urbanization*]: Irving M. Zeitlin, *Liberty, Equality, and Revolution in Alexis de Tocqueville* (Little, Brown, 1971), pp. 12, 58.

[*Commager on everyday social equality*]: Henry Steele Commager, *The American Mind* (Yale University Press, 1950), p. 14.

356 [*Tocqueville on self-respecting servants*]: Tocqueville, Vol. 2, p. 183.

[*John Quincy Adams to Tocqueville on legal equality*]: quoted in Pessen, p. 50.

[*Richard Wade on class lines in western cities*]: quoted in *ibid.*, p. 53.

[*Caste system in the Tombs*]: Dickens, *American Notes*, p. 68.

[*American classes*]: of the "revisionist" literature on stratification, see esp. Lloyd A. Fallers, *Inequality* (University of Chicago Press, 1973).

[*Tocqueville on Americans as born equal*]: quoted in Louis Hartz, *The Liberal Tradition in America* (Harcourt, Brace, 1955), p. i.

357 [*Tocqueville on American abundance*]: quoted in David M. Potter, *People of Plenty* (University of Chicago Press, 1954), p. 92.

[*Tocqueville on most rich men as having formerly been poor*]: quoted in Pessen, p. 51.

[*Tocqueville's belief that unadulterated democracy ruled in America*]: Zeitlin, p. 11.

[*Tocqueville on "God's will" about more equality*]: Tocqueville to M. Stoffels (Paris), Feb. 21, 1835, quoted in Tocqueville, Vol. 1, p. xx. [*Tocqueville on egalitarianism, majority rule, leveling, etc.*]: *ibid.*, Vol. 1, Chs. 15, 16; Vol. 2, passim.

[*Tocqueville on great parties, ambition, and leadership*]: *ibid.*, Vol. 1, pp. 174 ff.; Vol. 2, p. 247.

358 [*Workingmen's politics*]: Walter Hugins, *Jacksonian Democracy and the Working Class* (Stanford University Press, 1960); Nathan Fine, *Labor and Farmer Parties in the United States, 1828–1928* (Rand School of Social Science, 1928); Pessen, pp. 191–215.

359 [*Question of employer as a "working man"*]: quoted in Pessen, p. 210.

[*Radical leaders*]: J. R. Pole, *The Pursuit of Equality in American History* (University of California Press, 1978), Ch. 5; Arthur M. Schlesinger, Jr., *The Age of Jackson* (Little, Brown, 1945), passim; Hugins, passim; Dumas Malone, ed., *Dictionary of American Biography* (Charles Scribner's Sons, 1936).

360 [*Walt Whitman on Frances Wright*]: quoted in Schlesinger, *Age of Jackson*, p. 181.

[*Wright as "Red Harlot"*]: New York *Courier and Enquirer*, quoted in Schlesinger, *Age of Jackson*, p. 182.

361 [*Samuel Clesson Allen on the "natural limit of production"*]: quoted in *ibid.*, p. 153.

[*Robert Rantoul*]: Marvin Meyers, *The Jacksonian Persuasion* (Stanford University Press, 1957), Ch. 10.

363 [*The jackass as voter*]: story told by a delegate to the Massachusetts constitutional convention, 1853, cited in James MacGregor Burns and Jack Walter Peltason, *Government By the People*, 2nd ed. (Prentice-Hall, 1954), p. 251.

[*Blackstone on property qualifications*]: quoted in Chilton Williamson, *American Suffrage from Property to Democracy, 1760–1860* (Princeton University Press, 1960), p. 11.

364 [*Pessen on the suffrage situation before the Jacksonian era*]: Pessen, p. 155.

364 [*James Kent and the conservative rearguard action against the "tyranny of numbers"*]: John T. Horton, *James Kent: A Study in Conservatism, 1763–1847* (Appleton-Century, 1939), pp. 256–57. [*Randolph on "King Numbers"*]: Robert Dawidoff, *The Education of John Randolph* (W. W. Norton, 1979), p. 276.

365 [*The Dorr Rebellion*]: Arthur M. Mowry, *The Dorr War* (Preston & Rounds, 1901); Williamson, Ch. 13.

366 [*First issue of* Liberator]: John L. Thomas, *The Liberator: William Lloyd Garrison* (Little, Brown, 1963), p. 128. [*Massachusetts Anti-Slavery Society denounces Constitution*]: quoted in Russel B. Nye, *William Lloyd Garrison and the Humanitarian Reformers*, Oscar Handlin, ed. (Little, Brown, 1955), p. 143.

[*Weld on abolitionism*]: quoted in Richard Hofstadter, *The American Political Tradition* (Alfred A. Knopf, 1948), p. 144.

[*Frances Wright's experiment in emancipation*]: Cecilia Helena Payne-Gaposchkin, "The Nashoba Plan for Removing the Evil of Slavery: Letters of Frances and Camilla Wright, 1820–1829," *Harvard Library Bulletin*, Vol. 23, No. 3 (July 1975), and No. 4 (October 1975). See also William Randall Waterman, "Frances Wright," *Studies in History, Economics, and Public Law*, Vol. 115, No. 1 (Columbia University Press, 1924), pp. 92–133.

State Politics: Seedbed of Party

370 [*Pre- and post-Revolutionary New York State politics*]: Patricia U. Bonomi, *A Factious People* (Columbia University Press, 1971); Carl Lotus Becker, *The History of Political Parties in the Province of New York, 1760–1776* (University of Wisconsin Press, 1960); Alfred F. Young, *The Democratic Republicans of New York: The Origins, 1763–1797* (University of North Carolina Press, 1967).

[*The rapid rise of De Witt Clinton*]: quotation from *Dictionary of American Biography*, Vol. 2, p. 221; see also, on Clinton, Dixon Ryan Fox, *The Decline of Aristocracy in the Politics of New York* (Columbia University Press, 1919).

371 [*New York State party development*]: Michael Wallace, "Changing Concepts of Party in the United States: New York, 1815–1828," *American Historical Review*, Vol. 7, No. 2 (December 1968), pp. 453–91. See, in general, Edward Pessen, "Reflections on New York and Its Recent Historians," *New-York Historical Society Quarterly*, Vol. 63, No. 2 (April 1979), pp. 145–56; John W. Taylor Papers, New-York Historical Society.

[*The Albany Regency*]: Robert V. Remini, "The Albany Regency," *New York History*, Vol. 39, No. 4 (October 1958), pp. 341–55; A. C. Flagg Papers, Columbia University Library and New York Public Library; Charles H. Ruggles Papers, New York Public Library.

[*Submission to party by the* Advocate's *Mordecai Noah*]: Wallace, pp. 464–65, quoted at p. 465.

[*The "martyrs'" banquet*]: *ibid.*, p. 465.

372 [*Close association of Regency families*]: quotation from James Gordon Bennett, in Remini, pp. 350–51.

[*Regency leaders' conception of political party*]: Wallace, pp. 481–91, Throop quoted at p. 488.

[*Regency conservatism*]: Lee Benson, *The Concept of Jacksonian Democracy* (Princeton University Press, 1961), pp. 30, 39, 66.

373 [*Benson on the Regency strategy*]: quoted in *ibid.*, p. 55.

[*Early Massachusetts state politics*]: Van Beck Hall, *Politics Without Parties* (University of Pittsburgh Press, 1972); Paul Goodman, *The Democratic-Republicans* (Harvard University Press, 1964); manuscript sources: Massachusetts Historical Society; Boston Public Library; Widener Library, Harvard University; Library of Congress.

373 [*Aspects of political transition of Massachusetts*]: Arthur B. Darling, "Jacksonian Democracy in Massachusetts, 1824–1848," *American Historical Review*, Vol. 29, No. 2 (January 1924), pp. 271–87; Pessen, *Jacksonian America*, pp. 238–40.

374 [*David Henshaw*]: Schlesinger, *Age of Jackson*, pp. 146–47; *Dictionary of American Biography*, Vol. 8, pp. 562–63.

[*Kentucky political developments*]: Lynn L. Marshall, "The Genesis of Grass-roots Democracy in Kentucky," *Mid-America*, Vol. 47, No. 4 (October 1965), pp. 269–87; Thomas B. Jones, "New Thoughts on an Old Theme," *Register of the Kentucky Historical Society*, Vol. 69, No. 4 (October 1971), pp. 293–312; Billie J. Hardin, "Amos Kendall and the 1824 Relief Controversy," *ibid.*, Vol. 64, No. 3 (July 1966), pp. 196–208; Duff Green Papers, Nicholas Trist Papers, Library of Congress.

375 [*Historians on rational, popular demands and aspirations in Kentucky*]: Marshall, pp. 273, 284, quoted at p. 284.

On party development in the South as a whole, see Burton W. Folsom II, "Party Formation and Development in Jacksonian America: the Old South," *Journal of American Studies*, Vol. 7, No. 3 (December 1973), pp. 217–29.

Majorities: The Flowering of the Parties

376 [*Chambers on the building of parties*]: William Nisbet Chambers, *Political Parties in a New Nation* (Oxford University Press, 1963), p. 49.

377 [*Role and decline of deference in early politics*]: Ronald P. Formisano, "Deferential-Participant Politics: The Early Republic's Political Culture, 1789–1840," *American Political Science Review*, Vol. 68, No. 2 (June 1974), pp. 473–87.

[*"Party in office" as distinguished from national party organization and affiliation among the electorate*]: Frank J. Sorauf, "Political Parties and Political Analysis," in William Nisbet Chambers and Walter Dean Burnham, eds., *The American Party Systems* (Oxford University Press, 1967), pp. 33–55, esp. pp. 37–38.

378 [*The congressional caucus*]: Noble E. Cunningham, Jr., "The Ascendance and Demise of the Congressional Caucus, 1800–1824," paper prepared for conference, "The American Constitutional System Under Strong and Weak Parties," sponsored by Project 87 (Washington, D.C.), April 27–28, 1979, pp. 1–36 (typescript).

379 [*McCormick on the "hidden revolution"*]: Richard P. McCormick, *The Second American Party System* (University of North Carolina Press, 1966), p. 343.

[*Intellectual attitudes toward the party system*]: Richard Hofstadter, *The Idea of a Party System* (University of California Press, 1969); see also Austin Ranney, *The Doctrine of Responsible Party Government* (University of Illinois Press, 1962).

[*Berlin on Archilochus' hedgehog*]: Isaiah Berlin, *The Hedgehog and the Fox* (Simon and Schuster, 1970).

[*Van Buren's view of party*]: Martin Van Buren to Thomas Ritchie, Jan. 13, 1827, Martin Van Buren Papers, Library of Congress; see also Hofstadter, *Idea of a Party System*, pp. 223–26.

[*Chase on intellectual failure in party organization*]: James S. Chase, *Emergence of the Presidential Nominating Convention, 1789–1832* (University of Illinois Press, 1973), p. 17.

380 [*Inter-party balance in the states*]: McCormick, p. 341.

381 [*Party and constitution*]: Theodore J. Lowi, "Party, Policy, and Constitution in America," in Chambers and Burnham, pp. 238–76.

11. THE MAJORITY THAT NEVER WAS

383 [*Revolutionary, radical, and reformist movements, their emergence, non-emergence, and suppression*]: Ted Robert Gurr, *Why Men Rebel* (Princeton University Press, 1970); Barrington Moore, Jr., *Injustice: The Social Bases of Obedience and Revolt* (M. E. Sharpe, 1978); James Chowning Davies, ed., *When Men Revolt and Why* (Free Press, 1971); Bob Jessop, *Social Order, Reform and Revolution* (Herder and Herder, 1972); the works of Marx, Weber, Dahrendorf, and other theorists from which much of the recent analysis is drawn.

384 [*Tocqueville on revolution in America*]: quoted in Irving M. Zeitlin, *Liberty, Equality, and Revolution in Alexis de Tocqueville* (Little, Brown, 1971), p. 41.

[*The slave trade*]: John R. Spears, *The American Slave-Trade* (Charles Scribner's Sons, 1900); W. E. Burghardt Du Bois, *The Suppression of the African Slave-Trade* (Longmans, Green, 1904); Julius Lester, *To Be a Slave* (Dial Press, 1968).

[*Voyage of* La Fortuna]: Brantz Meyer, ed., *Captain Canot, an African Slaver* (Arno Press, 1968), pp. 99–106. [*Canot's accounting*]: ibid., p. 101.

Blacks in Bondage

385 [*Description of Montevideo*]: Robert Manson Myers, ed., *The Children of Pride* (Yale University Press, 1972), pp. 17–19; for another large plantation (Georgia), see Pierce Butler Papers, Pennsylvania Historical Society.

[*Letter of Cato to Charles Colcock Jones, Sept. 3, 1852*]: Robert S. Starobin, ed., *Blacks in Bondage* (New Viewpoints, 1974), pp. 47–50.

386 [*Statistics on number of slaves living on large plantations and small farms*]: Kenneth M. Stampp, *The Peculiar Institution* (Alfred A. Knopf, 1956), p. 31.

[*Cato to Charles Colcock Jones*]: Starobin, pp. 47–50.

387 [*Reverend Jones on religion for slaves*]: Eugene D. Genovese, *Roll, Jordan, Roll: The World the Slaves Made* (Pantheon Books, 1974), p. 208. [*Importance of religion and black preachers to slaves*]: John W. Blassingame, *The Slave Community* (Oxford University Press, 1972), pp. 64–76.

[*Genovese on proportion of house servants*]: *Roll, Jordan, Roll*, p. 328.

[*Charles Colcock Jones Jr.'s letter about his body servant, George*]: Myers, pp. 306–7.

388 [*Behavior of house servants*]: Blassingame, pp. 200–1.

[*Letter of Cato to Charles Colcock Jones, March 3, 1851, on behavior of Phoebe and Cassius*]: Starobin, p. 54.

[*Rose Williams and Rufus*]: quoted in Herbert Gutman, *The Black Family in Slavery & Freedom, 1750–1925* (Pantheon Books, 1976), pp. 84–85.

390 [*Statistics on infant mortality and increase of slave population*]: Stampp, pp. 318–21.

[*Charles Colcock Jones to Charles C. Jones, Jr., Oct. 2, 1856, on pricing of blacks for eventual sale*]: Myers, p. 244.

391 [*Charles Colcock Jones to Charles C. Jones, Jr., Nov. 17, 1856, on purchase of new cloth for better appearance of family for sale*]: ibid., pp. 263–64.

[*Phoebe to children, March 17, 1857*]: Starobin, p. 57.

[*Early life of Nat Turner*]: Stephen B. Oates, *The Fires of Jubilee* (Harper & Row, 1975), pp. 28–41.

392 [*Capture and hanging of Nat Turner*]: ibid., pp. 125–26.

[*Restrictions on free blacks in the South*]: Allan Nevins, *Ordeal of the Union* (Charles Scribner's Sons, 1947), Vol. 1, pp. 518–32.

392 [*Restrictions of northern states on civil rights of blacks*]: Leon F. Litwack, *North of Slavery* (University of Chicago Press, 1961), pp. 63–91. See, in general, Ira Berlin, *Slaves Without Masters* (Pantheon Books, 1974).

393 [*Restrictions on blacks in Boston*]: *The Liberator*, March 16, 1860, and quoted in Litwack, p. 110.

[*Escape to liberty*]: Larry Gara, *The Liberty Line: The Legend of the Underground Railroad* (University Press of Kentucky, 1967); Samuel Ringgold Ward, *Autobiography of a Fugitive Negro* (John Snow, 1855).

[*Frederick Douglass' early career*]: *Life and Times of Frederick Douglass, "Written by Himself"* (Collier Books, 1962); Nathan Irwin Huggins, *Slave and Citizen: The Life of Frederick Douglass* (Little, Brown, 1980); Dickson J. Preston, *Young Frederick Douglass* (Johns Hopkins University Press, 1980); Benjamin Quarles, ed., *Frederick Douglass* (Prentice-Hall, 1968).

Women in Need

394 [*Household tasks of women*]: R. Carlyle Buley, *The Old Northwest* (Indiana Historical Society, 1950), p. 223.

395 [*Statistics on the size of families*]: Julie Roy Jeffrey, *Frontier Women* (Hill & Wang, 1979), p. 57.

[*Millicent Hunt's discontent*]: quoted in Horace Adams, "A Puritan Wife on the Frontier," *Mississippi Valley Historical Review*, Vol. 27, No. 1 (June 1940), pp. 67–84; see also, on "custom," Anne Firor Scott, "Women's Perspective on the Patriarchy in the 1850's," *Journal of American History*, Vol. 61, No. 1 (June 1974), p. 55.

[*Infant mortality*]: Scott, p. 55.

396 [*The* Lowell Offering]: Philip S. Foner, *The Factory Girls* (University of Illinois Press, 1977), pp. 26–29.

397 [*"Fictional" account of first day at work*]: quoted in Thomas Dublin, "Women, Work, and Protest in the Early Lowell Mills: 'The Oppressing Hand of Avarice Would Enslave Us,' " in Milton Cantor and Bruce Laurie, eds., *Class, Sex, and the Woman Worker* (Greenwood Press, 1977), p. 45.

[*Mill worker's letter*]: quoted in Lise Vogel, "Hearts to Feel and Tongues to Speak: New England Mill Women in the Early Nineteenth Century," in Cantor and Laurie, pp. 65–66.

[*H. E. Back's letter*]: ibid., pp. 66–68.

[*Sarah Bagley on* Lowell Offering]: quoted in Foner, p. 57.

[*Mehitable Eastman on denial of liberty*]: address to Manchester Industrial Reform Association, Sept. 1846, quoted in Vogel, p. 70.

398 [*"The Factory Bell"*]: author unknown, quoted in Lise Vogel, "Their Own Work: Two Documents from the Nineteenth-Century Labor Movement," in *Signs Journal of Women in Culture and Society*, Vol. 1, No. 3 (Spring 1976), pp. 793–94.

[*Lucy Larcom's initial liking for factory*]: ibid., p. 778.

[*Sarah Bagley on mutual dependence*]: Foner, p. 172.

[*Lowell strike of 1834*]: Dublin, pp. 51–55.

399 [*Lowell Female Labor Reform Association*]: ibid., pp. 57–61.

[*Schouler concludes that "the remedy is not with us"*]: W. Elliot Brownlee and Mary M. Brownlee, *Women in the American Economy* (Yale University Press, 1976), p. 169.

400 [*"Female fragment societies"*]: Richard D. Brown, "The Emergence of Urban Society in Rural Massachusetts, 1760–1820," *Journal of American History*, Vol. 61, No. 1 (June 1974), p. 39.

[*Emma Willard and the Troy Female Seminary*]: Anne Firor Scott, "What, Then, Is the American: This New Woman?" *Journal of American History*, Vol. 65, No. 3 (December 1978), pp. 679–703.

[*Women at Oberlin*]: Jill K. Conway, "Perspectives on the History of Women's Education in the United States," *History of Education Quarterly*, Vol. 14, No. 1 (Spring 1974), pp. 1–11.

[*Emergence of women's rights movement within abolitionism*]: Aileen S. Kraditor, *Means and Ends in American Abolitionism* (Pantheon Books, 1967), pp. 11–39.

[*Lucretia Mott and National Anti-Slavery Convention*]: Otelia Cromwell, *Lucretia Mott* (Harvard University Press, 1958), p. 58.

[*Exclusion of women from World's Anti-Slavery Convention*]: Mari Jo and Paul Buhle, *The Concise History of Woman Suffrage* (University of Illinois Press, 1978), pp. 78–87.

401 [*Seneca Falls convention*]: Eleanor Flexner, *Century of Struggle* (Harvard University Press, 1975), Ch. 5. [*Seneca Falls declaration*]: text in Miriam Schneir, ed., *Feminism: The Essential Historical Writings* (Vintage Books, 1972), pp. 77–82.

[*Lucretia Mott*]: Margaret Hope Bacon, *Valiant Friend* (Walker, 1980); Anna Davis Hallowell, ed., *James and Lucretia Mott, Life and Letters* (Houghton Mifflin, 1884).

402 [*Legal status of wives*]: Richard B. Morris, *Studies in the History of Early American Law* (Columbia University Press, 1930), Ch. 4; Mary R. Beard, *Woman as Force in History* (Macmillan, 1946), pp. 113–21; Peggy Rabkin, "The Origins of Law Reform: The Social Significance of the Nineteenth-Century Codification Movement and Its Contribution to the Passage of the Early Married Women's Property Acts," *Buffalo Law Review*, Vol. 24, No. 3 (Spring 1975), pp. 683–760; Linda K. Kerber, *Women of the Republic* (University of North Carolina Press, 1980), Ch. 5.

[*Difficulty of divorce*]: Kerber, Ch. 6.

[*Millicent Hunt*]: diary quoted in Adams, pp. 67–84.

[*Lydia Maria Child*]: Patricia G. Holland and Milton Meltzer, eds., *The Collected Correspondence of Lydia Maria Child, 1817–1880*, Guide and Index to the Microfiche Edition (Kraus Microform, 1980); "Biography of Lydia Maria Child," *ibid.*, pp. 23–38; Collections of Lydia Maria Child papers and correspondence in the Schlesinger Library, Harvard College, and in the New York Public Library.

403 [*Women's rights and blacks' rights*]: see, in general, Gerda Lerner, *The Majority Finds Its Past* (Oxford University Press, 1979); Kerber.

[*Mehitable Eastman on "hearts to feel"*]: quoted in Vogel, "Hearts to Feel and Tongues to Speak," p. 64.

Migrants in Poverty

404 [*Frances Wright's voyage to America*]: Alice J. G. Perkins and Theresa Wolfson, *Francis Wright: Free Enquirer* (Harper & Brothers, 1939), quoted at pp. 26–29.

[*Voyage of the* Oxford]: Edwin C. Guillet, *The Great Migration* (Thomas Nelson, 1937), p. 78; Thomas W. Pate, "The Transportation of Immigrants and Reception Arrangements in the Nineteenth Century," *Journal of Political Economy*, Vol. 19, No. 9 (November 1911), pp. 732–49.

[*Reception of immigrants at docks*]: Guillet, pp. 185–86; Nevins, Vol. 2, p. 285.

405 [*Irish emigration after 1835*]: Oscar Handlin, *Boston's Immigrants* (Harvard University Press, 1959), p. 51. [*Statistics on immigration*]: David Ward, *Cities and Immigrants: A Geography of Change in Nineteenth Century America* (Oxford University Press, 1971), p. 63.

[*Concentration of immigrants in tenement neighborhoods*]: Ward, p. 107.

[*Incident of doctor and canal worker*]: Rudolph J. Vecoli, *The People of New Jersey* (Van Nostrand, 1965), p. 81.

406 [*Swindling of immigrants*]: Nevins, Vol. 2, pp. 282–85.

[*Irish in New Jersey*]: Vecoli, passim.

[*Competition between Irish and blacks*]: Robert Ernst, *Immigrant Life in New York City* (King's Crown Press, 1949), pp. 66–68.

407 [*Bellevue*]: Raymond A. Mohl, *Poverty in New York, 1783–1825* (Oxford University Press, 1971), pp. 84–85.

[*Work as deterrent to welfare*]: ibid., p. 225.

408 [*Mike Walsh and Tammany*]: William V. Shannon, *The American Irish* (Macmillan, 1963), pp. 51–54. [*Walsh on "negro slaves and white wage slaves"*]: quoted in Arthur M. Schlesinger, Jr., *The Age of Jackson* (Little, Brown, 1945), p. 490.

409 [*Poor whites of the rural South*]: Clement Eaton, *The Growth of Southern Civilization, 1790–1860* (Harper & Row, 1961), pp. 168–76; J. Wayne Flynt, *Dixie's Forgotten People* (Indiana University Press, 1979).

[*Franklin Plummer*]: Reinhard H. Luthin, "Some Demagogues in American History," *American Historical Review*, Vol. 57, No. 1 (October 1951), pp. 22–46, esp. pp. 25–26; Edwin A. Miles, "Franklin E. Plummer: Piney Woods Spokesman of the Jackson Era," *Journal of Mississippi History*, Vol. 14 (January 1952), pp. 2–34.

Leaders Without Followers

410 [*Protest of "Unlettered Mechanic"*]: quoted in Howard Zinn, *A People's History of the United States* (Harper & Row, 1980), p. 216; [*handbill against the "rich"*]: ibid., p. 218.

[*Protest of Sojourner Truth*]: quoted in Schneir, pp. 94–95.

411 [*Lydia Maria Child on drawing up her will*]: Lydia Maria Child to Ellis Gray Loring, Feb. 24, 1856, reprinted in *Letters of Lydia Maria Child* (Houghton Mifflin, 1882).

[*Staughton Lynd on the Declaration of Independence*]: Staughton Lynd, *Intellectual Origins of American Radicalism* (Pantheon Books, 1968), p. 4.

[*Barrington Moore on the recurring sense of injustice*]: Moore, p. 77.

412 [*Angelina Emily Grimké and Sarah Moore Grimké*]: Gerda Lerner, *The Grimké Sisters from South Carolina* (Houghton Mifflin, 1967); Gilbert H. Barnes and Dwight L. Dumond, eds., *Letters of Theodore Dwight Weld, Angelina Grimké Weld, and Sarah Grimké, 1822–1844*, 2 vols. (Peter Smith, 1965).

[*Theodore Weld*]: Benjamin P. Thomas, *Theodore Weld* (Rutgers University Press, 1950).

413 [*Frederick Douglass in the* North Star *on the Seneca Falls convention*]: quoted in Schneir, p. 85.

[*Lydia Maria Child on Fanny Kemble and Pierce Butler*]: Lydia Maria Child to Ellis Gray Loring, Dec. 5, 1838, Lydia Maria Child Papers, New York Public Library.

[*Exchanges at the Akron meeting*]: Schneir, pp. 93–95.

414 [*Seneca Falls declaration and economic issues*]: ibid., p. 82.

[*FLRA "Factory Tract"*]: reprinted in Vogel, "Their Own Work," p. 795.

414 [*Frances Wright*]: Perkins and Wolfson; William Randall Waterman, "Frances Wright," *Studies in History, Economics, and Public Law*, Vol. 115, No. 1 (Columbia University Press, 1924), pp. 92–133; Cecilia Helena Payne-Gaposchkin, "The Nashoba Plan for Removing the Evil of Slavery: Letters of Frances and Camilla Wright, 1820–1829," *Harvard Library Bulletin*, Vol. 23, No. 3 (July 1975), and No. 4 (October 1975).

12. WHIGS: THE BUSINESS OF POLITICS

419 [*The Whig rally in Dayton*]: *Ohio State Journal*, Sept. 16, 1840, p. 2; Dayton *Log Cabin*, No. 12, Sept. 18, 1840, p. 1.

[*William Henry Harrison's speech, Dayton, Ohio, Sept. 10, 1840*]: Cincinnati *Gazette*, Sept. 12, 1840; Dayton *Log Cabin*, No. 12, Sept. 18, 1840; text published by the Whig Republican Association, reprinted in Arthur M. Schlesinger, Jr., ed., *History of American Presidential Elections* (Chelsea House, 1971), Vol. 1, pp. 737–44. The version quoted is paraphrased from Schlesinger, pp. 678–79.

420 [*Harrison's "first presidential campaign speech"*]: Robert Gray Gunderson, *The Log-Cabin Campaign* (University Press of Kentucky, 1957), pp. 164–65.

[*John Quincy Adams on "itinerant speech-making"*]: John Quincy Adams, *Memoirs* (Lippincott, 1876), Vol. 10, p. 352, entry for Sept. 24, 1840.

421 [*Invective*]: Schlesinger, pp. 671–74; Gunderson, passim.

[*Voter turnout, 1840*]: William Nisbet Chambers, "Election of 1840," Schlesinger, p. 680; see also William Nisbet Chambers, *Political Parties in a New Nation* (Oxford University Press, 1963), Ch. 1.

The Whig Way of Government

422 [*Harrison's inaugural*]: Robert Seager II, *And Tyler Too* (McGraw-Hill, 1963), p. 144. [*Harrison's illness*]: Glyndon G. Van Deusen, *The Jacksonian Era: 1828–1848* (Harper & Brothers, 1959), p. 153.

423 [*Tyler on Whig factions*]: Seager, p. 149.

[*Clay's anger*]: *ibid.*, p. 134.

424 [*Dilemma of the Whigs in Congress*]: John E. Fisher, "The Dilemma of a States' Rights Whig," *Virginia Magazine of History and Biography*, Vol. 81, No. 4 (October 1973), pp. 387–404.

[*Ewing's bank bill*]: Clement Eaton, *Henry Clay and the Art of American Politics* (Little, Brown, 1957), p. 146. [*Clay's reaction*]: *ibid.*, p. 147.

[*Tyler's retort to Clay*]: Seager, p. 154.

["*Corporal's Guard*" *of Virginians*]: *ibid.*, p. 159.

[*Tyler on Clay's compromise*]: *ibid.*, p. 155.

425 [*Veto celebration and protest*]: *ibid.*, p. 156.

[*Crittenden's warning*]: *ibid.*, p. 159.

[*Webster and Tyler*]: Van Deusen, p. 159.

426 [*Van Deusen on "logrolling"*]: *ibid.*, p. 161. [*Tyler welcomes Democratic victory of 1842*]: Seager, p. 171.

[*Whigs nominating generals*]: James MacGregor Burns, *The Deadlock of Democracy* (Prentice-Hall, 1963), pp. 60–61.

427 [*Politics of Whiggery*]: William R. Brock, *Parties and Political Conscience: American Dilemmas, 1840–1850* (KTO Press, 1979); Daniel Walker Howe, *Political Culture of the American Whigs* (University of Chicago Press, 1979); Lynn L. Marshall, "The Strange Stillbirth

of the Whig Party," *American Historical Review,* Vol. 72, No. 2 (January 1967), pp. 445–68; Sydney Nathans, *Daniel Webster and Jacksonian Democracy* (Johns Hopkins University Press, 1973).

428 [*Marshall on Whig nostalgia for a "heroic era" of leadership*]: "Stillbirth of the Whig Party," p. 463.

The Economics of Whiggery

429 [*Frederic Tudor, the "Ice King"*]: Daniel J. Boorstin, *The Americans: The National Experience* (Random House, 1965), pp. 11–16; Dumas Malone, ed., *Dictionary of American Biography* (Charles Scribner's Sons, 1936), Vol. 19, pp. 47–48.

[*Nathan Jarvis Wyeth*]: Boorstin, pp. 13–14.

430 [*Solomon Willard*]: ibid., pp. 18–19; *Dictionary of American Biography,* Vol. 20, pp. 241–42.

[*Du Pont Company*]: Alfred D. Chandler, Jr., and Stephen Salsbury, *Pierre S. du Pont and the Making of the Modern Corporation* (Harper & Row, 1971).

[*Samuel Finley Morse*]: *Dictionary of American Biography,* Vol. 13, pp. 247–51.

431 [*Railroad development and leadership*]: Thomas C. Cochran, *Railroad Leaders, 1845–1890: The Business Mind in Action* (Harvard University Press, 1953); Roger Burlingame, *March of the Iron Men* (Charles Scribner's Sons, 1938); Alfred D. Chandler, Jr., ed., *The Railroads* (Harcourt, Brace & World, 1965).

432 [*Railroad expansion*]: Chandler, p. 13.

[*Boston and New York City railroad promoters and magnates*]: Cochran, pp. 263–64.

[*Schuyler-Pond exchange*]: Robert Schuyler to Charles F. Pond, Dec. 1, 1848, reprinted in Cochran, p. 457.

433 [*Population growth and economic growth*]: Stuart Bruchey, *The Roots of American Economic Growth, 1607–1861* (Harper & Row, 1965), p. 91.

[*Adams on Whigs*]: Arthur M. Schlesinger, Jr., *The Age of Jackson* (Little, Brown, 1945), p. 279.

[*Whigs and economic development*]: Robert Kelley, *The Cultural Pattern of American Politics* (Alfred A. Knopf, 1979), pp. 154–55.

434 [*Hare on unity of interests*]: Schlesinger, *Age of Jackson,* p. 270.

[*Everett on "wheel of fortune"*]: ibid., p. 271. [*Channing on hardships of the rich*]: ibid., p. 272.

["*Ode to the Factory Girl*"]: ibid.

[*Channing on "Elevation of Soul"*]: ibid., p. 273.

435 [*American politics a "romance"*]: Louis Hartz, *The Liberal Tradition in America* (Harcourt, Brace, 1955), p. 140.

[*Van Deusen on Ohio Whigs*]: Van Deusen, p. 96.

[*Wealth of Boston Whiggery*]: Robert Rich, " 'A Wilderness of Whigs'," *Journal of Social History.* Vol. 4 (Spring 1971), pp. 263–76

436 [*Justice Story*]: Hartz, p. 104. [*Shaw and "fellow-servant rule"*]: Richard B. Morris, ed., *Encyclopedia of American History,* rev. ed. (Harper & Brothers, 1961), p. 778.

[*Everett on "Numbers against Property"*]: Schlesinger, *Age of Jackson,* p. 110.

437 [*Lawrence's loan to Harrison*]: Seager, p. 145.

[*Daniel Webster as typical Whig*]: Irving H. Bartlett, *Daniel Webster* (W. W. Norton, 1978).

Experiments in Escape

438 [*Sophia Ripley letter*]: Sophia Willard Dana Ripley to John S. Dwight, Aug. 1, 1840, in Zoltán Haraszti, *The Idyll of Brook Farm* (Trustees of the Boston Public Library, n.d.), pp. 12–13.

439 [*Jefferson on laboring in the earth*]: Thomas Jefferson, *Notes on Virginia*, Thomas P. Abernethy, ed. (Harper & Row, 1964), p. 157.

[*Owenite and other communitarian associations*]: Arthur Eugene Bestor, Jr., *Backwoods Utopias* (University of Pennsylvania Press, 1950); John F. C. Harrison, *Quest for the New Moral World* (Charles Scribner's Sons, 1969); V. F. Calverton, *Where Angels Dared to Tread* (Bobbs-Merrill, 1941); William E. Wilson, *The Angel and the Serpent* (Indiana University Press, 1964); Everett Webber, *Escape to Utopia* (Hastings House, 1959); Donald E. Pitzer, ed., *Robert Owen's American Legacy* (Proceedings of the Robert Owen Bicentennial Conference) (Indiana Historical Society, 1972).

440 [*Owen's goals*]: quoted in Calverton, p. 180. [*Evil of individualism*]: Bestor, p. 8.

[*New Harmony purchased*]: Harrison, p. 164.

[*New Harmony members*]: Webber, p. 139.

[*"Pecuniary inequality"*]: Bestor, p. 120.

[*Regulations for members*]: Wilson, p. 118.

441 [*Arrival of Philanthropist*]: *ibid.*, p. 138.

[*Pelham is "free"*]: quoted in Bestor, p. 167.

[*"Persons of color"*]: Wilson, p. 118.

[*Mrs. Pears on equality*]: Bestor, p. 175. [*Bestor on paradox of experiment*]: *ibid.*

442 [*Brown denounces Owen*]: *ibid.*, p. 188. [*Decline of New Harmony*]: *ibid.*, pp. 197–201.

[*Fourier and Fourierism*]: Nicholas V. Riasanovsky, *The Teaching of Charles Fourier* (University of California Press, 1969); Mark Poster, ed., *Harmonian Man* (Doubleday, 1971); Charles Gide, Intro., *Design for Utopia: Selected Writings of Charles Fourier* (Schocken Books, 1971).

[*Fourier on commercial world*]: Poster, p. 3.

443 [*Fourierist associations in America*]: Bestor, pp. 238–40.

[*Brook Farm*]: Edith Roelker Curtis, *A Season in Utopia* (Thomas Nelson, 1961); Haraszti.

[*Failure of communal societies*]: Maren L. Carden, *Oneida: Utopian Community to Modern Corporation* (Johns Hopkins University Press, 1969), p. 20.

[*Intellectual leaders who could not plan*]: Webber, pp. 192–99.

444 [*Greeley's admiration*]: quoted in Bestor, p. 10. [*Marx and Engels*]: quoted in *ibid.*, p. 11.

13. THE EMPIRE OF LIBERTY

445 [*Adams on peace and prosperity*]: quoted in Thomas A. Bailey, *A Diplomatic History of the American People*, 9th ed. (Prentice-Hall, 1974), p. 191.

[*Jackson denounces French*]: *ibid.*, p. 195. [*Refusal to apologize*]: *ibid.*, p. 197.

446 [*Andrew Jackson Pageot*]: *ibid.*, p. 198.

[*Rochester Democrat demands revenge*]: *ibid.*, p. 200.

[*Vow to liberate Canada*]: *ibid.*, p. 201.

448 [*Ashburton pays Sparks's "expenses"*]: Samuel F. Bemis, *A Diplomatic History of the United States*, 5th ed. (Holt, Rinehart and Winston, 1965), p. 263.

Trails of Tears and Hope

449 [*Frontier ruffians*]: Ray A. Billington, *Westward Expansion* (Macmillan, 1960), p. 482. [*Tocqueville's pioneer*]: Theodore R. Fehrenbach, *Lone Star* (Macmillan, 1968), pp. 103–4.

450 [*Immigrant population*]: Billington, pp. 301–2, 308. [*Steamboat fares*]: Richard B. Morris, *Encyclopedia of American History*, Bicentennial Edition (Harper & Row, 1976), p. 602.

[*Economy of the Northwest*]: Malcolm J. Rohrbough, *The Trans-Appalachian Frontier* (Oxford University Press, 1978), pp. 293–95, 321–46.

[*"King Whirl"*]: Wilbur J. Cash, *The Mind of the South* (Alfred A. Knopf, 1960), pp. 11–12. [*Plantation house*]: ibid., pp. 15–16. [*Items bought by Southerners*]: Rohrbough, pp. 309, 315; Thomas D. Clark, *Three American Frontiers*, Holman Hamilton, ed. (University Press of Kentucky, 1968), p. 33.

451 [*Emerson on West*]: quoted in Frederick J. Turner, *The United States, 1830–1850* (Henry Holt, 1935), p. 378.

[*Three waves of settlers*]: Frederick J. Turner, "The Significance of the Frontier in American History," in George R. Taylor, ed., *The Turner Thesis Concerning the Role of the Frontier in American History*, rev. ed. (D. C. Heath, 1956), pp. 9–10.

[*Everyone involved in politics*]: Stanley Elkins and Eric McKitrick, "A Meaning for Turner's Frontier, Democracy in the Old Northwest," in Taylor, p. 104. [*Slick law*]: Rohrbough, p. 307.

[*Jefferson's toast*]: Katharine C. Turner, *Red Men Calling on the Great White Father* (University of Oklahoma Press, 1951), p. 39. [*Mary Rapine and Petalesharo*]: ibid., pp. 51–57.

452 [*Henry Clay on Indians*]: Diary of John Quincy Adams, cited in Frederick Merk, *History of the Westward Movement* (Alfred A. Knopf, 1978), p. 186.

[*Black Hawk and Easterners*]: Katharine C. Turner, p. 90. [*Massacre of Indians*]: Billington, pp. 300–1; see also Milo M. Quaife, ed., *Life of Black Hawk* (Lakeside Press, 1916).

[*Cherokee wealth*]: Billington, p. 314. [*Indian spiritual values*]: Eufaula Harjo, a Creek sage, quoted in Angie Debo, *A History of the Indians of the United States* (University of Oklahoma Press, 1970), p. 4.

453 [*Ross's eloquence*]: Grant Foreman, *Advancing the Frontier, 1830–1860* (University of Oklahoma Press, 1933), p. 322.

[*Mistreatment of tribesmen*]: Grant Foreman, *Indian Removal* (University of Oklahoma Press, 1932), pp. 131, 114, 272; see also Flora W. Seymour, *Indian Agents of the Old Frontier* (Appleton-Century, 1941), pp. 13–14. [*Army private's account*]: Debo, pp. 108–9.

[*Choctaw government*]: Grant Foreman, *The Five Civilized Tribes* (University of Oklahoma Press, 1934), pp. 32–33. [*Choctaw Academy*]: ibid., p. 66.

454 [*Austin's arrangement*]: Fehrenbach, pp. 135–37. [*Austin in Mexico City*]: Eugene C. Barker, *The Life of Stephen F. Austin* (Lakeside Press, 1949), pp. 43–44. [*Jeffersonian paradise*]: Fehrenbach, p. 166.

[*Houston's call*]: Llerena Friend, *Sam Houston: The Great Designer* (University of Texas Press, 1954), p. 63.

455 [*Travis' appeal*]: Fehrenbach, p. 208.

[*"El Bostono"*]: David M. Pletcher, *The Diplomacy of Annexation: Texas, Oregon, and the Mexican War* (University of Missouri Press, 1973), p. 92.

455 [*California description*]: Bernard De Voto, *The Year of Decision: 1846* (Houghton Mifflin, 1942), p. 45.

456 [*Wagon train election*]: Frederick Turner, *United States*, p. 367.

[*Larkin's scheme for Californian independence*]: Billington, pp. 570–72. [*Sutter and the new arrivals*]: Julian Dana, *Sutter of California* (Macmillan, 1936), passim.

Annexation: Politics and War

457 [*"Manifest Destiny"*]: Frederick Merk, *Manifest Destiny and Mission in American History* (Alfred A. Knopf, 1963), p. 24. [*Douglas on "area of liberty"*]: ibid., p. 28. [*"American multiplication table"*]: ibid., p. 29.

[*"Who is Polk?"*]: Eugene I. McCormac, *James K. Polk* (University of California Press, 1922), p. 248; see also Charles Sellers, *James K. Polk: Continentalist, 1843–1846* (Princeton University Press, 1966), p. 105.

458 [*Benton on Oregon*]: Bailey, p. 224.

[*Claim to Oregon "unquestionable"*]: ibid., p. 225.

[*Looking John Bull in the eye*]: ibid., p. 228.

459 [*"Reannexation of Texas" in Democratic platform*]: quoted in Charles Sellers, "Election of 1844," in Arthur M. Schlesinger, Jr., ed., *History of American Presidential Elections* (Chelsea House, 1971), Vol. 1, p. 773.

460 [*Slidell's status*]: George Meade, *The Life and Letters of George Gordon Meade* (Charles Scribner's Sons, 1913), Vol. 1, p. 65.

461 [*Sequence of events on Rio Grande*]: George W. Smith and Charles Judah, *Chronicles of the Gringos* (University of New Mexico Press, 1968), pp. 61–62.

[*Polk's decision for war*]: Allan Nevins, ed., *Polk: The Diary of a President, 1845–1849* (Longmans, Green, 1929), pp. 81–83. [*War message*]: Pletcher, p. 386.

462 [*Mexican prisoners*]: Ulysses S. Grant, *Personal Memoirs of U. S. Grant* (Webster, 1885), Vol. 1, pp. 117–18.

[*Mexicans at Buena Vista*]: Justo Sierra, *The Political Evolution of the Mexican People*, Charles Ramsdell, trans. (University of Texas Press, 1969), pp. 241–42.

[*Liberty cap*]: soldier quoted in Lloyd Lewis, *Captain Sam Grant* (Little, Brown, 1950), p. 194. [*Amphibious assault described*]: *Correspondence of John Sedgwick, Major-General* (De Vinne Press, 1902), Vol. 1, p. 71.

463 [*Valley of Mexico*]: Lewis, p. 225.

463–4 [*Scott's choice*]: De Voto, pp. 489–90. [*Scott on Chapultepec assault*]: quoted in *Sedgwick*, p. 113.

464 [*American casualties*]: K. Jack Bauer, *The Mexican War, 1846–1848* (Macmillan, 1974), p. 397. [*Grant's lament*]: Lewis, p. 261.

The Geometry of Balance

464 [*Post-Mexican War politics in general*]: William R. Brock, *Parties and Political Conscience: American Dilemmas, 1840–1850* (KTO Press, 1979); Roy Franklin Nichols, *The Democratic Machine, 1850–1854* (Longmans, Green, 1923); Arthur M. Schlesinger, Jr., ed., *History of U.S. Political Parties* (Chelsea House, 1973), Vol. 1; Roy F. Nichols, *The Stakes of Power, 1845–1877* (Hill & Wang, 1961).

465 [*John Quincy Adams on internal Whig divisions*]: Charles Francis Adams, ed., *Memoirs of John Quincy Adams* (Lippincott, 1877), Vol. 12, p. 274.

465 [*John Quincy Adams on three-fifths rule as fatal drop of prussic acid*]: quoted in Brock, p. 233.

466 [*Justice Taney on community rights*]: quoted in Dumas Malone, ed., *Dictionary of American Biography* (Charles Scribner's Sons, 1936), Vol. 18, p. 292.

[*Dalzell on balance as organic*]: Robert F. Dalzell, Jr., *Daniel Webster and the Trial of American Nationalism, 1843–1852* (W. W. Norton, 1972), p. 14.

467 [*Strategic questions facing antislavery movement*]: Aileen S. Kraditor, *Means and Ends in American Abolitionism: Garrison and His Critics on Strategy and Tactics, 1834–1850* (Pantheon Books, 1969).

[*Liberty party*]: Theodore C. Smith, *The Liberty and Free Soil Parties in the Northwest* (Longmans, Green, 1897), Vol. 6 of Harvard Historical Studies; Joseph G. Rayback, "The Liberty Party Leaders of Ohio: Exponents of Antislavery Coalition," *Ohio State Archaeological and Historical Quarterly*, Vol. 57 (April 1948), pp. 165–78; Betty Fladeland, *James Gillespie Birney: Slaveholder to Abolitionist* (Cornell University Press, 1955).

468 [*Liberty party in New York election of 1844*]: Lee Benson, *The Concept of Jacksonian Democracy* (Princeton University Press, 1961), pp. 134, 209–13.

[*Conscience Whigs*]: Kinley J. Brauer, *Cotton versus Conscience* (University Press of Kentucky, 1967); Martin B. Duberman, *Charles Francis Adams, 1807–1886* (Houghton Mifflin, 1961); David Donald, *Charles Sumner and the Coming of the Civil War* (Alfred A. Knopf, 1960); Frank Otto Gatell, *John Gorham Palfrey and the New England Conscience* (Harvard University Press, 1963); and biographies of Conscience Whig leaders.

[*Cotton Whigs*]: Thomas H. O'Connor, *Lords of the Loom: The Cotton Whigs and the Coming of the Civil War* (Charles Scribner's Sons, 1968).

469 [*Free-Soil party*]: Frederick J. Blue, *The Free Soilers* (University of Illinois Press, 1973); Joseph G. Rayback, *Free Soil: The Election of 1848* (University Press of Kentucky, 1970); Theodore C. Smith; Aileen S. Kraditor, "The Liberty and Free Soil Parties," in Schlesinger, *History of U.S. Political Parties*, Vol. 1, pp. 741–61 and appendices.

[*Eric Foner on Free-Soil party evasion of Negro rights issue*]: Eric Foner, "Politics and Prejudice: The Free Soil Party and the Negro, 1849–1852," *Journal of Negro History*, Vol. 50, No. 4 (October 1965), p. 239.

[*1848 presidential election*]: Flagg Papers, Columbia University Library, esp. correspondence with John A. Dix.

[*Lewis Cass*]: Frank B. Woodford, *Lewis Cass* (Rutgers University Press, 1950).

470 [*1848 election results*]: Svend Petersen, *A Statistical History of the American Presidential Elections* (Frederick Ungar, 1963), pp. 31–32.

[*The Southern Address*]: Charles M. Wiltse, *John C. Calhoun Sectionalist, 1840–1850* (Bobbs-Merrill, 1951), quoted at p. 385.

471 [*Gold discovered*]: Dana, pp. 296–302. [*Population hurries to mines*]: Col. Richard B. Mason, letter in John C. Frémont, *The Exploring Expedition to the Rocky Mountains, Oregon and California* (Derby, 1851), p. 427. [*Prospectors' methods*]: Milo M. Quaife, ed., *Pictures of Gold Rush California* (Lakeside Press, 1949), pp. 192–234.

[*Gold rush*]: Quaife, *Pictures*, pp. xx–xxv. [*San Francisco*]: Dana, p. 353.

472 [*Statehood convention*]: Dana, pp. 342–49. [*Slavery prohibition*]: ibid., pp. 347.

[*Remarks on slavery by Representatives Allen and Hilliard*]: *Congressional Globe*, 31st Congress, 1st session (Appendix), Dec. 12, 1849 (speeches of Dec. 12, 1849, and Dec. 13, 1849), pp. 33–35.

[*Extremist feelings in 1849–50*]: Claude M. Fuess, *Daniel Webster* (Da Capo Press, 1968), Vol. 2, pp. 201–2.

472 [*Clay's meeting with Webster on omnibus proposal*]: *ibid.*, pp. 204–5; Dalzell, p. 173; Glyndon G. Van Deusen, *The Life of Henry Clay* (Little, Brown, 1937), p. 399.

473 [*Clay "never before arisen to address any assembly . . . so anxious"*]: *Congressional Globe*, Feb. 5 and 6, 1850, p. 115.

[*Clay's presentation of his omnibus proposal to the Senate*]: *ibid.*, pp. 115–27, quoted at p. 127.

[*Calhoun's speech*]: quoted in Dalzell, p. 174 (March 4, 1850).

[*Webster's speech*]: *Congressional Globe*, March 7, 1850, pp. 269–76, quoted at pp. 269, 276.

475 [*Philip Hone on post-Compromise rejoicing*]: quoted in Brock, p. 315.

[*California lawlessness*]: Dana, pp. 367–68 and passim.

14. THE CULTURE OF LIBERTY

476 [*Emerson on the limited culture of Massachusetts*]: *The Journals of Ralph Waldo Emerson*, eds. E. W. Emerson and W. E. Forbes (Houghton Mifflin, 1912), Vol. 8, p. 339 (Oct. 1852).

[*John Adams on the generational sequence of studies*]: James T. Adams, *The Adams Family* (Literary Guild, 1930), p. 67.

[*New England cultural development in general*]: F. O. Matthiessen, *American Renaissance* (Oxford University Press, 1941); Vernon L. Parrington, *Main Currents in American Thought* (Harcourt, Brace & World, 1958), Vol. 2: *The Romantic Revolution in America;* Van Wyck Brooks, *The Flowering of New England* (E. P. Dutton, 1936); Russell Blaine Nye, *The Cultural Life of the New Nation* (Harper & Brothers, 1960); Perry Miller, *The Life of the Mind in America* (Harcourt, Brace & World, 1965).

477 [*Harvard conflict over religion*]: Samuel Eliot Morison, *Three Centuries of Harvard* (Harvard University Press, 1936), pp. 187–90.

[*Parrington on Washington Irving's detachment from literary America*]: Parrington, p. 203.

[*Parrington on William Cullen Bryant's "self-pollenizing nature"*]: Parrington, p. 239.

478 [*Harvard in the early nineteenth century*]: Morison, pp. 224–30; Brooks, Ch. 2.

479 [*William Ellery Channing on experience and experiment*]: Allen Johnson and Dumas Malone, eds., *Dictionary of American Biography*, Vol. 4 (Charles Scribner's Sons, 1930), p. 7.

[*Channing on the "great nature" and "divine image" of man*]: quoted in Parrington, p. 334.

[*Oliver Wendell Holmes on Channing's "bland, superior look"*]: quoted in Brooks, p. 43.

The Engine in the Vineyard

The title of this section is adapted from Leo Marx, *The Machine in the Garden* (Oxford University Press, 1967), which is a major source of ideas for this chapter.

479 [*Emerson's return to Concord with Lidian*]: Ralph L. Rusk, *The Life of Ralph Waldo Emerson* (Charles Scribner's Sons, 1949), pp. 222–24.

480 [*The Emersons' home in Concord*]: Stephanie Kraft, *No Castles on Main Street* (Rand McNally, 1979), Ch. 11.

[*Emerson's early life*]: Rusk, Chs. 1–10; *Dictionary of American Biography*, Vol. 3, pp. 132–34.

481 [*Emerson on moving "from the Unconscious to the Conscious"*]: quoted in Rusk, p. 66.

[*Emerson's return to Concord in 1834, with his mother*]: *ibid.*, pp. 208–9.

481 [*Emerson's Nature*]: Ralph Waldo Emerson, *Nature* (Munroe, 1836). Quoted on nature, pp. 77, 9, 12, 53, 79; quoted on man, pp. 14, 41, 50–51, 80.

482 [*Emerson on man's talent and genius*]: quoted in Perry Miller, ed., *The American Transcendentalists* (Anchor Books, 1957), p. 58, from Emerson's lecture, "The Method of Nature," Waterville College, Maine, Aug. 11, 1841.

[*Emerson on man's magnetic needle*]: quoted in Brooks, p. 206.

[*Emerson on self-reliance*]: "Self-Reliance," in Mary A. Jordan, ed., *Essays by Ralph Waldo Emerson* (Houghton Mifflin, 1903), quoted at pp. 86, 88, 111.

483 [*Theodore Parker on worshipping with no mediator between people and the father of all*]: quoted in *Dictionary of American Biography*, Vol. 7, pp. 239–40.

[*Margaret Fuller as "unsexed version of Plato's Socrates"*]: Barrett Wendell, *A Literary History of America* (Charles Scribner's Sons, 1901), p. 300; see also Marie Mitchell Olesen Urbanski, *Margaret Fuller's "Woman in the Nineteenth Century"* (Greenwood Press, 1980).

[*Harriet Martineau on Margaret Fuller's circle of women intellectuals*]: quoted in *Dictionary of American Biography*, Vol. 4, p. 64.

[*Emerson on a "foolish consistency"*]: Jordan, p. 93.

484 [*Emerson on technology*]: quoted in Marx, p. 230.

[*"Things are in the saddle . . ."*]: Ralph Waldo Emerson, "Ode Inscribed to W. H. Channing," Richard Ellmann, ed., *The New Oxford Book of American Verse* (Oxford University Press, 1976), pp. 67–69. On Emerson and his circle, see also Joel Porte, *Representative Man* (Oxford University Press, 1979).

[*Henry Thoreau at Walden Pond*]: Henry D. Thoreau, *Walden* (Princeton University Press, 1971), pp. 114–16; see also Marx, pp. 249–55; R. W. B. Lewis, *The American Adam* (University of Chicago Press, 1955), pp. 20–27; Henry Beetle Hough, *Thoreau of Walden* (Archon Books, 1970); James McIntosh, *Thoreau as Romantic Naturalist* (Cornell University Press, 1974).

[*Thoreau on the railroad*]: *Walden*, pp. 115–22.

485 [*Lerner on Thoreau*]: Max Lerner, "Thoreau: No Hermit," from Max Lerner, *Ideas Are Weapons* (Viking Press, 1939), p. 45.

[*Thoreau on the railroad as an Atropos*]: *Walden*, p. 118.

486 [*Thoreau's description of his house*]: *Walden*, p. 48.

[*Thoreau's "experiment in human ecology"*]: so described by Stanley Edgar Hyman, "Henry Thoreau in Our Time," in Sherman Paul, ed., *Thoreau* (Prentice-Hall, 1962), p. 26; this essay, p. 26, is also the source of Thoreau's statement about living deep. See also Sherman Paul, *The Shores of America* (University of Illinois Press, 1958).

[*James Russell Lowell on Thoreau's "experiment"*]: quoted in Leon Edel, *Henry D. Thoreau* (University of Minnesota Press, 1970), p. 29.

[*Sam Staples on Thoreau's jailing*]: quoted in Milton Meltzer and Walter Harding, *A Thoreau Profile* (Thomas Y. Crowell, 1962), p. 158.

487 [*Thoreau's exchange (apocryphal) with Emerson*]: ibid., pp. 161–62.

[*Sherman Paul on Thoreau's means of self-emancipation*]: Sherman Paul, "A Fable of the Renewal of Life," in Paul, p. 103.

[*Emerson on Thoreau's "Excursions on Concord & Merrimack Rivers"*]: Emerson to Charles K. Newcomb, July 16, 1846, Emerson Papers, Concord Free Public Library.

488 [*Emerson on communicating across seventeen miles*]: Emerson to Newcomb, Aug. 16, 1842, ibid.

488 [*Nathaniel Hawthorne on Sleepy Hollow*]: Randall Stewart, ed., *The American Notebooks by Nathaniel Hawthorne* (Yale University Press, 1932), pp. 102–4.

[*Hawthorne's life*]: Nina Baym, *The Shape of Hawthorne's Career* (Cornell University Press, 1976); Newton Arvin, *Hawthorne* (Little, Brown, 1929); Hyatt H. Waggoner, *Nathaniel Hawthorne* (University of Minnesota Press, 1962).

[*Van Wyck Brooks on the ghosts and legends of Salem*]: Brooks, p. 212.

489 [*Hawthorne on the "supremely artificial establishments"*]: Nathaniel Hawthorne, *Passages from The American Note-Books* (Houghton Mifflin, 1900), p. 156.

[*Hawthorne interpretation*]: Harry Levin, *The Power of Blackness* (Alfred A. Knopf, 1958); A. N. Kaul, ed., *Hawthorne* (Prentice-Hall, 1966).

490 [*Ethan Brand on humanity as the subject of an experiment*]: Nathaniel Hawthorne, "Ethan Brand," in *Hawthorne's Works* (Houghton Mifflin, 1887), Vol. 3, p. 495.

[*Melville on his "Whale" and Hawthorne's "Unpardonable Sin"*]: Melville to Hawthorne, June 1?, 1851, in Merrell R. Davis and William H. Gilman, eds., *The Letters of Herman Melville* (Yale University Press, 1960), pp. 126–31.

[*Melville on "cruel cogs and wheels"*]: quoted in Marx, p. 286.

491 [*Leavis on Melville*]: Q. D. Leavis, "Melville: The 1853–6 Phase," in Faith Pullin, ed., *New Perspectives on Melville* (Kent State University Press, 1978), p. 214.

[*Marx on the American hero*]: Marx, p. 364.

[*Philosophical themes and dualities in Emerson, Thoreau, Hawthorne, and Melville*]: works cited above, esp. Levin, Marx, Parrington; Quentin Anderson, *The Imperial Self* (Alfred A. Knopf, 1971); Lewis, *The American Adam;* Stephen E. Whicher, *Freedom and Fate* (University of Pennsylvania Press, 1953).

Religion: Free Exercise

492 [*Finney's sermon*]: Bernard Weisberger, *They Gathered at the River* (Little, Brown, 1958), pp. 101, 109, 239.

[*Concern of eastern ministers about lack of religion on the frontier*]: Theodore Dwight Bozeman, "Inductive and Deductive Politics: Science and Society in Antebellum Presbyterian Thought," *Journal of American History*, Vol. 64, No. 3 (December 1977), p. 708.

[*Timothy Dwight*]: Clifford S. Griffin, *Their Brother's Keepers: Moral Stewardship in the United States, 1800–1865* (Rutgers University Press, 1960), p. 17.

493 [*"Very wintry season" for religion after the Revolution*]: R. Carlyle Buley, *The Old Northwest: Pioneer Period, 1815–1840* (Indiana Historical Society, 1950), Vol. 2, p. 420.

[*Tocqueville on everywhere meeting "a politician where you expected to find a priest"*]: Alexis de Tocqueville, *Democracy in America* (Alfred A. Knopf, 1960), Henry Reeve Text, Phillips Bradley, ed., Vol. 1, pp. 306–7.

[*Dependence of American ministers on laity for support after disestablishment*]: Sidney E. Mead, "The Rise of the Evangelical Conception of the Ministry in America (1607–1850)," in H. Richard Niebuhr and Daniel D. Williams, eds., *The Ministry in Historical Perspectives* (Harper & Brothers, 1956), p. 217.

[*Timothy Dwight on uncertainty of voluntary contributions for support of ministry*]: Timothy Dwight, *Travels in New England and New York*, 4 vols. (T. Dwight, 1821–22), Vol. 3, p. 131.

494 [*Dominant religious groups in colonial America*]: Sidney E. Mead, "Denominationalism: The Shape of Protestantism in America," *Church History*, Vol. 24 (December 1954), p. 294.

494 [*Early missionary work of Presbyterians on the western frontier*]: William Warren Sweet, *Religion in the Development of American Culture, 1765–1840* (Charles Scribner's Sons, 1952), pp. 148–49.

495 [*Cane Ridge revival described*]: Buley, p. 421.

[*Presbyterian split into Old School and New School*]: Edward Pessen, *Jacksonian America: Society, Personality, and Politics* (Dorsey Press, 1969), p. 82.

[*Methodist circuit riders*]: Buley, pp. 450–52.

496 [*Description of camp meeting*]: John Allen Krout and Dixon Ryan Fox, *The Completion of Independence, 1790–1830* (Macmillan, 1944), p. 173.

[*Peter Cartwright's account of frontier proselytizing*]: Sydney E. Ahlstrom, *A Religious History of the American People* (Yale University Press, 1972), pp. 443–44. [*Ahlstrom on dramatic confrontation over "infant sprinkling"*]: ibid., p. 444.

497 [*Membership statistics of churches in 1850*]: Will Herberg, *Protestant-Catholic-Jew: An Essay in American Religious Sociology* (Doubleday, 1955), p. 119.

[*Second Great Awakening in New England*]: Ahlstrom, p. 417.

[*Timothy Dwight's asceticism*]: Ann Douglas, *The Feminization of American Culture* (Avon Books, 1977), p. 173.

498 [*Numbers of Roman Catholics in America in colonial era*]: Herberg, p. 151. [*Numbers of Roman Catholics in America in 1850*]: Ahlstrom, p. 542.

[*Issue of "trusteeism" in Roman Catholic Church*]: Herberg, pp. 152–54.

[*Anti-Catholic rioting in 1830s and 1840s*]: Ray Allen Billington, *The Protestant Crusade, 1800–1860: A Study of the Origins of American Nativism* (Macmillan, 1938), pp. 68–70; see also Herberg, p. 155.

499 [*The beginning of the Mormon Church*]: Leonard J. Arrington and Davis Bitton, *The Mormon Experience: A History of the Latter-day Saints* (Alfred A. Knopf, 1979), p. 204.

[*Mormons expelled from Missouri and Illinois*]: Bernard De Voto, *The Year of Decision: 1846* (Houghton Mifflin, 1942), pp. 75–101, 327–30.

500 [*Brigham Young growing up amidst "fiery" Methodist revivals*]: in Arrington and Bitton, p. 86.

[*Mead on competition*]: Mead, "Denominationalism," p. 316.

[*Evangelical antislavery activities of Lane rebels*]: Buley, p. 617.

501 [*Whittier on antislavery*]: quoted in Anne C. Loveland, "Evangelicalism and 'Immediate Emancipation' in American Antislavery Thought," *Journal of Southern History*, Vol. 32 (1966), pp. 187–88.

Schools: The "Temples of Freedom"

501 [*George Washington on the need for "general diffusion of knowledge"*]: "Farewell Address," John C. Fitzpatrick, ed., *The Writings of George Washington* (Government Printing Office, 1940), Vol. 35, p. 230.

[*Thomas Jefferson on need for education*]: Jefferson to Charles Yancey, Jan. 6, 1816, in Paul L. Ford, ed., *The Writings of Thomas Jefferson* (G. P. Putnam's Sons, 1899), Vol. 10, p. 4.

[*The need to educate jurors, etc., in the "first interest of all"*]: Charles Stewart Davis, "Popular Government," reprinted in Joseph L. Blau, ed., *Social Theories of Jacksonian Democracy* (Hafner, 1947), pp. 45–46.

501 [*Edward Everett on "the utmost practicable extension . . . to a system of education"*]: Lawrence A. Cremin, *The American Common School* (Bureau of Publications, Teachers College, Columbia University, 1951), p. 32.

502 [*Schools as "Temples of Freedom"*]: J. Orville Taylor, quoted in Rush Welter, *Popular Education and Democratic Thought in America* (Columbia University Press, 1962), p. 43.

[*William Manning on "larning"*]: William Manning, *The Key of Libberty* (The Manning Association, 1922), pp. 20–21.

[*Welter on republican and democratic educational institutions*]: Welter, p. 57.

503 [*Leaders and goals of the Common School Awakening*]: Robert L. Church and Michael W. Sedlak, *Education in the United States: An Interpretive History* (Free ,Press, 1976), pp. 55–57.

[*Undermining of status of skilled craftsmen and the decline of the apprenticeship system*]: Merle Curti, *The Social Ideas of American Educators* (Charles Scribner's Sons, 1935), p. 25.

[*Leadership of Robert Dale Owen in Working Men's party demands for education*]: Richard William Leopold, *Robert Dale Owen: A Biography* (Octagon Books, 1969), p. 93; Joseph G. Rayback, *A History of American Labor* (Macmillan, 1959), p. 66; Welter, p. 45.

[*Owen on need for national system of education*]: Cremin, p. 33.

[*Leadership of Thaddeus Stevens in passage of common school law in Pennsylvania*]: Carl Russell Fish, *The Rise of the Common Man, 1830–1850* (Macmillan, 1927), p. 217.

504 [*Colonial education*]: Bernard Bailyn, cited in Carl F. Kaestle, *The Evolution of an Urban School System* (Harvard University Press, 1973), p. viii.

[*Estimates of number of children without education in middle Atlantic states*]: Curti, p. 28.
[*Statistics on free education in Massachusetts, New England, and the middle Atlantic states*]: ibid., pp. 27–28.

[*Complaint of school board member on a teacher's lack of dedication*]: Stanley K. Schultz, *The Culture Factory: Boston Public Schools, 1789–1860* (Oxford University Press, 1973), p. 76. See also Michael B. Katz, *The Irony of Early School Reform* (Harvard University Press, 1968).

505 [*Henry Barnard's estimates on better funding of private schools in Connecticut*]: Curti, p. 27.

[*Horace Mann on the money value of education*]: ibid., p. 112.

506 [*Views of Henry Barnard on education*]: ibid., pp. 139–68, and in *Dictionary of American Biography*, Vol. 1, p. 623.

[*Leaders of the Common School Awakening in the South*]: Church and Sedlak, pp. 123–27.

507 [*Calvin Wiley on universal education*]: Curti, p. 71.

[*Educational effort of the South before the Civil War*]: Church and Sedlak, pp. 122–23.

[*Teacher training program of Catharine Beecher*]: Kathryn Kish Sklar, *Catharine Beecher: A Study in American Domesticity* (Yale University Press, 1973), p. 183.

508 [*Missionary effort of New England ministers "swarming out" to save the West*]: Fish, p. 224.

[*Caleb Mills and the founding of the Indiana school system*]: R. E. Banta, *Indiana Authors and Their Books, 1816–1916* (Wabash College, 1949), p. 221; Charles W. Moores, *Caleb Mills and the Indiana School System* (Indiana Historical Society *Publications*, Vol. 3, No. 6, 1905), pp. 363–78; Emma Lou Thornbrough, *Indiana in the Civil War Era, 1850–1880* (Indiana Historical Bureau and Indiana Historical Society, 1965), pp. 461–65.

[*Mills on advisability of meeting the expense of "proper education"*]: Thornbrough, pp. 462–63.

508 [*John Pierce and the establishment of the Michigan educational system*]: Buley, Vol. 2, p. 368, and in *Dictionary of American Biography*, Vol. 14, p. 583.

509 [*Religious leaders' founding of public schools described*]: Timothy L. Smith, "Protestant Schooling and American Nationality, 1800–1859," *Journal of American History*, Vol. 53, No. 4 (March 1967), pp. 679–95.

[*Religious issues in New York City schools*]: Church and Sedlak, pp. 158–68.

[*Conflict of purposes in common school movement*]: ibid., pp. 186–89. See also Selwyn K. Troen, *The Public and the Schools* (University of Missouri Press, 1975); Kaestle.

510 [*High school movement*]: Church and Sedlak, p. 182. [*School attendance figures*]: Fish, p. 224.

[*Mann on the need to be free before being educated*]: Curti, p. 136.

Leaders of the Penny Press

511 [*Hamilton on liberty of the press*]: Federalist No. 84.

512 [*Rise of the penny press*]: Frank L. Mott, *American Journalism* (Macmillan, 1962), Ch. 12; Edwin Emery, *The Press and America* (Prentice-Hall, 1972), Ch. 11; Sidney Kobre, *Foundations of American Journalism* (Florida State University, 1958), Ch. 13.

[*Newspapers dependent on big-city environment*]: Allan R. Pred, ed., *The Spatial Dynamics of U.S. Urban-Industrial Growth, 1800–1914* (MIT Press, 1966), pp. 174–175, 202–3.

[*Police-court reports of the* Sun]: Mott, p. 223.

513 [*Bennett's New York* Herald]: Kobre, Ch. 15, quoted at p. 259; Mott, pp. 229–35.

[*Hoe's "lightning press"*]: Emery, pp. 201–2. [*Impact of cost of large presses*]: Kobre, p. 289.

[*Telegraph dispatch*]: Mott, p. 247.

514 [*Papers in every tavern*]: ibid., p. 241.

[*Refusal of southern postmasters to deliver abolitionist papers*]: ibid., p. 306.

[*New papers in the East*]: Kobre, pp. 302–3; Mott, pp. 238–41. [*New papers in the West*]: Mott, Ch. 16, quoted at p. 282.

515 [*Attacks on Bennett*]: Kobre, pp. 269–71.

[*Coverage of the Mexican War*]: Emery, p. 194.

516 [*Horace Greeley's description of himself*]: Greeley Papers, New York Public Library, 1844–47 folder.

[*Greeley's boss's desire for "decent-looking men"*]: Mott, p. 219 n.

[*Greeley's ideal of a paper*]: Horace Greeley, *Recollections of a Busy Life* (J. B. Ford, 1868), p. 137.

[*Greeley on reform*]: Mott, p. 272. [*Criticism of "libertines"*]: ibid., p. 271. [*Advice to Emerson and other young writers*]: Greeley Papers, 1844–47 folder.

517 [*Readership of the* Tribune]: Kobre, p. 285.

[*Parrington's description of Greeley*]: Parrington, *Main Currents in American Thought*, Vol. 2, p. 257.

[*Young reporters' income*]: Kobre, p. 291.

[*Melville's source of income*]: Matthew J. Bruccoli, ed., *The Profession of Authorship in America, 1800–1870: The Papers of William Charvat* (Ohio State University Press 1968), p. 196.

517 [*The penny press in a democratic market society*]: Michael Shudson, *Discovering the News: A Social History of American Newspapers* (Basic Books, 1978), pp. 43–60.

[*Subscribers to* Godey's Lady's Book *and* North American Review]: Douglas, p. 275.

[*Domestic novels*]: John T. Frederick, "Hawthorne's 'Scribbling Women,' " *New England Quarterly*, Vol. 47 (June 1975), pp. 231–40.

[*The special journal devoted to reform*]: Bernard A. Weisberger, *The American Newspaperman* (University of Chicago Press, 1961), p. 86.

518 [*Elijah Lovejoy*]: Buley, p. 623.

Abolitionists: By Tongue and Pen

518 [*Reactions of Adams,* New York Evening Post, *and Channing to murder of Lovejoy*]: Lawrence Lader, *The Bold Brahmins: New England's War Against Slavery, 1831–1863* (E. P. Dutton, 1961), p. 82.

[*Lovejoy as bigot*]: Louis Filler, *The Crusade Against Slavery* (Harper & Brothers, 1960), p. 78.

[*Faneuil Hall protest meeting*]: Lader, pp. 82–85; Irving H. Bartlett, *Wendell Phillips* (Beacon Press, 1961), Ch. 4.

[*Attorney General's castigation of blacks*]: Lader, p. 83.

519 [*Phillips joining antislavery cause*]: Bartlett, Ch. 3.

[*Speech of Phillips*]: Wendell Phillips, *Speeches, Lectures, and Letters* (Negro Universities Press, 1968, orig. pub. 1884), pp. 1–10, quoted at p. 3.

[*Garrison on Phillips*]: Bartlett, p. 51.

[*Early antislavery sentiment*]: David B. Davis, *The Problem of Slavery in the Age of Revolution, 1770–1823* (Cornell University Press, 1975).

[*Questions of goals, strategy, and tactics*]: Aileen Kraditor, *Means and Ends in American Abolitionism* (Pantheon Books, 1967), passim; Gerald Sorin, *Abolitionism* (Praeger, 1972), passim; Staughton Lynd, *Intellectual Origins of American Radicalism* (Pantheon Books, 1968), Chs. 4–5; William M. Wiecek, *The Sources of Antislavery Constitutionalism in America, 1760–1848* (Cornell University Press, 1977).

520 [*Garrison on the Constitution*]: Filler, p. 216.

[*Wendell Phillips on government and the safety of the Republic's liberties*]: Wendell Phillips, "Public Opinion," speech of Jan. 28, 1852, reprinted in *Speeches*, pp. 53–54; Richard Hofstadter, *The American Political Tradition* (Alfred A. Knopf, 1948), Ch. 6.

[*Phillips on roles of reformer and politician*]: Hofstadter, p. 136.

[*Lydia Child on moral influence and party action*]: Lydia M. Child, "Talk About Political Party," reprinted from *The National Anti-Slavery Standard* in *The Liberator*, Aug. 5, 1842, quoted in Kraditor, p. 163.

[*Characterization of abolitionists*]: Sorin, Ch. 1; see also Gerald Sorin, *The New York Abolitionists* (Greenwood, 1971), Ch. 1.

[*Lewis Tappan*]: Bertram Wyatt-Brown, *Lewis Tappan and the Evangelical War Against Slavery* (Atheneum, 1969), p. viii.

521 [*The Grimké sisters*]: Gerda Lerner, *The Grimké Sisters from South Carolina* (Houghton Mifflin, 1967), passim.

[*Kraditor on abolitionists*]: Kraditor, p. x.

[*Influence of Phillips' wife*]: Hofstadter, p. 139.

521 [*Lydia Child on changing public opinion*]: Kraditor, p. 160.

522 [*James Russell Lowell*]: Martin Duberman, *James Russell Lowell* (Houghton Mifflin, 1966), passim.

[*Hildreth, and antislavery themes in American literature*]: Lorenzo D. Turner, *Anti-Slavery Sentiment in American Literature Prior to 1865* (Kennikat Press, 1929).

[*Harriet Beecher Stowe*]: Robert Forrest Wilson, *Crusader in Crinoline* (Lippincott, 1941). [*Sales figures for* Uncle Tom's Cabin]: Filler, p. 210; Wilson, pp. 281, 341.

[*John Brown in Ohio*]: Stephen B. Oates, *To Purge This Land with Blood* (Harper & Row, 1970), pp. 41–42.

15. THE RIPENING VINEYARD

525 [*Webster's death*]: George Ticknor Curtis, *Life of Daniel Webster* (D. Appleton, 1870), Vol. 2, pp. 664–705; Claude M. Fuess, *Daniel Webster* (Little, Brown, 1930), Vol. 2, Ch. 30; Peter Harvey, *Reminiscences and Anecdotes of Daniel Webster* (Little, Brown, 1878), Ch. 12.

[*Description of Webster*]: Harvey, p. 432.

["*Any thing unworthy of Daniel Webster*"]: Curtis, p. 698.

[*Webster's determination to resign*]: Webster to Fletcher Webster, July 4, 1852, Edward Everett Papers, Massachusetts Historical Society.

[*Webster's prediction that "the Whigs are ended"*]: Curtis, p. 693.

[*Calhoun's death*]: Gaillard Hunt, *John C. Calhoun* (George W. Jacobs, 1907), Ch. 20; Margaret L. Coit, *John C. Calhoun* (Houghton Mifflin, 1950), Ch. 28.

[*Calhoun on "two peoples so different"*]: J. Franklin Jameson, ed., *Correspondence of John C. Calhoun*, Annual Report of the American Historical Association for the Year 1899 (Government Printing Office, 1900), Vol. 2, p. 784.

[*Clay's death*]: Glyndon G. Van Deusen, *The Life of Henry Clay* (Little, Brown, 1937), Ch. 25.

526 [*Emerson's musings on Webster*]: *Journals of Ralph Waldo Emerson*, eds. E. W. Emerson and W. E. Forbes (Houghton Mifflin, 1912), entry for Oct. 25, 1852, Vol. 8, pp. 335–36.

The Cornucopia

526 [*John Muir's boyhood life in Wisconsin*]: John Muir, "Scotch Pioneers in Wisconsin," in David B. Greenberg, ed., *Land That Our Fathers Plowed* (University of Oklahoma Press, 1969), pp. 87–95, quoted at pp. 88, 89.

[*Nevins on the Northwestern Surge*]: Allan Nevins, *Ordeal of the Union: A House Dividing, 1852–1857* (Charles Scribner's Sons, 1947), Vol. 2, p. 160.

527 [*Population growth of states in the Northwest*]: U.S. Civil War Centennial Commission, *The United States on the Eve of the Civil War, as Described in the 1860 Census* (Government Printing Office, 1963), p. 61.

[*The farmers and the land*]: Allan G. Bogue, *From Prairie to Corn Belt* (University of Chicago Press, 1963).

[*Introduction and improvement of farm machinery*]: Percy Wells Bidwell and John I. Falconer, *History of Agriculture in the Northern United States* (Carnegie Institute of Washington, 1925), Part IV; Leo Rogin, *The Introduction of Farm Machinery in Its Relation to the Productivity of Labor in the Agriculture of the United States During the Nineteenth Century* (University of California Press, 1931).

[*James Baldwin's farm life*]: summarized in Nevins, p. 162.

528 [*Production of corn, wheat, and livestock*]: ibid., pp. 169–71.

[*Stockman B. F. Harris*]: ibid., p. 171.

[*Agricultural change in New England*]: Percy W. Bidwell, "The Agricultural Revolution in New England," *American Historical Review*, Vol. 26, No. 4 (July 1921), pp. 683–702.

529 [*Ephraim Bull of Concord*]: Nevins, p. 174.

[*South Carolinian on southeastern farming*]: J. Foster Marshall, pamphlet, Nov. 11, 1857, quoted in Nevins, pp. 182–83.

[*Relative size of wheat and corn crops*]: *The United States on the Eve of the Civil War*, pp. 70–71.

[*Southern farming*]: Lewis Cecil Gray, *History of Agriculture in the Southern United States to 1860* (Peter Smith, 1958), originally published by the Carnegie Institution of Washington, Publication No. 430, Vol. 2.

530 [*Prosperity under "King Cotton"*]: *The United States on the Eve of the Civil War*, pp. 43, 45.

[*Farming, general aspects*]: Paul W. Gates, *The Farmer's Age: Agriculture*, Vol. 3 of *The Economic History of the United States* (Holt, Rinehart and Winston, 1960).

531 [*Denunciations of the railroads*]: quoted in Stewart H. Holbrook, *The Story of American Railroads* (Crown, 1947), pp. 40–41.

[*Transportation changes*]: George Rogers Taylor, *The Transportation Revolution*, Vol. 4 of *The Economic History of the United States* (Holt, Rinehart and Winston, 1951); Caroline E. MacGill, *History of Transportation in the United States Before 1860* (Carnegie Institution of Washington, reprinted by Peter Smith, 1948).

[*Mortgaging of property by Wisconsin farmers for railroad investment*]: Taylor, p. 98.

[*Railroad development*]: Albert Fishlow, *American Railroads and the Transformation of the Ante-Bellum Economy* (Harvard University Press, 1965); Robert W. Fogel, *Railroads and American Economic Growth* (Johns Hopkins University Press, 1964); Paul Wallace Gates, *The Illinois Central Railroad and Its Colonization Work* (Harvard University Press, 1934).

532 [*Nevins on lake vessels*]: Nevins, p. 228.

[*Nevins on Mississippi riverboats*]: ibid., p. 214.

533 [*George Cable on the New Orleans dock scene*]: George W. Cable, *Dr. Sevier* (Charles Scribner's Sons, 1887), p. 52.

[*Industrial innovation and enterprise*]: Joseph and Frances Gies, *The Ingenious Yankees* (Thomas Y. Crowell, 1976); Thomas C. Cochran and William Miller, *The Age of Enterprise* (Macmillan, 1947).

534 [*Interchangeable parts*]: Gies, Ch. 13.

[*Hawthorne on the "scribbling women"*]: quoted in John T. Frederick, "Hawthorne's 'Scribbling Women,'" *New England Quarterly*, Vol. 48, No. 2 (June 1975), pp. 231–40, at p. 231.

[*Economic expansion of the 1850s*]: Stuart Bruchey, *The Roots of American Economic Growth* (Harper & Row, 1965); Douglass C. North, *The Economic Growth of the United States* (Prentice-Hall, 1961); Charles H. Hession and Hyman Sardy, *Ascent to Affluence* (Allyn and Bacon, 1969).

535 [*Differences among economic historians as to period of greatest expansion*]: Bruchey, Ch. 4.

[*Inequality in the 1850s*]: Lee Soltow, "Economic Inequality in the United States in the Period from 1790 to 1860," *Journal of Economic History*, Vol. 31, No. 4 (December 1971), pp. 822–39; Edward Pessen, *Riches, Class, and Power Before the Civil War* (D. C. Heath, 1973).

535 [*Workers' wages*]: Edgar W. Martin, *The Standard of Living in 1860* (University of Chicago Press, 1942), p. 409 (Appendix).

[*Inequality as constant*]: Soltow, p. 839.

The Cornucopia Overflows

535 [*American exhibits at the Crystal Palace*]: *National Intelligencer*, Feb. 3, 1852, quoted in Nevins, p. 254.

536 [*"Floating palaces" in the coastal trade*]: William H. Ewen, "Steamboats to New England," *The Log of Mystic Seaport*, Vol. 32, No. 2 (Summer 1980), pp. 43–50.

[*Eastern ports, relative standing*]: Robert Greenhalgh Albion, *The Rise of New York Port* (Charles Scribner's Sons, 1939), Appendix I, p. 389.

[*American ships*]: Taylor, Ch. 6.

[*Marcy's instructions on diplomatic dress*]: Thomas A. Bailey, *A Diplomatic History of the American People* (F. S. Crofts, 1941), pp. 282, 283. [*America's cup*]: "Yachts and Yachting," in *Encyclopedia Americana*, International Edition (Americana Corporation, 1977), Vol. 29, p. 635.

[*Young America*]: Merlo E. Curti, " 'Young America,' " *American Historical Review*, Vol. 32, No. 1 (October 1926), pp. 34–55.

[*Support for those "who had suffered in the cause of liberty"*]: *ibid.*, p. 48.

537 [*Kossuth's reception in New York Harbor*]: Bailey, p. 286.

[*Seward on democracy and markets*]: quoted in William Appleman Williams, *The Roots of the Modern American Empire* (Random House, 1969), p. 99.

[*Punch cartoon*]: reproduced in Bailey, p. 283.

538 [*Pierce on expansionism*]: James D. Richardson, ed., *A Compilation of the Messages and Papers of the Presidents* (Washington, D.C.: Bureau of National Literature, 1913), Vol. 4, p. 2731.

[*Marcy on the spoils system*]: quoted in Dumas Malone, ed., *Dictionary of American Biography* (Charles Scribner's Sons, 1933), Vol. 12, p. 275.

[*Cuba and the Black Warrior incident*]: Nevins, Ch. 10.

[*Soulé*]: Amos A. Ettinger, *The Mission to Spain of Pierre Soulé, 1853–1855* (Yale University Press, 1932).

539 [*Tribune on Ostend Manifesto*]: quoted in Nevins, p. 362.

[*U.S. diplomacy as a "singular profession"*]: London *Times*, March 24, 1855; see also Ettinger, pp. 406–10, for other foreign commentary.

[*Incidents in Central America*]: Bailey, pp. 290–95.

540 [*American whalers*]: Elmo Paul Hohman, *The American Whaleman* (Longmans, Green, 1928); Edward A. Ackerman, *New England's Fishing Industry* (Chicago: University of Chicago Press, 1941); Marshall B. Davidson, *Life in America* (Houghton Mifflin, 1951), Vol. 1, pp. 340–45.

[*Whaling statistics*]: Hohman, Appendixes.

541 [*Melville on the whale chase*]: Herman Melville, *Moby-Dick* (Hendricks House, 1962), pp. 222, 223–24.

542 [*Chinese trade*]: John King Fairbank, *Trade and Diplomacy on the China Coast*, 2 vols. (Harvard University Press, 1953); Hallett Abend, *Treaty Ports* (Doubleday, Doran, 1944).

542 [*The Matthew Perry expedition to Japan*]: Francis L. Hawks, comp., *Narrative of the Expedition of an American Squadron to the China Seas and Japan* (D. Appleton, 1856); Official Report, "Commodore Perry's Landing in Japan, 1853," *Old South Leaflets* No. 151 (Directors of the Old South Work, n.d.), Vol. 7, pp. 1–28; Arthur Walworth, *Black Ships off Japan* (Archon Books, 1966).

[*Japanese lament about the black ship*]: quoted in Bailey, p. 330.

"It Will Raise a Hell of a Storm"

543 [*Stephen Douglas*]: Robert W. Johannsen, *Stephen A. Douglas* (Oxford University Press, 1973); Robert W. Johannsen, ed., *The Letters of Stephen A. Douglas* (University of Illinois Press, 1961).

[*Douglas' Nebraska bill*]: Johannsen, *Stephen A. Douglas*, pp. 405–8.

544 [*"It will raise a hell of a storm"*]: quoted in David M. Potter, *The Impending Crisis, 1848–1861* (Harper & Row, 1976), p. 160.

545 [*Douglas on leaving slavery to the laws of climate, etc.*]: quoted in *ibid.*, p. 172.

[*Salmon P. Chase*]: Albert B. Hart, *Salmon P. Chase* (Houghton Mifflin, 1899).

[*Charles Sumner*]: David Donald, *Charles Sumner and the Coming of the Civil War* (Alfred A. Knopf, 1960).

[*Longfellow, Lieber, and Winthrop on Sumner*]: quoted in *ibid.*, pp. 214, 227, 212, resp.

546 [*"Appeal of the Independent Democrats"*]: see the New York *Times*, Jan. 24, 1854, p. 2.

[*Douglas on the storm soon spending its fury*]: Stephen A. Douglas to Howell Cobb, April 2, 1854, in Johannsen, ed., *Letters of Stephen A. Douglas*, p. 300.

547 [*Greeley on the Kansas-Nebraska bill*]: Jeter Allen Isely, *Horace Greeley and the Republican Party* (Princeton University Press, 1947), p. 49.

[*Press reaction to Kansas-Nebraska bill*]: Nevins, Ch. 9; Isely, passim.

[*Rise of the Know-Nothings*]: Michael F. Holt, "The Politics of Impatience: The Origins of Know Nothingism," *Journal of American History*, Vol. 60, No. 2 (September 1973), pp. 309–31.

[*Know-Nothing party's stated purpose*]: quoted in Paul Kleppner, *The Third Electoral System, 1853–1892* (University of North Carolina Press, 1979), p. 68.

548 [*Anti-Negro prejudice, 1850s*]: Kenneth M. Stampp, *The Imperiled Union* (Oxford University Press, 1980), esp. Ch. 4; C. Vann Woodward, *American Counterpoint: Slavery and Racism in the North-South Dialogue* (Little, Brown, 1971), Ch. 5; Nevins, passim; Leon Litwack, *North of Slavery: The Negro in the Free States, 1790–1860* (University of Chicago Press, 1961); Eugene H. Berwanger, *The Frontier Against Slavery: Western Anti-Negro Prejudice and the Slavery Extension Controversy* (University of Illinois Press, 1967).

[*Early fusion and Republican meetings*]: Hans L. Trefousse, "The Republican Party, 1854–1864," in Arthur M. Schlesinger, Jr., ed., *History of U.S. Political Parties* (Chelsea House, 1973), p. 1145; Isely, p. 84.

549 [*Douglas' speeches like "cannon-balls"*]: Carl Schurz, *Reminiscences* (McClure, 1907), Vol. 2, p. 30.

[*Burns incident in Boston*]: Nevins, pp. 150–52.

550 [*Seward on competition for Kansas*]: *Congressional Globe*, 33rd Congress, 1st session, Appendix, p. 769.

550 [*The struggle for Kansas*]: James C. Malin, *The Nebraska Question, 1852–1854* (University of Kansas Press, 1953); James A. Rawley, *Race & Politics: "Bleeding Kansas" and the Coming of the Civil War* (Lippincott, 1969).

551 [*John Brown at Pottawatomie*]: Stephen B. Oates, *To Purge This Land with Blood* (Harper & Row, 1970), Ch. 10.

   [*Sumner on Congress as a "godless place"*]: quoted in Donald, p. 278.

   [*Sumner's speech "The Crime Against Kansas"*]: *Congressional Globe*, 34th Congress, 1st session, Appendix, pp. 529–47. [*Exchange of insults between Sumner and Douglas*]: ibid., p. 547.

552 [*Brooks's assault on Sumner*]: Avery O. Craven, *The Growth of Southern Nationalism* (Louisiana State University Press, 1953); see also Robert L. Meriwether, ed., "Preston S. Brooks on the Caning of Charles Sumner," *South Carolina Historical and Genealogical Magazine*, Vol. 12, No. 2 (April 1951).

The Illinois Republicans

553 [*Potter's listing of diverse rivals of the Republicans*]: Potter, p. 249.

554 [*Edward Everett's admonition to nativist leader*]: Edward Everett to W. B. Weiss, Feb. 14, 1853, Reel 14, Edward Everett Papers, Massachusetts Historical Society.

555 [*Antebellum Springfield*]: Paul M. Angle, *"Here I Have Lived": A History of Lincoln's Springfield* (Abraham Lincoln Book Shop, 1935), pp. 1–84; Carl Sandburg, *Abraham Lincoln: The Prairie Years* (Harcourt, Brace, 1926), Vol. 2, passim.

   [*The Lincoln-Herndon law office*]: David Donald, *Lincoln's Herndon* (Alfred A. Knopf, 1948), p. 72; Sandburg, passim.

556 [*Lincoln riding circuit*]: Benjamin P. Thomas, *Abraham Lincoln* (Alfred A. Knopf, 1952), Ch. 5; Sandburg, passim.

   [*David Davis*]: Willard L. King, *Lincoln's Manager, David Davis* (Harvard University Press, 1960).

   [*Lincoln's law practice*]: Stephen B. Oates, *With Malice Toward None* (Harper & Row, 1977), esp. pp. 95–105.

   [*Lincoln on acquiring property*]: quoted in Williams, p. 296.

   [*Lincoln "swallowed up" in greed for office*]: from Herndon's lectures on Lincoln, quoted in Donald, *Lincoln's Herndon*, p. 202. [*"Ambition was a little engine that knew no rest"*]: William H. Herndon and Jesse W. Weik, *Abraham Lincoln* (D. Appleton, 1917), Vol. 2, p. 44.

   [*Reaction of Whig junto to passage of Kansas-Nebraska bill*]: Donald, *Lincoln's Herndon*, pp. 81–82.

557 [*Lincoln to Speed on his political views*]: quoted in Thomas, pp. 163–64.

   [*Douglas-Lincoln confrontations, 1854*]: Johannsen, *Stephen A. Douglas*, pp. 456–59; Oates, *With Malice Toward None*, pp. 113–18. [*Douglas journeys home "by the light of my own effigy"*]: Johannsen, *Stephen A. Douglas*, p. 451.

558 [*The Republican "third cadre" in Illinois*]: Victor B. Howard, "The Illinois Republican Party," *Journal of the Illinois State Historical Society*, Vol. 64, No. 2 (Summer 1971), Part I: "A Party Organizer for the Republicans in 1854," pp. 124–60. See also Paul Selby, "Genesis of the Republican Party in Illinois," *Transactions of the Illinois State Historical Society*, 1906, No. 11 (Springfield, Ill., 1906), pp. 270–83, and Paul Selby Collection, Illinois State Historical Society. Dee Ann Montgomery conducted field research in Illinois on the Illinois Republicans.

558 [*Meeting of anti-Nebraska editors*]: Howard, Part II: "The Party Becomes Conservative, 1855–1856," pp. 297–99.

[*Lincoln's response to Herndon in regard to the call*]: quoted in Thomas, p. 165; see also Donald, *Lincoln's Herndon*, p. 84.

[*Bloomington convention*]: Howard, Part II, p. 303.

559 [*Douglas' situation in the Democratic national convention, 1856*]: Johannsen, *Stephen A. Douglas*, pp. 515–22.

[*Republican platform*]: Nevins, p. 461.

560 [*Nevins on Frémont as a candidate*]: ibid., p. 462; see also Allan Nevins, *Frémont, Pathmarker of the West* (D. Appleton, 1939), pp. 425–32.

[*Benton opposes Frémont*]: Nevins, *Pathmarker of the West*, p. 448.

[*The Whigs' last hurrah*]: Roy F. Nichols and Philip S. Klein, "Election of 1856," in Arthur M. Schlesinger, Jr., ed., *History of American Presidential Elections, 1789–1968* (Chelsea House, 1971), Vol. 2, pp. 1007–33.

[*Republican reporter's comment on Whigs*]: ibid., p. 1031.

[*1856 campaign*]: Schlesinger, *Elections;* Nevins, *Ordeal of the Union;* Don C. Seitz, *Lincoln the Politician* (Coward-McCann, 1931); Kleppner.

561 [*Mrs. Emerson and the Republican delegation*]: Report of the Wayland, Mass., delegation to the Republican National Convention, 1856, from the 8th Congressional District meeting at Concord, Mass., June 2, 1856, Emerson Papers, Concord Free Public Library.

[*The Republicans' battle song*]: Wilfred E. Binkley, *American Political Parties: Their Natural History* (Alfred A. Knopf, 1947), p. 219.

562 [*Lincoln's Galena speech*]: quoted in Thomas, p. 168.

16. THE GRAPES OF WRATH

563 [*Washington at the time of Buchanan's Inaugural Address*]: Constance M. Green, *Washington, Village and Capital, 1800–1878* (Princeton University Press, 1962), Ch. 7, "The Eye of the Hurricane, 1849–1860."

[*Description of Washington*]: Frederick Law Olmsted, *A Journey in the Seaboard Slave States* (Dix & Edwards, 1856), Ch. 1; Daniel D. Reiff, *Washington Architecture, 1791–1861* (U.S. Commission of Fine Arts, 1971), pp. 113–18; Green; Robert Sears, *Pictorial Description of the United States* (Robert Sears, 1849), p. 282, 301; John Hayward, *A Gazetteer of the United States of America* (Case, Tiffany, 1853), pp. 612–15; John W. Reps, *Monumental Washington* (Princeton University Press, 1967).

564 [*Olmsted's black servant*]: Olmsted, pp. 4–5.

[*Arrest of "genteel colored men"*]: ibid., pp. 16–17; Green, pp. 186–87.

[*Marriage of Jefferson Davis and Sarah Taylor*]: Holman Hamilton, *Zachary Taylor: Soldier of the Republic* (Bobbs-Merrill, 1941), Vol. 1, Ch. 7.

[*Carl Schurz on Jefferson Davis*]: Carl Schurz, *Reminiscences* (McClure, 1907), Vol. 2, p. 21.

565 [*Seward on "higher law than the Constitution"*]: quoted in Thornton K. Lothrop, *William Henry Seward* (Houghton Mifflin, 1896), p. 86.

566 [*Green on the "eye of the hurricane"*]: Green, p. 180.

South Carolinians: The Power Elite

566 [*Preston Brooks's assault and vindication*]: David H. Donald, *Charles Sumner and the Coming of the Civil War* (Alfred A. Knopf, 1960), pp. 297–311; Avery O. Craven, *The Growth of Southern Nationalism, 1848–1861* (Louisiana State University Press, 1953), pp. 228–36.

[*South Carolina*]: Louis B. Wright, *South Carolina* (W. W. Norton, 1976); Rosser H. Taylor, *Ante-Bellum South Carolina: A Social and Cultural History* (University of North Carolina Press, 1942); William A. Schaper, "Sectionalism and Representation in South Carolina," *Annual Report of the American Historical Association for the Year 1900* (Government Printing Office, 1901), Vol. 1, pp. 245–58; William W. Freehling, *Prelude to Civil War* (Harper & Row, 1965), Ch. 1; Olmsted, Ch. 6.

567 [*Freehling's portrait of planters*]: Freehling, pp. 11–13.

[*Slaves' lives*]: Robert W. Fogel and Stanley L. Engerman, *Time on the Cross* (Little, Brown, 1974), esp. pp. 202–9, 220–21.

568 [*Savannah River planter (Hammond) on slave mortality*]: Freehling, p. 71.

[*Olmsted's description of slave scene*]: Olmsted, p. 388.

[*Patriarchal nature of planter families*]: Michael P. Johnson, "Planters and Patriarchy: Charleston, 1800–1860," *Journal of Southern History*, Vol. 46, No. 1 (February 1980), pp. 45–72.

568–9 [*Mary Boykin Chesnut on planters and "their concubines"*]: quoted in *ibid.*, p. 45. [*On feeling "like a beggar"*]: *ibid.*, p. 51. [*On "hideous black harem"*]: *ibid.*, p. 71. This diary was rewritten after the Civil War.

569 [*Columbia*]: Freehling, p. 20; Wright, *passim*. [*Intellectual life in Columbia*]: Wright, Ch. 8.

[*Charleston*]: George C. Rogers, Jr., *Charleston in the Age of the Pinckneys* (University of Oklahoma Press, 1969), pp. 147–48 and passim; William Oliver Stevens, *Charleston* (Dodd, Mead, 1939), passim; Hayward, p. 321.

[*Death of cultural adornments during nullification crisis*]: Rogers, p. 160.

570 [*Attempt to require test oath*]: Freehling, pp. 310 ff.

[*Unique ideological solidarity and structure of government in South Carolina*]: James M. Banner, Jr., "The Problem of South Carolina," in Stanley M. Elkins and Eric McKitrick, eds., *The Hofstadter Aegis* (Alfred A. Knopf, 1974), pp. 76–78 and passim. [*Doctrine of "virtual representation"*]: Kenneth S. Greenberg, "Representation and the Isolation of South Carolina, 1776–1860," *Journal of American History*, Vol. 64, No. 3 (December 1977), pp. 723–43. [*Weakness of local government*]: Ralph A. Wooster, *The People in Power* (University of Tennessee Press, 1969), pp. 88, 92.

571 [*Definition of ideology*]: James MacGregor Burns, *Leadership* (Harper & Row, 1978), pp. 249–50.

[*Wiltse on Calhoun's concept of liberty*]: Charles M. Wiltse, *John C. Calhoun: Sectionalist, 1840–1850* (Bobbs-Merrill, 1951), p. 425. See also Charles G. Sellers, Jr., "The Travail of Slavery," in Charles G. Sellers, Jr., ed., *The Southerner as American* (University of North Carolina Press, 1960), pp. 40–71.

572 [*Intellectual leaders in the defense of slavery*]: William S. Jenkins, *Pro-Slavery Thought in the Old South* (University of North Carolina Press, 1935); Drew Gilpin Faust, *A Sacred Circle: The Dilemma of the Intellectual in the Old South, 1840–1860* (Johns Hopkins University Press, 1977); David Donald, "The Proslavery Argument Reconsidered," *Journal of Southern History*, Vol. 37, No. 1 (February 1971), pp. 3–18; Kenneth S. Greenberg, "Revolutionary Ideology and the Proslavery Argument: The Abolition of Slavery in

Antebellum South Carolina," *Journal of Southern History,* Vol. 42, No. 3 (August 1976), pp. 365–84; Eugene D. Genovese, *The World the Slaveholders Made* (Pantheon Books, 1969); Clement Eaton, *The Mind of the Old South* (Louisiana State University Press, 1964); Jesse T. Carpenter, *The South as a Conscious Minority* (New York University Press, 1930).

572 [*Hammond on slavery as "cornerstone"*]: letter to Thomas Clarkson, Jan. 28, 1845, printed in *The Proslavery Argument* (Walker, Richards, 1852), p. 109.

[*Calhoun on people not being all "equally entitled to liberty"*]: John C. Calhoun, "A Disquisition on Government," in Richard K. Cralle, ed., *The Works of John C. Calhoun* (D. Appleton, 1854), Vol. 1, p. 55. [*Simms on liberty*]: William Gilmore Simms, "The Morals of Slavery," in *The Proslavery Argument,* pp. 256, 258; Faust, pp. 84, 120.

573 [*Contradictions in states' rights doctrine*]: Greenberg, "Representation and the Isolation of South Carolina," passim; William W. Freehling, "Spoilsmen and Interests in the Thought and Career of John C. Calhoun," *Journal of American History,* Vol. 52, No. 1 (June 1965), p. 38. [*Control of state legislature over local officials*]: Wooster, pp. 88, 92.

[*Rejection of Jeffersonian moral philosophy*]: Louis Hartz, *The Liberal Tradition in America* (Harcourt, Brace, 1955), passim.

[*Fitzhugh on destructiveness of liberty and equality*]: George Fitzhugh, "Sociology for the South," in Eric L. McKitrick, ed., *Slavery Defended* (Prentice-Hall, 1963), p. 40.

[*Bledsoe on slavery and liberty*]: quoted in Jenkins, p. 113.

[*Hammond's repudiation of Jefferson's dictum*]: letter to Clarkson, in *The Proslavery Argument,* pp. 109–10.

[*Southern abrogation of freedom of discussion*]: Clement Eaton, *Freedom of Thought in the Old South* (Duke University Press, 1940); Russell B. Nye, *Fettered Freedom* (Michigan State University Press, 1963).

[*Hammond's "one way" to silence talk of abolition*]: Nye, p. 177.

[*Suppression of the* True American]: Eaton, *Freedom of Thought,* pp. 185–93.

[*Chapel Hill professor (Hedrick) forced to leave*]: ibid., pp. 202–5; Nye, pp. 92–94.

[*Eaton on southern intellectual blockade*]: Eaton, *Freedom of Thought,* pp. 209, 316.

[*For a survey of other defenses of slavery*]: see Donald, "Proslavery Argument." See also Jenkins, passim.

574 [*Hammond's "mud-sill" address*]: U.S. Senate, March 4, 1858, *Congressional Globe,* 35th Congress, 1st session, Part I, pp. 952–62. [*Trescot's assertion that blacks were not fit for education*]: Greenberg, "Revolutionary Ideology," p. 372.

[*Donald on "pastoral Arcadia"*]: Donald, "Proslavery Argument," p. 16.

[*"A Carolinian" (Edward J. Pringle) on slave as compared to wage worker*]: "A Carolinian," *Slavery in the Southern States* (J. Bartlett, 1852), pp. 25–27, quoted in Greenberg, "Revolutionary Ideology," p. 383.

[*Fitzhugh on "wage slavery"*]: George Fitzhugh, *Cannibals All! Or, Slaves Without Masters,* C. Vann Woodward, ed. (Belknap Press of Harvard University Press, 1960). See also Stanley M. Elkins, "The Right to Be a Slave," *Commentary,* Vol. 30, No. 5 (November 1960), pp. 450–52.

The Grand Debates

The main source for the Dred Scott decision is Don E. Fehrenbacher, *The Dred Scott Case* (Oxford University Press, 1978), and major works cited therein.

575 [*Chief Justice Taney*]: Carl Brent Swisher, *Roger B. Taney* (Macmillan, 1935); Samuel Tyler, *Memoir of Roger Brooke Taney, LL.D* (John Murphy, 1876). [*Other Justices*]: Carl B. Swisher, *History of the Supreme Court of the United States*, Vol. 5: *The Taney Period, 1836–1864* (Macmillan, 1974), pp. 46–48, 53–55, 58–70, 229–40, 242–44.

576 [*Headlines reporting the Dred Scott decision*]: cited in Allan Nevins, *The Emergence of Lincoln* (Charles Scribner's Sons, 1950), Vol. 1, p. 92.

[*New York* Tribune *comment on Dred Scott decision*]: quoted in Fehrenbacher, p. 3.

[*Procedural aspects of Dred Scott*]: Walter Ehrlich, "Was the Dred Scott Case Valid?" *Journal of American History*, Vol. 55, No. 2 (September 1968), pp. 256–65; F. H. Hodder, "Some Phases of the Dred Scott Case," *Mississippi Valley Historical Review*, Vol. 16, No. 1 (June 1929), pp. 3–22.

[*Buchanan informed by Justices as to probable nature and timing of Dred Scott decision*]: Fehrenbacher, pp. 311–14.

577 [*Importance placed on "massing the court" against Missouri Compromise*]: David M. Potter, *The Impending Crisis* (Harper & Row, 1976), p. 274.

[*Taney's rage against the antislavery movement*]: Fehrenbacher, pp. 311, 388, 557, 561.

578 [*Taney's legal errors in Dred Scott decision*]: ibid., pp. 337–64, 367–88.

[*Everett's hope for a "vigorous and conciliatory administration"*]: Edward Everett to James Buchanan, Jan. 19, 1857, Edward Everett Papers, Reel 16, Massachusetts State Historical Society.

579 [*Kansan on Lecompton constitution vote*]: Nevins, Vol. 1, p. 236. Emporia *Kansas News: ibid.*

580 [*Douglas querying validity of Lecompton constitution*]: Robert W. Johannsen, *Stephen A. Douglas* (Oxford University Press, 1973), pp. 581–82.

[*Exchange between Buchanan and Douglas*]: ibid., p. 586.

[*Douglas' rejection of the Lecompton constitution and reaffirmation of popular sovereignty*]: ibid., pp. 590–91.

[*Machinations of Republicans and Democrats concerning Douglas in 1858*]: Potter, p. 331.

581 [*Herndon to Greeley on "selling out" Illinois Republicans*]: William H. Herndon to Horace Greeley, April 8, 1858, Greeley Papers, New York Public Library. See also Abraham Lincoln to Elihu B. Washburne, April 26, 1858, in Roy P. Basler, ed., *The Collected Works of Abraham Lincoln* (Rutgers University Press, 1953), Vol. 2, pp. 443–44; Abraham Lincoln to Elihu B. Washburne, May 27, 1858, ibid., p. 455.

[*Nomination of Lincoln at state party convention*]: Don E. Fehrenbacher, *Prelude to Greatness: Lincoln in the 1850's* (Stanford University Press, 1962), Ch. 3. [*Herndon on wanting to see "old man Greely's" notice of the convention*]: ibid., p. 50.

[*Lincoln's preparations for speech*]: Stephen B. Oates, *With Malice Toward None* (Harper & Row, 1977), p. 142.

582 [*Opening of Lincoln's "House Divided" speech*]: Basler, Vol. 2, p. 461.

[*On the "House Divided" speech*]: Fehrenbacher, *Prelude to Greatness*, Ch. 4; Harry V. Jaffa, *Crisis of the House Divided* (Doubleday, 1959), passim.

["*Ultimate extinction" or victory of slavery in "all the States"*]: Basler, Vol. 2, pp. 461–62. [*"Another Supreme Court decision" preventing a state from outlawing slavery*]: ibid., p. 467. [*Douglas, Taney, Pierce, and Buchanan conspiring "before the first lick was struck"*]: ibid., pp. 465–66.

583 [*Lincoln following Douglas around the state*]: Johannsen, p. 662.

[*Theatrics of the debates*]: ibid., pp. 631, 655.

584 [*Douglas on Lincoln*]: *ibid.*, pp. 640–41.

[*Douglas on inequality of blacks*]: Basler, Vol. 3, p. 10.

[*Douglas on diversity as the "safeguard of our liberties"*]: Johannsen, p. 642.

[*Lincoln's views on the rights of blacks*]: Basler, Vol. 3, pp. 16, 145, 222.

[*Lincoln's accusation that Douglas held a "care not" attitude*]: *ibid.*, pp. 233–34.

[*Audience participation in the debates*]: *ibid.*, passim.

585–6 [*Lincoln asking if Douglas could be "on all sides"*]: Basler, Vol. 3, p. 298. [*Republican party view of slavery as "a moral, social and political wrong"*]: *ibid.*, pp. 312–13. [*Solution of providing that slavery "grow no larger"*]: *ibid.*, p. 313.

586 [*Lincoln on "physical difference" between blacks and whites*]: *ibid.*, pp. 145–46. [*On the equality of the black to "every living man" in right to fruits of his labor*]: *ibid.*, p. 16.

[*Lincoln on economic rights basic to liberty*]: Eric Foner, *Politics and Ideology in the Age of the Civil War* (Oxford University Press, 1980), pp. 10, 21, 32.

[*"Because I do not want a negro woman for a slave I must necessarily want her for a wife"*]: Basler, Vol. 3, p. 146.

587 [*Lincoln on waiting for the harvest*]: *ibid.*, p. 334.

The Politics of Slavery

588 [*Intense trading on the New York Stock Exchange*]: Nevins, Vol. 1, p. 181.

[*Verses on ladies' trips to Paris*]: *ibid.*, pp. 179–80.

[*Emerson on American materialism*]: *The Journals of Ralph Waldo Emerson,* ed. Edward Waldo Emerson (Houghton Mifflin, 1911), Vol. 5, p. 285.

[*Vitality of American literary life in the 1850s*]: Nevins, Vol. 1, Ch. 2.

590 [*Frederick Douglass' refusal to join John Brown*]: Stephen B. Oates, *To Purge This Land with Blood* (Harper & Row, 1970), p. 283.

[*Lydia Maria Child's request to visit John Brown*]: Lydia Maria Child to Henry A. Wise, Oct. 26, 1859, Lydia Maria Child Papers, Schlesinger Library.

[*Northern acclaim for John Brown*]: Oates, *To Purge This Land with Blood,* p. 318; "A Plea for John Brown," Henry David Thoreau, *The Writings of Henry David Thoreau* (Houghton Mifflin, 1893), Vol. 10, p. 234; "Harper's Ferry," speech of Nov. 1, 1859, Wendell Phillips, *Speeches, Lectures, and Letters* (Negro Universities Press, 1968), p. 263.

[*Brown on his martyrdom*]: Oates, *To Purge This Land with Blood,* p. 335. [*On the need to purge "with Blood"*]: *ibid.*, p. 351.

591 [*Repudiation of Brown by Republican notables*]: Nevins, Vol. 2, pp. 105–6; Oates, *With Malice Toward None,* p. 168; Oates, *To Purge This Land with Blood,* p. 353.

[*Unity of South in "sentiment and feeling"*]: Nevins, Vol. 2, p. 110.

[*Background on the opening session of the 36th Congress*]: *ibid.*, Ch. 4.

592 [*Hinton Rowan Helper*]: Hinton Rowan Helper, *The Impending Crisis of the South: How to Meet It* (Burdick Brothers, 1857), quoted at p. 120.

[*Democratic convention of 1860*]: Robert W. Johannsen, "Douglas at Charleston," in Norman A. Graebner, ed., *Politics and the Crisis of 1860* (University of Illinois Press, 1961), pp. 61–90; Austin L. Venable, "The Conflict Between the Douglas and Yancey Forces in the Charleston Convention," *Journal of Southern History,* Vol. 8, No. 2 (May 1942), pp. 226–41.

593 [*Dilemmas facing Republican party in shaping an identity in 1860*]: Don E. Fehrenbacher, "The Republican Decision at Chicago," in Graebner, pp. 32–60; Foner, *Politics and Ideology*, Chs. 1–3; Hans L. Trefousse, "The Republican Party, 1854–1864," in Arthur M. Schlesinger, Jr., ed., *History of U.S. Political Parties* (Chelsea House, 1973), Vol. 2, pp. 1141–72.

[*Seward's attempts to appear conciliatory at convention*]: Potter, p. 420.

594 [*Lincoln on how to defeat the enemy*]: Basler, Vol. 3, pp. 460–61.

595 [*Reaffirmation of the Declaration of Independence at 1860 Republican convention*]: Nevins, Vol. 2, p. 254. [*The convention in general*]: Fehrenbacher, "Republican Decision at Chicago," passim.

[*"Lincoln ain't here . . ."*]: Henry C. Whitney, *Lincoln the Citizen* (Current Literature, 1907), p. 288. The authenticity of this quotation is questionable, however.

596 [*Lincoln informed of nomination*]: Oates, *With Malice Toward None*, p. 179.

[*Friend on Lincoln's view of southern "political game of bluff"*]: Donn Piatt, *Memories of the Men Who Saved the Union* (Belford, Clarke, 1887), pp. 28–30.

[*William Cullen Bryant on maintaining Lincoln's image*]: Nevins, Vol. 2, p. 278.

596–7 [*Douglas' presidential campaign*]: Johannsen, *Stephen A. Douglas*, Ch. 29. [*Douglas in the South*]: Robert W. Johannsen, "Stephen A. Douglas and the South," *Journal of Southern History*, Vol. 33, No. 1 (February 1967), pp. 26–50. [*Douglas' attempt to "save the Union"*]: Johannsen, *Stephen A. Douglas*, pp. 797–98.

597 [*Election results of 1860*]: Ollinger Crenshaw, "Urban and Rural Voting in the Election of 1860," in Eric F. Goldman, ed., *Historiography and Urbanization: Essays in American History in Honor of W. Stull Holt* (Johns Hopkins University Press, 1941), pp. 43–63; Peyton McCrary, Clark Miller, and Dale Baum, "Class and Party in the Secession Crisis: Voting Behavior in the Deep South, 1856–1861," *Journal of Interdisciplinary History*, Vol. 8, No. 3 (Winter 1978), pp. 429–57; cf. Robert P. Swierenga, "The Ethnic Voter and the First Lincoln Election," in Frederick C. Luebke, ed., *Ethnic Voters and the Election of Lincoln* (University of Nebraska Press, 1971), pp. 129–50; Paul Kleppner, *The Third Electoral System, 1853–1892* (University of North Carolina Press, 1979), passim; Walter D. Kamphoefner, "St. Louis Germans and the Republican Party, 1848–1860," *Mid-America*, Vol. 57, No. 2 (April 1975), pp. 69–88.

[*South Carolina secession ordinance*]: quoted in French Ensor Chadwick, *Causes of the Civil War, 1859–1861* (Harper & Brothers, 1907), p. 138.

[*Douglas on America as the "last hope of freedom"*]: Johannsen, *Stephen A. Douglas*, p. 789.

598 [*Explanations of advent of the Civil War*]: Swierenga; McCrary, Miller, and Baum; Crenshaw; Albert C. E. Parker, "Beating the Spread: Analyzing American Election Outcomes," *Journal of American History*, Vol. 67, No. 1 (June 1980), pp. 61–87.

[*Theories of causes of the Civil War*]: Foner, *Politics and Ideology*, Chs. 1–2.

599 [*The southern ideology*]: Carpenter; Craven; David M. Potter, *The South and the Sectional Conflict* (Louisiana State University Press, 1968), Part I; Rollin G. Osterweis, *Romanticism and Nationalism in the Old South* (Yale University Press, 1949); Foner, *Politics and Ideology*, passim; cf. C. Vann Woodward, *American Counterpoint* (Little, Brown, 1964), esp. Ch. 5; Kenneth M. Stampp, *The Imperiled Union* (Oxford University Press, 1980), esp. Ch. 4.

[*General sources on the politics of slavery*]: Foner, *Politics and Ideology;* Eric Foner, *Free Soil, Free Labor, Free Men: The Ideology of the Republican Party Before the Civil War* (Oxford University Press, 1970); Potter, *The South and the Sectional Conflict;* Potter, *Impending Crisis;* Woodward, *American Counterpoint;* Craven; Don E. Fehrenbacher, "Comment on 'Why the Republican Party Came to Power,'" in George H. Knoles, ed., *The Crisis of the Union* (Louisiana State University Press, 1965), pp. 21–29; Carpenter; Staughton

Lynd, *Class Conflict, Slavery, and the United States Constitution* (Bobbs-Merrill, 1967); James MacGregor Burns, *The Deadlock of Democracy* (Prentice-Hall, 1963), Chs. 3–4; Steven Channing, *Crisis of Fear: Secession in South Carolina* (Simon and Schuster, 1970); William J. Cooper, Jr., *The South and the Politics of Slavery, 1828–1856* (Louisiana State University Press, 1978); James A. Rawley, *Race and Politics* (Lippincott, 1969); Edward Pessen, *Riches, Class, and Power Before the Civil War* (D. C. Heath, 1973); Harold S. Schultz, *Nationalism and Sectionalism in South Carolina, 1852–1860* (Duke University Press, 1950).

17. THE BLOOD-RED WINE

601 [*Davis' journey to Montgomery*]: Shelby Foote, *The Civil War, A Narrative: Fort Sumter to Perryville* (Random House, 1958), p. 17; Hudson Strode, *Jefferson Davis, American Patriot: 1808–1861* (Harcourt, Brace, 1955), pp. 401–7.

[*Montgomery convention*]: Ellis M. Coulter, *The Confederate States of America, 1861–1865* (Louisiana State University Press, 1950), pp. 19–26. [*Confederate Constitution*]: text in Edward A. Pollard, *The First Year of the War*, reprinted from the Richmond corrected edition (Charles B. Richardson, 1863), pp. 363–78.

602 [*Public "approbation" of Davis*]: Jefferson Davis to Varina Davis, Feb. 20, 1861, in Dunbar Rowland, ed., *Jefferson Davis, Constitutionalist: His Letters, Papers and Speeches* (Mississippi Dept. of Archives and History, 1923), p. 54. [*Davis' speeches*]: Strode, p. 406.

[*Yancey introduces Davis*]: Strode, p. 407. [*Inaugural address*]: text in Rowland, pp. 49–53.

603 [*Davis on reception of address*]: Rowland, p. 54.

[*Lincoln's journey to Washington*]: Foote, pp. 35–37; Benjamin P. Thomas, *Abraham Lincoln* (Alfred A. Knopf, 1952), pp. 239–44; Carl Sandburg, *Abraham Lincoln: The War Years* (Harcourt, Brace, 1939), Vol. 1, Ch. 2.

[*Lincoln's farewell to Herndon*]: William H. Herndon and Jesse W. Weik, *Abraham Lincoln* (D. Appleton, 1917), Vol. 2, p. 194.

[*Buchanan's hopes and indecision*]: Thomas, pp. 228–29.

604 [*Indianapolis, Cincinnati, and Pittsburgh speeches*]: see Roy P. Basler, ed., *The Collected Works of Abraham Lincoln* (Rutgers University Press, 1953), Vol. 4, pp. 194, 199, and 211, resp.

[*Speech at Independence Hall*]: ibid., p. 240.

[*Lincoln before the inauguration*]: see Sandburg, Ch. 3. [*Greeley on peaceful acquiescence*]: quoted in David M. Potter, *The Impending Crisis, 1848–1861* (Harper & Row, 1963), p. 524.

[*Lincoln's feelings for the Union*]: George B. Forgie, *Patricide in the House Divided: A Psychological Interpretation of Lincoln and His Age* (W. W. Norton, 1979), passim.

605 [*Lincoln's Inaugural Address*]: Basler, Vol. 4, pp. 262–71.

[*Richmond Enquirer reacts to Inaugural Address*]: Sandburg, p. 137.

The Flag That Bore a Single Star

605 [*General sources on Sumter*]: Frank Barnes, *Fort Sumter*, No. 12 in the National Park Service Historical Handbook Series (Government Printing Office, 1962), passim; Robert U. Johnson and Clarence C. Buel, eds., *Battles and Leaders of the Civil War* (Century, 1884), Vol. 1, pp. 40–83; William A. Swanberg, *First Blood* (Charles Scribner's Sons, 1957), passim.

[*Charleston rooftop scene*]: Barnes, opposite p. 1.

605 [*Sumter as a symbol*]: Potter, p. 541.

606 [*Conflicting counsels in Washington*]: Sandburg, Ch. 7.

[*Pryor's exhortation*]: quoted in Sandburg, p. 207.

[*Pryor's reluctance*]: *Battles and Leaders*, Vol. 1, p. 76. [*Ruffin fires the first shot*]: Sandburg, p. 209. (There is some controversy on this point, however.)

607 [*New York farmer choosing sides*]: quoted in Fletcher Pratt, *Ordeal by Fire* (William Sloane Associates, 1948), p. xvi.

[*The "Bonnie Blue Flag"*]: Richard Crawford, ed., *The Civil War Songbook* (Dover, 1977), pp. 18-19.

[*Sherman on end to indecision*]: John Sherman to William T. Sherman, April 12, 1861, in Rachel Sherman Thorndike, *The Sherman Letters* (Charles Scribner's Sons, 1894), p. 110. [*Nevins on "purifying hurricane"*]: Allan Nevins, *The War for the Union*, Vol. 1: *The Improvised War* (Charles Scribner's Sons, 1959), p. 75.

[*Disparity between northern and southern resources*]: Charles P. Roland, *The Confederacy* (University of Chicago Press, 1960), pp. 34-37.

608 [*Confederate volunteers*]: Bell I. Wiley, *The Life of Johnny Reb* (Bobbs-Merrill, 1943), pp. 15-27, 108-10; William C. Davis, *Battle at Bull Run* (Doubleday, 1977), pp. 18-28.

609 [*Battle of Bull Run*]: Davis, passim; Frank Moore, ed., *The Rebellion Record* (G. P. Putnam, 1862), Vol. 2, pp. 36-37, Documents pp. 1-116; William K. Scarborough, ed., *The Diary of Edmund Ruffin* (Louisiana State University Press, 1976), Vol. 2, pp. 68-75; Edward P. Alexander, *Military Memoirs of a Confederate* (Charles Scribner's Sons, 1907), pp. 13-51.

[*Union advance a "picnic"*]: see Alfred S. Roe, ed., *The Fifth Regiment, Massachusetts Volunteer Infantry* (Blanchard Press, 1911), pp. 79-80; also Charles C. Coffin, *Four Years of Fighting* (Ticknor and Fields, 1866), pp. 17-21; *Rebellion Record*, Vol. 2, p. 55. [*Greeley's masthead*]: Harlan H. Horner, *Lincoln and Greeley* (University of Illinois Press, 1953), p. 226.

[*Ruffin on southern morale*]: Scarborough, pp. 69-77.

610 [*Doherty on Union courage in attack*]: *Rebellion Record*, Vol. 2, p. 90.

[*Sherman's frustration*]: Mark A. D. Howe, ed., *Home Letters of General Sherman* (Charles Scribner's Sons, 1909), pp. 205-6.

[*Bee's rallying cry*]: quoted in Alexander, p. 36. [*Cummings' order to charge*]: James I. Robertson, Jr., *The Stonewall Brigade* (Louisiana State University Press, 1963), p. 40.

611 [*The Union retreat*]: Oliver O. Howard, *Autobiography of Oliver Otis Howard* (Baker and Taylor, 1907), Vol. 1, pp. 159-62.

[*Carnage on the battlefield*]: Scarborough, pp. 92-93. See also Howe, p. 208.

612 [*Greeley's letter to Lincoln*]: Horner, pp. 233-34.

[*Southern braggadocio*]: Nevins, p. 222.

[*General sources on the Confederacy*]: Coulter; Clement Eaton, *A History of the Southern Confederacy* (Macmillan, 1954); Frank L. Owsley, *States Rights in the Confederacy* (University of Chicago Press, 1925); Roland.

[*Florida governor on central control of army*]: quoted in Roland, p. 59. [*Benjamin on need to centralize*]: quoted in Owsley, pp. 30-31.

613 [*"Executive usurpation" by Davis*]: Pollard, p. 265. [*Printing of Confederate money*]: Sandburg, pp. 239-40.

[*Stephens on liberties coming first*]: quoted in Coulter, p. 402.

613 [*Brown on conscription*]: quoted in James G. Randall and David Donald, *The Civil War and Reconstruction*, 2nd ed. (D. C. Heath, 1969), p. 269. [*Roland on "deadliest conflict"*]: Roland, p. 59.

[*Attitude of Rhett*]: Roland, pp. 53, 58.

Men in Blue and Gray

614 [*Lincoln watching soldiers return from Bull Run*]: Thomas, p. 272. [*Whitman on Lincoln recovering himself*]: Richard M. Bucke, Thomas B. Harned, and Horace L. Traubel, eds., *The Complete Writings of Walt Whitman* (G. P. Putnam's Sons, 1902), Vol. 4, p. 36.

615 [*Lincoln on limited presidential power*]: fragment of House speech, 1848 (July 1?), in John G. Nicolay and John Hay, eds., *Complete Works of Abraham Lincoln*, enlarged edition (Century, 1894), Vol. 2, p. 56.

[*Randall on Lincoln's use of arbitrary power*]: James G. Randall, *Constitutional Problems under Lincoln* (D. Appleton, 1926), p. 513. See also Wilfred E. Binkley, *President and Congress* (Alfred A. Knopf, 1947), p. 126.

[*Lincoln on choice between life and limb*]: Nicolay and Hay, Vol. 10, p. 66.

[*Anna Ella Carroll*]: Sandburg, pp. 410-11.

[*Lincoln's program for action*]: Basler, Vol. 4, pp. 457-58.

616 [*Union sympathizers in Virginia and Tennessee*]: Carleton Beals, *War Within a War: The Confederacy Against Itself* (Chilton Books, 1965), passim.

[*McClellan in Washington*]: Sandburg, pp. 314-20; Nevins, pp. 237-39. [*Captain on military panorama*]: quoted in Nevins, p. 239.

617 [*Cameron and the War Department*]: A. Howard Meneely, *The War Department, 1861* (Columbia University Press, 1928), esp. Ch. 9; Fred A. Shannon, *The Organization and Administration of the Union Army, 1861-1865* (Arthur H. Clark, 1928), Vol. 1, passim; Sandburg, pp. 425-35.

[*Washington neglects the West*]: Nevins, Ch. 16. [*Union gunboat fleet*]: *Battles and Leaders*, Vol. 1, pp. 358-61; Allan Nevins, *The War for the Union*, Vol. 2: *War Becomes Revolution* (Charles Scribner's Sons, 1960), pp. 70-73.

[*Sam Grant in peace and war*]: Lloyd Lewis, *Captain Sam Grant* (Little, Brown, 1950), Chs. 17-23; Bruce Catton, *Grant Moves South* (Little, Brown, 1960), Chs. 1-3. [*Cairo in 1861*]: Coffin, pp. 52-53.

[*The Union Navy*]: Bern Anderson, *By Sea and by River: The Naval History of the Civil War* (Alfred A. Knopf, 1962), pp. 3-66; *Battles and Leaders*, Vol. 1, pp. 611-91.

618 [*The Trent affair*]: *Battles and Leaders*, Vol. 2, pp. 135-42. [*"Wrap the whole world in flames"*]: Sandburg, p. 363. [*"One war at a time"*]: ibid., p. 365.

619 [*Writ of habeas corpus for Merryman*]: Sandburg, p. 279.

[*Taney's opinion in* Ex parte Merryman]: Randall, p. 121. [*Taney calls upon Lincoln to perform his duty*]: ibid., p. 162; Sandburg, p. 280.

[*Madison on ambition*]: Federalist No. 51.

619-20 [*Congress grudgingly approves emergency acts*]: Randall, pp. 128-29. [*Committee on Government Contracts*]: Sandburg, pp. 425-27. [*Sanitary Commission*]: Nevins, *Improvised War*, p. 283.

620 [*Joint Committee on the Conduct of the War*]: Nevins, *Improvised War*, p. 387. [*Soldier bitter at government suspicion*]: General Charles F. Smith, quoted in Bruce Catton, *America Goes to War* (Wesleyan University Press, 1958), p. 99.

620 [*Cameron and the antislavery radicals*]: Burton J. Hendrick, *Lincoln's War Cabinet* (Little, Brown, 1946), pp. 219–35.

621 [*Course of the war in 1862*]: Foote; Nevins, *War Becomes Revolution; Battles and Leaders,* Vol. 2, pp. 22–89.

622 [*Boys in blue*]: Bell I. Wiley, *The Life of Billy Yank: The Common Soldier of the Union* (Bobbs-Merrill, 1951).

[*Boys in gray*]: Wiley, *Johnny Reb.*

[*Fair on naïveté of Civil War soldiers*]: Charles Fair, *From the Jaws of Victory* (Simon and Schuster, 1971), p. 223.

[*Composition of Illinois regiments*]: Victor Hicken, *Illinois in the Civil War* (University of Illinois Press, 1966), pp. 7–8.

623 [*Elected officers*]: see Catton, *America Goes to War,* p. 38 and passim.

[*"Purge" in Wisconsin regiment*]: Nevins, *Improvised War,* p. 280.

[*Soldier complaining about Jackson*]: quoted in Davis, *Battle at Bull Run,* p. 18. [*"Old Blue Light"*]: *ibid.*

[*Grant as the "quiet man"*]: Lewis, p. 428. [*"Go to your quarters!"*]: *ibid.,* p. 430.

[*Northern soldiers and blacks*]: Wiley, *Billy Yank,* Ch. 5; Catton, *America Goes to War,* pp. 24–25. [*Ohio soldier on blacks*]: quoted in Wiley, *Billy Yank,* p. 109.

[*Holocaust of Shiloh*]: Leander Stillwell, *The Story of a Common Soldier* (Franklin Hudson, 1920), p. 48.

624 [*Antietam*]: Bruce Catton, *The Army of the Potomac: Mr. Lincoln's Army* (Doubleday, 1951), Part VI; John W. Schildt, *Drums Along the Antietam* (McClain Printing, 1972).

The Battle Cries of Freedom

625 [*Lincoln on the war as a people's war*]: Message to Congress in Special Session, July 4, 1861, in Basler, Vol. 5, p. 438.

[*Greeley's "Prayer of Twenty Million"*]: Horner, pp. 263–67.

[*Lincoln on putting the Union first*]: Lincoln to Horace Greeley, Aug. 22, 1862, in Basler, Vol. 5, pp. 388–89.

[*Early congressional measures for emancipation*]: Harman Belz, "Protection of Personal Liberty in Republican Emancipation Legislation of 1862," *Journal of Southern History,* Vol. 42, No. 3 (August 1976), pp. 385–400.

[*Seward on the "last shriek on our retreat"*]: quoted in Thomas, p. 334.

626 [*Frederick Douglass on the proposed emancipation proclamation*]: quoted in Stephen B. Oates, *With Malice Toward None* (Harper & Row, 1977), p. 320.

[*The December cabinet crisis*]: Hendrick; Thomas, pp. 352–54.

627 [*Lincoln on "the dogmas of the quiet past"*]: Annual Message to Congress, Dec. 1, 1862, in Basler, Vol. 5, p. 537.

[*Lincoln's dream the night before the signing of the Emancipation Proclamation*]: quoted from Oates, pp. 331–32.

[*Lincoln: "if my name ever goes into history"*]: Oscar and Lillian Handlin, *Abraham Lincoln and the Union* (Little, Brown, 1980), p. 159.

627 [*Final Emancipation Proclamation*]: Philip Van Doren Stern, ed., *The Life and Writings of Abraham Lincoln* (The Modern Library, 1940), pp. 746–48 (capital letters added). [*Gathering in front of the White House*]: Oates, p. 333.

628 [*Battle songs of freedom*]: Irwin Silber, ed., *Songs of the Civil War* (Columbia University Press, 1960), pp. 17–20, 26.

Sections of this chapter were drafted jointly by the author and Jeffrey P. Trout.

ACKNOWLEDGMENTS

In my studies in political history I have found it useful to conceive of three levels of leadership: the galaxy of presidents, nationally known senators and governors, intellectual and economic and cultural power wielders at the top; a second level of influential state and metropolitan notables, editors, preachers, heads of state and national interest groups, issue groups, and idea groups; and a third layer of grass-roots activists in government, political parties, interest groups, racial, religious, and ethnic organizations, and economic and social enterprises who serve as crucial transmission links between the upper echelons and the mass public. Volumes—sometimes whole libraries—are written about the galaxies; the intermediate notables often make their way into the *Dictionary of American Biography* or *Notable American Women;* the activists at the third level down are lucky to win biographical coverage in the local obituary pages.

While the "third cadre" of activists is, in my view, the one most crucial to democracy, the "second cadre" offers by far the most fascinating personalities. At least, this seems to have been true during the seventy-five-year period the present work covers, from the great constitution-making years of the 1780s to the crises of 1862. I doubt that any country has produced a more brilliant array of men and women leaders in politics, literature, women's rights, business enterprise, from such a small population during such a short period. I wish I could have done justice to this creative second cadre, but then the present work would be far more encyclopedic than it is.

Instead, I have examined certain personages—Lydia Maria Child, for example—at some length, as exemplars of countless other second-cadre leaders. I have tried also to reach into especially important subcultures to give some sense of the smell and feel and sound of the place as representative of certain sections of the country at certain times. In order to sink these historical drill holes into particular areas, and in order to capture significant personages in the second cadre of leadership, I have benefited from researches undertaken at the following archives and libraries, to whose staffs I express appreciation: Albany State Library, California Historical Society, Columbia University Library, William R. Perkins Library of Duke University, Emory University Library, Filson Club of Louisville, Library of Congress, Louisiana State University Library, Massachusetts Historical Society, New-York Historical Society, New York Public Library, Pennsylvania Historical Society, Schlesinger Library at Radcliffe, South Carolina Historical Society, South Carolina Library of the University of South Carolina, Tulane University Library, Virginia State Library, University of Virginia Library, Widener Library, Earl Gregg Swem Library of the College of William and Mary, Williams College Library, and a number of local archives and libraries as indicated in the notes. Dee Ann Montgomery conducted research also at the Illinois State Historical Library and other libraries in Illinois.

I was privileged, in writing key sections of this work, to have the collaboration of exceptionally gifted research associates and the benefit of the work they have done in particular fields of study. Stewart Burns collaborated in planning and drafting material on major aspects of black history and of social history more broadly; Dee Ann Montgomery, in social history, especially women's history, and in political party history; and Jeffrey P. Trout, in military history—particularly the Civil War—and political history. I am responsible for the final writing, including any errors of omission and commission; I would be grateful to be informed of any such errors at Williams College, Williamstown, Mass., 01267. David Coolidge, Virginia Earll, Ann F. Hickey, and Ellen Yager also assisted with research. Robert A. Burns investigated Shays's Rebellion in western Massachusetts libraries and archives. Peter A. Meyers assisted me on conceptualization and data on some major theoretical problems. Michael Beschloss, Maurice Greenbaum, and Lisl Cade helped me in important ways. Deborah Burns designed the endpapers in collaboration with Betty Anderson. Jay Leibold worked intensively on manuscript preparation.

Because I have ranged through many periods and dimensions of American history, I solicited critical reviews of the manuscript from scholars far more expert than I. Linda K. Kerber, Ronald P. Formisano, Robert M. Johnstone, Jr., and Robert F. Dalzell, Jr., generously responded with stringent and constructive criticism on the basis of their diverse areas of scholarship. Richard B. Morris and Charles B. Dew kindly reviewed portions of the manuscript. I am grateful to these scholars for taking time from their own teaching and writing.

I am indebted to Ashbel Green and his colleagues at Alfred A. Knopf for constant encouragement on this long-term project, and to Ashbel Green also for wise editorial suggestions. I am also grateful to the National Endowment for the Humanities for financial support of the national, state, and local political party research and analysis that was indispensable to the work. My longtime editorial friend and critic, Jeannette Hopkins, helped significantly in clarifying both the ideas and the language in the work.

Deborah Burns, Milton Djuric, Daniel Frank, Jack Lynch, Melvin Rosenthal, and Wendy Severinghaus provided indispensable help in guiding the manuscript through its final stages. My wife and fellow author, Joan Simpson Burns, was as always the source of unending support and encouragement.

J.M.B.

Index

PERMISSION ACKNOWLEDGMENTS

The following illustrations have been reproduced with the kind permission of the institutions indicated:

[FRONT ENDPAPER] *Courtesy of the American Antiquarian Society:* "Spooler and Stand," advertisement for E. C. Cleaveland & Co. *Courtesy of the New-York Historical Society: The New-York Packet,* April 7, 1789; *The New-York Packet,* Federalist #51, February 8, 1788; View of boats navigating the Mohawk; View from Rushonga Tavern, 5 miles from Yorktown on the Baltimore Road. *Courtesy of the New York Public Library:* American Log-House, 1826 (Rare Books & Manuscripts Division); Federal Hall, 1790 (Phelps-Stokes Collection of American Historical Prints); "Join, or Die," *Pennsylvania Gazette,* May 9, 1754 (Rare Books & Manuscripts Division); "Mad Tom in a Rage" (Prints Division); Map of the United States in 1783 (Map Division); Map of Kentucky in 1784 (Map Division); Second Street North from Market Street, Philadelphia (Phelps-Stokes Collection); Se-Quo-Yah (Rare Books and Manuscripts Division).

[BACK ENDPAPER] *Courtesy of John Deere & Co.:* Advertisement for Centre-Draft Plow. *Courtesy of the New-York Historical Society:* Advertisement for *Uncle Tom's Cabin; Charleston Mercury Extra:* "Union Dissolved"; Clipper Ship *Flying Cloud*; Group of Workmen on the Union Pacific Railroad; "Ho! for the Gold Mines!"; Principal Street of San Francisco. *Courtesy of the New York Public Library:* "Am I not a man and a brother?" (Prints Division); Clinton Line Barge (Prints Division); Kansas City, 1853 (Phelps-Stokes Collection); The Modern Balaam and His Ass, 1837 (Prints Division). *Courtesy of the Worcester Art Museum:* "Conquering Prejudice, Fulfilling a Constitutional Duty with Alacrity."

The endpapers were designed and executed by Deborah Burns and Sara Reynolds.

[PART TITLE ILLUSTRATIONS] *Courtesy of the American Antiquarian Society:* "Spooler and Stand," advertisement for E. C. Cleaveland & Co. *Courtesy of the Bettmann Archive, Inc.:* "Am I not a woman and a sister?," Garrison's *Liberator,* 1849; The Modern Balaam and His Ass, 1837. *Courtesy of John Deere & Co.:* Advertisement for Centre-Draft Plow. *Courtesy of the New York Public Library:* Federal Hall, 1790 (Phelps-Stokes Collection).

The map of the United States in 1783 that follows page 10 is reproduced with the kind permission of the New York Public Library. The map of the United States in 1857 by J. H. Young, Philadelphia, that follows page 416 is reproduced with the kind permission of the Newberry Library, Chicago.

A NOTE ABOUT THE AUTHOR

JAMES MACGREGOR BURNS is one of America's most prominent scholars and biographers. Born in Melrose, Massachusetts, he received his B.A. from Williams College in 1939, and his M.A. and Ph.D. from Harvard University. He has been a member of the political science department at Williams since 1941, and a professor of political science since 1953. Among his numerous books are *Roosevelt: The Lion and the Fox* (1956), *John Kennedy: A Political Profile* (1960), *The Deadlock of Democracy* (1963), *Roosevelt: The Soldier of Freedom* (1970), which was awarded both the Pulitzer Prize and the National Book Award, and *Leadership* (1978). He is currently co-director of Project 87, an interdisciplinary study of the American Constitution during the Bicentennial Era.